THE S. MARK TAPER FOUNDATION

IMPRINT IN JEWISH STUDIES

BY THIS ENDOWMENT
THE S. MARK TAPER FOUNDATION SUPPORTS
THE APPRECIATION AND UNDERSTANDING
OF THE RICHNESS AND DIVERSITY OF
JEWISH LIFE AND CULTURE

The publisher gratefully acknowledges the generous support of the
Jewish Studies Endowment Fund of the University of California
Press Foundation, which was established by a major gift from
the S. Mark Taper Foundation.

Tales of High Priests and Taxes

HELLENISTIC CULTURE AND SOCIETY

General Editors: Anthony W. Bulloch, Erich S. Gruen,
A. A. Long, and Andrew F. Stewart

I. *Alexander to Actium: The Historical Evolution of the Hellenistic Age*, by Peter Green

II. *Hellenism in the East: The Interaction of Greek and Non-Greek Civilizations from Syria to Central Asia after Alexander*, edited by Amélie Kuhrt and Susan Sherwin-White

III. *The Question of "Eclecticism": Studies in Later Greek Philosophy*, edited by J. M. Dillon and A. A. Long

IV. *Antigonos the One-Eyed and the Creation of the Hellenistic State*, by Richard A. Billows

V. *A History of Macedonia*, by R. Malcolm Errington, translated by Catherine Errington

VI. *Attic Letter-Cutters of 229 to 86 B.C.*, by Stephen V. Tracy

VII. *The Vanished Library: A Wonder of the Ancient World*, by Luciano Canfora

VIII. *Hellenistic Philosophy of Mind*, by Julia E. Annas

IX. *Hellenistic History and Culture*, edited by Peter Green

X. *The Best of the Argonauts: The Redefinition of the Epic Hero in Book One of Apollonius' Argonautica*, by James J. Clauss

XI. *Faces of Power: Alexander's Image and Hellenistic Politics*, by Andrew Stewart

XII. *Images and Ideologies: Self-definition in the Hellenistic World*, edited by Anthony W. Bulloch, Erich S. Gruen, A. A. Long, and Andrew Stewart

XIII. *From Samarkhand to Sardis: A New Approach to the Seleucid Empire*, by Susan Sherwin-White and Amélie Kuhrt

XIV. *Regionalism and Change in the Economy of Independent Delos, 314–167 B.C.*, by Gary Reger

XV. *Hegemony to Empire: The Development of the Roman Imperium in the East from 148 to 62 B.C.*, by Robert Kallet-Marx

XVI. *Moral Vision in The Histories of Polybius*, by Arthur M. Eckstein

XVII. *The Hellenistic Settlements in Europe, the Islands, and Asia Minor*, by Getzel M. Cohen

XVIII. *Interstate Arbitrations in the Greek World, 337–90 B.C.*, by Sheila L. Ager

XIX. *Theocritus's Urban Mimes: Mobility, Gender, and Patronage*, by Joan B. Burton

XX. *Athenian Democracy in Transition: Attic Letter-Cutters of 340 to 290 B.C.*, by Stephen V. Tracy

XXI. *Pseudo-Hecataeus, "On the Jews": Legitimizing the Jewish Diaspora*, by Bezalel Bar-Kochva

XXII. *Asylia: Territorial Inviolability in the Hellenistic World*, by Kent J. Rigsby

XXIII. *The Cynics: The Cynic Movement in Antiquity and Its Legacy*, edited by R. Bracht Branham and Marie-Odile Goulet-Cazé

XXIV. *The Politics of Plunder: Aitolians and Their Koinon in the Early Hellenistic Era, 279–217 B.C.*, by Joseph B. Scholten

XXV. *The Argonautika*, by Apollonios Rhodios, translated, with introduction, commentary, and glossary, by Peter Green

XXVI. *Hellenistic Constructs: Essays in Culture, History, and Historiography*, edited by Paul Cartledge, Peter Garnsey, and Erich S. Gruen

XXVII. *Josephus's Interpretation of the Bible*, by Louis H. Feldman

XXVIII. *Poetic Garlands: Hellenistic Epigrams in Context*, by Kathryn J. Gutzwiller

XXIX. *Religion in Hellenistic Athens*, by Jon D. Mikalson

XXX. *Heritage and Hellenism: The Reinvention of Jewish Tradition*, by Erich S. Gruen

XXXI. *The Beginnings of Jewishness: Boundaries, Varieties, Uncertainties*, by Shaye D. Cohen

XXXII. *Thundering Zeus: The Making of Hellenistic Bactria*, by Frank L. Holt

XXXIII. *Jews in the Mediterranean Diaspora: From Alexander to Trajan (323 B.C.E.–117 C.E.)*, by John M. G. Barclay

XXXIV. *From Pergamon to Sperlonga: Sculpture and Context*, edited by Nancy T. de Grummond and Brunilde S. Ridgway

XXXV. *Polyeideia: The Iambi of Callimachus and the Archaic Iambic Tradition*, by Benjamin Acosta-Hughes

XXXVI. *Stoic Studies*, by A. A. Long

XXXVII. *Seeing Double: Intercultural Poetics in Ptolemaic Alexandria*, by Susan A. Stephens

XXXVIII. *Athens and Macedon: Attic Letter-Cutters of 300 to 229 B.C.*, by Stephen V. Tracy

XXXIX. *Encomium of Ptolemy Philadelphus*, by Theocritus, translated with an introduction and commentary by Richard Hunter

XL. *The Making of Fornication: Eros, Ethics, and Political Reform in Greek Philosophy and Early Christianity*, by Kathy L. Gaca

XLI. *Cultural Politics in Polybius's Histories*, by Craige B. Champion

XLII. *Cleomedes' Lectures on Astronomy: A Translation of The Heavens*, with an introduction and commentary by Alan C. Bowen and Robert B. Todd

XLIII. *Historical Fictions and Hellenistic Jewish Identity: Third Maccabees in Its Cultural Context*, by Sara Raup Johnson

XLIV. *Alexander the Great and the Mystery of the Elephant Medallions*, by Frank L. Holt

XLV. *The Horse and Jockey from Artemision: A Bronze Equestrian Monument of the Hellenistic Period*, by Seán Hemingway

XLVI. *The Hellenistic Settlements in Syria, the Red Sea Basin, and North Africa*, by Getzel M. Cohen

XLVII. *Into the Land of Bones: Alexander the Great in Afghanistan*, by Frank L. Holt

XLVIII. *Mediterranean Anarchy, Interstate War, and the Rise of Rome*, by Arthur M. Eckstein

XLIX. *Hellenistic Egypt: Monarchy, Society, Economy, Culture*, by Jean Bingen. Edited and introduced by Roger S. Bagnall

L. *Jewish Perspectives on Hellenistic Rulers*, edited by Tessa Rajak, Sarah Pearce, James Aitken, and Jennifer Dines

LI. *The Image of the Jews in Greek Literature: The Hellenistic Period*, by Bezalel Bar-Kochva

LII. *From Alexander to Jesus*, by Ory Amitay

LIII. *Lost World of the Golden King: In Search of Ancient Afghanistan*, by Frank L. Holt

LIV. *The Hellenistic Settlements in the East from Armenia and Mesopotamia to Bactria and India*, by Getzel M. Cohen

LV. *Creating a Common Polity: Religion, Economy, and Politics in the Making of the Greek Koinon*, by Emily Mackil

LVI. *Tales of High Priests and Taxes: The Books of the Maccabees and the Judean Rebellion against Antiochos IV*, by Sylvie Honigman

Tales of High Priests and Taxes

The Books of the Maccabees and the Judean Rebellion against Antiochos IV

Sylvie Honigman

UNIVERSITY OF CALIFORNIA PRESS

University of California Press, one of the most distinguished university presses in the United States, enriches lives around the world by advancing scholarship in the humanities, social sciences, and natural sciences. Its activities are supported by the UC Press Foundation and by philanthropic contributions from individuals and institutions. For more information, visit www.ucpress.edu.

University of California Press
Oakland, California

© 2014 by The Regents of the University of California

First Paperback Printing 2021

Library of Congress Cataloging-in-Publication Data

Honigman, Sylvie.
   Tales of high priests and taxes : the books of the Maccabees and the Judean rebellion against Antiochos IV.
      p. cm.
   Includes bibliographical references and index.
   ISBN 978-0-520-27558-4 (cloth: alk. paper); 978-0-520-38314-2 (pbk. : alk. paper); 978-0-520-95818-0 (ebook)
    1. Bible. Apocrypha. Maccabees, 1st—History of Biblical events.
2. Bible. Apocrypha. Maccabees, 2nd—History of Biblical events.
3. Antiochus IV, King of Syria, approximately 215 B.C.–164 B.C.
4. Jews—Kings and rulers—Brothers. 5. Maccabees. 6. Jews—History—586 B.C.–70 A.D. 7. Jewish high priests—History. I. Title.
BS1825.55.H66   2014
229′.7095—dc23   2013044076

CONTENTS

Preface and Acknowledgments   xi

General Introduction   *1*

PART I. *IOUDAÏSMOS*: 1 AND 2 MACCABEES AS DYNASTIC HISTORY

    Methodological Introduction: The Modern Semantic Categories of "Religion" and "Politics" and Ancient Societies   *51*

1. 2 Maccabees as Dynastic History   *65*
2. Temple Foundation and Royal Legitimacy: A Narrative Pattern and Its Message   *95*
3. *Ioudaïsmos* as the Legitimate Social Order Founded by Judas Maccabee   *119*
4. Royal High Priests and Temple Foundation: The Narrative Pattern and the Hasmonean Political Order   *147*

    Conclusion   *183*

PART II. *HELLĒNISMOS*: THE CAUSES OF THE REBELLION ACCORDING TO THE AUTHORS OF 1 AND 2 MACCABEES

    Methodological Introduction: Symbolic Universe, Cultural Codes, and Causal Analysis in 1 and 2 Maccabees   *189*

5. *Hellēnismos:* The Social Order of the Wicked Rivals in 1 and 2 Maccabees — 197

6. The "Religious Persecution" in the Light of Ancient Judean Cultural and Narrative Codes — 229

7. The Causes of the Rebellion according to 1 and 2 Maccabees — 259

Conclusion — 287

PART III. HISTORY: THE JUDEAN REBELLION IN HISTORICAL PERSPECTIVE, 200–164 B.C.E.

From Literary Analysis to History: A Summary of the Conclusions of Parts I and II — 291

8. Judea and Koilē Syria and Phoinikē under Antiochos III, 200–187 B.C.E. — 297

9. Seleukos IV Philopator and the Revision of Antiochos III's Settlement in Judea, 187–175 B.C.E. — 316

10. Judea under Antiochos IV Epiphanes: The Reforms, 175–ca. 172 B.C.E. — 345

11. Judea under Antiochos IV Epiphanes: The Suppression of the Rebellion, 169/8–164 B.C.E. — 378

Appendix A. The Literary Composition of 1 Maccabees — 405
Appendix B. The Literary Composition of 2 Maccabees — 409
Abbreviations — 413
General Notes — 417
Bibliography — 513
Index Locorum — 533
Subject Index — 539

PREFACE AND ACKNOWLEDGMENTS

I was first introduced to 1 and 2 Maccabees when, as a visiting student, I attended Daniel R. Schwartz's advanced seminars at the Hebrew University of Jerusalem. I remember the charisma of a great scholar, amazing teacher, and immensely generous man, who with his dry humor welcomed foreign students to his classes, inviting us to comment on the Greek of the ancient sources in our hesitant Hebrew. Daniel Schwartz related to all of us as though we were formal research students of his, sharing his knowledge and encouraging personal investigation. This book is greatly indebted to him, and I am glad to pay homage to him here—especially as I suspect he will strongly disagree with most of its arguments. These were also the years when I came to know Noah Hacham, who as a fellow student was always there to help, either with Hebrew or with such unfamiliar material as Jewish Halakhah; and Katell Berthelot, who by then was another visiting student from France. In time, both were to become friends and colleagues, and numerous strands of our ongoing intellectual conversations have found their way into this book in one form or another.

The intellectual encounters that proved most decisive for this book were those I had with biblical scholars working on Persian times. I first heard of Victor Hurowitz's book on the central place of the narrative pattern of temple foundation in the royal ideologies of the ancient Near East and the Bible from Arnaud Sérandour, when the two of us spent one year in Jerusalem as PhD students and shared our working pauses. When thereafter I discovered 1 and 2 Maccabees, I was intrigued by what by then struck me as vague similarities between the Hanukkah narrative and ancient Near Eastern stories of kings and temple foundations. However, it took several years for that issue to crystallize into a proper research project, and eventually the present book. And as it did, I benefited from more encounters with biblical scholars whose help was invaluable. First and foremost among these are Christophe Nihan and Ehud Ben Zvi, who generously shared with me their knowledge of biblical texts of Persian times and were open to discuss ideas.

My project also led to a close collaboration with Gilles Gorre, which gave us the opportunity time and again to share views about Hellenistic kings and Judean and Egyptian priests. Laetitia Graslin-Thomé and Philippe Clancier were open to discussions about Jerusalem and Seleukid Babylonia, and Hannah Cotton about the Olympiodoros inscription. I also benefited from conversations with John Ma, Maurice Sartre, and Erich Gruen on 2 Maccabees and Antiochos IV, as well as with Gali Shapira on structural semiotics, and Frank Pollack on ethnopoetics. In the framework of a common research group I could share more conversations on Qumran with Jonathan Ben Dov and on Bickerman with Albert Baumgarten. On a less formal front, my many conversations over coffee with Susan Weingarten at Tel Aviv University were both delightful and intellectually rewarding.

Gilles Gorre, Erich Gruen, Christophe Nihan, Frank Pollack, Maurice Sartre, and Gali Shapira read earlier drafts of chapters, and Katell Berthelot and John Ma the entire manuscript. Their comments and corrections have been invaluable in helping me improve the book, and I warmly thank them for their time and interest. Ehud Ben Zvi kindly prepared a detailed list of intertextual references to biblical texts in 1 Maccabees, for which I am most grateful. This document helped me to substantially improve the literary analyses expounded in Chapters 3 and 4; my commentary on Simon's Eulogy in 1 Maccabees 14, in particular, is heavily indebted to this document. All remaining errors are mine alone. I also wish to thank U.C. Press's referees and committee reader, whose comments have been most helpful.

I wish to thank the scholars who offered me the opportunity to present aspects of my investigation on 1 and 2 Maccabees in academic forums: Claire Clivaz and Sabrina Inowlocki; Lester L. Grabbe and Oded Lipschits; Jonathan Ben Dov and Albert Baumgarten; Yuval Rotman; Noah Hacham; Marie-Françoise Baslez and Olivier Munnich; Silvia Bussi; and Laetitia Graslin-Thomé and Christophe Feyel.

My thanks also go to scholars who shared unpublished papers and bibliographical references with me: Damien Agut, Marie-Françoise Baslez, Laurent Capdetrey, Philippe Clancier, Tobias Funke, Gilles Gorre, Laetitia Graslin-Thomé, Christophe Michels, Julien Monerie, Olivier Munnich, Christophe Nihan, Andrea Rotstein, Maurice Sartre, Loren Stuckenbruck, Rolf Strootman, Daniel R. Schwartz, and Caroline Waerzeggers, with special thanks to Ehud Ben Zvi, who made available to me his unpublished draft of a book of collected papers.

Andrew Ellis and Jonathan Orr-Stav edited the final manuscript, while Doron Narkiss and Susan Weingarten edited earlier drafts of various chapters. Rotem

Avineri Meïr, Roii Ball, Michal Molcho, and Kristjan Sinkec provided most useful technical help. I warmly thank them for their aid. My thanks go also to Paul Psoinos, who copyedited the manuscript.

Finally, I thank Avital, Melvyn, Daniel, Nittay and Maor, Aryeh, Taly, Colette, and Danièle for their presence and support.

General Introduction

SUMMARY

The first and second books of Maccabees narrate events that occurred in Judea from the 170s through the 150s and eventually led to the rise of the Hasmonean dynasty: the toppling of the last high priest of the Oniad dynasty, the transformation of Jerusalem into a Greek polis, Antiochos IV's storming of Jerusalem, his desecration of the temple and his so-called persecution of the Jews, the liberation of the city and rededication of the temple altar by Judas Maccabee, the foundation of the commemorative festival of Hanukkah, and the subsequent wars against Seleukid troops. 1 Maccabees covers the deeds of Mattathias, the ancestor of the Maccabean/Hasmonean family, and his three sons, Judas, Jonathan, and Simon, taking its story down to the establishment of the dynastic transmission of power within the Hasmonean family when John, Simon's son, succeeded his father; whereas 2 Maccabees, which starts from Heliodoros's visit to Jerusalem under the high priest Onias III, focuses on Judas and the temple rededication, further displaying a pointed interest in the role of martyrs alongside that of Judas. Because of this difference in chronological scope and emphasis, it is usually considered that 1 Maccabees is a dynastic chronicle written by a court historian, whereas 2 Maccabees is the work of a pious author whose attitude toward the Hasmoneans has been diversely appreciated—from mild support, through indifference, to hostility. Moreover, the place of redaction of 2 Maccabees, either Jerusalem or Alexandria, is debated. Both because of its comparatively flamboyant style and the author's alleged primarily religious concerns, 2 Maccabees is held as an unreliable source of evidence about the causes of the Judean revolt. While modern scholars (erroneously) believe that the ancient author emphasizes religious and cultural issues, allegedly depicting the revolt as a struggle between Judaism and Hellenism, they are convinced that the causes of the revolt were a mix of religious and political factors (the family feud between the Oniads and the Tobiads, and how this interlocks with geostrategic tensions between the Ptolemies and the Seleukids), and perhaps also economic ones. However, for want of a reliable account, a detailed back story continues to elude us.

The present book questions these assertions both about the nature of 1 and 2 Maccabees and their depiction of the causes and essence of the Judean revolt, and, on the basis of its revised literary analysis of the two works, offers a new historical interpretation of these events. I argue that when 1 and 2 Maccabees are read with the proper attention to their culturally conditioned narrative codes, they appear to tell a completely different and perfectly rational story, albeit one with a heavy political bias. Far from being opposed in nature and purpose, these two Maccabees books are parallel works; despite their undeniable differences in narrative scope and style, both tell the founding myth of the Hasmonean dynasty. This, indeed, is what the story of the rededication of the temple altar by the Maccabees, the ancestors of the Hasmonean dynasty, is: a variant of the narrative pattern of temple foundation (or refoundation) that, in the Judean political tradition, was instrumental to any claim to political legitimacy. When we trace the evolution of the narrative pattern from the days of native kingship, through Persian, to Hellenistic times, it appears that the specific variant found in 1 and 2 Maccabees was precisely crafted to suit the specific shape of the Hasmoneans' power, which combined priestly and kingly prerogatives—a clear indication that both texts were crafted by court historians. As parallel works, they complement rather than duplicate each other: whereas 1 Maccabees narrates the run-up to the establishment of the dynastic principle, 2 Maccabees, by dwelling on the events that took place prior to the revolt, highlights the temple refoundation theme. Moreover, by focusing each on a different set of events—those that occurred before and after the temple refoundation, respectively—they appropriate the memory of both to the Hasmoneans' benefit.

While the two Maccabees authors offer strongly biased accounts of the events owing to their political allegiance, they can be shown to have a perfectly rational understanding of the causes and nature of the Judean rebellion against Antiochos IV. In particular, the modern view that 2 Maccabees presents the revolt as a struggle between Judaism and Hellenism is a misrepresentation and fails to recognize the cultural and narrative codes shaping the text. Both ancient authors expressly point out political causes—not only the wide-ranging consequences of the transformation of Jerusalem into a Greek polis, which have been abundantly commented upon by modern scholars, but also the political destabilization that resulted from Antiochos IV's deposition of Onias III, whose key role is usually overlooked—and furthermore they denounce the fiscal crisis that preceded (and largely explains) the revolt in far more explicit terms than modern students seem willing to acknowledge. Conversely, a proper literary analysis of 1 and 2 Maccabees, the book of Daniel, and Josephus, shows that there was no religious persecution. What we have are complex literary elaborations of a military suppression whose genesis can be reconstructed, once again, by being attentive to the ancient authors' culturally conditioned narrative codes. In turn, interpreting the "persecution" stories as accounts of a military suppression implies that the popular rebellion was the cause and not the consequence of Antiochos IV's crackdown on Jerusalem and therefore must have broken out during the king's second campaign in Egypt in 168 B.C.E. This must mean that religious issues were not in fact the primary cause of the rebellion, if a cause at all.

The revised literary analysis of 1 and 2 Maccabees offered in this book—and in particular the revised interpretation of how the ancient authors themselves understood the causes and nature of the revolt—provides fresh material for the historical reconstruction of the events themselves. For a proper understanding, this must start from Antiochos III's conquest of the region in 200/198 B.C.E. In Part III of this book I argue that the Judean revolt, which as just stated broke out during Antiochos IV's second campaign in Egypt, was primarily a reaction, first, to the wide-ranging administrative reforms implemented at the end of Seleukos IV's reign and the beginning of Antiochos IV's; second, to the political destabilization entailed by Antiochos IV's brutal ousting of Onias III; and third, to the seemingly sharp tax increase imposed by this king. As it appears, this interpretation of the decisive factors of the revolt is very close to the causal analysis offered by the author of 2 Maccabees himself. Reinstated thus from a bigoted account of little use to modern students of the rebellion, through the revised literary analysis offered in this book the text becomes a reasonably dependable source of evidence for modern historians to employ—provided we remain aware of its political bias. The historical reliability of 2 Maccabees as it is read in this book may be further supported by documentary evidence. In particular the recently published Olympiodoros inscription, which documents Seleukos IV's administrative reform of 178 B.C.E. aiming at a tighter control over the temples of the satrapy of Koilē Syria and Phoinikē, casts new light on the story of Heliodoros's visit to the Jerusalem temple that is told in 2 Maccabees 3.

The historical scenario sketched out in this book relies on the comparative approach, adducing documentary evidence from elsewhere to cross-check the literary accounts of the Judean events. However, whereas most adepts of the comparative approach since Elias Bickerman have primarily explored the relations between Seleukid kings and Greek cities for parallels, in this book the principal emphasis is on the relations between Hellenistic kings and temples. By this logic there is no reason to restrict our search of parallel material to the Seleukid empire, all societies of the ancient Near East in which temples had a status similar to that in Jerusalem being potentially relevant. For practical reasons, our main focus here is on Ptolemaic Egypt and Seleukid Babylonia.

Rather than simply offer a fresh historical reconstruction of the causes, nature, and unfolding of the Judean revolt against Antiochos IV, this book aims to make a methodological contribution by examining how the authors of 1 and 2 Maccabees, as Judean scribes of Hasmonean times, elaborated the relation between historical experience and the literary transcription of it. It is now a well-established tenet of scholarship that before we can use literary works as sources of evidence for historical investigation, we need to clarify their internal narrative logic. This does not merely entail unmasking the authors' calculated use of rhetoric for ideological purposes suiting their political biases. More crucially, as far as possible we need to identify the cognitive and narrative codes of the culture in question, which determined the perception of reality of the contemporary social actors in the context, and also establish the ways in which ancient authors, as professional scribes, intuitively understood how to put this perceived experience into words and give it appropriate, meaningful literary form. This is not a matter of rhetorical manipulation on the part of the authors, or of consciously motivated bias, but of ethnopoetics, both generated by and catering to the basic values of the respective authors' society. I will refer to the way the authors of 1 and 2 Maccabees perceived reality as a "symbolic universe." What is more, the intentional distortions resulting from political biases—in which 1 and 2 Maccabees are not lacking—are inescapably shaped by these basic cultural codes.

First and second Maccabees have too often been, and still are, read as though their accounts were shaped by the same semantic categories as our own, as if certain words and concepts had the same connotations for their original audience as they do for us. In particular, a recurrent source of misinterpretation is the projection of the present-day categories "religion" and "politics" on these texts. But whereas according to modern Western semantic categories, 2 Maccabees' high interest in the temple is taken as evidence for its author's religiousness, according to ancient Judean criteria it is actually a token of political side-taking. The issue is not that the temple was desecrated and reinaugurated, but who did it. Admittedly, even a greater awareness of the cultural codes informing the Maccabees books (as well as other contemporary literary sources) will not solve all the uncertainties of these texts, because in practice while these cultural codes condition the authors, they do not prevent them from manipulating their material by selecting, rewriting, distorting, or accordingly omitting material as they think fit. That said, if we are more mindful of how cultural codes shape a given author's discourse, we will have more accurate parameters of interpretation for our historical reconstructions of the events in Judea. This is now the actual pressing matter, and this book primarily aims to contribute to its advance.

1. BOOKS 1 AND 2 OF THE MACCABEES

1.1. The Literary Sources Documenting the Judean Rebellion

The sources covering the Judean rebellion against Antiochos IV in the 160s B.C.E. are essentially of a literary nature: in chronological order, the book of Daniel, 1 and 2 Maccabees, and Josephus's *Jewish Antiquities* and *Jewish War*. Although the book of Daniel is held to be contemporary to the revolt, its allusive tone, typical of the apocalyptic genre, makes it problematic as a source of historical data. Moreover, Daniel was written in response to the disruption of the daily sacrifices,[1] and the range of information it offers is limited: only the few verses covering Antiochos IV's reign (Dan. 11:21–35) are usually deemed relevant to historical study, and they bear on what is traditionally described as Antiochos IV's "religious persecution."

Josephus wrote his *War* ca. 75 C.E. and *Antiquities* ca. 94 C.E. in Rome. The section of *Antiquities* that interests us is 12.237–56: starting from Antiochos IV's appointment of Jason, whom Josephus calls "Jesus," it describes his replacement with Menelaos (whom Josephus calls "Onias"), the ensuing party strife between the Oniads and the Tobiads (237–40), Menelaos's and the Tobiads' petition to Antiochos to build a *gymnasion* (241), Antiochos's campaign in Egypt (242–45) and his attack on Jerusalem on his way back (246–47); and the king's second attack on Jerusalem "two years later," during which he plundered the temple, prohibited the Judean customs, and persecuted the people (248–56). Starting from *Antiquities* 12.241, Josephus follows 1 Maccabees from 1:11 on. After a protracted debate about whether or not Josephus interspersed his paraphrase of it with additional sources exploitable by modern scholars, it is now established that the discrepancies between 1 Maccabees and *Antiquities* are owed to Josephus himself.[2] The summary of Antiochos's Egyptian campaign inserted at 12.242–45 is a typical example of his technique: although he did not paraphrase any specific source, he compiled from other works the missing information he thought was indispensable to his own account and composed the passage himself.

From *Antiquities* 12.241 on, therefore, Josephus's account has been discredited as an independent source of evidence. So what about the preceding sections, 12.237–40? The question is of interest, since they form the most ancient source mentioning the civil strife between the Oniads and the Tobiads (the second and last one being Jerome, *Commentary on Daniel* 11:14). In contrast with the prevailing tendency to hold this account as an independent source, I see it as much more plausible that, like the rest, it is Josephus's own composition.[3] If we turn to Josephus's *War*, the few sections covering Antiochos IV's reign (1.31–40) add no information. In contrast with Daniel and Josephus, the first two Maccabees books offer a firsthand and detailed account of the events. The present book focuses primarily on these, as the most important sources on the Judean rebellion.

1.2. Dating 1 and 2 Maccabees

Although there can be no doubt that 1 and 2 Maccabees were written in the days of the Hasmonean dynasty, their precise dating is debated.[4] Moreover, investigations of this issue partly hinge on questionable criteria, which range from the emphasis on specific "facts" whose authenticity is far from ascertained to questionable distinctions between the "original" works and later interpolations, and the alleged dependence of one work on the other. The literary analysis of 1 and 2 Maccabees put forward in this book questions the viability of this positivistic method. But while it corroborates the works' dating to the days of the Hasmonean dynasty, reliable landmarks for narrowing down this time-span are scant. John Hyrkanos, the last character mentioned in 1 Maccabees, ruled in 134–104 B.C.E., providing a rough terminus post quem for this work. The date of the first letter prefixed to the account of 2 Maccabees, which supposes its completion, exhibits the date of 124 B.C.E., and to the extent that it is reliable, this may set a terminus ante quem. If these data are tenable, then the two works are roughly contemporary. Actually, the issue of their relative dating is secondary, since there is no reason to conclude that one is dependent upon the other. As I shall argue below, they simply betray a common tradition, and they will be treated as parallel works in this book.

1.3. 1 Maccabees

This proposal certainly runs against the common view, since 1 and 2 Maccabees are still widely regarded as markedly different because of their respective styles, scope, (alleged) subject matter, political (and religious) sensitivity, and possibly place of redaction. Notably, 1 Maccabees is a translation from a Hebrew original, and moreover imitates Septuagint Greek.[5] Following the survey of the rule of the Seleukid dynasty from Alexander's succession to Darius on in the first ten verses, the account starts from the establishment of the *gymnasion* under Antiochos IV (at 1 Macc. 1:11) and seemingly chronicles the ensuing events until the establishment of the dynastic principle within the Hasmonean family, with the first succession from father to son. Set in the shadow of the Seleukid dynasty, the first chapter surveys the time of disruption, culminating in a detailed account of the disruption of the temple cult and of the massacre of the Judeans faithful to their ancestral customs (the so-called religious persecution of 1 Macc. 1:41–64). The high priests Jason and Menelaos, who are explicitly identified in 2 Maccabees, are nowhere named in the corresponding account in 1 Maccabees. The rest of the book successively surveys the deeds of four heroes, Mattathias (1 Macc. 2:1–70), Judas (3:1–9:22), Jonathan (9:23–12:53), and Simon—the last of these by himself first (13:1–15:41) and then in association with his sons (16:1–22)—and closes with a short conclusion summarizing John Hyrkanos's reign after his father's death (16:23–24).

Because of this chronological pattern, 1 Maccabees is unanimously defined as dynastic history. Indeed the unmistakable bias of the account leaves no doubt that its author was a Hasmonean supporter, most probably a court historian. Although the most recent studies of the literary composition of the work depart from the old view that 1 Maccabees is a plain linear chronicle,[6] no structuring principle lending the work its inner coherence has yet been identified in a satisfying way. As a palliative, scholars persistently fall back on attempts to show that the extant work is composite.[7]

1.4. 2 Maccabees

The issues raised by 2 Maccabees are more complex. In particular, the literary structure of the work continues to baffle commentators. In its present form, the work includes two prefixed letters (2 Macc. 1:1–10a; 1:10b–2:18), the first enjoining the Judeans of Egypt to celebrate the Festival of the Dedication (Hanukkah), while the second narrates how Nehemiah rekindled the temple altar with hidden fire, and further evokes the divine fires that consumed Moses' and Solomon's sacrifices. The main body of the work begins with the proem (2:19–32), which famously describes the work as the abridged version of a longer historiographical opus allegedly written by one Jason of Cyrene—about whom, however, nothing is known. The main account itself is composed of four units. The first of these, the Heliodoros story (3:4–4:6), narrates the attempted plunder of the temple by Heliodoros, Seleukos IV's senior official, in the time of the high priest Onias III. The second unit (4:7–10:9), usually regarded as the principal one, tells the etiological story of the Hanukkah festival. It covers Antiochos IV's reign, successively narrating Onias III's deposition by Jason, Jason's foundation of the *gymnasion*, and his eviction by Menelaos (4:7–50); the king's campaign in Egypt and his assault on Jerusalem caused by the civil war between Menelaos and Jason, as well as the desecration of the temple, the disruption of the sacrificial rites, and the massacre of the Judeans (5:1–6:11). In 6:18–7:42 a lengthy description of the exemplary deaths of the faithful Judeans (the so-called martyrs) suspends the narrative. Closing this section are Judas Maccabee's first victories (8:1–36), Antiochos's death (9:1–18), and the temple rededication (10:1–8). The third unit (10:10–13:26) is entirely devoted to Judas's wars, lumping them all together in Antiochos V Eupator's reign. Finally, the fourth unit (14:1–15:37a) narrates the institution of a second festival commemorating Judas's victory over Nikanor and the latter's death. The narrative ends before the death of Judas Maccabee.

A. *Literary Structure*. The unifying principle of the literary structure of 2 Maccabees is not immediately apparent, to say the least, and this problem is further complicated by the fact that the work either is or purports to be an epitome. The combination of these two difficulties has encouraged the hunt for additions, interpolations, and displacements, as well as suspicions about cuts.[8] Many would elide the first and last units (the Heliodoros story and the Nikanor's Day story) altogether from what they suppose Jason's original to have been; there is unanimous agreement that the third unit (the wars section) lumps together different campaigns in complete disregard of chronology, although the question whether this unit is conceptually linked to the preceding or following one is debated; the martyrs stories inserted in 6:18–7:42 are almost unanimously seen as a late interpolation; the account of Antiochos IV's death should be chronologically located after the temple rededication, and Daniel Schwartz has pointed to this seemingly illogical order to argue that the story of the temple rededication is a secondary insertion that was added at the same time and by the same author as the prefixed festal letters.[9] Moreover, scholars disagree whether the epitomator is responsible for the current (apparent) lack of coherence, some seeing him as a mere abbreviator, others as a genuine author. Recently Schwartz has reconciled his view of the work as composite with the affirmation that the writer was a genuine author in claiming that he not only abbreviated Jason of Cyrene's work but inserted the extant additions.[10]

Schwartz's drastically segmented reading of 2 Maccabees was published almost three decades after Robert Doran's detailed review of earlier source theories, in which the latter had concluded: "The application of the methods of source-criticism ... has failed to turn up 'sources' in the technical sense. The epitome, therefore, must be considered as a whole and analysed accordingly."[11] Doran's conclusion is fully supported by the literary analysis of the main account of 2 Maccabees presented in this book, which admits of one possible addition alone, namely the so-called martyr stories of 6:18–7:42. With due respect to the prevailing view, the overall coherence of the text's literary structure leaves no doubt that its writer is a genuine author. For these reasons I will refer to 2 Maccabees as a work, and not as an epitome.

B. Subject Matter and Purpose: The Location Issue. Given this wide disagreement about the original form of the work, it is not surprising that its subject matter and purpose continue to elicit diverging appraisals. To begin with, the problem of the relation between 2 Maccabees and the original book by Jason of Cyrene has some bearing on this issue. Jason's place of origin prompted scholars of the late nineteenth and early twentieth century to surmise that he lived and wrote in the diaspora.[12] This implied a diasporan viewpoint in 2 Maccabees as well, which at that time was regarded as a mere epitome, the perfectly fluent Greek of the work even fostering the assumption that this too was written in the diaspora, most probably in Alexandria.[13] Recently Schwartz has revived the Alexandrian or diasporan hypothesis on the argument that the author's religious sensitivity is not primarily centered on the temple and is therefore typically diasporan in approach. According to him, the subject matter of 2 Maccabees is the city of Jerusalem and not the temple.[14] Doran now concurs, taking "the author's passionate dissent from the practice [of Jews (sic) going to *gymnasia*]" to be a diasporan concern.[15] In contrast, scholars relying on arguments of intertextuality point to a Judean setting, a conclusion that I substantiate in the present study.[16]

C. Subject Matter and Purpose: Further Aspects. The location issue is not the only cause of disagreement about the subject matter of 2 Maccabees. At first sight, it is easy to draw a reasonably agreeable list of the work's major topics: the temple, the exemplary dead, divine epiphanies, Judas Maccabee (and the omission of Judas's brothers), the sin-retribution (or measure-for-measure) motif illustrating God's righteousness, and the (alleged) conflict between "Hellenism" and "Judaism." Yet the controversy revolves not around the list per se but around the relative weight of each topic in the overall economy of the work. For instance, is the main focus on the temple or on the so-called martyrs? Schwartz's claim that the narrative betrays a diasporan "religious and political orientation" has led him to revive the old claim that 2 Maccabees is more concerned with the martyrs than with the temple.[17] However, in contrast with Schwartz, virtually all recent critics agree that the temple is the central motif of 2 Maccabees.[18] Accordingly, there is some consensus about the (assumed) purpose of the work: to promote the celebration of the Hanukkah festival by recounting its etiological story, namely the desecration of the temple by Antiochos IV and its liberation.[19] This indeed is patently the objective of the prefixed letters.

Disagreements resurface when we turn to secondary aspects. In particular, what is the relative weight granted to the martyrs and Judas Maccabee in liberating the temple? In George Nickelsburg's view the martyrs are given prominence, whereas Judas Maccabee's heroism is downplayed—an opinion shared by Doran (1981), whereas Jan Willem van Henten tends to concede equally important roles to the martyrs and Judas Maccabee.[20] In contrast, John Kampen puts the emphasis on the conflict between "Judaism" and "Hellenism," and not the martyrs.[21] Nonetheless, all commentators agree that the sin-retribution scheme, by which the oppressors of Israel are punished by God, is a major theme in the narrative, whether or not it is associated with the story of the temple's desecration and liberation.[22]

Virtually all critics are aware of the major shortcomings of their analyses: if the central topic of 2 Maccabees is the etiological story of Hanukkah, which is told in the second narrative unit of the work, what role does the Heliodoros story (the first unit) play? And the last unit? And why is the long unit about Judas's wars (the third one) necessary? In other words, how does this definition of the subject matter and purpose explain the extant literary composition of the work?

D. The Author's Religious and Political Sensitivity. The accepted definition of the subject matter and purpose of 2 Maccabees—to which I do not subscribe[23]—further impinges on a scholarly appreciation of the author's religious and political sensitivity. Although the authors of both 1 and 2 Maccabees are routinely described as "pious," only in the latter case does this characterization effectively influence the way many scholars perceive the nature of the work. Thus whereas 1 Maccabees is considered "dynastic history," 2 Maccabees is seen as "theological history."[24] This definition, as well as the insistent characterization of the author of 2 Maccabees as a "pious" (or "devout") man, is upheld even in the most recent scholarship, among both biblical scholars and historians of the rebellion.[25]

This ingrained position explains the enduring opinion that the two authors display quite distinct political stances. The view that the author of 2 Maccabees kept his distance vis-à-vis the Hasmoneans continues to prevail in most recent studies, either explicitly or implicitly. In earlier scholarship, clues to this stance were sought in isolated verses allegedly critical toward Simon Maccabee; in the fact that the narrative breaks off before Judas's death, whereas 1 Maccabees takes its story down to John Hyrkanos;[26] and in the omission of the figure of Mattathias.[27] It was even contended that 2 Maccabees was a learned response to 1 Maccabees' pro-Hasmonean "propaganda," to use the term then accepted.[28] With the emergence of the theory that 2 Maccabees is "theological history," the author's supposed piety became the main ground for setting the works in opposition to each other. Nickelsburg opined that the author sided with the Hasidim, the Hasmoneans' "pious" opponents.[29] Doran also found in what he saw as the author's "religious" perspective a clue to his critical stance vis-à-vis the Hasmoneans.[30] In recent studies this perception seems to persist out of tradition rather than well-thought-out arguments, being sometimes simply implied, although outright statements that one is "dynastic history" and the other "theological history" have by no means disappeared.[31] Nevertheless, some dissent is finally emerging, if only sporadically.[32]

The idea that 2 Maccabees is "theological history" was first aired in the 1970s,[33] with the aim of salvaging the work from its previous appraisal as "pathetic [i.e., bad] historiography." However, while this new label opened fresh avenues of investigation into the properly literary composition of the work, it did little to improve its value in the minds of modern historians scouring ancient literary works primarily for hard facts on which to base "pragmatic" interpretations. If characterizing 2 Maccabees as "theological history" means that the author's primary interest is to demonstrate God's power at rescuing His temple and to show how sinful Gentiles are punished and Israel brought back to God's path, this is of no interest to historians of the Judean rebellion—or so it was perceived.

The gap between what modern historians consider viable evidence for reconstructing the history of the Judean rebellion, and what they believe the author of 2 Maccabees has to say about it, is made no narrower by the complementary—and no less ingrained—view that he perceived and described these events in terms of a conflict between "Judaism" and "Hellenism."[34] In fact although the conviction that this is indeed the ancient author's view is seldom challenged, for some time now modern students of the rebellion have been convinced that the key to comprehending the events in Judea lies in the political, economic, and institutional aspects, whereas the supposedly religious aspects of the crisis were an unintentional by-product.[35] In short, for these critics our author was somewhat blind to what was actually happening in his days, and as additional proof of the man's lack of perspicacity, they quote the fact that despite his pointed hostility toward "Hellenism," he himself was thoroughly Hellenized, as his remarkable command of Greek rhetoric betrays.[36]

The fact that literary students of 1 and 2 Maccabees have so far failed to unravel the connection between form and content in these works; the enduring conviction that the interpretive framework set by the author of 2 Maccabees is worthless to modern historians; the parallel conviction that the "pro-Hasmonean bias" of the author of 1 Maccabees is transparent enough to be easily emended, and that 1 Maccabees is "on the whole factual and objective,"[37] may partly explain why modern historians investigating the Judean rebellion continue to read these works in a basically positivistic way. By this, I mean that the two books are treated as linear accounts from which hard facts may be freely extracted and recomposed into "pragmatic" narratives suiting the modern criteria of rational historical explanation. To take a comparison, the history of the Judean rebellion against Antiochos IV continues to be written like the history of tyranny in archaic Greece was in the 1970s, on the basis of a literal reading of Herodotus. That said, it may be that the sustained influence of Bickerman's groundbreaking study of the Judean rebellion (and to a lesser extent that of Tcherikover) on virtually all subsequent scholarship is also responsible for the persistently unsophisticated handling of the literary sources by modern historians. Before proposing an alternative literary interpretation of the works that opens the way to alternative historical investigations, I will examine the consequences that the current literary appraisal of the two books has on the contemporary historical research on the rebellion.

2. THE MODERN HISTORIOGRAPHY OF THE JUDEAN REBELLION SINCE BICKERMAN

2.1. Bickerman

Published in 1937, Elias Bickerman's *Der Gott der Makkabäer* (*The God of the Maccabees*)[38] marks a watershed in the modern study of the Judean rebellion against Antiochos IV. Bickerman's pioneering methodological claim was that this episode must be investigated in the context of the Seleukid empire, and the historical reliability of the ancient literary sources cross-checked with documentary evidence. In particular, inscriptions casting light on the legal and institutional status of subject communities in the Seleukid empire, as well as on the state practices of the king and the central administration of the empire, provide precious comparative material.[39] For the first time, *Der Gott der Makkabäer* put forward a comprehensive, genuinely historical interpretation of the Judean crisis.

Bickerman starts his historical survey from Antiochos III's conquest of southern Syria from the Ptolemies in 200/198 B.C.E., seeing the legal settlement granted to Jerusalem by Antiochos III on this occasion (*Ant.* 12.138–44) as "the cornerstone for any reconstruction of the fate of Seleucid Jerusalem."[40] At each step of his analysis, Bickerman contextualizes the Judean events against Seleukid political history. The financial strictures of the Seleukid dynasty entailed by the treaty of Apamea (188 B.C.E.), by which the Romans imposed heavy war indemnities on Antiochos III, are used to explain several episodes: Heliodoros's visit to Jerusalem (2 Macc. 3), interpreted as Seleukos IV's attempt to abolish the financial autonomy of the Jerusalem temple, and similarly Antiochos IV's successive replacements of Onias III by Jason and of Jason by Menelaos, explained as Antiochos's will to award the office of high priest to the highest bidder. Likewise the allegations that Menelaos stole and sold temple vessels and helped Antiochos IV plunder the temple to procure the money he owed the king (2 Macc. 4:27–28, 39; 5:15–16) are taken at face value and read in the light of the Apamea treaty; and finally Antiochos's plunder of the temple is made the last repercussion of Antiochos's financial strictures. Next, Bickerman used wide-ranging comparative material to offer a detailed analysis of the legal aspects of Jason's foundation of the *gymnasion* (2 Macc. 4:7–15).[41] He famously identified the "Antiochenes of Jerusalem" as a *politeuma*, an institution known from other cities and denoting an organized community of foreign residents. The resulting legal situation was, in his view, the coexistence of a "sacred city" (a "temple-state") side by side with a polis, a situation he compares with that of Comana in Cappadocia. Finally, Bickerman draws on his knowledge of the Hellenistic *gymnasia* to explain why and in precisely what way Jason's *gymnasion* was offensive to "pious Jews."

Bickerman took advantage of his comparative standpoint to substantially depart from the version of his sources in several instances,[42] relying on his sole intuition as a guide to build his own sequence of events from details plucked by turns from 2 Maccabees, Josephus, Jerome, and Polybius. His basic contention that Antiochos IV's attack on Jerusalem was motivated by the civil strife between Jason and Menelaos follows 2 Maccabees 5:1–14. However, whereas this source blames the episode solely on the personal ambitions of Jason and of Menelaos, Bickerman turns it into a nexus of personal ambition, family rivalries, and the local repercussions of the geostrategic conflict between the Seleukids and the Ptolemies, laying down his immensely influential theory of the Seleukid and Ptolemaic "parties." Drawing on Jerome's *Commentary on Daniel* and Josephus's *Antiquities*, he argues that the Seleukid party in Jerusalem was represented by the Tobiads, who supported Menelaos, whereas the Oniads (i.e., Jason) had been driven to associate themselves with the Ptolemaic party.

This questionable use of the sources is responsible for another highly influential legacy of Bickerman's, namely his dividing the atrocities that occurred under Antiochos IV into three neatly differentiated sequences. First, Antiochos's plunder of the temple is treated as a separate episode,[43] which Bickerman dates to the aftermath of Antiochos's first Egyptian campaign—that is, to the autumn of 169 B.C.E. Next, Bickerman points to a military and political repression,[44] presented as the consequence of the civil strife between Jason and Menelaos reinterpreted as an attempted rebellion of the Ptolemaic party triggered by Antiochos's second invasion of Egypt. This sequence of political revolt and military reaction to it started in the autumn of 168 and lasted till the summer of 163, and was marked by the legal annihilation of the "temple-state," the incorporation of the Jerusalem temple into the polis of the Akra, and the transformation of the "Jewish" community into a subordinated population incorporated within the territory of the polis.[45] Finally the "religious persecution" forms the third sequence, which started in December 167 and lasted till March 164.[46] Bickerman's analysis of Antiochos IV's "political repression" (i.e., the second phase) hinges on his definition of Antiochos III's decree for Jerusalem as a charter by which he had granted the Jews the right to live according to their ancestral laws. But whereas in a Greek city the ancestral constitution determined the political system, "for the Jews 'the laws of the fathers' meant Torah. Only Torah and nothing but Torah." In other words, Antiochos III's "charter" transformed the Mosaic laws into Jerusalem's legal constitution.[47] Therefore when Jason first endowed his *politeuma* with a Greek constitution, he had to apply to Antiochos IV for derogation, since Mosaic law was the valid public statute in Jerusalem under royal guarantee.[48] Next the political repression comprised the abolition of the "charter" and the replacement of Mosaic law with a Greek constitution. In turn, its restoration by Antiochos V in 163 B.C.E. marked the end of the crisis. In contrast, Bickerman famously blames the "religious persecution" on the local authorities, by which he means both Jason and Menelaos, whom he dubs "renegades," "Hellenists," and "reformers."[49] The Maccabean revolt was a reaction to this specific episode.[50]

2.2. Tcherikover

By demonstrating that it was possible to propose a coherent and rational interpretation of the Judean events by contextualizing them in their Seleukid setting, Bickerman allowed a new start. An important complement to his monograph was Victor Tcherikover's *Hellenistic Civilization and the Jews*, which was published in 1959.[51] Tcherikover took the rational reinterpretation of the events further still by questioning Bickerman's idealistic conception of religious matters, and his own reconstruction departs from Bickerman's in several key aspects. First, against

Bickerman's view that the Antiochenes of Jerusalem formed a *politeuma* coexisting with the "temple-state," he argued that the entire city of Jerusalem was turned into a polis as Antiocheia of Jerusalem. However, this polis had an aristocratic character, and therefore full-fledged citizen rights were restricted to the wealthy.[52] Second, he argued that "the conversion of the theocracy to a *polis*" did not entail the "abolition of the Jewish religion," thereby refuting Bickerman's assessment of the impact of Jason's *gymnasion* on "the Jewish faith."[53] Moreover, Tcherikover nuanced Bickerman's appreciation of Jason and Menelaos by defining the former as a "moderate" and the latter as an "extreme Hellenizer." Jason's leading motive was to put an end to the "self-differentiation from the Gentiles" in the political sense alone, given that "the Greek *politeia* ('way of government') was not a religious concept, but a political one."[54] Tcherikover identifies the "privileges [that] were to fall to the lot of Jerusalem as a result of the reform" as being of a primarily political and economic nature.[55]

Finally, Tcherikover put forward a distinctly rationalized interpretation of Antiochos IV's "religious persecution" that departs from the sequence of events found in the sources as boldly as Bickerman's.[56] As he summarizes it, in 1 and 2 Maccabees (in fact, in 2 Maccabees), the events unfolded in the following order:[57] First, collisions between parties or personalities among the Jews; second, the military intervention of Antiochus in the affairs of Judea; next, the persecution; and last, the rebellion of the Hasmoneans. According to this order, the rebellion came as an answer to the persecution. In contrast, Tcherikover argued that the popular rebellion antedated, and hence explained, Antiochos IV's attack: "It was not the revolt which came as a response to the persecution, but the persecution which came as a response to the revolt."[58] This inversion restored the "political purpose" of Antiochos's decrees, but it required additional changes. First, it was necessary to pinpoint an alternative trigger to the rebellion, and accordingly Tcherikover pointed to Menelaos's theft of the temple vessels shortly after his appointment as high priest in 172 B.C.E., the earliest manifestation of popular anger being the ensuing murder of Lysimachos, Menelaos's brother and accomplice, by the mob. Tcherikover further intertwined the religious and cultural issue with an underlying class conflict. He equated the Hellenizers with the citizens of Jason's polis, who belonged to the upper class, whereas the popular movement comprised the poorer sections of the urban plebs who had been excluded from the citizen body, along with the agricultural population of the villages around the city, and the lower priesthood. Moreover, whereas the Maccabees effectively became leaders of the revolt only after the persecution, as the sources claim, in its early stage the popular movement was led by the Hasidim, the "pious." Therefore the king's crackdown on the "Jewish observances" was a rational act dictated by the identity of the rebels' leaders.

Subsequent scholarship viewed Tcherikover's analysis of the class conflict with reservation, and his claim that the rebellion preceded and therefore explained

Antiochos's "prohibition of the Jewish religion" won few adherents. However, by stressing Menelaos's alleged religious cynicism as well as the Hellenizers' economic motivations, Tcherikover paved the way for a strictly rationalized type of interpretation that prevailed in the scholarly circles of the 1970s and 1980s.

2.3. Bringmann

In his *Gott der Makkabäer*, Bickerman had achieved the scholarly ideal of putting forward a comprehensive historical interpretation that was both entirely plausible by the standards of his time and faithful to the testimony of the ancient authors themselves—albeit at the cost of arbitrarily reshuffling their data.[59] In contrast, the approach that crystallized in the 1970s and 1980s, and whose influence is felt to this day, generated a yawning gap between ancient and modern narratives.[60] As the biblical scholars redefined 2 Maccabees as "theological history," this was interpreted by historians of the revolt as a license to disregard the author's frame of interpretation—and all the more eagerly since, like most historians of their generation, they were convinced that the "real" driving forces of history were to be sought in the economic and political motivations of the leading actors. The main proponent of the "pragmatic school," as we may dub it, was Klaus Bringmann with his *Hellenistic Reform and Religious Persecution in Judea*, which was published in 1983. Bringmann's interpretation has been described as a combination of Bickerman's and Tcherikover's works,[61] with the specific twist that he systematically selected from their propositions those most compatible with his extreme instrumentalist conception of religious matters.

Bringmann exploited Bickerman's theme of Antiochos IV's financial strictures further by adding the king's need to secure his position at the court at the beginning of his reign through bribes and by attributing his prospective Egyptian campaign to the war indemnities owed to the Romans.[62] Antiochos supported Jason and Menelaos both because of his money needs and in order to put an end to the internal Judean conflict between Onias III and Simon. The incentive for Jason's "Hellenizing reform" was primarily economic, Jason seeking to promote commerce. Moreover, it is excluded that this reform affected the "traditional Jewish" cult, because it was Jason's and the priests' personal interest to maintain the purity of the temple, as their main source of revenue.[63] Menelaos put an end to Jason's Hellenizing reform for narrow political reasons, the Hellenizers being Jason's partisans.[64] Like his predecessors, Bringmann endorses 2 Maccabees' claim that Menelaos stole temple vessels in order to pay off the tribute arrears to Antiochos, magnifying the episode by arguing that it opportunely replenished the king's coffers on the eve of his Egyptian campaign.[65] In contrast with Tcherikover, he further reverts to 2 Maccabees' (and Bickerman's) version that Antiochos's attack on Jerusalem was caused by the civil strife between Jason and Menelaos, and maintains the distinction between Antiochos's military steps—in particular, his establishment of a colony in Jerusalem—and the "religious reform."[66] The latter was instigated by Menelaos for political reasons: by instituting a new cult in Jerusalem, Menelaos hoped to weaken the hereditary priesthood and strengthen his own power.[67] Logically, because the military colonists were Syrian, he opted for a Syrian cult.[68] Antiochos accepted Menelaos's religious reform because he had no choice and, moreover, did not realize that such a move would be seen as sacrilegious by "pious Jews."[69] The Maccabean rebellion was the outcome of this tragic misunderstanding.

Bringmann's monograph constituted a new turning point in the scholarly investigation of the Judean rebellion. To a large extent, Bickerman and Tcherikover have been read through Bringmann's lens ever since. At the same time, there is a sense that the classical model Bickerman and Tcherikover had put forward was being transformed into a paradigm, by which I mean a set of interconnected assumptions that together form a binding conceptual framework of analysis.[70] The outline of historical facts, the questions asked, and the underpinning theoretical premises that constitute the "Bickerman-Tcherikover paradigm" are interdependent.[71] This is precisely why substantial changes are difficult to introduce in isolation.

For three decades the Bickerman-Tcherikover paradigm has determined the scholarly agenda on the Judean rebellion.[72] This consists exclusively in finding ever more refined rational explanations to the same set of recurrent issues, using the same methodological premises—a positivist reading of the sources, endorsing and discarding the ancient authors' version at will, a rigidly legalistic conception of both the local institutions and the interaction between the king and the local rulers, and an instrumentalist conception of religion—despite the fact that these premises are increasingly outdated. We may pursue our historiographical survey with a review of the salient issues that have been debated in the last three or four decades. Our following step will be to show how questionable the theoretical premises on which the Bickerman-Tcherikover paradigm is based have become. I will take advantage of this survey of topics to situate my own views.

3. THE MODERN HISTORIOGRAPHY OF THE REBELLION: AN OVERVIEW OF THE TOPICS INVOLVED

3.1. The Chronological Issues

The first debated issue bears on the chronological frame. Because of contradictions between the book of Daniel and 1 and 2 Maccabees, it is still disputed whether Antiochos IV attacked Jerusalem at the outcome of his first Egyptian campaign, which lasted from November 170 to autumn 169 B.C.E., or after his second one, in the ensuing summer of 168. The matter is further complicated by uncertainty about the question whether the book of 1 Maccabees uses a coherent dating system or mixes the Syrian-Macedonian and Babylonian time-reckoning systems of the Seleukid era. In the former the first year begins in Tishri (autumn) 312; in the latter, in Nisan (spring) 311.[73] The chronological issue is crucial to scholars who accept Bickerman's argument that Antiochos IV's attack on Jerusalem was a response to the strife between Jason and Menelaos, and endorse Bickerman's distinction between the "political repression" and the "religious persecution." If the "persecution decree"—the "prohibition of the Jewish religion," as scholars now say—was issued in December 167, as Bickerman believed, this means that more than one year elapsed between the two, compelling scholars to speculate about the possible causes of the aforesaid "prohibition."[74]

In my view, on the basis of my literary analysis of the works, the very terms of the debate need modification. On the one hand, all three literary sources may be equally suspected of distorting the number of Antiochos IV's Egyptian campaigns, and there is no means to know whether he attacked Jerusalem in 169 or 168 B.C.E. On the other, I argue that Antiochos's plunder of the temple, his "political repression," and his "religious persecution" are actually three aspects of the same episode. Therefore the chronological framework of my historical reconstruction is based on the following landmarks: thanks to the Babylonian astronomical diaries it is now firmly established that Antiochos IV became king in September 175 and died in November 164 B.C.E.;[75] it is impossible to determine with certainty whether he attacked Jerusalem in 169 or in 168; nor is it possible to precisely date his decree, which meted out punishments in the wake of the rebellion. (While the temple cult was disrupted, it was not "prohibited" by this decree.) Antiochos V's decree (2 Macc. 11:23–26) rescinding his father's decree of suppression probably dates to early 163 B.C.E.,[76] immediately after Antiochos Eupator's accession to the throne.

Likewise it is unclear whether the Jerusalem temple was rededicated before or after Antiochos IV's death. In the former case, 25 Kislev (i.e., the commemorative date of Hanukkah) refers to December 165 B.C.E.; in the latter, to December 164.[77] This issue partly interlocks with the delicate dating of the four official letters clustered in 2 Maccabees 11:16–38. According to Christian Habicht's reconstruction, to which most scholars subscribe, an amnesty was granted to the rebels by Antiochos IV, to take effect on 30 Xanthikos (i.e., March 164 B.C.E.; 2 Macc. 11:27–33).[78] It is therefore likely that Judea was in a state of war in December 165, meaning that the temple rededication at this date is improbable. As the royal inscriptions of the ancient Near East make clear, the restoration of peace was a precondition to the foundation or refoundation (or rededication) of a temple, and there is no reason to doubt that this conception was reflected in actual practice.[79] On this account the date of December 164 B.C.E. for the temple rededication seems more plausible, although no certainty is possible.

John Ma has recently questioned not only Habicht's reordering and dating of these letters but indeed the very version of 1 and 2 Maccabees regarding the circumstances of the temple's rededication.[80] According to him it is implausible that the Maccabees won major victories against Seleukid armies in the years 167–166, because at this time Antiochos IV was gathering his military forces in the region of Antioch, not far away from Judea, in preparation for his Eastern expedition.[81] Therefore, the temple was recovered not through the Maccabees' reconquest of Jerusalem but through negotiations between Menelaos and the Seleukid administration after Antiochos IV's death, Menelaos acting as the head of the Judean elites who had remained faithful to the Seleukids during the time of unrest. By this logic, the four letters of 2 Maccabees 11 date to Antiochos V's first year and respond to Menelaos's petition. The amnesty negotiated by Menelaos must be situated in March 163, and the date of the temple's rededication is uncertain—perhaps 25 Kislev of 163 B.C.E.[82]

3.2. Issues Relating to the Period Prior to Antiochos's Assault on Jerusalem

The debated issues may be reviewed in their chronological order. A first series relates to the period prior to Antiochos's attack on Jerusalem.

A. *The Assault on the City.* As we saw earlier, Bickerman and Tcherikover analyzed the reason for Antiochos IV's assault on Jerusalem in very different ways. Tcherikover sees it as the consequence of the popular rebellion that had started earlier; and Bickerman, of the civil strife under way between Jason and Menelaos. While most scholars accept Bickerman's view, the Olympiodoros inscription, to my mind, now substantiates Tcherikover's belief that Antiochos began his crackdown in reaction to a popular rebellion.[83]

B. *The Plunder of the Temple.* Following Bickerman, some scholars see the theft of the temple's treasures as a distinct episode that occurred in 169 B.C.E. (cf. 1 Macc. 1:20–24), the motive being Antiochos's need to replenish his coffers after his Egyptian campaign.[84] Alternatively, others explain the act of plunder in the context of the military repression that followed the civil strife (cf. 2 Macc. 5:15–21).[85] On the basis of my literary analysis, I argue that the three items distinguished as separate episodes by Bickerman—the temple plunder, political repression, and religious persecution—are actually three aspects of the same event.

C. *The Deposition of Onias III.* According to 2 Maccabees 4:7–10, Antiochos IV deposed Onias III upon Jason's initiative. Bickerman endorsed this version, contending that kings were entitled to depose the high priests at their discretion.[86] While he has been followed by Fergus Millar, who quotes *Antiquities* 12.237–38 in support, other scholars have instead emphasized Jason's personal initiative in the matter.[87] As shown below in Chapters 7 and 10, a closer literary analysis reveals that the presentation of events offered in 2 Maccabees is patently biased. Although Jason did play an active role, it was Antiochos IV who actually took the initiative.

D. Jason's Legal Reform: The Antiochenes. The question continues to be debated whether Jason's reform turned the whole of Jerusalem into a Greek city under the name Antiocheia (Tcherikover's thesis) or whether he instituted a *politeuma* within the city (Bickerman's view).[88] Technically, the problem revolves around the translation of a phrase in 2 Maccabees 4:9 referring to Jason's creation of a list of "Antiochenes." While a minority has reaffirmed Bickerman's view, most scholars have accepted Tcherikover's philological demonstration that "Antiochenes" stands as a predicate accusative: that is, that Jason had received the king's permission to inscribe "those of Jerusalem *as* Antiochenes." Tcherikover's analysis is usually endorsed, together with his mitigating commentary that in actuality full citizenship was restricted to prominent families.[89] Fine-tuning Tcherikover's arguments, Maurice Sartre has suggested that, to judge from attested Hellenistic practice, Jason must have founded a city of Greek type and named it Antiocheia, after Antiochos IV. At the same time, the fact that Jason drew up the list of the new citizens implies that not all Judeans were automatically enfranchised.[90] Recently, Nigel Kennell confirmed afresh Tcherikover's translation, basing his philological analysis on epigraphic parallels, in particular the recently published Tyriaion inscription. While objecting to the translation itself, Doran upheld the view that Jason's reform turned the whole city into an "Antioch-in-Jerusalem."[91] Arguably these technicalities have only a limited bearing on the issue of the social impact of Jason's reform, because even though the fate of the underprivileged urban population is open to question, by far most commentators agree that some segments of the population of Judea—in particular the nonurban one—were not enfranchised, and presumably suffered a degradation of both legal and economic status. In my view, this aspect is decisive for understanding the subsequent troubles. In recent years the foundations of poleis in native cities and temple-states have been adduced as parallels that may cast light on the nature and impact of Jason's reform.[92] In this book I pay particular attention to the polis founded in Babylon under either Antiochos III or Antiochos IV.

E. The Legal and Economic Implications of Jerusalem's Politicization. A related issue concerns the legal implications of Jason's politicization of Jerusalem,[93] which commentators have interpreted in diametrically opposed ways. As summarized above, Bickerman was convinced that Antiochos III's decree of 200/198 B.C.E. had turned Mosaic law into the official *politeia* of Jerusalem, with the consequence that when Jason founded his polis in 175 B.C.E.—which in Bickerman's mind was necessarily endowed with a constitution of Greek type—he needed a derogation from Antiochos IV. Moreover the creation of the polis entailed religious changes. With varying nuances, this view became a basic tenet of the Bickerman-Tcherikover paradigm and in its most extreme form—Bickerman's own—has been recently revived by John Ma.[94] Conversely, Doran has defended the view that Jason's reform had no real legal implications, denying the tenet that the politicization of a native city necessarily meant its adoption of a Greek type of government and institutions, citing as evidence the retention of indigenous titles for officials in various cities of Phoenicia, Syria, and Babylonia.[95] Likewise, Sartre has stressed that Jerusalem's previous political institutions—namely the *gerousia,* priests serving as officials, and the high priest—remained unchanged.[96] I follow Sartre's viewpoint. Moreover, I hold as implausible that Antiochos III's decree endorsed anything but the political institutions of Judea.[97] No less important, several scholars have pointed out that alongside the religious and political factors, the increased tax burden that accompanied Jason's reforms must have played a part in the rebellion.[98] In my view the Olympiodoros inscription brings additional clues to the fiscal aspect of the rebellion, although it invites a modification of its chronology. (See above, §3.1.)

F. The Religious Implications of Jason's Reforms.   Bickerman's thesis that Jason and Menelaos were intent on effecting a Hellenizing religious reform of the temple cult was famously endorsed by Martin Hengel,[99] and more recently also by George Aperghis.[100] Alternatively, Tcherikover and Bringmann emphasized the underlying political and economic motivations, whereby the religious changes were rather the consequence and not the motive driving the reform.[101] Subsequent studies tend to combine the religious and instrumentalist explanations.[102] As shown in this book, the surmise that Jason's reform involved specifically "religious" problems is erroneous.

G. The Gymnasion.   Initiated by Bickerman, the debate aimed at clarifying why the institution of the *gymnasion* was deemed offensive by "pious Jews" seems to be coming to an end, as recent studies now argue that the practices of the *gymnasion* need not have entailed major breaches of religious tradition.[103] In a fundamental study of 2 Maccabees 4:7–15, our main source of evidence on the *gymnasion,* Kennell established that, as elsewhere in the Hellenistic world, the main purpose of the Jerusalem *gymnasion* was the physical training of ephebes.[104] As shown in Chapter 5 below, the question why in 1 and 2 Maccabees the *gymnasion* is described as an "abomination" is a typical example of how a revised literary analysis of the texts may change the very terms of the question.

H. The Plunder of the Sacred Vessels by Menelaos.   So far as I am aware, the overwhelming majority of commentators accept outright 2 Maccabees' claim that Menelaos stole temple vessels to pay the tribute; their disagreement is limited to whether this deed was sacrilegious or not.[105] To my mind, this claim is merely a case of slandermongering, the far-reaching ideological resonances of which are analyzed below in Chapter 5.

3.3. Issues Relating to the Military Repression and the "Religious Persecution"

A second set of issues concerns the military repression and the alleged "religious persecution" (or "prohibition of the Jewish religion," to quote the favored alternative phrase).

A. *Those of the Akra.* In Bickerman's wake, there is a wide consensus that the fortress of the Akra housed both a military garrison and civilians, the latter variously called "renegades" or "Hellenized Jews."[106] Recently, John Ma refined Bickerman's view by sketching out a precise legal procedure that may aptly support it, whereby the polis that had been founded by Jason in 175 B.C.E. was refounded by Antiochos IV following the Judean revolt. The refoundation involved a *synoikismos* (synoecism): that is, the merging of a group of foreigners with privileged locals. The polis received new laws, which were written by a lawgiver, the "Geron the Athenian" of 2 Maccabees 6:1, as well as fortifications (the Akra).[107]

An additional issue concerns the ethnic identity of the foreign settlers, some endorsing Bickerman's view that they were ethnic Syrians, while one scholar has argued they could only be Greeks.[108] This dispute was generated by Bickerman's claims that the Jerusalem patron deity was identified with a Syrian god by the foreigners and that some of the rites described in the persecution accounts are of Syrian origin.

B. *The Identity of the Instigators of the "Prohibition of the Jewish Religion" and their Motivations.* In the wake of Bickerman and Bringmann,[109] some scholars put the blame for the so-called prohibition on the "Jewish Hellenizers," who by deception incited the king to promulgate his decree of prohibition.[110] Others put the blame on the king alone.[111] Strikingly, those who indict the "Jewish Hellenizers" explain Antiochos IV's support for their measures by invoking a tragic misunderstanding: the king supported the prohibition of the "Jewish laws" because he was unaware of their specificity—prompted not so much by hostility as by ignorance.[112] In contrast, those imputing the initiative to the king are sometimes reduced to concede that his motivations remain obscure.[113] John Ma has recently contended that the cultic reforms were but the logical consequence of what in essence was a purely administrative reform, namely Antiochos's refoundation of the polis of Antiocheia, which had originally been founded by Jason.[114]

The settlers have also been assigned some responsibility in the cultic changes. Thus, although most scholars identify Zeus Olympios as a Greek deity promoted by Antiochos, Bickerman argues that this Greek name actually refers to the Syrian god Baalshamin, an identification made by the settlers, who moreover instituted Syrian rites. (This line of argument was recently revived by Aperghis.)[115] Through the literary analysis expounded here, I argue instead that this so-called "prohibition of the Jewish religion" has no historical basis whatsoever and that what is being described in the sources is in fact a literary elaboration of the symbolically more sensitive aspects of the military repression that followed the popular rebellion.

C. *The Authenticity and Actual Tenure of Antiochos IV's Decree (1 Macc. 1:41).* According to 1 Maccabees, a royal decree ordered all the king's subjects to forsake their customs and become one people. In the earlier modern historiography, this generated the tenet that Antiochos IV carried out an active Hellenizing policy, which was allegedly demonstrated by his exceptionally active policy of city foundations as well as his promotion of the cult of Zeus Olympios.[116] Alongside the ongoing discussions regarding Antiochos's policy in these two matters, the actual content and very existence of this decree remain controverted.[117] Ma has recently advocated anew, in a slightly modified form, the old view that Antiochos IV's active policy of state centralization included questions of worship.[118] Through active interventions in the cities of Syria and Cilicia, among them his promotion of Zeus Olympios as a unifying cult, Antiochos IV aspired to create a homogeneous imperial culture within a metropolitan area. Ma suggests that the description of Antiochos's "universal edict" in 1 Maccabees could be a distorted echo of this policy.

The literary analysis proposed below in Chapter 6 supports the conclusion that the notion of a decree "prohibiting the Jewish customs" has no historical basis. That said, it is plausible that Antiochos promulgated a decree with a totally different purpose whose content was either severely distorted by the popular Judean memory or reinterpreted in a contentious way by the author of 1 Maccabees. I contend that the actual decree announced punishing measures following the crushing of the popular rebellion. Alternatively, in tune with John Ma's hypothesis that Geron was the lawgiver of the refounded polis, 1 Maccabees may contain a distorted echo of the foundation decree.

Despite the ongoing debates over these issues, the very framework of discussion changed very little from the publication of Bringmann's monograph in 1983 till the early 2010s. By this I mean that neither the critical machinery used to verify the reliability of the literary sources nor the underpinning picture of the Hellenistic world was revised in any substantial way, even though in the meantime studies of the Hellenistic world at large were anything but static. In particular, our comprehension of the relations between the central power and local communities was thoroughly modified.[119] As a result the tenets of the Bickerman-Tcherikover paradigm have become untenable by the current scholarly standards of investigation of the Hellenistic world, making its interpretations of the rebellion in question increasingly implausible. Since the 2000s, and more clearly since the early 2010s, research on the Judean revolt seems to be taking a new start.[120] To allow a better appreciation of this turn, here follows a discussion of the more questionable premises of the paradigm in light of the current standards.

4. THE BICKERMAN-TCHERIKOVER PARADIGM: A REVIEW OF ITS FLAWED THEORETICAL PREMISES

The main methodological premises of the Bickerman-Tcherikover paradigm may be summarized as follows:

1. The ongoing positivist reading of the ancient literary sources, coupled with an arbitrary handling of their versions; details are either retained as hard facts or discarded, according to the scholar's preconceived frame of analysis, and not as the result of a comprehensive literary analysis of the works.
2. The conception of institutions remains legalistic, and the relations between central government (the Seleukid king and administration) and subject communities are for the most described as top-down processes.
3. Discussions about the Hellenization of Jerusalem in general, and the *gymnasion* in particular, are persistently underpinned by an essentialist view of culture, turning the focus on the wrong questions.
4. The conception of religion remains instrumentalist, with two main consequences: on the one hand, the implications of the steps taken by Antiochos IV, Jason, and Menelaos on the "Jewish religious customs" are downplayed by invoking political and economic motivations. Scholars usually overlook the alternative approach, namely to start anew with an in-depth literary analysis of the ancient sources to reassess what really happened. On the other hand, the various semantic fields of religion, politics, economy, and culture are implicitly understood to be coterminous with ours: hence the way ancient actors and ancient historians are regularly defined as either "pious" or "Hellenized," the latter term being synonymous with either "liberal" or "skeptical" for many commentators. This system of categorizing misrepresents the Judean society.
5. Because of these combined questionable premises, the very criteria guiding the selection of the comparative documentary material employed to support the scholar's case also remain positivist. The legalistic approach, in particular, explains the persisting tendency to overemphasize the parallels with the world of the old Greek cities, although recent efforts to integrate material

from Babylonia must be noted. And while each one of these flawed premises has a specific effect on modern analysis, in some instances they combine and reinforce each other, resulting in a "paradigm" generated by their cumulative effect.

4.1. Positivist Reading of the Sources

In a typically positivist manner, Bickerman crafted his historical outline with details gleaned selectively from diverse sources, treating them as though they were complementary factual databases, in complete disregard for their respective intrinsic literary qualities. Similarly, in line with his *Quellenforschung* training, he explained the differences between the various sources, as well as what he thought were inner contradictions within each, as evidence that the ancient authors themselves had combined several sources in their accounts. Although scholars now pay greater attention to the specificities of each work, as a rule the ancient sources are still basically read in a literal way. As noted above, the most striking product of Bickerman's *Quellenforschung* method is his influential theory about the Seleukid and Ptolemaic "parties."[121] But of the ancient authors, only Josephus and Jerome talk of "parties," and it is no coincidence that they wrote in imperial times.[122] Since Bickerman, students of Roman historiography have demonstrated the extensive authorial interventions of Roman historians in their sources,[123] and we may reasonably think that Josephus and Jerome reread their Hellenistic sources (1 Maccabees and Daniel, respectively) through the lens of the Roman civil wars of late Republican and imperial times. Their Judean "parties" therefore do not reflect independent evidence but denote their mistaken projections from one context to the other. While Dov Gera has questioned their existence by reexamining each case empirically, I argue that these alleged parties may be dismissed altogether, both on the basis of literary arguments and because they have no place in the current understanding of the political culture of Hellenistic societies outside the context of the Greek poleis.[124]

The enduring positivist reading of 1 and 2 Maccabees (and Josephus) may partly be related to the disciplinary background of historians of the Seleukid period. Until recently it was admitted that the analysis of inscriptions and authors like Diodorus Siculus and Strabo did not require sophisticated literary tools.[125] Significantly, the recent impetus toward applying the technique of discourse analysis to the study of inscriptions has prompted Seleukid scholars to propose discourse analyses of 2 Maccabees as well.[126] It is the purpose of this book to show that the tools required for analyzing that text are of a totally different nature. In a recent study, Ian Moyer has demonstrated that the Delian Sarapis aretalogy, recounting how a certain priest won a trial against his own enemies and those of the god, is informed by the Egyptian mythical pattern of the struggle between Osiris and Seth.[127] I argue that this sort of inquiry into the non-Greek intertextual references of texts written in Greek is what is needed in our case, which obviously requires some acquaintance with the local cultures of the Hellenistic world, as I shall explain below (§6).

4.2. The Legalistic Conception of Institutions: The "Charter" Theory

Among the Hellenistic scholars of his generation, Bickerman was a leading proponent of the legalistic conception of the relations between kings and local communities. According to his surrender-and-grant theory,[128] local communities automatically lost their political identity by right of conquest and were reinstated through royal charters. He believed that this is what happened in Judea in 200/198 B.C.E. and identified Antiochos III's decree about Jerusalem (*Ant.* 12.138–44) as one such "charter."[129] As we saw above, this means that this legal document transformed "Jewish" cultic customs into the constitution (*politeia*) of Jerusalem. Precisely because Mosaic law had acquired legal validity, Jason needed a royal derogation to install his *politeuma*, endowed with a Greek "constitution." Moreover the Mosaic law was abolished overnight when Antiochos IV created the polis of the Akra and was then restored overnight by his successor.

Bickerman's charter theory has enjoyed enduring popularity because it enables scholars to rationalize away a wide range of "religious" issues[130]—from the imputed consequences of Jason's Hellenizing reform to Menelaos and Antiochos IV's supposed "prohibition of the Jewish observances." However, not only has the surrender-and-grant model, of which the charter theory is part, been questioned at root, but the legalistic approach underpinning it has also come under sharp criticism by an increasing number of Hellenistic scholars because it unthinkingly apprehends the nature of the Hellenistic kingdoms through the lens of the modern Western state.[131] In its ideal description, this state model is characterized by centralized and standardized administrative structures that are independent from the local social networks. In addition, the relations between the central power and local elites are mediated by a set of objectively defined laws, and the central government makes decisions according to rational motivations and implements them through top-down procedures.[132] In contrast, the stately culture of the Hellenistic kingdoms was closer to what Joseph Manning has called the "bureaucratic premodern state,"[133] wherein the administrative and political structures were organically embedded in the social system, law was customary, and decision making was the outcome of pragmatic negotiations framed by local custom between the central (imperial) power and the local elites, a procedure neatly encapsulated by the phrase "empire as negotiation."

In recent years students of the Hellenistic kingdoms have insisted that no attempt was made to standardize their provincial organization according to a preconceived model. In each province the local political and administrative traditions were respected insofar as they were compatible with the interests of the central power. At the same time they were progressively modified for adaptation to the political culture of the central power. Not only were changes negotiated, but it was the primary interest of the local elites to adapt to the imperial culture, so as to ensure good relations with the imperial power and strengthen their leverage in local affairs. Parenthetically, the process of Hellenization of the Hellenistic East is now analyzed according to this model.[134] In addition, although kings could meddle brutally with local affairs to protect their own interests, their interventions most often consisted in replacing recalcitrant local leaders with more compliant rivals, without modifying the local anatomy of the political order.[135] Only in the old Greek poleis were royal interventions likely to entail a change of *politeia*, in particular from oligarchy to democracy, because of the specific political culture of Greek society. Otherwise, kings by no means meddled with those local customs that regulated the relations between men and gods.[136]

Bickerman's charter theory is underpinned by the modern delineation of the semantic field of politics—an order defined by an objective set of laws regulating the public sphere and liable to modifications by rational decision: that is, precisely the substance of the legalistic approach. It is now the widely shared view that the latter is inadequate for fully comprehending not only the Hellenistic kingdoms but also the Greek polis.[137] If we accept these revised premises, we must exclude the supposition that the Mosaic law became a "political constitution" that could be canceled and restored overnight by royal fiat. In other words, the current perception of the ancient political culture rules out the path posited in the frame of the Bickerman-Tcherikover paradigm as the best means for rationalizing the "religious persecution." Furthermore, the model of "empire as negotiation" also precludes the tragic-misunderstanding thesis. Precisely because of the negotiation process, kings were necessarily aware of the implications of their decisions on the local social order—and this must surely include their effects on what we today call religion.

4.3. *The Essentialist View of Culture: Hellenization*

As just suggested, the concept of empire as negotiation has bearings on our understanding of the process of institutional Hellenization—that is, the transformation of a city of non-Greek political tradition into a Greek polis (or politicization). According to our revised paradigm, instances of institutional Hellenization were mostly if not always initiated by the local elites, and rather than follow a standardized model, they accommodated local traditions.[138] This was true in particular in the realm of the relations between men and gods. Recently Rolf Strootman has analyzed the institutions of poleis in Babylon and Jerusalem according to this revised model.[139] But in order to refute the modern comments about the cultural and institutional Hellenization of Jerusalem in a comprehensive manner, we need to add the issue of religion.

4.4. The Instrumentalist Conception of Religion: Piety versus Impiety and "Hellenism" versus "Judaism"

The instrumentalist conception of religion is the natural complement of the legalistic conception of the Hellenistic state culture. In the case of the Bickerman-Tcherikover paradigm, it is furthermore inseparable from the essentialist conception of culture, because it upholds that the author of 2 Maccabees saw the crisis as a conflict between "Judaism" (a "religion") and "Hellenism" (a "culture").

In the wake of theoretical studies in the anthropology of religion, students of the ancient Mediterranean and Near Eastern religious systems have long since admitted that these were neither a matter of beliefs nor of private choice,[140] in contrast to the religious experience of modern Western societies. Most scholars dealing either with 1 and 2 Maccabees or with the Judean rebellion tend to reason with this modern conception in mind. The differences between the two models and their consequences for the study of the ancient literary works and the historical events are examined in detail elsewhere in this book,[141] and so I will only summarize the issue here. In a nutshell, the basic question concerns the different ways in which the semantic fields of religion, politics, economy, and culture are construed in modern Western and preindustrial societies.

The modernist approach typically involves an instrumentalist conception of religion, whereby the social elites and political leaders manipulate religion as a tool of political, social, and economic control. By this logic, Jason and Menelaos are presented as exclusively concerned with furthering their political and economical interests, and whatever religious measures they take are therefore subordinated to these goals or are merely unintentional consequences.

Moreover, scholars endorsing the instrumental approach have gone so far as to claim that the "Jewish Hellenizers" willfully embraced Greek religious rites in becoming citizens of the polis of Antiocheia and undid their circumcision in order to attend Jason's *gymnasion*. Their behavior was the natural consequence of what instrumentalists see as their "cultural" choice to become Hellenized, which shocked "pious Jews" because it contravened the Mosaic laws.[142] This contention not only rests on a blend of legalistic and instrumentalist assumptions but moreover equates Hellenism with the enlightened and rational "religion of the philosophers." This indeed was what Bickerman claimed, overlooking the fact that in Hellenistic times the Greek themselves were very conservative in their religious praxis.[143] No Greek city—let alone the partisans of Jason and Menelaos—ever embraced the "religion of the philosophers."[144] In particular, it is inconceivable that a significant number of the Judeans who attended the *gymnasion* undid their circumcision for "cultural" reasons—most certainly not the priests, Jason and Menelaos included. Even Bringmann's instrumentalist logic rules out this possibility. By dissimulating their circumcision, priests would have been debarred from entering the temple *temenos* because their new state made them impure, and therefore they would have lost their main source of income—unless we want to claim that such subjects had no scruples about trespassing basic rules of purity; but this requires taking the instrumentalist argument very far indeed, although we have evidence that rules of purity were scrupulously respected by the citizens of the Greek poleis themselves.[145]

The alternative construction of the semantic fields of religion and politics proposed in this book pivots on the idea that in ancient Judea the notions of piety and impiety had political connotations. Therefore in 1 and 2 Maccabees, the systematic characterizations of Judas and Simon Maccabee as pious men, and accordingly of Jason and Menelaos as impious, are contentious constructs on the part of the authors and not objective descriptions of reality. To claim that one leader is pious and another impious was to acknowledge the former as a legitimate ruler and denounce the latter as illegitimate. In light of this, there is no reason to believe that Jason and Menelaos were not likewise dutiful in their roles as high priests, at least in the minds of their partisans.

Finally, if we reject the modernist construction of the semantic fields of religion and culture, problems arise with the custom among scholars of translating *Ioudaïsmos* and *Hellēnismos* as "Judaism" (a religion) and "Hellenism" (a culture).

4.5. Using Documentary Sources as Comparative Evidence: Greek Cities versus Babylonian and Egyptian Temples

From the above it becomes clear that these outdated premises—legalism, essentialism, and instrumentalism—form a nexus coherent enough to offer a paradigm. Hence, the alternative paradigm of the bureaucratic premodern state, with its own nexus of methodological assumptions, entails revising some aspects of the comparative method in use since Bickerman to contextualize the testimony of the ancient literary works. In particular, the nature and geographical scope of the comparative data needs to be redefined.

For Bickerman the Judean events constituted a case study to test his propositions for Seleukid institutions.[146] Accordingly, he focused primarily on documentary evidence from the Seleukid empire to validate the historical plausibility of the literary sources on the rebellion, making only few references to Ptolemaic papyri. Furthermore, despite his tenet that Greek poleis and native *ethnē* (polities) were treated differently by Hellenistic kings, his claim that Antiochos III's "charter" turned Mosaic law into Jerusalem's *politeia* in the (erroneous) sense of a "political constitution" may explain why he chose inscriptions concerning the old Greek cities as his main source for comparison.[147] Bickerman's premises are questionable, however. Although it is undeniable that the world of the Greek poleis may provide useful comparative material, the legalistic approach tends to blur pivotal differences between the cultural traditions of an old Greek polis and those of a non-Greek society centered on its temple—the point being that political institutions themselves are part and parcel of any society's cultural tradition. If instead we shift our focus from the formal definition of the "constitution" to the identity of the elites who were the king's interlocutors, a more interesting source of parallels becomes other non-Greek societies in which temples and priestly elites had a similar status. In this perspective, Ptolemaic Egypt becomes as relevant as Seleukid Babylonia.

As it happens, in the last decade studies have been paying greater attention to non-Greek political models as sources of comparison. Already in the late 1970s, Fergus Millar had made a pioneering use of non-Greek material for comparative purposes. In tune with the scholarly concerns of his days, however, his focus was the impact of Hellenization on the cultural and religious life of non-Greek communities,[148] and the geographical scope of his survey was accordingly the Syrian area, of which the Judean cultural and cultic system is considered a subgroup. In recent years, the availability of studies on Hellenistic Babylon accessible to non-Assyriologists has enabled scholars to realize that that city is particularly relevant to the study of Jerusalem, given their striking similarities of sociopolitical organization and the presence of a Greek polis in both.[149] Since Millar's days, the shift of focus from "culture" to institutions reflects a change in the understanding of the processes of cultural encounter that are lumped under the term "Hellenization."

As noted above, Ptolemaic Egypt cannot be overlooked if our goal is to cast light on the relations between the kings and temples. Recent studies on the relations between the Ptolemaic dynasty and Egyptian temples greatly facilitate comparison with Jerusalem.[150] In my historical reconstruction of the relations between the Seleukids and the Jerusalem temple under Antiochos III, Seleukos IV, and Antiochos IV, I appeal to both Babylonia and Egypt for comparison.[151]

It is of course no coincidence that the ancient Near East as a whole—long adopted by biblical scholars to contextualize their research—rather than the Seleukid empire is the geographical area that, in my view, constitutes the natural social and cultural environment from which comparative material for the study of Seleukid Judea should be drawn.

A. *The Olympiodoros and Tyriaion Inscriptions.* As noted, a shift of focus to the ancient Near East does not invalidate the relevance of Greek inscriptions, as confirmed by two recently published texts that shed outstanding light on the events of Judea on the eve of the rebellion. One is a fragmentary inscription from Marisē (the capital of Idumea) documenting Seleukos IV's appointment of one Olympiodoros as provincial high priest (or some equivalent title) in the satrapy of Koilē Syria and Phoinikē in 178 B.C.E., which sets Heliodoros's visit to Jerusalem (2 Macc. 3) in a new context, vindicating the intuition of several scholars that this episode had to do with taxes.[152]

The Tyriaion (or Toriaion) inscription from Asia Minor for the first time documents the concrete process of raising the status of what was a military settlement and its adjacent village to that of a polis in its own right. The inscription's discovery offered revealing material for the study of Jason's reforms, particularly as the document attests to the prominent role played by the *gymnasion* in the organization of the nascent civic body.[153] At the same time, it has been used to emphasize the military character of Jason's *gymnasion*, which signals a substantial innovation relative to prevailing commentaries.[154]

Conversely, recent studies have raised questions over whether the war indemnity paid to the Romans by the Seleukids caused financial strictures to the dynasty, thereby challenging one of Bickerman's most influential contributions to the analysis of the economic causes of Seleukos IV's and Antiochos IV's behavior in Judea.[155]

4.6. The Paradigm: From Innovation to Impracticality

The continued preference for the Greek poleis as a useful parallel is not the most problematic legacy of the Bickerman-Tcherikover paradigm, whose heuristic limits are made evident by two other factors.

First, the lack of a thorough literary analysis of the ancient works continues to hamper a full understanding of the nature and causes of the Judean rebellion. Because of this omission, in too many cases scholars seize on any comparative evidence that they can explain what is actually likely to be a literary construct mistaken for a hard fact. As a result, some of the basic aspects of the historical outline proposed by the paradigm are becoming increasingly inexplicable in light of our growing understanding of the Hellenistic world and of the Seleukid empire in particular. The most blatant deficiencies of the paradigm are the implicit belief that "Hellenized" means "religiously liberal" and the ensuing claim that Menelaos purloined sacred vessels to pay tribute arrears; and the further claims that Antiochos IV plundered the temple of his peaceful subjects simply to replenish his coffers, that the Judean cultic customs were the object of a formal prohibition by decree, that the Judeans were forced to participate in Greek rites, and that Antiochos was unaware of the consequences of his decisions on his subjects (the popular tragic-misunderstanding thesis).

The limits of the paradigm's practical application are particularly well illustrated by two articles published in the early 2010s by Robert Doran and John Ma, whose reflections respectively make a genuine attempt to incorporate aspects of the updated picture of the Seleukid empire while at the same time keeping within the parameters of the old paradigm.[156] In particular, the two articles are predicated on Bickerman's view that the Mosaic laws were transformed into Jerusalem's "constitution" by Antiochos III's grant of a "charter," and in a way they exemplify the potential pitfalls of basing a comparative approach on epigraphic material stemming from old Greek cities while sticking to legalistic premises.[157] Within these constraints, the two authors seek to break the current deadlock regarding who instigated the "prohibition of Jewish rites" by proposing rational interpretations of the "prohibition" while at the same time refraining from imputing responsibility for it to Antiochos IV. As we saw above, so far all the rationalized (and instrumentalist) interpretations have put the blame on the "Jewish Hellenizers." Eventually, however, both Doran and Ma seem compelled to maintain the implausible argument of the tragic misunderstanding to explain the king's behavior.[158] This is not to say that the attempt to decode and make sense of the persecution accounts is mistaken in itself. My point is that these attempts will remain fruitless as long as they are framed by the Bickerman-Tcherikover paradigm.

The second aspect of the paradigm's counterproductiveness is that available documentary evidence that might undermine the paradigm's premises tends to be overlooked. Thus Bickerman claimed that the military settlers installed in the Akra by Antiochos IV merged with the "Jewish Hellenists" to form the new civic body controlling the territory of Judea during the years of the "political repression," a contention that is readily accepted[159] because it provides an explanation of how the colonists could have access to the temple, and thus makes them ostensibly responsible for introducing foreign rituals. However, not only is there no epigraphical evidence that military colonists received the same status as the local privileged elite upon their arrival, but there is plenty to indicate the contrary—a fact simply disregarded in order to keep the Bickerman-Tcherikover paradigm viable.[160]

The second factor involves a blend of Bickerman's heritage and the enduring prejudice about the ability of the author of 2 Maccabees to understand the world in which he lived. In 2 Maccabees 4:11, we read that Jason "pushed aside the royal concessions [*philanthrōpa basilika*] to the Judeans which were put in place through John the father of Eupolemos."[161] Since Bickerman, the consensus has been that the cancelled *philanthrōpa basilika* were those granted by Antiochos III's decree (Bickerman's charter). But precisely what concessions were granted? As we saw above, Bickerman's charter theory led him to focus on the political significance of Antiochos III's decree, and moreover to contend that the latter concerned the laws of Moses. Yet, in papyri and inscriptions from the Ptolemaic and Seleukid realms, the phrase *philanthrōpa basilika* primarily refers to tax privileges: that is, either exemptions or remissions granted by kings. Although Bickerman was perfectly aware of this meaning—he completed his *Institutions des Séleucides* shortly before his monograph on the Maccabean rebellion—he somehow dismissed its pertinence in 2 Maccabees 4. In subsequent years, the usefulness of Bickerman's charter theory for rationalized (instrumentalist) reconstructions of the Judean events explains why, instead of discarding Bickerman's thesis on the basis of the documentary evidence, scholars have continually attempted to adjust it apace with our changing comprehension of the relations between Seleukid kings and local communities[162]—in my view with scant success.

I believe an additional reason why the fiscal connotation of *philanthrōpa basilika* is persistently overlooked in the context of 2 Maccabees is the ingrained conviction that the work in question is theological history. Moreover, the *philanthrōpa basilika* are mentioned in the very passage (2 Macc. 4:7–15) in which the author speaks of the conflict between *Ioudaïsmos* and *Hellēnismos*. That said, this is also the passage in which he denounces Jason's (in his view) outrageous proposal to Antiochos IV to increase the tribute rate (4:7–9). Moreover, the main topic of Antiochos III's decree is not "constitutional" arrangements but tax exemptions. To my knowledge, the place of the fiscal issue in the present episode has never been seriously explored,[163] but even to begin such an inquiry one must accept the idea that the author of 2 Maccabees did in fact pay attention to fiscal issues and was not concerned exclusively with "religious" matters. This requires a proper understanding of his use of rhetoric—in other words, our inquiry must start with a comprehensive literary analysis of the work, using the appropriate literary and sociolinguistic tools.[164]

5. THE LITERARY ANALYSIS OF 1 AND 2 MACCABEES: A HISTORIOGRAPHICAL SURVEY

Of course, numerous available literary analyses of 1 and 2 Maccabees by biblical scholars have disclosed scores of intertextual connections between these works and earlier Judean traditions,[165] implying that their authors were not impervious to contemporary techniques of literary elaboration. One therefore wonders why these literary investigations have had such a limited impact on those commentators who have mined 1 and 2 Maccabees for their historical reconstruction of the uprising. While the disciplinary gap between biblical scholars and Seleukid historians is obviously a factor, this cannot be the whole answer.

On the positive side, there are two particular fronts on which the identification of intertextual motifs in our texts has had an impact on the work of modern historians. One is the theme of temple plunder central to the story of Heliodoros's visit to Jerusalem (2 Macc. 3): ever since this theme was identified as a well-documented literary topos in pre-Hellenistic and Hellenistic times, historians have been more willing to read a matter of tax litigation into the Heliodoros episode.[166] Similarly, it is now well established that the accounts of the Maccabean wars in 1 and 2 Maccabees cross-refer to tales of war known from the Judean tradition. And while biblical scholars continue to debate whether the template is Joshua's conquest of the Promised Land, or David's wars, few historians today would take the accounts of 1 and 2 Maccabees at face value.[167]

While these particular issues have a fairly narrow focus, other topics with farther-reaching implications for the interpretation of the Judean events as a whole continue to receive a literal reading. This is particularly true of the persecution accounts, but the continued conviction that the author of 2 Maccabees perceived the crisis as a conflict between "Judaism" and "Hellenism" also plays its part. Moreover, as the case of the *philanthrōpa basilika* above suggests, items of information volunteered by the ancient authors that could be of interest to historians get lost because the literary dimension of the works is overlooked. This enduring divide between literary and historical investigations is in part due to the historians' insistence on 1 and 2 Maccabees as linear Hellenistic historiography, like Diodorus Siculus.[168] That said, to my mind the major obstacle to a mutually beneficial dialogue between biblical scholars and historians lies in the working premises of the former. First, it seems that many biblical scholars themselves do not believe their investigations in 1 and 2 Maccabees can have any bearing on historical inquiries: they see literary and religious traditions as one thing and history as quite another. An extreme example is Steven Weitzman's downplaying of the potential implications that his remarkable literary analysis of the persecution accounts could have on historical reconstructions of the period. Although he demonstrated that these accounts are essentially an elaborate literary construction, he framed his literary analysis with a reference to Hayden White's theory of "text as a literary artifact,"[169] and he concluded that his analysis[170]

> does not solve the enigma of Antiochos' persecution.... The real Antiochus almost certainly acted in ways that justified his reputation. But that Antiochus remains inaccessible, his behavior impossible to understand within the political and cultural norms of the Hellenistic world.

This position is clearly conditioned by the scholar's familiarity with the entrenched paradigm, when instead his shrewd literary deconstruction of the accounts should invite a fresh inquiry into the underlying events and break the current deadlock afflicting their historical investigation.

The reason for this critical divide between the literary and historical studies of 1 and 2 Maccabees is, I repeat, the absence of a thorough analysis of their literary composition. Basically, it is essential to identify the structural coherence of a given work in order to understand its author's intentions correctly. Together with the correct identification of the author's rhetorical codes, identifying a structural logic is in turn a prerequisite for assessing whether or not the descriptions found in the sources are reliable facts, and ultimately for reevaluating the factual outline on which modern historical reconstructions are predicated. Before proposing my alternative interpretation of 1 and 2 Maccabees, I will give an overview of the current state of research into their respective literary composition. (See Chapter 1 for a fully detailed discussion of 2 Maccabees.)

5.1. A Brief Overview of the Literary Composition of 2 Maccabees

The first breakthrough in the literary analysis of 2 Maccabees came in the early 1970s, when George Nickelsburg demonstrated that the main unit of the work

(3:1–15:36) was informed by a narrative pattern well known to biblical scholars from the book of Deuteronomy, which includes the four components of sin, retribution, reconciliation, and salvation.[171] This "Deuteronomic" pattern, as it was then called, was the ground to Nickelsburg's innovative classification of 2 Maccabees as "theological history," which quickly became a premise widely shared among scholars. Subsequently, Robert Doran improved Nickelsburg's investigation by arguing that the work is composed of three successive stories of temple liberation (3:1–40, 4:1–10:9, 10:10–15:36), each one structured by the narrative pattern identified by Nickelsburg. Arguing that the sin-retribution motif at the core of the narrative pattern is also found in the Greek culture, Doran further compared 2 Maccabees with accounts of miraculous temple liberations stemming from major Greek temples, and dubbed 2 Maccabees "temple propaganda."[172] Finally, Jan Willem van Henten combined his forerunners' insights, applying further fine-tuning to argue that 2 Maccabees comprises two (and not three) successive and symmetrical stories of liberation (3:1–10:9, 10:10–15:36).[173] Each of these, he asserted, comprises a story of martyrdom and culminates in the institution of a commemorative festival, and moreover is subdivided into two parts, each subsection corresponding to a different Seleukid king.

It would seem, therefore, that advances are being made in the research into the literary composition of 2 Maccabees. However, as we saw from my historiographical overview, the equivocal definition of 2 Maccabees as "theological history" (or "temple propaganda") has hindered fruitful interaction between biblical scholars and historians. Since this classification is based on the author's use of both the sin-retribution (or measure-for-measure) theme and the four-part narrative pattern deriving from it, we need to examine these closer. According to the modernist understanding of "religion" as a separate semantic field, being a "pious-minded" or "theologically"-minded person means to be primarily engaged in speculations about the relations between the divine world and men in such matters as idolatry, purity, sacrifices, and the like, and to be indifferent to the "political" and "social" matters that are of concern to modern historians. As our case study of the *philanthrōpa basilika* above aimed to suggest, this is a misrepresentation. Because the measure-for-measure equation apparently presupposes "belief" in God, and moreover seems to us a naive form of causality, we tend to imagine that ancient authors exclusively used it to reflect upon abstract religious tenets.[174] But in the ancient Near East—or in the Greek cultural area, for that matter—there was no need to demonstrate God's (or the gods') power in history.[175] In societies in which not to believe in God (or the gods) was not an option,[176] that was stating the obvious, and ancient authors knew better. Rather, the measure-for-measure scheme was a weapon in polemics. Admittedly, biblical scholars working on 1 and 2 Maccabees have finally acknowledged this polemical function in the last decade, but they still tend to restrict its scope to the realm of "theological" concerns. Thus

József Zsengellér has argued that the purpose of 2 Maccabees was to promote "the sole legitimacy of the Jerusalem temple," its author—described as a "skilled theologian"—using as his theological basis three Judahite texts that "together presuppose the coexistence of potentially different understandings of the temple." 2 Maccabees "is a special case of temple propaganda, [in that] it proclaims the holiness of the temple, but is dependent upon the holiness of the temple."[177] In turn, Beate Ego has argued that the author wrote at a time when it was necessary to proclaim anew that "the God of Israel is the only true God," in the face of "Antiochus IV's claim of being a god."[178] Again, this is far too restrictive.

Let us take the subtheme of God's chastisement of the villains. If its intention is not to demonstrate God's righteousness, then the focus of the story is not God but the villain.[179] This means that the aim of the author is either to show that *NN* is a villain or to show that even God—and not only *NN*'s human opponents—deems him to be a villain. Going one step further, we may assume that this pattern was not used only negatively, to stigmatize evildoers, but could also be employed positively, to show who enjoyed God's support: that is, to indicate who was the legitimate ruler. Indeed this narrative function is documented in conjunction with the Judahite[180] royal ideology.[181] In conclusion, I argue that in 2 Maccabees the narrative pattern that numerous scholars mistake for "theological history" is instead put at the service of dynastic history, which means that, like 1 Maccabees, it is effectively dynastic history.

5.2. *The Literary Composition of 1 Maccabees*

While biblical scholars seem to readily accept that the author of 1 Maccabees was a "pro-Hasmonean" historian and yet had "theological" concerns, to my knowledge no one has made the leap toward concluding that these two facets are also interconnected in 1 Maccabees.[182]

According to a view accepted since the early days of modern historiography, 1 Maccabees is a linear chronicle composed of four parts: first, the introduction, which is taken to include the section on Mattathias in chapter 2 (1 Macc. 1–2); second, the Judas section (3:1–9:22); third, the Jonathan section (9:23–12:53); and fourth, the section on Simon (chs. 13–16).[183] The fact that the Mattathias section is lumped together with the introduction exposes the *extratextual* viewpoint from which the text structure is analyzed, since only the supposedly historical careers of the three Maccabean brothers are accorded the status of separate sections.[184]

Since the 1980s three scholars have tackled the literary composition of 1 Maccabees and the related question of its purpose. Using a *Quellenforschung*-inspired method, Nils Martola distinguished between the author's original scheme and the extant one, which derives from subsequent additions.[185] In its original state, the work told the story of the liberation of Jerusalem. After a short prologue (1 Macc. 1:1–10), 1 Maccabees 1:11–64 forms the first main section, exposing the "origin of an imbalance" due to the apostasy of the people. The second section runs through 1 Maccabees 2:1–14:15. Once the supposed later additions are removed, the "original" work can be seen to recount the restoration of balance, whose main focuses are, first, the liberation of the temple (4:36–59), and second, the liberation and purification of the citadel (13:49–52).[186] In sum, in Martola's view the pro-Hasmonean slant of the book stems from the additions.

In his turn, David Williams employed rhetorical criticism to divide the work into three sections. The first runs from the beginning to Antiochos IV's death (1:1–6:17), and the second to the end of Simon's Eulogy (6:18–14:15), whereas the third (14:16–24) may be an addition.[187] Williams reveals three interlaced themes in the first and second sections: the pro-Hasmonean stance and the "theological focus" of the work, which he dubs "double causality" (i.e., human and divine), in both sections, whereas the liberation of the temple and citadel[188] appear in sections one and two, respectively. Next, the third section focuses on the establishment of Simon's high-priestly line. The theme of double causality in the two first sections furthers the "pro-Hasmonean advocacy" of the book, since God cooperated in the Hasmoneans' victories. In contrast, the liberation theme is a distinct thread of its own.

As we can see, while both Martola and Williams identify the same two motifs, namely the temple liberation and the pro-Hasmonean slant (i.e., dynastic history), they keep them distinct. Martola's distinction between two redaction layers is an extreme way of maintaining the divide between religion (the apostasy, the temple, and the purification of the citadel) and politics (the Hasmoneans). Although Williams's "double causality" yokes "theology" and the Hasmoneans, the temple remains a distinct theme. By observing that "authorial intention [may] account for only a part, and not the whole, of a text's meaning,"[189] Williams insinuates that the author may have had a unitary purpose in mind—that is, either the temple or the Hasmoneans—but inadvertently ended up with two.

Moreover, while the sections delineated by Martola and Williams, respectively, cut across the basic narrative units structured around the Maccabean characters, neither scholar addresses the question of how the two composition principles might be articulated with each other. Finally, Williams explains that the structure of the second section is more complicated to grasp than that of the first, because the historical material becomes more complex: "For instance, there is only one king [Antiochos IV, in the first] but several royal figures in the latter part of the book."[190] Thus, in his mind, the text is a transparent window on extratextual reality, and neither Martola nor Williams seems to suspect a literary pattern structuring the work's composition; nor does either one of them veer from the notion that 1 Maccabees is a linear chronicle.

The first genuine breakthrough came in 2007, when a short paper by Zsengellér suggested a connection between temple liberation and the Hasmoneans.[191] Drawing on Martola's and Williams's studies of 1 Maccabees and also on Doran's definition of 2 Maccabees as temple propaganda, Zsengellér delineates three sections in 1 Maccabees. These respectively deal with, first, the defilement of the temple (1 Macc. 1); second, its purification and restoration (chs. 2–4); and third, "how the religious restoration inspired the liberation of the people and the country, the installation of a new priesthood" (chs. 5–16).[192] In contrast with earlier studies emphasizing the "theological" divergences between 1 and 2 Maccabees,[193] he argues that the two promote the belief in "the sole legitimacy of the Jerusalem temple" (monotemplism), and as a consequence 1 Maccabees is as much "temple propaganda" as 2 Maccabees. Served by the fact that 1 Maccabees is almost unanimously held as a work of political (pro-Hasmonean) propaganda, he combines the two threads, arguing that[194]

> this monotemplistic commitment also reinforces the pro-Hasmonaean propaganda of the book. The repetition of the heroic deed of Phinehas, the intervention for the sake of the people in time of battle and need, and the restorers of the genuine cult in the sole legitimate temple help to prove the legitimacy of the new high priesthood of the Maccabees/Hasmoneans. This could have been the main purpose of the book.

Whereas Doran was unwilling to contemplate the potential political implications of defining 2 Maccabees as temple propaganda, Zsengellér goes much further here. Nonetheless, he stops short of claiming that both 1 and 2 Maccabees are at the same time "temple propaganda" and have a genuine political content.[195] His depiction of how the temple theology promoted by the two works served the "propagandistic efforts" of the Hasmoneans has an instrumentalist overtone: its purpose was to emphasize "the holiness of the Jerusalem temple . . . as a symbol of holiness and unity [in order to] bring together the different religious groups" around the dynasty, but this aim ultimately failed.[196] In short, whereas the content is theological, the political intent is extratextual. Moreover, Zsengellér eschews the question of the unitary structure of 1 Maccabees. His literary analysis fails to explain how the apparent linear structure of 1 Maccabees, with its units depicting the deeds of the successive Maccabean leaders, and the structure of "temple propaganda," combine to form a well-integrated work.

Thus, at this point in the research on the literary composition of 1 and 2 Maccabees—and hence the basic purpose of both works—two key questions remain unsolved: How do the themes of dynastic and temple history merge? And how are the literary units corresponding to each combined in the overall composition of the two works? The answer I develop in this book is that the two themes may be brought together seamlessly by replacing the concept of temple liberation instead with that of temple foundation—or rather, in our case, refoundation. Second, I argue that the narrative structures of both 1 and 2 Maccabees are cyclical and not linear. These are the premises on which my literary analysis of the two works is predicated.

6. THE LITERARY ANALYSIS PROPOSED IN THIS BOOK

The narrative pattern of temple foundation is well known from Mesopotamian royal building inscriptions and from the Judahite/Judean traditions relating to the foundation of the Jerusalem temple by King Solomon and its refoundation in Persian times. I argue that it informs both 1 and 2 Maccabees, by which I mean that the story of the liberation and purification of the temple central to the Jewish Festival of Hanukkah (the "Dedication") is recast in these two works as a narrative of temple refoundation. It has long been established that the narrative template of temple building was an important vehicle of royal ideology both in Mesopotamia and Judah, the act of building (or rebuilding) the House of the patron deity having an intrinsic legitimizing function—for aspiring kings and usurpers alike. Being thus shaped by the same narrative pattern, 1 and 2 Maccabees must have the same basic subject matter, namely the Hanukkah story recast as a temple refoundation account, which in this specific narrative form necessarily has a legitimizing function. In other words, 1 and 2 Maccabees recount the charter myth of the Hasmonean dynasty. Moreover, the fact that the account of 2 Maccabees is informed by a traditional Judahite narrative pattern is a clear indication that the work was written in Jerusalem, and more precisely within the Hasmonean court itself. I argue that 1 and 2 Maccabees are not opposed, as has been widely surmised until now, but parallel, complementary works that can only gain from being studied together.

There are wide-ranging implications to this identification of the scheme of the temple-building account in 1 and 2 Maccabees. First, we must definitively discard the implicit premises in most modern analyses of 2 Maccabees that religion and politics are distinct matters and that focusing on the temple is the hallmark of a religiously minded individual. Founding the temple was a royal prerogative, and therefore all discourse about the temple necessarily bore political implications. In particular, recounting an act of temple foundation (or refoundation) was an expression of political allegiance toward the founder. In parallel, the way that the books' authors employ the notions of piety and impiety needs to be read in the same light. In both 1 and 2 Maccabees, praising the piety of a leader (Judas and Simon Maccabee) is a token of their respective authors' political support, while imputing impiety or wickedness to a leader (in our case, both the rival high priests and the Seleukid kings) is tantamount to denying his political legitimacy. Such descriptions are tendentious arguments therefore, and not intended as objective descriptions of reality. The modern belief that the Judean civil strife opposed "Jewish Hellenizers" and "pious" opponents is based on a misreading of the rhetorical devices inherent to the two works and must be jettisoned altogether, along with the notion that Jason or Menelaos was a religious reformer, or that both were. Finally, with regard to the cultural devices employed in the texts, the persistent description of the author of 2 Maccabees as "pious" must likewise be discarded:

insofar as not being "religious," in the sense that we today understand this word, was not an option in any society of the time in the entire Mediterranean and Near Eastern area, describing an individual as "religious" (or "pious") has poor heuristic value. If anything, not only does it thoroughly misrepresent the author's intellectual and political project, but it blinds us to what is a distinctly rational analysis of the Judean crisis. As just noted, his focus on Judas's piety actually exposes him as a Hasmonean partisan: it is evidence of his political agenda and has nothing to do with being "pious" in the modern sense of the word.[197]

Second, the primary function of a set narrative pattern is to encode (emplot)[198] and communicate a message. The fact that 1 and 2 Maccabees are informed by a distinct narrative pattern signifies that they cannot be read as linear descriptive accounts like those of Diodorus. First, the use of a narrative pattern turns the entire work into a coherent semantic field. All the narrative components of 1 and 2 Maccabees, and certainly all the important ones, fulfill a function within this pre-set pattern and therefore need to be read in this light. Moreover, the authors of 1 and 2 Maccabees use the cultural and narratives codes that were commonly accepted in the Judean literate circles of both pre-Hellenistic and Hellenistic times to give a meaningful interpretation of the events narrated—for instance, that piety is a condition of the ruler's legitimacy. These codes were underpinned by a symbolic perception of reality by which the world was centered on the Jerusalem temple. By this logic, only events related to the temple—and by extension to the way of life linked to the temple—were deemed meaningful and therefore worth recounting. (While this perception of reality is indeed the hallmark of religious conservatism, it connotes Judean society as a whole and not specific individuals.) However, as I will contend, this perception of reality does not preclude our authors' having a thorough understanding of the world around them. It merely implies that the literary translation of their experience was mediated by more elaborate narrative codes than is the case in the modern Western discourse about reality—and in modern historiography.[199] To some extent, these narrative codes are also different from those familiar from Greco-Roman historiography and therefore demand an even greater process of estrangement from modern scholars. Finally, my claim that our authors' construction of causes and effects is basically rational does not automatically mean it is also objective: political bias is always present, but the same may be said for Polybius and Tacitus.

Although our two authors had equally rational perceptions of the causes and nature of the rebellion against Antiochos IV, their respective accounts diverge in their chronological and topical emphases. With its focus on the origins of the crisis prior to the rebellion, 2 Maccabees points to three decisive "causes" (or at least what the author sees as such): the destabilization of the high priesthood that followed from Onias III's deposition and the correlative pretension of the Seleukid kings to meddle with the appointment of the new high priests (a political issue);

Antiochos IV's demand for an increased tribute rate (an economic issue); and the establishment of the *gymnasion,* which obliquely refers to a comprehensive reform in the status of Jerusalem (primarily a political issue, probably also an economic issue, and possibly also a matter of purity). For its part, 1 Maccabees more specifically foregrounds issues related to the later establishment of a military settlement in Judea: the presence of foreigners in Jerusalem (a political issue as well as, apparently, a matter of purity); the construction of the Akra (a political and military issue, alongside a matter of purity); and the land confiscations (an economic issue, alongside a matter of purity). 1 Maccabees also repeatedly stigmatizes the tax demands of the Seleukids, the issue being apparently political rather than strictly economic. (Paying the tribute was a mark of subjection; and refusing to pay it, a claim to autonomy.) Conversely, addressing the cultural and literary conventions informing the ancient accounts greatly facilitates the task of debunking the myth of religious persecution—and its delusively rationalizing recasting as "prohibition of the Jewish observances." What has been perceived as religious persecution in the later tradition (of which Josephus is an early witness) is, I argue, actually a description of a military repression, written according to the required narrative codes of the time. These various topics will be tackled in detail in this book.

The above outline aims to show how the perception that the ancient authors themselves had of the causes and nature of the rebellion does not detract from the historical understanding that we might expect from the finest Greek historians of the time. What distinguishes the accounts of 1 and 2 Maccabees is the literary means that each employs, and not the analytical capacity of its author. The purpose of this book is to present a historical reconstruction of the Judean rebellion against Antiochos IV that takes as its starting point the testimony of the authors of 1 and 2 Maccabees themselves, as it emerges from my revised literary analysis of these works. The analysis of the events that is put forward by these authors turns out to be perfectly compatible with a pragmatic interpretation of the causes, nature, and course of the rebellion, and may be validated by documentary material (in particular, the Olympiodoros inscription).[200] My thesis is that the decisive factors that triggered the rebellion were the policy of tax increase implemented successively by Seleukos IV and Antiochos IV, as well as the political destabilization that ensued from the toppling of the Oniad dynasty under and at the initiative of Antiochos IV (and not of Jason, as we shall see). Whereas the latter factor explains the power struggle between leading priestly families, the former explains the popular participation in the rebellion itself. In contrast, since the alleged "prohibition of the Judean customs" has no factual basis, it must be removed from the list of factors. Moreover, although the initial stage of the rebellion seems to have been followed by a massacre and harsh repressive measures (the historical core underpinning the persecution accounts), it is hard to determine whether this wave of repression sparked the rebellion anew, or whether the resistance to the Seleukid reaction was continuous. In the former case, the repression may be seen as a secondary factor of the rebellion, but not in the latter.

. . .

When Bickerman wrote his *Gott der Makkabäer* his challenge was to use the Maccabean episode as a case study to test his picture of the organization and operation of the Seleukid state adumbrated in his *Institutions des Séleucides*. Presently, the new challenge is to devise a genuinely interdisciplinary approach incorporating the updated insights not only of biblical scholarship and Hellenistic studies but also of literary criticism and the anthropology of religion. The scope of the comparative material must be widened from the Seleukid empire to the entire ancient Near East, with a privileged emphasis on Babylonia and Egypt. Moreover, the need to explore the cultural and rhetorical codes that were familiar to ancient Judeans, in particular those related to royal ideology, means that the corpus of comparative material cannot be limited to works dated to Hellenistic times but must reach back to Achaimenid and pre-Achaimenid times. Incidentally, given that the literary pattern of temple building and its organic association with royal ideology are familiar to biblical scholars, one wonders why it has not yet been identified in 1 and 2 Maccabees. The possible reasons for this omission are dealt with elsewhere in this book.[201]

Taking up Bickerman's lead, my own historical analysis will hinge on a revised literary analysis of the ancient sources, mainly 1 and 2 Maccabees, cross-checked against our knowledge of the Hellenistic world.[202] Bickerman achieved the scholarly ideal of offering a historical reconstruction that was both plausible for his time and faithful to the ancient sources. The instrumentalist school that, since Bringmann, has created and promoted what I call the "Bickerman-Tcherikover paradigm" doubts the analytical skills of the ancient authors—in particular that of 2 Maccabees—while showing complete disregard for their interpretive frameworks. Although Bickerman's ideal of a perfect coincidence between a modern historical reconstruction and its literary sources is nowadays considered illusory, I aim to show that the interpretations of the crisis proposed by the authors of 1 and 2 Maccabees themselves are eminently tenable starting points for historians seeking a "rational" explanation for the rebellion. Moreover, the emended factual outline that automatically results from my revised literary analysis will make it much easier to propose a historical reconstruction based on the updated methodological premises of our current understanding of the Seleukid empire: the workings of empire as negotiation (and not the legalistic conception of institutions); the new understanding of the process of Hellenization, in particular of institutional Hellenization (and not the essentialist view of culture); a view of religion integrating its political and economic dimensions (without being instrumentalist).

As a study appealing to an interdisciplinary inquiry, this book is aimed both at Seleukid (Hellenistic) historians and at biblical scholars interested in the texts of

Achaimenid and Hellenistic times. I define myself as a Hellenistic historian. For biblical studies, especially of pre-Hellenistic times, I benefited tremendously from private conversations with scholars trained in these fields. They generously shared their knowledge with me and guided me toward the most recent bibliographical material. Although I have no illusions of having overcome all the pitfalls of interdisciplinary inquiry, it is my hope that the outcome of the revised approach presented in this book will open the way for a new paradigm and prompt fresh debate among scholars in the field.

Moreover, the present study aims to make a contribution to the cultural study of the Hellenistic world. Studies of the last decades have pointed to an increasing number of literary texts that, albeit written in Greek and apparently following Greek conventions of style and genre, were shaped by intertextual references to non-Greek literary and cultural traditions.[203] It is my contention that 1 and 2 Maccabees must be added to this growing corpus.

7. SUMMARY OF THE BOOK

The present book is divided into three parts, each opening with a methodological introduction. Part I, "*Ioudaïsmos:* 1 and 2 Maccabees as Dynastic History," examines the central subject matter and purpose of 1 and 2 Maccabees, which, I argue, is to validate the legitimacy of the Hasmonean dynasty—as argued in Chapter 3, the word *Ioudaïsmos* in 2 Maccabees designates the political order of the Hasmoneans. Part II, "*Hellēnismos:* The Causes of the Rebellion according to the Authors of 1 and 2 Maccabees," investigates how the two Maccabees authors themselves present and analyze the causes and nature of the rebellion—as we shall see in Chapter 5 the word *Hellēnismos* refers to the situation of total disruption that was caused by Jason, Menelaos, and Alkimos, the political rivals of the Maccabees who are made responsible for the crisis. Whereas parts I and II offer a literary analysis of 1 and 2 Maccabees, Part III, "History: The Judean Rebellion in Historical Perspective, 200–164 B.C.E.," puts forward a historical interpretation of the causes and nature of the rebellion that is based on it.

The Methodological Introduction to Part I tackles the issue of the relation between religion and politics, with the view to clarify how the notions of piety and impiety in 1 and 2 Maccabees have a political connotation. On the basis of anthropological studies of religion as well as case studies chosen in cognate religious systems from the ancient Mediterranean and Near Eastern area, a critical discussion of the modernist definition of religion is offered, and an alternative definition proposed. The proposed axiom is that the ancient semantic fields coincided with occupational and social functions. Instead of talking of the "political and religious prerogatives of the king" and "the political functions of the high priest," we should delineate the operative semantic categories of ancient Judea in such a way as to define the "royal powers and privileges" alongside "priestly powers and privileges" as two semantic categories. The theoretical discussion is accompanied by 6 concrete assessment of the respective consequences of the old and the new definition on the investigation of 1 and 2 Maccabees on the one hand and the Judean rebellion on the other. In particular, I argue that the new delineation of the semantic fields may help us understand how the narrative pattern of temple building, which was originally coined as royal ideology, came to be employed in conjunction with the high priest in Hellenistic times. This proposed definition will be the operative tool of analysis used in the rest of the book.

Chapter 1 analyzes the literary composition of 2 Maccabees. The main purpose of this chapter is to substantiate my claim that 2 Maccabees is dynastic and not "theological" history. It is argued that the measure-for-measure scheme is used as a polemical weapon at the service of dynastic interests. The analysis of the narrative structure of 2 Maccabees is complemented by a discussion of the concept of cyclical time. I show that the hypothesis of a cyclical composition casts light on the overall structural coherence of the work, which all attempts based on a linear reading have thus far failed to do.

The three remaining chapters of Part I are concerned with the narrative pattern of temple foundation. Chapter 2 may be seen as a complement to the theoretical Introduction to Part I, in that it offers a detailed investigation of the pattern. Through a topical analysis of the formal structure of its classical form, it is shown how the narrative pattern of temple foundation brought together speculations about the cosmic order and an ideal representation of kingship and the social order, the temple and the king serving as mediators between the two. The function of the pattern was to assert the legitimacy of kingship, or rather, of the ruling king, by showing that the social order of which he was the guarantor was the mirror of the cosmic order. When native kingship was replaced by alternative forms of political and social organization, the narrative pattern retained its validating function for the new orders thanks to the gradual adaptation of its narrative components to the new social reality. The chapter includes a diachronic survey of this progressive adaptation, first to the division of power between a provincial governor and a high priest of hereditary right under the Achaimenids and later to the establishment of the high priest as sole ruler in early Hellenistic times. Cultural considerations substantiate my claim that 2 Maccabees stems from Judea and not the Greek-speaking diaspora. Whereas the narrative pattern of temple building is documented in Mesopotamia, northern Syria, and Judah/Judea, it was alien to Greek traditions of political thought. In particular the description of Jerusalem and Judea found in the Letter of Aristeas, a work written in Alexandria, follows a distinct, typically Greek scheme.

The last two chapters of Part I further make clear that both 1 and 2 Maccabees could have been written only at the Hasmonean court. Chapter 3 analyzes how the literary pattern of temple building informs the two stories of the temple rededication in 1 and 2 Maccabees. Furthermore, it is argued that, far from meaning "Judaism"—a translation that anachronistically presupposes that the concept of religion constituted a separate semantic field in the Judean society of Hellenistic times as it does in modern Western societies—the concept of *Ioudaïsmos* is used in 2 Maccabees to capture in a single word the entire semantic field covered by the traditional narrative pattern. Whereas set narrative patterns traditionally used to be epitomized by a synecdoche, one component of the pattern standing for the whole, the author's choice of encapsulating it in an abstract term such as *Ioudaïsmos* was a remarkable intellectual innovation. In addition, whereas the message of the narrative pattern summarized in the term *Ioudaïsmos* is fundamentally political, *Ioudaïsmos* also colors it with an ethnic slant.

Chapter 4 examines the closing narrative units of 1 and 2 Maccabees, namely Simon's conquest and purification of the Akra (whose impurities were a threat to the temple) in 1 Maccabees and what is presented as Judas's "second refoundation" of the temple in 2 Maccabees. It will be argued that these sections are also informed by the narrative pattern of the temple-building account, albeit in an untypical way, with the narrative of 1 Maccabees further hinging on the basically similar narrative pattern of palace building (Simon establishing his palace in the Akra). As might be expected, the closing sections are where the two authors emplotted what most probably was their main political message: to legitimize the combined exertion by the Hasmoneans of the high priesthood and royallike prerogatives (in particular military power). The specific episodes selected by each author to encode this message—Simon's purification of the Akra in 1 Maccabees and Judas's "second temple refoundation" in 2 Maccabees—seem to be the decisive factor explaining the diverging topical emphases of the two works. In particular, it explains why each work stresses a distinct chronological phase (1 Maccabees on the consequences ensuing upon the establishment of a military *katoikia* [settlement] and 2 Maccabees on Onias III's deposition and the politicization of Jerusalem prior to the rebellion). Thus the discrepancies between the two works hinge on a distinct narrative focus rather than on a genuine difference in political or religious sensitivity (or both).

Part II of the book investigates how the authors of the two works themselves present and to some extent analyze the causes and nature of the crisis, from Onias III's eviction to the military repression. The Methodological Introduction to Part II deals with the correlation between historical experience and the literary transcription of it from a theoretical point of view, using the notions of cultural and narrative codes borrowed from structuralist semiotics. These codes were determined by the perception of reality that the Maccabees actors shared with the rest of their society, which may be described as a "symbolic universe." This is a matter not of rhetorical manipulation, nor of consciously motivated bias, but of ethnopoetics. Specifically, this approach explains why the temple is so prominent in 2 Maccabees. Chapter 5 examines the narrative and rhetorical tools that the authors used to delegitimize Jason, Menelaos, and Alkimos, the political rivals of the Maccabees, by making them the embodiment of all the misfortunes that befell the Judeans. As might be expected, their portrayals exploit the same ideological paradigm as that used to assert the political legitimacy of the Maccabees/Hasmoneans, namely the narrative pattern of the temple-building account: whereas Judas refounds the temple and Simon completes its refoundation by cleansing the Akra threatening its purity, the rival high priests contribute to its destruction, Jason by founding an antitemple (the *gymnasion*) and Menelaos by stealing the holy vessels. The term *Hellēnismos* will be read anew in light of this new interpretation of the symbolic meaning of the *gymnasion*: whereas *Ioudaïsmos* means "the legitimate social order attuned to the divine order of things that was founded by the pious Judas when he refounded the temple, and in which the dynasty of the Hasmoneans ruled," *Hellēnismos* means "the illegitimate social order opposed to the divine order of things that was instituted by the wicked Jason when he founded the *gymnasion*."

Chapter 6 tackles the myth of the "religious persecution." The books of Daniel and 1 and 2 Maccabees are identified as primary accounts, whereas Josephus is derivative. The literary analysis discloses the elements of literary elaboration and argues that the historical events lying at the core of the persecution accounts are the atrocities of the military repression. What have been taken as two separate episodes—a military suppression and a religious persecution—were actually one and the same.

Chapter 7 reviews the causes of the rebellion pointed out by the authors of 1 and 2 Maccabees, respectively, as summarized above. Methodologically, this chapter has a pivotal function between the literary analysis of the two works and the historical reconstruction of the causes and unfolding of the rebellion that is the object of Part III of the book. It aims to demonstrate that the two Maccabees authors had a fairly rational understanding of the factors of the crisis by applying to the decoding of their respective causal analyses the notions of cultural and narrative codes discussed in the Methodological Introduction to Part II.

Part III puts forward a historical interpretation of the causes and the unfolding of the Judean rebellion under Antiochos IV. In order to adumbrate its context properly, it is necessary to start our inquiry from Antiochos III's settlement for Jerusalem in 200/198 B.C.E. After a summary of the relevant data from parts I and II of the book in the Introduction to Part III, Chapter 8 surveys the Seleukid conquest and domination of Koilē Syria and Phoinikē under this king (200–187 B.C.E.). The political and fiscal bearings of Antiochos III's decree are discussed in detail. A survey of the leading Judean families is also included, with the view to refuting both Bickerman's influential thesis of the Ptolemaic and Seleukid parties and the theory that there were social and cultural differences between the Maccabees and the "Hellenizers."

Chapter 9 tackles Seleukos IV's policy in Judea and Koilē Syria and Phoinikē (187–175 B.C.E.). This king initiated wide-ranging revisions of Antiochos III's fiscal settlement in the province, which were pursued under Antiochos IV. A preliminary discussion refutes the accepted view that the policies of Seleukos IV and Antiochos IV were determined by the financial burden of the Apamea treaty. The main thrust of the chapter is to propose a new interpretation of the Heliodoros story of 2 Maccabees 3 in the light of the Olympiodoros inscription (the Heliodorus Stele), which documents Seleukos's appointment of a provincial high priest. It is argued that the inscription provides a decisive clue that Seleukos IV engaged in a major administrative and fiscal overhaul in the satrapy. On the basis of recent studies arguing that Josephus's story of Joseph the Tobiad genuinely documents the fact that Antiochos III had conceded the right to levy the provincial tribute to the Ptolemies in the early second century B.C.E., it is argued that the primary purpose of Seleukos's fiscal revamping was to put his grip back on the tribute revenues. This move may have been coupled with a reform aimed at drawing new taxes from the temples' revenues, as suggested by the nomination of the provincial high priest. These aspects seem variously to form the background of the Heliodoros story. In particular, the quarrel between Onias III and Simon the temple *prostatēs* (an official of sorts) that forms a subplot in it most probably reflects the tensions that arose from the new fiscal demands, with Onias III—who as the high priest was responsible for paying the tribute—apparently refusing to comply with the tax increase.

Chapter 10 argues that the reforms that occurred in the early years of Antiochos IV's reign (175–ca. 172 B.C.E.) are the direct follow-up to Seleukos IV's bold fiscal policy. The intrinsic connection between Onias III's deposition and the increased tribute demands are analyzed in detail, and contrary to what the author of 2 Maccabees claims, it is argued that both moves were instigated by Antiochos IV, and not Jason. This interpretation is supported by comparative material from Ptolemaic Egypt, where Ptolemy II implemented a complex set of reforms that tightened the royal grip on the revenues of the temples while involving a progressive change of the priestly personnel. The establishment of Jerusalem as a polis is also examined in detail. The Tyriaion inscription documenting the establishment of a polis in Asia Minor and the evidence relating to a community of *politai* (citizens) in Seleucid Babylon are surveyed, with the view to assess whether they may cast light on Jason's reforms in Jerusalem.

Chapter 11 tackles the Judean rebellion and the phase of repression that followed it, down to Antiochos IV's death (169/8–164 B.C.E.). The reconstruction of the events is based on the premise that a genuine popular rebellion broke out during Antiochos IV's campaign in Egypt. That is, Antiochos IV's assault on Jerusalem was a response to the revolt, and not the cause of it. Therefore the conflict must be described as a "Judean rebellion," and not as "Maccabean uprising." The existence of this rebellion was erased from the record of 1 and 2 Maccabees because of the authors' pro-Hasmonean bias: their conceding that Antiochos's attack was justified would have weakened the legitimacy of the Hasmonean usurpation of power. The chapter puts forward an outline of the rebellion based on a revised reading of 1 Maccabees 1:20–2:48 and 2 Maccabees 5:1–6:11. The fate of the temple is discussed separately. No detailed chronological outline is proposed, since it is impossible to determine whether Antiochos stormed Jerusalem after his first campaign in Egypt or after his second. Nonetheless the preliminary section of the chapter suggests a new methodological approach to the chronological issue, concluding that the second campaign offers a somewhat more plausible context.

8. TECHNICAL ISSUES

A few words are necessary about the translations used and spelling matters.

A. Translations. Unless otherwise stated, all the English quotations from 1 and 2 Maccabees follow Goldstein's translations,[204] first as an homage to a scholar who by his comprehensive introductions to his translations gave a new impulse to the study of these texts, and second because Goldstein elegantly assumes the inescapable fact that all translation is interpretation. Precisely because of that assumption he helped me understand these texts better, even when I disagreed. The quotations from biblical texts follow the New Revised Standard Version. In all translations borrowed from other sources, modifications in the spelling of names for the sake of consistency with the present text will not be pointed out.

B. Spelling. I speak of "Judeans" (and not "Jews") both for the inhabitants of Judea and for their diasporal communities. This is consistent first with my standpoint that history of the ancient Judeans needs to be normalized and next with my working premise that "religion" (which the term "Jews" connotes) is not a separate semantic field in Hellenistic times. Similarly, "Jerusalem temple" is written lowercase, as a sign of normalizing its status. Finally, "Law" is capitalized when it is equivalent to the Hebrew Torah and lowercased in other instances.

The name of the territory of the Judeans changed over time. I speak of "Judah" (adj. "Judahite"), "Yehud" (adj. "Yehudite"), and "Judea" (adj. "Judean") to refer to the pre-Persian, Persian, and Hellenistic eras, respectively. The combinations "Judah/Judea" ("Judahite/Judean") and "Yehud/Judea" ("Yehudite/Judean") are used to refer to transperiod time spans.

The spelling of most ancient Greek personal and geographical names uses a mixed system, as this is increasingly customary in Hellenistic scholarship. The usual Latinized spelling is upheld for names that are part of the general knowledge of educated modern classes. Thus, "Herodotus," "Josephus," "Polybius," "Cyrus," "Darius," and likewise "Nabonidus." For toponyms, note "Dura-Europos" and "treaty of Apamea." In contrast, names falling within the purview of specialized scholarship are transliterated. Note in particular "Antiochos" (not "Antiochus"), "Seleukos," "Menelaos," "Alkimos," "Ptolemaios" (but "Ptolemy" for kings of Egypt), "Hekataios" of Abdera, "Seleukids," "Achaimenids" and also *gymnasion*. Finally, an Anglicized spelling is adopted for the following names: "Maccabee" (not "Makkabaios"), "Jason" (not "Iason"), "Ptolemy" (referring to a king). Note the mixed system used for "Judas Maccabee" in order to avoid possible confusion between the personal name and the name of the Kingdom of Judah. A mixed system will also be used for a few other names (e.g., "John Hyrkanos").

The interdisciplinary scope of this book brings together methodological tools and sources familiar either to historians of the Seleukid empire or to biblical scholars but not necessarily to both. Since it potentially addresses readers from various disciplines, the need was felt to provide basic explanations in all the fields.

PART I

Ioudaïsmos

1 and 2 Maccabees as Dynastic History

METHODOLOGICAL INTRODUCTION

The Modern Semantic Categories of "Religion" and "Politics" and Ancient Societies

A Matter of Semantic Fields

The modern Western conception of religion is based on two tenets: First, religion is a separate semantic field endowed with an essence of its own that exists alongside (and is distinct from) the fields of politics, law, science, and culture; this essence is universal—in particular, it is transhistorical and transcultural. Second, this essence consists in a set of beliefs and rites, in which the former (as thoughts, representations) have primacy over the latter (as actions, praxis).[1] Anthropological studies of religion remained predicated on this double premise well into the 1980s.[2] To this day, most literary commentaries of 1 and 2 Maccabees—and all the historical reconstructions based on these texts that subscribe to the Bickerman-Tcherikover paradigm[3]—are informed by this conception of religion. It informs opinions about the ancient authors and the nature, structure, and purpose of 2 Maccabees; about the roles of Jason and Menelaos, as well as the nature of the civil strife between them and the Maccabees; about what *Ioudaïsmos* and *Hellēnismos* mean; and more. The perceived opposition between 1 Maccabees as dynastic history and 2 Maccabees as theological history is predicated on the modern perception of religion and politics as two separate spaces. The purpose of this Methodological Introduction is threefold: to provide a theoretical discussion analyzing the premises on which the modern definition of religion is based, and exposing in what ways it is inadequate to the study of ancient Mediterranean and Near Eastern societies in general, and Judea in particular; to point to the practical consequences of reading 1 and 2 Maccabees with this modernist definition in mind; and to suggest an alternative definition of the ancient semantic fields that might overcome the misleading tendency to treat religion and politics as separate or even antithetical realms. One major benefit of the present investigation will be to establish that the notions of piety and impiety as used in 1 and 2 Maccabees actually have a political significance. Before exploring an alternative operative construction of the ancient semantic fields, I will first examine the notions of religion and ritual.

I.1. RELIGION AND POWER: THE THEORETICAL VIEW

To reconcile their empirical data with the premise that religion has a universally valid essence, until the 1980s anthropologists of religion asserted that the social extension and function of religion may diverge from one society to the next, and from one period to another.[4] Moreover, the domain of religion may overlap with other domains, in particular politics. For instance, kings of the ancient Near East performed both "political" and "religious" functions. However, as Talal Asad points out, the very statement that religion overlaps with politics presupposes that the two are distinct domains endowed with their own essences.

I.1.1. Religion as a Matter of Beliefs

Clifford Geertz, who was a late and influential proponent of the modernist view of religion, defines its essence as a "system of symbols," a symbol being "any object, act, event, quality, or relation which serves as a vehicle for a conception—the conception is the symbol's 'meaning.'"[5] While there are many symbolic systems, that of religion consists in a set of beliefs—that is, cognitive processes—that may be articulated either as myths or as theological doctrines. More precisely, symbols are religious when they "affirm something about the fundamental nature of reality."[6] The primary function of religious symbols (beliefs) is to provide the cognitive means for people to cope with perceived threats to order (intellectual, moral, and physical, such as life and death).[7]

According to Geertz, symbolic systems belong to the cultural sphere, which in his structuralist scheme interacts with but is separate from the social and psychological spheres. According to this threefold division, religious beliefs induce religious actions (rituals and rites) at the social level by investing these actions with meaning, and produce religious dispositions (emotions) at the psychological level. Ritual per se is meaningless, and acquires significance only in relation to its respective set of beliefs. Moreover, being merely a secondary expression of religious ideas, ritual per se is unable to produce emotive responses; hence, the primacy of the attendant beliefs.[8] Conversely, belief itself is a state of mind, which per se does not constitute any activity in the outside world.[9]

This assumed priority of beliefs (thoughts) over rites (actions) exemplified by Geertz is responsible for the widely shared tendency to overstate the contrast between Judaism (as a monotheistic "religion") and all other ancient "religions," defined as polytheistic. If, in contrast, stress is laid on the ritual system, the distinctiveness of "Judaism" becomes far less obvious.[10] As we shall see in Chapter 5 below, this focus on beliefs has been a major hindrance to the elucidation of why the authors of 1 and 2 Maccabees so virulently attack Jason's *gymnasion*. Moreover, the diffuse view that the purpose of 2 Maccabees is to exemplify God's power down through history, and thereby encourage "Jews" to participate in the Hanukkah festival,[11] is in line with the conception of religion as a state of mind, which does not constitute activity in the real world. If, in contrast, we accept that beliefs are linked to social activity, the purpose of 2 Maccabees may be seen in a totally different light. This brings us to the relation between religion and social power.

I.1.2. Religion and Social Power

The conception of religion as being primarily a matter of beliefs that lend meaning to but remain distinct from the domain of social practices (i.e., belief as a pure state of mind) further implies that as a social phenomenon religion is separate from power. As Asad points out, Geertz eschews the question of how religious symbols are formed, and how and why specific symbols become authoritative in a certain society at a certain time.[12] It is as though "religious symbols possess a truth independent of their effectiveness," to which he objects that the process by which some symbols become authoritative—in other words, how the accepted definition of truth in a certain society is shaped—depends on the institutions of power within that society.[13]

As Asad argues, this "modest view of religion"—namely religion as a state of mind severed from social processes—is the product of historical conditions, and not a universally valid proposition. Its "genealogy" (in Foucault's sense) may be traced to the status of Christianity in Western Europe in the post-Enlightenment era and is the outcome of a drastic shift in the conditions of knowledge production in modern society. In medieval times the Church was the only source of knowledge. Not only was Christian belief built on this knowledge, but the latter perforce embraced the whole domain of social life and was eminently practical.[14] Familiarity with it was "a precondition for normal social life, and belief (embodied in practice and discourse) an orientation for effective activity in it."[15]

With the rise of modern science, industrial forms of production, and the modern state, new sources of knowledge (science) and new forms of institutional power (central government; secular legal courts; and secular schools) began competing with what used to be the exclusive province of the Church. From the moment that knowledge was produced by a secular science and rooted in a-Christian everyday life in which social power stemmed from and was regulated by a-Christian institutions, belief ceased to be the end point of the knowledge process. As a result, the space in which the Church was able to preserve its authority and enforce truth became increasingly restricted: "The churches ... shift[ed] the weight of religion more and more onto the moods and motivations of the individual believer." From being the exclusive source of knowledge, religious space gradually became the space of "'[individual] belief,' 'conscience,' and 'sensibility.'"[16] Religion had become a particular state of mind.

As in medieval Europe, belief was the conclusion of knowledge in ancient societies. There is no word in classical Latin corresponding to our "religion," and I take this to mean that religion did not exist altogether as a semantic category in ancient Rome. The so-called fertility rites were part of agricultural knowledge; rites carried out in wartime belonged to the semantic category of warfare; and so on. Knowing which divinities needed to be invoked, when, where and how, who was to do and say what, using which instruments, and wearing which clothes, was as indispensable to harvesting as knowing when to sow what and which sorts of plow and hoe to use for which plant.[17] In this sense the whole civic community, and not the peasants alone, contributed to its collective prosperity, each category—the Arval Brethren, the *flamen*, the youths of senatorial rank and public slaves who assisted them, and peasants—according to its social competence.[18]

The practical nature of religious knowledge is demonstrable in all ancient societies. In ancient Greek cities, laws governing cult activity were the purview of the civic assemblies. Those meticulously regulated the conditions of ritual purity, stipulating (for instance) how many days must elapse for a man to become pure (*hagnos*) again after the death of a kinsman, or after having sex with his wife or with a prostitute, because being pure was a requirement for citizens to participate in communal ritual activities.[19] In Judea, the distinction between pure and impure animals not only defined cognitive categories but practically determined which animals were fit for human consumption.[20]

I.1.3. The Option to Believe or Not: Piety as Devoutness

From the moment that science and not doctrine became the source of social (practical) knowledge, religious knowledge and belief became optional. In this situation, piety denotes an intensity of beliefs: to be pious means being devout, and the opposite is being liberal or atheist. It is only from this standpoint that 2 Maccabees' description of Jason and Menelaos as impious (*asebeis*) can give rise to Tcherikover's theory about moderate and extreme Hellenizers and to Bringmann's portrayal of Menelaos as a religious skeptic.[21] Analogously, the ancient descriptions of Judas Maccabee and his supporters as pious have earned them a reputation for being backwatered conservatives among modern commentators.[22] When the divine is the only source of knowledge, it makes little sense to define someone as a religious or pious person. In such a system, belief is rooted in the social construction of reality (that is, in the common idea of truth), and in this sense there is no alternative to it. In such a configuration we must reconsider the meanings of *eusebēs* and *asebēs* (pious and impious) in 2 Maccabees. To this end, we must start from an alternative definition of ritual.

I.2. RITUAL AS PERFORMANCE: REDEFINING PIETY AND IMPIETY

The pre-1980s conception of religion as primarily a cognitive process (that is, a set of beliefs expressed both in myths and theological doctrines and in rites) perforce influenced theories on ritual. Rites were conceived as goal-oriented: a rite is performed in order to achieve an effect in the external world (such as to bring rain or to avert a plague).[23] This instrumental conception of ritual could further be loaded with an additional slant of cynicism, all the more so since it also presupposes a disjunction between ritual and private emotions. Speculation about Jason and Menelaos using religious matters to further "extraneous" purposes, such as securing their political position and increasing their revenues, which is so central to the Bickerman-Tcherikover paradigm, falls precisely into this niche.[24] At this point, a brief survey of the premises of this instrumentalist outlook will be useful to situate the alternative theories by contrast.

I.2.1. The Instrumentalist Conception of Ritual, and the Disjunction between Ritual and Emotion

In the modern Western tradition, human emotion (feelings and thoughts) is held to belong to the inner self, whereas proper behavior required by social conventions belongs to the outer persona[25]—a scheme that squares with Geertz's distinction between the social (collective) and psychological (individual) levels. This binary view posits an unbridgeable moral distance between private thoughts and feelings, and public forms of behavior, and it is precisely this tension between inward and outward that enables ritual to be conceptualized as instrumental.

As Asad argues, this posited tension is the product of a radical shift in the perception of the moral economy of the self that occurred in the Renaissance. With the emerging distinction between mind and body (representation and praxis) at that time, the notion of a distance between inner self and outer persona became the object of systematic knowledge:[26]

> When the display of "proper" behavior is disconnected from the formation of a virtuous self and acquires the status of a tactic, it becomes the object of a different kind of theorizing—a meditation not on virtue but on power. But in this case behavioral signs need to be seen as representations conceptually detachable from what they represent; only then can they invite readings in a game of power, a game in which the "true" self is masked by its representations.

Clearly, the instrumentalist view sees ritual as representation. In contrast, in premodern times external behavior was regarded as the visible sign of the inner self, and not something divisible from it.[27] From this standpoint, alternative definitions for ritual may be articulated.[28] Inasmuch as rituals *have* a purpose, this is primarily to articulate the hierarchy between gods and men, and further to accord God or the gods a proper share of honor.[29] Ritual also often, albeit secondarily, serves to "remember" a founding event, which is either commemorated by or reenacted in the rite itself. Conversely, purposes such as achieving an effect in the world, or expressing theological doctrines, are of far less importance, if any at all. The primary concern of the participants, both as individuals and as a collective, is to perform the ritual with scrupulous attention to procedure.[30] Any deviation from prescribed rites is therefore perceived as a reform of sorts. From this standpoint there were many ways by which the foreign settlers of Jerusalem might have caused distress to the local Judeans, even if we rule out that the newcomers sacrificed swine.[31] One instance would be the introduction of a new festival into the ritual calendar. Similarly, as documented elsewhere in the Hellenistic East, the "Hellenization" of local rites simply consisted in borrowing some Greek way of honoring the gods: for instance, by organizing a procession in the Greek style or by wearing a cloth identified as Greek.[32] In this sense, Bickerman's contention that Jason and his partisans adopted the religion of the philosophers, which assumes a shift from a "religion" of *rites* to one of *beliefs,* is totally implausible.

Rituals are also quite simply a form of collective activity—a shared experience.[33] They are the most important form of festivity in preindustrial societies, being an occasion for gathering, rejoicing, eating specific foods, or fasting for contrition. In this function "the identity of the [participating] actors is just as important as the acts which they are called on to perform."[34] Even if the foreign settlers did not do anything reprehensible, the fact that they had access to the Jerusalem temple per se was outrageous to Judeans because of its political significance: they, and not the Judeans, were the legitimate owners of the temple and the territory linked to it. At the individual level, performance may also be oriented toward generating particular moral dispositions and capacities by subjecting the body to systematic practices.[35]

According to this view of ritual, it is primarily a matter of doing, not of believing. In this sense it may be described as performance, and more precisely as apt performance—both in utterance and behavior.[36] This is the notion to bear in mind for our elaboration of an alternative definition of piety.

I.2.2. Piety as Apt Performance

There is an evident link between the apt performance of ritual, the definition of knowledge, and the distribution of power in society. To be effective, rites need to be executed in precisely the way prescribed.[37] This requires discipline, meaning systematic instruction and training. Such training may be articulated either in treatises (like the Community Rule of Qumran) or in a narrative form providing a model to imitate, be that the deity himself or herself or a human exemplum;[38] but first and foremost, mastery is transmitted in the ritual performance itself.

However, the notion of instruction also raises the question whether and wherein rituals differ from other forms of codified social behavior. As recent studies have emphasized, any skilled physical operation serving for daily purposes may become a ritual (for instance, weaving a *peplos* for Athena or preparing sacrificial meat). At the same time, daily actions acquire distinguishing features when these are turned into rituals, a change of status that hinges on the particular circumstances and cultural strategies that generate rituals and not on the intrinsic separateness of the rites themselves. In turn, the acquisition of the practical mastery needed for a specific ritual performance empowers participants to the execution of the corresponding activity in its daily-life setting. The notion of ritualization is used to denote "the way in which certain social actions strategically distinguish themselves in relation to other actions."[39]

This conception of ritual as ritualized daily activity is pivotal to understanding the meaning of piety in ancient Mediterranean and Near Eastern societies. Amélie Kuhrt has stressed that the personnel who took part in the service of the gods in Babylon and Uruk included not only lamentation chanters, liturgy singers, and exorcists, but also "cooks, bakers, brewers, oil-pressers, fishermen, herdsmen (of two types), gatekeepers and those responsible for supplying first-quality dates for divine offerings."[40] Like exorcists, these held land allotted to them by the temple as income associated with their office, and they were enjoined to recite precise prayer formulas when carrying out their task in the service of the gods. As she concludes,[41]

> Clearly people with these mundane-seeming designations were knowledgeable, not just in a specific activity such as butchering or baking bread, but also in the ritual for which they were supplying the temple: they had to be aware of what to supply (the regulations are very precise), at what hour and in what section of the temple it was required and precisely what prayers to recite over which items of prepared foodstuff.

Similarly, the Athenian decree known as Kallias's decree that was voted in the second half of the fifth century B.C.E. to regulate financial matters stipulated that those chosen as treasurers of the Opisthodomos in the Parthenon were to administer the funds of the gods "capably and piously" (*dynaton kai hosion*).[42] The notion of piety sanctions the apt performance of ritualized skilled knowledge. In societies in which outward behavior is the visible sign of the essential self, skillfulness in execution is the token of the performer's inner disposition.

I.2.3. Impiety as a Political Motif: The Contentious (and Political) Use of the Notions of Righteousness and Wickedness

When social power is widely distributed in society, multiple channels of instruction in both intellectual and disciplined knowledge coexist to produce competing forms of knowledge. In ancient Egypt each temple possessed its own Creation myth featuring its patron deity as demiurge. In Judea priestly traditions—both about narratives and practical skills—were a matter of family lore. Distinct family and group traditions about calendars, gestures, prayer wording, garments to wear, and rules of purity could easily become points of contention in power conflicts, given that each side could contend that its own way of performing ritual was the only valid one—that is, the truly pious one. In this air of one-upmanship, it is not hard to see how pretensions of piety might fuel struggles over social and political leadership. Instrumentalist comments on ancient arguments over piety misrepresent their nature, presuming that the choice is between "religion" and rationality (between believing and not believing) when effectively the choice lies between two Creation stories, two calendars, and two sets of purity rules. This kind of polemic crops up in the Qumran text known as 4QMMT,[43] which is cast in the form of a letter addressed (probably) by the Teacher of Righteousness to the "ruler in Jerusalem" and exposes some contested ritual laws that the ruler in Jerusalem is urged to adopt.

When they concerned kings and their competitors or opponents, such claims over piety and impiety were particularly prone to escalating into political arguments. This political slant is well documented in the Egyptian priestly rhetoric of Ptolemaic times. For example, the trilingual decrees issued by the gathered priests in honor of several Ptolemaic kings employ the traditional nomenclature of the pharaoh, representing the king as a religious figure.[44] The decree of 196 B.C.E. celebrating Ptolemy V's victory over the rebels of Lykopolis depicts the latter as *impious* men.[45] Being enemies of the king, they are enemies of the gods: that is, Sethians or Typhonians.[46] As I argue in the chapters included in Parts I and II of this book, the terms "piety" and "impiety" are used as political arguments in 1 and 2 Maccabees. They respectively denote the rightful claim to rule and the lack of requisite legitimacy.

The moment qualifications of piety and impiety become political arguments, they are necessarily contentious—but political bias is not equivalent to instrumentalism. Ironically, a serious approach to ancient religious feeling may allow a more critical reading of their rhetoric than the instrumentalist approach admits. For example, the claim in 2 Maccabees 4:39 that Lysimachos stole "many sacred articles . . . with the connivance of Menelaos" has been mistaken for a factual description by those scholars who have an instrumentalist conception of religion.[47] If we take ancient religion seriously, and also allow that it has political ramifications, it becomes clear that this type of accusation is largely a form of defamation.[48]

I.3. A PROPOSITION FOR AN ALTERNATIVE DEFINITION OF SEMANTIC FIELDS

In this Methodological Introduction my concern so far has been to show how a reappraisal of the theoretical definition of religion and ritual casts new light on our comprehension of 1 and 2 Maccabees and of the nature of the Judean crisis under Antiochos IV. Central to this shift in perspective is a revised understanding of the significance of piety and impiety conveyed in the ancient texts, which shows that the modernist construction of religion and politics as separate semantic categories is totally inadequate to their analysis. To complete this inquiry we now need to explore an alternative definition for these semantic categories, which will serve as a fresh analytical tool for the study of Hellenistic Judea. To this end we may take as a starting point the conclusions of scholars who have investigated cognate religious systems within the realm of the ancient Mediterranean and Near East.

I.3.1. From "Overlapping Political and Religious Functions" to "Royal Functions"

Classical Latin had no word for "religion," an omission that may prompt the deduction that in ancient Rome, fertility rites and rites performed in wartime belonged to the semantic categories of agriculture and warfare. Similarly, in Akkadian there was no term corresponding to our general category "priests." After surveying the different groups of temple staff documented in Babylon and Uruk, Kuhrt concludes that the "only clear distinctions in temple-hierarchy that can be arrived at" correspond to the social classes known from the relative civic context as well:[49]

1. In the upper echelon we find "the small group of temple administrators who between them were responsible for directing all temple affairs": from Nabonidus on (556–539 B.C.E.) this category also included officers appointed by the king.[50]
2. The "officiants of all types": lamentation chanters, liturgy singers, cooks, bakers, and the like.
3. And "below these, temple oblates and employees such as shepherds, cowherds and tillers of the soil."[51]

Those who composed the two higher levels seem to have been drawn "from a specific juridically defined group, the *mār banê* sometimes described as 'citizens.'" A survey of their various activities and sources of income "might indicate that temple and civic community were not easily separable entities."[52]

While there are innumerable examples showing the need to deconstruct the modern dichotomy between civic (or political) and "religious" in ancient societies, Kuhrt's comments point toward an alternative pattern that may be of interest for Judea as well. By means of extrapolation, I propose to delineate a set of operative semantic categories applicable in both ancient Mesopotamia and Judea along the lines of social and occupational categories. Rather than speaking of the "political and religious powers of the king," and of the "political functions of the high priest," I identify the "royal functions" (or "royal powers and prerogatives") and the "priestly functions" as two constitutive and separate semantic categories.[53] The principle I propose is vindicated by both theoretical and empirical arguments: on the empirical side, my alternative semantic categories fit the semantic delineation of existing terms, unlike the modernist divided categories of religion and politics.⁵⁴ A good case in point is the eminently *royal* virtue of righteousness.

I.3.2. A Case Study: Royal Righteousness

The Akkadian and Hebrew texts of pre-Hellenistic and Hellenistic times dealing with royal ideology affirm that the royal virtue par excellence is righteousness (Hebrew ṣedeq). A king is defined either as righteous (just) or as wicked (unjust), and the symmetrically opposed semantic fields of righteousness and wickedness leave no doubt that they encompassed what in modern terms we would distinguish as secular and religious activities. For instance, the Babylonian literary text dubbed the "crimes and sacrileges of Nabû-šuma-iškun" by its modern editor S. W. Cole catalogues "the crimes and sacrileges that a single ruler committed against the inhabitants and shrines of several of Babylonia's principal cult centers."⁵⁵ The king's wide-ranging misdeeds include a change to the ritual calendar ("he turned Festival Vigil and Festival Day into one day"); the violation of a food taboo ("Leek—a thing forbidden in Ezida—he brought to the temple of Nabû and gave to the *ērib biti* personnel to eat"); the introduction of a divine seat belonging to a god from another's temple ("Ea, god of wisdom, whose seat was founded with pure heaven and earth, he made get up from (this) seat befitting his great divinity and makes him reside in the 'Exalted Gate' of Bēl"); the "killing, pillaging, murdering, and imposition of forced labor upon the citizens of Babylon, Borsippa, and Kutha"; the destruction of quarters and streets of Babylon that he turned into royal property; the violation of a sworn treaty; the appropriation of the possessions of the Esagila temple, which he used to make offerings to foreign gods and adorn the women of his palace.⁵⁶ This litany of wrongdoing might seem composite according to modern semantic categories, but actually its contents are consistent if we adopt my revised category of royal functions. It squares with Kuhrt's comments about the Babylonian king's⁵⁷

> personal involvement and close interest in the functioning of temples. . . . The temple represented one of the communal institutions by which royal control of city communities could be maintained.

The same mixture of "secular" and "religious" activities is attested in the corpus of Hebrew literature of pre-Hellenistic and Hellenistic times.⁵⁸ The following excerpt from the Apocalypse of Animals further illustrates how the notions of righteousness and wickedness intertwine the dual aspect of congruity (or not) with social norms and faithfulness (or not) to divine orders (1 Enoch 89:59–62):⁵⁹

> Then he summoned seventy shepherds and threw the sheep and their care to them. And he told these shepherds and their assistants: "From now on, each one of you will individually tend the sheep. Do everything I command you to do. I will hand them over to you duly numbered, and I will tell you which of them are to be destroyed.

Destroy these." ... Next he summoned another one, and told him this: "Be alert and watch everything that the shepherds do to these sheep, because they will destroy far more of them than I have commanded. Record every excess and the destruction done by the shepherds.... Make a record against each individual shepherd of the destruction he causes."

The underlying concept is that divine will and the law of the righteous king are identical. By destroying the "sheep" in compliance with YHWH's command (that is, by punishing "sinners"), the righteous king (the shepherd) acts as YHWH's arm in society. Conversely, destroying more sheep than instructed by YHWH's law is the hallmark of the wicked king. Here, departure from YHWH's path and arbitrary cruelty are one and the same. Social and what we would call ritual precepts are inextricably bound in YHWH's law. The concluding words of 4QMMT are underpinned by the related axiom that by following the (true) law of God, the ruler achieves prosperity for all the people, whereas its neglect will entail punishment for all.[60]

In 4QMMT the addressee, who in all likelihood was a Hasmonean high priest, is compared with David, symbolically assimilating his status to that of a king.[61] Similarly, he is credited with the eminently royal virtues of wisdom, knowledge, and righteousness. This apparently entire transfer of the traditional royal prerogatives onto the high priest is of particular interest. At first sight, this transfer may seem to contradict my proposed redefinition of the two semantic categories of royal and priestly functions, but actually the opposite interpretation is also possible, given that in Hellenistic Judea, the high priest exercised what we call political power. The nomenclature used by modern scholars to describe this situation— "theocracy," "temple-state"—denotes what is seen as an anomaly, in that political power should be exercised by a secular leader, and a temple-state is a different sort of state from a kingdom. In contrast, by my proposed logic the situation is one in which the high priest (partly) fills the slot traditionally denoting the king. In this way, the prerogatives that are merged in the person of the high priest are not religious and political functions but priestly and *royal* functions. Although the anomaly is patent in both patterns of definition, in the former it consists in the overlap between two state structures, and in the latter between two functions—and this interpretation explains why in 4QMMT the high priest may be referred to using the semantic category of the royal functions.

The shift from one template to the other is essential to my argument in the first part of this book, namely that 1 and 2 Maccabees are shaped by the narrative pattern of temple building, which in monarchic Judah was used to denote royal legitimacy. One might argue, however, that native kingship had disappeared from Judea for several centuries, and a narrative pattern so closely associated with royal ideology had no reason to outlive the royal institution.[62] Instead, if we accept my scheme that the high priest filled a slot that traditionally defined the king, it is easier to understand how a narrative pattern articulating royal ideology could eventually be applied to a high priest.[63]

A. Righteousness (ṣedeq) *versus piety* (eusebeia).   One further semantic objection to my proposed identification of the narrative pattern of temple building that informs 1 and 2 Maccabees might be that in these works Judas and Simon Maccabee are praised for their *eusebeia*—a Greek term regularly translated "piety"— whereas the royal virtue connoting royal legitimacy in the Hebrew version of the narrative pattern is "righteousness" (*ṣedeq*).[64] This apparent gap in nomenclature can be explained by the fact that in Judea specifically, *eusebeia* was occasionally used to render the Semitic semantic field of *ṣedeq*. This semantic overlap is worth looking at straight away, since it completes our inquiry into the meaning of piety and impiety in 1 and 2 Maccabees.

The Hebrew equivalent of *eusebēs* (pious) is usually considered to be *ḥasid*, a word found in transliteration in 1 Maccabees to refer to a group of people who joined the Maccabees (the Hasidim, or Asideans). However, a philological inquiry into the Septuagint shows that translations of the root *ṣdq* are not so clear-cut. While the common noun (*ṣedeq*) is regularly translated as *dikaiosynē* (justice), in three occurrences the adjective *ṣadiq* is rendered as *eusebēs*.[65] Yet in turn, *eusebeia* is used to translate a distinct expression, "God's fear" (*yir'at YHWH*).

Although this word-to-word inquiry remains inconclusive, some additional clarity can be had from comparing the vocabulary associated with the good high priests in 2 Maccabees and that of the early rabbinic tradition. Whereas in 2 Maccabees the emblematic virtue of Onias III is his piety (*eusebeia*, 2 Macc. 3:1), in the rabbinic tradition the emblematic virtue attributed to a high priest is his being "righteous" (*ṣadiq*), as illustrated by the nickname "Simeon the Just" (*Šim'on ha-ṣadiq*), which is all the more telling since the identity of the man himself remains unspecified, indicating that he is an archetype rather than a historical character.[66] Moreover, the name of the family of the high priests, the Zadoqites, is related to the same root, endorsing righteousness as intrinsic to the family identity.

Finally, the contextual use of the vocabulary of piety and impiety in 1 and 2 Maccabees further confirms the conceptual equivalence between *ṣedeq* and *eusebeia*.[67] The contrast between the pious Maccabees and their impious enemies in the Greek texts strikingly recalls the distinctions drawn between the righteous and the wicked kings in the Babylonian inscriptions and Judean literary texts. The first thing we learn about Judas Maccabee in 2 Maccabees is his concern for purity (5.27).[68] In Hebrew, Judas's behavior would qualify him as a righteous man (*ṣadiq*). In 2 Maccabees, he is deemed pious. The counterpart to Judas's piety is the wickedness (*asebeia*, "impiety") of his enemies. Thus Simon is called "impious" (*dyssebēs*, 3:11). Lysimachos, Menelaos's brother and deputy, is a "temple robber" (*hierosylos*, 4:42). Menelaos is accomplice to Lysimachos's robbery of the holy vessels (4:39) and later guides Antiochos IV into pillaging them (5:15); hence, he deservedly meets the death reserved for temple robbers (13:6). Alkimos had defiled himself (*memolysmenos*, 14:3) the first time he was high priest. These distinctions clearly show that actions connoting the concepts of righteousness and wickedness in Hebrew correspond to the semantic field of piety and impiety in 2 Maccabees.

I.3.3. Defining Semantic Fields: Hellenization and the Social Structures of Judea

My proposal to replace the modern semantic fields of religion and politics with alternatives that coincide with the sets of royal and priestly prerogatives implicitly rejects the view shared by some scholars that the changes in the social structures of Judea that occurred in Hellenistic times prompted the emergence of a realm of secular activity alongside that of priestly activity. This assumption, which equates Hellenization with modernity and liberalism, used to be especially popular among students of the sapiential books of Ben Sira and Qohelet (Ecclesiastes), which reputedly document the rising class of scribes. Albeit not consensual any longer, the supposition endures even in recent studies.[69] Since, moreover, the portrayals of Jason and Menelaos in the Bickerman-Tcherikover paradigm are informed by the same outdated social model—even though they were priests—I will conclude this introductory chapter with a brief discussion of the question. After the empirical case study of the semantic field of righteousness, this discussion will provide a more theoretical ground for my revised definition of the ancient semantic fields.

According to this model, allegedly explaining the social location of Ben Sira and Qohelet, the traditional social organization of Judea (which was dominated by hereditary priestly elites) was thoroughly shattered as the newly founded Greek-speaking dynasties encouraged the rise of new, secular elites. Trained to Greek literacy, rhetoric, and literature in the *gymnasia*, their members were employed as scribes in the royal administration and successfully competed with the entrenched priestly aristocracies, who by essence were conservative and opposed to the new way of thinking. Alongside the authors of Qohelet and Ben Sira,[70] Joseph the Tobiad (employed as a tax farmer by the Ptolemies) is another paradigmatic figure of this rising "secular" milieu.

Projecting onto Hellenistic Judea the schema of the rise of the bourgeoisie in modern Europe at the beginning of the Industrial Revolution, this model is irreconcilable with the picture of Hellenistic kingdoms as premodern bureaucratic states that is increasingly proposed by today's scholars of the Hellenistic world.[71] From this anachronistic viewpoint, Hellenization anachronistically stands for the emergence of secular knowledge (Greek rhetoric and literature) put at the service of the modern state (the Greek administration of the Hellenistic kingdoms), a development that allegedly relegated the old, priestly aristocracies (like the Church in modern Western Europe) to a defensive position. Alongside modernity and social mobility, Hellenization is also seen to be coterminous with liberalism, in particular liberal religiosity ("Hellenized Judaism").

Recent studies have basically disproved all the key components of this previously established formula. Thus it has been demonstrated that in Hellenistic times the *gymnasion* essentially remained an institution for physical and military training.[72] All recent studies on Greek religion in this period insist on continuity with archaic and classical times, and there is no ground to assume that "Hellenized Jews" were more "liberal" in religious matters than the Greeks themselves.[73] Fresh studies on the stately culture unanimously stress that the native temples remained the privileged interlocutors of the Seleukid and Ptolemaic royal administrations.[74] Although in some cases the old, entrenched priestly families were removed, they were replaced either by other priestly families or by Greek administrators, and not by new, secular native elites.[75] Finally, the traditional priestly elites of Egypt and Babylon were the first to incorporate the study of Greek literacy, rhetoric, and literature in their educational curriculum.[76] Against this background the view that a space of secular knowledge borne by new elites developed in Hellenistic Judea alongside the religious sphere of the temples is untenable.

As a consequence, the depictions of Jason and Menelaos as Hellenizers must be discarded. Moreover, in the absence of any semantic field that could correspond to our categories of religion ("Judaism") and culture ("Hellenization"), the question of what *Ioudaïsmos* and *Hellēnismos* mean in 2 Maccabees arises.[77] The answer requires a detailed analysis of how the old narrative pattern of temple building was exploited by the author of 2 Maccabees. This will be our concern in Part I of this book.

1

2 Maccabees as Dynastic History

INTRODUCTION

For decades, modern scholars have tended to stress contrasts between 1 and 2 Maccabees. In the late nineteenth and early twentieth centuries, this conviction of their divergences was based on stylistic considerations. The sober style of 1 Maccabees fostered confidence in the reliability of the information it contains. In contrast, the stylistic flourishes of 2 Maccabees and the author's indulgence in heavenly apparitions earned it scant esteem.[1] A renewed interest in 2 Maccabees was triggered by several innovative literary analyses published in the 1970s and 1980s, which advocated a wholly different interpretation of the work's nature, based on a greater attention to narrative structure over style. One of these authors was George Nickelsburg, who pointed out that 2 Maccabees was structured by what was then inappropriately called the Deuteronomic scheme of history, whereby the evolution of events was explained through a four-part sequence composed of sin, retribution, reconciliation, and salvation.[2] From this new standpoint, 2 Maccabees was now seen as theological history, rather than as a case of bad historiography. Nickelsburg's recategorizing of the work, which soon became the new consensus,[3] only reinforced the conviction that 1 and 2 Maccabees are opposed in tenor and purpose. In Nickelsburg's view the main clue to the generic difference between the two was the scope and focus of their respective narratives, although he still read the two works as linear chronicles narrating the same events. As he pointed out, 1 Maccabees covers the whole span of time from the causes of the rebellion against Antiochos IV (starting from 1 Macc. 1:11) down to the establishment of the dynastic principle within the Maccabean family and the birth of the Hasmonean dynasty.

Recounting the stories of the three brothers Judas, Jonathan, and Simon, sons of Mattathias, the narrative ends with John Hyrkanos succeeding his father, Simon. In contrast, 2 Maccabees deals with Judas's time alone, and does not follow its story even up to his death, focusing instead on the fate of the Jerusalem temple and the establishment of the Hanukkah festival. Further, the author is fond of "martyr" stories and epiphanies, and foregrounds the role of the martyrs as instruments of reconciliation and salvation, at the expense of Judas's personal role in liberating the temple. In consequence, the ancient author was either indifferent to political concerns (in Nickelsburg's view) or, as others thought, kept his distance vis-à-vis the Hasmoneans in spite of his admiration for Judas Maccabee.[4] In the last few years scholars have become more cautious about the political ideas of the author of 2 Maccabees, but no consensus has emerged—except, perhaps, for the notion that politics was not his main concern.

In the following decades students of 2 Maccabees essentially engaged in refining the new tenet that 2 Maccabees is theological history. Robert Doran defined it as "temple propaganda," while Jan Willem van Henten asserted that 2 Maccabees embodies a theology of martyrdoms.[5] More important, in 1981 Doran was the first to genuinely depart from the tenet that 2 Maccabees is a linear chronicle, by interpreting its structure as a catalogue of three stories of temple liberation.[6] Although in the last few years such heavily loaded phrases as "theological history," "pious author," and the like have tended to disappear from many of the studies on 2 Maccabees (albeit not all: far from it),[7] the real question is not so much nomenclature as the repercussion on how scholars apprehend the work's subject matter and purpose. From this perspective it is not certain that any real shift has occurred since Nickelsburg. As used by students of 2 Maccabees, the concept of theological history is predicated on the modern delineation of the semantic field of religion.[8] This means that the religious and political conceptions expressed in 2 Maccabees are taken as evidence of the author's personal insights. Insofar as he sought any performative effect, scholars argue, this belongs to the interpersonal register alone—such as inculcating moral principles in "Jews" and encouraging them to observe newly founded festivals.

It is striking that this same tacit perspective informs two recent comprehensive commentaries on 2 Maccabees despite their notable surface differences.[9] Daniel Schwartz has advocated the heterodox view that 2 Maccabees was originally meant solely to encourage the observance of the Nikanor's Day festival, celebrating "the establishment of stable Jewish rule in the city [of Jerusalem]." Whereas the sections related to the Hanukkah festival commemorating the temple purification—the festal letters prefixed to the work and 2 Maccabees 10:1–8, containing its core episode—were purportedly added at a secondary stage.[10] In the same line, Schwartz has argued that the subject matter of 2 Maccabees is "the history of the *city* of Jerusalem from the beginning of institutionalized Hellenization under the high priest Jason around 175 B.C.E. and until Judas Maccabaeus's victory over the Seleucid general Nicanor in . . . 161 B.C.E."¹¹ Jerusalem is of interest to the author as the "Jews' capital city and also . . . the capital of its territory, Judaea."¹² In contrast he had no particular interest in the temple, as he was a diasporan Jew.¹³ In short, Schwartz rejects the accepted tenets that 2 Maccabees is about the Jerusalem temple and that the Hanukkah story is its original core, reverts to the old view that 2 Maccabees is a linear chronicle, and revives the diasporan hypothesis. That said, he does not question the view that the temple is a matter of "religion"— claiming only that, in the author's diasporan religious sensitivity, the people is more important than the latter. Hence the work's focus on martyrdom, a "typically diasporan" subject matter.¹⁴ And so he believes are the author's political concerns: "Our diasporan author insists repeatedly that Gentiles and their rulers respect the Jews and Judaism and are benevolent toward them. . . . And as for the Jews, all they want to do is keep the peace."¹⁵ Despite this diasporan relocation, Schwartz's analysis does not veer from the implicit premise that the author writes as a private man addressing fellow "Jews."

In his new commentary on 2 Maccabees, Doran has judiciously substituted the concept of theomachy for that of temple propaganda to describe the subject matter of what he sees as a subgenre of local history, namely "epiphanies of the patron god/goddess in defense of the city."¹⁶ As we shall see in this chapter, he has thoroughly revised his analysis of the narrative composition of 2 Maccabees with regard to his 1981 monograph, so as to incorporate new insights of his own and those of others.¹⁷ In substance, however, his definition of the work's subject matter and purpose remains unchanged. In his new phrasing he states that "the author intended to move his audience both to follow the ancestral traditions of the Jews by narrating how the ancestral God of the Jews had defended his temple in Jerusalem against attackers, and also to celebrate the new festivals inaugurated in honor of this defense."¹⁸ In short, encouraging "Jews" to celebrate festivals is a religious issue; and as such, a private matter.

The literary analysis that will be elaborated in this chapter and the three that follow has close affinities with Doran 1981, in that it sees 2 Maccabees primarily as a succession of self-contained stories in which meaning is communicated through a set narrative pattern. However, although the temple *is* the main signifier in which the meaning of the text is rooted, the narrative pattern that informs the second and main temple story (the Hanukkah story) is identified as a temple-foundation account (in our case, a refoundation), such as is well documented in several areas of the ancient Near East, including Judah/Judea, but is alien to the Greek cultural world. This contrasts with the pattern of temple liberation described by Doran, which is culturally common to both. The implications of this shift regarding the meaning and purpose of the narrative pattern informing 2 Maccabees, and hence of the work itself, are far-reaching. Basically, this alternative identification eschews the modernist delineation of the semantic fields of religion and politics, and places the temple *within* the realm of dynastic history. Moreover, the present analysis of

2 Maccabees' composition departs from Doran in claiming that the narrative pattern used is not consistent throughout, and therefore Doran's suggested scheme of catalogue form is inadequate. In its place, I propose the literary composition of the work as five discrete periods forming a cyclical (as opposed to linear) structure, the cyclical organization of time being another template rooted in ancient Near Eastern traditions—in particular, albeit not exclusively, in the genre of historiography.

As we shall see in this chapter, the cyclical structure of 2 Maccabees is complex, since it is based on the combination of three primary elements: the three successive temple stories, four kings, and four high priests—all three threads brought together in the last period of time.[19] The first cycle is the story of Heliodoros (3:1–4:6), dominated by Seleukos IV and the pious Onias III; the Hanukkah story (4:7–13:26), is a double unit (comprised of 4:7–10:9 and 10:10–13:26) featuring Antiochos IV Epiphanes and his son Antiochos V Eupator on the one hand and the wicked high priests Jason and Menelaos on the other;[20] the fourth cycle is Nikanor's Day (14:1–15:37a), built around Demetrios I and the wicked Alkimos; and the final cycle, contained in the last verse but one of the work (15:37b), refers to the Hasmonean period, in which the dynasty fulfills the two functions of pious high priests and royallike rulers together. The result is best regarded as a dynastic history that, like 1 Maccabees, was written to champion the Hasmonean dynasty.

The revised understanding of the literary composition and of the nature, meaning, and purpose of the narrative that will be explored in detail in this and the three following chapters is predicated on several fundamental premises that depart from the common view just presented. First, 2 Maccabees is situated in an exact geographical and cultural environment. This situation means that although in its *form* 2 Maccabees is written in Greek and is akin to Greek Hellenistic historiography, its *content* is the product of local literary traditions and local intertextuality,[21] these time-old traditions being adapted to reflect on the one hand the political and social conditions of Seleukid and Hasmonean times and on the other the cultural and religious changes of this period. Second, it is essential to establish the social and cultural environment of the work in order to determine the precise connotations of the words and institutions referred to, in particular the institution of the temple. Under the native monarchies of the ancient Near East, including the old Kingdom of Judah, the temple of the patron deity of the city (as in Babylon), or alternatively of the dynasty (as in Jerusalem), was closely linked to the reigning dynasty. This close association between deity and king meant that, as an institution, the temple was to a large extent located *within* the sphere of the royal power, a fact that left its hallmark on the subsequent social and political status of ancient Near Eastern temples as well as on their symbolic representation.[22] In particular, the temple's foundation itself was a royal prerogative. In subsequent times, the motif of temple building remained a major vehicle of ruler ideology. If we situate 2

Maccabees in this cultural context, the assumption that a literary work about temples and martyrs is theological history is clearly unsustainable, especially if theological history is conceived as a genre alternative to dynastic history. Not only is 2 Maccabees a work of dynastic history, but—in line with the Near Eastern and Judahite/Judean traditions of historiography—it also patently employs an ideological argument for dynastic legitimization: namely temple foundation. In other words, the narrative schemes of sin-retribution-reconciliation-restoration and of temple foundation (or refoundation) are actually subordinated to and even put at the direct service of dynastic legitimization.

The classic format of the temple-building account and the way this informs the narrative of 2 Maccabees—and incidentally also that of 1 Maccabees—will be explored in detail in the next three chapters. The present chapter will be devoted to refuting the currently prevailing view that 2 Maccabees is theological history and its implied consequences for the analysis of the work's subject matter and purpose.

Our first step must be to examine the proem, since this is the place where the subject matter of the book is introduced. My basic hypothesis that 2 Maccabees is *not* structured as a linear chronicle necessarily impinges on the analysis of the proem, since it precludes the usual implicit assumption that the latter refers to the content of the book in a linear way. If, in contrast, we accept that it is not organized in a linear, sequential order, the fact that the proem not only gives primacy of place to Judas but moreover takes pains to stress his close connection with the temple becomes an unambiguous token of political support for the Hasmoneans.[23]

Our next step will be to disprove the modern illusion that the sin-retribution (or measure-for-measure) motif was a naive form of causality used to demonstrate God's power in history.[24] No one needs the obvious to be explained, and in societies in which the existence and workings of God (or the gods) in human destiny is a matter of knowledge and not belief,[25] divine righteousness per se was a nonissue, and therefore no material for historians. What was of interest for the ancient was to know *who* and *what* caused the community's divine patron to get angry against His or Her people to the point of letting enemies invade their territory and attack His or Her temple; *how* the reconciliation was obtained, and, most important, by *whom*. In other words, who the sinner (or sinners) was (or were) and what was his (or their) sin, and who was chosen as the new legitimate leader by the people's divine patron. That is to say, the two alternative interpretations of the function of the measure-for-measure motif—either demonstrating God's righteousness or indicating who is the sinner and who the divinely elected leader—are precisely what makes the difference between "theological" and dynastic history. In truth, the author of 2 Maccabees exploited his rhetorical tools—and particularly the retribution theme—in a far less ingenuous manner than is usually assumed. Like Polybius, he used them as an effective rhetorical weapon at the service of partisan

70   PART I: *IOUDAÏSMOS*

opinions, although he acclimated them to the cultural conventions of his own society. In terms of the latter, the meaningful hints to disclose his opinions do not stem from a fondness for epiphanies and martyrs; again, when divine powers are implicated as a pervading source of causality in worldly affairs, these are intended as clues of something else, and not an issue per se. The key lies in the way the moral qualities of piety and impiety are distributed among the characters involved. Quite simply, to describe some leading figure as a pious man is an expression of the author's political endorsement, whereas the opposite allegations of wickedness (impiety) indicate authorial opposition. In our case, the pious hero is clearly Judas Maccabee, whereas the vocabulary of impiety swiftly identifies Jason and Menelaos as his main opponents. The author employed the measure-for-measure pattern of causation to reinforce his case against Judas's main rivals, the "wicked" high priests Jason and Menelaos.

The last two sections of the chapter will deal with the literary composition of the work. First, I will summarize the conclusions of the most incisive analyses produced to date (those of Nickelsburg, Doran 1981, and Henten). As we shall see, Henten was the first to note that the main narrative units coincide with specific units of time, namely the reigns of four Seleukid kings. However, to make the central political agenda of 2 Maccabees apparent requires taking a fifth time unit into account and observing that the five time units comply with a cyclical rather than a linear construction of time. My last section will therefore be devoted to a detailed analysis of how time is delineated in 2 Maccabees.

The main contribution of this chapter will be to reinstate the author of 2 Maccabees, both as an individual and as a writer: far from being a pious, naive believer in divine justice, or a historian careless of the chronology of Judas's military campaigns, he was a highly skilled writer. It may even be contended that the author is a worthy heir to the tradition of the editors whose work is so well known to biblical scholars—indeed, we should not forget that editorial work on the Hebrew texts that were later gathered into the biblical canon of the Massoretic text and the Septuagint was still under way in the author's day.

1.1. THE SUBJECT MATTER OF 2 MACCABEES: THE PROEM'S EMPHASIS ON JUDAS AND THE TEMPLE

2 Maccabees is a work of historiography, as its introduction and conclusion make clear (2 Macc. 2:19–32 and 15:37b–39).[26] The introduction is indeed the place where our inquiry into the subject matter of the work must start. The author's statement of intentions is put forward in a list (2:19–22):[27]

> Jason of Cyrene narrated the history[28] of Judas Maccabee and his brothers, of the purification of the greatest of temples and the dedication of the altar, and also of the wars against Antiochos Epiphanes and his son Eupator, and of the epiphanies from

Heaven in favor of those who vied with one another in fighting bravely and gloriously for the sake of *Ioudaïsmos;* few though they were, they took the spoils of the whole country and expelled the numerous Barbarians, recovered the temple famous in the whole world, freed the city and restored the laws which were on the point of being abolished. All this they accomplished because the Lord in the fullness of His grace became merciful of them.

The content of this list has essentially been scrutinized for what it omits. The seeming discrepancy between the topics spelled out and the extant scope of the narrative has often intrigued commentators and continues to do so.[29] The list has repeatedly been used as evidence that the Heliodoros story in Chapter 3 and the story of the battle against Nikanor culminating in the institution of Nikanor's Day in chapters 14 and 15 are interpolations. The main argument on which the interpolation theory is based is that only two kings, Antiochos IV Epiphanes and Antiochos V Eupator, are mentioned in the proem, but the events associated with their reigns span 2 Maccabees 4:7–13:26. In contrast the Heliodoros story (2 Macc. 3:4–4:6) dates to Seleukos IV's days, and chapters 14 and 15 to the time of Demetrios I. However, as D. Schwartz conceded, the authorial reflections at 5:18 suppose that the Heliodoros story "was part of the book that our author prepared."[30] More important, Doran's thorough literary analysis of 2 Maccabees led him to conclude that there is an inner coherence to the work in its extant form, against earlier claims that different sources and additions can be identified.[31] The new interpretation of the meaning and purpose of the work proposed in Chapters 3 and 4 below will vindicate my proposition that the three temple stories that compose 2 Maccabees (3:1–4:6; 4:7–13:26, and 14:1–15:37a) were conceived as a whole from the outset.

To this end, the list of topics that prefaces 2 Maccabees at 2:19–22 must be considered from the perspective of how it is organized and not in terms of what it lacks. Prima facie we may easily get the impression that it prefigures the sequential order of the full narrative, starting with the purification of the temple (4:7–10:9), continuing with the wars (10:10–13:26), and finally relating the reconquest of the temple (14:1–15:37a). However, several details alert us that this is not the case: the wars against Antiochos Epiphanes are bracketed with those against Eupator, although strictly speaking they belong in the earlier section (4:7–10:9, especially chapter 8). Wedged between the wars and the recovery of the temple, the epiphanies are misplaced. Clearly, the list is not intended to be sequential and is instead organized by topic and in a decreasing order of importance: Judas Maccabee and his brothers are mentioned first, and are immediately followed by the purification of the temple and the inauguration of the altar (2:19), after which come the wars (20), and last the epiphanies (21). This arrangement offers an effective literary device for making the association between the Maccabean family and the temple clear right from the outset. It does not substantiate D. Schwartz's claim that the subject matter of 2 Maccabees is the *city* of Jerusalem.[32] Likewise, the statement that Judas and his partisans fought "for the sake of *Ioudaïsmos*" can be read only as a legitimizing claim.

At the same time, the emphasis, properly speaking, is laid on the purification of the temple and the inauguration of the altar, and not on the institution of the Festival of the Tabernacles of Kislev (Hanukkah), contrary to what we would expect if the purpose of the work were to narrate the etiology of the festival. The difference between the two is fundamental, as these items signify different narrative patterns.[33] Emphasis on the festival would point to the pattern found in Greek stories of temple liberation culminating in the institution of a commemorative festival, as studied by Doran and Henten.[34] In contrast, the allusion to the purification of the temple and the inauguration of the altar that we have in the proem (2:19) recalls the narrative pattern used for describing the foundation and refoundation of temple and altar in the books of Kings, Chronicles, Ezra, and LXX 1 Esdras. (In the following chapter we shall see how the rest of the list [2:20–22] introduces secondary narrative components of the same narrative pattern.) If we accept that the list of events exposed in the proem is not a linear summary of the book, it is no evidence of later additions. The omission of the Heliodoros story may be taken as showing that the narrative function of this episode is subordinated to the main account, the rededication of the temple after its desecration by Antiochos Epiphanes. This will indeed be the conclusion of our detailed analysis of the narrative pattern of 2 Maccabees below in Chapters 3 and 4.

Thus the introduction provides important clues to the author's intention. The role of Judas is highlighted, and his association with the refoundation of the temple and the altar is not only stated explicitly but also points to a narrative pattern whose political implications have been overlooked. The author's use of the sin-retribution pattern of causality buttresses these preliminary observations.

1.2. THE SIN-RETRIBUTION PATTERN AS A POLITICAL TOOL

In Greek as well as in Judean historiographical tradition, works were written not simply to narrate events but to explain them: that is, to give them meaning.[35] Ancient historians made it their task to enlighten their readers about the true, deep meaning of past events beneath the superficial, deceptive appearances—"deep causes" behind "pretexts." Intentions and meaningful patterns could and had to be deciphered behind apparently random events. The author of 2 Maccabees was no exception.

The specific pattern of causality imposed by the author of 2 Maccabees on his "hard facts"[36] has been variously labeled by modern scholars as a matter of sin-retribution, *lex talionis*, measure-for-measure, just retribution, and just deserts.[37]

This pattern of attributing causality is widely documented both in the ancient Near Eastern cultural area, including Judea, and in the Greek one, down to Hellenistic and Roman times.[38] In its simplest form, the sin-retribution equation posits a balance between cause and consequence by which people are rewarded when they behave appropriately and punished when they do not. Moreover, retribution is not arbitrary but is proportionate to sin in both quantity and quality.

The pattern may be used in its simple, binary form or may be expanded into a more complex, sequential pattern comprised of four basic elements: sin, punishment, *repentance, and reconciliation* between a patron deity and His or Her people. Reconciliation, further, implies the punishment of the wicked who had served as the human agent (or agents) of divine wrath. Like the binary sequence, the more complex one is widely documented in the ancient Near Eastern and the Greek cultural areas alike. Doran and Henten identify it in the Greek pattern of temple and city liberations;[39] and as we shall see in the next chapter, it underpins the ancient Near Eastern pattern that was used to relate the destruction and rebuilding of temples.

There is some paradox in stating that the presence of this scheme—in both its two-part and its four-part sequences—in 2 Maccabees evinces the author's theologically oriented view of history, at the same time insisting that it is found in Greek authors of Hellenistic times such as Polybius. Polybius saw himself and is seen by modern scholars as the quintessential representative of "pragmatic history," and the *political* function of the *lex talionis* in his work may easily be demonstrated. Thus in a passage quoted and commented on by Doran, Polybius uses this scheme against Philip V of Macedon, his most hated political figure.[40] When Philip V planned war on Rome, he was led by "Furies" to conduct wide deportations of people as part of his strategic preparation, and he had the children of slain citizens imprisoned in order to suppress growing unrest. But resentment against him only increased and eventually drove him mad. Retaliation finally came when Furies induced Philip to kill his own son. Formally speaking, the measure-for-measure equation applies to the deaths of the children, but the political overtone of the moralizing story can hardly be missed. Philip's real mistake, in Polybius's view, was to plan war on Rome. As a commentator, Polybius uses the measure-for-measure equation as a form of divine endorsement of his own political (and military) opinions, a tactic that is by no means exceptional. In tune with the need to posit harmony between men and gods in ancient societies, the measure-for-measure equation was employed in narrative texts as a heavenly confirmation that human feelings are correct. Villains are enemies not of men alone but also of the gods. Put differently, political enemies are (always) sinners too. For our discussion, it is important to stress the formula's correct logical order: it was not assumed that sinners become political enemies qua sinners, but political enemies were denounced as sinners before the gods (or before God) as well. Why would things be different in 2 Maccabees?

1.2.1. The Sin-Retribution Pattern in 2 Maccabees

Applications of the *lex talionis* are found throughout 2 Maccabees, and most examples are straightforward, showing how sins incur measured retributions. Their repetitiveness can easily lull the reader into believing that its author has a naively pious perception of reality. To take a few examples,[41] Lysimachos, who had stolen vessels from the temple treasure, is killed by the crowd near the treasure room (4:42); those who had set fire to the sacred doors are burned alive (8:33); Antiochos IV's general Nikanor son of Patroklos, who thought badly of the Judeans, ends up a fugitive slave running for his life (8:34–36, echoing 8:9–11); Demetrios I's general Nikanor, who had stretched out his hand against the temple in blasphemy, has his right hand cut off by Judas Maccabee (15:32–33); Antiochos is struck by two successive measure-for-measure retributions: first, his belly is inflicted with an incurable ill, "in all justice" (*panu dikaiōs*), since he tormented the bellies of others (9:5–6). Yet Antiochos's real sin was his *hybris* against God, and thus he falls to the ground, he who "had been thinking of giving orders to the waves of the sea and had been planning to weigh the peaks of the mountains in a balance" (9:8). Conversely, God is merciful both to the Judeans and to Antiochos V in thwarting the latter before he could do the same (13:20–24)—and Antiochos V does not suffer divine retribution.

While the examples just listed refer to incidents of limited scope, the measure-for-measure equation informs the author's reading of major events as well, as Nickelsburg, Doran, and Henten have duly pointed out. All instances are easy to spot, since they are punctuated by authorial comments making the correlation between sin and punishment explicit. Three particularly long digressions are frequently identified as evidence that the author of 2 Maccabees wrote his historiographical account to illustrate his theological view that the Jews were being punished for their sins.[42] This is only part of the picture, however. Contrary to what is usually assumed, the author does not conceive the people as a social congregation enjoying unmediated relations with its divine patron, but he is definitely interested in its leadership—that is, interested in political affairs.

A. Political Use of the Sin-Retribution Pattern: Identifying the Cause . . . and the Culprits. When calamities occur, the pattern of causality was triggered in the reverse order.[43] Insofar as calamities were held to be the direct consequence of God's wrath against His people because of their sins, the first thing to do in order to bring the calamities to an end was to identify the offending acts and atone for them. The author of 2 Maccabees proceeded by similar induction. For him, the desecration of the temple and the persecution of the Judeans under Antiochos IV were unequivocal signs of God's ire. Consequently, the sin that triggered these calamities is what the author set out to disclose in his work. Given that retribution is always measured in both quantity and quality, he needed to clarify in what the *lex talionis* consisted in this case, hence the long reflection concluding the account of setting up the *gymnasion* (2 Macc. 4:16):

> For that very reason, grievous troubles came upon them: the Greeks, whose way of life they admired and whom they wished to ape in every way, became their enemies and the executors of their punishment.

Thus the talionlike equivalence is encapsulated in the concept of Greekness: that is, the Judeans' sin was having adopted purportedly Greek customs, and the retribution was the desecration of the altar at which these supposedly Greek rites were performed in honor of an alien god.[44]

But what about the leading sinner, Jason? Intriguingly, the measure-for-measure principle is applied in the most unsatisfying way precisely when it comes to the two characters about whom the author might be expected to be most cautious: Jason and Menelaos, the two wicked high priests. Although Jason receives a "just desert" twice, his punishments are surprisingly lenient given the gravity of his sins: he is first thrown out of the office of high priest, just as he had dismissed his brother (4:26), and finally, he who had banished so many Judeans and left so many men without a grave, meets his death in exile and has no place in the tomb of his forefathers (5:10). Menelaos's fate is no less puzzling, since his measure-for-measure retribution seems somewhat contrived. As one who has committed sacrilege, Menelaos appropriately suffers the punishment of the ashes (13:8), but an authorial comment introduces an unexpected connection between the ashes that killed Menelaos and the ashes of the temple altar (13:8).[45] This verse is the only passage in 2 Maccabees to link Menelaos with the desecration of the altar. The disruption of the sacrifices (6:5) was foreshadowed by the priests' neglect of the sacrifices in their haste to attend the *gymnasion* set up by *Jason*, as the authorial comment in 4:16–17 makes unmistakably clear, yet Menelaos himself had no part in this.[46]

The author's eagerness to link Menelaos back to this major misdemeanor provides a key to the author's overall organization of his narrative. In particular, it would explain his creating a double unit around two paired high priests and two paired kings. As Henten has shown (see below), 2 Maccabees describes two successive crises, each culminating in the establishment of a respective commemorative festival. The second one is unproblematic, since the high priest Alkimos is shown outright as responsible for launching the second, minor crisis. But why not have two different sequences of sin and measured retribution for Jason and Menelaos respectively? Why was the author keen to associate Menelaos with the sin of the *gymnasion* alongside Jason? If we take 2 Maccabees to be theological history that lays the stress on commemorative festivals, the structure of Jason's and Menelaos's respective measured retributions has little sense. Conversely, it becomes meaningful when read as dynastic history informed by the narrative pattern of temple building: just as building the temple is a legitimizing act, harming it is delegitimizing. And as the *lex talionis* application rules help us realize, the creation of the *gymnasion* is presented in 2 Maccabees as a threat to the proper operation of the temple. Hence the author's reason for associating both Jason and Menelaos with this act by turning Jason and Menelaos into a topical pair, and have Menelaos undergo the talion retribution that actually suited Jason, and should have been brought upon him. In this way, the balance of one sin to one retribution was maintained. Apart from this ultimate rereading of Menelaos's deeds, nowhere else in 2 Maccabees is he presented as a Hellenizer.[47] On the basis of his talionlike punishment, there are grounds to believe that the author of 2 Maccabees saw Menelaos as the Maccabees' most dangerous political adversary.

1.2.2. Disingenuous Authorial Comments

Before we pursue this inquiry by examining the composition of the work, an additional case of the disingenuous use of authorial comments in 2 Maccabees needs discussing because of its implications on modern historical reconstructions. As proof that its author did not intervene in his narrative merely to enlighten readers about the causes of divine punishments, and that his use of this device was all but ingenuous, there are several instances in which he can be seen skillfully exploiting the distinction between deep causes and pretexts.[48] The device of interpolating authorial comments in historical descriptions of events goes back to the times of Herodotus. It enabled Greek historians to present factual descriptions collected from witnesses or earlier written sources as faithfully as possible, and supplement these supposed plain facts with their own interpretation of events. In this way, authors could nudge their readers toward a "correct" evaluation of events without compromising their intellectual honesty. There are three such examples from 2 Maccabees that can be seen adopting this system.

At the beginning of the Heliodoros story (2 Macc. 3) we are told that Heliodoros arrived in Jerusalem on a "tour of inspection of the cities of Koilē Syria and Phoinikē." At which point the author promptly informs us that this tour was a "pretext" (*emphasis*), and reveals that Heliodoros's "deeper" purpose was to confiscate monies kept in the temple, because of Simon's denunciation (3:8). Because the source used by the author (which source does not concern us here) described Heliodoros's visit in a light that was not to his taste, he gave a twist to that version (the alleged pretext) through an authorial comment (the deeper cause) that puts a completely different slant on the original situation. The literary device is subtle enough to avoid censure perhaps, but the more critical reader is left wondering why, in times of peace, would an army led by someone of the rank of Heliodoros, second to the king in the Seleukid Empire, be marching throughout the province of Koilē Syria and Phoinikē. Odd indeed, unless things were less peaceful than the author would have us believe.[49]

The second example is equally curious. After Heliodoros has been set upon by angels, his friends request Onias to pray for the dying man's life (2 Macc. 3:31). The justification given for Onias's assent is particular (3:32, my emphasis):

> The high priest, indeed, was apprehensive *lest the king come to the conclusion that Heliodoros had been the victim of foul play perpetrated by the Jews.* Hence he offered up a sacrifice for the man's recovery.

Onias may indeed have had good reason to fear the king's "misunderstanding," and even better reasons to make the journey to Antioch in a last-ditch attempt to appease him (4:5–6). Onias's reasons for accepting the request may have been far less innocent than the author insists.

The last example brings us to the eve of Antiochos's second campaign against Egypt (2 Macc. 5:1–11), in which the author's deft montage has proved particularly detrimental to modern historical studies. Everyone, we are pointedly told in a long section, duly prayed for the success of the king's expedition. Even heavenly apparitions are enlisted to endorse the people's good will and utter loyalty to the king (5:1–4). Nonetheless, the king *mistakenly* thought that Judea was rebelling and promptly seized Jerusalem, "treat[ing] it as enemy territory captured in war" (5:11).[50] In Bickerman's wake, modern commentators have been keen to accept this version.[51] Yet the entire scenario is doubtful. By definition, unsolicited protestations of loyalty are suspect,[52] and it is hard to believe that the king had no reliable informers in his provinces, all the more so in wartime.

As these three examples show, the author of 2 Maccabees is occasionally able to tweak the historical significance of events simply by inserting comments into the descriptive part of his narration, and in this way turning causes into pretexts that enable him interpose new causes of his own devising. Since the literary technique he uses is relatively unobtrusive compared to his reiterations about God's ways, his ploy may easily be overlooked. Given that all three examples concern tensions between the king and the local community, this inevitably compromises the historical reconstructions.

1.3. THE NARRATIVE STRUCTURE OF 2 MACCABEES: THE STATE OF THE QUESTION

The narrative structure of 2 Maccabees continues to be heavily debated. As noted in the opening section of this chapter, in the last four decades major breakthroughs were achieved by the interrelated works of Nickelsburg, Doran (1981 and 2012), and Henten. If we combine their results, their analysis of the literary structure of 2 Maccabees essentially hinges on pinpointing two distinct narrative patterns, the sin-retribution-reconciliation-salvation sequence identified by Nickelsburg and the stories of the liberation of Greek sanctuaries, which are Doran's contribution.

In addition, a scheme of division according to four Seleukid reigns has been identified. The two narrative patterns are recognized as the product of a piously minded view of history, which is taken to imply that political concerns were of secondary importance to the author, if of any at all. In view of the earlier discussions of the present chapter, corrections to this approach are necessary, but this does not mean rejecting the authors' reconstruction of the narrative composition of the work—far from it—and the analysis I advocate here may be seen as a further refinement of their considerations.

1.3.1. Nickelsburg's Sin-Retribution Pattern

Nickelsburg was the first to see that the composition of 2 Maccabees is based on the composite pattern of sin-retribution-repentance-reconciliation, whereby he argued that 2 Maccabees was composed of a single narrative sequence that could be divided into five stages, as follows:[53]

1. *The blessing* of Jerusalem under Onias (3:1–40).
2. *The sin* of Hellenization under Jason and Menelaos (4:1–5:10).
3. *Punishment* through Antiochos's persecution (5:11–6:17).
4. *A turning point* constituted by the deaths of the martyrs and prayers of the people (6:18–8:4).
5. *Judgment and salvation,* materialized in Judas's victories (8:5–15:36).

The disproportionate length of the fifth stage (8:5–15:36) and the narrative imbalance that results from it are typical of the bewildered response of scholars to those last chapters of 2 Maccabees, which comprise the account of the liberation of the temple and the institution of the Festival of Hanukkah ending in 10:9, while the status and function of the closing segment of 10:10–15:36 remained obscure.[54] For lack of a better explanation the extant composition was explained in terms of assorted interpolations—that is, until Doran put forward his pioneering proposition that 2 Maccabees was composed of *several* narrative units, thereby finally offering a workable alternative to Nickelsburg's somewhat faltering theory.

1.3.2. Doran's Narrative Pattern of Temple-Liberation Accounts

Doran's starting point in his monograph of 1981 was his identification of what he saw as close similarities between 2 Maccabees and a well-documented type of account narrating how a deity defended His or Her sanctuary or city against assailants. Although this literary topos belongs to a wider cultural stock, Doran and later Henten noted that it was particularly well documented in the Greek cultural realm through inscriptions and literary sources throughout classical and Hellenistic times.[55] Despite varying literary forms, these stories have a few basic components in common, as Doran observed: "The attackers approach, the defenders ask help of the deity, the deity responds, the attackers are repulsed, and the defenders rejoice."⁵⁶ In his study of 1981 Doran identified three different stories bearing "all the hallmarks of [these] accounts" in 2 Maccabees,⁵⁷ and on the basis of this observation concluded that the narrative of 2 Maccabees has a threefold structure:

I. 3:1–40: The repelling of Heliodoros.
II. 4:1–10:9: The profanation of the temple and its renewal, subdivided into:
   A. 4:1–7:42: The assault of evil.
   B. 8:1–10:9: The restoration of the temple.
III. 10:10–15:36: The defense of the temple, subdivided into:
   A. 10:10–13:26: Two symmetrical sequences of warfare (chs. 10–11 and 12–13).
   B. 14:1–15:36: The final Seleukid campaign against the holy temple and its territory.

According to Doran, the Greek Hellenistic context supplies two further important parallels to 2 Maccabees. First, the liberations of sanctuaries accomplished by the epiphany of their patron deities were commemorated through the institution of festivals. In a similar way, the second and third stories of liberation in 2 Maccabees culminate in the institution of a festival, the first one commemorating the purification of the sanctuary of Jerusalem (Hanukkah) and the second the victory against Nikanor (Nikanor's Day), with the festal letters included before the proem of the work (1:1–2:18) bringing additional support for this comparison. Second, the Greek sanctuaries edited collections of stories of epiphanies and published them in the form of inscriptions erected within the sanctuary precincts in tribute to their patron gods or goddesses.⁵⁸ Doran pointed to this practice of collecting epiphanies in the form of catalogues as a way of explaining how 2 Maccabees could be composed of three successive stories of temple liberation (or, as he now dubs it, theomachy).⁵⁹

Notwithstanding the major breakthrough of Doran's analysis, his comparison between 2 Maccabees and the stories of epiphanies (or stories of temple liberation) contains two major flaws. First, it is true that the narrative sequence of the temple-liberation stories as summarized by Doran ("The attackers approach, the defenders ask help of the deity, the deity responds, the attackers are repulsed, and the defenders rejoice") fully matches up with the Heliodoros story (2 Macc. 3) and corresponds reasonably well to the etiological account of Nikanor's Day (2 Macc. 14:1–15:36). However, the etiological story of Hanukkah includes two components that deviate from this pattern (the desecration of the temple and its purification), variants that are too important, symbolically speaking, to be treated as merely secondary. Rather, they should be seen as the principal signifiers of a narrative pattern of its own. In other words, in this case the narrative sequence of the story of Hanukkah does *not* correspond to the narrative scheme of temple liberation.

Second, Doran is obliged to conflate two epigraphic literary genres to justify his comparison: etiological accounts of festivals and catalogues of epiphanies. Cases of epiphanies that were considered important enough to be commemorated by an annual festival were written down in the form of independent memoirs or records that were carefully kept in the civic archives. Not only were these records engraved on steles set up in the sanctuaries themselves, but their contents were also used in interstate diplomacy, when the city ambassadors who were sent to invite foreign cities, leagues, and kings to acknowledge the Panhellenic status of the commemorative festival and participate in the games, would quote them in support of their request.[60] It is this function in interstate diplomacy that is echoed, in Doran's view, in the festal letter that prefaces 2 Maccabees. In contrast, the catalogues of epiphanies simply recorded the time and circumstances of the events in a concise form. The catalogues listed the occurrences of all recorded epiphanies whether or not commemorated in festivals, but without the detailed etiological accounts. Like the monographs, the catalogues were kept in the archives and engraved on inscriptions but must have had a limited function, if any at all, in interstate diplomacy.

The literary form of 2 Maccabees is therefore clearly *not* that of a catalogue. Thus while Doran's analysis of 1981 considerably improved our understanding of the work's composition and inner coherence, his comparison with Hellenistic collections of epiphanies fails to explain the rationale of its threefold narrative sequence. The first story, that of the repulse of Heliodoros in 2 Maccabees 3, in particular, does not lead to the institution of a festival, and the prefixed letters of 2 Maccabees refer to the Festival of Hanukkah, namely that related to the second story, exclusively.

1.3.3. Henten's Synthesis

The lack of a commemorative festival in the first story was Henten's main reason for proposing a revised analysis of the composition of the work.[61] His solution was to combine Doran's temple epiphanies and Nickelsburg's sin-retribution scheme in a fourfold overall composition. Studying 2 Maccabees from the perspective of what he calls the author's theology of martyrdom, Henten distinguishes two (and not three) successive and symmetrical stories of liberation, each one including a story of martyrdom and culminating in the institution of a commemorative festival. The first story provides the full etiology of the festival of the purification of the temple and inauguration of the altar (Hanukkah) on 25 Kislev (2 Macc. 3:1–10:9), while the second tells of the Day of Nikanor on 13 Adar, one day before Purim (2 Macc. 10:10–15:36). Each story in turn is subdivided into two parts, and the resulting fourfold division corresponds to the four Seleukid reigns under which the account of 2 Maccabees unfolds:[62]

I. 3:1–4:6 corresponds to Seleukos IV's time.
II. 4:7–10:9 corresponds to Antiochos IV Epiphanes.

III. 10:10–13:26 corresponds to Antiochos V Eupator.
IV. 14:1–15:36 corresponds to Demetrios I.

The second and fourth parts of the composition are the most important sections, since they spell out in full the two stories of oppression, liberation, and foundation of the festivals. The two unfold according to similar patterns of six successive steps:

1. The betrayal by a Judean leader (Jason and Menelaos, and Alkimos).
2. An attack on the temple, city, and people by a king or his general.
3. The statement of faith by martyrs (the Mother and Her Seven Sons, and Razis).
4. The rescue by Judas Maccabee and the Lord.
5. The revenge on the wicked enemies.
6. The institution of a new festival (10:5–8 and 15:36).[63]

Henten's study offers the most convincing analysis of the composition of 2 Maccabees thus far. His decisive contribution is the premise that the narrative pattern (or patterns) structuring the account on the one hand, and the compositional divisions of the work on the other, must coincide. Nonetheless, here too Henten's proposal does not entirely satisfy, because of two unsolved questions.

First, only the second and fourth parts of the composition fully match his scheme, leaving unaddressed the question of what function is played by the story of Heliodoros's visit to Jerusalem (3:1–4:6). Second, Henten's interpretation of the purpose of 2 Maccabees really relates to the second part (4:7–10:9) alone. Henten has continued Doran's comparison between 2 Maccabees and the Hellenistic Greek practice of founding Panhellenic festivals to commemorate the deliverance of sanctuaries through divine intervention. According to this comparison, the first festal letter (1:1–10a), urging Egyptian Judeans to celebrate the Hanukkah festival, has the same function as the formal letters of invitation that Greek ambassadors delivered to foreign cities requesting their participation in the games held in their cities. In turn, the account of 2 Maccabees is a detailed etiological story that, like the Greek sacred records kept in civic archives, was used by the Judean ambassadors sent to Alexandria to prepare a display speech supporting their formal invitation to the games. However, this hypothesis would be better applied to a *secondary* use of 2 Maccabees, since the letter refers only to the festival of Hanukkah. Such a definition of the book's purpose leaves out three of its four parts entirely.

In short, neither Doran (1981) nor Henten has convincingly explained why 2 Maccabees comprises more than one liberation story—three according to Doran, and two according to Henten.[64] Doran's proposed correlation with epigraphic catalogues is not appropriate to the literary genre of 2 Maccabees, and Henten's interpretation of the work's purpose fails to tally with his four-part division of the work. Subsequent studies have not brought substantial improvement.[65]

As I shall now argue, the hypothesis of 2 Maccabees as a dynastic history explains the presence of *three* successive temple stories, and moreover casts light on how these three can be successfully combined with the *four* narrative units based on the royal reigns.

1.3.4. Second Maccabees as Dynastic History: A Revised Analysis of Its Literary Composition

The formal criteria determining the construction and definition of 2 Maccabees' narrative units are more complex than Henten's scheme assumes. Actually, the four main time units do not coincide simply with the reigns of Seleukid kings but also involve the associated figures of four high priests (Onias, Jason, Menelaos, and Alkimos). Moreover, the threefold sequence based on the triad of temple stories imposed the merging of the two units identified with Antiochos IV and his son Antiochos V to produce a double unit, corresponding to the Hanukkah story. For political bias,[66] the author relocated Menelaos in the unit dominated by Antiochos IV (the time of disruption), striking him out of the narrative unit of Antiochos V. Finally, the epilogue of 2 Maccabees refers to a fifth and successive time unit (2 Macc. 15:37b): "From that time on the city has been held by the Hebrews." This last time unit is that of the Hasmonean dynasty, in which rulers were both kings and high priests, and is implicitly yet unambiguously presented as succeeding Demetrios I's reign.

Overall, the temple stories vary in weight and import. Thus the Hanukkah story is clearly the core narrative, and is moreover twice as long as the other two (4:7–13:26). It is informed by the narrative pattern of temple foundation and not by that of temple liberation identified by Doran and Henten. The key episode of the temple refoundation is located at the very end (10:1–8) of the Antiochos Epiphanes time unit (4:7–10:9) and constitutes the turning point in the overall narrative. This pivotal function explains why the tone and content of the Antiochos Eupator time unit (10:10–13:26) differs from the preceding one. In turn, the Heliodoros and Nikanor's Day stories (3:1–4:6 and 14:1–15:37a), which are located on either side of the core narrative, correspond to one another. Doran's proposition that they are informed by the same literary pattern is partly correct, but while the Heliodoros episode is a pure story of temple liberation, the Nikanor's Day one is a curious blend of the narrative patterns of temple liberation and temple foundation.[67] If we turn to the narrative function of the three temple stories, we find a parallel distinction. As shown in detail in Chapter 2 below, the narrative pattern of temple foundation was originally linked to royal ideology and was used to assert the legitimacy of ruling kings. In 2 Maccabees, the story of temple refoundation (Hanukkah) narrates what must be seen as the founding myth of the Hasmonean dynasty. In turn, the narrative function of the two subordinate stories of temple liberation is to create a symmetry between Onias III's action in rescuing the temple from the intended assault of Heliodoros and Judas's action in rescuing the temple from the intended assault of Nikanor. As argued in detail in Chapter 4 below, the symmetrical benevolence of Onias and of Judas designates Judas—and through him, the Hasmoneans—as Onias III's legitimate heirs.

On this basis, the composition of 2 Maccabees may be summarized as follows:[68]

    I. 3:1–4:6: *Ideal state.* Narrative pattern of temple liberation and time unit of Onias III and Seleukos IV, the pious high priest and pious king. Under Onias III, the pious high priest, kings honor the temple, and the latter is protected from the assault of Heliodoros, the wicked royal officer. (How the Heliodoros episode fits in this definition of Seleukos IV as good king will be justified in a moment.)

II–III. 4:7–13:26: *First cycle of disruption and reconstruction.* Narrative pattern of temple foundation and time unit of Jason, Menelaos, Antiochos IV, and Antiochos V, wicked high priests and wicked kings.

    II. 4:7–10:9: *Disruption.* Under Jason and Menelaos, the wicked high priests whose fates are lumped together in one measure-for-measure retribution, the temple is first successfully attacked by the wicked king, Antiochos IV Epiphanes, until the reconciliation between the Judeans and their patron deity that makes the refoundation of the temple possible.

        IIa. The subsection 4:7–5:26 is dominated by the wicked actions of Jason and Menelaos (and Antiochos IV).

        IIb. 5:27–10:9: *Turning point.* Judas's first appearance (in 5:27) cues the beginning of the turning point that is finally achieved with the temple refoundation. This subsection focuses on the process of reconciliation with the patron deity, in which both Judas and the Judeans murdered for their faithfulness are instrumental.

    III. 10:10–13:26: *Reconstruction.* The refoundation of the temple makes victory possible under Judas's leadership.

    IV. 14:1–15:37a: *Second cycle of disruption and reconstruction.* Narrative pattern combining elements from temple foundation and temple liberation, and time unit of Alkimos and Demetrios I, wicked high priest and wicked king. The malevolent influence of Alkimos and Demetrios is successfully counterbalanced by the pious action of Judas. As a result, the temple is saved from the assault of Nikanor, the wicked royal officer.

    V. 15:37b: *Return to the ideal state* under the leadership of the Hasmoneans, good high priests and kinglike rulers.[69]

This synopsis will be validated in the course of the three forthcoming chapters, in which the temple stories are analyzed in detail, but it is presented in advance here to show how interpreting 2 Maccabees as a dynastic history provides a comprehensive explanation for the extant narrative structure of the work. While many commentators have taken the far shorter time span covered by 2 Maccabees to mean that its author was not interested in manifesting open support to the Hasmonean dynasty,[70] that argument holds only if we see the work as a linear chronicle. Instead, if it is seen as a cyclical account, the length of the time span it covers is of secondary importance. Whereas 1 Maccabees is concerned with asserting the kinship and symbolic link between Judas, the refounder of the temple, and the Hasmonean dynasty through Simon, Judas's brother and the father of John Hyrkanos, with whom the dynastic principle was established, 2 Maccabees focuses on the founding myth of the dynasty, the refoundation of the temple, and is moreover concerned with asserting or reasserting that the Hasmoneans are legitimate heirs to Onias III.

Given that the construction of the four time units framing the literary composition of 2 Maccabees is far from straightforward, it is vital to obtain a clearer picture of the author's intense editorial work as a first step toward grasping the intricate relation between historical reality and its literary transcription in 2 Maccabees. To do this we must first examine the author's conception of time. Modern commentators have often been bewildered by the numerous chronological inaccuracies that may be imputed to the author. Fortunately, Doran's thorough literary and narrative analysis of the work has amply shown that these alleged errors are in fact the fruit of the author's deliberate rearrangement of his historical material. In 1981 Doran explained this through the author's literary concerns, emphasizing how the reordering of the material allowed for a more finely balanced account. Subsequently, in 2012 Doran illustrated how this reordering was motivated by the need to use the narrative pattern of temple liberation more effectively.[71] Doran's rehabilitation of the author can be pursued on two fronts. Principally, what has been perceived as careless handling of time actually stems from the author's *cultural relation* to the concept of time itself. In parallel, he also knowingly *manipulated* time to serve his political purposes. From this perspective, the idea of editorial work used in biblical scholarship may aptly describe the author's modus operandi: time, which has an intrinsically ethical quality, becomes a tool in the construction of meaning.

1.4. EMBEDDED TIME, CYCLICAL TIME, AND DYNASTIC HISTORY

The narrative composition of 2 Maccabees pivots on combined elements: three temple stories and four (developed) time units pairing four Seleukid kings and as many high priests. There can be little doubt that this pairing of kings and high priests is intentional, as it clearly involves chronological manipulations in the cases of Menelaos and Alkimos, and possibly of others too. Note that there is no mention of Onias IV, Onias III's son and legitimate heir. Moreover, this pairing is not merely chronological but has a moral basis as well. Not only does the ethical (either pious or impious) behavior of the kings and high priests coincide within their shared time unit, but to a large extent the high priest's action seems to foreshadow that of the associated king. For instance, Jason's partial disruption of the sacrifices by establishing the *gymnasion* prefigures their ensuing total disruption by Antiochos IV. Doubtless it was this type of authorial montage that encouraged Bickerman and others to affirm that Jason and Menelaos (the leaders of the so-called Hellenizers) took an active part in the desecration of the temple—what modern historians have converted into a cult reform—some commentators going so far as claiming that they fomented the subsequent atrocities.[72] If, in contrast, we accept that the neat slotting together of the narrative material within the time units is a deliberate editing ploy, we may infer that the supporters of the Hasmoneans (and the author of 2 Maccabees is one) saw the main political adversaries of the dynasty as the high priests who succeeded Onias III, and not the Seleukid kings, and accordingly considered it vital to denigrate them as they fashioned their account of the dynastic foundation myth. Given how the author's construction of the time units has repeatedly thrown modern historical reconstructions off course, we need to examine the text anew in order to clarify the author's original intentions.

1.4.1. Objective and Linear versus Embedded and Cyclical Time

Anthropological and historical studies have demonstrated how human perception of time is historically conditioned and differs from one society to another.[73] While modern Western society has evolved a conception of time as something abstract, neutral, objective, continuous, and homogeneous, in ancient societies time was embedded in the social actuality.[74] For them, time was not a homogeneous continuum but a succession of discrete cyclical units. These cycles were constituted by the units of day and night, of the year, and of groups of years. The daily and yearly cycles were punctuated, indeed defined, by rites, and in particular by specific sacrifices and festivals. To keep account of the passing of the years, Greek cities and the Romans appointed officials, sometimes priests and priestesses, whose name was given to the year of their office. Hence, counting the years meant counting eponymous officials.[75] In monarchies, time was computed according to the reigning years of rulers; hence, the advent of a new king brought the reckoning of time back to year one. Similarly, successive reigns were grouped into dynasties and empires. And of course the notion of the succession of the empires that emerges in Daniel, Herodotus, and Roman historians is related to this custom of sectioning time into cycles.[76] Greek literature also confirms this cyclic logic, which in the Greek case was based on the succession of political systems (*politeiai*) and empires.[77]

In much the same way, the successive phases marking the fate of temples offered their priestly personnel a yardstick for periodization. Thus the destruction of the temple of Athena Lindia by fire in 392/1 B.C.E., and its rebuilding probably soon thereafter, was used for periodizing the list of gifts to the goddess in the long Lindos inscription of 99 B.C.E.[78] In a similar fashion, the ancient Judeans' system for periodizing the past was directly linked to the history of their temple. Thus Josephus sequenced Judean history according to the changing fate of the temple, distinguishing between the period of Solomon's temple, the period of destruction, the rebuilding by Zerubbabel and Joshua, and the destruction by the Romans.[79] In the ancient Near East even the Creation itself was considered cyclical, whereby in Mesopotamia and Judah the world was created anew at each festival of the New Year and at each reconstruction of a temple.[80] Although linear systems of time reckoning started emerging in the Greek world in late classical and early Hellenistic times, they never quite eclipsed the traditional, cyclical modes of periodization.[81] As for 2 Maccabees, its author doubtless conceived time as socially embedded and cyclical.

A. Kings' Reigns as Discrete Units of Time. The capacity of rulers to embody discrete units of time was not merely an abstract, intellectual representation but hinged on concrete social and political practices that were still current in the Hellenistic world. Since the king embodied the state, his edicts, decrees, and laws were only valid as long as he ruled.[82] Upon the accession of a new king to the throne, society began anew, as it were, and the social order needed to be restarted. Theoretically at least, formal confirmations were needed for virtually all the decisions that had been taken by the late king, and a similar rule applied to settlements negotiated with subject cities and *ethnē*. In most cases, such confirmations must have gone smoothly. However, the advent of a new king was an ideal opportunity for cities and *ethnē* to try to negotiate more advantageous fiscal and military settlements, and for the new king to impose reforms conforming to his own interests. Similarly, a new reign potentially entailed changes in the administrative personnel serving in the court and the provinces. The persons who served as high-ranking officials in the Hellenistic kingdoms were men with whom the kings had personal ties, which were reflected in such court titles as *philoi* or *syngeneis*.[83]

The author of 2 Maccabees exploited this social reality to its utmost. As a rule, most characters in his work feature in one narrative unit alone. This is particularly well illustrated in the sequences dealing with military campaigns, and each campaign is differentiated through its Seleukid general (or generals).[84] Even Lysias's two campaigns are not doublets, since Lysias led on his own in the first but accompanied Antiochos V in the second (2 Macc. 11:1–13 and 13:9–26, paralleled by 1 Macc. 4:26–35 and 6:28–63).[85]

Because of this custom of reformulating all prior agreements at the start of a new reign, previously arranged settlements and appointments required the new king's approval.[86] In this sense, mere confirmations of past agreements could easily be transformed by our author into original decisions, without particularly compromising the (Greek) historiographical standards of reliability.[87] Manipulation of this sort can be seen in our author regarding Lysias when compared with the equivalent piece in 1 Maccabees,[88] which reports that Lysias had been left in charge of affairs in the part of the empire west of the Euphrates when Antiochos IV departed to the eastern satrapies in the spring of 165 B.C.E. On the king's death in the East, he became regent, since Antiochos V was a child at the time (1 Macc. 3:32–34 and 6:5–6). In 1 Maccabees, Lysias's first campaign against the Judeans is dated to the time of Antiochos IV's anabasis (1 Macc. 3:31–37), whereas his second campaign took place after Antiochos IV's death, and Lysias accompanied Antiochos V as the regent (1 Macc. 6:18–63). In contrast, the author of 2 Maccabees claims that Lysias was *appointed* by Antiochos V (2 Macc. 10:11), and the two campaigns are placed in Antiochos V's time unit (2 Macc. 11 and 13).[89]

As we shall see, the author employed the sophisticated rhetorical devices of anticipation (prolepsis) and hindsight (analepsis) to generate the impression in the audience that the rules of high priests and kings coincided. Quite simply, by means of these devices a given character might be mentioned for the first time (say, in an authorial comment) either ahead of time or delayed, so as to have his name conveniently associated with the desired time unit.[90]

1.4.2. Kings and High Priests: The Construction of Cycles of Time in 2 Maccabees

The aforementioned embedded systems of time reckoning become more complex in an imperial situation. From the period of Achaimenid domination, a system of dual command prevailed in Yehud/Judea, whereby the imperial king ruled alongside the local leader—in Persian times the governor and in Hellenistic times the high priest.[91] Ideological constructions had to come to terms with this dual power structure. The device found in 2 Maccabees is radical yet simple: kings and high priests are made to coincide in time, with the past ordered by a succession of clear-cut, discrete sequences of action in which the kings are usually introduced first, their names and reigns tending to define the chronological boundaries of their time units.

This schematic solution had an apparently well-established tradition. For example, the narrative composition of LXX 1 Esdras juxtaposes three time units in a cyclical arrangement, and each narrative cycle is characterized by a different pair of leaders, one Persian king and one leader of the Returning Exiles: Cyrus and Sheshbazzar in the first narrative cycle (1 Esd. 2); Darius and Zerubbabel and Joshua (the two are functionally linked together) in the second cycle (1 Esd. 3–7); and Artaxerxes and Ezra in the third (1 Esd. 8–9). Thanks to this turnover of characters, 1 Esdras can rehearse the story of the Return of the Exiles to their land three times, creating both a sense of repetition (endorsing legitimacy) and a chronological progression.[92] As we shall see, the same device is exploited in the symmetrically opposite way in 2 Maccabees, to create contrasts and not repetition.[93]

In 2 Maccabees the rules of kings and high priests coincide a little too neatly to be a tenable account of events. Hence Onias III and Seleukos IV are introduced together at the beginning of the Heliodoros story: two verses apart, to be precise (2 Macc. 3:1–3; see below). Similarly, Antiochos IV and Jason are introduced in the same verse (4:7).[94] Antiochos IV's death neatly marks off his time unit. In a chronological montage that has flummoxed modern commentators,[95] the author depicts Antiochos IV's agony in detail in chapter 9, but announces his death only in 10:9, meanwhile inserting the description of the refoundation of the temple and the institution of the commemorative festival (10:1–8). The next verse (10:9) starts Antiochos V's rule.

New reign, new content. The most blatant case of chronological manipulation is that of the fourth time unit, linking Demetrios I and Alkimos (14:1–15:37a). The unit begins with the start of Demetrios's rule (14:1), and almost immediately mentions Alkimos (14:3), expressly using the device of analepsis (or flashback).[96] This trick of providing a back story for Alkimos upon his first mention enables the author to maintain historical accuracy (compare *Ant.* 20.235) while keeping his time units homogeneous.[97]

This brings us to the deviating case of Menelaos's appointment as high priest. Effectively, Jason is ousted by Menelaos under Antiochos IV Epiphanes (2 Macc. 4:24), yet the circumstances of his appointment only superficially break up the synchronization of the time units in 2 Maccabees. First, the author would have us believe that Menelaos met his death at the very end of Antiochos V Eupator's reign (13:3–8). As a result the inner chronological and topical coherence of the sequence beginning with Antiochos IV's accession to the throne is only rounded off at the end of Antiochos V's reign, creating the double unit.[98] Moreover, Menelaos is not merely introduced but is entirely relocated in the course of Antiochos IV's time unit. Although he dies at the end of Antiochos V's time unit, we do not hear about him until this fatal moment. There is only one exception to Menelaos's narrative relocation to Antiochos's time unit, which will be examined below. At this point it must be said that the synchronization between kings and high priests in the successive time units is a little too systematic to be natural, and as such carries meaning.

1.4.3. *The Qualitative Essence of Time*

The perception of time as something embedded in social life means not only that time is conceived as a succession of discrete units but, moreover, that periods of time are differentiated by distinct qualities. For example, time could be either sacred or profane, *fastus* or *nefastus*, and this difference in quality accordingly required men to behave differently. However, there were various other ways by which time might acquire a distinct quality. Rulers not only framed these divisions of time into periods, but they also influenced the qualitative essence of time. For instance, in a time unit associated with a good ruler—or alternatively with the proper operation of the local temple—society is seen to flourish, and harmony reigns. In contrast, a wicked ruler imprints dark colors on his associated time unit. As a result, the fluctuation of good and wicked rulers produces alternating eras of serenity and disruption.

This mode of thought was not alien to Greek historiography. Indeed, the *Histories* of Polybius are riddled with ideal rulers and wicked kings, and their reigns are painted in black or white, whereby Antiochos III commands a high place on the ladder whereas Ptolemy VIII is the very embodiment of the iniquitous king. In the Greek historiography of Hellenistic times, however, this schematization is softened by the concomitant drive to realistic writing. In contrast, this stereotyping endured in Mesopotamian historiography of Seleukid times, in which the tendency to conceive history cyclically is more blatant. For instance, the early Seleukid text known as the Uruk Prophecy is comprised of a succession of reigns, each one forming a discrete unit within a pattern of alternating times of idyll and disruption, the reign as a whole being evaluated in the light of the king's behavior toward one or several cult centers.[99] In this sense, 2 Maccabees is more akin to the Mesopotamian tradition than to Polybius.

A. The Ethical Overlap: Pairing Kings with High Priests in 2 Maccabees. In keeping with the principle that the discrete time units in 2 Maccabees are framed by sets of paired kings and high priests, making them coincide chronologically alone was not sufficient: they were required to have the same ethical behavior also. But while it is the king who frames the period, the qualitative essence of the unit appears to be defined by its high priest; hence, a pious high priest entails a pious king, and not the other way round. The clearest example of the ethical slant stemming from the high priests is the Heliodoros episode (2 Macc. 3:1–4:6), in which Seleukos IV and Onias III are not only introduced together but the short opening section also spells out the blissful state of affairs defining this time unit (2 Macc. 3:1–3):

> Under the high priest Onias the inhabitants of the holy city enjoyed undisturbed peace, and there was the strictest observance of the laws, because of his piety and hatred of wickedness. It also frequently happened that even the kings honored the Place and contributed to the glory of the temple with the most sumptuous gifts. In fact, Seleukos, king of Asia, provided for all the expenses of the sacrificial cult out of his own revenues.

In short, under the pious Onias III, not only does the imperial king piously honor the temple with gifts, but the wicked maneuvers of Onias's enemy Simon are held in check in spite of everything (3:4–7 and 4:1–6), while the attempt by Heliodoros, the king's wicked official,[100] to enter the temple and plunder its money deposits is successfully repelled. The lesson is simple: under a pious high priest, society is blessed with political rewards and is spared misfortunes. If, as argued in this book, the specific purpose of 2 Maccabees was to illustrate the Hasmoneans' claim that they were Onias III's legitimate heirs through Judas, it is not hard to read a political intention in this construction of the relationship between the (native) high priest and the (foreign, imperial) king.

To understand the overall organization of 2 Maccabees, it may be worth comparing it with a small group of contemporary texts from Mesopotamia, labeled Akkadian Prophecies by modern scholars, which offer examples of predictions coming after the events. As Beaulieu noted:[101]

> They were intended to provide sanction to an event contemporary with their composition, such as the restoration of a cult or the rise of a new dynasty. This crucial event is always announced in the closing prediction of the prophecy and constitutes, in a manner of speaking, its historical climax. The narration which leads up to this climax includes a succession of historical events carefully selected for their illustrative value and assembled into a dramatic progression of cycles of "good" and "bad" heralding the establishment of a final era of bliss. The prophecy contains the implicit message that this era of bliss is brought about by the realization of the event which it is the purpose of the text to vindicate.

In this sense, 2 Maccabees follows a similar scheme, opening with the description of the state of bliss that characterized the city of Jerusalem and its temple under the pious Onias, coming round in a full circle with the last time unit, when the quality of time has changed radically after two intervening cycles of disruption (4:7–13:26 and 14:1–15:37a), and the initial state of bliss is finally reestablished (15:37b): "From this time on, the city has been held by the Hebrews."[102] And at that point the account can reach its conclusion (37c–39).

While the second cycle of disruption (Nikanor's Day story, 14:1–15:37a) requires no specific comment, the question of the ethical nature of cycles of time brings us back to the construction of the double unit comprising the first cycle of disruption (4:7–13:26). The cycle as a whole is constructed around a frame of continuity, within which a turning point brings about a radical change in intrinsic quality. The element of continuity is supplied by the two kings, Antiochos IV Epiphanes and Antiochos V Eupator, whose relationship as father and son was to the advantage of the author of 2 Maccabees since the kinship between the other succeeding kings was less direct: Seleukos IV was succeeded by his brother Antiochos IV, while Antiochos V was succeeded by Demetrios, his cousin and Seleukos IV's son (14:1). Generally speaking, in ancient thought individuals were primarily apprehended as members of a family, a concept documented in both Near Eastern and Greco-Roman traditions.[103] Thus the direct descent between Epiphanes and his son Eupator, which is specified from the outset in the proem (2:20), could be treated as a factor of continuity not only in time but also in ethical bearing. Indeed, Antiochos V is first ushered on stage as "the son of the impious king" (10:10), and following this inauspicious start things could only get worse (13:9).[104]

At the same time, the familial and ethical linkage between the two kings allowed the author to underscore not only continuities but also contrasts. Under Antiochos IV the temple was defiled and the Judeans persecuted, but Antiochos V's time unit was colored by victories. This means that a turning point has occurred at the end of Antiochos IV's time. Contrary to what might be expected, the precise nature of this turning point is controverted by modern scholars, some stressing the martyrs and others the temple. Actually it is orchestrated through a *progression*, moving from the exemplary deaths of the faithful Judeans (the so-called martyrs, 2 Macc. 6–7) through Judas's first victory (2 Macc. 8) to the refoundation of the temple (10:1–8). Far from competing with each other, these various items have a cumulative power. In Chapter 3 below they will be shown to correspond to basic narrative constituents (reconciliation, initial victory, and temple refoundation) of the literary pattern of the temple-building account. In addition the death of the wicked king in 2 Maccabees 9 is part of the reconciliation process. However, the sequence of the turning point does not start with the exemplary deaths in 6:1. By the device of prolepsis (anticipation), Judas's first mention heads the entire sequence in 5:27. The next mention of Judas arises in 2 Maccabees 8, when his military actions are depicted, and his moral qualities are stated from the outset: "Judas, also known as Maccabee, in a group of about ten, withdrew to the mountains, where he and his men eked out a living like beasts. There they stayed, eating herbs for food, in order to keep clear of defilement" (2 Macc. 5:27). The piety of Judas is in sharp contrast with the way Antiochos V (10:10) and Alkimos (14:3) are first introduced. Similarly, the first action ascribed to Jason is his eviction of the pious Onias and usurpation of his power. The author insists that Onias III's deposition was the result of Jason's approaching the king (2 Macc. 4:7–10).

1.4.4. Menelaos and Judas Maccabee

We now have a better view of how the author constructed the double time unit corresponding to the Hanukkah story. As we saw, the figure of Menelaos is closely associated with Jason's sin and retribution. The narrative section of 2 Maccabees to which the two men are confined is contained in verses 4:7–5:26, corresponding precisely to the time of disruption. In contrast, Judas Maccabee is first mentioned in 5:27 and is placed at the head of the reconciliation sequence culminating in the refoundation of the temple (2 Macc. 5:27–10:8). Moreover, being entirely relocated to the time of disruption under Antiochos IV, Menelaos is denied any connection with the cycle of victories related as the fortunate consequence of the temple's refoundation.

The purpose of linking Jason and Menelaos in the same subunit may be analyzed further. The first event following the mention of Antiochos's accession and Jason's usurpation at 4:7 is Jason's establishment of the *gymnasion* (4:8–15), an act explicitly said to entail the disruption of the sacrifices (4:14), long before the desecration of the altar by Antiochos's men takes place. By shifting the figure of Menelaos entirely to Jason's subunit of disruption, and by claiming that his death is just retribution for Jason's sin, the author has neatly turned Menelaos into the coinstigator of the first disruption, namely the setting up of the *gymnasion* and the ensuing defilement of the ashes of the altar. Given that in 2 Maccabees the *gymnasion* is depicted as an antitemple,[105] the purpose of this shrewd montage was to paint Jason and Menelaos as temple destroyers, and hence the antithesis of Judas the temple builder. In the context of the narrative account of temple foundation, the political slant is clear: Jason and Menelaos were illegitimate rulers, whereas Judas is the legitimate founder of the Hasmonean dynasty. Bickerman and Tcherikover were misled by the author's apparent reordering of events and notoriously saw Menelaos as a Hellenizer alongside Jason.[106]

As we can see, the narrative construction of Antiochos IV's time unit (or subunit) is skillfully balanced: it opens with a (partial) disruption of the sacrifices instigated by Jason (and Menelaos), passing through their total disruption by Antiochos IV,[107] and thence to their resumption—thanks to Judas Maccabee, who dominates the reconciliation subsection. The insertion of the section describing the rededication of the temple at the end of the unit (10:1–8) is the result of the author's editing and not a later interpolation.[108] Moreover, it is really only after the temple has been reclaimed and the perpetual sacrifices renewed that victories can follow, and the Antiochos V time unit is thus characterized throughout by Judas's victorious battles.

A. Usurping Menelaos's Credit: Judas as the Peace Negotiator Under Antiochos V. The systematic reordering of the narrative material in 2 Maccabees focuses on blackening the names of Jason and Menelaos (as well as Alkimos in the second cycle of disruption) while highlighting Judas Maccabee's pious actions. To this end, however, the author has found a further way to exploit the topical arrangement of the material.

Christian Habicht has shown that the chronology of the four official letters grouped together in 2 Maccabees 11:16–38 has been distorted by the simple fact that this section is inserted in the Antiochos V unit. These decrees concern the negotiations between the Judeans and the Seleukids for putting an end to the revolt. Besides agreeing to an amnesty, it seems that the previous status quo was basically restored and the Judean *ethnos* recovered most of its earlier privileges. According to Habicht, while letter 2 was indeed written by Antiochos V upon his accession to the throne, the other three letters were written in the last year of the reign of Antiochos IV, during his anabasis to the eastern satrapies.[109] The original chronological distribution of the letters would therefore indicate that Antiochos IV had already put an end to the repression and reestablished the previous status quo in Judea before his death.[110]

Technically, the grouping of these four letters under Antiochos V may simply be the author's choice to organize his material topically rather than chronologically. Notably, the author of 1 Maccabees does the same, and in fact the topical ordering of historical material at the expense of chronological accuracy is a common feature of Greek historiographical writing.[111] That said, in 2 Maccabees this arranging of the material by topic also had an ideological purpose: first, by bracketing the letters dealing with peace negotiations under Antiochos V (after the altar's rededication) the author preserved the atmosphere of doom characterizing the period prior to this pivotal event. More critical is letter 3, originally issued under Antiochos IV and implying that Menelaos was instrumental in obtaining the royal decree of amnesty (2 Macc. 11:27–33).[112] Thanks to its displacement, the negotiations for peace are credited to Judas. While Menelaos's activities are barely recorded in the section of 2 Maccabees identified with Antiochos V's time, "Maccabee" is the leader who is granted an audience by the king in 13:24. In conclusion, through the literary device of presenting Eupator's reinstatement of Lysias as a first appointment, the author of 2 Maccabees was able to enhance Judas's role and downplay Menelaos's at the same time. Like the author's narrative manipulations, this artful chronological editing is put at the service of dynastic history.

. . .

The reinterpretation of 2 Maccabees as dynastic history and not theological history or temple propaganda is predicated on the different status of temples in the Greek world and in the ancient Near East in general, and in Judah/Judea in particular. In the ancient Near East, temple building was royal prerogative at the time of native monarchies, and this old reality had left its hallmark on symbolic representations. Whereas 2 Maccabees was written in Greek and is a good example of the literary techniques deployed in Hellenistic Greek historiography, the narrative pattern that shapes it is of Judean stamp.

As we have seen in this chapter, now that it is clear how 2 Maccabees implements a discourse about piety and impiety at the service of political goals, our appreciation of the nature and purpose of our author changes decisively. Far from the allegedly pious theologian who employs his literary skills to praise God's ways, our author is revealed to be putting his vision of history at the service of partisan interests. Consequently, we must reexamine the function of the entire range of literary devices—the measure-for-measure equation, authorial comments, the chronological rearrangement of the material, prolepsis and analepsis—regularly employed throughout the text.

The most remarkable instance of the author's reshaping of his material is his construction of the four (actually five) time units composing the work. The fact that the latter not only are discrete units but are endowed with a specific ethical quality of their own has a twofold purpose: the first, to construct an affiliation between Onias and Judas, and through Judas with the Hasmoneans; the second, to paint their rivals, especially the high priests, as utterly wicked. This practice of besmirching the image of rivals for political reasons is typical of dynastic history, as in the case of Jason and Menelaos, who are plainly identified as Judas's direct political rivals. However, Bickerman's reinterpretation of the wicked high priests as "Hellenists" has led many modern commentators to take the political bias at face value.

In addition to the cyclical pattern of the four narrative units of 2 Maccabees, this chapter discusses other elements that largely support the claim that our author had a political agenda. To make them all fall into place, however, we must examine the narrative pattern of temple foundation (or temple building), which is essentially what gives 2 Maccabees its meaning. This analysis will come in the next chapter, which describes the narrative components and the function of this pattern, tracing its evolution in time from the days of the native monarchy through Persian times to Seleukid Judea. Chapter 3 will in turn track how this scheme is applied in both 1 and 2 Maccabees, which each introduce it twice. The first time it is used to shape the account of the refoundation of the temple desecrated by Antiochos IV. Forming the etiological account of the Hanukkah festival, this passage patently constitutes the foundation myth of the Hasmonean dynasty. However, as Chapter 4 below will show, the second time the device is used it serves to interweave an additional dynastic claim, though this additional claim differs in the two texts under study, and this employment of the temple-building account to support quite different but complementary claims appears to be the underlying reason for the parallel redactions of 1 and 2 Maccabees.

2

Temple Foundation and Royal Legitimacy

A Narrative Pattern and Its Message

INTRODUCTION

In his book *Temple Propaganda* (1981), Robert Doran made the pioneering proposition that 2 Maccabees is informed by a narrative pattern centered on the temple.[1] In substance, the stories that follow this pattern narrate how a given temple came under threat of the pending assault of enemies, and how it was liberated thanks to the epiphanic intervention of its divine patron.[2] Greek cities evolved a particular predilection for this sort of story, which in Hellenistic times was used to assist diplomatic efforts to persuade other Greeks to acknowledge the Panhellenic status of their commemorative festivals and to recognize their sanctuaries as places of *asylia* (inviolability). In contrast, Doran was able to trace only few documentary instances of temple-liberation accounts outside the Greek world, and the biblical stories he adduces—in the book of Esther and 3 Maccabees—stem from a diasporan and not a Judean setting,[3] and could reflect local influences. Moreover, as we saw in Chapter 1 (§1.3.2), while the Greek examples of temple-liberation accounts offer convincing parallels to the Heliodoros story (2 Macc. 3:1–4:6), their structure fails to make sense of manifestly constitutive elements of the Hanukkah story (2 Macc. 4:7–13:26). In particular, the narrative unit of the temple rededication (10:1–8), which gives its name to the Hanukkah festival (Festival of the Dedication [or Rededication]), is paradoxically out of place in this scheme. To my mind, the fact that the temple-liberation scheme only partially maps with the Hanukkah story is evidence enough of its different narrative pattern. In this and the next two chapters I show that the account of the Hanukkah story in both 1 and 2 Maccabees is informed by the narrative pattern of temple foundation rather than of temple liberation, with the dedication presented in them actually acquiring the status of a refoundation. Unlike Doran's pattern of temple liberation, this pattern is typical of the ancient Near East, being particularly well documented over a long span of time in three cultural areas: Mesopotamia (Sumerian, Old Babylonian, Assyrian, Neo-Assyrian, and Neo-Babylonian cultures), the northwest Semitic cultures of Ugarit, at Ras Shamra (in northern Syria), and Judah/Judea.[4]

The formal literary structure of temple-building accounts has been the object of a comprehensive study by Victor Hurowitz.[5] On the basis of an extensive corpus of texts stemming from the three areas just cited above, he outlined a basic six-part literary pattern corresponding to the six successive phases of the building process and, further, showed how each part in turn comprised a few preset elements. The full six-part structure surfaces only in some of the texts, and likewise the elements composing the individual parts do not systematically recur in all of them. However, while inner components—and even entire parts—are on occasion omitted, there are few variations in those narrative elements that do appear in the texts, and the corpus as a whole displays a remarkable conformity to the basic template. Yet the pattern could be used in connection with the construction of buildings other than temples. In particular, accounts of palace building follow a similar narrative pattern, which can also apply to other items of urban architecture, such as the repairing of Jerusalem's wall and gates recounted in the book of Nehemiah.[6]

The parallel between the construction of temples and palaces immediately situates the ideological connotations of the narrative pattern in a very different register, in comparison with the Greek accounts of temple liberation. Both in the eastern Semitic cultures of Mesopotamia and in the northwestern Semitic cultures of Ugarit and Judah/Judea, the narrative template of the temple-building accounts was originally devised as a vehicle of royal ideology. It may be reasonably supposed that it emerged in conjunction with the ideology of divine election of the king (i.e., of sacral kingship) that was shared by the native kingships of these cultural areas.[7] Stories of temple building could also prove useful in situations of contested power: for instance, to legitimize usurpers who were unable to rely on heredity to warrant their seizure of power. These texts regularly proclaim that the deposed king had neglected his duties toward the deity and allowed His or Her temple fall into ruin—undeniable proof of the ruler's wickedness.[8] The deity therefore seeks a righteous servant to replace the wicked one, and the new, divinely elected king proclaims his justness and loyalty by restoring the dilapidated temple and instituting social reforms. With the demise of native kingship in Judah, the narrative proceeds to articulate the legitimacy of the rulers who inherited the royal prerogatives, in particular the royal privilege of building the temple (and the palace) and, through the rulers, the social orders they instituted. When placed in this cultural context, the story of Antiochos IV's desecration of the temple of Jerusalem—and its subsequent purification and refoundation related in 1 and 2 Maccabees—emerges as the founding myth of the Hasmonean dynasty: that is, the event on which the dynasty based its legitimacy.[9] The very fact that 2 Maccabees tells the story of the rededication of the temple by the family from which the Hasmoneans were descended confirms that our author, very much like the author of 1 Maccabees, was an avowed supporter of the Hasmonean dynasty.[10]

The six-part pattern identified by Hurowitz occurs in a wide range of literary genres. In Mesopotamian literature, for example, one finds royal inscriptions, in particular the subgenre of so-called building inscriptions; additional types of building accounts;[11] and mythical accounts depicting the building of temple-palaces by god-kings (e.g., Enuma Eliš). In contrast, the Ugaritic corpus is almost exclusively mythical (the Baal epic).[12] In turn, the Judahite/Judean corpus of texts dealing with temple building is both extensive and composite in nature.[13] Witness Solomon's original construction of the temple in the lengthy pericope of 1 Kings 5:15–9:25 (NRSV 5:1–9:25),[14] which must be read together with Nathan's prophecy in 2 Samuel 7.[15] A parallel account is found in 1 Chronicles 17 to 2 Chronicles 8; and related elements surface in the group of psalms called Psalms of Enthronement.[16] Similarly, the narrative pattern of temple building informs the detailed account of the building of the Tabernacle in the desert (Ex. 25–31, 35–40; Lev. 8–10; Num. 7)[17] and those of the rebuilding of the temple in Persian times found in Ezra 1–6 and 1 Esdras, while the prophetic books of Haggai-Zechariah 1–8 (hereafter HZ) and Deutero-Ezekiel 40–48 deal with related issues.[18] Together with the story of Nehemiah's restoration of Jerusalem's wall, a noncanonical tradition about the temple's refoundation is echoed in 2 Maccabees 1:18–2:18, whereas Josephus's description of Herod's rebuilding of the temple in *Antiquities* 15.380–425 follows the classical narrative pattern.[19]

The main purpose of Hurowitz's argument was to demonstrate that the account of Solomon's building of the temple in 1 Kings 5:15–9:25 (NRSV 5:1–9:25; together with Nathan's prophecy in 2 Samuel 7) is informed by the same six-part narrative template as the Mesopotamian and Ugaritic literary material; and as a consequence he only briefly dealt with the rest of the Judahite/Judean corpus. Hurowitz's lead was taken up by subsequent scholars, however, such as Diana Edelman, who has shown that the prophetic unit of HZ matches the temple-building template by identifying in it five of the six parts that the classical model contains.[20] She has further argued that Ezra 1–6 is a derivative account elaborated on the basis of HZ that, possibly because of its very artificiality, displays the full six-part sequence accurately.[21]

The two authors of 1 and 2 Maccabees were fully conversant with the six-step narrative pattern that Hurowitz elaborates. Their thorough acquaintance with its formal structure is evidenced by their ability not only to reproduce its classical form but also to creatively rework it while keeping within its constitutive boundaries. Thus the core story of 2 Maccabees (the Hanukkah story) as I proposed to delineate it in Chapter 1 (§1.3.4) turns out to follow the scheme in a fairly classical way. First, the comparison with Hurowitz's corpus of texts confirms that the section of the military victories corresponding with the reign of Antiochos V (2 Macc. 10:10–13:26) must be joined with the preceding unit (4:7–10:9), forming a long narrative unit encompassing the two time units of Antiochos IV and his son (4:7–13:26).[22] Moreover, applying Hurowitz's pattern to the Hanukkah story clarifies why the episode of the temple purification and rededication is inserted at the very end of the first time unit (in 10:1–8). The pattern indeed designates it as the climactic narrative element of the whole sequence, and its location at a turning point from both a compositional and a narrative point of view within the double unit reflects and reinforces its importance. Similarly, the inner section of 2 Maccabees 10:1–8, which forms a self-contained narrative cluster depicting the episode of the refoundation, closely tallies with Hurowitz's proposed outline. In contrast, the parallel account of 1 Maccabees 4:36–61 displays bold variants, although it is recognizably modeled on the pattern Hurowitz identifies. However, the boldest creative variations of the template are found in the last literary units of 1 and 2 Maccabees, respectively, which unexpectedly turn out to duplicate the narrative pattern, albeit in noncanonical versions. In 2 Maccabees the section corresponds to the third temple story (Nikanor's Day, 14:1–15:37a); and in 1 Maccabees, to Simon's time unit (1 Macc. 13:1–16:24).

The detailed analysis of how the temple-building pattern shapes 1 and 2 Maccabees, as well as the function of its duplication in the two works, will be analyzed in the next two chapters.[23] The present chapter is devoted to answering a preliminary question: How could a narrative pattern originally coined to relay royal ideology not only outlive the demise of native kingship but eventually be used to extol the origins of a dynasty that contested for the high priesthood, and not kingship? We already have examined the theoretical terms of this question.[24] Therefore the purpose of this chapter is to complement the discussion with a concrete inquiry into the narrative pattern, which will not only outline the formal narrative elements that compose the complete pattern sequence and elucidate the generic message it emplots but will also trace their gradual transformation over time.

The presentation of the narrative scheme in the next section of this chapter will require an exploration of the two basic literary genres most narrowly associated with it, namely the myths of creation and the chroniclelike accounts of the construction of temples (and palaces) by kings. These two corpora of texts must be considered together if we wish to understand the meaning of the narrative pattern in a comprehensive way. The temple-building account enshrines an entire range of associations that revolve around four closely interlocking narrative morphemes, namely the king, the temple, the ordering of the divine cosmos (and law), and the ordering of society. It is this fourfold framework that served as the vehicle of royal ideology, since individual rulers were associated with specific forms of social order, and the organization of society had to replicate the order of the cosmos in order to be legitimate.

In the ancient Near East, power was never grasped in an abstract form but through its embodiment in specific kings and dynasties. This way of thinking explains why kingship could become a metaphor for all forms of power. With the demise of native kingship, the symbolic representations originally related to native kings came to denote any embodiment of political power. As part of this process, the narrative pattern of the temple-building account was accommodated to the forms of political and social organization that began to replace native kingship. In section 2.2 of this chapter, a historical survey will trace the evolution of the narrative pattern of the temple-building account in the cultural realm of Judah/Judea. My purpose here is to investigate how the details of the narrative framework were successively modified in order to adapt to the evolving configuration of rule that Judahite/Judean society went through up until Hellenistic times. Notwithstanding this process, throughout its adaptation the temple-building account retained the four fundamental poles and its legitimizing function. In light of this historical perspective, it will seem only natural that the temple-building account continued to adapt itself likewise in 1 and 2 Maccabees.

2.1. TEMPLE BUILDING, ORDERING OF THE WORLD, AND ORDERING OF SOCIETY: THE ANCIENT NEAR EASTERN TRADITION OF POLITICAL LEGITIMIZATION

In the ancient Near East the building of a temple was not a material process alone. As the abode of the deity on earth, the temple was the fulcrum between earth and heaven. Simple though it may seem, this proposition encapsulates a broad set of interconnected concepts. By linking heaven and earth while maintaining their perpetual separation, the temple preserved the order established at Creation and held chaos at bay.[25] At the same time, it ensured the survival and orderly functioning of its society. Effectively, according to the ancient Semitic conception, gods physically inhabited their temples and therefore could not dwell amid their peoples unless these shrines were built and operated properly—and society could not function without this divine presence.[26] Next, the construction of the temple required a king, because temple building was a royal privilege, and it was the king's task to provide the temple personnel with the necessary supplies for sacrifices.[27] Finally, carrying out this royal task presupposed that the king had imposed social justice and social order among his people, the guarantee of economic prosperity.

The various aspects of this close-knit vision of society are precisely brought out in the narrative pattern of temple foundation. Out of the wide range of literary texts that both reflect this vision and conform to the narrative pattern, two are particularly relevant to our concern, namely the myths of creation, which talk of the building of temples by the gods themselves, and texts describing the building of temples by kings (royal building inscriptions in Mesopotamia, prophetic and historical texts in the Judahite/Judean literary corpus). Thanks to their complex narrative sequence unfolding from the creation of an ordered cosmos through the establishment of structured human society to the foundation of the temple, myths of creation are particularly helpful for clarifying the conceptual status of the temple, the physical interface between the cosmos and human society. Not only does this representation offer one more example that the modern separation between religion and political and social matters proves inept for grasping ancient constructions of social reality,[28] but it indirectly provides a decisive clue to why the narrative pattern of temple foundation—with which, we may insist, myths of creation share the same set of underlying concepts and formal narrative structures—retained its conceptual cogency after the demise of native kingship. Whatever its form, in order to be validated, the existing social order needed to be associated with the rest of the conceptual and narrative items that clustered around the temple in a complex albeit coherent semantic field. Therefore the myths of creation deserve a short survey before we turn to texts featuring human kings.

2.1.1. *The Semantic Field of Ancient Near Eastern Cosmogonies*

Although in some areas of the ancient Near East myths of creation also included theogonies, we are primarily concerned with their cosmogonies, which focused on the ordering of the cosmos and human society out of chaos.[29] To put this more precisely: the narrative sequence of the cosmogony brings together the ordering of the cosmos, the ordering of society, the building of the temple-palace,[30] and the institution of kingship, revealing the conceptual link connecting these notions together.[31] The full sequence may be illustrated by the Akkadian myth of Enuma Eliš (second millennium B.C.E.) and the "Baal cycle" of Ugarit (fourteenth century B.C.E.), whereas in the ancient Hebrew literature the themes are quoted in shorter sequences of more allusive tone.[32] These are found in the psalms sometimes called Psalms of Enthronement as well as in passages of the Pentateuch and the Prophets.[33]

In the ancient Near Eastern cosmogony, order is achieved through a cosmic battle between order and chaos. In this battle, the storm god, who is also a king deity, slays either a sea monster or Death, or the Desert, all embodiments of chaos, of a world in which life is not possible.[34] What emerges out of the victory of the king-deity over chaos is an ordered human society.[35] In Enuma Eliš, Marduk is enthroned in his temple-palace, and the implication seems to be that kingship and temple are indispensable institutions to guarantee the existence of an ordered society.[36] As king, Marduk will look after the sanctuaries of his fathers, the elder gods, and will care for food offerings for them. In the last sequence of the myth, mankind is created in order to relieve the gods of their work and serve them, especially Marduk in his temple of Babylon. This, we need to understand, is the final purpose of society—that is, of humanity itself. In the Baal cycle of Ugarit, following his victory over the principle of chaos Baal asks to build his temple-palace and receives permission from El, the supreme god. As soon as his temple-palace is built, Baal invites the gods to a banquet to assert his power over them and proclaims his kingship.[37] As in Enuma Eliš, the building of the temple-palace and the establishment of Baal's kingship represent the birth of organized society.[38] Last, as with Marduk and Baal, YHWH's victory over chaos entitles Him to kingship and enthronement,[39] and the Psalms of Enthronement present the emergence of Israel as a people (that is, as an organized human society) as the result—and final act—of the cosmogony.

The Ugaritic mythical cycle of Baal dates to the fourteenth century B.C.E., and the Hebrew psalms and passages from the Pentateuch referring to cosmogonic themes are usually held to be ancient. Prima facie, the chronological gap seems to preclude the relevance of this mythical material for the analysis of 2 Maccabees. However, the gap between these early traditions and the time of the Hasmoneans may be bridged in two ways. First, the continued cultural vitality of the themes belonging to the semantic complex of the cosmogony is evidenced by their resurgence in Deutero-Isaiah, which is usually dated to Persian times, as well as in Daniel 7, a chapter belonging to the part of the book of Daniel (chs. 7–12) whose final edition, if not actual redaction, is contemporary with the days of the Judean revolt against Antiochos IV.[40] Likewise, the ongoing adaptation of the myths of creation in texts that were produced in Judea in Hellenistic times and were eventually left out the canon of the Hebrew Bible, like 1 Enoch (Ethiopic Enoch), is well researched.[41]

The second channel bridging between early traditions and Hellenistic Judea is the liturgical setting of the Psalms of Enthronement. The combined themes of Creation and YHWH's kingship are associated with the Festival of the Booths (or Tabernacles, or Sukkoth), which is conceptually linked to the Festival of the New Year.[42] Because of this liturgical connection there can be little doubt that the semantic association between the birth of the temple, the birth of the world, the birth of human society, and YHWH's kingship continued to be part of the cultural heritage of the Judeans—at least, the learned Judeans—down to Hellenistic times.[43] To anticipate the discussion of 2 Maccabees 10:1–8, it is certainly no coincidence that the ceremony of the rededication of the temple carried out by Judas Maccabee and his followers was modeled after the Festival of Sukkoth (2 Macc. 10:6). Before them, according to the Judahite/Judean tradition, Solomon had celebrated the dedication of his newly built temple during this festival (1 Kgs 8; 2 Chr 5–6), and the dedication of the rebuilt wall of Jerusalem by Nehemiah also coincided with the Sukkoth celebrations.[44] Moreover, the references to the refoundation of the temple by Zerubbabel and Joshua in HZ are interlaced with typical cosmogonic images.[45]

If we extrapolate from the ancient Near Eastern cosmogonies and their cultic setting to actual royal practice, it is not difficult to conclude that founding or refounding the temple of the chief deity of the society was an assertion of (royal) power. However, in order to fully understand the complex framework of social and political ideas that explain why the Maccabees modeled their commemorative festival upon that of Sukkoth, it is necessary to turn to our second corpus, namely the accounts of temple building featuring human kings.

2.1.2. Human Kings and Temple Building

A. *Hurowitz's Six-Part Narrative Pattern.*   Although Hurowitz showed that the fully fleshed-out cosmogonies are informed by the same six-part narrative pattern as temple building, the material dealing with mortal kings is inevitably more abundant. The pattern structures not only the royal building inscriptions of Mesopotamia but also the Hebrew texts that narrate the foundation of the temple of Jerusalem by Solomon and its refoundation in Persian times.[46] Each of the six parts of the template is in turn subdivided into a limited set of elements, which may or may not be found in individual inscriptions. Variants either may be characteristic of a specific time and culture (e.g., Neo-Assyrian, Neo-Babylonian) or may be specific to one king or even one inscription. The basic six-part outline of the pattern is presented here together with the main subtopics, since a minimal acquaintance with the latter will be helpful when we turn to analyze the topical sequence of 1 and 2 Maccabees in the next two chapters.[47]

1. *Decision to build and divine approval.* This step may spell out the *circumstances* that led to the project of building the temple; the *initiative* may stem from either the king or the deity. In the former case, divine approval must be sought, and it is obtained either through divination or through a dream. When the text concerns a refoundation, background information is offered about the *earlier history of the temple* that is being restored. Insofar as the destruction of a temple was perceived as the consequence of the wrath of the deity who yielded His or Her people to enemies, the story of the restoration often includes the account of the *defeat of the enemy* and the people's *reconciliation* with their patron deity.[48]
2. *Preparations for the building.* The preparatory phase may combine material and social aspects. On the material side, the *gathering of building materials*, the *drafting of workers*, and the laying of foundations are likely to be mentioned. In addition, the establishment or *restoration of peace* and *social justice* is a prerequisite to the construction of the temple.
3. *Description of the construction process* and of the buildings and furnishings.

4. *Dedication rites and festivities.* This part recalls how the god, goddess, or divine couple entered the temple, the inception or resumption of *sacrifices,* the accompanying *music* and popular festivities, and the installation of the temple personnel. *Social justice* is imposed.
5. *Blessing of the king by the deity, or prayer of the king to request this blessing, or both.* The themes of the divine blessing include a promise of prosperity and long life, together with the promise of a stable dynasty.
6. *Divine promises, or revelation, or both; blessings and curses on future generations.* Blessings for the king, or those who will preserve the temple and remain faithful to its divine dweller, or both, are balanced with curses on trespassers. Norms are established.⁴⁹

Two aspects of the semantic field of this narrative pattern require particular attention, namely the association between the king and the temple, and the association between the temple and social justice (i.e., the social order corresponding to the cosmic order of the Creation). The former is essential to understand the political significance of the Hanukkah story in both 1 and 2 Maccabees, whereas the latter provides the background to reexamine the meaning of *Ioudaïsmos* in 2 Maccabees.⁵⁰

B. King and Temple: Temple Building as the Prerogative of Victorious Gods and Kings. The association of king and temple first comes to the fore in step 1, which associates the victory over the enemy and the decision to build the temple. In concept, and probably also in actuality, the construction of a temple followed a victory—or at least, a claim to victory, as though to manifest that the candidate was genuinely entitled to be a king and therefore a temple (and palace) builder.⁵¹ The primordial victory was the cosmic victory of the demiurgic god over the principle of chaos. In the myth, as we saw, Marduk asks the great gods' permission to build the temple of Ešarra for them after slaying Tiamat.⁵² But of course gods also won worldly battles through the arms of their elected kings. Therefore victory had the twofold consequence of entitling the king to build a temple for his god or goddess (or a palace for himself) and of entitling the god or goddess to receive His or Her house.

The motif of victory preceding the decision to build a temple is particularly recurrent in Assyrian and Neo-Babylonian royal inscriptions.⁵³ The Hebrew traditions associated with David and Solomon express a similar ideology, and likewise the defeat of the enemy is presented as a prelude to the refoundation of the temple in HZ.⁵⁴ Cyrus's toppling of the Neo-Babylonian empire is credited to YHWH, justifying Cyrus's proclamation that YHWH's temple should be rebuilt and His people sent back to their land—that is, to the temple site—as the appropriate workforce.⁵⁵ In Babylon, Cyrus ascribes his victory to Marduk, claiming that he was chosen by Marduk to restore order in Babylon and rebuild the god's temple, which had fallen in ruins.⁵⁶

C. *Temple Building and Kingship of Divine Election: The Dynastic Promise.* Cyrus's example shows how, from a royal privilege associated with victory, temple building could easily be turned into a sign that the winner was entitled to kingship. Another striking historical instance of the connection between temple building (or rebuilding) and royal legitimation is offered by Alexander's conquest of Babylon, proving that the traditions inherited from the time of native kingship were all but forgotten in Babylonia at the inception of the Hellenistic era. After the negotiated surrender of the city, the conqueror was ceremoniously received by the priests of Bel, the city leaders, and the population. If Alexander's first step was to take possession of the royal palace, immediately after this he ordered the refoundation of the temples destroyed by Xerxes, especially the temple of Bel, "whom the Babylonians honor before all gods."[57] Later, Alexander performed the sacrifices according to the instructions of the local priests.[58]

This function of royal legitimization is rooted in the long tradition of dynastic promises that crown the ceremonies of temple dedication. According to Hurowitz's six-step pattern, the last part of the building accounts consists of a divine blessing upon the king, including a promise of dynastic stability. In the Hebrew traditions about David and Solomon, the divine blessing unambiguously becomes a dynastic pledge. The promise is first bestowed to David in anticipation and later renewed to Solomon after YHWH has properly entered His temple.[59] The promise is part of a contract of reciprocity between the deity and the king: the king builds a house to YHWH, and YHWH builds a great house—that is, a lasting dynasty—in honor of the king.[60] This was the essence of the ancient Near Eastern ideology of sacral kingship that was shared by Judahite society.

D. *Temple Building, Cosmic Harmony, and Social Justice.* As we saw, the procession that brought the statues of the god and his consort into the temple at the inauguration of the newly built (or rebuilt) edifice formed the climax of the dedication rites, and the same is true of the ushering of the Ark of the Covenant into the temple of Jerusalem under Solomon. By dwelling in His temple, YHWH not only places His name in it but also institutes cosmic harmony ("peace").[61] Hence the need for *peace* to be reestablished prior to the commencement of building. Reestablished indeed, since the decision to build a temple (or a palace) is ideally both the consequence and the reward of victory. Thus David and Solomon successively declare their intention to build the temple when they are at rest from their enemies.[62] Likewise Zechariah 1:11 proclaims that earth is at peace at the beginning of the building works.[63] Subsequently, peace is restored after temporary disruption by revolt, and building works are resumed.[64]

That said, peace involves more than just a final victory over chaos (for divine kings) and over enemies (for mortal ones). In myths, the definitive victory over chaos entails the establishment of a new cosmic and social order. Whereas in the world of men the restoration of peace after the defeat of the enemies is coupled with the preliminary restoration of *social justice*—a staple topos that can be traced back as early as the Sumerian cylinder of Gudea (ca. 2000 B.C.E.), the *ensi* (ruler) of Lagaš. Before commencing building works for Eninnu (Ningirsu's temple), Gudea not only brought peace upon the city but took pains to ensure social equity among its population.[65] Closer in time to the period under study, similar steps were undertaken by Nabonidus.[66] Zechariah 5:1–4 announces the imposition of justice in society, symbolized by a Torah scroll.[67] In other cases, temple building was the *prelude* to the institution of social harmony.[68] In the book of Ezra, the story of the refoundation of the temple is placed at the beginning of the book by way of a preface to the ensuing description of Ezra's reforms.[69]

The sequential association between temple building and the establishment of social order so clearly articulated in myths of creation reflects the idea that the legitimate social order—social justice—mirrors the grand cosmic order.[70] It follows, therefore, that the agency of the king in imposing this justice is fundamental—be it divine or human. Insofar as the (human) king is the vicar of the demiurgic god-king on earth, his righteousness consists in mapping the divine order onto society; and alongside his building of the temple, establishing justice and equity in society is his main task. In both cases, he is guided by his wisdom. It is noteworthy that in Sumerian and Old Babylonian inscriptions, kings are granted wisdom by the gods to build the temple[71] *and* to govern with justice and equanimity, and the character of Solomon in the book of Kings uses his wisdom for the same two purposes.[72]

The fundamental correspondence between the cosmic and social orders implies that the element at stake in the worldly side of the equation was not righteousness merely as one aspect of kingship but righteousness—the imposition of proper social order—as the very *essence* of kingship. This nexus explains why a change of dynasty, and all the more so a change in the form of rule, needed to be rooted in a temple refoundation and hence a symbolic recreation of the cosmic order, exactly as if the refoundation of a temple embodied the recreation of the world. This general reshuffling was precisely what ensured the continued harmony between the cosmic and social orders. Thus, in cultures that generally condemned innovation as sinful, any social reforms—let alone usurpations of power—were represented as restorations of social justice epitomized in physical restorations; no wonder, then, that usurpers hastened to rebuild the local temples. To anticipate our detailed discussion below in Chapter 3, the concept of proper social order established by the legitimate ruler at the foundation (or refoundation) of the temple was captured in the neologism *Ioudaïsmos* by the author of 2 Maccabees.[73]

To trace the transformation of the concept of social justice—or proper social order—however, we need to start from the king. The notion of kingship may be seen as a metaphor for all forms of power. Indeed, power was grasped never in abstract form but through its embodiment in specific rulers and dynasties; and similarly, the notion of ideal rule was not explored through theoretical treatises but was emplotted and embodied in a concrete biography, which was idealized for this purpose. By analogy, rulers who were not kings could be objects of the same type of stereotyped emplotment. The Hebrew literary traditions patently illustrate how the various narrative components of the temple-building pattern were progressively modified over time, keeping abreast of changing configurations of rule. With the demise of native kingship, symbolic representations originally related to native kings came to denote any embodiment of political power. As part of this symbolic transfer, the narrative pattern of the temple-building account—and, to some extent, the associated cosmogonic speculations—were accommodated to the emerging forms of political and social organization that began to replace native kingship. This happened first under the Achaimenids with the division of power between the Persian governor and the native high priest, and later with the assumption of royal competences by the high priest—in all likelihood after the fall of the Persian empire.

2.2. SYMBOLIC REPRESENTATIONS OF POWER IN YEHUD/JUDEA FROM THE RETURN TO HELLENISTIC TIMES

The literary material that mirrors the ongoing political evolution of Judah in Persian and early Hellenistic times is remarkably abundant.[74] Two successive organizations of the society are documented. In the first, power is divided between the Persian governor and the high priest. In the second, the high priest alone stands in the place of the king. These two political orders, moreover, are reflected through different angles. Five issues will be surveyed here: the rebuilding of the Jerusalem temple under the Achaimenids and the legitimization of the division of power between the Persian governor and the high priest as it is construed in HZ; the catalogues inserted in Ezra-Nehemiah and 1 Esdras as a refoundation of society; the link, according to the book of Nehemiah, between Ezra's reforms and Nehemiah's reconstruction of Jerusalem's wall; the depiction of the royal prerogatives of the high priest in Ben Sira's Praise of the Fathers; and the translation of the political status of the high priest of Judea in Greek political idiom as a *theokratia* in Hekataios of Abdera and in the Letter of Aristeas.

2.2.1. *Yehudite/Judean Traditions about the Rebuilding of the Jerusalem Temple by Zerubbabel and Joshua*

The traditions relating to the refoundation of the Jerusalem temple in Persian times are preserved in the Massoretic books of Ezra and Nehemiah (usually treated as a single unit, Ezra-Nehemiah, henceforth EN), and LXX 1 Esdras, as well as in Haggai-Zechariah 1–8 (HZ). In a detailed study of the ideological and religious conceptions encapsulated in HZ, Arnaud Sérandour has shown how the replacement of native kingship with a new distribution of power, in which a governor and a high priest coexisted, led to the alteration not only of political but also of cosmological representations.[75] The intrinsic coherence of this complex set of variants—introduced in particular through the editorial framework of HZ—reveals how deeply interconnected the various conceptual elements contained in the temple-building template were felt to be.

A. The Governor and the High Priest: Probable Historical Background. Recently, students of Persian Yehud have become skeptical about the historical accuracy of the account of the Return from the Babylonian exile as it is transmitted in the literary texts now gathered in the Hebrew Bible and the Septuagint.[76] These scholars support an alternative chronological framework resulting from a comparative analysis of the literary texts against archeological evidence and the Aramaic papyri from Elephantine (in Upper Egypt).[77] Although Judah remained a distinct administrative entity in the aftermath of Nebuchadnezzar II's conquest of 586 B.C.E., its capital was moved to Mizpah.[78] The date when Jerusalem recovered its ancient glory, with the reconstruction of its temple and the relocation of the administrative center there, remains conjectural, although the Passover papyrus, a letter dated to 419/418 B.C.E. enjoining the Judean settlers of Elephantine to adopt the customary law of the Jerusalem temple for the Passover festival, provides a terminus ante quem.[79] Given the link between the office of high priest and the Jerusalem temple, the former was most probably instituted either in the context of the refoundation of the temple or the relocation of the administrative capital in Jerusalem.

The institution of the high priest was an innovation. In the days of the native monarchy each temple was administered independently, and the king either appointed or confirmed the persons who stood at the head of each. In contrast, the high priesthood of Jerusalem was a hereditary office, and the governor had no say in the appointment of the incumbent. In addition, the high priest of Jerusalem exercised his jurisdiction over all the sanctuaries of Yehud and even those located outside it, such as the temple of Yaho in Elephantine.[80] Thus the institution of the high priesthood resulted in the innovative juxtaposition of two spheres of jurisdiction.[81] While the powers of the hereditary high priest extended over all the sanctuaries and their personnel, as well as family cult and specific social institutions, the governor—who was appointed by the Persian administration and was the representative of the Persian king—inherited the main royal competences, in particular that of building the temple and other urban monuments, imposing order and justice, and ensuring the regular payment of the tribute to the central Persian treasury.[82]

B. The Symbolic Translation of the New Order in the Yehudite/Judean Literary Tradition about the Time of the Return: The Joined Election. Ancient societies were averse to the idea of change. Social order was legitimate insofar as it was an accurate reflection of the cosmic order and was therefore considered as immutable as the latter. Therefore, although the division of power between the governor and the high priest was the fruit of reform—and was probably not established prior to the second half of the fifth century B.C.E.—the social memory of the early times of the Return collected in HZ, EN, and 1 Esdras antedates this division to the very days of the Return, and naturally situates the reconstruction of the Jerusalem temple much earlier in time than historical circumstances allow. In HZ, the royal prerogative to initiate the refoundation of the temple is shared by the governor and the high priest. This has no parallel in the Mesopotamian corpus, in which the status of high priests is never equated with that of kings. In contrast, in HZ, YHWH's order to rebuild the temple, which is transmitted through the prophet Haggai, is jointly addressed to Zerubbabel son of Shealtiel, the Persian governor of Davidic descent, and to Joshua son of Jehozadak, the high priest.[83] Similarly, the divine promise of prosperity that accompanies the injunction to rebuild is addressed to both Zerubbabel and Joshua.[84] However, the transfer of the royal prerogatives to the high priest is limited to the temple refoundation, and the dynastic promise is addressed to Zerubbabel alone.[85] (See below, §2.2.1C.)

At the same time, the demise of genuine native kingship is duly accounted for and, notwithstanding Zerubbabel's Davidic descent, Darius alone is granted the title "king" in dating formulas.[86] Strikingly, the demise of native kingship entails one further change, the collectivization of the royal responsibility to rebuild the temple, now entrusted to the people of Israel as a whole. Thus the "remnant of the people" (i.e., the Returnees) is systematically included alongside Zerubbabel and Joshua as the recipient of both the divine injunction to rebuild and of the divine promise.[87] Nonetheless, the two leaders are singled out by name, and the collectivization of the order is made compatible with the existing social hierarchy.[88] As we shall see in the next chapter, the people as a collective participate in the refoundation of the temple by the Maccabees in 1 and 2 Maccabees, and the collectivization of the royal competences in these texts must be seen as an inheritance of earlier times.

C. Temple Refoundation, Recreation of the World, and the Division of Power: The Twofold Division of the World at Creation. The victory that was won by YHWH and that justified the restoration of His house was not only an earthly victory—secured through the hands of either Cyrus or "Darius"—but also a cosmic one, as in the Psalms of Enthronement.[89] The first relevant passage is the second part of the oracle urging Zerubbabel, Joshua, and the people to begin the works of reconstruction in Haggai 2:6–9.[90] The literary construction of these verses mimics the violent reordering of the universe that accompanies YHWH's installation in His temple-palace. The image of the earthquake—"I will shake the heavens and the earth"—is a well-known theophanic motif, while the precious materials that the temple is made of are gathered from the far corners of the world, turning the divine house into a symbolic epitome of the whole of Creation.[91] Yet the most striking detail of the prophecy is the double division of the cosmos that accompanies the refoundation of the temple: "I will shake the heavens and the earth *and* the sea and the dry land." The realm on which YHWH establishes His rule is divided twice, vertically and horizontally. The establishment of the cosmic order at Creation consists in a process of separation: that is, of division. However, the primitive division is usually what separates heaven and earth. As it turns out, this constitutive division of the cosmos was perceived as a cosmic guarantee of the rule of a single king. Consequently, in the present prophecy the process of primitive division is duplicated to affect not only heaven and earth but also the sea and dry land. This duplication of the constitutive act of Creation is the counterpart of the division of power between the Davidic governor and the Zadokite high priest.[92] As we saw above, the legitimate social order is what replicates the cosmic order on earth. To be legitimate, the division of power must be shown to be rooted in the process of cosmic Creation.

The epiphanic image of shaking the heavens and the earth that closes the book of Haggai is associated with the promise of victory over the enemies and the promise of divine election that are uttered to Zerubbabel the governor as the builder of the temple.[93] These verses put forward the conditional dynastic promise handed down from the traditional royal ideology. In effect, the promise constitutes a renewal of the dynastic pledge that had once been uttered to David and Solomon.[94] Thus it appears that the refoundation of the Jerusalem temple by Zerubbabel and Joshua reaffirms the original foundation by Solomon and acknowledges the same symbolic status. At the same time, the dynastic promise to Zerubbabel brings together the refoundation of the temple by Zerubbabel the governor, the recreation of the universe through divine epiphany—"I am about to shake the heavens and the earth and to overthrow the throne of kingdoms" (Hag. 2:21)—the promise of the defeat of the enemies,[95] the election of the temple builder, and finally a renewed covenant with the people, manifested by cosmic harmony and material wealth.[96] This promise, like the rest of the prophecies collected in HZ, leaves no doubt that the traditional construal of the building of the temple as the ultimate purpose and climax of Creation remained lively in Persian Yehud and was knowingly associated with the rebuilt edifice. As for the cultic reality with which this nexus of representations is associated, it is made explicit by the framing dates. Both the day of the ceremony of laying the founding stone (2:18)—that is, the very day of the foundation of the temple and the utterance of the dynastic promise (2:20)—fall on the twenty-fourth day of the (ninth) month. This is the date of the Sukkoth festival, whose specific association with rites of kingship and rites of temple foundation were noted above.[97]

D. *The Refoundation of Society: The Catalogues of Ezra-Nehemiah and 1 Esdras*   As we saw above, the primary function of men in Enuma Eliš, the Babylonian myth of creation, is to care for the gods and build their temples. Because of their literary genre, neither EN nor 1 Esdras makes explicit reference to the cosmic aspect of the refoundation of the temple, in contrast with the prophetic text of HZ. Nevertheless, their accounts of the Return bring further confirmation that the refoundation of the temple was construed as the recreation of human society. Thus when Cyrus orders the reconstruction of YHWH's house following his victory, his first step is to send the Returnees back home, since the latter, as in Enuma Eliš, constitute the appropriate workforce needed for this task.

The account of 1 Esdras is particularly explicit in allocating a common fate to YHWH's temple and YHWH's people. Temple and society had been destroyed together by Nebuchadnezzar, and the holy vessels and the people deported together to Babylon.[98] Not only do holy vessels and people return together, but their joined restoration is made in an orderly way. Catalogues of vessels and Returnees are inserted in 1 Esdras as well as in EN, and their function is clearly to manifest the orderly division of both vessels and men. The two are named by categories (forms and metal for the vessels; Israel, priests, Levites and temple servants, tribes and families, clean and unclean, for the Returnees) and are counted to the last unit.[99] Inasmuch as creation is the process by which the unshaped chaos is ordered into its fitted categories through the process of division, an undifferentiated throng of men and heaps of objects cannot form a society. Therefore their ordered cataloguing may be seen as a statement that the Return was a recreation of society.

The association between Creation of the world and construction of the temple on the one hand and the vital need to harmonize the cosmogonic account with the representation of the political power in society on the other shows that the modern tendency to define the Yahwistic "religious" system as a set of abstract beliefs alone ("monotheism") is far too reductive.[100] In reality, the political and social order of Persian Yehud is part and parcel of the cosmological representations put forward by the texts relating to the refoundation of the Jerusalem temple under the Achaimenids. At the same time, the lack of any explicit reference to these cosmological speculations in EN and 1 Esdras reminds us that the literary genre of each text also had a determining influence on its specific content. Myths of creation, psalms, prophetic texts, and narrative accounts dealing with human society (the historical works) emphasize different aspects. As far as their literary genre is concerned, 1 and 2 Maccabees are closer to EN and 1 Esdras. The absence of explicit reference to cosmological ideas in these texts is a generic feature and cannot support the view that their authors differentiated between "religion" and "politics."

Defining the Yahwistic religious system of Persian times as integrating the conception of the political and social order within its cosmological representation invites us to question the common modern understanding of the meaning of *Ioudaïsmos* in 2 Maccabees. If we read the text with this Persian heritage in mind, it is far from certain that *Ioudaïsmos* means "Judaism" in the modern sense of the word (that is, a set of beliefs in God associated with a set of ritual practices carried out by individuals in the private and social realms—as opposed to the "public" spheres of their homes and synagogues). Insofar as the narrative pattern of temple-building accounts informs the narrative of 2 Maccabees, our working hypothesis must be that the semantic field of *Ioudaïsmos* in this work encompasses the entire framework of interrelated political and cosmological representations that characterized the Yahwistic system in earlier times. At the same time, there is no reason to doubt that these representations went through further modifications in order to adapt them to the cultural, religious, social, and political conditions that prevailed at the time of the redaction of 2 Macabees, namely the period of Hasmonean rule.

Before we turn to 2 Maccabees, however, it is appropriate to pursue our historical survey of the reshaping of the temple-building account. This historical inquiry will show how the gap was gradually bridged between the ideological needs of the native kingship that dictated the original configuration of the narrative pattern of temple building and the needs of the Hasmonean dynasty.

2.2.2. Nehemiah's Reconstruction of Jerusalem's Wall and Ezra's Refoundation of the Social Order

Our next step is Ezra's reforms in Persian times. Remembered as the most important reformer in the subsequent Judean tradition, Ezra promoted the Pentateuch as the Law of Israel, promulgating the Prophets alongside the Torah, and renewed the covenant between Israel and its God that was to endure in subsequent generations. Despite this, no temple refoundation is reported in his days, which entailed finding a conceptual equivalent with which to associate Ezra's social reforms (his "restoration of social justice"). In the present case, this symbolic function was fulfilled by Nehemiah's repair of Jerusalem's wall and gates, and it was signified that by the fact that Nehemiah's act is informed by the narrative pattern of the temple's building. As a matter of fact the reconstruction of the wall could easily be seen as a symbolic extension of the temple, since after its completion it marked the physical boundary separating the in-group from outsiders. On Sabbaths and festival days members of the in-group alone were allowed in through the city gates, which were closed to foreign women and their sons, and to all merchants from outside.[101] Moreover, the temple and the wall of Jerusalem were associated by another vital link in the social memory of the Judeans, since Solomon, the first builder of the temple, was also the first to build the city wall.[102] The two, alongside Solomon's edification of the royal palace, are precisely associated in the book of Kings.[103]

According to Nehemiah's memoirs (Neh. 2:1), he was sent to Jerusalem "in the twentieth year of king Artaxerxes" at his own request in order to rebuild the city wall. However, the reliability of this chronological notation is dubious, and the date of his mission and its chronological relation to Ezra's reforms are debated, such that the very historicity of these events has been questioned.[104] This notwithstanding, it is widely agreed that the conflation of Nehemiah's reconstruction of the city and Ezra's refoundation of the social order was the work of later editors.[105] In light of numerous notations aiming to equate the rebuilding of the city wall with the rebuilding of the temple, it is tempting to think that a traditional need for social reforms to correspond to the rebuilding of a temple—the concrete sign of a cosmic refoundation—was part of the editorial rationale, if not its main motivation.

Hurowitz identifies the account of Nehemiah's restoration of Jerusalem's wall and gates (Neh. 1–6, 12) as a topical variant of the narrative template.[106] Indeed its successive steps are easily traced in the book of Nehemiah if we allow for necessary variants that the difference between a temple and a city wall imposes:[107]

1. *Decision to build.* Nehemiah 1 relates the *circumstances* in which Nehemiah took the decision to go to Jerusalem and rebuild the city wall. Since he lives in "Susa, the capital" (1:1), he is informed by men arriving from Yehud that the wall and the gates lie in ruins (1:2–3). Nehemiah first turns to his God in a prayer of *reconciliation,* in which the city to be rebuilt is explicitly identified as the place chosen by YHWH to establish His name: that is, as the place of YHWH's temple (1:9). Next Nehemiah requests King Artaxerxes to send him on a mission to Yehud (2:1–9). Once there, he inspects the wall (2:11–16), and his call to the people to rebuild it is met with an enthusiastic response, despite the opposition of the neighbors (2:17–20).

2. *Preparations for the building.* Before departing from Susa, Nehemiah requests a letter from the king instructing the keeper of the king's forest to give him "timber to make beams for the gates of the temple fortress, and for the wall of the city, and for the house that I shall occupy" (Neh. 2:8). Chapter 3 of the book of Nehemiah is a *list of workers,* which offers striking literary affinities with the catalogues of Returnees that occur elsewhere in EN and 1 Esdras (e.g., Neh. 7:5–73). The workers are posted to the different wall sections and gates to be rebuilt according to their status (priests, Israelites, and Levites) and according to their families and dwelling places, rather than according only to their professional skills.[108] (Compare Neh. 5:70.) Thus the building works are the occasion for reasserting—in fact refounding—the social organization of the community. The setting up of guardians to protect the building works from hostile neighbors assumes the same function (Neh. 4:13–14).

This material aspect of the preparation is accompanied by the restoration of *social justice* by Nehemiah, who is the governor (5:1–19).

3. The *description of the construction process* is dramatized by the account of the intrigues plotted by the hostile neighbors (Neh. 4; 6:1–14). Their defeat is a sign

that the work has been accomplished "with the help of YHWH" (6:16), as would suit a temple. Finally the wall is completed, and the date of the event duly recorded (6:15).

4. *Dedication rites and festivities.* Nehemiah's first step is to appoint "the gatekeepers, the singers, and the Levites" (7:1), as though the temple itself were being refounded and the temple personnel needed to be appointed anew. (Compare 12:44–47.) A catalogue of Returnees is inserted at this point (7:5–73), and the contribution that they bring includes priestly robes (vv. 70, 72), clearly for temple service. Thus, the refoundation of society goes hand in hand with the refoundation of the temple as an institution, if not as an edifice. In addition, the construction of the city wall makes one further contribution to the reordering of the people, since the wall reifies the separation between the community of those who are bound by YHWH's covenant and the foreigners, who are not (10:28–31; 13:1–3).[109] Division, as we already saw, is the key concept of Creation, be it the separation of heaven from earth or the proper divisions of society.

The completion of the wall is also the occasion for Ezra's reading of the Law (8:1–12) as a prelude to the celebration of the Festival of Booths (Sukkoth: 8:13–18), which is depicted as a founding celebration.[110] Thus, the rebuilding of the city wall, which was completed shortly before (6:15), allowed the reading of the Law and the resumption of the regular celebration of the festival, thereby playing a role similar to that of the rededication of the altar and the temple in the days of Zerubbabel and Joshua.[111] To remind us: Sukkoth was the very festival celebrating the dedication of the temple in Solomon's days and the dedication of its refoundation in the days of Zerubbabel and Joshua; and as noted above, the festival instituted by the Maccabees and the people to commemorate their own refoundation of the temple was modeled after it. A collective confession of sins, whose function is to refound the social order in conformity with YHWH's Law, also takes place during the Festival of Booths ("on the twenty-fourth day of the seventh month," 9:1), and Ezra's prayer celebrates YHWH in his demiurgic function (9:6–15).

Whereas the completion of a temple allows the deity to come and dwell in it, the completion of the city wall, as it were, allows the people to come and dwell in the city. Following the confession of sins, lots are cast in order to bring one Israelite out of ten to live in the holy city of Jerusalem (11:1). The catalogue of these Israelites is duly listed (11:3–24) and is followed by a catalogue of priests and Levites (12:1–26) to ensure the presence of samples of the three components indispensable for the society to be complete.

As with a temple's refoundation, a ceremony of dedication of the city wall can now take place (12:27–43). The ceremony is similar to that of a temple dedication, including "rejoicing, thanksgiving, and singing," the Levites playing the music of "cymbals, harps, and lyres" (12:27), the priests' trumpets (12:41), and sacrifices (12:43).[112] According to a scheme that is now familiar to us from HZ, the *division of power* between the priest Ezra and the governor Nehemiah is accounted for in the division into two processions (12:31, 40):[113] one led by Ezra (12:31–37) and the other by Nehemiah (12:38–39). Finally, further reforms imposing *social justice* are implemented (ch. 13).

The final steps (5–6) in Hurowitz's scheme are borne out. The prayer is uttered by Ezra (9:6–37), and the divine promise takes the form of a renewal of the covenant (ch. 10).

Pinpointing Hurowitz's six-step narrative pattern in the book of Nehemiah is particularly relevant to our concerns for three reasons. First, its application to the rebuilding of the city wall shows its (relative) topical flexibility. To anticipate our discussion below in Chapter 4 (§4.2), the case of Nehemiah's (and Solomon's) foundation (or refoundation) of the wall facilitates the identification of Hurowitz's narrative pattern in the account of Simon's liberation of the Akra in 1 Maccabees 13:1–16:24. As we shall see, it is the theme of the rebuilding of the city wall and the cleansing of the Akra that serves as the narrative vehicle of legitimation in the case of Simon. Second, while the status of Zerubbabel as governor is ambiguous, since several sources acknowledge his Davidic line,[114] Nehemiah's is unequivocal. Therefore his character offers the first unambiguous example of the transfer of sovereign prerogatives to nonroyal rulers. With the demise of native kingship, the symbolic representations that were originally associated with native kings now come to signify any embodiment of power. Third, a group of scholars working on EN dates the final edition of the text to Hasmonean times.[115] If this later date is accepted, it implies that the modeling of the book of Nehemiah after the six-part narrative pattern, which belongs to the editorial frame, is roughly contemporary with the redactions of 1 and 2 Maccabees.[116]

2.2.3. The Holding of Royal Competence by the High Priest: Ben Sira

The innovative division of power between the high priest and the governor that seems to have come into existence in the second half of the fifth century B.C.E. prompted the need to adapt the details of the symbolic discourse to the changing social reality further and further. As the interference of the high priest in the traditional sphere of royal power increased, the ideological construction that had originally crystallized to define the status and powers of the king came to color the way the high priest was depicted. The vision of Zechariah 8 depicts a symbolic coronation of the high priest, although the royal prerogatives of the dynastic alliance and of building the temple are bestowed upon Zerubbabel alone.[117] The comprehensive transfer of royal competences to the high priest seems to date to the early Hellenistic period.[118] The traditional set of associations combining Creation, temple foundation, social restoration, and kingship was revised once again to articulate the full transfer of royal status to the high priest in meaningful terms. The continued use of this traditional mode of thinking and talking about the ruling power is illustrated in the Praise of the Fathers in Ben Sira (Ecclesiasticus) 44–50. This text, usually dated to circa 200 B.C.E., revisits the past through a carefully selected catalogue of prominent figures. The list mixes kings, prophets, and three high priests, Aaron (45:6–22), Phineas (45:23–26), and Simon (50:1–21). The eulogy of Phineas is the occasion to draw a now perfect equation between the covenant established with Phineas the high priest and the covenant established with David the king, and this is the very context in which Phineas is acclaimed as the "leader of the sanctuary and of his people" (24a).[119] In turn, the transfer of the royal prerogative of temple and monument builder is spelled out in the final eulogy of the high priest Simon son of Onias.[120]

With Ben Sira, the symbolic assimilation of the high priest to a king has been taken to its logical conclusion. This evolution of representations must have matched contemporary social reality to some extent. As a matter of fact, Josephus's story of Joseph the Tobiad (*Ant.* 12:156–222 and 228–36) and the books of 1 and 2 Maccabees bear evidence that the high priest assumed the function of a local representative in Hellenistic times. In hindsight, his ruling position was imagined as harking back to the earliest times of the Hellenistic era. In Josephus's description of Alexander's visit to Jerusalem, the high priest is unambiguously depicted as the leader who stands at the head of the welcoming delegation made up of the city's prominent men (*Ant.* 11:325–39).[121]

2.2.4. Theokratia; or, The High Priest in Greek Garb: Hekataios of Abdera and the Letter of Aristeas

Ben Sira is clearly affiliated to the Judean tradition, offering a landmark between the temple-building accounts that articulate the division of power of Persian times and 1 and 2 Maccabees. However, we are lucky to possess two further texts dating to Hellenistic times that depict the high priest as the political leader of Judea: an excerpt from Hekataios of Abdera (*ap.* Diodorus Siculus 40.3) and the Letter of Aristeas.[122] The importance of the excerpt from Hekataios has been unanimously recognized, because the author is known to have lived in the days of Ptolemy Soter and to have flourished around 300 B.C.E.[123] Consequently his testimony provides a chronological marker for dating the elimination of the figure of the governor and the appropriation of his powers by the high priest. That said, in the present case Hekataios's passage is relevant for a different reason and should be read together with the description of Jerusalem and Judea arising in the Letter of Aristeas 83–120, in particular the section that refers to the temple (100–104).[124] Hekataios's excerpt and the Letter of Aristeas both comment on the political and social organization of Judea through the lens of the *politeia,* the literary genre that had been the preeminent vehicle of expression of Greek political thought since the fifth century B.C.E. In this sense they provide a useful foil to Ben Sira, which, as we just saw, testifies to the ongoing vitality of Judahite/Judean political culture.

Basically, a *politeia* describes the political and social organization and way of life of a city or a foreign land;¹²⁵ and the constraints of the genre are evident in Hekataios, in which Judea is conventionally depicted as an autonomous polity, and any reference to foreign domination is omitted, as required by the genre. Moses is featured as the founder of a colony, and the influence of topics borrowed from the Lakedaimonian *politeia* in Hekataios has long since been noted. In this genre, of course, a cosmogony is out of place.¹²⁶

What interests us here is the depiction of the high priest standing alone at the head of the *politeia* of the Judeans—undoubtedly an unconventional feature for this genre. Greek political thought knew of only three basic *politeiai*, distinguished by the number of citizens wielding power—either one, a few, or many—and an additional distinction between the correct and incorrect forms of *politeiai* entailed a subdivision into six as early as Herodotus.¹²⁷ In the old Greek world, further political speculations seem to have been limited to the possibility of blending the positive constituents of the *basileia*, the *aristokratia*, and the *dēmokratia*. The best-known depiction of a mixed *politeia* is of course that of Polybius.¹²⁸ The substitution of a high priest for a king in the position of single ruler in the description of the Judean *politeia* constitutes a remarkable variant compared with the standard seven (including the mixed constitution).

But to what extent is this innovation genuine—that is, an unmediated reflection of an eyewitness report of the *politeia* of the Judeans? Modern scholarship has made much of Hekataios's use of local informants, and the quotation resembling a citation from the Bible that commands attention in Diodorus Siculus 40.3.6¹²⁹ does indeed support the contention that Hekataios used either eyewitnesses or a written report of such witnesses. However, his use of a direct report by no means precludes the possibility that his field information was filtered by a preexisting model of *theokratia*.¹³⁰ Temple-states headed by high priests were a familiar reality in Asia Minor and northern Syria; hence, the Greeks from Asia Minor must have been aware of their existence long before Alexander's days. Thus it is possible that the earliest instances of *theokratiai* were written there and that the model of the *theokratia* was formalized soon after Alexander, when the curiosity of Greek philosophers about non-Greek political systems increased. At the turn of the fourth and third centuries B.C.E., Euhemeros of Messene wrote a travelogue in which he imagined an island ruled by priests.¹³¹ Euhemeros's *theokratia* is thus contemporary with Hekataios's but differs in that his derives from the model of the *aristokratia*, since it was headed by a priestly class, whereas Hekataios's was an adaptation of the *basileia*, since it stresses a single high priest.¹³²

The literary formalization of Judea's political regime according to the rules of the *politeia* genre is fully accomplished in the Letter of Aristeas. In sections 100–104 the author continues Aristotle's speculation about the localization of the system of defense of the territory appropriate to each of the three basic *politeiai*.¹³³

Thus he singles out the fortress assigned to protect the temple as the unique defensive monument of the city, and this picture perfectly fits the *politeia* of the *theokratia*. Since in the latter power is exercised by the high priest and therefore localized in the temple, it follows that the main site to be protected is the temple.[134]

The numerous literary reminiscences of the genre of the *politeia* in Hekataios's description of Judea—most notably his suggestion that the polis of the Judeans enjoyed independence—together with the fact that Euhemeros depicted a *theokratia* at about the same time as Hekataios wrote his description of Judea are far more significant clues to Hekataios's working method than his quotations of genuine Judean traditions. The extensive differences between Ben Sira and the rest of the literary texts affiliated with the native Judean tradition on the one hand and the works affiliated with Greek political thought on the other are evidence that the distinct generic constraints of the Near Eastern temple-building account and the Greek *politeia* reshaped the living experience of each writer according to preestablished reading templates. In consequence, the descriptions of the social and political organization of Judea in Hekataios and in the Letter of Aristeas may act as foils against which to appreciate the intertextual references of 1 and 2 Maccabees. Although 2 Maccabees was written in Greek and purports to be the epitome of a longer Greek work written by one Jason of Cyrene, its depiction of the social and political organization of Judea owes nothing to the genre of the *politeia*. In contrast, as we shall now see, its affinities with the narrative structure of the temple-building account inherited from pre-Hellenistic Hebrew tradition are outstanding.

. . .

We have seen in this chapter that the narrative pattern of temple foundation enshrines a range of associations that revolve around four closely interlocking narrative morphemes, namely the king (or kinglike rulers), the temple, the order of the divine cosmos, and the order of society. For the ruler to be legitimate, the social order of which he is the ward needs to mirror the divine order, his foundation (or refoundation) of the temple being the concrete sign for this reflection. The temple played this function not only because it was the interface between heaven and earth, but also because of the prescribed conditions of its foundation. In a preliminary phase the ruler, as founder, had secured the agreement of his patron deity to build (or rebuild) His or Her house—that is, a temple—by reinstating social justice—that is, the social order mirroring divine law, will, and order—and thereby manifested his righteousness. Moreover, the foundation involved a double pledge between the ruler and his divine patron, the former building a house for the latter, who in return promised a house—that is, a dynasty—to his servant. The message relayed by the six-part narrative pattern of temple foundation was the most fundamental tenet of ancient Near Eastern and Judahite/Judean political thought.

Although the template retained its four fundamental poles and its legitimizing function throughout, it underwent successive modifications in the Judahite/Judean tradition in order to keep its functional cogency. The figure of the temple founder, in particular, was modified—from king to governor and high priest and to high priest alone—in order to reflect the changing forms of political organization. If we consider the narrative pattern in this dynamic aspect, the natural question becomes how, and not whether, the Hasmoneans imprinted their hallmark on this tradition. 1 and 2 Maccabees are the works in which the answer must be sought. Seeking it will be the purpose of the next two chapters.

3

Ioudaïsmos as the Legitimate Social Order Founded by Judas Maccabee

INTRODUCTION

As we saw in Chapter 2, the narrative pattern of temple foundation, which in its classical form was linked to native kingship, underwent successive alterations in the Judahite/Judean literary tradition in keeping with changes in the political structure of the region. A first set of changes endorsed the division of power between the governor and the high priest in Persian Yehud, while another reflected the grip on power of the high-priestly dynasty of the Oniads in early Hellenistic times. 1 and 2 Maccabees evince the new set of alterations that responded to the advent of the Hasmoneans, and their account of the dynasty's founding myth bears out the remarkable plasticity of the narrative template. This chapter and the next will investigate in detail how the template was refashioned in these parallel works.

The most striking innovation they introduce is the duplication of the template. The first time, it is used to encode the story of Judas Maccabee's rededication of the temple as a full-blown temple refoundation. In 2 Maccabees, as we saw in Chapter 1 (§1.3.4), the corresponding section is 4:7–13:26, whereas in 1 Maccabees it comprises Judas's time unit (1 Macc. 3:1–9:22). Within the two units, the subsections specifically depicting the "refoundation" (2 Macc. 10:1–8 and 1 Macc. 4:36–61) are again structured by the six-part pattern that Victor Hurowitz described,[1] generating a *mise en abyme*. The second occurrence corresponds to the last narrative unit of each work, respectively: that is, the last temple story in 2 Maccabees (Nikanor's Day, 14:1–15:37a) and Simon's time unit in 1 Maccabees (13:1–16:24). As will be argued below in Chapter 4, this duplication was the device that enabled the two ancient authors not only to legitimize the Hasmonean dynasty per se but also to endorse the specific form of rule that the dynasty aspired to, namely their merging of the office of high priest with that of king.

Despite their common partisan concerns, however, the parallel works modulate their political message in slightly diverging ways, thanks to their different modes of duplication, which effectively makes their accounts complementary rather than redundant. Moreover, both embark on demonstrating not only the legitimacy of the Hasmoneans but also the illegitimacy of their rivals—the "wicked" high priests Jason, Menelaos, and Alkimos on the one hand and the Seleukid kings on the other—and each author chooses a different emphasis in this respect as well. However, the most remarkable difference has to do not with topic but with form: the author of 2 Maccabees engages in an intellectual speculation that has no equivalent in 1 Maccabees, recasting traditional concepts in an innovative nomenclature.

As we saw extensively above in Chapter 2, traditionally the narrative template of temple foundation served to assert the legitimacy of specific rulers and forms of political and social organization. This is consistent with its usage on the part of the literati of the ancient Near East to expound their political viewpoints in narrative guise rather than through abstract treatises. Alongside the temple-foundation template, for instance, the concept of ideal kingship was explored in the form of biographies of historical kings, which were stereotyped by ascribing stock inventories of righteous or wicked actions to them, thus transforming their reigns accordingly into archetypal embodiments of ideal kingship or its opposite.[2] In their use of the temple-foundation template, our two Maccabees authors are unquestionably heirs to this tradition. However, the author of 2 Maccabees went one step further by conflating it with an alternative thread of political discourse that was rooted in the memory of the Return from the Babylonian Exile. Whereas the former tradition focused on the figure of the leader (either the king or his substitute), the latter referred to the community as a whole. Hence, the Returnees equated themselves with the whole of "Israel," despite their forming only one social group within the population living in Yehud/Judea and treating the other social groups as distinct *ethnic* groups. The purpose of the present chapter is to show that the neologism *Ioudaïsmos*, far from referring to "religious" issues in the narrow Western sense of the word,[3] is the fruit of our author's conflation of these two traditions, and its meaning must accordingly be determined on their basis. I argue that it denotes the social order of the Judeans that the author deemed legitimate, namely the one established by Judas Maccabee when he refounded the temple, and in which the Hasmoneans ruled.[4] By social order, we must understand the entire range of cosmological[5] and sociopolitical concepts traditionally emplotted together in the narrative pattern of temple building. In short, in a single word *Ioudaïsmos* encapsulates a particular variant of the temple-building template devised to validate the legitimacy of the Hasmonean dynasty.

The word has two features of particular interest: first, being an abstract term it contrasts with the type of metaphoric image routinely used in the prophetic and apocalyptic literature to refer to kings and empires (e.g., the four great beasts, the ram, and the male goat; and the King of the South and the King of the North in the book of Daniel, etc.), but it also departs from the traditional procedure of using a single, concrete, narrative component (e.g., thunder in cosmogonies and the temple in the temple-building template) of a set narrative pattern to stand for the whole sequence in a synecdochic relation.[6] In addition, the term itself is a case of ethnicized political nomenclature that aims to associate the political order established by the Hasmoneans with the very essence of the ethnic group, thereby "otherizing" all political rivals of Judas Maccabee outright. Logically, therefore, the ethnic term *Hellēnismos* must be understood in the same way: in 2 Maccabees, it embodies the impious cosmological and sociopolitical order headed by Jason the high priest (2 Macc. 4:13–15), whereas *allophylismos,* more speculatively, may refer to the Seleukid order.

The present chapter deals with the first occurrence of the temple-foundation account in 1 and 2 Maccabees, namely the Hanukkah story. Although the two works need to be considered together, for three reasons the following detailed analysis will give precedence to 2 Maccabees. In the first place, the description of the refoundation in 2 Maccabees 10:1–8 offers a fairly classic example of the six-step pattern identified by Hurowitz, whereas the variant in 1 Maccabees 4:36–61 is less conventional. Second, in 2 Maccabees this pivotal section is organically linked both to the broader narrative unit hosting it (the Hanukkah story, 4:7–13:26) and to the final narrative unit, the Nikanor's Day story (14:1–15:37a). In particular, key legitimizing elements of the template that we might expect to find in the Hanukkah story are instead postponed to the last unit, thereby lending structural coherence to the book as a whole. For this reason, the analysis of 2 Maccabees discloses the very principle and the function of the duplication of the template in a much clearer way than the parallel work. Last, the wider narrative unit of 2 Maccabees 4:7–13:26 presents the additional interest of using the innovative political nomenclature of *Ioudaïsmos* and *Hellēnismos* to denote the legitimate and illegitimate social orders.

In the first section below (§3.1) I will analyze the parallel descriptions of the temple refoundation (2 Macc. 10:1–8 and 1 Macc. 4:36–61) in the light of Hurowitz's six-part pattern. The second section of this chapter (§3.2) will focus on the wider narrative units of 2 Maccabees 4:7–13:26 and 1 Maccabees 3:1–9:22. In the final section (§3.3) I will dwell on the semantic field of the concept of *Ioudaïsmos* and, more succinctly, *Hellēnismos* in 2 Maccabees. The literary composition of the second occurrences of the temple-building pattern (the Nikanor's Day story in 2 Maccabees and Simon's time unit in 1 Maccabees), along with the rationale of the aforesaid duplication, will be examined in Chapter 4. As for *Hellēnismos,* by definition it has no place in the legitimate social order founded by Judas. Whereas *Ioudaïsmos* denotes the restoration of the legitimate order after the disruption, *Hellēnismos* defines the very time of disruption in which the wicked high priests ruled. As numerous commentators have noted, in 2 Maccabees the two terms are never used together—and for good reason. Nor either are the wicked priests and Judas referred to in the same section, let alone the same sentence. In line with the logic of the ancient author, the detailed analysis of the notion of *Hellēnismos*, along with the portrayal of the wicked rivals, will be postponed to Part II of this book (Chapter 5, §5.1), which deals with the causes of the rebellion according to the authors of 1 and 2 Maccabees.

3.1. THE NARRATIVE PATTERN OF TEMPLE BUILDING IN THE HANUKKAH STORY: 2 MACCABEES 10:1–8 AND 1 MACCABEES 4:36–61

As we saw in Chapter 2, the narrative template of temple building was regularly reworked at different historical moments to generate new variants that captured the changing patterns of political organization in Jerusalem. This ongoing adjustment was indispensable, of course, if the accounts were to retain their function of legitimizing the existing rule. But at the same time, there cannot be clearer proof that, throughout, the institution of the temple retained the symbolic associations that had originally crystallized in the context of sacral kingship: founding and refounding the temple, or alternatively founding and refounding an urban monument that could in some way or other be associated with the temple (such as the city wall), remained the main channel through which rulers could articulate their claim to legitimacy. The desecration of the temple in Antiochos IV's days, its rededication by the Maccabees, and the rise to power of a new dynasty descended from the temple's refounders generated ideal conditions for yet another reactivation of the traditional pattern of discourse articulating temple foundation (or refoundation) and legitimacy. As a starting point for our inquiry, I wish to explore to what extent the description of the rededication of the temple found in 2 Maccabees 10:1–8 fits the classical narrative pattern of temple-building accounts. I suggest that it fits strikingly well.

3.1.1. *Identifying the Temple-Building Narrative Pattern in 2 Maccabees*

The analysis of the literary structure of 2 Maccabees in Chapter 1 (§1.3) concluded that the episode of the rededication of the temple inserted in 2 Maccabees 10:1–8 is a pivotal point in the narrative. Its key location in the structural organization of the work is a decisive hint that from the outset alerts us to the possibility that the entire episode may either cross-refer with, or even be informed by, the traditional narrative pattern known from other temple-building accounts. My working hypothesis that the story of Hanukkah is fundamentally one of temple refoundation will now be explored in detail. Its adherence to Hurowitz's pattern and its intertextual connections with the Judahite/Judean texts relating to the building of the temple by Solomon, and (what is more crucial) with its Persian refoundation told in the books of Ezra-Nehemiah (hereafter EN), 1 Esdras, and Haggai-Zechariah (hereafter HZ), require closer examination.

However, before embarking on this inquiry, we must address a potential formal objection.[7] As noted in the opening section of this chapter, some key components of the narrative pattern are missing in the core section of 2 Maccabees 10:1–8. Some are distributed throughout 2 Maccabees 5:27–13:26, and others (no doubt deliberately) postponed to the last narrative cycle (14:1–15:37a). As a result the projection of the six-step pattern onto this short unit might seem contrived, and it might be argued that the passage's construction, as indeed the parallel passage of 1 Maccabees, is merely a compilation of reminiscences plucked from other texts describing Solomon's building and Zerubbabel's and Joshua's refoundation of the temple, while their symbolic significance is ignored. While I believe that this alternative possibility is ultimately overruled through my detailed analysis of the text,[8] it may be pointed out from the outset that Hurowitz's comments on the narrative template of temple building caution against evolving too rigid an image of it. The full six-part pattern that he describes is an archetype, while Hurowitz emphasizes that its concrete applications are flexible.[9] This feature can be verified in the corpus of Hebrew texts. Thus, although the account of Solomon's building of the temple preserved in 1 Kings 3–9:9 conforms very closely to the ideal pattern, the divine promise enunciated in Nathan's prophecy was addressed to David, and not Solomon, and is inserted in an earlier chapter (in 2 Samuel 7).[10] Likewise the account of the rebuilding of the temple extending through Ezra 1–6 is split in two: the stories of the laying of the founding stone of the temple and of the building of the altar are located in Cyrus's time, whereas the building of the temple per se is dated to Darius's reign.[11] Moreover, the background information about the history of the site, which is normally part of step 1, is postponed to Ezra 5:11–13.[12] In other words, whereas the short building inscriptions of Mesopotamia tend to relate the six-step process of the building in a standardized order, with little room for variation in narrative order, longer literary texts lend themselves to greater flexibility in the overall organization of the narrative material. Therefore the nonlinear order of the narrative components in 2 Maccabees is not an oddity, and the fact that the core section of 2 Maccabees 10:1–8 cannot be read separately from the rest of the work is not an obstacle to reading Hurowitz' pattern in it.

3.1.2. The Rededication of the Temple and Altar in 2 Maccabees 10:1–8 and 1 Maccabees 4:36–61: A Synoptic Table

Despite the extreme concision of the section, the literary structure of 2 Maccabees 10:1–8 easily breaks down into the six-step format outlined by Hurowitz.[13] Its conformity to the classical pattern may be further enhanced by a synoptic comparison with the parallel text of 1 Maccabees 4:36–61,[14] and the seemingly greater abundance of pertinent details in 1 Maccabees ultimately turns out to be deceptive. In Table 3.1 the divisions of the two parallel texts comply with Hurowitz's prescribed sections. The numbers and titles reproduced are also his.[15]

As Table 3.1 shows, the six stages envisaged in the archetypal template are identifiable in the two parallel accounts, despite the laconic treatment of some items in 2 Maccabees. At the same time, the comparison highlights the differences between the two texts. In general terms, the discrepancies are largely due to the differing lengths of the two descriptions. The extreme concision of the unit of 2 Maccabees means that certain themes are drastically reduced, in particular the purification of the temple, which here replaces the gathering of material in the phase of preparation (step 2; see below), and the construction of the new altar (step 3). In both cases, 1 Maccabees yields far more details: Judas's selection of priests to carry out the purification rites (4:42) and their careful disposal of the profaned altar (4:43–46) in step 2, with step 3 including successively the reinstatement of the altar, the sanctuary, and the holy vessels (4:47–49). The only details slightly more fleshed out in 2 Maccabees are the descriptions of the festivities (step 4) and the prayers (step 5). But in reality the concise account of 2 Maccabees 10:1–8 is partly deceptive, since some themes are treated elsewhere in the work. Thus the themes of reconciliation, entitling victory, and the restoration of social justice are treated in the section inserted before the episode of the temple refoundation (5:27–9:29), and the rewarding victories are treated later (10:10–13:26).

There are, however, other differences beyond the stylistic nuances, and these also require explanation. The synoptic comparison that follows will review them according to the set order of the narrative sequence. The first purpose of this survey is to show that the refoundation account of 2 Maccabees does not introduce any thematic elements alien to the canonical topics of the temple-building pattern. Note that this is not the case with the description provided by 1 Maccabees. That said, the synopsis does reveal an oddity of 2 Maccabees, namely the blurring of the figure of Judas Maccabee in 10:1–8, as against his unambiguous status of leader in the parallel account. This contrast is no less striking if we compare 2 Maccabees 10:1–8 to 2 Maccabees 15:29–37a, since Judas is pointedly shown to assume the leading role in the "second" refoundation. This matter is worth investigating in more detail.

3.1.3. Step 1: The Preliminary Restoration of Peace and Justice—1 Maccabees 4:36–41; 2 Maccabees 10:1–8 and 5:27–9:29

Although the building (or rebuilding) of a temple must be preceded by a victory, it can be carried out only once peace has been restored.[16] In 1 Maccabees, Judas and his brothers effectively take the decision of refounding the temple only after their

TABLE 3.1. A comparison of 1 and 2 Maccabees in view of the six-step narrative pattern of temple-building accounts according to Hurowitz 1992.

2 Maccabees 10:1–8	1 Maccabees 4:36–61
Step 1. Preliminary phase: The circumstances of the project and the decision to build (10:1) Maccabee and his men, with the Lord leading them, recovered the sanctuary and the city.	*Step 1. Preliminary phase: The circumstances of the project and the decision to build* (4:36–38) Thereupon Judas and his brothers said, "Now our enemies have been defeated. Let us go purify the sanctuary and restore it." The entire camp assembled, and they went up to Mount Zion. They saw the temple laid desolate and the altar profaned and the gates burned and the courts overgrown with plants as "in a thicket" or like "one of the mountains" and the chambers laid in ruins.
	Intrusive item: Rite of lamentation (4:39–40) They rent their garments and made great lamentation and put on ashes. They prostrated themselves upon the ground and sounded the signal trumpets and cried out to Heaven.
	Intrusive item: Continued warfare (4:41) Then Judas assigned soldiers the duty of fighting the men in the Akra while he purified the sanctuary.
Step 2. Preparations for the building: gathering materials, drafting workmen, laying foundations (10:2–3a) They destroyed the illicit altars which the foreigners had built around the marketplace and also the illicit shrines. After purifying the temple, . . .	*Step 2. Preparations for the building* (4:42–46) He appointed unblemished priests, lovers of the Law, who purified the sanctuary and removed the stones of the loathsome structure to an unclean place. They deliberated over what they should do with the profaned altar of the burnt offering, and they came up with the good idea of dismantling it lest the fact that the peoples had defiled it should be held to their disgrace. Accordingly, they dismantled the altar, and put its stones away on the temple mount in a suitable place until a prophet should come to give an oracle concerning them.
Step 3. Description of the construction process and the buildings and furnishings (10:3b) . . . they made another altar.	*Step 3. Description of the construction process and the buildings and furnishings* (4:47–49) Taking uncut stones as prescribed by the Law, they built a new altar after the pattern of the old. They repaired the sanctuary and sanctified the interior of the house and the courts. They also

(continued)

TABLE 3.1. *(Continued)*

2 Maccabees 10:1–8	1 Maccabees 4:36–61
	made new sacred vessels, and they brought the candelabrum and the altar of incense and the table into the nave.
Step 4. Dedication rites and festivities (10:3c) Using fire they got by igniting stones, for the first time in two years they offered sacrifices and incense and installed the lights and set out the showbread.	*Step 4. Dedication rites and festivities (4:50–54)* They burned incense on the altar and kindled the lights on the candelabrum so that they illumined the nave. They set loaves upon the table and hung the curtains and brought to completion all the work which they had done. They rose early on the morning of the twenty-fifth day of the ninth month (that is, the month of Kislev), in the year 148, and they brought a sacrifice according to the Law upon the new altar of burnt offerings which they had built. At the very time of year and on the very day on which the peoples had profaned the altar, it was dedicated to the sound of singing and harps and lyres and cymbals.
Step 5. Blessing, or prayer of the king, or both (10:4) That done, they prostrated themselves and prayed to the Lord that they never again would come to suffer such disasters. Rather, if they should ever sin, let them be chastised by the Lord himself, with clemency, and not delivered over to the hands of blasphemous and barbarous peoples.	*Step 5. Blessing, or prayer of the king, or both (4:55)* The entire people prostrated themselves and bowed and gave thanks to Heaven Who had brought them victory.
Step 4. Dedication rites and festivities (10:5–7) "On the very same date on which the temple was profaned by foreigners occurred the purification of the temple, on the twenty-fifth of the ninth month (that is, Kislev). Joyfully they held an eight-day celebration, after the pattern of Tabernacles, remembering how a short time before they spent the festival of Tabernacles like wild beasts, in the mountains and in the caves. Therefore, holding wreathed wands, and branches bearing ripe fruit, and palm fronds, they offered songs of praise to Him Who had victoriously brought about the purification of His Place."	*Step 4. Dedication rites and festivities (4:56–58)* They celebrated the dedication of the altar for eight days, joyfully bringing burnt offerings and sacrificing peace offerings and thank offerings. They decorated the front of the nave with golden cornices and bosses and restored the gates and the chambers and fitted them with doors. The people were overjoyed as the shame inflicted by the gentiles was removed.

Step 6. Divine promises or revelation; blessings and curses of future generations; setting of norms (10:8)	Step 6. Divine promises or revelation; blessings and curses of future generations (4:59)
By vote of the commonwealth they decreed a rule for the entire nation of the Jews to observe these days annually.	Judas and his brothers and the entire assembly of Israel decreed that the days of the dedication of the altar should be observed at their time of year annually for eight days, beginning with the twenty-fifth of the month of Kislev, with joy and gladness.
	Intrusive item: Continued warfare (4:60–61) At that time they also fortified Mount Zion, surrounding it with a high wall and strong towers to prevent the gentiles from ever coming and trampling it as they had done before. He posted a special force there to guard it, and he fortified ... Beth-Zur so that the people might have a fortress facing Idumea.

enemies have been defeated (4:36), and yet the context of this refoundation is not entirely peaceful. Whereas the inclusion of the rite of lamentation (1 Macc. 4:39–40) might be read as a variant called for by the circumstances of Judas's refoundation—a desecration rather than a destruction—the allusion to the continued military operations in 4:41 and again in the immediate closure of the passage (4:60–61) is strikingly incongruous, as is the explicit identification of the congregation that carried out the purification and rededication as a "camp," a "company of soldiers" (*parembolē*, 4:37) battling (*polemein*) against the garrison of the Akra at the very same time as the sanctuary is being cleansed (4:41).

In contrast, in 2 Maccabees the episode of the refoundation is carefully isolated from the surrounding context of warfare. Furthermore, the account of Judas's military operations at the close of 2 Maccabees 8 gives way to a new chapter that dwells at length upon Antiochos IV's agony. Not only does this hiatus mark a suspension in time, opportunely diverting our attention from the theater of war at home and transferring us to the Upper Satrapies, where Antiochos met his death. As the accomplishment of divine justice, the demise of the wicked king also manifests the reconciliation of God with His people. The striking down of the wicked, the instrument of God's wrath against His people, further constitutes a crucial element in the restoration of the proper order of things. This act is appropriately completed before the work begins on the refoundation of the temple—the climactic event of the restoration of order.[17]

On its own, the brevity of the narration in 2 Maccabees 10:1–8 fails to explain the suppression of references to warfare. It would have sufficed for the author to mention the themes in half a sentence, as he does for the building of the new altar (10:3b). Instead, he suppresses all mention. Their total omission, along with the careful selection of the details reported at 10:1–8, are evidence enough that our author used the legitimizing temple-building scheme wittingly and with intent. Because, moreover, all extraneous elements are systematically discarded, there is little plausibility in the alternative possibility that might come to mind, by which the passage's construction is a random compilation of intertextual reminiscences with no particular symbolic significance. Such a possibility seems even more unlikely when we consider further the intertextual connections between Hurowitz's pattern and the passage in question.

How, then, are we to understand the intrusive elements in 1 Maccabees? As just noted, they are not merely untypical: their evocation of warfare is in blatant contradiction with the entrenched expectation that peace must reign before building works can commence. The motives for their inclusion cannot be explained by the immediate context alone and will be discussed below in Chapter 4 (§4.2), when we tackle the second occurrence of the narrative pattern of temple building in 1 Maccabees (13:1–16:24). What should be stressed from the outset is that these intrusive elements are the fruit neither of authorial oversight nor of the author's failure to grasp the ideological potential of the temple-building account. Quite the contrary. The author's reference to the need to fight the men of the Akra for the purification of the temple to be complete (4:41) and his mention of the fortification of the Temple Mount and Beth-Zur at the end of the ceremony (4:60–61) are details carefully selected with the purpose of creating a thematic link with the second episode, which is informed by the temple-building narrative pattern, in particular the liberation and purification of the Akra by Simon (1 Macc. 13:49–52). In other words the description of Judas's rededication of the temple in 1 Maccabees 4:36–61 must be seen as an unconventional variant of the classical narrative template, and not as a random literary product.[18]

3.1.4. Step 2: Purification as a Variant of the Phase of Preparations— 2 Maccabees 10:2 and 1 Maccabees 4:42–46

The topical variants of the phase of preparations in both books are clearly imposed by the special circumstances of the rededication. There are relatively few stereotyped situations in the Mesopotamian royal inscriptions and the Hebrew material that provide reasons for the undertaking of building works. The three most common ones that occur are the need to build a temple ex novo, the need to carry out renovations on a temple, and temple-enlargement schemes.[19] In the first two cases, step 1 records the divine approval to build (or rebuild) along with the entitling victory, while step 2 narrates the gathering of material and the levying of manpower through corvée (1 Kgs 5 about Solomon; 1 Esd. 5:54–55 about Zerubbabel and Joshua; Neh. 2:8 and 3:1–32 about Nehemiah's repairs to the city wall). When the inscription commemorates a restoration scheme, the building's history is given, including its current state of decay. When works of enlargement are involved, justifications are given for the existing building's replacement with a larger one. The situation that the Judeans were faced with in Antiochos's days was clearly different, owing to the fact that the temple and its altar had been not destroyed but desecrated.

In 2 Maccabees the account of the building's historical background is omitted in the passage in question, since it has been treated in detail earlier (2 Macc. 5:11–16 and 6:1–7). Less expectedly, the topics usually included in the phase of preparation (step 2)—for example, the assembling of the necessary materials and workforce—are replaced with a description (10:2) of the cleansing of the city through the destruction of the unlawful altars and shrines.[20] For a change, 1 Maccabees actually follows Hurowitz's pattern in a more classical way than its counterpart (4:42–46). Indeed, the description focuses on the purification of the sanctuary and furthermore on the dismantling of the profaned altar. The reference to the prophet thereafter in 1 Maccabees 4:46 is worthy of note, since a similar idea will surface anew in the decree instituting Simon's powers (1 Macc. 14:41); and so its mention here establishes an additional intertextual connection between this passage and the final narrative unit of the work (13:1–16:24).

3.1.5. Step 4: Dedication Rites and Festivities—Reenacting the Heritage of Solomon, Zerubbabel and Joshua, and Nehemiah

The description of the rites and festivities that accompanied the purification of the temple and the building of the new altar introduces important themes. Once again, divergences arise between the two parallel accounts.

A. *The Date Formulas.* First, although the two versions concur in their mention of the dedication day, stressing that the sacrifices were resumed on the very same day as the temple was profaned (2 Macc. 8:5 and 1 Macc. 4:53), they differ in how they reckon the year: whereas 1 Maccabees records the year accurately by the Seleukid era (148 S.E., 4:52), the usual annalistic system of the period, 2 Maccabees untypically uses a relative form of dating by mentioning the time elapsed since the sacrifices had been interrupted ("[for the first time] in two years," 10:3c).[21] The interest of this dating device is to underscore that the ceremony indeed is a *refoundation:* that is, it marks the resumption of the normal course of things after a period of chaos and disruption. A similar device is employed to conclude the account of the renewed performance of the Festival of Passover under King Josiah in 1 Esdras (1:20–21): "No Passover like it had been kept in Israel since the times of the prophet Samuel; none of the kings of Israel had kept such a Passover as was kept by Josiah and the priests and Levites and the people of Judah and all of Israel who were living in Jerusalem." By recalling earlier ceremonies and leading figures, this dimension of refoundation conveys legitimation to the leading figure associated with the performance of the ceremony. In order to be genuine, the refoundation must be a reenactment.

B. *The Reference to Sukkoth, the Festival of Tabernacles.* That the ceremony carried out by Judas's men was intended as a reenactment is attested by the format chosen for its celebration: an eight-day festival, "after the pattern of Tabernacles" (10:6). As already noted, the Festival of Tabernacles (Sukkoth) was felt to be particularly appropriate for celebrating and commemorating the historical foundation and refoundations of the temple.[22] Tradition recorded that the dedication of the temple in Solomon's days had been held during this festival, and likewise the refoundation and rededication of the altar by Zerubbabel and Joshua together with the Returnees had been followed by the celebration of the Festival of Tabernacles.[23] It has been suggested on the basis of the precise wording of HZ that the Festival of Tabernacles included a ritual commemoration of the foundation of the temple. The ritual setting turned the foundation that was celebrated into an archetypal event that attracted and fused together all the historical refoundations.[24] Therefore it was natural for Judas's partisans to model their celebration after the pattern of Sukkoth, despite the different date. The ceremony that they perform becomes in turn a founding festival to be reenacted annually in the future, as stipulated by the people's decree voted at the end of the festival (2 Macc. 10:8; 1 Macc. 4:59).

2 Maccabees goes much farther than its parallel source in stressing that the new ceremony was a reenactment. One could expect the festival to be an occasion of unalloyed joy, as indeed 1 Maccabees presents it ("*joyfully* bringing [sacrifices].... The people were *overjoyed* as the shame inflicted by the gentiles was removed," 4:56–58). However, 2 Maccabees introduces a contrasting note by adding the remembrance of days of sorrow ("joyfully they held an eight-day celebration, after the pattern of Tabernacles, *remembering how a short time before they spent the festival of Tabernacles like wild beasts, in the mountains and in the caves,*" 10:6).[25] There is probably more than the inclination for sharp contrasts typical of Hellenistic Greek writing in this blending of contrasted feelings. In effect, in the Yehudite/Judean tradition the ceremony of the refoundation of the temple in Zerubbabel's and Joshua's days was also recorded as a day of mixed feelings.[26] Admittedly, the relation between remembrance and cause of sorrow is inverted in 2 Maccabees compared with Ezra and 1 Esdras, since in the latter the weeping is prompted by the remembrance of brighter days, whereas in our text it is caused by the memory of dark times. Notwithstanding this difference, it seems reasonable to surmise that the theme of joy mixed with sorrow in 2 Maccabees hints at the tradition recorded in Ezra and 1 Esdras.

C. *The Celebrating Community: Judas's Partisans as the New Returnees.* The author's concern for presenting the new festival as the reenactment of the founding events of Persian times may further provide at least a partial explanation for the diverging depictions of the community of celebrants in the parallel works. 1 Maccabees goes into many details about their identity: we successively come across "Judas and his brothers" (4:36), soldiers (4:37, 41), and priests appointed by Judas (4:42), and the decree is passed by "Judas and his brothers and the entire assembly of Israel" (4:59). The absence of a prophet is also deplored (4:46). In 2 Maccabees, at the very beginning of the passage, the community of celebrants is only once referred to as "Maccabee and his men" (10:1);[27] the successive actions cited are simply carried out by a collective of otherwise unspecified men. Yet this collective is twice contrasted with the impious "foreigners" (*allophyloi*, 10:2, 5). This emphasis on the opposition between insiders and outsiders is apparently intended to replicate the confrontation between the community of the Returnees headed by Zerubbabel and Joshua on the one hand and on the other the "people of the country," who were denied the right to participate in rebuilding the temple because they were deemed unfit and imputed with hampering the works (Ezra 4:1–4; 1 Esd. 5:66–73). As at Creation, the Returnees refound their society by *separating* themselves from the "peoples of the land."[28]

D. *The "Continuity Motif": Nehemiah's Fire.*   One of the ways adopted to manifest a concrete link between the old building and the new one was to point to cultic items. In Solomon's dedication, for instance, this function is fulfilled by the "Ark [of the Covenant], the tent of meeting, and all the holy vessels that were in the tent" (1 Kgs 8:4). These items connect the temple to the Tabernacle of the Desert built by Moses. In turn the continuity between Solomon's temple and the new edifice of Persian times was manifested by the holy vessels as well as, to a secondary extent, the people themselves. The books of Ezra and 1 Esdras both specify that the holy vessels that Cyrus gave to the Judean leaders to be deposited in the rebuilt temple were the same holy vessels that Nebuchadnezzar had removed from Solomon's temple when he destroyed it, which were taken away to Babylon.[29] These cultic items function as tangible signs[30] that the new building exists as a continuity of the former one, continuity being the main claim to authenticity and legitimacy. (In conservative societies, innovation is tantamount to sin.) The insistence on the theme of "fire"[31] in 2 Maccabees (10:3c) appears to fulfill a similar function. In contrast, no reference to fire is made in 1 Maccabees, although the resumption of the divine service is treated in far greater detail (4:50–54); nor either does any other object seem to function as a sign of continuity. The author of 1 Maccabees seems interested in downplaying the symbolic importance of Judas's rededication, whereas the author of 2 Maccabees highlights it.[32]

The intertextual connection that casts light on the identity of the fire of 2 Maccabees 10:3c points to a tradition about Nehemiah's rekindling of the altar, which was left out of the later biblical canon but is recounted in detail in the second epistle prefacing the main narrative of 2 Maccabees (1:18–22, 31–36).[33] While the first prefixed epistle (2 Macc. 1:1–10a) invites the Judeans of Egypt to celebrate the "days of Tabernacles in the month of Kislev" (the Festival of Hanukkah), the purpose of the second is to bring support to this demand by situating the rededication that the new festival commemorates in relation to a long chain of earlier events, of which it is the reenactment.[34] To underscore this chain, the festival is dubbed by the double name of "Days of Tabernacles and Days of the Fire," the latter explicitly referring to the days "when Nehemiah, the builder of the temple and the altar, brought sacrifices" (1:18). By validating the link between the original altar and the rebuilt one, the fire guarantees that the new altar is ritually fit for use and not a sinful innovation. Moreover, through Nehemiah the chain of legitimizing reenactments is taken further back to Solomon and Moses, whose respective sacrifices were consumed by fire sent from heaven (2 Macc. 2:9–13a).

Although the episode of Nehemiah's kindling of the altar is dwelt upon most extensively, no less than four items function as signs of continuity between Solomon's, Nehemiah's, and Judas's ceremonies of foundation (or refoundation): the fire that had been hidden by the priests and found by Nehemiah, a fragment of which was also taken into exile on Jeremiah's order (2:1); the Law that was taken into exile by the priest at Jeremiah's order (2:2–3); and the tabernacle and the ark that had been hidden by Jeremiah and will be found at the end of the days (2:4–8), and which the new altar replaces. In addition, alongside the chain of reenactment linking the altar of the Hasmonean temple through Nehemiah to Solomon and Moses, a second one links the books reassembled by Judas through Nehemiah's library (2:13–14) to the Law taken into exile by the priests (2:2–3). Inasmuch as the epistle evinces how the pro-Hasmonean circles staged their own history as the reenactment of founding deeds in their contacts with the Judean community of Alexandria, it makes sense that their memory of the rededication of the temple and the altar by the Maccabees was also shaped by the same narrative template as the accounts of these earlier dedications. The intertextual references in 2 Maccabees (and in the parallel works) to the refoundations of Solomon and Zerubbabel and Joshua are not accidental but deliberate and meaningful.

This conclusion has further implications. As we saw extensively in Chapter 2 (§2.1), the Festival of Sukkoth, absorbing the memory of all historical dedication ceremonies, celebrated not only the creation of the cosmos (which each temple foundation reenacted), but also kingship, both human (1 Kgs 8:1–2) and divine, because founding (or refounding) a temple was a royal prerogative. In assimilating the newly founded festival of rededication of the temple with Sukkoth, the partisans of the Maccabees (or of the Hasmoneans) cannot possibly have ignored this royal association. As a matter of fact, the refoundation of the temple cleansed of Antiochos's abominations not only prompted the resumption of the sacrifices after a three-year disruption (2 Macc. 10:3) but also marked the "restoration of social justice"—that is, in modern terms, the inception of a *new* social and political order in the guise of restoration. Moreover, it is narrated that the celebrants assembled to take a decree (to "fix a norm," in Kapelrud's terms) at the end of the festival (2 Macc. 10:8, 1 Macc. 4:59).[35] These are royal acts. But who exactly was the new ruler in this "restored" (in truth new) order? And—perhaps a more crucial question—What was his status? Was he a high priest, like Phineas and Simon in Ben Sira's Praise of the Fathers? A governor, like Nehemiah? A king, like Solomon? A tandem, like Zerubbabel and Joshua? Or something else? It is astounding that there is no ruler in 2 Maccabees 10:1–8.

3.1.6. Steps 5 and 6: Which Social Order, and Which Ruler?

A. *Collectivization of the Prayer, or Vacancy of Royallike Power?*   In the Mesopotamian royal inscriptions, as in the Judahite/Judean traditions relating to David and Solomon, the king is the recipient of the divine injunction to build the temple and, respectively, the one who must seek divine approval when the initiative to build is his own (step 1; cf. 2 Sam. 7 and 1 Kgs 5:3–5). This is the very principle on which the ideology of kingship of divine election is based. The king alone is granted wisdom, because possessing wisdom is necessary to build the temple and accordingly govern with righteousness (1 Kgs 9:1–9 with 3:4–15 and 4:29–34); in some instances, the design of the temple is revealed to him in dream (step 1). He is the one who drafts men and has building material brought in from far away (1 Kgs 5); he utters the prayer to the deity in his name and in the name of the entire people after building works are complete (step 5; cf. 1 Kgs 8:22–53); and he is the addressee of the divine blessings (step 6; see 1 Kgs 9:1–9).

In 1 Maccabees the divine approval is deferred to a later date (4:46), and the lack of a prophet to make an authoritative decision about what to do with the dismantled altar is seemingly matched by the absence of a kinglike ruler able to speak the prayer in the name of the people. 1 and 2 Maccabees concur in stating that the prayer was uttered by the people as a whole (1 Macc. 4:55; 2 Macc. 10:4), and similarly the new norm fixing the annual commemoration of the rededication in the month of Kislev is decreed by a vote of the people (2 Macc. 10:8; 1 Macc. 4:59). As we saw in Chapter 2 (§2.2.1B), the collectivized performance of the new refoundation is at least in part the result of a long evolution. With the demise of native kingship, the people had already been narrowly associated with the refoundation process of Persian times. Haggai's oracles urging to start on the reconstruction are consistently addressed to the "remnant of the people": that is, the entire community, alongside Zerubbabel and Joshua (Hag. 1:12, 14; 2:2, 4). Likewise, in ordaining the reconstruction, YHWH recalls His Covenant with the *people* he led out of Egypt, and His pledge of prosperity is obviously intended for the entire community (Hag. 2:5, 9). Similarly, Ezra's renewed Covenant is with the assembly of the people of Israel in their entirety (Neh. 9–10).

However, there still remains an obvious difference between the works on the Achaimenid period and our two texts. As just noted the remnant of the people is always mentioned alongside the leading figures of Zerubbabel and Joshua in Haggai's prophecies, and in Nehemiah 9–10 the collective confession, the prayer, and the renewal of the Covenant is unambiguously led by Ezra. Each time, there *are* kinglike leaders[36] in charge. Diana Edelman has described the collectivization of YHWH's interlocutor in Haggai as "democratization."[37] As far as our two authors are concerned, it is far from certain that this label captures their intention accurately. At the end of the two works, there will be a leader in charge again— Judas in 2 Maccabees, and Simon in 1 Maccabees. The function of the ultimate narrative unit in each work will be precisely to identify the kinglike leader. Therefore, it seems that the collectivization of the ceremony and the prayer in 1 Maccabees 4:55 and 56–58 and 2 Maccabees 10:4–5 carries a slightly negative slant, potentially pointing to the want of a leader and to a wished-for reversal of this situation.

B. Vacancy of Power and the Denial of Menelaos's Legitimacy as High Priest. In 1 Maccabees Simon is bestowed his royallike privileges (*hēgemōn,* high priest, and *stratēgos,* in perpetuity and with hereditary rights, 1 Macc. 14:41–42, 47, 49) through a decree voted collectively by the people (1 Macc. 14:41). The context is propitious for this procedure, with the process of investiture devolving upon the populace: the former leader Jonathan has just died; Demetrios II has sent a letter exempting the Judeans from the tribute and conceding their right to have their own fortresses, thereby acknowledging their autonomy (13:36–40), and the Judeans have started a new era based on Simon's years of rule to date official documents (13:41–42). Moreover, Demetrios had already recognized Simon as high priest and Friend of Kings (*philos,* 13:36), and therefore the decree of the people involves a reappointment necessitated by the start of the new era,[38] not a genuine election. In contrast, in the context of the temple refoundation, Judas is not acknowledged as a royallike leader. In a sense, there is a vacancy of royallike leadership.

The same is true in 2 Maccabees 10:1–8, but in that text the assertion of the vacancy of power is even more telling, because there formally *was* a high priest, Menelaos. The circumstances that allegedly generated this vacancy of power are the topic of the earlier part of the narrative unit of the Hanukkah story (2 Macc. 4:7–5:26). Recounted there are the many deeds of impiety through which the successive high priests Jason and Menelaos disqualified themselves. From 5:27 (that is, the first appearance of Judas Maccabee) to the account of his death in 13:3–8, Menelaos simply vanishes from sight, except for two incidental references in one of Antiochos V's letters (11:29, 33). The artificiality of this alleged vacancy of power and the seeming collectivization of the decision-making process is most clearly exposed in the naming of the addressees of the Seleukid letters in 9:19–27 and 11:16–33. In 9:19, 11:16, 11:27, and including 11:24, the high priest in charge is absent. Although the portrayal of Menelaos in 2 Maccabees will be discussed more fully in Chapter 5 below (§5.2), it is worth noting here that Menelaos, like Jason, implicitly rules in the impious order of *Hellēnismos* that is centered upon the *gymnasion* and can have no place in the new order of "restored social justice" that is instituted with the temple refoundation. Yet Judas is not acknowledged in the position of the royallike leader in the ceremony of the refoundation. That acknowledgment is postponed until the last narrative unit, wherein Judas's dream, the site of his formal proclamation (2 Macc. 15:12–16), will be followed by a new "temple refoundation" in which he will definitely hold the part of the kinglike ruler (15:29–37a).

The image of the vacant place of the kinglike ruler is even more evident in 2 Maccabees than in the parallel account. In 1 Maccabees, Judas is depicted as the one in charge: the decision to purify the sanctuary is taken by "Judas and his brothers" (4:36); Judas assigns tasks to soldiers and priests (4:41–42, 61); the decree is voted by "Judas and his brothers and the entire assembly of Israel" (4:59). In contrast, in 2 Maccabees 10:1–8, Judas is mentioned through his nickname alone at the beginning of the section (10:1) and thereafter is swallowed up in the plural "they." Thus it seems that, whereas the second episode modeled upon the temple-building template (2 Macc. 15:29–37a) is used to hail God's new champion and, through Judas, proclaim the legitimacy of the Hasmonean dynasty, the first episode (10:1–8) is used quite unconventionally as the site for a *negative* statement about power, to denounce a vacancy of legitimate leadership.

C. *Denouncing Imperial Rule? The Prayer of Judas's Men in 2 Maccabees: Step 5.* The refoundation may further have been used as a juncture to denounce the imperial domination of the Seleukids as illegitimate. The strange phrasing of the collective prayer uttered by Judas's men in 2 Maccabees demands attention (2 Macc. 10:4):

> They prostrated themselves and prayed to the Lord that they never again would come to suffer such disasters. Rather, if they should ever sin, let them be chastised by the Lord himself, with clemency, and not delivered over to the hands of blasphemous and barbarous gentiles.

The theme of reconciliation is traditionally required when a temple is rebuilt after its destruction. The ruin of the edifice (whether by collapse or by enemy assault) was a consequence of the deity's wrath, and therefore He or She needed to be reconciled with His or Her king, city, and House, to agree to the latter's reconstruction and the restoration of "peace": that is, the reinstatement of cosmic and social harmony.[39] Admittedly though, a prayer of reconciliation had already been offered on the eve of the victorious battle, opening the way to the refoundation (2 Macc.

8:2–4) and successfully turning God's wrath into mercy (8:5). Therefore, the verbatim repetition of this topic was superfluous in the ceremony of refoundation, and some variation could be allowed. It may even be conceded that the alternative topic retained for the prayer is to some extent appropriate, since it evokes the theme of measure-for-measure punishment that runs throughout the narrative of 2 Maccabees.

Yet some details seem odd. To begin with, the comparison with the prayer inserted in 1 Maccabees suggests that the topic of reconciliation was not the sole possible option. In 1 Maccabees, the prayer is quite appropriately concerned with thanking God for victory (4:55). The prayer uttered by Solomon provides a better point of comparison,[40] but the differences are no less telling than the similarities. While Solomon conventionally asks God to forgive His people if they repent, Judas's men take it upon themselves to instruct God about which punishment will suit them should they sin again. This plea addressed to God in the very ceremony of the refoundation is quite unheard of and might be taken as insolence toward God. However, we must consider the extraordinary element of the entreaty to be punished by the Lord himself rather than through the hands of the Seleukid king and his armies. Seen in a political perspective, this means that they are acknowledging God, and not the Seleukids, as their legitimate overlord. In the context of a prayer of reconciliation uttered in a ceremony of refoundation, there could be no more outspoken way to plead for political independence. If this interpretation is correct, it may further explain why the resumption of the sacrifices is dated only relatively ("[for the first time] in two years," 10:3c), and why the expected dating by the year of the Seleukid era is suppressed, in contrast with 1 Maccabees.

3.2. THE PATTERN OF TEMPLE BUILDING IN THE LONGER NARRATIVE UNITS: 1 MACCABEES 3:1–9:22 AND 2 MACCABEES 4:7–13:26

The classical form of the narrative pattern of temple foundation advises us that the account of the reconstruction of the divine abode is part of a wider sequence of actions, some of which constitute the preliminary steps indispensable to the realization of the temple-building project itself. On the one hand the building works presuppose material preparations, and on the other the construction of a divine house requires the explicit agreement of its inhabitant. Similarly, the building of the temple enables more actions to be carried out, such as the restoration of social justice, and further victories. Consequently, the wider narrative units in which the descriptions of the rededication of the temple are inserted in 1 and 2 Maccabees can reasonably be expected to comply with the more ample sequence of Hurowitz's pattern. This working hypothesis is indeed easily verified.

3.2.1. *The Preliminary Phase: Reconciliation in 1 and 2 Maccabees*

A. Reconciliation in 2 Maccabees 5:27–9:29. As the detailed outline of Hurowitz's pattern presented in Chapter 2 (§2.1.2A) records, the temple-building template comprises a series of conditions that must be fulfilled before the foundation or refoundation can be undertaken: the deity's reconciliation with His or Her king, people, city, and temple; the victory over the enemies that entitles the deity to receive a House, and a specific person endowed with royal powers to rebuild it; the restoration of peace and justice; and the gathering of material and drafting of a workforce. Applying this interpretative grid to the chapters in 2 Maccabees preceding the refoundation of the temple offers dual rewards. On the one hand, it indeed appears that the lengthy section stretching from Judas Maccabee's first apparition in 2 Maccabees 5:27 to the refoundation of the temple in 10:1–8 is exclusively devoted to these preparatory actions. On the other hand, the comparison with the classical model of temple-building accounts reveals that in our text these topics are treated in an unconventional way. The preliminary actions described are as follows:

- 2 Maccabees 5:27: Judas's first presentation marks the turning point from the time of disruption (4:7–5:26) to the process of reconciliation that will eventually lead to the refoundation of the temple and the resumption of the sacrifices;
- 2 Maccabees 6–7: The reconciliation is enacted by the sacrifice of the faithful, who are ready to die for their righteousness (the so-called martyrs);
- 2 Maccabees 8 recounts the first victorious military operation led by Judas. The context of the first battle and first victory is also the occasion to deal with enrolling the manpower and the first deeds of the restoration of social justice and order;
- 2 Maccabees 9 offers an additional sign of reconciliation, since Antiochos's dreadful death manifests divine justice, an important element in the restoration of order.

The originality of the treatment of these actions in 2 Maccabees seems to derive from three combined factors: the cultural evolution of Judean society, the adaptation of the template to the specific historical circumstances, and the personal ideological motivations of the author.

Cultural evolution seems to impinge on the theme of reconciliation, since the instrument of reconciliation that turned God's wrath into mercy is the torture and murder of the faithful ones. Their fate is narrated in the colorful section of 2 Maccabees 6:18–7:42;[41] moreover, the prayer inserted at the beginning of 2 Maccabees 8 (2–4), along with the short authorial comment of 8:5 that follows, both explicitly state that it was the sufferings of the faithful that brought about divine reconciliation. Thanks to the faithful who chose an exemplary death, God's wrath has turned into mercy, and the sign for this change is of course victory.

The second variant is dictated by the specific circumstances of the account, but also by the ideology of the author. It consists in the conflation of three distinct identities in Judas's men: the very men who are drafted as warriors and secure the victory are also those who are bound to carry out the work of "refoundation," and furthermore constitute the collective in whose name the work is done in the absence of a legitimate ruler. The third variant bears the hallmark of the political ideology of the author, and concerns the treatment of the theme of leadership in conjunction with victory. This last topic will be discussed further below in Chapter 4.

B. The Preliminary Sequence in Judas's Time Unit: 1 Maccabees 3:1–4:35. Upon close examination, the section of Judas's time unit inserted before the refoundation of the temple in 1 Maccabees (3:1–4:35)[42] seems to comply with Hurowitz's pattern, albeit its literary composition is far less schematic than its counterpart's. In particular, it is remarkable that no fewer than four battles resulting in four victories are said to be fought by Judas prior to the temple purification,[43] whereas according to the classical pattern victories are the consequence of the foundation, which seals the reconciliation between the deity and His or Her servants. This seemingly deviant arrangement of the material in 1 Maccabees may be explained partly by the author's notation that Judas and his followers made a covenant in Mizpah, as Samuel had done in the time of the Judges (1 Macc. 3:46–54), and they go off to wage their wars only after the ceremony.[44] The episode of the covenant at Mizpah seems to fulfill the same narrative function as the story of the torture and murder of the faithful in 2 Maccabees 6–7, namely to assert the initial reconciliation between God and the community of the faithful warriors.[45] Thus, despite appearances, the two authors were concerned with a single question: How could victories be won while the temple lay in ruin? Although emplotted in different ways, their answers embody the same concept: the initial victories were made possible by the preliminary reconciliation with God. It may be added that the acts signifying the restoration of social justice are assigned to Judas in 1 Maccabees 3:56: "He ordered all who had built houses or betrothed wives or planted vineyards or were timid to go home *as required by the Torah.*"

However, two victories are located before the episode of Mizpah (1 Macc. 3:10–12, 13–26), suggesting that they are associated with a different context. Throughout 1 Maccabees 3:1–26, the wicked king and his sinful supporters take the initiative, and Judas's victories must apparently be read together with the description of Antiochos's ensuing reaction (3:27–37). In particular, Antiochos, who departs for the Upper Satrapies, prepares for Jerusalem and its inhabitants to be destroyed and replaced by a military settlement (3:34–36). This context would put Judas in the position of waging a defensive and therefore legitimate war. The reconciliation at Mizpah opened the way to offensive warfare.

Thus the periodization of the wars seems to follow a threefold sequencing in 1 Maccabees, the ceremony of reconciliation at Mizpah and the rededication of the temple prompting turning points:

1. Unprovoked attacks and legitimate war (3:1–37).
2. Causality is switched a first time after the Mizpah covenant and the restoration of social justice (3:46–54); from this point on, Judas's victories drive the infuriated king into sending new armies *in reaction* (4:1–36; see 3:27).
3. The restoration of the temple, in turn, launches a new series of reactions, prompting the neighboring peoples to attack the Judeans (5:1)[46] and Antiochos IV to realize that the cause of his death lies in the wicked deeds he perpetrated in Jerusalem (6:6–8, 12–13). Thus, as in 2 Maccabees, the course of events is modified by the resumption of perpetual sacrifices. The restoration of the temple marks the major turning point in this work too, since it operates as a new source of causality.

3.2.2. The Entitling Victory in 2 Maccabees 8

Victory and temple foundation are closely interconnected in traditional ancient Near Eastern and Judahite ideologies of kingship. Their relation is reciprocal. In the first instance, victory is a preliminary condition to the building (or rebuilding) of a temple, since it entitles the deity to receive a House and the victor to act as a king (or assume royal prerogatives) by carrying out the erection of the divine abode. In turn, the king is rewarded with more victories. Victory, it appears, is a sign of divine election, along with the building of the temple. In keeping with this cultural background we can expect the theme of warfare to be loaded with ideological references in both 1 and 2 Maccabees. Indeed, an attentive perusal of the details confirms that the two works share a similar ideology of warfare. For example, the preliminary instances of the restoration of justice occur in the context of the inaugural battles in the two works (1 Macc. 3:55; 2 Macc. 8:28).[47] However, 2 Maccabees deserves particular attention, since the author takes care to underline the ideological coherence of the various elements involved in warfare and temple building by grouping them all under a single denomination, *Ioudaïsmos*. Therefore our examination of the ideology of warfare in 2 Maccabees is preliminary to our study of the concept of *Ioudaïsmos* below.

Chapter 8, depicting Judas's entitling victory in 2 Maccabees, is important in several ways.[48] First, with the exception of the first presentation of Judas in 5:27, the preliminary victory offers the author the occasion to specify who Judas and his men are. Likewise, for victory to be legitimizing—that is, to entitle the victor to divine election and give him the right to rebuild the temple—war must be waged in such conditions as to confirm the victor's piety and justice.[49] It is no coincidence that Judas's first victorious military operation provides the occasion for several deeds restorative of justice (i.e., of the righteous social order) that "validate" his pious warfare. Not only is God's alliance solicited and secured before the battle (2 Macc. 8:2–4; see 24), but the amassing of war booty is interrupted by Judas in order to observe the Sabbath (8:26–27), and he shares out the spoils to the surviving victims of atrocities (the "martyrs") and to the widows and orphans (8:28). Finally, it is openly declared that Judas intends to restore the broken Covenant with God (8:29). The author's remarking upon widows and orphans is particularly worth noticing, because caring for widows and orphans (i.e., the fatherless) is an emblematic topic of royal justice in the ancient Near Eastern ideology of kingship.[50]

Last, the inaugural battle against Nikanor, which covers most of chapter 8 (8:10–36), to a large extent serves as the narrative template for all the subsequent battles related. Major themes are introduced in the context of this battle, and discussed in utmost detail, with concise references recurring in the other battles variously related in the narrative section of 10:10–13:26. The repetitiveness from one battle description to the next, despite some literary attempts at variation, enhances the peculiar status of the inaugural battle. The main topics receive more detailed treatment again in the battle of the last narrative unit of 2 Maccabees (15:1–29); here the war against the second Nikanor duplicates fairly accurately the narrative structure of 2 Maccabees 8 along with the general's name. The inaugural battle of 2 Maccabees 8 successively introduces the following motifs:

The specification of the enemy (8:10–11).

Judas's placing his trust in God (8:13–14a). The topic is here dramatized through the expulsion from Judas's ranks of those who are not trustful enough and through the remainder's selling their possessions.[51] Thereafter, the theme of the pious warriors placing their trust in God recurs in 10:28.

The initial prayer (8:14b–15). Its function is to secure God's help (8:24). In the subsequent scenes the theme of the prayer may be either complemented by or substituted with a rite of supplication performed on the eve of battle.[52] The inaugural performance of the rite of supplication takes place at the altar (10:25–26), where it further illustrates the theme of collectivized[53] communication between the pious warriors and their God. The venue of later ceremonies is unspecified (11:6, 13:12, 14:15). In the subsequent episodes, the depiction of the prayers as well as the mentions of God's assistance are basically repeated (10:16, 26; 12:6, 11, 16, 28, 36; 13:10, 13, 14, 17; 14:15), albeit occasionally with notable variation (e.g., 12:22).

Judas's harangue to his men illustrates the efficient outcome of trusting God with historical examples (8:16–20). It includes the founding passage

(8:18–20) that introduces the topics of *the few against the many* and of their victory.⁵⁴ This topic is important enough to be announced in the proem of the work (2:21). Following Judas's harangue, the theme promptly becomes reality in the form of battle against Nikanor (8:24; see already 8:6–7). The topos of the few against the many recurs formulaically thereafter (10:23, 31), finally regaining some vitality in 15:27.⁵⁵

The *sacred books are read* to extract the password (8:23; cf. the selection of the password in 13:14).

The restoration of social equity. War operations are interrupted to respect the Sabbath (8:26–27; cf. 12:38–39 and the celebration of the Festival of Weeks in 12:31–32), and Judas cares for the widows and orphans.

The prayer to God after the victory (8:29, 33) here takes the form of a supplication for complete reconciliation. Exceptionally, the standard hymns of praise for victory are introduced only in the account of a subsequent battle (10:38).

Finally, *the vanquished enemy acknowledges God's might* (8:36). In 11:13 Lysias's peace overtures are assigned to his acknowledgment that God fought on the side of Judas and his men.

3.3. IOUDAÏSMOS

What is the identity of those who wage these wars? What are their goals, and what does the rededication of the temple entitle warriors to do if they are pious? To say it differently: What do those "remaining faithful to *Ioudaïsmos*" (8:1) have at heart? What does their remaining faithful to *Ioudaïsmos* inspire them to fight for with divine approval?

3.3.1. Fighting for Ioudaïsmos: 2 Maccabees 8

Above in Chapter 1 (§1.4) we saw how our author made use of the narrative techniques of prolepsis and analepsis to delineate meaningful narrative units by making characters appear at the desired places. Judas's first entrance in 5.27 is a prolepsis whose purpose is to place him at the head of the narrative subunit that is properly centered on the rededication of the temple (5:27–13:26). To some extent, Judas's first mention marks a watershed in the work: before he appears onstage (4:7–5:26), disruption and chaos rule; but as he begins to intervene, things begin to change for the better. Despite its brevity, 2 Maccabees 5:27 condenses two important sets of information: first, Judas withdraws from Jerusalem to continue fighting alongside his men; second, he is a pious leader from the onset, eating herbs to avoid defilement.⁵⁶ After this, Judas does not show up again until chapter 8, when his first initiative is to enlist men as his followers: it is his very capability and willingness to enlist the right men that qualifies him as a pious and therefore legitimate leader. Like Judas himself, his followers have remained faithful to *Ioudaïsmos* and are willing to fight for what it represents, just as the murdered pious were ready to die for it.[57]

Ioudaïsmos is not one item among others but subsumes all others. The author is quite explicit about which elements it comprises, spelling them out in lists time and again in 2 Maccabees, with particular emphasis in chapter 8 when Judas's men utter a prayer in the wake of their enrollment, calling God to look upon His people, temple, and city, and the exemplary dead (8:2–4). Mentioned hereafter are God's earlier covenants with the forefathers and the divine name (8:15); temple, city, and the ancestral social order (*proginikē politeia*, 8:17); laws (*nomoi*) and territory (*patris*, 8:21). The same items recur elsewhere: Law (*nomos*), territory (*patris*), and holy temple (*hieron hagion*, 13:10); and laws, temple, city, territory, and the social order (*politeia*, 13:14). It is no surprise that these themes are precisely those spelled out in the summary of the subject matter of the book that the author includes in his proem: the "greatest of temples," the altar, land (*chōra*), city, and laws.[58]

Ioudaïsmos is also a set of personal practices, especially when it comes to those who choose an exemplary death (chs. 6–7 and 14:37–46). Thus Razis is said to "have been brought to trial on a charge of practicing *Ioudaïsmos* in the preceding time of war" (14:38). Judas too, of course, is faithful to *Ioudaïsmos* in refraining from eating impure foods (5:27), restoring social justice (8:28), collecting money from his soldiers to atone for the sin of idolatry in Jamnia (12:43–44), waging war in a pious way, destroying the sites of idolatry (12:26, a shrine of Atargatis), and punishing the blasphemous (10:36).

3.3.2. *The Semantic Field of* Ioudaïsmos

The list of elements of *Ioudaïsmos* to be defended by Judas's faithful warriors is wide but finite: patron deity, temple, city, territory, and laws. In the same way as ideal kingship is defined through stock inventories of good actions, I take this list to be the defining catalogue of *Ioudaïsmos*. It is striking that it matches the constitutive components of the temple-building template fairly well. Moreover, the motif of fighting for *Ioudaïsmos* reinforces the similarity, since it can easily qualify as a variant of the theme of "victory as restoration of the righteous social order" that lies at the core of the template. The rescue of the temple from the negligence of a wicked ruler—in our case, both an impious high priest, Menelaos, and an impious imperial king, Antiochos IV—by waging a pious war against him, restoring social justice (the ancestral *nomoi*; and *politeia* in the sense "social order," caring for the widows and orphans of war, keeping the festivals, avoiding impure foods)—all these are precisely what usurpers of royal power claim that they have done in Mesopotamian royal inscriptions. To say it differently: the complex semantic field covered by the neologism *Ioudaïsmos* in 2 Maccabees dovetails (to a more than reasonable extent) with the range of political, social, and cosmological concepts that were traditionally clustered together in the narrative template of temple building. Insomuch as in 2 Maccabees the temple-building pattern is used to emplot the idea that the rule of the Hasmoneans is legitimate, I understand *Ioudaïsmos* to be the righteous social order founded by Judas, the ancestor of the Hasmonean dynasty, when he refounded the temple, which his "descendants" ruled after him.[59] In the specific variant of the traditional narrative crafted in 2 Maccabees, Judas emerges as the sole legitimate leader in the Nikanor's Day story. As a leader, Judas is assimilated with the very order of *Ioudaïsmos*, and his main legitimizing virtue, piety, is stressed time and again.

A. *The Term* Ioudaïsmos *as a Contentious Ethnicization of Partisan Political Ideology.* The neologism *Ioudaïsmos* not only captures in a single abstract term the entire semantic field of ruler legitimacy that the temple-building template traditionally relayed by telling a story; it also ethnicizes it in a deliberately tendentious way. To understand this process we need to widen the scope of our inquiry. As a word, *Ioudaïsmos* is a cultural hybrid. The fact that the author coined a specific label to denote the order embodied by the Hasmonean dynasty and the abstract nature of the term he chose[60] both point to Greek influence. However, *Ioudaïsmos* cannot be understood through the lens of the Greek political traditions alone, given that the political nomenclature used by the Greeks—including *tyrannis* (tyranny), *aristo-kratia, demo-kratia, ochlo-kratia* (Polybius's "rule of the mob"), *mon-archia, olig-archia,* and the latecomer *theo-kratia*—denotes configurations of power. It is obviously not the same to describe Hasmonean rule as *basileia* and as *Ioudaïsmos*. Notwithstanding its abstract nature, *Ioudaïsmos* is semantically more in tune with the Judahite/Judean tradition of political culture, hinging on the temple-building template, than with any Greek one. As that template discloses, local political thought tended to assimilate social order with the essence of society, the righteousness of the king purportedly mirroring the divine plan of cosmic order. At the same time, abstract concepts were always explored through specific instances—in the case of "ideal kingship," through biographies of particular kings. To capture the essence of society, the author of 2 Maccabees started from the ethnic label of the social group, the *Ioudaioi* ("Judeans"), and he summarized the idea of the "righteous social order of the *Ioudaioi*" by coining the abstract noun *Ioudaïsmos* after it. The next step, namely to apply this term to the rule of the Hasmoneans and thereby to equate their partisans with the ethnic group, looks to me deliberately tendentious.

The knowingly contentious use of the name of an entire social group in Judea as a definition benefiting one particular segment of it harks back to the intergroup tensions that marked the early postexilic era in Persian Yehud. These tensions involved hostilities between the Returnees and the descendants of those who had remained in Judea after the fall of Jerusalem in 586 B.C.E., and those tensions came to the fore on the occasion of the reconstruction of the altar and the temple, when the Returnees refused to include the other group in this pivotal symbolic undertaking. Likewise the new Covenant that they struck with YHWH was for their group alone.[61] Proclaiming themselves "the remnant of Israel," they considered themselves ethnically distinct from all other groups.[62] Yet there is a difference between the epithet "remnant of Israel" and the term *Ioudaioi*. Whereas the former stresses the Covenant with YHWH, the latter applies a distinctly ethnic slant on the group definition. The process of otherizing outsiders analyzed in relation to the Qumran community, for instance, was far more traditional and involved equating group membership with the Covenant.[63] In this case, however, the ethnicization of the group definition appears to have been a response to the *self-description* of Jason's and Menelaos's partisans as "Greeks." On this topic, further supporting arguments will be presented elsewhere in this book.[64]

The conceptual equivalence established by the author between the act of "remaining steadily in [or "faithful to"] *Ioudaïsmos*" (8:1) and the act of becoming Judas's partisan in 2 Maccabees 8 is confirmed by a detail in his proem, in which he asserts that those who "behaved bravely and gloriously for the sake of *Ioudaïsmos* were blessed with epiphanies": that is, they were granted signs of divine support. Given that such epiphanies occur mainly and repeatedly on the battlefield, by this association these men are unambiguously designated by the author as Judas's warriors.

B. *Judas's Partisans as* Ioudaioi. These considerations raise the further question what Judas's partisans should be called. In a conversation with King Demetrios, the wicked high priest Alkimos calls them *Asidaioi* (14:6). Modern scholarship has read a lot in this term,[65] but in 2 Maccabees it is never put into the mouth of Judas himself. To the contrary: it seems that neither Judas nor the author of 2 Maccabees cares about distinguishing groups among Judas's followers, let alone categorizing Judas's warriors as a particular group among others. They are those who have remained loyal to *Ioudaïsmos* and are ready to fight for it, to the death if necessary. These are the true *Ioudaioi,* the New Returnees, who distance themselves from the abominations of the *Hellēnes* and the *allophyloi*. The vocabulary and images used throughout the work to refer to Judas and his men on the one hand and Judas's rivals to power on the other leave no doubt about the author's contentious ploy of hijacking definitions common to the community of Judeans at large (piety, faithfulness to the forefathers' traditions, and the like) and repurposing them for the exclusive benefit of Judas and his partisans. That ploy also includes his labeling of Judas's men.[66]

C. Hellēnismos. To appreciate the term *Ioudaïsmos,* it must be considered alongside its counterparts *Hellēnismos* and *allophylismos*. I propose that the semantic fields of *Hellēnismos* and *allophylismos* follow the same logic as that of *Ioudaïsmos*. If the latter can be said to ethnicize Judas's royallike righteousness—and through

Judas, Hasmonean rule in general—the other two terms logically give an ethnic slant to the notion of wickedness and embody it in Judas's enemies.

A closer look at the text bears out the scheme proposed above. As set forth in Chapter 1 (§1.3.4), the idea of Judas's legitimacy is emplotted in the part of the narrative starting at 5:27 through to the end of 2 Maccabees, whereas the preceding section (4:7–5:26) is concerned with delegitimizing his competitors.[67] Both the high priests who succeeded Onias III (Jason and Menelaos) and the two Seleukid kings (Antiochos IV and Antiochos V) are vilified as impious and therefore unworthy to rule through the systematic inversion of the main legitimizing themes used to enhance Judas's deeds as part of the semantic field of *Ioudaïsmos*. From this perspective, the contrasted pairing of *Ioudaïsmos* and *Hellēnismos* in 2 Maccabees can be seen to have a political connotation. The concept of *Hellēnismos* appears as an updated (and similarly ethnicized) variant of the denunciation of the overthrown ruler. *Allophylismos* may denote the political order embodied by Antiochos IV, the king of imperial standing.[68]

In a sense, the closest parallels to the use of the traditional narrative in 2 Maccabees from a generic point of view may arguably be found in the royal inscriptions belonging to usurpers—for example, the Cyrus Cylinder of Babylon or the literary traditions contrasting Alexander's benevolence with the Persians' insulting behavior toward the gods.[69] As a rule, the inscriptions of usurpers take care not only to praise the royal virtues of the new ruler in order to justify his seizure of kingship but also to denounce the overthrown king or dynasty as evil. The striking innovation of 2 Maccabees is this ethnicization of the traditional political concepts of piety and wickedness. Incidentally, this interpretation explains why *Ioudaïsmos* and *Hellēnismos* never appear together in 2 Maccabees—a fact that has puzzled modern commentators.[70] In the royal inscriptions, the time and actions of the deposed king and those of the victor are described separately, which is precisely how they are handled in 2 Maccabees: the time of disruption equated with *Hellēnismos* is described in 4:7–5:26, whereas Judas's time, which is equated with *Ioudaïsmos*, runs from 5:27 on, and therefore separately.

· · ·

Although both 1 and 2 Maccabees provide the ruling dynasty with a legitimizing account by coining a new, full-fledged variant of the traditional narrative pattern, the second of the two books is further distinguished for introducing an innovative political nomenclature. The outcome is a cultural hybrid: on the one hand recounting a meaningful story—the royallike leader building or rebuilding the temple—is in line with the local tradition of political discourse; on the other, coining a specific label to denote a social order in a single word betrays Greek influence. Add the fact that the label (*Ioudaïsmos*) refers to the rule of a particular dynasty, and not to the configuration of power per se (as *basileia* does), and again we have the hallmark of the local political tradition; conversely, if my suggestion that it is a response to the self-description of the rival high priests as Greeks is correct, its ethnicized nature may be seen as due to Greek influence.

Incidentally, the goals of the heroes and their struggles are depicted in very similar images in 1 Maccabees. They too fight for the Law and for the Covenant of their fathers.[71] And although the word *Ioudaïsmos* itself is never used, these similarities suggest parallel concerns. In subsequent discussions in this book, *Ioudaioi* will be used subjectively, to designate Judas's followers, whereas "Judeans" will be used objectively, to refer to *all* the members of the *ethnos*.

But Near Eastern traditions did not necessarily need the influence of Greek thought to remain creative, and 1 and 2 Maccabees are also evidence of the continued vitality of the narrative pattern of temple foundation in Hasmonean times. In the classical version, the building of the temple is justified by an entitling victory, thereby authorizing the builder to undertake more victories. David was a king and could wage war and win the entitling victory, whereas Solomon alone enjoyed the peace necessary to carry out his building project. In Persian times, the royal prerogatives of temple building are inherited by the governor and the high priest and later grasped by the high priest alone, as Ben Sira's Praise of the Fathers shows. In contrast, the royal prerogative of victory has been transferred onto the imperial kings, first Cyrus (Ezra 1:2) and subsequently the Macedonian kings. 1 and 2 Maccabees offer an entirely different picture, in which the temple builder, Judas, is also the one who fights and obtains the victories, both before and after the temple's rededication. Despite extensive hijacking of royal privileges by the high priests of the Oniad dynasty in Hellenistic times, the definition of high-priestly prerogatives inherited from them could not accommodate this new modification. The pointed interest of our two authors in military matters may convey more than their sense of fulfilling their chronographic duty. As will be argued below in Chapter 4, the two narratives of 1 and 2 Maccabees equally echo the pretensions of the Hasmoneans to be at once kings *and* high priests.

4

Royal High Priests and Temple Foundation

The Narrative Pattern and the Hasmonean Political Order

INTRODUCTION

Tobias Funke has argued that the figure of Phineas was appropriated by the Hasmoneans to legitimize the connection between priestly and royal prerogatives, and in particular the military privileges,[1] in the office of the Maccabean/Hasmonean high priest.[2] 1 Maccabees 2:15–26 narrates how the king's men came to the town of Modein (Mattathias's place) to coerce the Israelites living there to perform sacrifices. The simile (comparison) that ends the passage (2:26) equates Mattathias's zealous slaying of the Judean man who dared to make the impure sacrifice with Phineas's killing of Zimri son of Salom (Num. 25:1–15). This episode from the book of Numbers is explicitly the reason why Phineas is presented as "our ancestor" in Mattathias's Eulogy of the Fathers (1 Macc. 2:54), where it is specified that "through his act of zeal, [Phineas] received the covenant of everlasting priesthood."[3] Phineas is also praised in very similar terms in Ben Sira's Praise of the Fathers (45:23–25), to which Mattathias's Eulogy is often compared.

Equating the actions of contemporary characters with those of traditional prototypes was a frequent ploy by which ancient authors could reflect upon the ethical value of recent events. The deeds assigned to these prototypes were coded as either positive or negative, and equating actions that had been done either in the present or in the recent past with these deeds of old made the contemporary themes more easily decipherable for the intended audience. To some extent, the use of such similes in literary works reflected actual social practice: the Greco-Roman cultural sphere in particular offers documented instances in which political and social leaders knowingly employed exempla to shape their personas, but this practice was not exclusively Greco-Roman.⁴ If we accept that exempla encapsulate social values, the fact that the Hasmoneans co-opted Phineas as their ancestral prototype means that the idea Phineas stood for—a priest using armed violence—was a key concern for their dynastic image. Beside Phineas, we may surmise that they used other forms of symbolic expression to justify their simultaneously holding priestly and royal (military) functions.

As outlined in Chapters 2 and 3, the narrative template of temple foundation legitimized not only individual rulers and dynasties but also the specific form of their rule. The historical overview in Chapter 2 (§2.2) traced how the details of the template were continually modified in the Judahite/Judean tradition to keep pace with the ever-changing status of successive local rulers—native king, combined governor and high priest, or high priest alone. The contention of the present chapter will be that 1 and 2 Maccabees were written not merely to legitimize the accession of the Hasmoneans to power by recounting the founding act of the dynasty, namely the rededication of the Jerusalem temple by the Maccabees, but also to legitimize the specific form of rule the Hasmoneans were identified with. Their simultaneous exercise of the prerogatives of the high priest and the military functions that were associated with their titles as governors, and, later, kings,⁵ made it necessary to adapt the narrative template again to suit the new configuration of their rule.

The narrative device adopted by the two Maccabees authors to translate this new political reality consisted in duplicating the narrative scheme of temple building within a single work, in the first instance to emplot the sphere of competence of the high priest and in the second to emplot the sphere of "royal," and in particular military, prerogatives. Despite the authors' common ploy of duplication and similar messages, the stories they devised differ in several respects. The author of 1 Maccabees split the two sets of prerogatives by embodying each one in a different character: the first story featuring Judas's rededication of the temple (1 Macc. 3:1–9:22) legitimizes the descendants of Judas's family as high priests;⁶ the second story, instead, features Simon (1 Macc. 13:1–16:22) and presents him as builder of the city walls and the palace, whose prototype was Nehemiah the governor.⁷ Conversely, the author of 2 Maccabees not only managed to condense the two forms of power in a single character—Judas—but also employs a similar frame story, namely that of temple refoundation. In his case, although particularly complex, this specific narrative solution is highly efficient in endorsing the twofold legitimacy (as high priests and kinglike rulers). As shown in Chapter 3 (§3.1.6B), in the first cycle (2 Macc. 4:7–13:26) the place of the leader is essentially vacant.⁸ In the second (14:1–15:37a), Judas is first acknowledged simultaneously as high priest and king by the late Onias III and Jeremiah, after which the Ptolemaic image of the king-pharaoh is used to depict him as performing the ceremony of refoundation as a king.

The first section of the present chapter will track the narrative elements of 2 Maccabees that flesh out the regal portrait of Judas. While numerous details of the Hanukkah story (5:27–13:26) already hint in this direction, Judas's enthronement is properly achieved in the second refoundation, the Nikanor's Day story (2 Macc. 14:1–15:37a), which requires a detailed analysis. The second section will turn to Simon's time unit in 1 Maccabees (13:1–16:24). Finally, the last section will show how the preliminary units of the two works—Mattathias's time unit in 1 Maccabees 2 and the Heliodoros story in 2 Maccabees (3:1–4:6)—cross-refer with these related narrative units.

4.1. JUDAS'S ROYAL ENTHRONEMENT: THE SECOND REFOUNDATION OF 2 MACCABEES 14:1–15:37a

As we saw in Chapter 3 (§§3.1 and 3.2.2), the portrayal of Judas as the legitimate heir to Onias III starts with his first appearance in 2 Maccabees (5:27). The hero gradually emerges as a king of divine election, chosen by God to bring the Seleukid imperial yoke to an end, to revive autonomous rule in the tradition of the old native kingship, and to strike a new covenant with God, as Ezra had done before him (8:15).[9] Along with his piety (5:27),[10] the firmest ground for Judas's entitlement to the royal (or royallike) status is his record as unchallenged military victor, which is evidence of divine support. This is all the more true since all Judas's campaigns (10:10–13:26), which occur after the temple rededication, are a consequence of the ceremony, and hence a sign of divine approval of the men who performed it. One more sign that Judas's victories are God-sent is the fact that they are won against enemies who outnumber the *Ioudaioi*[11] (8:18–20; 10:23, 31; 15:27).[12] Moreover, they are abetted by heavenly apparitions, like Onias III's defense of the temple against Heliodoros.[13]

Judas's rise to royal status also sees a gradual widening of his civil decision-making. As we saw in Chapter 3 (§3.2.2), his first royal act is the distribution of the spoils of war to widows, orphans, and the tortured faithful who have survived (2 Macc. 8:28).[14] Showing increasing assertiveness, in 2 Maccabees 10:21–22 Judas acts as a judge,[15] assembling the leaders of the people to prosecute a certain Simon and his men for receiving bribes from the enemy, and has them executed. While the royal letters inserted in 2 Maccabees 11:16–33 are (artificially) addressed to all the Judeans,[16] collective representation comes to a halt when idols are discovered on the bodies of the *Ioudaioi* fallen in battle at Jamnia (12:40). At first, the entire community of *Ioudaioi* "turn[s] to supplication, praying that the sin which had been committed might be entirely blotted out" (42a). However, Judas soon takes the lead and after his exhortation to the people he collects money from each man present and sends the money "to Jerusalem to be used to bring a sin offering" (42b).

From this point onward, Judas is increasingly acknowledged as the Seleukids' interlocutor. In the context of Philip's attempted usurpation in Antioch, Antiochos V sends messages to the "Judeans" as a whole but grants an audience pointedly to Judas (13:23–24). At the beginning of the last narrative unit, it is Judas who negotiates the peace treaty with envoys from Nikanor, Demetrios I's new governor of Judea (14:12, 19–22), after which Nikanor begins to deal with him exclusively (14:23–24), even appointing him to a semiofficial position (26).[17] In a crescendo of events, Judas's position as unchallenged royal leader is finally reached in the ensuing war with Nikanor and in the new "quasi temple refoundation" in which the last narrative unit culminates.

The Nikanor's Day story is a carefully crafted passage that neatly brings together all the legitimizing themes deployed in the earlier narrative sections of the work. Although earlier commentators have pinpointed each of the main intratextual connections,[18] the systematic clustering of these links in the last narrative cycle prompts a rereading of them as a coherent whole. In marked contrast with the parallel account in 1 Maccabees 7, the Nikanor's Day story has been devised to fit into the classic temple-building narrative pattern. Similarly, while the related chapter of 1 Maccabees winds through structurally devious details, the construction of the last two chapters of 2 Maccabees focuses exclusively on the narrative components of the legitimizing pattern: the victory entitling temple founding (or refounding); Judas's dual acknowledgment as heir to Onias III the high priest and to the ancient kings of Israel; and the new temple refoundation, this time unambiguously performed under Judas's leadership. None of the elements featured in 1 Maccabees 7 that depart from these constitutive motifs are found in 2 Maccabees, in particular the episodes of Bacchides' campaign to reinstate Alkimos and the latter's subsequent fight for power (1 Macc. 7:8–26). A detailed analysis of the narrative unit will help clarify its congruity with the narrative pattern of the temple-building account.

4.1.1. *The Preliminary Phases: The Entitling Victory*

Structurally speaking, the battle waged against Nikanor in 15:1–29 is the counterpart of the battle of the *Ioudaioi* against (the other) Nikanor in 8:10–36, and the point-by-point narrative symmetry of the two battles reveals their common function. Before examining it, let us review the details.[19]

> Both in the time of Antiochos's abomination and in that of Nikanor's, the battle led by Judas is preceded by the exemplary death of faithful *Ioudaioi* (2 Macc. 14:37–46; cf. 2 Macc. 6–7).
>
> Not only do the two Seleukid generals bear the same name, but they are disgraced with the same epithet, *trisalitērios*, "thrice-accursed"[20] (2 Macc. 15:3; cf. 2 Macc. 8:34).

Judas puts his faith in God (15:7; cf. 8:13–14) and wages war with divine help.

The books of the Law and the Prophets are consulted as part of the preparations for the new battle (15:9), as they had been earlier in the paradigmatic model (8:23).

Judas's men fight for *Ioudaïsmos* and not out of self-interest (15:17–18; cf. 8:14–15).

The contrast between the *Ioudaioi*'s piety and the Seleukids' wickedness is pointedly noted. In one of the rare elements of the battle that refers back to a different section than 2 Maccabees 8, Nikanor is reported to have planned an attack on the day of the Sabbath (15:1–5). This treacherous design finds its antecedent in Apollonios's assault on Jerusalem in the days of Antiochos IV (5:24–26). Nevertheless, Nikanor's wicked scheme remains at the level of verbal intention alone.[21]

Nikanor indulges in the supreme sin of equating himself with God when he replies to the Judean men who dare to object to his sinful plan of launching an attack on the Sabbath day (15:5). Thus Nikanor's behavior echoes Antiochos Epiphanes' *hybris*, since the latter believed he could modify the order of nature (9:8, 10). As a consequence, their talionlike punishment is similar, except that Antiochos's body is ravaged by a God-sent disease (9:5, 9–10), whereas Nikanor's body is wrecked by Judas (15:30, 33). In the former case, the divine punishment is inflicted in a supernatural way (disease), because the high priest's (Menelaos's) wickedness leaves the *Ioudaioi* leaderless, whereas in the latter case Judas acts as the arm of God.

Judas's harangues to his men are featured in these two battles alone, albeit with an important variation. The historical precedents that form part of the first harangue (8:19–20) are transposed in the last unit to the prayer that Judas raises before the battle (15:22–23), whereas in his speech to his men Judas relates his dream (15:11–16). The symbolic importance of the harangues and the dream justifies a separate examination below.

Thus the two battles mirror each other in both structure and detailed content, and from their parallel construction it can reasonably be deduced that they are equated in symbolic function too. Given that the function of the first battle is to entitle Judas and his warriors to the refoundation of the defiled temple, the like must also be the function of the second. The symmetrical depiction of the two battles is a literary device through which the author transforms the events commemorated by Nikanor's Day into a full-fledged temple-building account. His purpose in so doing is to provide the appropriate narrative setting for his final proclamation of Judas's status as a high priest and "king" of divine election. The inclusion of Judas's dream leaves no doubt that this status is indeed the issue at stake.

4.1.2. The Anticipated Divine Promise, or Hurowitz's Step 5: Judas's Dream, 2 Maccabees 15:12–16

Judas's vision prior to entering battle (2 Macc. 15:12–16) is the culminating point in a series of similes employed in 2 Maccabees to evoke prestigious characters of the Judahite past. The first instance comes in Judas's initial harangue (8:19–20); the second, in his supplication before the assault against Kaspin (12:15); and the last, in his prayer before the final battle (15:22–23). In Hellenistic Greek historiography, the recollection of past events is a set topos of battlefield harangues;[22] however, these are mainly rhetorical adornments, whereas the three similes in 2 Maccabees seem to serve the more precise function of incorporating Judas's military feats within the line of tradition, as if to assert that the warriors could fight for *Ioudaïsmos* only if they drew their inspiration from the deeds of their forefathers.

A. *Preparing the Ground for the Dream: The Three Similes Evoking Glorious Victors of the Past.*   The legacy of the past is primarily cited to highlight the theme of the wars fought by the few against the many. Thus, Judas's harangue before the inaugural battle (2 Macc. 8:19–20) juxtaposes one such deed of the forefathers—Hezekiah's victory against Sennacherib—and a more recent one that occurred when the Seleukids were already in power, the victory over the Galatians.[23] The second simile occurs with Judas's prayer during the siege of Kaspin and references Joshua's sack of Jericho (Josh. 6:1–21)—an appropriate choice, given that both cities were encircled by walls (12:13–15).[24] Significantly, 2 Maccabees 12 also lists all the battles fought by Judas and his men in the neighboring regions, and these references to Joshua are perhaps intended to suggest that Judas's expeditions are a reenactment of Joshua's Conquest of Canaan.[25] Note also that shortly before, Judas had indeed acted as a judge (10:21–22).[26] Finally, the third reference, in the prayer Judas raises on the eve of the final battle, equates Judas's feats with a royal victory (2 Macc. 15:22–23). Surprisingly, the victory over Sennacherib is evoked here for a second time.

Why disregard the principle of literary variation and quote the same battle twice?[27] The repetition is probably part of the author's endeavor to construct an equation between the two battles of 2 Maccabees 8 and 15, since the first instance is located in the former and the second in the latter; but it may also have aimed to highlight a distinguishing detail, namely the mention of King Hezekiah in Judas's last speech but not in his first. Because of the omission of the king's name, the emphasis in 8:19–20 is shifted to the number of enemies slaughtered, along with the identity of the vanquished king. As a result, the prestige of the victory is assigned to the army of fighters as a whole, in line with the systematic collectivization of decision making that colors Judas's early career. (Witness the first account of temple refoundation.)[28] In the final battle, the Judahite king Hezekiah is explicitly named as Sennacherib's victor, and as a result the simile implies that Judas's final battle resumes the warring tradition of the kings of Judah. Accordingly, the temple refoundation that follows is explicitly assigned to him.

The similes strongly suggest a political subtext. In ancient Mesopotamia, usurpers would make up for their lack of hereditary legitimacy by presenting themselves through narrative patterns that brought alternative sources of legitimacy into play. In the same way, likening Judas's battles with those fought by illustrious predecessors of undisputed legitimacy was a shrewd exploitation of Judas's military record—his main if not sole source of prestige. Judas's warmongering continued the native tradition of the Judges and Kings, and furthermore in Hellenistic times victories over the Galatians were a source of outstanding prestige.[29] In this context, the observation that after their final liberation of the temple the *Ioudaioi* praised God "in the language of their forefathers" (2 Macc. 15:29; cf. 12:37) may be interpreted as an additional legitimizing device: in antiquity, a people's language carried a keen sense of cultural identity,[30] and so the reference here links up the historical tradition of Judas's prestigious predecessors with his loyalty to *Ioudaïsmos*. Whereas Antiochos Epiphanes changed the name of the patron deity of the Jerusalem temple to Zeus Olympios (2 Macc. 6:2), altering the cult at the same time as the name, Judas's addressing God "in the language of the forefathers" is another way of saying that he addressed Him in accordance with the tradition: that is, faithfully.

B. *Judas's Dream.*   Thus the chain of tradition is what entitles Judas to establish a new Covenant, in continuation of the covenants of the forefathers invoked by Judas's men in 8:15. While the political implications of the three similes remain allusive, Judas's vision before the final battle is wholly unambiguous (2 Macc. 15:12–16):[31]

> His vision was as follows: he saw Onias, the late high priest, a good man and true, of modest bearing and mild manner, . . . [and] stretched forth his hands to pray for the whole assembly of the *Ioudaioi*. Thereafter . . . there appeared a man remarkable for his white hair and his dignity. . . . On being asked, Onias replied, "This lover of his brethren, who offers many prayers for our people and for the holy city, is Jeremiah, the prophet of God." Jeremiah stretched forth his hand to give Judas a golden sword, and as he gave it to him, he addressed him as follows: "Take the holy sword as a gift from God, and with it shatter our enemies."

On the eve of the legitimizing victory that opens the account of Judas's second "temple refoundation," Judas is jointly sanctioned as high priest and king by Onias and Jeremiah.

C. *Judas, Legitimate High Priest: Onias's Blessing.*   Judas's enthronement as the legitimate heir to Onias the high priest comes as no surprise, not only because it is envisaged from an early stage in 2 Maccabees, but also because it is staged with full intensity from the beginning of the Nikanor's Day narrative unit. Indeed, the tale of treachery related in 14:3–13 is a reenactment of the drama played out in Onias III's time. Here, the king's wicked officer Nikanor is a new Heliodoros, likewise jeopardizing the integrity of the temple; while Alkimos, who acts as a traitor against Judas in the new episode, may be likened to Simon, the man who betrayed Onias III (3:4–7, 4:1–4).[32] At the same time, of course, Judas is equated with Onias, who here operates as the prototype of the pious leader who falls victim to treachery at the very moment when he is defending his temple and people.[33]

As we shall see below (§4.1.3), the symmetry of the first and last narrative cycles of 2 Maccabees goes even further: Judas's "second refoundation" is the story of an "averted refoundation," so to speak. Nikanor's threat to raze the temple, destroy the altar, and build a shrine to Dionysos in their place (14:33, with 36) will eventually be averted (15:34) thanks to Nikanor's military defeat by Judas—events that mirror what happened when Heliodoros was miraculously prevented from defiling the temple in Onias III's days. Pious leaders are able to act as efficient intercessors. As in the days of Onias, there now *is* a leader in Israel enjoying divine favor, and therefore God has no reason to abandon His temple and allow the enemy to violate it, unlike what happened as a result of Jason's and Menelaos's wickedness. Thus, whereas the Hanukkah story is a classical account of temple refoundation, the Nikanor's Day story combines elements of Hurowitz's scheme of temple building and Doran's narrative pattern of temple liberation.[34]

The close link between Judas and Onias implied by their symmetrical positions in the two stories of betrayal culminates accordingly in Judas's dream and is proclaimed by Onias himself. By appearing before Judas to bless the army (2 Macc. 15:12), Onias III, the last legitimate Oniad, acknowledges Judas as the new protector of the temple—and through him, the Hasmoneans as legitimate successors.[35] Unsurprisingly, no mention whatsoever is made of Onias III's having a son, who would logically have succeeded his father (as Onias IV).[36]

D. Judas, King of Israel: Jeremiah's Sword. While the literary construction of Onias's message in the dream is relatively straightforward, Jeremiah's piece is more elaborate. The prophets of earlier times were abundantly commented on in the literature of Persian Yehud and Hellenistic Judea, each prophet being associated with a specific period of the past. Therefore, as Ben Zvi pointed out, "imagining a prophet was often imagining a period too."[37] While Jeremiah was identified with the last days of monarchic Judah, he was also remembered as the prophet who had foretold the rebuilding of the temple.[38] Although the two connotations seem relevant to Judas's dream, Jeremiah's prophecy seems to reference Nathan's prophecy to David (2 Sam. 7) rather than those delivered by Haggai and Zechariah in the days of Zerubbabel and Joshua. Whereas the latter urged the reconstruction of the temple, Nathan's prophecy principally relates to the divine election of the pious warrior as king, and not to the temple refoundation per se. This is the topic of Jeremiah's prophecy as well, as the comparison between the Heliodoros story and the Nikanor's Day story reveals—the structural symmetry between the two passages highlighting the differences as well as the similarities. To forestall Heliodoros's pending impiety, Onias turned to prayer, and God answered by sending heavenly horse riders to stop Heliodoros. Likewise, Judas steadily turns to prayer, God hearkening to his requests and periodically sending celestial warriors to buttress him on the battlefield.[39] Unlike Onias, however, Judas fights and vanquishes Nikanor by his own hand. More accurately, Judas serves as God's hand, whereas Onias did not. Jeremiah's presence at Onias's side in Judas's vision underscores the fact that the pious high priest can administer only a partial blessing upon Judas, because as a warrior, Judas inhabits a sphere of competence that is actually wider than his own. Finally, like Nathan's prophecy, the joint announcement by Jeremiah and Onias is made in anticipation of the temple refoundation, on the very eve of the entitling battle.

Essentially, Jeremiah's prophecy is delivered not by word but by the deed of his consignment of the sword to Judas. In contrast with what we have seen so far, the significance of his gesture cannot be understood through reference to native Judean traditions alone. As Jan Willem van Henten has shown, the image of a god bestowing a sword upon the king harks back to ancient Egyptian royal ideology, where it emphasized the theme of victory and was sometimes combined with another traditional scene in which the pharaoh holds the sword in one hand and in the other a tuft of hair or the arm of a kneeling captive enemy he is about to slaughter.[40] The sword motif was still used in Egyptian priestly circles of Ptolemaic times in reference to the Macedonian dynasty. It is documented in four trilingual priestly decrees honoring Ptolemaic kings that were voted on the occasion of priestly meetings summoned by the kings, by the pictures found on the steles on which the decrees are engraved and in temple reliefs.[41] Both the texts and the images date to the third and the second centuries B.C.E., and some of them are therefore coeval with the Ptolemaic domination of Koilē Syria in the third century, whereas the close economic and cultural ties between Koilē Syria and Egypt are known to have continued under Seleukid domination in the second century. Consequently, there can be little doubt that the links between the sword motif and Ptolemaic royal ideology were as familiar to the literati of Judea as they were to the Egyptian subjects of the Ptolemies.[42]

That said, in 2 Maccabees the moment of Jeremiah's yielding the sword to Judas takes place prior to the battle and not after it, suggesting a reworking of the borrowed cultural motif, since this timing would be nonsensical in its original cultural setting—the pharaoh cannot slay prisoners before a battle has taken place. In 2 Maccabees the Egyptian theme of the sword is conflated with the traditional Judean motif of dynastic promise, the hallmark of divine election; the two could easily be merged, since they have the same function of linking victory and kingship. Nonetheless, in the Judahite/Judean tradition the motif of divine election manifesting itself through victory is an integral part of the temple-building account, into which the pharaonic motif of the sword is also incorporated. Indeed the interest for the author of 2 Maccabees to borrow the pharaonic motif may become more apparent if we consider the narrative pattern as a whole. As we saw in Chapter 2 (§2.2.3), in Hellenistic times this narrative pattern had come to signify entitlement to high priesthood, not kingship. As a specifically royal motif, the sword shifted its connotation back to entitlement to kingship. Moreover, it draws attention to two additional allusions to kingship in Judas's dream. First, the anticipated deliverance of the prophecy must be seen as an additional allusion to Nathan's prophecy, which as we have just seen delivered YHWH's promise of a dynasty to David prior to the building of the temple. Second, Judas's dream may reference Solomon's dream at Gibeon, in which the king asked YHWH for and was granted wisdom (2 Kgs 3:4–15).[43]

Strikingly, as Henten has shown, the final scene of 2 Maccabees—the ceremony of "temple refoundation" that is carried out after the victory over Nikanor—also incorporates Ptolemaic themes.

4.1.3. The New Temple Refoundation: 2 Maccabees 15:29–37a

In 1 Maccabees' version of Nikanor's visit to the temple, the wicked general is held responsible for a physical act of defilement, namely spitting in the face of the priests (7:34), a detail absent from 2 Maccabees, in which the profanation remains verbal only: he curses the priests and threatens to raze the temple and build a shrine to Dionysos in its place (14:33–34). The horrified priests refer to Nikanor's blasphemies in their prayer, beseeching the Lord to "preserve forever from defilement this newly purified house" (14:36). Last, the *Ioudaioi* evoke them in their prayer closing the ceremony of "refoundation," praising the Lord in thanks for preserving His temple from further defilement (15:34).[44] Altogether, we hear about Nikanor's threats no less than three times.

But these are only threats. As a consequence, Judas performs a ceremony of refoundation in the apparent wake of a profanation that has not actually happened. But, curious as it may be, a temple refoundation is what we have in 2 Maccabees 15:29–37a, the final scene of the work.[45] More precisely, the scene oddly intertwines three motifs: first, topics belonging to the temple-building pattern, which create a conceptual link between the new ceremony performed by Judas and the rededication in the Hanukkah story (10:1–8). Second, the contradictory note of the "averted threat," which signals that there was actually no need to rebuild the temple but must be included because it references Onias III. Finally, the Ptolemaic representations of royal victory precisely connote kingship (and not high priesthood). Thanks to this disorienting montage, the ceremony is turned into a founding event whose significance is symbolically equivalent to the rededication of the temple in Antiochos IV's time. In contrast, the concise description of the ceremony in 1 Maccabees 7:47–49 ignores the pattern of temple refoundation and ostensibly invokes more remote (and vague) precedents (1 Macc. 7:41–42). The synoptic Table 4.1 shows how the passage of 2 Maccabees compares with the parallel account of 1 Maccabees, revealing their congruity to and divergence from Hurowitz's six-step pattern of the temple-building template.[46]

The first meaningful difference between the two Maccabees books is the setting. It is clear from 1 Maccabees 7:47b that the severed parts of Nikanor's body were not brought to the temple—the last place where mutilated human body parts should be found. Hence, while the setting of the scene in 2 Maccabees is utterly unrealistic, this oddity offers a hint of our author's intention: by moving the scene of Judas's butchering of Nikanor's body from the battlefield to the temple precinct, the author aimed to incorporate the deed within the familiar semantic field of the temple-building pattern, and in this way to inject the symbolic connotations that are normally associated with it. Henten has cogently argued that the slaughter of Nikanor here echoes the pharaonic ritual of shaming the leader of the defeated enemy. However, although Egyptian reliefs depicting this theme show the king holding the sword in one hand and the arm of a kneeling captive in the other,[47] neither pharaohs nor Ptolemaic kings performed this gory ceremony in a temple. Hence, the account of Judas's displaying the enemy's blasphemous arm in the Jerusalem temple occupies the customary slot of the "dedication rites and ceremonies" (Hurowitz's step 4).

There is, however, another major difference between our passage and the description of the first refoundation in 2 Maccabees 10:1–8: there, Judas's role was toned down, and in the absence of a legitimate leader the prerogative of decision making was held collectively by the community of the performers. In the last narrative unit, 14:1–15:37a, Judas's leadership has been legitimized by his vision prior to the new "refoundation." Accordingly, the description of the preparations carried out on the battlefield for the ceremony involving Nikanor's body is wrapped in authorial words of praise singling out Judas (15:30), who thereafter emerges as the unchallenged leader throughout the temple ceremony (15:29–37a). Thus Judas is now the one who summons the people (15:31a), dispatches orders (33, 35), and performs the "rites" (31b–33). Judas's new status explains why the "prayer of the king" (step 5) is omitted. Its usual object was the king's request for divine election and the grant of a dynasty, but the promise has already been delivered in the vision of 15:12–16. For distinct reasons, the prayer of the king was omitted in 10:1–8 and replaced by the collective prayer. Last, 15:37b confirms that the promise of a dynasty—the essence of divine election—has been fulfilled.[48] The final scene of 2 Maccabees culminates with Judas's full accession to the status of king.

It has long been recognized that in 1 Maccabees the figure of Judas is likened to David.[49] The comparison between Jeremiah's prophecy of 2 Maccabees 15:12–16

TABLE 4.1. A comparison of 2 Maccabees 15:28–37 with 1 Maccabees 7:47–50 in light of Hurowitz's (1992) six-step pattern of the Near Eastern temple-building template.

2 Maccabees 15:28–37	1 Maccabees 7:47–50
Step 1. Preliminary phase: The circumstances of the project [and decision to build]	
28–30. [After the battle, Judas's men] recognized the fallen body of Nikanor in full armor. There was shouting and tumult, and then they began to praise the Lord in the language of their forefathers. The man who in every way had played the chief role [*proetaxen*], body and soul, in the struggle of his fellow citizens, the man who had throughout maintained his youthful love for his fellow *Ioudaioi* [*homoethneis*], ordered that Nikanor's head and his arm up to his shoulder be cut off and brought to Jerusalem.	47a. Taking the spoils and the booty, the victors cut off the head of Nikanor and his right hand, which had so presumptuously raised in oath, . . .
Step 2. Preparations for the building (gathering materials, drafting workmen, laying foundations)	
31a. On [Judas's] arrival [in Jerusalem], he called together his fellow *Ioudaioi* [*homoethneis*] and had the priests stand before the altar.	47b. . . . and brought and raised them where they could be viewed from Jerusalem.
[Step 3. Description of the construction process and the buildings and furnishings]	
—	—
Step 4. Dedication rites and festivities? (Or Step 3?) *Ptolemaic motif of the slaughtered enemy*	
31b–33. Then he summoned the men from the Akra and showed them the head of the abominable Nikanor and the hand of the blasphemer, which he had boastfully stretched forth against the sacred house of the Almighty. Cutting out the tongue of the impious Nikanor, he said he would feed it to the birds, bit by bit, and he ordered that the arm be hung opposite the temple as retribution for Nikanor's mad audacity.	[Cf. 1 Macc. 4:41: Then Judas assigned soldiers the duty of fighting the men in the Akra while he purified the sanctuary.]
Step 5. Blessing or prayer of the king	
34. All offered praises toward heaven, to the Lord Who had manifested Himself, saying, "Blessed is He Who has preserved His place from defilement."	47c. The people were overjoyed and observed the day as a day of great rejoicing.
Step 4. Dedication rites and festivities *Ptolemaic motif of the slaughtered enemy*	
35. He had the severed head of Nikanor hung from the Akra as a clear and evident token for all of the Lord's succor.	

	Step 5. Blessing or prayer of the king
[Omitted here, since the promise of divine election has already been received in 15:12–16]	

	Step 6. Divine promises or revelation; Blessings and curses of future generations; Setting of norms
36. By a unanimous vote of the people they decreed that they would by no means let that day pass unmarked but that they would keep as a special day the thirteenth of the twelfth month, called Adar in Aramaic, the day before the Day of Mordechai."	49. They decreed that the day, the thirteenth of Adar, should be observed annually.

	[Fulfillment of the promise of dynasty implicitly contained in the divine election]
37. Such was the outcome of the affair of Nikanor. From that time on, the city has been held by the Hebrews.	50. There followed a brief period of peace for the land of Judah.

and Nathan's prophecy to David proves that—in this matter as in many others—the claim that 1 and 2 Maccabees contradict or stand in contrast to each other is wholly mistaken.

A. *The Absence of the Leader and the Martyrs in the Hanukkah Story.* The fact that in 2 Maccabees the second refoundation account assumes the status of Judas's major feat, whereas his personal part is downplayed in the account of the Hanukkah story, contradicts the Hasmonean tradition that emphasizes the etiological story of the Hanukkah festival as Judas's main exploit. This dislocation of Judas's figure from the Hanukkah story to the second episode is certainly the most disconcerting feature of the literary construction of the work. It leaves the account of the rededication leaderless, and it may be tempting to see this "vacancy of leadership" as a narrative flaw: the author of 2 Maccabees failed to cope with the constraint of the duplication adequately, and his own variant of the story remains incompletely fleshed out. A more positive interpretation is possible, however, prompted by the insertion of two stories of the exemplary death of faithful Judeans in the preliminary phase of the two temple-building accounts (2 Macc. 6:18–7:42 and 14:41–46). Whereas Judas's power is legitimized in the second story, the absence of a leader in the first refoundation is used to enhance the part played by the faithful Judeans who died for the temple and the Law. By inserting the topic of the faithful dead into the narrative template that served to legitimize rule in the Judahite/Judean tradition, the author granted legitimacy to certain innovative concepts emerging at the time, such as the belief in life after death.

4.2. THE SECOND EMPLOTMENT OF THE TEMPLE-BUILDING TEMPLATE IN 1 MACCABEES 13:1-16:24

Whereas the account of Nikanor's campaign in 1 Maccabees 7 is not encoded through a narrative template as such, in contrast with its counterpart, meaningful patterning in 1 Maccabees returns in the last narrative cycle, namely Simon's time unit (1 Macc. 13:1–16:24). Here, however, the legitimizing pattern is used to inform not a story of temple refoundation but two relative topics, Simon's fortification works—of the walls of the temple, Jerusalem, and the fortresses of Judea—and his transformation of the Akra into his residence. As we saw in Chapter 2 (introductory section and §2.2.2), the themes of building a wall and a palace are both closely bound with that of building a temple. Thus in Mesopotamian royal inscriptions, accounts of building palaces and temples—and potentially other urban works as well—were informed by the same narrative pattern. Within the Judahite/Judean literary tradition, Solomon unites the three features, since he was remembered as simultaneously building YHWH's House, his own palace, and the city walls.[50] As shown in Chapter 2 (§2.2.2), the account of Nehemiah's repair of the walls and gates of Jerusalem is informed with a legitimizing narrative pattern, and this is the model on which Simon's building of the city walls more specifically hinges. As was argued there, Nehemiah's rebuilding of the city walls was indispensable to the safeguarding and correct operation of the temple. Likewise, we shall see in this section how the author of 1 Maccabees turned Simon's liberation and purification of the Akra into the necessary final step in the progressive liberation and purification of the temple itself.

As with the parallel work, in 1 Maccabees there seem to be deliberate *intra*textual references between the first and the second occurrences of the narrative pattern. Thus the preliminary phases are constructed in a symmetrical way, like the two entitling victories of 2 Maccabees 8:10–36 and 15:1–29. Moreover, foreshadowings of the Akra, the fortification of Jerusalem, and the fortresses of Judea are scattered through the run-up to Judas's refoundation of the temple (see further §4.2.2D below) and, even more significant, are slotted into the description of the rededication itself.[51] Finally, as in 2 Maccabees, the second application of Hurowitz's pattern is used to make a statement about power. Five sections are particularly worth highlighting in the composition of Simon's unit, as follows:

I. The first forms the *preliminary phase* (13:1–42): As in 2 Maccabees (see Chapter 4, §4.1.1), it is centered on the entitling battle—actually a cluster of battles—and the assertion of Simon's personal piety. The preliminary wars eventually culminate in the (alleged?) achievement of autonomy from the Seleukid empire, which is expressed in an (alleged?) exemption from tribute and the right to uphold the fortresses of the country, as well as the dating of official documents by Simon's ruling years as a high priest and *stratēgos*.

II. The second section corresponds with the *central phase of monumental building* (13:43–53), consisting in Simon's building of two palaces, one for himself (in the Akra) and one (in Gazara) for his son John, whom he thereby associates with his rule.
III. The last three sections are part of the *subsequent blessings:* first, Simon's Eulogy (14:4–15); second, his official appointment by the sovereign people acting in the place of a prophet (14:25–49); and third, the dynastic transmission of his rule to his son (16:23–24).

While these sections are constitutive elements of the template, others of minor structural importance are interwoven with them to meet various narrative needs. Thus Simon's "refoundation" is immediately followed by the mention of Demetrios II's military disaster in the Upper Satrapies (14:1–3), a mention that is symmetrical with Antiochos's defeat and death in the Upper Satrapies after Judas's victory and refoundation of the temple in the first occurrence of the template (1 Macc. 6:1–17). Simon's "victorious negotiation" with Antiochos VI the son of Demetrios II (15:1–36) completes his achievement of autonomy, which closes the preliminary phase (13:36–42), since the exemption from tax and the right to uphold the fortified cities of Joppe, Gazara, and the Akra are reiterated, and moreover the right to strike coinage is granted. Chapter 16 is devoted to demonstrating John's entitlement to succeed his father. The first part of the chapter shows how Simon's son came to be associated with his rule and narrates John's military prowess (16:1–10); whereas the second depicts Simon's treacherous assassination (16:11–22). These two episodes logically lead to the transmission of Simon's powers and titles to his son. Last, Simon's renewal of alliances with the Romans and the Spartans (14:16–24 with 15:15–24) provides the necessary cyclical symmetry between the three respective time units of Judas, Jonathan, and Simon, and therefore does not require specific attention here.[52] As with 2 Maccabees 14:1–15:37a, the system by which Simon's ruling legitimacy is gradually built up will come to light through a linear analysis of the text.[53]

4.2.1. The Preliminary Phase: 1 Maccabees 13:1–42

As noted above, the preliminary phase is constructed in close symmetry with the lead-up to Judas's rededication of the temple. This symmetry is demonstrated in the synoptic Table 4.2, comparing Judas's and Simon's entitling battles.

The comparison casts light on both the meaningful similarities and divergences. The crucial similarity between the accounts of Judas's and Simon's initial battles is their respective preliminary restoration of social justice, one of the set components of Hurowitz's classical scheme, whose function is to underscore the leader's justice (or piety). While Judas presides over a ceremony in Mitzpah and subsequently exonerates specific categories of Israelites from military service "as required by the

TABLE 4.2. A comparison of the legitimizing battles led by Judas (1 Macc. 3:1–4:35) and Simon (1 Macc. 13.1–42).

1 Maccabees 3:1–4:35: Judas	1 Maccabees 13:1–42: Simon
The appointment of the kinglike leader	*The appointment of the kinglike leader*
3:1–9. Judas's appointment	13:1–9. Simon's appointment
1. Judas Maccabee succeeds his father (dynastic principle).	1–9. Simon is appointed by the people in replacement of Jonathan, whom Tryphon has made prisoner.
2. Judas gathers his brothers and the followers of his father to fight Israel's war.	9. Simon is appointed as their leader to fight their war.
3–9. Hymn praising Judas.	
Preliminary minor victories	*Preliminary minor victory*
3:10–26. Judas defeats Apollonios and Seron.	13:10–11. The conquest of Joppe.
Themes of piety and impiety	Theme of the fortification
15. Seron enrolls impious men.	10. Simon completes the walls of Jerusalem and strengthens the fortifications around her.
17–22. Theme of the few against the many winning with God's support because of their just war.	11. Simon expels Joppe's inhabitants and occupies the town.
The main campaign	*The main campaign*
3:27–4:25. Nikanor's and Gorgias's sinful campaign against Judas.	13:12–33. Tryphon's sinful campaign against Simon.
(Part: 3:35–36, 39–41, 42.)	(Part: 13:23, 31–32.)
26–27. Judas's fame reaches the king and every nation. When Antiochos hears of these events he angrily gathers an army against Judas.	12–14. When Tryphon receives the news that Simon has taken the place of his brother Jonathan and that he is ready to join in battle with him, he sends envoys (to deceive him).
Antiochos's sinful levying of the tribute	*Tryphon's sinful levying of the tribute*
28–29, 37. Antiochos realizes that his treasury has run out of money and that the tribute from his territories is small because of the dissension and disorder that he caused in his land by abrogating the laws that had been in force from the earliest times. He decides to go to Persis and gather a large sum of money by collecting the tribute of the territories (by unlawful plunder: see 6:1–4).	15–39. "Because of money which your brother Jonathan owed the royal treasury in connection with his official capacities we are now holding him under arrest. Accordingly, send now a hundred talents of silver and two of [Jonathan's] sons as hostages. . . ." Simon sends the money and the hostages but Tryphon refuses to release Jonathan.
	Theme of the fortifications
	21. The men of the Akra turn to Tryphon for help because they are besieged by Simon. (Cf. 4:2.)
3.35–36, 39–41, 42. The Seleukid commanders intend to destroy Israel, sell them as slaves, and settle foreigners in their territory.	23. Tryphon puts Jonathan to death and buries him in the Galaaditis.
Judas's piety	*Simon's piety*
46–54. The ceremony at Mitzpah.	25–30. Simon has the bones of his brother Jonathan collected and gives him a lavish burial in Modein, the town of his ancestors.
56. Judas sends some men back as required by the Torah.	

55, 57–59. Judas's men prepare to fight for their people and their sanctuary. (Cf. Simon's harangue, 13:3–9.)

31–32. Tryphon becomes king by treacherously killing Antiochos VI; he is a bad king.

Theme of the fortifications
33. Simon built up the fortifications of Judea, constructing circuits with lofty towers and big walls and gates and bars; he placed stores of food in the fortresses.

Anticipated theme of the Akra
4:2. Gorgias is helped by the men of the Akra, who serve him as guides. (Cf. 13:21.)

Theme of piety
4:8–11. Theme of the few against the many winning with God's support.
4:24. Hymns of thanksgiving after the victory.

Foil to the theme of the tribute?
4:23. Judas and his men take spoils and booty—that is., money justly won. (Cf. 6:6.)

The last preliminary campaign 4:26–35. Lysias against Judas and Israel.	*Toward autonomy* 13.36–42. Demetrios acknowledges the autonomy.
Theme of piety 4:30–33. Judas's just war. Judas invokes the Lord. Simile of David and Jonathan son of Saul.	*Theme of the tribute* 34. Simon writes to King Demetrios to ask that the country be made tax-exempt, because all Tryphon's exactions were acts of robbery. 37. In his reply, Demetrios acknowledges the gifts (golden crown and palm branch) and grants the tax exemptions . . . *Theme of the fortifications* 38. . . . and acknowledges the right of the Judeans to keep their fortresses. 41–42. End of Seleukid domination in 170 S.E.; first year of Simon's rule as high priest, *stratēgos*, and *hēgemōn* of the Judeans.

Torah" (4:55), Simon offers a magnificent burial to his murdered brother in the town of his forefathers (13:25–30), this pious act enhanced by the fact that Jonathan had already been hastily buried by Tryphon's men in Galaatidis (13:24).

The differences between the two accounts are no less important to emphasize. A blatant one concerns Judas's and Simon's respective modes of accession to leadership. Mattathias hailed Judas as his successor upon his deathbed (1 Macc.

2:66), and in a sense Judas's smooth succession to his father anticipates the eventual establishment of the dynastic principle with John's succession to Simon, his father, recounted in the last two verses of the work (1 Macc. 16:23–24). In contrast, the circumstances of Simon's promotion to power are delicate, since Jonathan is not dead but a prisoner to Tryphon. Therefore a formal act of appointment is indispensable, and Simon's pledge to lead the people to "take vengeance for my nation and our sanctuary and wives and children" is approved by the people in lieu of a genuine prophet.[54] Thanks to this equation between collective and prophet, Simon's provisional appointment in this scene cross-references with two highlighted episodes of the work, the provisional decision concerning the fate of the desecrated altar that had been taken by the priests in the absence of a prophet (1 Macc. 4:44–46) and Simon's definite appointment as leader, which will be formalized in the solemn decree of the people (14:41) following Simon's purging of the Akra.[55]

Further differences are noteworthy. The main legitimizing motif of Judas's preliminary actions is his pious warfare. Thus Judas and his men wage war against more numerous troops and win because they call for help upon the Lord, who hearkens because their war is just (3:17–22; 4:8–11, 30–33); and after the victory, the pious warriors thank the Lord with hymns (4:24). In contrast, the themes that dominate Simon's preliminary deeds prepare the ground for the eventual acknowledgment of the Judeans' autonomy by Demetrios II (13:36–40). These are, on the one hand, the Seleukids' illegitimate requirement of tribute (13:15–19; see 13:34) and settlement of the Akra (13:21), and on the other, Simon's works of fortification in Jerusalem (13:10) and in the countryside (13:33). Not coincidentally, the topics of taxes and Seleukid control of the Akra are foreshadowed in Judas's unit (3:28–29, 37 + 6:1–17; and 4:2).

4.2.2. Simon's Entitling Building Activity: 1 Maccabees 13:43–53

As in Judas's unit, and as required by Hurowitz's scheme, the sequence of the preliminary steps of Simon's unit is immediately followed by the core episode of the refoundation: that is, the legitimizing act. Nonetheless, the transition is not clearly signposted (contrast 1 Macc. 4:36), and in a sense its precise delineation becomes clear only in hindsight, the hymn singing and praises of 1 Maccabees 14 cueing the start of the "subsequent blessings." In between, Simon's legitimizing building activity not only involves constructing a palace rather than a temple but is moreover duplicated. Quoting the passage in two columns, as in Table 4.3, will make the parallel construction of Simon's capture of Gazara and of the Akra apparent.

A. *The Palaces of Gazara and the Akra: 1 Maccabees 13:43–53.* The conquest of Gazara (13:43–48, 53) and the capture of the Akra (13:49–52) combine to prompt

TABLE 4.3. A comparison of the accounts of Simon's building of the palaces of Gazara and of the Akra (1 Macc. 13:43–53).

1 Maccabees 13:43–48, 53. The ruler's palace of Gazara	1 Maccabees 13:49–52. The ruler's palace of the Akra
43–44. At that time Simon besieged Gazara, surrounding it with camps. He built a movable tower, and by bringing it up against the city he overwhelmed an enemy tower and took it. The men in the movable tower surged into the town, where panic began to reign.	49. The men of the Akra in Jerusalem were now blocked from leaving it to go out into the country to buy and sell. They suffered grievously from hunger, and a considerable number of them died of starvation.
45–47a. The townspeople with their wives and children came up onto the wall with their garments torn and cried out loudly, imploring Simon to grant them a truce. They begged, "Look not to our wickedness in treating us, but to your mercy." Simon came to terms with them and ordered his men to cease hostilities.	50a. They cried out to Simon for a truce, and he consented, . . .
47b. However, he expelled the people from the city and saw to the purification of the buildings in which there were idols.	50b. . . . expelling them from the citadel and purifying it of the impurities.
47c. Having accomplished all that, he entered the city singing hymns and praises.	51–52a. Simon's men entered the citadel on the twenty-third day of the second month, in the year 171 S.E., with utterances of praise and palm branches and to the music of lyres and cymbals and lutes and hymns and songs, because a great enemy had been smashed and driven out of Israel. He decreed that the day be observed annually with rejoicing.
48a. After removing all impurity from the city, he resettled it with men who observed the Law.	
48b. He also improved the fortifications . . .	52b. He also improved the fortifications of the temple mount running along the Akra . . .
48c. . . . and built himself a residence within it.	52c. . . . and began to dwell there himself with his retinue.
53. Observing that his son John had reached maturity, Simon appointed him chief of the entire army. John began to reside at Gazara.	

the edification of a "royal" house, the Akra becoming Simon's residence and his son John receiving the palace of Gazara. Set in the context of the legitimizing narrative pattern, the creation of the two royal residences symbolizes the dynastic transmission of power, and in this sense the core episode of the narrative unit prefigures Simon's associating his son to his rule in 1 Maccabees 16. In Judean memory, Gazara (Gezer) had been captured and destroyed by Pharaoh, who had endowed it to his daughter when she married Solomon. Solomon's reconstruction of the city is mentioned alongside his building of the temple of YHWH and his own house (the palace).[56] By building two palaces in Jerusalem and Gezer, the historical Simon most probably took King Solomon as his model.

Why does our author have Simon build palaces? While in Hellenistic Judea the image of the temple builder had come to signify entitlement to the office of high priest, that of the palace builder had apparently remained unaffected by the semantic shift. It retained its original value, which means that it defines Simon as a "king." Thus as a signifier, the palace of 1 Maccabees is equivalent to Jeremiah's sword in 2 Maccabees. This interpretation may further explain two odd details arising in 1 and 2 Maccabees, respectively, as we shall now see.

B. The Purification and the Sukkothlike Ceremony. While the depiction of Judas's rededication of the temple in 1 Maccabees 4:36–61[57] is untypically framed with references to war activities (4:41, 60–61), the violence of warfare is downplayed in the description of Simon's capture of Gazara and the Akra. The Akra falls without bloodshed (13:49–50), and the audience is spared the usual horrors of siege in Simon's assault on Gazara (13:43–47). This toning down of violence brings the account as close as possible to the peaceful atmosphere that is appropriate to the conduct of a ritual ceremony of foundation (or refoundation). As with Judas's refoundation (4:42–46), the phase of preparation for Simon's ceremony consists not in gathering building material but rather in the expulsion of the alien inhabitants and the erasure of all traces of the places' defilement (Gazara, 13:47b; the Akra, 13:50b). The subsequent ceremony that takes place in the Akra is described in particularly solemn terms. The date of the ceremony is specified (13:51), just as the date of Judas's ceremony of refoundation had been (4:52), and moreover Simon decrees an annual commemoration (13:52) that mirrors the institutions of both the festival of the rededication of the temple (1 Macc. 4:59; cf. 2 Macc. 10:8) and that of Nikanor's Day (1 Macc. 7:48–50; cf. 2 Macc. 15:36). Moreover, the content of the ceremony is reminiscent of the Festival of Sukkoth, which as we saw in Chapter 2 (§2.1.1) is a paradigm for all ceremonies of refoundation.

When the construction—or the purification—of a temple is completed, its patron deity normally takes possession of his or her new abode. In the case of cities, their appropriate inhabitants settle in (48a), and in turn rulers enter their palaces (13:48c, 52c, 53). The two refoundations of Gazara and the Akra end with the observation that Simon strengthened their fortifications (48b, 52b), and the narrative symmetry with the closure of Judas's temple rededication (4:60–61) is certainly not coincidental.

As we saw in Chapter 3 (§3.1.3), the intrusive elements of warfare inserted into—or rather, framing—the account of the temple's rededication in 1 Maccabees

(4:41, 60–61) constitute a most unconventional variation, since the building (or rebuilding) of a temple normally requires the preliminary restoration of peace. In hindsight, their insertion may have aimed at something more than creating a link between Judas's and Simon's legitimizing deeds. Whereas, as just noted, the narrative template of temple building had come to be identified with the province of the high priest,[58] warfare remained the exclusive province of the king and, in the absence of a king, of the governor. Therefore the intrusive hints at warfare in the rededication ceremony may be interpreted as signifiers of kingship. If this interpretation is correct, the hints at warfare in 1 Maccabees have the same function as the insertion of the pharaonic royal motif of humiliating the enemy's body in Judas's second ceremony of refoundation in 2 Maccabees, namely interlacing references to high priesthood and kingship. Within 1 Maccabees, they cross-refer to the theme of Simon's building palaces.

C. Simon's Purging of the Akra as the Final Step in Judas's Purification of the Temple. As shown in Chapter 2 (§2.2.2), the symbolic equation between Nehemiah's restoration of Jerusalem's walls and the canonical act of temple refoundation lies in the fact that the walls created a physical separation between the inner space of Israel, within which YHWH's Law ruled on Sabbath days and festivals, and the outer space, where the foreigners unbound by YHWH's Covenant were required to sojourn during these days. In the same way, the author of 1 Maccabees created an organic link between Simon's seizure and purging of the citadel of the Akra and the temple. This link is enunciated from the outset, in the passage that describes the fortification of the citadel by Antiochos IV's soldiers at the beginning of 1 Maccabees (1:33–40; emphases added):

> Thereupon they [the Mysarch and his army] fortified the City of David with a high strong wall and strong towers so as to have a citadel, the Akra. They stationed in it a breed of sinners, wicked men, who grew strong there. The *garrison* was provided with a store of arms and provisions and kept there under their hands the spoils of Jerusalem, which they had collected, *and became a dangerous menace.*
> *It was an ambush against the temple,*
> And continually a wicked adversary against Israel.
> *They shed innocent blood around the sanctuary*
> *And defiled the temple.*
> The rightful inhabitants of Jerusalem were put to flight by them,
> and she became a colony of foreigners; ...
> *Her temple was deserted like a desert,*
> Her *festivals* were turned into mourning,
> Her *Sabbaths* into cause for mockery,
> Her glory into cause for contempt.
> Her humiliation matched her former splendor,
> And her pride was turned into mourning.

This initial presentation of the Akra cross-refers in two ways to the account of its being wiped out by Simon. First, we are informed that the citadel is strong because its garrison has abundant provisions (1:34). Simon undid what Antiochos Epiphanes had done by starving the inhabitants of the Akra into surrender (13:49). Second, and more important, we learn that the Akra posed a constant threat to the temple; and more specifically, its impurities and the frequent bloodshed around the sanctuary that it occasioned were a constant source of defilement for the temple (1:36–37).[59] Even though Judas purified the temple and allowed the sacrifices of Sabbaths and festivals (1:39) to be resumed, the temple could not operate safely as long as the garrison of the Akra kept jeopardizing its purity. This is the message enacted by Judas's order to fight the men of the Akra while he, his brothers, and his men were carrying out the cleansing and rededication of the temple (4:41). Simon's purge of the Akra was the final step toward completing the temple's return to splendor.[60] Therefore, as with Nehemiah's walls, it is reasonable to identify Simon's conquest of the Akra as a form of temple refoundation.

D. Intratextual Connections and Historical Objectivity: The Akra in 1 Maccabees. The fact that Simon's purification of the Akra in 1 Maccabees occupies the symbolic slot of the legitimizing activity of building may explain why the author of 1 Maccabees included accounts of Judas's and Jonathan's ill-fated attempts to suppress the Akra in their respective time units.[61] The successive accounts of their failures keep the issue of the Akra constantly in sight, periodically reminding the audience that the Akra's presence posed a constant threat to the temple. Moreover, by underscoring that Simon succeeded where his brothers had failed, the recurrent episodes of the assaults on the Akra create a continuity of action between Judas, Jonathan, and Simon.

In other words, the need to establish links between the successive narrative units of the work may explain why 1 Maccabees includes accounts of military defeats, whereas 2 Maccabees tells a uniform story of victories. The accounts of military defeats in 1 Maccabees are by no means a token of the work's greater "historical" reliability over the parallel work, since they above all have an intratextual function.

We may pursue further this claim that the content of 1 Maccabees was primarily determined by intratextual and intertextual needs, not by the author's concern for historical objectivity. Thus the narrative string that runs from Judas's military failures through Jonathan's and thence to Simon's final victory further explains why the institution of Nikanor's Day is treated so lightly in 1 Maccabees, and why it is reported as followed by a brief period of peace (1 Macc. 7:50). Much remains for Judas's brothers to do before peace is finally established by Simon's "refoundation." Last, chapter 14, which immediately follows Simon's building of the palaces, opens with a short transitional section informing us that Demetrios was defeated and captured alive by Arsakes, the king of Persia and Media (14:1–3). The brief observation is functionally symmetrical to the report that Antiochos Epiphanes was humiliated during his anabasis to Persia, where he eventually met his death (1 Macc. 6:1–17), and the comparable fate of the kings is one more "sign" that Judas's and Simon's respective legitimizing deeds have an equivalent status and enjoy divine approval equally. The symmetry between Judas's and Simon's narrative cycles in 1 Maccabees is evidence that the book is underpinned by the same symbolic logic as the account of 2 Maccabees. The two Maccabees authors entertained the same relation to extratextual reality, and their conception of historical truth is equally different from that of modern historians.[62] Consequently, the modern view that 1 Maccabees is more reliable as a historical source than 2 Maccabees is unwarranted.

4.2.3. *The Subsequent Blessings: The Proclamation of Simon's Legitimate Kingship*

Commenting on the people's decree in honor of Simon (1 Macc. 14:25–49), Henten argued that this document offered a good instance of the adoption of Greek practices in Hellenistic Judea.[63] As far as the decree's generic form and vocabulary are concerned, Henten's conclusion is irrefutable. It remains, however, that it is also a structural component in a narrative pattern that owes nothing to Greek influence. Moreover, the decree is not the only passage in which Simon's powers are dealt with. The whole section extending from Simon's building of the palace (or palaces) through the end of the book in general, and chapter 14 in particular, is a reflection on Simon's status as the new legitimate ruler of Israel. 1 Maccabees 14 explores this issue through *two* successive sections: the hymn of 14:4–15 (Simon's Eulogy) and the vote of the decree. John Collins entitled the hymn "Simon's Reign as a Messianic Age," and the two components of this statement—that Simon is construed as a king and that his age is messianic—may equally be endorsed.[64] Thus, chapter 14 qualifies as a case of cultural bilingualism rather than one of Hellenization.[65] Furthermore, the image and status of Simon is explored in the section depicting John's association with his father's rule (1 Macc. 16), to which we may add the section on the negotiations with Antiochos son of Demetrios II (1 Macc. 15), although this unit is of secondary importance from a structural viewpoint. The content of all four sections corroborates the message that the core episode of Simon's building of the palaces enshrines, namely the royal (or royallike) status of the new ruler. Simon's Eulogy is particularly explicit in this sense, since it explores the status of Simon through the Judahite/Judean semantic field of ideal kingship.

A. Simon, King of Israel: The Eulogy of 1 Maccabees 14:4–15. The hymn of 1 Maccabees 14:4–15 is a montage of verses and images borrowed from contemporary Hebrew literature, in particular from the Prophets. This technique of "draw[ing] from a wide range of passages from the prophets and the psalms" for the portrayal of a leader is well documented for the cultural environment in which 1 Maccabees was written, thanks to the Hymns of the Teacher of Righteousness from Qumran.[66] The literary references comprised in the hymn convey a subtle interplay between transparent allusions to the intratextual context of 1 Maccabees and prototypical images linking the text to a wider cultural heritage. Thus, on the one hand, the portrayal of Simon has much in common with that of the Teacher of Righteousness.[67] On the other, the themes composing the hymn offer an inverted mirror to Mattathias's lament of 1 Maccabees 2:7–13, and the echo between the two frames the work with a cyclical construction, which Simon's royal proclamation rounds off by bringing the land to its final "rest." The parallel scheme outlined in Table 4.4 shows that behind the wide range of literary allusions, three themes emerge: (1) the establishment of peace and social harmony; (2) the conquest of the land; and (3) the good king.[68]

The three themes into which the verses may be grouped belong to the semantic field of ideal kingship.

1. "*Peace,*" in the sense of *cosmic and social rest* (4, 7bb,[69] 8, 9, 11, 12), is an essential prerequisite to building the temple, and the theme is a narrative component of the traditional pattern of temple building.[70] Similarly, the establishment of "peace" is a *consequence* of the building of the temple. The fact that peace (rest) is one of the recurring themes of Simon's Eulogy brings further confirmation that the conquest of the Akra plays a symbolic function equivalent to that of a temple foundation (or refoundation) in 1 Maccabees.
2. *The theme of the conquest of the land* or the extension of the community's territory is a reference to the theme of the military leader, either a "judge" or a "king." The relative set of images is more specifically drawn from the books of Joshua and Judges. The theme of conquest is treated both generically (6a, 6b) and specifically (5, 7a), with the explicit mention of Simon's four emblematic conquests: Joppe (5), Gazara, Beth-Zur, and the Akra (7a). The allusion to Simon's taking numerous prisoners of war is a reversal of the Mysarch's treacherous attack on Jerusalem (1 Macc. 1:32).
3. *The theme of the good king* breaks down into various subtopics that systematically cross-reference themes dealt with elsewhere in 1 Maccabees: the warrior-king (13); the conqueror-reformer (7ba), alluding to the theme of the Akra; the supplier of food and arms (10a; see also 14a), referencing by contrast the wicked king's officer supplying food and weapons to the Akra (1 Macc. 1:33–35); and the king's justice (or piety; 14b, 15). Moreover, the king's glorious renown reaches the ends of the earth (10b), which are located westward, in Rome and Sparta (1 Macc. 14:16–24 with 15:15–24;[71] see 14:40).

TABLE 4.4. Themes and intertextual and intratextual references in 1 Maccabees 14:4–15.

1 Maccabees 14:4–15	Themes and references
4a. The land had peace *as long as Simon lived.* He sought the good of his people.	Theme 1: Peace and social harmony accruing as a reward for the construction of the temple: *(E.g.) 2 Sam. 7:11, 1 Kgs 5:18.
4b. They welcome his rule And his glory as long as he lived.	Theme 3: The good king (A phrase typically used about Judges) *Judg. 3:11, 30. **Contrast Mattathias's lament (1 Macc. 2:7a, 13): Woe is me! Why was I born To see the ruin of my people And the ruin of the holy city? . . . . . . Why should we go on living?
5. By means of all his glory he captured Joppe to be a port And secured access to the islands of the sea.	Theme 2: Conquest of the land *Josh. 11:6. **Cf. 1 Macc. 13:11.
6a. He proceeded to extend the territory of his nation.	Theme 2: Conquest of the land *Exod. 34:24: For I will cast out nations before you, and enlarge your borders. *Isa. 26:15: But you have increased the nation, O YHWH, you have increased the nation; you are glorified; you have enlarged all the borders of the land. **Cf. 1 Macc. 5.
6b. After conquering the land, . . .	Theme 2: Conquest of the land *Josh. 11:6. **Contrast Mattathias's lament (1 Macc. 2:7b): The people sat idle there As the city fell into the hands of enemies, The sanctuary into the hands of foreigners."
7aa. . . . he collected large numbers of prisoners of war.	Theme 3: The good king Waging war **Contrast the Mysarch (1 Macc. 1:32). **Contrast Mattathias's lament (1 Macc. 2:8): Her people acted like a base coward
7ab. In conquering Gazara and Beth-Zur and the Akra, . . .	Themes 1 and 2 The link between the conquest of the land and the completion of the temple refoundation *Gazara: Cf. Solomon (1 Kgs 9:15–17) *Beth Zur: The Midianite woman killed by Phineas together with the Israelite man, was Cozbi, daughter of Zur (in Hebrew, *bath Zur*: Num. 25:15).
7ba. . . . he eliminated the unclean things from the Akra, . . .	Theme 3: The good king Who is a conqueror and a reformer *E.g., Josiah's cleansing of the temple (2 Kgs 23:4–7); Nehemiah's reforms (Neh. 13:9) **Cf. 1 Maccabees 13:50.

(continued)

TABLE 4.4. *(Continued)*

1 Maccabees 14:4–15	Themes and references
7bb. . . . and there was none to oppose him.	Theme 1: Peace and social harmony *Related to the motif of fulfillment (Deut. 7:24; 11:25). *Related to the motif of rest in 1 Kgs 5:18. **Cf. 1 Maccabees 15?

8. The people farmed their land in peace,
And the land gave forth its produce,
And the trees of the fields their fruit.
	Theme 1: Peace and social harmony
	*Lev. 26:3–4:
	  If you walk in my statutes and observe my commandments and do them, then I will give you your rains in their season, and the land shall yield its increase, and the trees of the field shall yield their fruit.
	*Hag. 1:3–11 links the divine promise of blessing to the rebuilding of the temple.[a]
	**Contrast Mattathias's lament (1 Macc. 2:9a):
	  Her glorious furnishings have gone into captivity.

9. The old people sat in the town squares,
All chatting about their blessings,
*While the young men put on the
  glorious raiment of war*
	Theme 1: Peace and social harmony
	*Zech. 8:4–5:
	  Old men and old women shall again sit in the streets of Jerusalem, each with staff in hand for very age. And the streets of the city shall be full of boys and girls playing in its streets.
	**Contrast Mattathias's lament (1 Macc. 2:9b):
	  Her babes have been killed in her squares,
	  Her young men by the sword of the enemy.

10a. Simon supplied the towns with food And *equipped them with weapons* for defense.	Theme 3: The good king *See Chronicles (e.g., 2 Chr 14:2–8). **Contrast with the Mysarch's supplies to the Akra (1 Macc. 1:33–35).

10b. So that *his glorious renown reached the end of the earth.*	Theme 3: The good king
	*Mic. 5:4:
	  And he shall stand and feed his flock in the strength of YHWH, in the majesty of the name of YHWH his God. And they shall dwell secure, for now he shall be great to the ends of the earth.
	*Ps. 48:10:
	  Your name, O God, like your praise, reaches to the ends of the earth. Your right hand is filled with victory.
	**Cf. 1 Maccabees 14:16–24 with 15:15–24,[b]14:40. Rome and Sparta are to Simon what the Queen of Sheba was to Solomon (1 Kgs 10:1–13; 2 Chr 9:1–12).
	**Contrast the wicked king in 1 Macc. 1:41.

11. He established peace *in the land,*
And Israel rejoiced exceedingly.
	Theme 1: Peace and social harmony
	*Lev. 26:6–7:
	  And I will give peace in the land, and you shall lie down, and none shall make you afraid. . . .
	  And you shall chase your enemies, and they shall fall before you by the sword.

12. Everyone sat under his own vine and fig tree, With none to make him afraid.	Theme 1: Peace and social harmony *Mic. 4:4: They shall sit every man under his vine and under his fig tree, and none shall make them afraid; for the mouth of YHWH of hosts has spoken.
13. No longer was there anyone on earth waging war against them. *The kings had been defeated in those days.*	Theme 3: The good king Waging victorious wars *Deut. 3:3: So YHWH our God also handed over to us King Og of Bashan and all his people. We struck him down until not a single survivor was left. *Josh. 11:22: None of the Anakim was left in the land of the Israelites.... *Josh 12:1: Now these are the kings of the land, whom the Israelites defeated. **Cf. 1 Maccabees 15. **Add 1 Maccabees 14:1–3? **Contrast Mattathias's lament? (1 Macc. 2:10): What nation has not inherited kingdoms and has not seized her spoils?
14a. Simon supported all the *poor* of his people.	Theme 3: The good king *Imitatio Dei* (e.g., Ps. 76:9). *See also the ideal future king (e.g., Isa. 11:3).
14b. *He sought to* fulfill the Law And *wiped out all the impious and wicked.*	Theme 3: The good king *Good kings and good people seek YHWH (i.e., YHWH's Torah) in Chronicles (e.g., 2 Chr 14:7, 15:4, 26:5, 34:3).
15. *He* glorified the temple And added to its *furnishing.*	Theme 3: The good king *Ezra 7:10: For Ezra had set his heart to seek the Law of YHWH. *Neh. 13:4–14. **Contrast Mattathias's lament (1 Macc. 2:11–12): All her ornaments have been taken away; From a free woman she has become a slave. Behold, our sanctuary, our beauty, our glory has been laid waste, And the gentiles have profaned it.

NOTE: Italics in left column signal clauses in which allusions to biblical themes are found. Single asterisks mark intertextual references to other (biblical) texts. Double asterisks mark intratextual references to other passages in 1 Maccabees.

[a]See Chapter 2, §2.2.1B.

[b]See Chapter 4 n. 52.

As already noted (§4.2.2A), the high priest had ascribed to himself part of the prerogatives traditionally incumbent on the king in early Hellenistic times, in particular the construction of the temple and other urban monuments but not the palace. Therefore, whereas the theme of peace and social harmony in Simon's Eulogy is an ambiguous signifier, which may refer to Simon's high priesthood,[72] the topic of the conquest of the land, as well as the essentially military topics that are grouped here under the heading "good king," remained outside the enlarged province of the high priest and are therefore unambiguous signifiers of kingship. In the hymn, Simon is portrayed as a new Solomon. The people's decree can definitely be interpreted in much the same way.

B. The People's Decree and Simon's "Election" as the New Ruler in Israel: 1 Maccabees 14:25–49. The Eulogy and the decree are separated by a short section depicting Sparta's and Rome's renewal of diplomatic ties with Simon (14:16–24 with 15:15–24); that section, on the strictly narrative side, creates an intermezzo between one highlight and the next. Thematically, as just noted, the inserted episode is a "sign" that Simon's renown had reached the very ends of the earth (14:10); in similar fashion, the Queen of Sheba had been attracted to Solomon's capital by his immense fame (1 Kgs 10:1–13; 2 Chr 9:1–12).

The honorary decree voted by the people in assembly is undeniably a narrative and thematic highlight (14:25–49). Simon had been in power for two years when the decree was issued ("on the eighteenth of Elul in the year 172, which is year 3 under Simon the high priest": 14:27), his first year of rule occurring when Demetrios II granted autonomy to the Judeans by exempting them from paying tribute and acknowledging their right to retain their strongholds (in 170 S.E.: 1 Macc. 13:36–40). Just as Simon built two palaces, one for himself and one for his son, Simon and his sons are the joint recipients of the decree (1 Macc. 14:25, 49).

Although 1 Maccabees offers numerous details regarding Simon's career, the inconsistency of the titles ascribed to him thwarts any attempt to discern a coherent progression. As announced in a previous episode, the private contracts and official documents of Simon's first year in office were dated by his threefold title as "high priest, *stratēgos,* and *hēgemōn* of the Judeans" (1 Macc. 13:42), implying that the powers decreed by the people two years later were effectively a reappointment (14:41–42).[73] However, in the historical overview that the preamble of the decree comprises,[74] Simon's status is presented as that of "high priest" alone (14:27), as was Jonathan's before him (14:30). In addition, it states that the people had already appointed Simon as their "*hēgemōn* and high priest" (14:35). This conflicting description of Simon's powers in the past is further aggravated by the nomenclature applied to the powers that were now decreed by the people, with Simon being awarded the titles of *hēgemōn,* high priest, and *stratēgos* (1 Macc. 14:41–42), whereas the episode concludes by saying that he agreed to serve "as high priest and to be *stratēgos* and *ethnarchēs* of the Judeans and of the priests and to preside over all [as *prostatēs*]" (1 Macc. 14:47).

The author's description of Simon's rise to power clearly does not follow the legal nomenclature of his official status but instead puts the emphasis on three particular issues. The first is the extension of his powers, moving from his priestly genealogy (priest of the clan of Joarib, 14:29) through his becoming high priest (14:27) in succession to Jonathan, his brother (14:30), to his simultaneous appointment to either two or three offices by the people's vote: as high priest, military chief commander (*stratēgos*), and governor (*hēgemōn, prostatēs, ethnarchēs*).[75] From the legal perspective, this seemingly casual alternation between his having two and three titles is at first perplexing, but if we consider the semantic context of the work, it becomes clear that the point being underscored is that Simon was not solely high priest, but *simultaneously* wielded two (or three) forms of power, which the text makes retroactive by projecting the people's decision onto the account of Simon's first year (13:42). In line with the royal significance of Simon's building of the palaces and the numerous references made to the "ideal king" in the Eulogy, we should understand that Simon's official titles above all point to his royallike status. If this is so, the alternation between two and three titles may simply reflect the author's wavering between the Judahite and Seleukid traditions. Whereas the latter tradition recognized a distinction between military and administrative officers,[76] this difference was alien to the semantic field of the Judahite "kingship."[77]

The second focus of the decree is the identity of the institutional body appointing Simon. Although the "great assembly of priests and people and chiefs of the nation and the elders of the land" (14:28) is formally sovereign in the era of autonomy, it acts only in lieu of a prophet ("until a true prophet shall arise": 14:41). This is the second time that the assembled people act in this capacity; the first occurred in their fateful decision to replace the defiled altar with a new one when they refounded the temple (1 Macc. 4:45–47).[78] In the absence of a prophet, therefore, the people collectively endorse the responsibility of building the new altar and appoint Simon as both high priest and *hēgemōn*-king. Not only does the people-prophet (i.e., the people in the place of a prophet) create a conceptual link between the temple rededication (refoundation) and Simon's enthronement, but the resolution of 14:41 comes glaringly close to proclaiming Simon as king and high priest of divine election—as close as it possibly could using Seleukid administrative nomenclature. If this is so, the "election" of Simon simultaneously to the offices of *hēgemōn*-king and high priest by the people-prophet is the functional counterpart to the vision of Judas in 2 Maccabees 15:12–16, which, as noted earlier (§4.1.2), sees Jeremiah the prophet and Onias III the late high priest, respectively, appointing Judas as pharaoh-king and high priest.

The third focus of the passage are Simon's sons, mentioned in the first and last sentences of the section, thereby bookending the decisions (14:25, 49). Their presence, of course, signifies the dynastic principle, which is endorsed afresh with the closing passage on the dynastic transmission of rule, and with it the establishment of the Hasmonean dynasty.

C. The Dynastic Principle: 1 Maccabees 16. As shown above, the more thematically charged sections of chapter 14 (4–15, 25–49) are interspersed with more restrained passages that offer a degree of narrative respite, so to speak. Similarly, 1 Maccabees 15, reasserting the autonomous status of the *ethnos* of the Judeans,[79] provides another breather of sorts. In a letter to Simon and the Judeans that adopts a notably lenient tone (15:1–9), Antiochos VII confirms the tribute exemptions already conceded (5) and in addition grants the Judeans the right to strike their own coinage (6), exempts Jerusalem and the temple from garrisoning (7), grants the right for the Judeans to use armaments and fortifications (7), and annuls their outstanding debts to the royal treasury (8). Soon afterward, however, Antiochos turns against Simon (15:27) and dispatches Athenobios to Jerusalem to seize Joppa, Gazara, and the Akra (15:27–30), a threat that Simon averts by offering money instead. Athenobios is duly astonished at the extent of Simon's riches (32), and as a result Antiochos opts not to push his provocation further (36). In this way, chapter 15 neatly fulfills the "prophetic picture" given in 14:13: "No longer was there anyone on earth waging war against them. The kings had been defeated in those days." The last chapter of 1 Maccabees returns to a fundamental aspect of the divine pledge accompanying the building of the temple and the palace: the promise of a dynasty. The chapter first narrates how Simon associated his sons with his rule (16:2–3) and concludes with the reign of John (16:23–24):

> As for the remainder of the history of John, his wars and his valorous deeds and his wall building and his other accomplishments, all these are recorded in the chronicle of his high priesthood, from the time he succeeded his father as high priest.

Once again, these symbolically loaded verses bring together the semantic fields of kingship and high priesthood. Technically, John succeeds his father as high priest (24); "the remainder of the history of John" denotes his royallike behavior. Like his father's, John's royallike status is demonstrated both by his wars and by his wall building—in his father's footsteps, John continues the line that harks back to the construction of the city walls by King Solomon and their repair by Nehemiah the governor.[80] Finally, the allusion to the remainder of John's deeds and in the chronicle of his high priesthood is a deft conflation of the two realms. The theme of the chronicle recording the rest of the deeds of a king is a common literary topos, and notations of this sort are abundantly present in the books of the Deuteronomic history.[81] The phrase that closes the annals of Hezekiah's reign is a particularly cogent model, since this king was remembered for his attention to urban installations.[82] A similar stereotyped formula concludes Judas's time unit (1 Macc. 9:22), offering another cross-reference between the two units.

2 Maccabees rounds off its narrative with a sentence linking the time of Judas to the time of the narrator, which is left unspecified and open-ended.[83] The impression generated by the last two verses of 1 Maccabees is similar, the sweeping reference to John's reign effectively signifying an indeterminate time gap between John's rule and the present. Thus the ideal era of the dynasty of the kings and high priests continues "into the present" and will continue forever.

4.3. THE PRELIMINARY UNITS IN 1 AND 2 MACCABEES: THE LEGITIMACY OF HERITAGE

There can be little doubt that by emplotting the notion that the Hasmoneans' simultaneous exercise of high-priestly and military functions was legitimate, the authors of 1 and 2 Maccabees addressed a particularly controversial aspect of their rule. However, the fact that the Hasmonean mode of government was controversial accentuated other problematic aspects of their dynasty: in particular, the fact that the Hasmoneans were usurpers. Although this question was far less weighty than the unprecedented manner in which they exercised the high priesthood, it needed to be addressed by their court historians. As seen in previous chapters, one means of securing their own legitimacy was to thoroughly delegitimize the dynasty's trio of initial rivals—Jason, Menelaos, and Alkimos.[84] But to fully vindicate the dynasty's claim to rule, it was also indispensable to insert the Hasmoneans, through the dynasty's founders, within a legitimizing chain of heritage. To do this the two Maccabees authors used a similar narrative device, namely to add a preliminary unit to their works. As we shall now see, the Heliodoros story featuring Onias III in 2 Maccabees (3:1–4:6) and Mattathias's time unit in 1 Maccabees (ch. 2) fulfill similar prefatory functions within their works' structures. Here too the authors diverge in method, implementing the same device but in different ways.

4.3.1. *The Heliodoros Story: 2 Maccabees 3:1–4:6*

The function of the Heliodoros story in the overall economy of 2 Maccabees has been partially explored already.[85] As we saw, it is a story not of temple refoundation but of temple liberation,[86] and the fact that the Nikanor's Day story (2 Macc. 14:1–15:37a) intertwines elements of the two narrative patterns generates an intratextual link between the first and the last units of the work. In particular, Onias III and Judas are equated through their similar actions, since each piously defended the temple against a pending threat from a wicked royal official, Heliodoros and Nikanor, respectively. This equation between the two men is the prelude to Onias III's acknowledging Judas as his legitimate heir in Judas's vision.[87] It has been pointed out that Judas's genealogy is never referred to in 2 Maccabees, in contrast with 1 Maccabees;[88] this omission is typical of the way usurpers constructed their representation. By erasing their blood link with a father of dubious credentials, they could co-opt themselves into a worthier genealogy. In 2 Maccabees, Judas's entitlement to rule hinges on his election by Onias III himself. The function of the Heliodoros story therefore is to situate Judas, and through him the Hasmoneans, in a legitimizing chain of continuity by asserting a privileged link between the last legitimate Oniad and the founder of a new dynasty.

4.3.2. Mattathias's Praise of the Fathers: 1 Maccabees 2:49–62

In contrast, given that the author of 1 Maccabees recounted the stories of the three Maccabean brothers, it made little sense for him to erase the memory of their father. Rather, he exploited it creatively. Thus, whereas in 2 Maccabees the preliminary unit features Onias, in 1 Maccabees it features Mattathias. Strikingly, the same range of literary techniques used by the author of 2 Maccabees to create the legitimizing link between Onias and Judas—the verbal utterance of the heritage in the dream, the illustration in deeds that the heir behaved in a way worthy of his model, and the use of similes—recurs in the parallel work, but with one necessary structural difference. Insofar as these features are transposed to the figure of Mattathias, they are transmitted onto both Judas and Simon. The passage that best illustrates this ploy is Mattathias's Eulogy of the Fathers (1 Macc. 2:49–62), which has rightfully been compared to Ben Sira's Praise of the Fathers:[89]

> Remember the deeds of our ancestors, which they did in their generations,
> And win for yourselves great glory and undying renown.
> Was not Abraham found to keep his faith under trial,
> And was it not reckoned to his merit?
> Joseph in his time of distress kept a commandment
> And became lord of Egypt.
> Phineas, our ancestor, through his act of zeal
> Received a pact of priesthood for all time.
> Joshua by fulfilling the Word became a Judge in Israel.
> Caleb by bearing witness before the congregation
> Received an inheritance of land.
> David for his piety received as his heritage a royal throne for ages.
> Elijah for his acts of zeal on behalf of the Torah
> Was taken up as if into heaven.
> Hananiah, Azariah, and Mishael because they maintained their faith
> Were preserved from the fire.
> Daniel through his guiltlessness was saved from the mouth of lions.
> In this manner consider the generations past:
> All who place their hopes in Him shall not falter.
> Have no fear of the words of a wicked man,
> For his glory is destined for dunghills and worms.

Given that Mattathias was not an especially memorable ancestor, he provides a bridge of sorts between his sons and a string of worthier "fathers," and more particularly Phineas. Although the figures of the past are collectively introduced as "fathers" (2:51), Phineas is singled out as *"our* father" in 2:54. Similarly, the first deed performed by Mattathias in the time of impiety was modeled after Phineas (Num. 23:1–15), since he slew a Judean about to offer an illicit sacrifice on the unlawful altar that the king's men had built in Modein (2:23–26), an equation openly stated in the text (26).[90] As Tobias Funke argues, Phineas offered a particularly apt paragon, since he belonged to a priestly line but used violence.[91] Thus, Phineas in 1 Maccabees and Onias in 2 Maccabees have similar functions, serving as the ultimate models of Simon and Judas, respectively. However, whereas the latter references the notion of pious defense of the temple, the former incorporates the figure of military high priest.

For his part, Jonathan Goldstein has contended that all nine characters or groups of characters listed in Mattathias's Praise in one way or another serve as prototypes for the latter's actions.[92] It is therefore worth examining how this list is composed. Topically, the Fathers can be divided into three categories.[93] First come the righteous men saved by their loyal piety in times of distress, who serve as models for the martyrs of the present day: Abraham (52),[94] Elijah (58), Hananiah, Azariah, and Mishael (59), and Daniel (60). These are followed by kings and kinglike conquerors: Joseph (53), Joshua (55), Caleb (56), and David (57).[95] Coming last is Phineas, the sole priest mentioned (54), as if his warring example alone were a worthy model for this office. In order then, the characteristics that these exempla embody are piety, kingship, and warring high-priesthood—qualities that coincide with the powers eventually assigned to Simon by the decree of the people.[96]

One more detail is worth pointing out in relation with the first category. Goldstein has proposed that the deed that likens Mattathias to David is the latter's escape to the mountains (1 Macc. 2:27–28; 1 Sam. 22:1–2 and 23:14). Like David, he loyally led his warring band to fight for the sake of Israel (1 Macc. 2:44–48; 1 Sam. 23:1–5 and 25:14–16), but both these escapes were also followed by a massacre of innocents (1 Macc. 2:29–38; 1 Sam. 22:7–19). The priests slaughtered at Nob in David's days belonged to a spurned line of high priests, and the parallel might suggest that God showed little favor for the *Asidaioi*, "who died in their nonresistance, . . . but gave victory to Mattathias, the zealot who dared to make defensive war even on the Sabbath" (1 Macc. 2:39–48).[97] Goldstein's interpretation would explain why 1 Maccabees includes no stories praising the faithful who died for the Law, in contrast with 2 Maccabees. The divergence between the two books results from a different narrative emphasis rather than from a genuine difference of views. Whereas the author of 2 Maccabees laid the stress on the exemplary dead, the other writer chose to justify the radical act of waging war on the Sabbath.[98]

Thus, despite the fact that the Maccabees' genealogy is mentioned in 1 Maccabees, the genuinely meaningful chains of continuity in *both* 1 and 2 Maccabees are first and foremost provided by the models of identification (the exempla). Beside

Onias III and Phineas, Nehemiah, the wall builder, was certainly a prominent model for the dynasty, and lurking farther behind Nehemiah was the figure of Solomon himself, who simultaneously built the temple, his palace, and the city walls. Intriguingly, though, whereas Simon's construction of the city walls in 1 Maccabees obviously derives its legitimizing power from Nehemiah's antecedent, the latter is mentioned by name only in the second epistle prefacing 2 Maccabees, where the text alludes to a different tradition.[99]

...

THE RELIGIOUS CENTRALITY OF THE TEMPLE IN HELLENISTIC TIMES

1 and 2 Maccabees were written with a similar purpose in mind, namely to tell a story emplotting the idea that the Hasmoneans' simultaneous holding of the high priesthood and of a royallike office involving military command was legitimate. This new configuration of power imposed a remodeling of the legitimizing narrative template of temple building, the device adopted by the two Maccabees authors being to duplicate the pattern within a single work. Although this narrative solution was definitely effective, it does not follow that it was the only one possible. Therefore, it begs the question how the two Maccabees authors came to employ the same device. The hypothesis that the one borrowed the idea from the other is hardly the most plausible, given that the two books betray significant differences. In particular, each author found his own way to transcribe the concept of kingship in a narrative form that could be compatible with the legitimizing pattern of monumental building works while at the same time taking for granted that the building of the temple per se denoted the legitimacy of the high priest. Thus, it is as though the principle of duplication framed the margin of creativity that our two authors allowed themselves, at once constraining them while allowing them to move freely within it. One may therefore argue that the notion of juxtaposing two accounts of monument building in order to articulate the idea of overlapping spheres of powers—those of the high priest and of kingship—had already crystallized among the literati of the Hasmonean court *before* the redaction of 1 and 2 Maccabees.[100] Nonetheless, whereas the events commemorated in the Hanukkah festival had become the founding myth of the Hasmonean dynasty, it seems that no event had imposed itself as an obvious site of memory. This may explain why the choice of a second topic to associate with the Hanukkah story was open to variation—provided that the principle of duplication was respected.

Throughout this chapter and the three preceding, the discussion has essentially focused on analyzing the formation and evolution of the narrative template of temple (and palace) building. Our purpose has been to show that the accounts of

1 and 2 Maccabees constitute but one variant of this traditional narrative pattern, and the discussion has been conducted at a strictly literary level. Insofar as we have made some incursions into the social reality underpinning the literary genesis of 1 and 2 Maccabees, the focus of our attention has been divided between the political ideology of the two authors—who were found to be partisans of the Hasmoneans—and the evolution of the status of the high priest in Judean society. It is now appropriate to add to these a few words about the continued importance of the temple in Judean society of the Hellenistic age. Studies of Second Temple "Judaism" usually insist on the emergence of personal piety, and the so-called theology of martyrdom that finds its earliest illustration in 2 Maccabees is regularly granted pride of place in this matter. More often than not, the emergence of personal piety is taken as a further symptom of a decline in the religious status of the temple. The literary analysis of 1 and 2 Maccabees proposed throughout these four chapters provides arguments against this assumption, showing that although the "martyrs" are granted an instrumental part in introducing divine reconciliation, their role is clearly subordinated to the temple's: the finality of their personal sacrifice is precisely to bring about the resumption of the regular temple service—exactly what divine reconciliation is needed for.

CONCLUSION

Contrary to the prevailing opinion, 1 and 2 Maccabees are parallel and complementary works. Their similarities do not result merely from the fact that they tell the same story, nor from their use of common sources; actually, their parallels concern their very narrative structure, which is put at the service of the same political message.

The literary forms of the two books combine the same two basic principles of composition.[1] First, the two works are structured by the duplication of the narrative pattern of temple foundation and, next, by the juxtaposition of cyclical time units. In 1 Maccabees these units are centered on the Maccabean characters (Mattathias, Judas, Jonathan, and Simon) from the second chapter through the end; and in 2 Maccabees they focus on paired high priests and Seleukid kings (Onias III and Seleukos IV; Jason and Menelaos and Antiochos Epiphanes and Antiochos Eupator; Alkimos and Demetrios I). In both works, time is divided in quality between moments of disruption and consequent restoration of order. In 1 Maccabees, the first chapter narrates the main time of disruption, followed by the four time cycles of Mattathias, Judas, Jonathan, and Simon, respectively. Moreover, the two time units of Mattathias and Jonathan are colored negatively by the evocation of the building and rebuilding of the Akra, the major cause of disruption; and each one is accordingly followed by a happy reversal in Judas's and Simon's time units. In 2 Maccabees, the times of disruption are internal to each one of the three narrative cycles (2 Macc. 3:1–14 in the time cycle of 3:1–4:6; 4:7–5:26 in the double time cycle of 4:7–13:26; 14:1–36 in the time cycle of 14:1–15:37a).

As regards their content, the two works share a common, central subject matter, namely, the Rededication (Hanukkah) of the temple by the Maccabees after the time of disruption. Given the ancient tenet that the founding act of a family ancestor determines the character of all his descendants, there can be no doubt that the Rededication commemorated in the Hanukkah festival was the deed from which the Hasmonean dynasty derived its claim to legitimate rule. In this respect, the very choice of this subject matter by the two authors is enough to conclude that they both were partisans of the Hasmoneans. Moreover, the duplicated structure of the temple-building pattern allowed the articulation of a more refined ideological message, which is evidently common to the two works. The purpose of the fellow writers was not only to recount the founding myth of the Hasmoneans but to assert the legitimacy of the simultaneous exercise of the function of high priest and of royal-like powers, in particular military leadership, which was a Hasmonean innovation.

One additional issue was addressed in parallel by the two authors and is responsible for one more shared compositional feature. The two authors posited in which chains of continuity the Maccabees were inserted, and through them the Hasmoneans. To do so, both authors used a complete narrative cycle, inserting this cycle (Mattathias's time unit in 1 Maccabees and that of Onias in 2 Maccabees) before the duplicated account of monumental building.

To summarize the analysis of the literary composition of 1 and 2 Maccabees that was put forward in Part I, the proposition that the two works carry similar political messages, and the related claim of an organic link between their political messages and their literary structures, is the most viable explanation for their overall literary coherence. Regarding 2 Maccabees in particular, the interpretation of its composition as detailed in the foregoing chapters makes it eminently possible to propose a balanced delineation of the inner narrative units and to show how the apparently disparate composition in fact ties up into a coherent narrative.

Further narrative tools are shared by the two authors of 1 and 2 Maccabees, and although they do not cast light on the compositional structure of the works, they indicate that the two works belong to the same cultural environment. Thus intertextuality with the Hebrew literary tradition is an important means of constructing meaning in the two works. Numerous instances have been pointed out throughout Chapters 1 to 4, and further examples would no doubt emerge from a more systematic analysis of the description of the battles in both 1 and 2 Maccabees.[2] Likewise, the fundamental means that the two works adopt to assess the actions of the characters as either good or bad, legitimate or illegitimate, is to compare the latter with the behavior of exemplary models from Israel's past. The equation between a given character and his relative ideal model is first and foremost expressed in deeds, his own actions reenacting those of his historical counterpart. In most cases, explicit similes provide the key to the symbolic signification of the heroes' actions. The presence of these formal features in 2 Maccabees, in particular, leaves no doubt that the work is rooted in a Judean social environment. In contrast, it displays no hint whatsoever of a possible diasporan extraction. Consequently the claim of the proem that the extant book is the digest of a longer work (2 Macc. 2:23) may be interpreted in two ways. Either the original work was also written in Judea or, conversely, the author of 2 Maccabees reworked his source so thoroughly as to erase all its original features.

The observation that the two authors explored the legitimacy of Hasmonean rule by informing their founding myth with a specific literary pattern and modeling the behavior of the Maccabean heroes upon the behavior of legitimizing prototypes further invites us to examine anew the purpose of the redaction of the two works and their mode of communication with their original intended audience. In 1981 Doran described 2 Maccabees as a work of "temple propaganda."[3] However, the two epistles prefixed to 2 Maccabees notwithstanding, 1 and 2 Maccabees cannot be seen solely in terms of their intent to reach out to new supporters.[4] Their use of the literary pattern of the temple foundation to inform the etiological event of the Hanukkah festival, and their choice of characters from Israel's past as prototypes of Judas (in 2 Maccabees) and Mattathias, Judas, and Simon (in 1 Maccabees), suggest that the two Macabees authors were engaged primarily in the self-serving construction of a communal identity. Insofar as the notion of innovation was anathema, it was vital to explain the present as the reenactment of traditional templates of actions validated by the community. Nonetheless, far from being static, these templates were constantly reinterpreted in order to accommodate what a modern observer would define as the novelties of the present. Inasmuch as they could be reread as reenactments of past actions, novelties became acceptable, even if the past needed to be "updated" in the process. Similarly, the sense of present misfortunes became possible to grasp when they were read as the return of a familiar scheme of misfortunes. This process of reinterpreting the present through the past is part of the mechanism of social or cultural memory. To borrow a definition of this concept from Ehud Ben Zvi:[5]

> Social memory is ... the public, integrated and socially integrative representation of the past that is held, shaped, negotiated within and which holds together a social group. Social memory is about the past that is constantly present within the community and *about the present of the community that is legitimized by that past.* Of course, different social groups have different cultural memories [of the same event or the same prototypical figure].

The mechanism of reshaping the present as a function of the past is furthermore determined by the social mindscape of the group. This latter concept explores how the behavior, the way of thinking and perceiving of individuals considered as members of a social group, is framed both by the way that the social group belonging to a specific culture and a specific historical period constructs its social categories—such as culture, religion, history and geography—through mental processes and by the way that these categories are perceived to interact.[6]

Two appendixes complement the analyses followed in the chapters of Part I. Appendix A summarizes the composition of 1 Maccabees, insisting on the delineation of the various components of the temple-building pattern in Judas's and Simon's time units, as well as on the cyclical construction of the four time units of Mattathias, Judas, Jonathan, and Simon. Appendix B similarly provides an overview of the composition of 2 Maccabees.

PART II

Hellēnismos

The Causes of the Rebellion according to the Authors of 1 and 2 Maccabees

METHODOLOGICAL INTRODUCTION

Symbolic Universe, Cultural Codes, and Causal Analysis in 1 and 2 Maccabees

The literary analysis of 1 and 2 Maccabees put forward earlier, in Part I, established that both books were written by court historians of the Hasmonean dynasty, each one accordingly employing the appropriate narrative form to encode the idea that not only was the dynasty's rule legitimate but so was the specific form of rule it adopted, namely the simultaneous exercise of priestly and royal powers.[1] Given that the narrative form and the conceptual message enshrined are closely correlated, it is logical that the two authors chose the same event—the rededication of the temple by Judas Maccabee—as the subject matter through which to argue their case of dynastic legitimacy. Contrastingly, however, they opted for different narrative solutions to emplot the idea of the simultaneous exercise of power, 1 Maccabees making Simon's liberation of the Akra and rebuilding of the city walls the subject matter of the second legitimizing account; whereas 2 Maccabees exploited the figure of Judas again, incorporating the institution of the Nikanor's Day festival into a full-fledged sequence of temple refoundation.

Because in both works the second legitimizing accounts are also the closing sections, their respective topics have a pivotal influence on the narrative construction of each work as a whole. Not only are they the natural point of convergence for all the loose ends, as the principle of internal narrative coherence requires,[2] but (what is more crucial) each determines the shape of the topical integration of its account as a whole. By "topical integration" I mean the process by which the two Maccabees authors constructed a link between three items: the initial cause or causes of the disruption of the sacrifices, the "proof" of the illegitimacy of the rival high priest (or high priests),[3] and the legitimizing deed of the founder of the Hasmonean dynasty (Simon in 1 Maccabees and Judas in 2 Maccabees). The primary function of this link is to ensure the topical coherence of the complete narrative sequence running from the initial cause of disruption marking the first legitimizing refoundation, through the second and final legitimizing act. If we shift the emphasis from narrative function to content, then because this running thread is also causal, we note that the requirement of internal narrative coherence prompted the Maccabees authors to present the causes and nature of the crisis in different ways, each one focusing on the matters cross-referring with the final act of refoundation. Thus, in 1 Maccabees, the thread linking the disruption of the temple service with the final restoration of order is determined by the double theme of Simon's legitimizing deed, his purification of the Akra and rebuilding of the city walls. By this logic, the initial causes of the disruption are Antiochos IV's fortification and garrisoning of the Akra, the latter being presented as a constant source of defilement for the temple; Alkimos, the wicked high priest of 1 Maccabees, supports those of the Akra and designs besides to tear down the wall of the sanctuary's inner court, a sacrilege for which, allegedly, he meets his death (1 Macc. 9:54–56); whereas the pious Simon rebuilds the city. In 2 Maccabees, Judas refounds the temple a second time. By this logic, the initial cause of the dysfunction of the temple sacrifices is Jason's establishment of the *gymnasion,* which is portrayed as an antitemple, while the wicked Menelaos contributes symbolically to the demolition of the temple by stealing its holy vessels.[4]

This brief overview prompts two observations. First, the two authors give different interpretations of the causes and nature of the Judean rebellion because their respective topical integrations pivot on different items (or, to use a semiotic term, different semes) and not because of any differing levels of religiosity. More important, the difference in topical emphases between 1 and 2 Maccabees actually corresponds to a chronological divide. Whereas 1 Maccabees covers the causes of the disruption that occurred in the wake of the rebellion (the Akra and Alkimos), 2 Maccabees focuses on the events that took place prior to its outbreak (the *gymnasion,* Jason, and Menelaos). This topical distribution substantiates my proposition that the two works were conceived as complementary accounts from the outset—their function was to bind the Hasmonean dynastic origins to these two phases of events, respectively, one symbolized by the *gymnasion* and the other by the Akra.[5]

That said, the topical integration of the narratives of 1 and 2 Maccabees around the Akra and the *gymnasion* respectively is not only a matter of chronological divide. More fundamentally, these two items operate as synecdoches by means of which the two authors develop their respective causal analyses of the Judean rebellion against the Seleukids. Without denying the intrinsic importance of the *gymnasion* and the Akra as factors of disruption, their symbolic functions are fundamental to understanding why they are granted such prominent attention in each work. As tangible landmarks in the cityscape the *gymnasion* in 2 Maccabees and the Akra in 1 Maccabees do not stand for themselves alone but are used as synecdoches[6] for a range of intangible issues (such as political and economic matters) seen to originate in the same circumstances as their creation. According to the aforementioned chronological split, they came to epitomize, respectively, the main factors of disruption that emerged on the eve of the rebellion and those that occurred at a later stage. Their status as synecdochic signifiers may be deduced from the fact that as a rule the material issues that the authors sought to allude to are mentioned only obliquely, by emphasizing their connection to the corresponding synecdoche (the *gymnasion* in 2 Maccabees and the Akra in 1 Maccabees). To take a well-known example, when talking about the transformation of Jerusalem into a polis, the author of 2 Maccabees stresses the place of the *gymnasion* in this episode while downplaying other aspects such as the political, social, and economic implications of this change, which from our modern standpoint are far more meaningful. In other words, the attention is shifted from (what in our view is) the core issue—the political, social, and economic implications of the politicization of Jerusalem—to the (again, in our view) secondary issue of the *gymnasion* (or the Akra in 1 Maccabees). While in the case of the politicization of Jerusalem the link with the *gymnasion* is relatively straightforward, since its creation was genuinely part of the reforms, in other cases the link between the pragmatic issue alluded to and either the *gymnasion* or the Akra is (in our view, at least) far weaker—although never arbitrary. I argue that this process of focal displacement (displacement, that is, as compared with what the modern mind may perceive as a realistic description of the causes of the troubles) is pervasive throughout 1 and 2 Maccabees alike, giving rise to the (erroneous) modern impression that their authors had no interest in political and economic issues. Instead, I suggest, we should ask why the Maccabees authors needed to use the *gymnasion* and the Akra as synecdoches to mediate their statements about the causes of the conflict with the Seleukids. The answer, I argue, is to be found in the social mindscape of the ancient Judahite/Judean literati, which informs the cultural and narrative codes used in 1 and 2 Maccabees.

The ancient Judahite/Judean literati conceived social life as reflecting the divine cosmos. This perception of reality (or mindscape) may be described as a "symbolic universe."[7] By this logic, the only viewpoint from which society could be examined was on the basis of whether or not it conformed to the divine order, because this was the way to establish whether or not the social order was legitimate.[8] An objective, so to speak, value-free description of reality would have been pointless, since it was culturally meaningless. Likewise historical events were worth remembering only insofar as they were relevant to this question. In concrete terms, the main focus of attention for Judean literati was the fate of the temple, because as the interface between the human and divine spheres, the temple operated as the synecdochic signifier of the Judean way of life and set of values that were centered on it.[9]

Therefore the way actions affected the temple was the yardstick by which such actions were evaluated as either worth remembering or irrelevant (depending on whether or not they had an impact on the temple) and as remembered in either a positive or a negative way. Accordingly, when a writer undertook to narrate events that affected society, the only question he cared about—because it was the only one that was meaningful and that therefore could sensibly be examined—was how these events affected the fate of the temple. This perception of reality as a symbolic universe informs the cultural and narrative codes used in literary works. In particular, it explains the topical focus of 1 and 2 Maccabees we described earlier.[10]

In structural semiotics, a code is "a general semantic model which enables one to pick out items as belonging to the functional space that the code designates,"[11] "the system of norms, rules, and constraints in terms of which the message signifies."[12] A "cultural code"—one of the five basic codes distinguished by Roland Barthes—"is constituted by the cultural background to which the text refers. It manifests itself as a 'gnomic,' collective, anonymous and authoritative voice which speaks for and about what it aims to establish as 'accepted' knowledge or wisdom."[13] If according to modern Western cultural codes—which are informed by a far more pragmatic perception of reality than what was held by ancient societies—a *gymnasion* denotes Greek culture and a fortress represents war, in 1 and 2 Maccabees these two objects were coded in relation to the temple (namely as antitemples), and as such they naturally served as synecdochic signifiers of the causes of disruption. To put it another way, they mediated the incorporation of the political, social, and economic aspects of the upheaval that the authors felt were in one way or another connected to either of them in the symbolic universe that centered on the temple—precisely because, as synecdochic signifiers, they mediated between those issues and the fate of the temple. This scheme, whereby the authors underline the association between a given incident and the *gymnasion* (or the Akra)—and through the *gymnasion* reveal how that incident affected the fate of the temple—may be designated a "semantic concatenation." Moreover, as we will see in Chapter 7 (§7.4), the authors occasionally used additional items as synecdochic signifiers of disruption (such as the illicit altars of the countryside in 1 Maccabees) to the same end, whereas alongside the temple other signifiers, such as the Sabbath, could bear a positive connotation. As a rule, the items selected as synecdochic mediators stood in an easily recognizable relationship to the temple, so that the semantic concatenation generated—from temple, through the synecdochic signifier, to political and economic matters—always remained eminently readable. Thus the altars of the countryside were equated with the Akra and opposed to the temple altar.[14] By this narrative means the Maccabees authors were able to turn any topic that they wished to talk about into a legitimate object of discourse—that is, of remembering.

That said—as implicit in the previous sentence—a note of caution may be in order. While the notion of a symbolic universe is perfectly suited to the perception of reality behind the redaction of Hebrew works of pre-Hellenistic times, it is less clear whether the authors of 1 and 2 Maccabees used the traditional codes of the symbolic universe strictly in good faith, or, to some extent at least, as a conscious archaism—with the aim of presenting the Hasmoneans (a dynasty of usurpers) as heirs to the kings of old. The author of 2 Maccabees, in particular, was well acquainted with Greek historiography, and must have been aware that there were other ways of narrating historical events. Therefore, we cannot entirely rule out some tension between genuine cultural conditioning and potentially manipulative construct in the manner in which the authors used the traditional codes and focused their accounts on the fate of the temple—although it is not easy to tell these two processes apart. Parenthetically, if their redaction was—in part or entirely—a construct, it served a political cause, and had nothing to do with what modern scholars call "temple propaganda." (See below in this chapter.) In either case, it must be emphasized that these cultural codes—rooted in the traditional social mindscape of the Judahite/Judean literati—not only operated as a filter, sifting facts worth remembering from facts that may be overlooked, but they also defined what part of those "facts" deemed worthy of attention was meaningful and therefore worth recording, and from which angle to apprehend them.[15] In keeping with the cultural rule that the fate of the temple was the only meaningful topic worth remembering, the Maccabees authors do not inquire into the causes of the rebellion per se (to adopt a modern viewpoint) but formally present them—and in all likelihood, genuinely saw them—as causes of the disruption of the temple service. The result is a way of apprehending and presenting things that is totally counterintuitive to modern Western readers and as such is a recurrent source of misunderstanding. Reading 1 and 2 Maccabees through our own cultural lens, we instinctively induce that the author of 2 Maccabees identified a cultural threat as the major cause of the rebellion—since this is how we construe the *gymnasion*—or, worse, that the Maccabees and their partisans themselves fought exclusively for the sake of identity symbols. Actually, once we understand this process of semantic concatenation we are able to realize that the ancient authors were perfectly aware of the rebellion's material causes. However, according to the cultural codes that conditioned their way of thinking and writing, the only conceivable way for them to address economic issues such as the tax increase and land confiscations was by showing how they adversely affected the temple. To this end, the material issues are mentioned only obliquely, as it were, by linking them to a symbolically charged signifier, such as the temple itself, or to its antitheses, the *gymnasion* and the Akra—which was a way of including them in the symbolic universe of the temple.

In other words, the widespread modern misreading of these narrative and cultural codes in 2 Maccabees as evidence of the author's being primarily concerned with theological issues—and hence supposedly uninterested in pragmatic matters—

is a case of mistaking the form for the content: that is, the culturally conditioned appeal to synecdoches standing in close relationship to the temple to mediate the analysis of events lacking intrinsic symbolic significance is mistaken for straightforward description. The moment we separate form from content, the way opens to a totally different understanding of what the Maccabees authors had to say about the causes and nature of the rebellion. The implication of this shift of approach on how their works may be used as sources for modern historical investigations of the rebellion barely needs comment. Far from describing this episode as a struggle between Judaism and Hellenism, the *two* Maccabees authors had a fairly rational analysis of the crisis. Although its material aspects are downplayed, or rather wrapped up in cultural and narrative codes that are thoroughly at odds with our own, they are by no means omitted and are there for modern historians to exploit, at the cost of some cultural estrangement. This is all the more true since the literary genre of 1 and 2 Maccabees, after all, considerably softens the alienating effect of these cultural codes and their narrative translation. Although their writers must have had much in common in terms of social mindscape with other learned Judeans of their day—the authors (or editors) of the book of Daniel as well as the Apocalypse of Animals now included in the first book of Enoch, and the authors (or editors) of the Qumran literature—unlike these, in 1 and 2 Maccabees the turmoil of the period is not narrated in a purely symbolic way. In congruity with the generic rules of Greek historiography, the two Maccabees authors give reasonably clear hints about the material issues involved in establishing the *gymnasion* and the Akra.

In addition to "theology," some modern scholars have read propaganda—"temple propaganda"—into the authors' discursive mode. Yet here again the tag is misleading, because essentially there is nothing inherently manipulative in our authors' culturally anchored concern for the impact of events on the temple—irrespective of whether their use of traditional codes was a genuine reflection of their personal mindscape or a case of archaizing: the codes themselves are not manipulative. It would be more profitable to see their way of sifting reality through this lens as a cultural tool aimed primarily at the self-assertion of group identity. This is not to say that this apprehension of reality ruled out differences of opinion. As long as there were different ways of implementing the cultural codes of the social group—such as various ways of playing with its constitutive values and accepting or rejecting innovations (e.g., waging war on Sabbaths)—there was ample room for disputes and the taking of sides. Manipulations, if they occurred, bore upon the selection of the issues incorporated in the symbolic universe. Moreover, the ancients were perfectly aware of the latent contentiousness of their statements about how specific events and deeds impacted the temple. Deciding who embodied the positive values and who was the villain clearly depended on the political orientation of the individual or social group in question. In other words, the examination of the fate of the temple neatly allowed for divergent and potentially conflicting narratives, because it was compatible with side-taking and political, social, and cultic antagonism. But it is one thing to say ancient social actors and writers were ready to exploit descriptions of reality for partisan goals and quite another to consider all discourse about the temple intrinsically as temple propaganda. Whereas the latter stance implicitly assumes this discourse about the temple was underpinned by a pragmatic, value-free perception of reality, and was but one among various pragmatic ways of presenting events, the former admits that this discursive slant was conditioned by a symbolic perception of reality. Thus there is a crucial difference between defining Menelaos as impious by imputing to him the theft of holy vessels—a slanderous accusation 2 Maccabees makes—and construing him as an extreme Hellenizer flirting with religious skepticism because of this misdeed, as numerous modern scholars have done. Whereas the statement of 2 Maccabees is a variant on a culturally conditioned mode of political polemic casting Menelaos into the conventional image of the utmost wrongdoer (who removes the holy vessels from the temple) in order to delegitimize him, its modern paraphrase presupposes that in second-century Judean society not being "religious" was an option—which is an anachronistic assumption.[16] Thus while our authors' political bias in favor of the Hasmoneans may potentially impair their analysis of the historical events they narrate, their personal religiousness is *not* a factor of distortion.

In Part I of this book, I offered a revised literary analysis of 1 and 2 Maccabees, whereas in Part III I will propose a historical reconstruction of the causes and unfolding of the Judean rebellion predicated on my revised reading of the ancient sources. Before undertaking that task, Part II of the book will investigate how the Maccabees authors themselves perceived the causes and nature of the crisis. This requires first understanding the two major factors of distortion that affect their ways of presentation, namely their social mindscape and their political bias in favor of the Hasmoneans. It was the purpose of the literary analysis of Part I to demonstrate that 1 and 2 Maccabees were written by partisans of the Hasmoneans, and logically therefore from a partisan standpoint. However, the analysis in Part I essentially focused on the positive portrayal of Judas and Simon Maccabee as well as on the narrative strategies that the two Maccabees authors deployed to emplot the idea that the rule of the Hasmoneans—the righteous political and social order that the author of 2 Maccabees describes as *Ioudaïsmos*—was legitimate. It remains for us now to investigate the negative side of the authors' political slant, namely their portrayal of the rival high priests Jason, Menelaos, and Alkimos. In the two works the handling of these figures is equally contentious and as a rule fiercely hostile. As the authors would have it, the rival high priests belong to the period of the disruption—the period of unrighteous political and social order that the author of 2 Maccabees describes as *Hellēnismos*; actually, these men are themselves *causes* of disruption. Their portrayal therefore will be dealt with first, as the principal topic of Chapter 5, completing the perception articulated in Chapter 1 (§1.4.4) that Menelaos in particular suffered from his fierce denigration in 2 Maccabees, a bias that modern reconstructions have uncritically endorsed. This discussion will also be the occasion to analyze the status of the *gymnasion* in 2 (and 1) Maccabees in detail, as a preliminary to investigating in Chapter 7 how the Maccabees authors phrased their views about the causes of the rebellion.

Indeed the second factor of distortion—which, in contrast with political bias, is "distortion" only from an outsider's perspective—is the rule whereby only those events and aspects of events affecting the temple are considered worth remembering and duly recorded, using as mediators synecdochic signifiers conceived as semantic extensions to the temple. By this logic, the item identified as the main cause of the revolt in each work—the *gymnasion* in 2 Maccabees and the Akra in 1 Maccabees—is also portrayed as the major threat to the integrity of the temple. Likewise, depending on how they are respectively related to the creation of the *gymnasion* and the Akra, the two works (to describe things from a modern viewpoint) overstate the relative importance of certain factors and downplay others. Chapter 7 will explore what the authors have to say about the causes of the crisis, paying particular attention to the process that I have described above as "semantic concatenation." Although the specific perspective of each account is the product of the combined lenses of political bias—identifying who the pious leader is, and who the wicked—and concatenation, it is vital to distinguish the two layers as best as we can. Before we come to this, however, Chapter 6 will analyze the passages in the ancient sources that are usually assumed to recount the supposed "religious persecution"—or, to use the phrase that has now become popular, the "prohibition of the Judean customs." The working premise of my alternative reading is that this "religious persecution" is in fact another instance of an account's being read at face value by modern scholars when instead it is a case of finding a place in the temple-centered symbolic universe for events that would otherwise not be symbolically charged and would therefore be unworthy of being remembered. Strictly speaking, the "religious persecution" is not a cause of the rebellion, since the purpose of the discussion will be to refute its existence; but it will be examined in Part II because of its resonance with modern historiography.

5

Hellēnismos

The Social Order of the Wicked Rivals in 1 and 2 Maccabees

INTRODUCTION

As a rule, Roman works of historiography were flagrantly partisan. A classic example is offered by Cicero, who in one of his letters to Lucceius exhorts his friend to write a long-planned book on his career and openly urges the writer to be as prejudiced in his favor as an *amicus* can be.[1] It may come as no surprise that lauding the feats of one's patron or friend inevitably entailed lambasting his social and political rivals. The practice of biased writing was so entrenched that in the Preface to his *Annals* (1.1.3), Tacitus penned the now-famous disclaimer that he would write "sine ira et studio" (with neither choler nor favor) toward anyone.

In this respect, 1 and 2 Maccabees were patently written with both choler and favor. And although their social and literary model was clearly not Roman, the content of ancient Near Eastern dynastic history—like its counterpart in Roman Late Republican historiography—frequently involved denigrating a current ruler's predecessor (or predecessors) to drive their message home. Other forms of ancient texts rely on traditional tirades against enemies, such as the Cyrus Cylinder of Babylon and the "Persian Verse Account," and their denunciation of Nabonidus; similarly, the historians of Alexander echo stereotyped defamations targeting either Darius III or the dynasty of the Achaimenids.[2] In our case, while the campaign of delegitimation adopted by the two Maccabees authors chiefly aims at the high priests who ruled in the interval between Onias III and the Maccabees—namely Jason, Menelaos, and Alkimos in succession—the Seleukids also come under attack.

Curiously, although our two authors were on the same political side and shared the same objective of denigrating the rivals of the Maccabees, the specific targets and topics they chose for their attacks differed notably. In 2 Maccabees the author's hostility is directed against Jason and Menelaos, whereas Alkimos is treated more concisely, albeit hardly more leniently. Conversely, in 1 Maccabees Jason and Menelaos are not even mentioned, and the focus is on Alkimos alone. As for the nature of the charges, in each case they are tailored to emphasize the contrast between the pious Maccabees and their wicked rivals: the Maccabean heroes are praised for rebuilding precisely what the wicked opponents have contributed to destroying. In 2 Maccabees all the sinful deeds of Judas's opponents are accordingly related to the temple that he refounds: the impious Jason builds an antitemple, the *gymnasion;* Menelaos steals the holy vessels; and Antiochos plunders and desecrates the temple itself. The list of the sins of the opponents is of course much longer, but it is through these actions that their wickedness is brought to the fore most significantly. In 1 Maccabees, Simon's legitimizing feat consists in his fortification of the defensive walls of the temple and the city, along with the expulsion of the garrison from the Akra. The actions of the wicked operate as an inverting mirror: Alkimos demolishes the wall; the Seleukid officers strengthen the fortifications that threaten the temple while installing and continuously supporting the garrison of the Akra. In both 1 and 2 Maccabees a sharp reversal marks the division between the time of the disruption and the time of the restoration of the righteous order of things. In 2 Maccabees the wicked deeds of Jason, Menelaos, and Antiochos are grouped into the section that forms the earlier part of the narrative unit of the Hanukkah story (4:7–5:26), after which Judas receives his first mention (5:27), marking the beginning of the restoration.[3]

Although our two authors showed creativity in modulating their respective campaigns of delegitimation, 2 Maccabees is particularly noteworthy for the new terminology that it adopts for describing the sins of the opponents. As argued in Chapter 3 (§3.3), the abstract term *Ioudaïsmos* was coined to capture in a single word the entire complex of ideas and concepts encapsulated in the narrative pattern of temple building. *Ioudaïsmos* means "the legitimate social order attuned to the divine order of things, which was established by the pious (or righteous) Judas when he refounded the temple, and in which the dynasty of the Hasmoneans ruled." To be precise, this was not the first time that a complex narrative sequence and its associated concepts were summarized in a single signifier. The traditional way to do this was to pick one of the central narrative components of the sequence, as for example a palace and thunder in a cosmogony or the temple in a temple-building account, and use them as synecdoches for the whole.[4] But the item so selected was a concrete image, whereas *Ioudaïsmos* is an abstraction. Furthermore, *Ioudaïsmos* ethnicizes a fundamentally political concept and in so doing reiterates the common Yehudite/Judean practice of appropriating the denomination of the entire social (or ethnic) group to the benefit of a partisan group within it, a practice well attested in the context of the Return.[5] The purpose of the present chapter will be to show that the semantic fields of *Hellēnismos* and *allophylismos* were revisited by the author of 2 Maccabees according to the same logic: that is, of capturing and ethnicizing an entire range of narrowly correlated concepts. Insofar as the ethnic connotations of *Hellēnismos* and *allophylismos* point to the author's intention to otherize the partisan groups referred to by these two terms, it may be readily assumed that both expressions were used to denote a wicked order of things. As will be argued in this chapter, *Hellēnismos* means "the illegitimate social order opposed to the divine order of things, established by the wicked Jason when he founded (so to speak) the *gymnasion*." In this reading, the *gymnasion* is an antitemple. In turn, *allophylismos* seems to denote the illegitimate order of the Seleukids, although this inference remains somewhat more speculative.

The present chapter will examine the literary means with which the opponents of the Maccabees are portrayed as the ultimate in wickedness. As this introductory survey has made clear, each character must be studied independently, and their respective portrayals in 1 and 2 Maccabees must be tracked separately. Pride of place will be granted to Jason's *gymnasion* and the semantic field of *Hellēnismos* in 2 Maccabees (§5.1). Next, the construction of the image of the *gymnasion* in 1 Maccabees (§5.1.3) and along with it the meaning of *allophylismos* in 2 Maccabees (§5.1.5) will be briefly examined before observing how Menelaos and Alkimos are depicted in both books (§§5.2 and 5.3 respectively).

5.1. *HELLĒNISMOS*: JASON'S *GYMNASION* AS AN ANTITEMPLE

The establishment of a *gymnasion* in Jerusalem during the reign of Antiochos IV is mentioned in both the Maccabees books and in Josephus's *Antiquities* (12.240–41).[6] In 2 Maccabees (4:7–15) the event is presented as the starting point of the crisis that eventually led to the rebellion against Antiochos IV.[7] In 1 Maccabees (1:11–15) the building of the *gymnasion* is the first matter mentioned after Antiochos's accession to the throne of the "kingdom of the Greeks" (1:10). It is followed by the latter's invasion of Egypt (16–19); his conquest of Jerusalem and plunder of the temple (20–28); the new Seleukid conquest of Jerusalem two years later, and the ensuing massacre of the population, the destruction of the city wall, and the building of the Akra (29–40); and the king's decree to become Greek and the persecution of the faithful (41–64). Thus the *gymnasion* is deemed one of the salient events of the time of disruption that coincides with Antiochos's early reign, and despite the paratactic arrangement of the chapter, its position at the head of the list seems to concur with the version of 2 Maccabees that the institution of the *gymnasion* heralded the onset of the troubles. Consequently, the primacy accorded to the event in the ancient sources leaves no doubt that its impact in real life was indeed tremendous.

The far-reaching social and economic implications of the establishment of the *gymnasion* in historical terms will be addressed below in Chapter 10 (§10.3). An important preliminary step is to analyze the echo of this event in our literary sources: that is, how the *gymnasion* was perceived at the time, which concepts and images were used in reference to it, to what extent the accounts of its establishment and operation are factual or contentious, and in the latter case to which ideological manipulations they were subjected. Modern historical reconstructions usually take the account of 2 Maccabees, by far the most detailed one, as their starting point, using 1 Maccabees for complementary data; while Josephus's muddled contributions are usually treated with reservation. That said, straightforward readings have missed the intention underlying the account of 2 Maccabees. The passage needs to be quoted integrally in Nigel Kennell's new translation before a revised commentary can be presented (2 Macc. 4:7–15):[8]

> [7] Upon the death of Seleukos and the ascension to the throne of Antiochos, called Epiphanes [175 B.C.E.], Jason, the brother of Onias, corruptly procured the high priesthood [8] by offering the king through a petition 360 silver talents and, from some other source of revenue, 80 talents. [9] In addition, he pledged to sign over another 150, if it be granted to him through his authority to establish a *gymnasion* and *ephēbeion* and to inscribe those in Jerusalem as Antiochenes.[9] [10] When the king gave his assent and he acquired the office, he immediately began to bring his people [*homophyloi*] over to the Greek style of life [*Hellēnikos charactēr*]. [11] And he pushed aside the royal concessions [*philanthrōpa basilika*][10] to the Judeans which were put in place through John, the father of Eupolemos, who conducted an embassy to the Romans concerning friendship and an alliance; and destroying the lawful social institutions [*nomimoi politeiai*], he brought in new customs contrary to the law [*paranomoi ethismoi*]. [12] He gladly founded a *gymnasion* under the very acropolis and, drawing up the strongest of the ephebes, led them under the *petasos*. [13] There was in this way a pinnacle of *Hellēnismos* and an advance in the adoption of alien ways [*allophylismos*] because of the overwhelming impurity of the impious anti-high priest [*asebēs kai ouk archiereus*] Jason, [14] so that no longer were the priests eager for service at the altar, but, despising the temple and heedless of the sacrifices, they hurried to share in the unlawful distribution [*paranomos chorēgia*] in the *palaistra*[11] at the call of the *diskos*, [15] and, setting their ancestral honors [*patrōioi timai*] at naught, held Greek forms of renown [*Hellēnikai doxai*] to be the finest.

Some confusion obtains regarding the initiative of setting up this *gymnasion*. 2 Maccabees explicitly names Jason (4:7–9), but Josephus ascribes it to Menelaos (*Ant.* 12.240–41), while 1 Maccabees is unhelpful, erasing the individual identity of those responsible but retaining the flavor of the event ("lawless sons of Israel," 1:11). Insofar as our purpose is to track the inner logic of the passage, contradictions of this sort must be kept in mind. In 2 Maccabees Jason's creation of the *gymnasion* is mentioned alongside that of an *ephēbeion* and the inscription of the inhabitants as

Antiochenes (or perhaps of a "list of the Antiochenes of Jerusalem": 4:9). The rest of the passage is a series of authorial comments about the negative effects of the reform, in particular the alleged neglect of the sacrifices by the priests hurrying to the distributions (of oil) in the *palaistra* and invectives against Jason, who is charged with impiety.

5.1.1. The Gymnasion in 2 Maccabees: The Current Modern Interpretation

2 Maccabees' account of Jason's establishment of the *gymnasion* has famously prompted the modern view that the author saw the revolt against Antiochos IV as a religious and cultural struggle between Hellenism and Judaism. Although the term *Ioudaïsmos* does not crop up in this specific section, and despite the fact that nowhere else in the work are *Ioudaïsmos* and *Hellēnismos* counterpointed in the same sentence,[12] the passage in question effectively claims that the neglect of the temple was a consequence of deeds described with the terms *Hellēnismos* and *allophylismos*, and related phrases (4:10, 13, 15). This supports the prevailing view that the author genuinely intended a counterpoint between the two—in fact, three— terms.[13] Nevertheless, further elucidation is required as to the meaning of *Hellēnismos*, both intrinsically and as a hypothetical antithesis of sorts to *Ioudaïsmos*. Moreover, it is also worth inquiring why the author coined two separate terms to contrast the notion of *Ioudaïsmos*, a fact that is usually ignored. The meaning of *allophylismos* will be tackled later in this chapter (§5.1.5).[14] The first step must be to pinpoint both the meaning of *Hellēnismos* in this specific passage and the sense of the counterpoint created between *Ioudaïsmos* and *Hellēnismos* throughout 2 Maccabees.

A. Ioudaïsmos *and* Hellēnismos: *The Need for Two Symmetrical Semantic Fields.* Modern commentaries have often imputed a somewhat paradoxical personality to the author of 2 Maccabees: notwithstanding the "fact" that he was a religious conservative who perceived Hellenism as a threat to Judaism, his Greek upbringing is generally deemed excellent. His rhetorical skills are praised,[15] and he is even credited with coining the term *Ioudaïsmos* and using its counterpart *Hellēnismos* in an innovative sense. Whereas *Hellēnismos* usually refers to the proper use of the Greek language, in 2 Maccabees it is employed for the first time to denote the "Greek way of life."[16] Even though the distinction between the earliest literary occurrence and the emergence of a linguistic practice must be kept in mind, it can safely be said that our author was responsible for the two neologisms (one morphological and one semantic),[17] because the opposition between *Ioudaïsmos* and *Hellēnismos* is a fundamental element of the work's literary construction, one that required an appropriate nomenclature. However, the conventional translation of *Ioudaïsmos* and *Hellēnismos* as "Judaism" and "Hellenism" posits a basic semantic asymmetry, since one refers to a "religion," and the other to a "culture." This linguistic lopsidedness is curious, given the author's known rhetorical skills. While some commentators have attempted to overcome this difficulty by translating the two terms respectively as "Jewish and Greek ways of life," the discrepancy soon resurfaces when the commentary enters the details. Thus, to quote Martha Himmelfarb:[18]

> 2 Maccabees, the first work to pose an opposition between Judaism and Hellenism, sees Hellenism as a new kind of threat in Jewish history. Previously, foreign cultures were perceived as dangerous because of the temptation posed by their gods. But *for 2 Maccabees, Hellenism involves a system of values distinct from idolatry, the values associated with the gymnasium*. 2 Maccabees condemns Jews who adopt these values even as they remain loyal to the God of Israel.

In fact, the passage of 2 Maccabees claims exactly the opposite: Jason and the priests did *not* remain "loyal to the God of Israel" (2 Macc. 4:13–15). Himmelfarb's quote typically shows how by casting an essentialist definition of what *Hellēnismos* and the *gymnasion* stand for on the text, modern commentaries are led to downplay certain key arguments of 2 Maccabees. Moreover, although her comment apprehends the opposition between Judaism and Hellenism at an abstract level, namely "conservatism" vs. "modernism," it still posits a semantic asymmetry between the "Jewish religion" traditionally opposed to idolatry, and a new system of values having nothing to do with idolatry. Nevertheless, Himmelfarb's observation that "foreign cultures were traditionally perceived as dangerous because of the temptation posed by their gods" provides an interpretative key to the way the author of 2 Maccabees constructed his denunciation of the *gymnasion*. As will be shown below (§5.1.1C), effectively 2 Maccabees presents Hellenism, or rather *Hellēnismos*, as a form of idolatry, and indeed it involves a ritual with no specific god. That said, our first step toward a revised interpretation of the passage is to discard the term "idolatry" itself, which stresses the notion of belief (belief in "pagan" gods) and approach the matter in terms of what was deemed appropriate in ancient societies, namely the proper performance of ritualized actions.[19]

B. *"Objective" Definitions of the* Gymnasion *and the Elusiveness of Jason's Sin of* Hellēnismos. The key to understanding the meaning of *Hellēnismos*—and therefore the semantic correlation between *Ioudaïsmos* and *Hellēnismos*—is predicated on a correct understanding of the attacks expressed against Jason and the *gymnasion* in 2 Maccabees 4. Jason is explicitly deemed impious and unworthy of being high priest (4:13), and this charge, which is articulated with considerable vehemence at the core of the passage on the *gymnasion,* has long puzzled modern commentators.

Asking what in a *gymnasion* could be a source of impiety, Bickerman typically resorted to an objective approach, cross-checking the accepted concept of a *gym-*

nasion with what was likely to offend "pious Jews." The result was a short list of items, *none of which* is actually mentioned in the text of 2 Maccabees: athletic contests in general and nakedness in particular; the cult of Hermes and Herakles, the traditional patrons of *gymnasia* in the Greek world; and last the royal cult, which was regularly associated with *gymnasia* in Hellenistic times.[20] Bickerman's method set the tone for later commentators, but perplexity gradually waned as the various lists of "potential infringements to the Jewish law" proposed were shown to lack correspondence with the text. Bickerman's imputations of nakedness and pagan worship were refuted by Lester Grabbe, using Bickerman's own criteria of objectivity.[21] In turn, Grabbe pointed to the mention in 1 Maccabees 1:15 that the "lawless men" removed the marks of circumcision.[22] To this Himmelfarb responded that "2 Maccabees does not mention the attempt to reverse circumcision . . . [and t]he failure to mention such behavior strongly suggests that 2 Maccabees did not believe it had taken place,"[23] adding:[24]

> Despite its tone and its insistence that the gymnasium brought with it behavior that violated the Torah, 2 Maccabees gives us no evidence for its view that Jason's followers were disloyal to the God of Israel.

It is one thing to argue that the charge of impiety against Jason is slanderous,[25] but it is quite another to claim that he was unable to make his case convincingly *within the text*. Yet this is precisely what most modern scholars do by stressing that our author has nothing to say about nakedness, idolatry, and the attempt to reverse circumcision. In short, not only is our author unable to construct a genuinely symmetrical counterpoint between the two terms *Ioudaïsmos* and *Hellēnismos*, and through them between the two camps of civil strife, but when he launches the singular accusation of impiety at the high priest, no less, he fails to substantiate the charge. How can these two literary oversights—which both bear upon focal issues in the text—be reconciled with the (correct) appreciation of the author's rhetorical skills? This paradox prompts a reexamination of the entire issue.

The issue requires tackling from two fronts simultaneously, starting with the semantics. The claim that the author of 2 Maccabees coined the two terms *Ioudaïsmos* and *Hellēnismos* entails two as yet underestimated implications: first and foremost, that the author invented the semantic field of the words together with their formation. The elementary rules of historical semantics speak against the modern assumption that the meanings of *Ioudaïsmos* and *Hellēnismos* in 2 Maccabees are coterminous with the modern sense of Judaism and Hellenism. Put simply, "religion" ("Judaism") and "culture" ("Hellenism") fail to match any recognizable semantic fields in the social and cultural environment of the author,[26] and therefore it is implausible that the author was restricting his own understanding of *Hellēnismos* to "cultural" aspects. The second implication involves the author's cultural viewpoint: given that he lived in Judea and not in Athens or Alexandria, the starting term of reference must be *Ioudaïsmos,* with the meaning of *Hellēnismos* being defined in relation to it, not the other way round. In other words, the processes of morphological and semantic formation of the two words are opposed. From a morphological point of view, *Hellēnismos* existed first, and there is no question that *Iouda-ismos* was forged after the model of *Hellēn-ismos.* In contrast, from a semantic point of view, *Ioudaïsmos* comes first, since it refers to the reality that was familiar to the author, whereas *Hellēnismos* must be derivative.

Beside the semantics, the internal logic of the text must be taken as a decisive guide to pinpoint the definition of the sin of *Hellēnismos* in the text and the nature of Jason's alleged impiety—"alleged," because it is an outright defamation, as will be seen below (§5.2). The widely shared opinion that the author failed to substantiate his allegation is simply untenable and exposes the shortcomings of the objective method of investigation inspired from Bickerman. Instead of applying an "outside" definition of what a *gymnasion* is, we must seek clues for the author's own definition of sin within the text itself. Clearly, the definition provided in the text is likely to involve an intentional distortion for the sake of polemics, since as we saw extensively in Part I of this book,[27] in 2 Maccabees the vocabulary of piety and impiety is used with distinctly political connotations.

The working hypothesis that will be adopted in the ensuing discussion is predicated on the semantic and literary premises just spelled out. Insofar as *Hellēnismos* implicitly offers a *symmetrical* counterpoint to *Ioudaïsmos* in 2 Maccabees, it may be surmised that the definition of the sin of *Hellēnismos*—with evident reference to the *gymnasion*—rests on a *symmetrical* opposition to what stands at the center of *Ioudaïsmos.* Indeed, an explicit reference to the latter occurs in the passage on the *gymnasion:* the allegation in 4:13–15 that Jason induced the priests to neglect the sacrifices ("so that no longer were the priests eager for service at the altar, but, despising the temple and heedless of the sacrifices, they hurried to [the *palaistra*]") charges the utmost impiety. If we situate this claim in the context of the wider narrative unit in which the section of Jason's setting up of the *gymnasion* is inserted—the Hanukkah story (2 Macc. 4:7–13:26)—Jason is held responsible for the initial disruption of the righteous order of things. On the one hand, Jason's *partial* disruption of the temple cult is a harbinger of the ensuing *total* interruption of the sacrifices caused by Antiochos's impiety (6:4–7).[28] On the other, the sacrifices were resumed "for the first time in two years" (10:3) by the *Ioudaioi,* the faithful warriors who had joined Judas.[29] In other words, whereas Judas refounded the temple, Jason played an instrumental part in its destruction, alongside Antiochos. By refounding the temple, Judas earned the right to be high priest, and Onias III himself acknowledged him as his worthy heir (15:12). When it is read in this context, the sense of the author's explicit accusation that Jason was unworthy of being a high priest (4:13) becomes crystal clear.

This reading may be taken one step further. Jason not only participated in the destruction of the temple by hampering the regular operation of the sacrificial service, but the harm he caused to the temple directly derived from his instituting the *gymnasion*. The insinuation methodically woven throughout the description of the operation of Jason's *gymnasion* is that it was set up as an institution to rival the temple: in short, in founding the *gymnasion* Jason founded an antitemple. The episode of the *gymnasion* is indeed a story of "idolatry"—or rather, of "unfaithfulness to YHWH."

C. Jason's Departure from YHWH's Path. Grabbe and Himmelfarb are undoubtedly correct in their observation that our author makes no reference to "pagan" gods in conjunction with the *gymnasion,* but the reason for this omission is less straightforward than it may seem. Intertextual references—which must have been immediately recognizable for their educated Judean audience—insinuate that "idolatry" *was* practiced, but the fact that this is not made explicit may have more to do with ideological motives than with factual reality. As we saw in Chapter 1 (§1.2), the pattern of causality that our author uses in his work imposes a measured balance between sin and retribution. Unfaithfulness to YHWH is the supreme sin, and its retribution is capital punishment for individuals and exile for collective foolishness. This is precisely the point of the anecdote about the idols of Jamnia found on the bodies of the fallen soldiers (2 Macc. 12:39–40), and likewise of YHWH's promise to Solomon (1 Kgs 9:1–10; see below in this section). Had the high priest in person indulged in introducing foreign gods in Jerusalem, the self-sacrifice of the faithful who preferred death to sin would have been to no avail. YHWH would have departed from His temple for good, and His people would have been sent into a new exile. Indeed, matters came very close to this doom-filled scenario, especially if the selling of the prisoners of war as slaves can be considered a new form of exile. However, God's eventual reconciliation was a "sign" that the most blatant aspects of the sin had been avoided. Our author found an ingenious way to "prove" Jason's personal attraction to foreign gods while exonerating Jerusalem itself: the sinful sacrifice is relocated to Tyre, and it is probably no mere chance that this episode is reported immediately after the passage dealing with the *gymnasion* (4:18–20). We are told that Jason dispatched a delegation of Antiochenes of Jerusalem to the games of Tyre with instructions to make a sacrifice to Herakles. However, the delegates eventually diverted the money intended for the sacrifice to pay for war galleys. The allegation is of a purely defamatory nature, since Jason's sin is cited as "intention" alone and never materialized. As Grabbe has suggested, the purchase of war galleys was most likely the intended purpose of the funds from the outset.[30] If we except the sacrifice itself, the description of operations performed in the *gymnasion* comes as close as possible to a portrayal of a foreign cult.

At first glance, the proposition that a cult, either righteous or foreign, may be envisaged without a god sounds self-contradictory. Yet it appears less absurd if we look more closely at how ancient Hebrew literature expressed the idea of what we dub "idolatry." A typical example is found in YHWH's promise and curse (1 Kgs 9:1–9) that closes the pericope of Solomon's building of the temple (1 Kgs 5:15–9:25; esp. 9:4–7):

> As for you, if you will *walk before me* as David your father *walked*, with integrity of heart and uprightness, *doing* according to all that I have commanded you, and *keeping* my statutes and my ordinances, then I will establish your throne over Israel forever.... If you *turn aside* from following me, you and your children, and do not *keep* my commandments and my statutes that I have set before you, but *go and serve* other gods and *worship* them, then I will cut Israel off from the land that I have given them; and the house that I have consecrate for my name I will cast out of my sight.

This passage says nothing of belief but rather speaks of "walking in and departing from YHWH's path" and doing and not doing certain things, and moreover of doing them either properly or not. Similar representations of the relation between men and the divine world are found in the Akkadian literature dealing with good and wicked kings. The wicked king not only removes the statue of the god (or goddess) and sets the statue of another god (or goddess) in a shrine "not belonging to Him [or Her]," as the Uruk Prophecy says, but moreover he fails to perform the rites correctly.[31] Both "faithfulness to YHWH" and "departure from YHWH's path" are a matter of deeds, deeds and words being the tangible signs of inner feelings.[32]

Moreover, "departure from YHWH's path" did not necessarily imply revering other gods but could also signify neglecting the apt performance of the rites honoring Him. Indeed YHWH's promise to Solomon is delivered in the context of the dedication ceremony of the temple, and this setting points to the underlying conceptual link that tied together the building and continued glory of the temple and the king's scrupulous respect of the divine commandments.[33] "Serving" YHWH was not a "spiritual" notion but very concretely referred to the service of YHWH in His House: that is, to the temple ritual, which it was the king's duty to endorse. Serving other gods meant both neglecting YHWH's temple—letting it fall into ruin—and building an alternative place to serve the other gods according to their own "statutes and ordinances" (1 Kgs 9:4).[34] In his capacity as high priest, Jason was primarily responsible for the correct performance of the temple service. Thus the accusation that Jason induced the priests to neglect the sacrifices (2 Macc. 4:14) must be taken very seriously. Not only is it a charge that Jason departed from YHWH's path, but because the culprit is the high priest, it is a claim that he is illegitimate.

5.1.2. The Service of the Temple and the Service of the Gymnasion

What happens when the service of the temple is not carried out properly? What type of dysfunction is induced by the destruction of the temple and the disruption of its ritual? As Francis Schmidt has suggested, the answer to this question may be sought in texts that addressed situations of crisis, such as the prophecy that opens the book of Haggai (1:3–11) and 1 Maccabees 3:46–59.³⁵ As he urges the people to get on with rebuilding the temple, which lies in ruins, Haggai is explicit about the consequences of failing to honor YHWH: drought and dearth. Haggai's prophecy explicitly articulates the link between temple, human community, and land.³⁶ The well-being and economic wealth of the community is directly dependent on the well-being of the temple. As we saw in Chapter 2 (§2.1), the building of the temple seals the process of creation. Thereafter, the temple rites form part of the constant task of maintaining the creation, and of preventing a relapse into chaos. The rebuilding of a temple is a new creation.

If this was the function of the temple, the claim that the wicked priests "despised the temple and were heedless of the sacrifices" in their eagerness to attend the distributions in the wrestling yard is tantamount to imputing to the priests an action that jeopardized the existence of the community.³⁷ This allegation is certainly a rhetorical manipulation, not to say a fierce abuse, and must not be taken literally in our assessment of Jason's action in historical terms. However, if we consider the intrinsic *literary* logic of the text, the author's claim that Jason was unworthy to be high priest is demonstrated with great precision. At the same time, the issue at stake, to use modern categories, is not a matter of "cultural" innovation, nor is it a "mere" religious issue either. The claim that Jason's and his supporters' behavior posed a threat to the community's survival has decidedly political overtones. Indeed, it is hard to think of a stronger rebuttal of legitimacy.

Thus the literary depiction of the episode of the *gymnasion* is shaped by the theme of the destruction and foundation of the temple. It is presumably no coincidence that the texts describing the founding ceremonies of the Jerusalem temple and the altar are precisely those that provide the key to the narrative codes by means of which the author of 2 Maccabees constructed his case against Jason as departing from YHWH's path. Through intertextual references to five topics that feature prominently in these traditional descriptions, he elaborates a detailed counterpoint between the ritual of the temple and the practices of the wrestling yard of the *gymnasion,* the latter being implicitly presented as "unlawful" (*paranomos,* 2 Macc. 4:14). These topics are, first, the ordering of time (i.e., the ritual calendar); second, possibly the music; third, the core ritual; fourth, the priestly vestments; and last, the division of the people of Israel into twelve tribes—that is, its social organization.³⁸ The original readers of 2 Maccabees will have been familiar with the rites that were associated with the foundation of the temple, since these were annually reenacted in the Festival of Sukkoth.³⁹ For modern readers, the most immediately relevant corpus of comparison is offered by the texts relating to the refoundation of the temple in Persian times, MT Ezra and LXX 1 Esdras.⁴⁰

A. *Sacrifices and the Ordering of Time.* Sacrifices regulate the divisions of time. The ritual and symbolic meaning of the resumption of the sacrifices is best understood in the description of the founding ceremony of the altar. As 1 Esdras 5:47–55 shows,[41] it signifies the restoration of the ritual calendar—that is, of time. From its undifferentiated state, time is restored to its orderly divisions, as it was established at Creation: day and night ("morning and evening"), sacred and secular (Sabbaths; new months and feasts; as opposed to "every day"), days, weeks, months; and yearly seasons. Time is henceforth governed again by the rhythm of sacrifices ("at proper times," "regular offerings").

In 2 Maccabees, the activities of the *gymnasion* are ordered according to a distinct temporality: instead of gathering in the temple at the required time for the regular performance of the sacrifices, the priests gather in the *palaistra* "at the call of the *diskos*," or gong (4:14), for the distribution of oil. In the order of the *gymnasion*, time is marked out at regular (probably daily) recurrences, as in the temple, but from now on the schedule of the priests is modulated by the sound of the *diskos*, not by the cycle of the daily sacrifices performed in silence[42] in the temple.

B. *Music.* Indeed the *diskos* produces a sound. In Cicero's *De Oratore*, Catullus complains that "the audience prefers to listen to the gong ["discum audire"] rather than to a philosopher; as soon as it sounds, they abandon the philosopher in the middle of his lecture to get some oil."[43] Therefore, in the description of the *gymnasion*, the *diskos* may have an additional function as a counterpart to the music played by the priests and the Levites in the temple ceremonies.[44] Parenthetically: music features in the account of Judas's refoundation of the temple in 1 Maccabees (4:54), but it is curiously omitted in the parallel passage of 2 Maccabees (10:1–8).

C. *Participating in the Distribution of Oil in the* Palaistra. However, the call of the gong, as just noted, seems to be primarily intended as a counterpoint to the silent unfolding of the sacrifices. Indeed, the ceremony it summons the priests to, "to share in the unlawful distribution of the *palaistra*,"[45] is an antisacrifice. In *Ioudaïsmos* too, of course, the priests and the Levites had a share in the sacrifices, and numerous passages in the Pentateuch and the Prophets as well as in Nehemiah precisely spell out which part of each sacrifice the priests were entitled to receive. In particular, the sin, guilt, and food offerings, the twelve showbreads, which were the most holy, had to be consumed in the temple.[46] Another contrast between the temple sacrifices and the distribution of the *gymnasion* relates to their origin. The goods used in the sacrifices were fetched purposely from all over Israel. In the book of Nehemiah the people make the solemn oath to "lay on ourselves the obligation to" bring one-third of a shekel, the first fruits of the fields and the trees, and the firstborn of their household and livestock (Neh. 10:32–39). These voluntary contributions define the relation between the various households and the temple, and through this, membership in the community. In contrast, the distribution of the wrestling yard of the *gymnasion* delineates a distinct community, that of the Antiochenes.

D. The Priestly Garments. Before pursuing this issue of the two antithetic definitions of the communities further, one more ceremonial detail needs to be considered. The texts dealing with the founding ceremonies specify that the priests were dressed in their priestly garments. Priestly vestments are mentioned in 1 Esdras 5:58 and Ezra 3:10,[47] which relate to the ceremony of laying the foundation stone. Similar mentions are found in the description of the ceremony of Passover that was celebrated by King Josiah in Solomon's temple (1 Esd. 1:1) and in the ceremony of temple dedication in Darius's time (1 Esd. 7:9).

The ritual and political importance of the ceremonial vestments of the high priest in Second Temple times is well known. It is reflected in numerous descriptions and references to these clothes that are found in Hellenistic and later rabbinic sources.[48] In particular, Ben Sira dwells at length on the priestly garments in the sections dedicated to praising Aaron, the original high priest, and Simon son of Onias (45:6–12, 50:11). Similarly, the reference to the vestments of the priests that is included in 2 Maccabees is telling precisely because of its brevity, which suggests that this image was a familiar topos. The context is that of Heliodoros's pretension to force his way into the temple, and in the midst of the confusion elicited by the prospective sacrilege, the priests have donned their ceremonial vestments and pray at the altar, this picture adding to the dramatization of the scene (2 Macc. 3:14–15).[49] In 1 Maccabees, Jonathan's advent to the office of high priest, to which he has been appointed by Alexander Balas (10:20), is marked by his putting on the ceremonial vestments (10:21).[50] The ritual importance of the high priest's garb was such that in Roman times the vestment seems to have become equated with Judean identity.[51]

In Jason's *gymnasion*, the ceremonial clothes prescribed by the Law[52] are replaced with the broad-brimmed felt hat of the ephebes, the *petasos* (2 Macc. 4:12). Moreover, in the *gymnasion* the priests are drawn up (*hypotassein*, 4:12) according to their physical strength and led under this hat by Jason.[53] In other words, they are not divided according to their families and classes as they are in the temple.[54] The issue of social organization definitely seems to run as an underlying thread throughout the text.

E. Sacrifices and Social Organization: The Twelve Tribes. One further function of the ceremonies that accompanied the performance of the sacrifices in the temple was to provide a representation of society. The right to participate in the rebuilding of the temple and the altar, like later the payment of the temple taxes, delineated the boundaries of the community. This tenet is illustrated in an inverted way by the rejection of the request to take part in the rebuilding of the temple that was made by the "people of the country" in Ezra's time, because the latter fulfilled none of the required criteria of legitimacy (1 Esd. 5:66–71 = Ezra 4:1–3).⁵⁵

The organization of society was played out time and again in the sacrifices that were carried out regularly, daily, monthly, and in the festivals. The social agents who took part in the ceremonies were organized according to two forms of division: the first separated priests, Levites, and Israel, and the second divided the people into twelve tribes, which were symbolized in the twelve victims sacrificed at the altar, as 1 Esdras 7:6–9 shows.⁵⁶ Jason's institution of the *gymnasion*, of course, was linked to a far-reaching reform in the social organization of the people in Jerusalem, as we read in 2 Maccabees 4:9. The translation of the reference to the Antiochenes in this verse is famously vexed, with some scholars understanding that the reform included all the inhabitants of the city and others, that the Antiochenes constituted a civic body within the native city of Jerusalem.⁵⁷ Whatever the correct interpretation, Jason's reform amounted to a social reorganization of the inhabitants of Jerusalem. The constitution of the Antiochenes—whatever their precise identity—disrupted the traditional division of the people into twelve tribes. Likewise, the setting up of the *ephēbeion* introduced an inner subdivision of the social group between seniors and juniors that canceled the traditional division between priests, Levites, and Israel.

Thus the unlawful ceremonies of the *gymnasion* are performed according to a distinct temporality, marked out by the distinct sound of the *diskos*, the gong. They are performed by distinct personnel, the young priests turned ephebes, who are led by a high priest wearing a distinct vestment, the *petasos*, and are performed for a distinct community, the Antiochenes. These people are not *homophyloi* (2 Macc. 4:10) with the rest of the Judeans any longer but form a distinct *ethnos* eager to become "like the Greeks" (*exomoiousthai*, 2 Macc. 4:17). The description of the *gymnasion* in 2 Maccabees 4 is an inverted discourse about the ritual of the temple.⁵⁸ From a literary point of view the passage cross-refers to texts describing the rituals of the temple. The details selected in the description are counterparts to the rituals of the temple, and their mention aims to accentuate the highly codified items composing the latter: gestures, garments, music, identity, and ordering of those participating in the ritual to varying degrees of active involvement, the priests and Levites on the one hand and the Israelites on the other.

5.1.3. The Gymnasion *in 1 Maccabees 1:11–15*

In comparison with 2 Maccabees, the treatment of the *gymnasion* in 1 Maccabees is concise (1:11–15):

> At that time, lawless men arose in Israel and seduced many with their plea, "Come, let us make a covenant with the gentiles around us, because ever since we have kept ourselves separated from them we have suffered many evils." The plea got so favorable a reception that some of the people took it upon themselves to apply to the king,

who granted them liberty to follow the practices of the gentiles. Thereupon they built a *gymnasion* in Jerusalem according to the customs of the gentiles and underwent operations to disguise their circumcision, rebelling against the sacred covenant. They joined themselves to the gentiles and became willing slaves to evildoing.

Modern commentaries have been inclined to focus on the allegation that the men who attended the *gymnasion* disguised their circumcision, partly because this detail is identified as the only factual notation of the passage, and partly because it is taken to substantiate the claim of 2 Maccabees that the *gymnasion* was a source of impiety. As a result, the symbolic implication of this allegation has tended to be sidelined.[59] Insofar as circumcision is the "sign" of the covenant, negating this sign amounts to "turning aside from following YHWH," and the men's longing for an unlawful covenant with the gentiles is the natural complement of their unfaithfulness to YHWH's covenant. The description of the lawless men seducing many in Israel into making a covenant with the gentiles blatantly borrows from certain expressions used in the Pentateuch to refer to "idolatry."[60] In contrast, Mattathias is portrayed as enforcing circumcision, thereby manifesting his faithfulness to YHWH's covenant (1 Macc. 2:45–46).[61]

Thus the passages referring to the *gymnasion* in 1 and 2 Maccabees draw on distinct literary schemes. 1 Maccabees borrows from the imagery of unfaithfulness to YHWH in an unmediated way, whereas in 2 Maccabees meaning is constructed through cross-references to the ceremonies of refoundation of the Jerusalem temple. The message of 2 Maccabees is more elaborated, combining the claim that Jason contributed to destroying the temple by inducing the priests to neglect the sacrifices with a carefully devised insinuation that the *gymnasion*, with its foreign rites, is an antitemple. Yet beyond their different encodings, the messages of the two works are similar: the *gymnasion* was a form of unfaithfulness to YHWH. But unfaithfulness to YHWH is not coterminous with "idolatry"—the modern use of this word implies a concept of religion as a separate realm primarily defined as a set of beliefs, which is certainly not how the ancient authors saw the problem.[62]

5.1.4. Gymnasion *and Temple as Synecdoches for* Hellēnismos *and* Ioudaïsmos

The two Maccabees versions about the *gymnasion* concur in one more way. As we saw in Chapter 1 (§1.4), the literary construction of 2 Maccabees establishes a link of causality between the *gymnasion* and the desecration of the temple by Antiochos IV. In 1 Maccabees, as just seen, the building of the *gymnasion* is the first episode in a series of juxtaposed events supposed to epitomize the period of disruption of Antiochos IV's reign. The paratactic construction of the first chapter of 1 Maccabees is particularly instructive, because it could make sense to the original audience only if the notion that the foundation of the *gymnasion* was the starting point of the entire crisis was common knowledge *at least* under the Hasmoneans, at the time when the text was written. In fact there is no reason to doubt that the perception that the *gymnasion* played a prominent role in the crisis crystallized in the very days of the rebellion.

In historical terms, the reason why the *gymnasion* was given such an echo in the sources has nothing to do with "culture." Far from becoming an institution of higher education, in Hellenistic times it retained its military function—the military function of the *ephēbeion* in Jerusalem was recently demonstrated by comparing the vocabulary of 2 Maccabees 4:7–15 with the Tyriaion inscription.[63] More to the point, the three accounts of the establishment of the *gymnasion* (2 Macc. 4:7-15, 1 Macc. 1:11–15, *Ant.* 12.240–41) use institutional terms that hint at the political and economic aspects of the reform, and this vocabulary is explicit enough to support reasonably plausible historical reconstructions. As Tcherikover rightly discerned, Jason's establishment of the *gymnasion* was part of a wider reform whose essence was political and apparently involved important economic aspects too.[64] The Tyriaion inscription has now confirmed the link between the establishment of a *gymnasion* and *ephēbeion*, and the politicization (the legal transformation into a polis) of a local community.[65] Institutionally speaking, the creation of the *gymnasion* was merely a side aspect of the political and fiscal changes instituted by Jason.

However, the literary treatment of Jason's reforms in 1 and 2 Maccabees does not aim at an emotionally distanced survey of the legal aspects of the settlement negotiated between Jason and Antiochos IV. The appearance of the *gymnasion* in the physical and social landscape of the city was made particularly conspicuous by its high symbolic value as a thoroughly alien institution. When popular emotions ran high because of the political and economic consequences of Jason's settlement, the *gymnasion* became the focal point of collective resentment—in disproportion to its effective institutional importance. There are many instances of this process of focal displacement,[66] by which resentment entailed by either an abstract or an intangible issue (in our case, the debased political status and economic situation of a large part of the Judean population) is projected onto a concrete symbol—even though (from a modern standpoint) the latter has only a tangential relation with the real problems at stake. In such cases, the object of popular outrage may be either a place, an institution, a person, or a scapegoated social group. Although this process per se is attested in many societies, the selection of the item turned into the concrete symbol of the immaterial problem depends both on immediate circumstances and on cultural conditioning. Here, the presentation of Jason's reform found in 1 and 2 Maccabees results from such a process of focal displacement. The choice of the *gymnasion* to symbolize the early stage of the crisis is the product of what I have dubbed the "semantic concatenation" in the Methodological Introduction to Part II of this book.

If we accept the hypothesis of a focal shift, the perspective of the primary sources (1 and 2 Maccabees) on the *gymnasion* in reference to "Jason's reforms" offers a remarkable similarity with the process of formation and operation of the synecdoche that we met in Part I of this book.[67] Through this process the complete sequence of a set narrative pattern and its associated conceptual message were evoked through the mention of a single component of the narrative sequence. As a rule the component selected was a material item, such as the temple, thunder, or a throne. The constructed counterpoint between *Ioudaïsmos* and *Hellēnismos* that underpins the account of Jason's creation of the *gymnasion* in 2 Maccabees is further evidence of how the *gymnasion* works as a synecdoche for a wider concept in this section of the work.

As argued in Chapter 3 (§3.3.2.), the term *Ioudaïsmos* was coined by the author of 2 Maccabees to capture the "righteous order of things that was established when Judas refounded the temple, the order in which the dynasty of the Hasmoneans ruled." To be more precise: *Ioudaïsmos* encapsulates the specific variant of the narrative template of temple building that was used to emplot the message that the Hasmonean dynasty was legitimate. The most remarkable feature of *Ioudaïsmos* is its abstract nature. Nonetheless, in addition to *Ioudaïsmos* the narrative sequence encoding the legitimacy of the Hasmoneans continued to be referred to by means of concrete synecdochic images. In 1 Maccabees this association was fulfilled jointly by the rededicated temple and the purified Akra, and in 2 Maccabees by the rededicated temple.

As observed earlier,[68] the consistent use of the temple as a synecdoche confirms the prestige that it continued to enjoy in Judean society of Hellenistic times. Because of its prominent political, social, judicial, economic, and religious functions, the temple stood both at the center of the entire social organization and of the Judean symbolic universe; and as the keystone of the Judean social system and symbolic universe, it stood for the entire system—as prophesied in the quote from Haggai above,[69] the fate of the temple reflected the fate of the social community as a whole: when the temple functioned properly, so did the society. Conversely, when the temple was destroyed, the community was dispersed and deported, and society could not be rebuilt unless the temple was likewise restored—this is the meaning of Cyrus's decree in Ezra 1:1–11.[70]

Second-century Judeans, accustomed as they were to using the temple as a representation of their entire society, organization, and history, must have instinctively sought an institution that would embody the essence of "Jason's reforms" and denote them synecdochically. It is doubtful whether a new architectural complex was built for the facilities of Jason's *gymnasion*, in particular the *palaistra*, let alone an edifice sumptuous enough to stand comparison with the temple.[71] However, in the description of 2 Maccabees as it was analyzed above—as an institution with its own way of marking time, its distinct music, clothing, "sacrifices" (*chorēgia*), and system of social division—the *gymnasion* was perceived as a rival to the temple. In 2 Maccabees, the *gymnasion* was chosen to represent the whole body of "Jason's reforms."

In other words, in 2 Maccabees the temple and the *gymnasion* denote two distinct, antithetical social systems within the symbolic universe centered on the temple. Insofar as the author of 2 Maccabees supplemented the concrete image of the temple with the abstract term *Ioudaïsmos*, it is logical that he would do the same with Jason's reforms. The term *Hellēnismos* per se may be explained in two ways. Given that the *gymnasion* was easily identified as a *Greek* institution, and that the political aspect of Jason's reforms in essence meant the institutional transformation of Jerusalem into a polis enjoying privileges comparable to those of any other Greek polis, the choice of the word *Hellēnismos* to denote Jason's reforms as a whole must have come to the author readily.[72] However, it is not excluded that Jason's partisans dubbed themselves "Greeks" in the first place.

To conclude, in 2 Maccabees the term *Ioudaïsmos* means "the righteous order of things that was established when Judas refounded the temple, the order in which the dynasty of the Hasmoneans ruled," whereas *Hellēnismos* means "the wicked [*paranomos*] order of things that was established when Jason founded his antitemple, the *gymnasion*, the order in which the wicked high priests Jason and Menelaos ruled."[73]

5.1.5. Allophylismos: *The Seleukid Kings and the Temple*

If *Hellēnismos* involves the ethnic otherization of the internecine enemy, how is the figure of the Seleukid king construed in 2 Maccabees? Although recent studies have insisted that the Greek ethnic identity of Hellenistic kings did matter,[74] it does not necessarily follow that in the mind of the author of 2 Maccabees Jason, Menelaos, and the Seleukid king and officers constituted an homogeneous ethnic category. Moreover, the king was defined not by his ethnicity alone but also, and perhaps primarily, by his behavior, whether righteous or wicked—or, to use 2 Maccabees' nomenclature, pious or impious.[75]

In 2 Maccabees the vocabulary of impiety is equally applied to all enemies from within and without.[76] The war waged by Judas against the neighboring people is a just one, because the latter are impious and blasphemous. The defenders of the fortress of Gazara use sinful words (10:34–35) and therefore rightfully incur punishment at Judas's hands (10:36). At some point, Judas marches against a shrine of Atargatis (12:26). In turn, the Seleukid officials are described as impious. Nikanor son of Patroklos, a royal official, is deemed *dyssebēs* because he fights an illegitimate war and has sold the *Ioudaioi* as slaves before battle (8:14; see 8:16). The impiety of his namesake—the central Seleukid figure of the Nikanor's Day story—hardly needs elaboration.[77] As one would expect, Antiochos IV is the most corrupt of all and is dubbed both *dyssebēs* (9.9) and *asebēs* (10.10). As for Antiochos V, he is a mere annex to his father's portrait (10:10).[78]

A. Royal Piety. This is not the whole story, however. The king, and by extension his officers, may also be characterized as pious. In 2 Maccabees the mutual duties between the king and the local communities are construed in terms of the king's (and royal officials') *piety* toward the local temple and the high priest's (and the whole community's) *loyalty* to the king. In this way, the semantic fields of piety and impiety serve to define the nature of relations between the imperial king and the local community. The king must be deemed to be pious to be acknowledged as legitimate.[79]

This representation of the legitimate king as pious was the product of a long tradition, harking back to the organic relations between kings and temples that were a common feature of all native kingships throughout the ancient Near East. In Persian and Hellenistic times, the king's attitude toward local temples was the means through which political relations between the imperial power and the local communities were channeled. Documents of Hellenistic times from Babylonia, Judea, and Egypt show how this ideology was variously revisited, but never quite relinquished, by both royal and priestly sides.[80]

In 2 Maccabees, piety toward the temple and loyalty to the king are closely related attributes in the characters of the high priests. Onias is both pious and loyal to the king: he prays when Heliodoros is struck to the ground by the angels, lest the king suspect the Judeans of disloyalty (*kakourgia,* "foul play," 3:32). When Antiochos prepares for his war against Egypt, supernatural beings appear in the air above Jerusalem, prompting "all" to pray that these apparitions should augur well for the royal enterprise (5:1–4). As this latter case shows, the entire community of the Judeans—not the high priest alone—display their political loyalty to the king, with divine approval. In contrast, when the impious Menelaos is unable to pay the sum that he had promised to the king (4:27), this forfeiture adds to his misdemeanors, until Lysias, Antiochos V's counselor, eventually charges Menelaos with being responsible for all the king's troubles (13:4). Last, the author pointedly stresses that it was not a local revolt that prompted Antiochos's attack on Jerusalem: the "wicked" Jason made an attempt to seize back power, which made the king *wrongly* believe that the Judeans were rising in revolt (5:11).

The realization that the author's point of view basically stays in line with the traditional Near Eastern conception of royal legitimacy helps us to further pinpoint the status of Antiochos IV in 2 Maccabees. Appropriate royal behavior was defined by a set of traditional rules, irrespective of whether the king was Greek, Persian, or of some other extraction. Therefore the scandal prompted by Antiochos IV's deeds arises from his impious behavior and not because, as a Greek, he has tried to impose a Greek way of life. Yet it seems that like Jason, Antiochos IV underwent a process of *ethnic* otherization in 2 Maccabees; but Antiochos is not included in the semantic field of *Hellēnismos*.

B. *Allophyloi and Allophylismos as the Ethnicized Definition of Imperial Rule?* One application of the semantic fields of piety and impiety to the alien enemies is found in the prayer uttered by the *Ioudaioi* during the ceremony of the rededication of the temple (2 Macc. 8:4; emphasis added):

> They prayed to YHWH that they never again would come to suffer such disasters. Rather, if they should ever sin, let them be chastised by YHWH himself, with clemency, and not delivered over to the hands of *blasphemous and barbarous peoples*.

On the basis of the traditional tenet that the enemy king and his army inflicting disasters upon YHWH's people act as His arm, the "blasphemous and barbarous *ethnē*" may be understood to refer to Antiochos and his men. Yet the author twice uses *allophyloi* to note the profaners of the temple and the city in describing the refoundation (2 Macc. 10:2, 5).[81] The word *allophylismos* is mentioned alongside *Hellēnismos* in the episode of the creation of the *gymnasion* (2 Macc. 4:13), and therefore it may be reasonably surmised that its semantic field was constructed in a way similar to the construction of *Ioudaïsmos* and *Hellēnismos*. Moreover, given the centrality of the temple and the *gymnasion*—as an antitemple—in the semantic fields of these two terms, respectively, it is hardly surprising to find the decisive clue to the identity of the *allophyloi* in the description of the ceremony of the temple's "refoundation." The *allophyloi* are those whose wicked values are Antiochos's, who carried out Antiochos's impious orders. Insofar as the attitude of the imperial king toward the temple is taken to express the nature of the relations between the imperial king and the local community, *allophylismos* may be taken to signify "the wicked order of things at the head of which Antiochos the wicked king stands."

Because it belongs to the genre of historiography, 2 Maccabees does not spell out any genuine cosmology.[82] Nevertheless, the infamy of Antiochos IV is given cosmic resonance upon the eve of his death: smitten by God, the king falls to the ground, he who "had been thinking of giving orders to the waves of the sea and had been planning to weigh the peaks of the mountains in a balance" (2 Macc. 9:8). Antiochos's pledge that he will turn *Ioudaios* in his ultimate confession (2 Macc. 9:17) acquires a much stronger signification if we admit that Antiochos heads the *allophyloi*. Whereas a pious king can be neatly incorporated into the system of *Ioudaïsmos*, Antiochos IV cannot.

As argued in Chapter 4, the political agenda of the authors of 1 and 2 Maccabees was twofold. The political legitimacy of the Hasmoneans needed to be supported not only against Jason, Menelaos, and Alkimos, their predecessors as high priests, but also against the imperial pretensions of the Seleukids. The fact that the author of 2 Maccabees coined the two terms *Hellēnismos* and *allophylismos* in opposition to *Ioudaïsmos* seems to substantiate this dual agenda, with *Hellēnismos* representing the impious order of Jason and *allophylismos* that of Antiochos. *Allophylismos* seems to be used to characterize—and stigmatize—the imperial yoke of the Seleukids over the Judeans.

5.2. MENELAOS AND THE HOLY VESSELS IN 1 AND 2 MACCABEES

Jason may have been Hellenized in the modern sense of the word, but this is not what the author of 2 Maccabees sought to stigmatize in claiming that Jason's way of life was *Hellēnismos*. What mattered from his point of view was that Jason was a temple destroyer. Moreover, his sin of *Hellēnismos* paved the way to Antiochos's own sin. By instituting the *gymnasion* and inducing the priests to neglect the sacrifices, Jason was responsible for the initial dysfunction of the temple cult. Shortly afterwards Antiochos was to cause the total interruption of the sacrifices. Similarly Menelaos in 2 Maccabees and Alkimos in 1 Maccabees contributed to destroying the buildings whose construction and repair operated as "signs" of political legitimacy. The intended message was certainly not lost on the original audience of the two works: the rival high priests were wicked and therefore had no legitimate entitlement to rule. However, the sins of Menelaos and Alkimos are distinct and require a separate examination, beginning with the former. Whereas Jason's misdeeds affected the sacrifices, Menelaos's sin consisted in stealing the holy vessels. Yet the offense is hardly lighter than Jason's, since the presence of the holy vessels in the temple was as vital to its proper functioning as the daily sacrifices.

5.2.1. The Symbolic Value of the Vessels

In the Judean cultic system, the holy vessels seem to have been invested with a symbolic value similar to that of the cult statues in other Semitic systems. In the absence of a cult statue, the fate of these vessels epitomized the destiny of the temple itself and therefore of the Judean community, which was organically linked to the temple. In a way, the holy vessels function as a "sign" for the temple as a whole, a synecdoche.

The way the holy vessels embodied the organic connection between the community and its temple in the symbolic universe of the Judahite/Judean literati is remarkably illustrated in 1 Esdras, and to a lesser extent in the parallel account of Ezra-Nehemiah (EN). The first chapter of 1 Esdras recounts the three successive deportations of kings of Judah to Babylon by Nebuchadnezzar: Jehoiakim (1 Esd. 1:39–42), Jehoiachin (1:43–46a), and Zedekiah (1:46b–57). All three times, the kings are banished together with the Israelites and the holy vessels, a sequence apparently aimed to match the threefold return of the Israelites thereafter: the first, under Cyrus, is led by Sheshbazzar (2:1–16); the second, under Darius, by Zerubbabel and Joshua (3–7:15); and the third, under Artaxerxes, by Ezra (8:1–9:55). Each time, the people and the holy vessels return in unison.

The Returnees constitute an exhaustive and orderly sample of society, not an undifferentiated throng of men. One function of the catalogues of people listed in 1 Esdras and EN[83] is to prove that the Returnees were organized according to the proper divisions of society. They are led by twelve leaders symbolizing the twelve tribes and are ordered according to their ancestral houses. Clans of lay people are listed first (1 Esd. 5:9–23), followed by the priests, Levites, temple servants, and descendants of Solomon's servants listed in descending hierarchical order (5:24–35), the unholy ones being listed apart from the holy ones (5:7–35, 36–43, 45–46; 8:68—9:36).

The catalogues of people are complemented by catalogues of the holy vessels.[84] The holy vessels that "return" together with the people are the selfsame vessels taken by Nebuchadnezzar when Solomon's temple was destroyed. Being deposited in the newly built temple, they function as emblems of the continuity between Solomon's destroyed temple and the new building.[85] The status of these vessels is spelled out in the story of their restitution by Cyrus (2:10–12, 15), and their identity is ascertained in the form of a brief inventory (2:13–14). Like the people, the holy vessels are divided into categories and counted to the unit. They are catalogued according to their shapes and precious materials, and the number of each category is specified, exactly as the people are counted by clans and houses. A second list of holy vessels appears in the narrative unit of Ezra's return (1 Esd. 8:55–57). As with the first time, the vessels are handed out by the Persian king to the leader of the Returnees (8:55), and their recording in the form of a catalogue establishes that the new set of holy vessels has the same history and therefore the same symbolic value as the first one.

The prominence given to the holy vessels in the accounts of the refoundation of the temple under the Achaimenids indicates that the symbolic implication of Menelaos's sacrilegious theft is no less dreadful than the charge of unfaithfulness to YHWH imputed to Jason in 2 Maccabees. Whereas Judas is depicted as the new refounder of the temple, purifying the temple and building a new altar as Zerubbabel and Joshua had done, his counterpart Menelaos is likened to Nebuchadnezzar, the Babylonian king who had removed the holy vessels from Solomon's temple (1 Esd. 1:39–57).

5.2.2. Menelaos's Theft of the Vessels in 2 Maccabees

Initially, the golden vessels stolen by Menelaos and sold off (2 Macc. 4:32) are not reported as being the holy vessels of the temple. However, this is done when Menelaos robs the temple a second time, with Lysimachos's complicity (4:39), and the charge of sacrilege is reiterated in the allegation that Lysimachos was lynched by the rioting people for absconding with the holy vessels (*hierosylos*, 4.42). Like Jason's sin before him, Menelaos's is later duplicated and amplified by one of Antiochos's misdeeds. Menelaos eventually became an accomplice of Antiochos IV's subsequent looting of the holy vessels, since he allegedly served as his guide (5:15–16).

A further aggravating factor was added to the charges made against Menelaos. The gifts made by kings to the temple form a recurrent theme in 2 Maccabees.[86]

These royal gifts are the "sign" both of the prestige of the sanctuary and of the ideal state of the relations obtaining between the local community and the imperial power. They are recorded, as one would expect, in the concise description of the ideal situation that prevailed in Judea under Onias III (2 Macc. 3:2). Likewise, the peace with Antiochos V is sealed by the king's resumption of offerings to the temple (13:23); whereas Antiochos IV, in his desperate attempt to dodge his destiny on the eve of his death, promised extravagant votive gifts to make up for the holy vessels he had stolen (9:16). In this context, the fact that royal gifts were found among the vessels plundered by Antiochos IV could only add to the king's sacrilege and through the king further indict Menelaos, who acted as the king's guide (5:16).[87]

Antiochos IV was not alone in stealing others' gifts from a sanctuary. In the Mesopotamian chronicle narrating the "Crimes and Sacrileges of Nabû-šuma-iškun," a similar charge is raised against this king, who is depicted as the embodiment of wickedness.[88] Comparison of these two texts strongly suggests that the account of Menelaos and Antiochos plundering the temple in 2 Maccabees fleshes out a historical event with much formulaic material. Antiochos IV's act of pillage is likely to be a real historical event, given that this episode is recorded in both 1 and 2 Maccabees, and nothing in the literary construct of 2 Maccabees hints at a purely symbolic montage. In contrast, the mention of the plunder of the royal gifts plainly shifts the account to a literary register. For the same reasons, every detail in the account of Menelaos's looting is suspect. To begin with, the symmetry between Jason's and Menelaos's sins, both of which are eventually amplified by Antiochos's evildoings, is a little too perfect. Second, the motivations assigned to Menelaos are suspiciously meaningful from a symbolic point of view. Menelaos allegedly steals the holy vessels to pay the increased rate of tribute that he (again allegedly) promised to the king in order to be appointed high priest in Jason's stead (2 Macc. 4:23–32). One may surmise there were plenty of items of precious metal in the temple chambers that Menelaos could have monetized before laying his hands on the holy vessels themselves if he indeed faced financial straits. Moreover, Menelaos is reported to have used some of the stolen vessels as a gift to Andronikos, whom Antiochos had left as his deputy in Antioch; and immediately after receiving this present, Andronikos was convinced by Menelaos to murder Onias III, because the latter had learned of his wicked actions and had denounced him (4:32–34). Thus Jason ousted Onias III from the high priesthood; Menelaos had him assassinated to eschew prosecution for his sacred robbery; and Judas was acknowledged by Onias III himself as his worthy heir (15:12–16).[89] The scheme is perhaps a little too neat.

5.2.3. The Holy Vessels in 1 Maccabees

It is striking that although the theme of the theft of the holy vessels is central in 1 Maccabees, that theft is used to incriminate Antiochos IV alone. The depiction of

Antiochos IV's attack on Jerusalem on his way back from Egypt almost exclusively focuses on the king's entering the temple and making off with the holy vessels (1 Macc. 1:20–24). Instead of 2 Maccabees' complaint that the king removed royal gifts, 1 Maccabees offers a catalogue of the plundered items (1:21–23), which is certainly intended as an intertextual allusion to the catalogues of holy vessels found in 1 Esdras and EN. Here, Antiochos and not Menelaos is depicted as the new Nebuchadnezzar, taking the vessels off to his home, just as Nebuchadnezzar had dispatched them to Babylon (1 Macc. 1:24b).[90] As in 1 Esdras, the massacre of the population goes hand in hand with the sacred looting, since the fate of the temple and the fate of the people are firmly interwoven (1 Macc. 1:24b).

This sacrilege plagues Antiochos throughout the rest of his life, and Antiochos himself eventually acknowledges that this sin is the genuine cause of his death (1 Macc. 6:12). In all this, no mention whatsoever of Menelaos is made. The target of 1 Maccabees is Alkimos, and Jason and Menelaos are omitted altogether.

5.3. ALKIMOS IN 1 MACCABEES

Unlike Jason and Menelaos, Alkimos is not a central target in 2 Maccabees, although his portrayal is hardly flattering.[91] In contrast, whereas Jason and Menelaos are not mentioned by name in 1 Maccabees, Alkimos is the main focus of the author's delegitimizing campaign.

5.3.1. Alkimos and the City Wall

In 1 Maccabees Alkimos features in three short passages (7:5–25; 9:1, 54–57) purporting to summarize his rule as a high priest, and the author spares no detail to paint him as the embodiment of wickedness. In the thirty-odd verses, we are told twice that Alkimos gathered all the sinful and wicked men of Israel around him, and together they lodged false accusations against Judas and their own people before the king (7:5–6, 21–25). Each time, Alkimos's wicked behavior is associated with his coveting the high priesthood (7:5, 21), and it is easy to understand that the two episodes are devised to define the essence of his priesthood. Alkimos's first ill-intentioned visit to the king effectively ends with his official appointment as high priest (7:9).

Beside his slanders against Judas and the people, the themes coloring Alkimos's high priesthood are his duplicity (7:10, 15–16), his falsification of justice (7:12–18), and his waging war against his own people (7:10, 20–23; 9:1). His wrongdoings cause more havoc than the gentiles, both in his denial of justice (7:17)[92] and in warfare (7:21–23). It is worth noting the fact that Alkimos meets the death of one guilty of blasphemy (9:54–56), like Antiochos IV (6:8–13). Antiochos was punished by dying far away from home because he had removed silver and gold vessels from the temple and ordered a massacre of the inhabitants of Judea "for no reason"

(6:12). Although Alkimos dies at home, he loses his voice and is unable to dictate a will, and thus dies an accursed death. However, Alkimos's sin consisted of words alone and not of actions, and his hideous death is punishment for having given the order to tear down the wall of the inner court of the sanctuary (9:54). It is as though the similarity between Alkimos's and Antiochos's deaths is what creates an equation between their sins in hindsight; but when the text is deconstructed, these allegations appear as outright slanders.

Alkimos's *intention* to tear down the wall of Jerusalem is the most important episode of his high priesthood from a symbolic point of view, and its symbolic significance is all the more evident since his wicked project in fact never materialized—in short, it is a mere invention.[93] The context of this "episode," or at least its literary construction, is carefully worked out. Whereas most of Alkimos's "career" unfolds in Judas's time, the episode of the wall is situated at the inception of Jonathan's time unit (9:23—12:53). Upon Judas's death, his (imperfect) restoration of order collapses anew: "After the death of Judas, 'the wicked sprouted' throughout the territory of Israel, 'and the evildoers flourished.'" (1 Macc. 9:23). In other words, a new cycle of disruption and restoration of order begins. This is why Jonathan is chosen by Judas's friends as their new leader "against our enemies and Bacchides, and against the foes of our people" (9:29). After an initial and inconclusive military episode, disruption returns in full (1 Macc. 9:50–56; emphases added):

> After returning to Jerusalem, Bacchides *fortified* several towns in Judea *with high walls, gates, and bars*. . . . He *stationed garrisons* in them to harass Israel. He also strengthened the *fortifications* of the town of Beth-Zur and Gazara and the Akra and *stationed* therein *troops* and stores of food. . . . In the year 153 [S.E.], in the second month, Alkimos issued an order to *tear down the wall of the inner court of the sanctuary, thus tearing down the work of the prophets*. Alkimos had already begun the work of having it torn down when he suffered a stroke, which put an end to his project. Unable to open his mouth and paralyzed, he could no longer speak or issue a will for his family. So died Alkimos in great agony on that occasion.

The disruption that marks the beginning of Jonathan's time unit is a precise reenactment of the disruption with which the crisis initiated by Antiochos IV's evildoing started in the first chapter of 1 Maccabees, when the king had sent a Mysarch against the towns of Judah (1 Macc. 1:29–35).[94]

Alkimos's sin equates to Jason's in 2 Maccabees in terms of their symbolic status, since their destructive actions—Alkimos's demolition of the wall and Jason's interference with the sacrifices—are the causes that galvanize Judas's and Simon's acts of refoundation. It is therefore not surprising that Alkimos and Jason are treated with the same hostility. Like Jason in 2 Maccabees, Alkimos is otherized.

A. Alkimos's Ethnic Otherization. Although the author of 1 Maccabees does not adopt the innovative ethnicized vocabulary—*Ioudaïsmos, Hellēnismos,* and *allophylismos*—that famously appears in 2 Maccabees, the difference between the two works may be more a matter of style than of ideology. The choice of the author of 1 Maccabees to emulate the style of the Septuagint in syntax and phrases necessarily restrained his use of neologisms, but he nevertheless expresses the same notion, albeit with different literary means.[95] Alkimos's destruction of the wall, for instance, exploits the device of the exemplum.[96] In fortifying the wall, Simon reenacts Nehemiah's act of foundation. In destroying it, Alkimos takes the "Mysarch," Antiochos's officer, as his model. Similarly, the theme of Alkimos waging war against his own people is straightforward enough (7:21–22) and is, moreover, punctuated by the explicit comment that Alkimos and his supporters had done much harm to Israelites, "far worse than anything the gentiles were doing" (7:23). Thus Alkimos and his followers are "the foes from within" and are deemed worse than the enemies from without. Alkimos and his wicked partisans on the one hand, and Judas and his faithful warriors on the other, fight each other for the same land, as though they belonged to two different peoples.[97]

Another intertextual device the author employs to otherize Menelaos is his quotation from Psalm 79:2–3, which inspires his description of the treacherous detention and execution of the sixty *Asidaioi* (1 Macc. 7:16–17):

> As soon as he had won their trust, however, he arrested sixty of them and had them executed all in a single day, in accordance with the verse which he himself wrote, "The bodies and blood of Your saints they have poured out around Jerusalem, and there is no one to bury them."

To understand the implication of this quote, we need to supplement the preceding verse, something the original audience of the work was undoubtedly able to do (Ps. 79:1; emphasis added):

> O God, *the nations* have come into Your inheritance;
> They have defiled Your holy temple;
> They have laid Jerusalem in ruins.

In 1 Maccabees the quote is contextualized in such a way as to change the identity of the enemy who has inflicted these misfortunes. Alkimos is construed as standing for "the nations."[98]

5.3.2. Alkimos and the Asidaioi

The justification for dwelling on Alkimos's unjust execution of the *Asidaioi* is primarily historiographic. From the perspective of the intrinsic logic of the narrative, this incident is secondary to tearing down the wall. However, it has played a major part in turning the *Asidaioi* into a "party" whose interests became distinct from those of the Maccabees at some point, and therefore its impact on modern historical reconstructions weighs more heavily. Modern commentators contend that so long as the

Maccabees fought for the liberation of the temple and the restoration of "religious freedom," all the supposedly religious parties were on their side. However, the reconquest of the temple and even more Antiochos V's and Lysias's rescinding of Antiochos IV's decree of "religious persecution" and their concession of a "freedom of cult" generated a rift in the ranks of the former allies, because from this moment on the aim of the struggle was not "preserving the Jewish religion" any longer but "the domination within Jewry itself of the pro-Greek faction or the nationalists."[99] The divergence of interests between the so-called parties came to the fore in the wake of Alkimos's appointment as high priest. Whereas Judas and his followers persisted in their opposition, the "representatives of the strictest branch of Jewry themselves— the scribes and the 'Devout' [*Asidaioi*, 1 Macc. 7:13]" rallied him.[100]

This assessment, which still surfaces in recent studies,[101] is based on a selective reading of the text typically guided by the conviction that "hard facts" may be sorted out from their rhetorical apparatus. Consequently, the semantic fields of piety and wickedness are rationalized so as to transform Alkimos into the head of the pro-Greek party and the Maccabees, the scribes, and the *Asidaioi* into religious parties. More specifically, the focus of the episode of the execution of the *Asidaioi* is drastically shifted so as to give weight to the emergence of a conflict of interests between the Maccabees engaging in a struggle for power and the most religious of their former partisans, in whose opinion the struggle ended with the Seleukid concession of "religious freedom."

As with Jason's *gymnasion* and Menelaos's theft of the holy vessels, paying attention to the literary construction of the passage is likely to thwart this interpretation. If the passage is read without an attempt to rationalize it, its thrust appears to be Alkimos's utmost wickedness as high priest, not the rift between the Maccabees and the *Asidaioi*. To understand the author's intention properly, however, a longer section of text must be taken into account (1 Macc. 7:5–20).

The text narrates how the "sinful and wicked men [*anomoi kai asebeis*] of Israel," led by Alkimos (who was still not high priest), brought charges "against their people" (in fact, Judas and his brothers) before Demetrios I. The king sent Bacchides and Alkimos, whom he appointed high priest, "with orders to wreak vengeance on the Israelites." Once in Judah, Bacchides makes a peace overture to Judas and his brothers, and whereas these turned it down, "an assembly of scribes gathered before Alkimos and Bacchides to seek justice." Despite his pledge to them that they might come in peace, Alkimos arrested sixty of them and had them executed in a single day, whereupon "the entire people ... said to one another, 'There is no truth or justice among them. They have violated their pledge and their sworn oath.'" Bacchides eventually returned to the king, after putting the country under the control of Alkimos. Although the episode of the execution of the *Asidaioi* stops here, the depiction of Alkimos's wickedness continues with the following summary (1 Macc. 7:21–25; emphases added):

224   PART II: *HELLĒNISMOS*

> Alkimos then faced a *struggle for the high priesthood,* in which, however, *all the troublers of their people rallied to him,* overran the land of Judah, and inflicted a great defeat upon Israel. Judas saw all the harm that Alkimos and his supporters had done to Israelites, *far worse than anything the gentiles were doing.* Accordingly, he went around the entire territory of Judea, punishing the turncoats so that they shrank from going out into the countryside. When Alkimos saw the growing strength of Judas and his men, knowing that he could not cope with them, he went again to the king and *accused them of misdeeds.*

1 Maccabees 7:5–25 is the main account of Alkimos's high priesthood in this book. Leaving aside the themes cited above (§5.3.1), we may note that the passage revolves around two closely linked issues, Alkimos's false word and injustice. As seen in Chapter 2 (§2.1.2A), the restoration of social justice is part and parcel of Hurowitz's pattern of temple foundation, and the same is true of the foundation of the palace, from which the theme of the construction and destruction of the wall more specifically draws.[102] Alkimos's injustice is fully consistent with his demolition of the temple wall. More generally, justice is the main duty of the king; and Simon, of course, seeks justice, as his Eulogy proclaims (1 Macc. 14:14).[103] In contrast, Alkimos gathers all the wicked men around him (7:5, 21–22) and slanderously accuses the faithful before the king (7:6, 25).

The parallels between the account of Alkimos's wicked deeds and Simon's Eulogy of 1 Maccabees 14:4–15 do not stop here.[104] The motif of "peace" is particularly prominent in the Eulogy. Therefore it is probably no coincidence that Alkimos is depicted so insistently as waging war against his own people:

> Under Simon, "No longer was there anyone on earth waging war against them. The kings had been defeated in those days" (14:13). Conversely, Alkimos is systematically associated with Bacchides (7:8–9, 19–20), thus waging war on the side of the "kings." The mention of Alkimos alongside Bacchides in 1 Maccabees 9:1 seems particularly slanderous, since he is not mentioned again in the rest of the account of Bacchides' campaign (9:1–22), which resulted in a defeat that saw the death of Judas (9:18–22), and the author was seemingly tempted to tie Alkimos's memory to this outcome.

> Under Simon, "The people farmed their land in peace, and the land gave forth its produce, and the trees of the fields their fruit" (14:8), whereas Alkimos "overran the land of Judah, and inflicted a great defeat upon Israel" (7:22).

> Simon also "sought the good of his people" (14:4a), whereas "Judas saw all the harm that Alkimos and his supporters had done to Israelites" (7:23).

> Finally, under Simon "everyone sat under his own vine and fig tree, with none to make him afraid" (14:12). The opposite resulted from Alkimos's unjust

execution of the sixty *Asidaioi*: "The fear and dread of them seized the entire people, as they said to one another, 'There is no truth or justice among them'" (7:18).

Thus the literary context in which the meeting between Alkimos and the *Asidaioi* is set throws doubt on its historical tenability, and such doubts increase when it is compared with an encounter related in 2 Maccabees 4:43–50. After the robbery of sacred vessels and the intended massacre of Jerusalemites by Lysimachos—who replaced Menelaos as high priest in the latter's absence—the *gerousia* of Jerusalem lodged a complaint against Menelaos, sending three elders to argue the case before the king in Tyre—to no avail, however: Menelaos bribed a courtier and was acquitted, whereas the three elders were put to death. The author concludes his account by informing his audience that Menelaos "retained his office . . ., having proved himself to be a plotter against his fellow Judeans" (4:50). The pattern of the two meetings is very similar: a delegation of "good" Judeans—the three elders in 2 Maccabees and the assembly of the scribes and the *Asidaioi* in 1 Maccabees—"seek justice" before the king and are unjustly executed. In 1 Maccabees, the cause of the injustice is Alkimos's breach of his pledge (1 Macc. 7:15, 18), whereas in the parallel account Menelaos corrupts a royal officer (2 Macc. 4:45). The fact that 2 Maccabees specifies the object of the case, whereas 1 Maccabees does not, may be explained by the different—but obviously parallel—context. In 2 Maccabees, Menelaos's sin has already been exposed in detail (2 Macc. 4:32). Moreover, the readers have already learned that Menelaos used the stolen holy vessels to have Onias III assassinated by another royal official (4:32–34), although in this particular case the culprit was punished by the king (4:35–38). In 1 Maccabees no particular sin is imputed to Alkimos, and therefore the precise description of the object of the meeting is replaced with a question over Alkimos's being worthy of the role of high priest (1 Macc. 7:14).

One last point is worth noting. The relation between the scribes and the *Asidaioi* is unclear in 1 Maccabees 7:12–13, and the extant text seems to conflate two stories, one involving the scribes and the other the *Asidaioi*. What may be left of the meeting between Alkimos and the *Asidaioi* in terms of historical reliability? Probably not much. What *is* certain, however, is that the episode does *not* intend to describe a rift between the *Asidaioi* and the Maccabees.

5.4. INTENTIONAL SINS: SOME READING GUIDELINES ABOUT THE RIVAL HIGH PRIESTS

Before drawing final conclusions from our revised portraits of Jason, Menelaos, and Alkimos, the literary device of what may be called the "intentional sin" is worth dwelling upon. When he lacks facts to substantiate his claims, the author of 2 Maccabees falls back on allegations about intentions. The intentional sins of the wicked characters in 2 Maccabees are numerous enough to foster the idea that they constitute a convenient literary device to blacken their portraits further at low cost.

> Jason intends to make a sacrifice to Herakles of Tyre (2 Macc. 4:19–20).
>
> Nikanor plans an attack on the Sabbath day (2 Macc. 15:1–5).
>
> Antiochos V fares as badly as his father, at least in words and intentions (2 Macc. 13:9–11).[105]
>
> Further, the first Nikanor intends to pay off the tribute owed to the Romans with the proceeds of selling the Judean prisoners of war (2 Macc. 8:10).
>
> And Lysias intends "to turn the city of the Judeans into a Greek settlement, to make their temple subject to tribute, . . . and to turn the high priesthood into an office to be put up for sale annually" (2 Macc. 11:2–3).

While the author of 2 Maccabees is particularly fond of this device, his fellow writer does not always resist the temptation to use it: Alkimos alleged orders that the wall of the inner court of the sanctuary is to be torn down (1 Macc. 9:54).

The sheer number of intentional sins in 2 Maccabees is noteworthy: while the moral character of an individual was generally held to be demonstrable in his actions, these were also considered closely related to his words. The author of 2 Maccabees overworked this common perception, perhaps counting on the cumulative effect of the negative notations in his portraits of Jason, Menelaos, and Alkimos to confound the critical sense of his original audience. Yet when the device of intentional sins is deconstructed, it casts doubts on the rest of the negative notations as well.

. . .

Our analysis of the delineation of the narrative units composing 2 Maccabees discussed in Chapter 1 showed that the portrayal of Menelaos in 2 Maccabees is heavily distorted, hinting at an alternative reconstruction of his actions that instead suggests the man was an able statesman.[106] Literary analysis of the account of his theft of the holy vessels confirms the need to rehabilitate him. Bickerman's depiction of Menelaos as an unscrupulous Hellenizer is an uncritical extrapolation from the claim of 2 Maccabees that the man was cynical enough to steal sacred vessels. But the portrayal of Menelaos in 2 Maccabees is not merely a case of literary montage; it is a web of distortions that turn him into a paragon of wickedness. Modern reconstructions need not endorse our author's campaign of denigration against the man who seems to have been Judas's most dangerous, and apparently most able, political rival.[107]

As argued repeatedly in Part I of this book (see the Methodological Introduction to Part I), qualifying a king (or a high priest) as either pious or impious was first and foremost a statement about the speaker's taking of a political side and has nothing to do with the alleged religiousness of the person thus qualified. Merely stating that someone was either pious or impious was not enough—it required demonstrating. In this respect, in both Maccabees books the roles are clearly distributed: the Maccabees themselves are pious, and their rivals duly impious. The literary analyses proposed in Chapters 3 and 4 showed how the portrayals of Judas and Simon are constructed from a literary point of view, employing devices that are partly specific to each author and partly similar between them. The same is true regarding the portrayals of Jason, Menelaos, Alkimos, and to some extent Antiochos IV. Through a careful handling of details, intertextual references, authorial comments, and rhetorical manipulations, the rivals of the Maccabees are deftly transformed into the utmost in wickedness, with elaborate correspondences linking their specific sins with the legitimizing actions of Judas and Simon. Once these literary devices are peeled away and the cultural codes underpinning their use are understood, what is left of the modern portraits of Jason, Menelaos, and Alkimos as moderate and extreme Hellenizers? Virtually nothing.

At the same time, in 2 Maccabees *Hellēnismos* and *allophylismos* are patently indicated as the sources of the disruption—and, to put it in modern terms, the main causes of the rebellion against Antiochos IV—but for the author this nomenclature has nothing to do with culture. Actually, acculturation is a tricky concept. In her analysis of the nomenclature used in 2 Maccabees to describe the narrative's heroes—Judas, Onias III, and the martyrs—Martha Himmelfarb has shown that the text makes use of "terms drawn from Greek culture." Thus whereas in their original context in Greek literature such terms as *gennaios* (noble), *eugenēs* (of noble birth), and *androdōs* (manfully) are applied to describe warriors, in 2 Maccabees they are repurposed for their new, Judean context.[108] In other words, elements borrowed from an alien culture are acclimated to the local context and become part of it. Once absorbed, they cease to be perceived as alien, and so there is no reason why the author should incriminate them as elements of *Hellēnismos*.

Works roughly contemporary with 2 Maccabees continued to reify their native culture and the cultures of others through lists of concrete items, which were inevitably selective. Two lists of this type in the first book of Enoch can be seen to reify Greek culture.[109] Similarly, as will be argued in Chapter 6 (§6.4), the so-called persecution account of 2 Maccabees (6:1–11) may to some extent be seen as an inverted list of items epitomizing Judean identity. Moreover, this traditional narrative code is akin to the use of synecdoche, by which one pivotal item can stand either for a range of abstract notions or for an overall narrative pattern. If we accept that the temple and the *gymnasion*, respectively, function as synecdoches for *Ioudaïsmos* and *Hellēnismos*, as argued in this chapter, we must conclude that the author of 2 Maccabees mixes two ways of reifying his own social and political experience as well as that of the other: the traditional narrative code that operates by focal shift along with the use of abstract, all-encompassing terms (*Ioudaïsmos, Hellēnismos* and *allophylismos*) that most probably he himself coined, certainly under the influence of Greek thought. Among his innovations, it is also worth noting that he dismissed the traditional dichotomy between respective inventories of righteous and wicked items, and instead painted *two* wicked orders side by side, namely those of Jason (*Hellēnismos*) and the Seleukid king (*allophylismos*). This deviation from tradition was doubtless inspired by a twofold political agenda: on the one hand, he needed to delegitimize those contending for power, and on the other, to denounce the Seleukid imperial yoke. In this regard, the trio *Ioudaïsmos, Hellēnismos,* and *allophylismos* are primarily concepts of a political nature, which is precisely why *Ioudaïsmos* and *Hellēnismos* are never referred to in the same sentence. For the author's purpose, they never coexisted side by side in Judean society but followed each other: Jason's *Hellēnismos* signified order disrupted; *Ioudaïsmos*, order restored.

The process of focal shift just noted is not limited to the *gymnasion* and the temple. In fact it is a pervasive means of constructing meaning, not only in 2 Maccabees but also in 1 Maccabees. The purpose of Chapter 7 will be to investigate these cultural and narrative codes in detail. Before that, however, one last point needs to be elucidated: the so-called religious persecution is an additional product of these said codes, by which the Maccabees authors and the authors (or editors) of the book of Daniel symbolically loaded signifiers to describe the military repression of the rebellion of the Judeans against the king, as a way to incorporate this event in their symbolic universe centered on the temple.

6

The "Religious Persecution" in the Light of Ancient Judean Cultural and Narrative Codes

INTRODUCTION

The wave of "religious persecution" imputed to Antiochos IV is without contest the most celebrated episode associated with the history of Judea in Hellenistic times. The earliest persecution accounts are found in Daniel 11:29–39, 1 Maccabees 1:41–64, 2 Maccabees 6:1–11, and Josephus's *Antiquities* (12.248–56) and *War* (1.1.32–35), and in the subsequent Jewish tradition its narrative became part and parcel of the celebration of the Hanukkah festival. For historians of the Seleukid empire, this episode remains something of a puzzle. Bickerman famously dubbed it a "unique" event, "the sole enigma in the history of Seleucid Jerusalem," and "the only attempt ever made to abolish the religion of Judaism."[1] This perplexity derives from the fact that the notion of a religious persecution is hard to reconcile with what we know of the behavior of Greeks in general, and Hellenistic kings in particular, toward foreign gods. Since Bickerman, various attempts have been made to make sense of the persecution accounts—or, to use the less onerous phrase now favored by most scholars, the "prohibition of the Judean observances," but the real breakthrough came from Steven Weitzman, who in a paper published in 2004 argued that the accounts of the "religious persecution" are informed by the same literary conventions as the portraits of wicked kings found in the Mesopotamian royal inscriptions of the Assyrian, Babylonian, Persian, and Seleukid periods.[2] In these inscriptions, the archetypal portrait of the wicked king uses the same topical components as that of the righteous king, merely inverting them.[3] More precisely, the accounts of Antiochos's persecution exploit the topics associated with the theme of the "king as agent of cultic restoration," his wicked counterpart being the cult disrupter.

As yet, Weitzman's analysis has not achieved much traction, partly because the pertinence of comparing the Mesopotamian and the Judean literary material has prompted reservations, and partly because the author has denied that his innovative literary analysis could be the basis for a new historical interpretation.[4] However, the reluctance to endorse Weitzman's comparison between the Mesopotamian and Judean literary corpora is unmerited, for three reasons. First, Weitzman points to several Judean texts of Hellenistic times for which affinities with Babylonian literature have been unquestionably demonstrated.[5] Texts from the Qumran library reflect Babylonian literary traditions about the Neo-Babylonian king Nabonidus and the mythical hero Gilgamesh.[6] Other cases of Mesopotamian influence have been variously indicated in the second book of Maccabees. Thus Doron Mendels has compared the account of Antiochos's death in 2 Maccabees 9:5–27 with the "Prayer of Nabonidus" from Qumran.[7] Inasmuch as the "Prayer of Nabonidus" has also been compared with Daniel 4,[8] this small corpus of related texts is evidence that the traditions about Nabonidus circulated in different Judean circles of literati in Hellenistic times. Therefore, comparisons between Judean and Babylonian material of Hellenistic times are not incongruous per se. Second, as Victor Hurowitz's study of the literary pattern of temple building demonstrates, Babylonian literary traditions about good and wicked kings were assimilated by Judean literati's circles long before Hellenistic times.[9] If the analysis of 1 and 2 Maccabees proposed in Part I of this book is correct, these two works are evidence that in Hellenistic times the custom of using the set literary patterns of good and wicked kings to shape the portrayal of political characters was firmly entrenched in native Judean tradition. The fact that Mesopotamian literary traditions had long been acclimatized to Judean needs made Judean literati's circles all the more receptive to new influences, since the latter struck a familiar chord. Moreover, the continued flow of Judeans migrating from Babylonia to Judea in Persian and Hellenistic times undoubtedly facilitated the circulation of traditions between the two regions, though merchants and soldiers may have played a role as well, especially after Judea was incorporated into the Seleukid empire. Third, as we shall see below, some of the literary topoi contained in the persecution accounts of Daniel and 1 and 2 Maccabees are genuinely Judean.

However, as just noted, the main reason why Weitzman's analysis has had a limited impact thus far is probably the author's reluctance to propose a new historical interpretation on the basis of his literary analysis. Ultimately, he seems to subscribe to the prevailing view that Antiochos IV's behavior remains unfathomable.[10] It will be the purpose of the present chapter to show that Weitzman's innovative reading of the texts paves the way for a fresh historical analysis of the two Maccabees accounts. The previously missing analytical tool for this leap is provided by our premise that the accounts of 1 and 2 Maccabees comply with cultural and narrative codes according to which all events deemed worth remembering must be narrated from the standpoint of their impact on the temple, and the same is true with the account of Daniel as well.[11] In a nutshell, the view that Antiochos IV perpetrated a religious persecution in Judea arises from mistaking narrative form for content. When the extant literary accounts are read with the appropriate literary tools, it appears that the persecution accounts actually relate an episode of military suppression. The genesis of the narratives involved two combined processes. First, the atrocities perpetrated in the context of the military suppression are recounted in such a way as to make them both meaningful and worth remembering for the social group who had undergone this traumatic experience. In conformity with the process of semantic concatenation defined in the Methodological Introduction to Part II,[12] the accounts focus on two assertions: that the atrocities had a negative impact on the temple and that people were slain because they were faithful to their ancestral traditions. In addition, as Weitzman demonstrated, the particular historical events are reshaped according to set topics and set narrative patterns whose function it was to make them meaningful. One of these is the wicked king acting as a cult disrupter, but others may be pointed out as well, in particular the genuinely Judean topic of the Suffering Servant.

Thus our premise will be that the historical core underpinning the persecution accounts is the military repression of a popular rebellion. The present chapter considers the literary analysis that endorses this claim, leaving the historical arguments to be examined in full in Chapter 11. The decisive argument supporting this premise relates to the nature of the ancient accounts' sequencing. Admittedly, when they are read in a linear way, the accounts of 1 Maccabees 1:20–64 and 2 Maccabees 5–7 (in fact, the section 2 Macc. 5–6:11 alone needs to be considered) may easily be read as three successive chronological phases, each one corresponding to a distinct narrative unit: Antiochos's assault on Jerusalem, the Mysarch's military repression, and the religious persecution. At a closer glance, it may be shown that the texts' sequencing is topical and not chronological, meaning that they refer to three different aspects of the same historical episode. This issue will be dealt with in section 6.1 of the present chapter. The sections thereafter will offer separate literary analyses of the three primary accounts of the "persecution," Daniel 11:29–39, 1 Maccabees 1:41–64, and 2 Maccabees 6:1–11, with the aim of pinpointing the historical core in each case.[13] Starting with a linear commentary, my analysis will first analyze the literary fabric of the text by identifying its literary topoi; the second step involves assessing whether the latter are pure narrative elaboration or plausibly hint at a corresponding historical fact. The linear commentaries will be followed by shorter sections recapitulating the data, verifying these against the parallel accounts.[14]

However, before embarking upon the detailed textual analysis of the primary accounts, from the outset we need to specify the method adopted for assessing the historical value of each text's narrative components. Taking as a starting point the proposition that the acts described refer to a military suppression, we can draw from descriptions of such suppressions found elsewhere in literary sources—in particular the work of Greek historians—in order to establish a list of the sorts of repressive measures a Hellenistic king would be likely to take, along with the behavior of Persian kings in similar situations. Typically, these may be divided in three phases. First, an immediate retaliation would likely have entailed a massacre of the population (principally all able-bodied males), enslavement of the women and children, plunder of the temple,[15] and in addition burning the entire city to the ground, along with the area around it. Second, this initial phase of retaliation would have resulted in mass deportation of the survivors, especially in regions in which land was scarce. Alternatively, in an underpopulated area, the pacified population would have been allowed to remain as an indispensable working force.[16] In this case, its status as a social community would be worsened. Moreover, a military settlement (*katoikia*) may have been installed on the territory of the suppressed rebels in order to keep watch over them, with their lands confiscated, particularly the lands of the known rebels and those of the dead. Part of the land seized would have been allotted to the military settlers, with other estates used to reward locally prominent men who remained loyal to the victor during the revolt. The third phase entailed rebuilding, either in cooperation with local figures of proven loyalty or with a new, compliant leadership. It was of major interest for the king to restore peace as soon as possible in order for economic activity to resume, and with it, taxation. As we shall see in Chapters 7 and 11, some of these features are detailed by the authors of 1 and 2 Maccabees. In particular, the former cites the installation of a *katoikia* and the related land confiscations as a cause of the upheavals (§§7.4 and 11.2). Our working hypothesis holds that the persecution accounts are another way of talking about the same events.

An additional interpretive framework indispensable for rationalizing the persecution accounts is the normative behavior of the Greeks with regard to foreign deities in general, and the behavior of Greco-Macedonian kings and their armies toward the gods and goddesses of vanquished peoples in particular. In instances of uprising, the gods of the rebelling people would usually be disgraced as part of the punishments inflicted, the fate of their gods being equal to their own. There are some exceptions, however, such as Alexander's sacrifice to Herakles of Tyre after storming the city (Arrian 2.24.5). The literature shows that after the initial phase of reconquest and punishment, attitudes changed, as it was vital to return to ordinary life as soon as possible. Among the immediate steps taken were the restoration of the local temples and the resumption of regular cult practices. Although the military settlers brought their own gods with them, they were aware of the need to honor the local deity as well, since he or she was the patron of the land. Moreover, it was acknowledged that each god or goddess required honoring with his or her traditional rites. Certain gods expected specific sacrificial victims, whereas other animals were abhorrent to them, so these ritual prescriptions needed to be scrupulously respected. In short, the victors' adherence to these principles serves as a yardstick for our assessment of the historical plausibility of the extant accounts of the sins perpetrated against the temple and the Judeans.

To what extent these principles were followed will be examined in the ensuing detailed analysis of our sources, by which I will demonstrate that most of the narrative items in the persecution accounts may be explained as violent acts typically associated with military repression. In the case of certain deeds that cannot be accounted for in this way, comparative material will be used to show that such passages are formal elaborations that agree with a series of traditional literary patterns and typified catalogues used by the ancient authors to relate such events. As we saw in Chapter 2 (§2.1.2), a literary pattern is composed of a set list of narrative components. The latter form a close-knit semantic field, creating such phenomena as the synecdoche, by which a single component of a given pattern evokes the whole. In a sense, typified catalogues are generated in the opposite way, starting from an isolated item. The isolated item is then turned into the synecdoche of a literary pattern, and by this process additional narrative elements usually associated with that particular literary pattern are incorporated into the account. The outcome is a preset inventory generated from a single historical detail. The use of these catalogues is well documented in portraits of righteous and wicked kings. When a historical king left a negative memory, he was remembered not for the specific evils that he had actually committed but for the entire index of archetypal wicked actions. Set catalogues of righteous and wicked actions associated with righteous and wicked kings unquestionably became part of the Judahite/Judean tradition. Several instances of the two types of catalogues are gathered in Isaiah 9–11. As Weitzman argued, the depiction of Antiochos IV's misdemeanors in the persecution accounts was typified. Thanks to comparative literary material, it will be shown that the actions of Antiochos IV that resist all rationalization may be analyzed as exemplary components of the archetypal portrait of the wicked king.

6.1. CHRONOLOGICAL SEQUENCING, OR TOPICAL?

Since Bickerman, no one has doubted that Antiochos IV led a military repression against Jerusalem and the Judeans.[17] However, a linear and positivist reading of the accounts of 1 Maccabees 1:20–64 and 2 Maccabees 5–6:11 can easily generate the impression that three distinct historical episodes occurred. The first was Antiochos's assault on his return from Egypt, in which the king is depicted massacring the population and plundering the temple (1 Macc. 1:20–24, 2 Macc. 5:11–16); the second relates that "shortly thereafter" (2 Macc. 6:1), or "two years later" (1 Macc. 1:29), a certain "Apollonios" or "the Mysarch"[18] was responsible for a second attack (1 Macc. 1:29–35, 2 Macc. 5:21–26 or 5:23b–26). And last, the evils committed against the temple and the faithful Judeans are presented as the direct consequence of the king's edict in 1 Maccabees (1:41–64, with 2 Macc. 6:1–11). On this basis, Bickerman believed that the military suppression was followed one year later by a spate of religious persecution. Since Fergus Millar, scholars have preferred to speak of a "prohibition of the Judean customs" and have tended to see this as the religious consequence of the political overhaul that followed the military crackdown;[19] but the notion of a series of distinct episodes remains. Given that Antiochos IV led two military campaigns in Egypt—the first one between November 170 and autumn 169, and the second in the summer of 168 B.C.E.[20]—scholars disagree only about the precise timeframe of the Judean events. According to the higher chronology sketched out by Bickerman,[21] Antiochos IV's plunder of the temple occurred when he returned from his first campaign—that is, in the autumn of 169—whereas the military repression followed Jason's rebellion during the second campaign, in the summer of 168, and the religious persecution started in December 168, resulting in three distinct waves of assaults altogether. Conversely, the lower chronology proposes that Antiochos plundered the temple in the aftermath of his second campaign, in the context of his crackdown against Jason's rebellion: that is, in the summer of 168 B.C.E. The decree of "religious persecution" was issued either shortly afterwards or one year later, and the temple was desecrated in December of either 168 or 167. Lately John Ma still endorses Bickerman's distinction between Antiochos's plunder of the temple in 169 B.C.E. and the assault on Jerusalem in 168, although he combines the "religious" and political aspects that followed the latter event.[22]

Whatever their variations, all these scenarios are based on a linear reading of the sources, and one that is questionable. Not only does Daniel 11:29–39 support a different reconstruction,[23] but no less important, Greek literature offers examples showing that two juxtaposed literary units may refer to the same chronological phase apprehended from two different perspectives.[24] In the present case, the organizing principle of the three sections is topical and not chronological, their delineation serving both an ideological purpose and the culturally conditioned need to highlight the fate of the temple in the narration—since both the way of life of the Judeans and the symbolic universe of their literati are centered on the temple, narrating harmful deeds against faithful Judeans is simply an extension of the temple theme. Whereas a linear reading of the accounts leaves us with an impression of a separate instance of a religious persecution, the alternative approach substitutes for this a series of violent acts typical of a military repression, positing that what took place was a single, if composite, event, recounted at length and in such detail as one might expect from such traumatic upheavals.[25]

Let us now take a closer look at the textual evidence. The modern thesis that the military suppression was soon followed by religious persecution embraces the chronological construction of 2 Maccabees, as against that of 1 Maccabees. The author of the former explicitly situates Jason's attack on Jerusalem and the civil strife between Jason and Menelaos during Antiochos's campaign (2 Macc. 5:5–10), therefore presenting Antiochos's strike on Jerusalem as the direct consequence of Jason's outrage. This is effectively the only precise chronological landmark provided in 2 Maccabees 5. Antiochos is depicted massacring the population and plundering the temple (2 Macc. 5:11–21), and it is further added that the king left an overseer (*epistatēs*) in Jerusalem and another one on Mount Gerizim, "as well as Menelaos" to dominate his fellow citizens (2 Macc. 5:22–23). Next we hear of Apollonios's attack on Jerusalem (5:24–26), whereupon Judas makes his first entrance (5:27). While the link between Jason's and Antiochos's assaults is emphasized, the chronological outline of 2 Maccabees 5:21–27 itself is deliberately muddled. In contrast, the author inserts a somewhat vague interval between this narrative sequence and the one following with the phrase "Not long thereafter" in 2 Maccabees 6:1. Despite the elusive timeline, the author delineates three clearly distinct episodes by coupling each one with a separate wicked character. Antiochos is responsible for the first attack and "Apollonios" for the second, whereas "Geron the Athenian" is associated with the section narrating the evils done against the temple and the faithful Judeans. Read at face value, the presentation of 2 Maccabees vindicates Bickerman's thesis that the military repression and the religious persecution (6:1–11) were two distinct matters, even though the phase of the military repression is not clearly delineated (5:21–26 or 5:24–26?).

A quite different impression is given by Daniel and 1 Maccabees, however. The former appears to distinguish two phases, but certainly not three: the first is Antiochos's own attack ("He shall turn back and pay heed to those who forsake the holy covenant," Dan. 11:30),[26] and the second corresponds to both Apollonios's attack and Geron's persecution ("Forces from him will arise and profane the sanctuary of the stronghold. They shall remove the daily offering and give the abomination of the appaller [in its stead]," Dan. 11:31).[27] In turn, although the account of 1 Maccabees is composed of three narrative units and includes the idea of an interval, as in 2 Maccabees, this gap is inserted between Antiochos's offensive (1 Macc. 1:20–24) and the assault of the Mysarch ("Two years later," 1 Macc. 1:29), giving the impression that they are unrelated. In this way, the second assault appears equally as arbitrary as the first. Both attacks were unprovoked and therefore unjustified:[28] the Judeans had done nothing to merit them. In a sense, the time gap is used to reinforce the idea of surprise (1 Macc. 1:30). Moreover, this narrative structure serves to highlight three symbolically meaningful things in turn: first, the heinous profanation of the temple and slaughter of the faithful; next, the building of the Akra, emphasized by the lament (1:36–40) that follows the factual description (1:29–35);[29] and finally the violation of the Law (1:41–64). As in 2 Maccabees, each episode is ascribed to a different figure, so as to separate them even more neatly: the first to the king in person, the second to the Mysarch, whereas the third is the direct upshot of the king's edict.

It seems that Josephus was aware of the problems of the sequencing in 1 Maccabees. Given that his persecution account in *Antiquities* 12.246–56 is derivative, it is of no use in identifying the historical core of the supposed persecution. That said, Josephus was a critical reader of his sources, constantly attentive to clarifying their obscurities and inconsistencies for the benefit of his own readers. Therefore the way he reshuffled the narrative material of 1 Maccabees suggests he suspected that something in his source was amiss. To uphold the idea that Antiochos perpetrated a massacre when he took Jerusalem, he duplicated the theme of the surprise attack (*Ant.* 12.246), whereas in both 1 and 2 Maccabees (1 Macc. 1:30, 2 Macc. 5:25) the element of surprise is linked to the attack of the Mysarch alone. Moreover, for the sake of clarity, Josephus substituted the king for the obscure Mysarch as the agent of the second attack, while favoring the time lapse cited in 1 Maccabees ("two years later," *Ant.* 12.248). What is more interesting for our present concern, he relocated the episode of the temple plunder to this second attack, adding a literary embellishment of his own (12.250), and further bracketed Antiochos's prohibition of the daily sacrifices (12.251) with his temple plunder. This rejigging of the narrative material of 1 Maccabees is proof of just how shrewd a reader Josephus was. Although his ploy of linking the temple plunder and the disruption of the sacrifices is a patent departure from both 1 and 2 Maccabees, it presents an ingenious rationalization of the material and reveals that, in his view, the account in 1 Maccabees fails to provide a satisfactory explanation for this disruption. It may be worth noting that Josephus's reconstruction in fact matches the overview provided in Daniel 11:30–31. This coincidence does not mean, however, that Josephus borrowed from Daniel; he could easily have reached this solution by reasoning alone. As an exception to the rule, in our specific case Josephus's rewriting is worthy of attention. As a rule, whenever his reworking aims to clarify *political* issues, the result is blatantly anachronistic, because the political world of Hellenistic Judea was very different from his own. In contrast, given that the religious conceptions of Hellenistic and Roman times were similar, in this particular case Josephus's critical reading of his source seems highly perceptive, since in all likelihood the sacrifices *were* interrupted, because the altar itself was defiled during the military assault.

To summarize: the timeline is not identical in Daniel and in 1 and 2 Maccabees. Unlike the latter two parallel texts, the account of Daniel does not distinguish between the acts of military repression and those of "religious persecution." Whereas 1 and 2 Maccabees share the notion of a time gap between two phases, the gap is located at a different point in each work. In 1 Maccabees, it comes between the offensives of Antiochos and the Mysarch, giving the impression that they are unrelated, in line with the author's use of paratactic style to suppress causality.[30] In 2 Maccabees, however, the time gap is used to sever the wrongdoings against the temple from the rest, and moreover the narrative construction imputes Antiochos's desecration of the temple to Jason and Menelaos. Furthermore, the different sequencing of 1 and 2 Maccabees serves to highlight different topics. In 1 Maccabees, these are the desecration of the temple, the building of the Akra, and the violation of the Law; whereas in 2 Maccabees, thanks to a prolepsis Judas's first act of defense is inserted in a separate section,[31] bracketed between the account of the desecration of the temple and that of the atrocities against the people and the Law. In this way, upon closer study the accounts of 1 and 2 Maccabees are seen to be carefully constructed, their respective literary montages serving two complementary purposes: first, to show that the Judeans were innocent and that Antiochos's aggressions were unjustified; second, to keep the account of the atrocities against the temple and the faithful Judeans separate from the rest. In both works the three narrative units are divided by topic. Hence the issue is one of essence and not of chronology.

6.2. THE ACCOUNT OF DANIEL 11:29-39

The premise that will guide the linear commentary of the three primary persecution accounts found in Daniel and in 1 and 2 Maccabees is that they are parallel versions, and therefore shed light on one another. On the basis of this premise, several verses of Daniel may be given a new interpretation.

6.2.1. Linear Commentary

DANIEL 11:29-30[32]

[29] At the time appointed he shall return and come into the south, but this time it shall not be as it was before. [30] For ships of Kittim shall come against him, and he shall lose heart and withdraw. He will return and rage against the holy covenant. He shall turn back and attend to those who abandon the holy covenant.

Commentary.[33]   Verse 29 is understood to refer to Antiochos IV's second campaign in Egypt, in 168 B.C.E. The "Kittim" (*Kitioi*) of verse 30 are the Romans. "He will return and rage against the holy covenant" seems to refer to Antiochos IV's assault on Jerusalem when he left Egypt. (Cf. 1 Macc. 1:20-24, 2 Macc. 5:11-16.) "Holy covenant" here may refer to the population, and therefore to a massacre, but more probably refers to both the components of the divine covenant, namely the people and the temple. If this is correct, the passage may well allude to the massacre and plunder. "He shall turn back and attend to those who abandon the holy covenant" may refer to the same event as 2 Maccabees 5:23, which claims that after his assault Antiochos appointed Menelaos as the local leader of the Judeans. The vocabulary used in this sentence recalls 1 Maccabees 1:11-15, which equates the Israelites who instituted the *gymnasion* with lawless men making a covenant with the gentiles. The prominent men who remained loyal to the king are deemed disloyal not only to their people but to the holy covenant, because people and deity cannot be dissociated.

DANIEL 11:31

Forces from him will arise and profane the sanctuary of the stronghold. They shall remove the daily offering and give the abomination of the appaller [in its stead].

Commentary. "Forces from him" may refer to the Mysarch's expedition to Jerusalem described in 1 Maccabees 1:29–40 and 2 Maccabees 5:24–26. If it is correct, Daniel's chronological outline differs from the two Greek sources". (See further below, §6.2.2.) Moreover, its chronological outline offers a plausible, rational context for the disruption of the daily offering:[34] the context of the military attack ("They shall remove the daily offering").

"Profane the sanctuary of the stronghold." According to John Collins, the temple was fortified. It is called a "fortress" in 1 Chronicles 29:1, 19.

"And give the abomination of the appaller." As Johann Lust demonstrated, Daniel's celebrated "Abomination of the Desolation" was a sacrifice and not a statue, whereas the Greek literal translation of the phrase in 1 Maccabees (1:54, 59) seems to denote the "idol altar" (*bōmos*), which was upon the temple altar (*thysiastērion*).[35] Moreover, when an "abomination" (*šiḳuṣ*) receives a further definition in the Hebrew literature, "it is always either a suffixed personal pronoun or a proper noun joined to *šiḳuṣ* in the construct state and referring to the collectivity of those who use or venerate the abomination in question in their cultic practices." According to this rule, "the Desolation" is a derogatory term for Antiochos and may be translated as "the appaller."[36] In truth, Lust's commentary leaves open the possibility that the term targets not only the king but also "the collectivity" of his partisans: that is, all the groups who in one way or another were associated with the settlement that followed the suppression. That would include Menelaos, the high priest. According to Lust, the daily offering was removed and replaced with an abomination, but his suggestion—on the basis of 1 Maccabees 1:47—that this abomination involved the sacrifice of swine is implausible: all the more so if we identify "the Desolation" as a collectivity potentially including the prominent Judean men who remained loyal to the king.[37]

DANIEL 11:32A

He will seduce those who violate the covenant with flattery.

Commentary. This image is a topos. Collins compares this clause with 1 Maccabees 2:18 and further points out that the expression "violators of the covenant" is found in 1QM 1:2.[38] However, the topos should perhaps be read as a narrative component of the theme of the Persecuted Servant, which appears in the following verse. On the basis of 1 and 2 Maccabees, the topos may be used here as a coded allusion to Menelaos and the Antiochenes, but this is uncertain.[39]

DANIEL 11:32B-35

[32b] But the people who know [i.e., are loyal to] their God shall stand firm and take action. [33] The teachers [maśkilim] among the people will instruct the common people ["the many"]; for some days, however, they shall fall by the sword and flame, and suffer captivity and plunder. [34] When they fall they will receive little help, and many will join them insincerely. [35] Some of the wise shall fall, to refine and purify and make them white, until the time of the end, for there is still an interval until the time appointed.

Commentary. This passage is a long reference to the theme of the Suffering Servant (or the Persecution of the Righteous), deriving from Isaiah 52–53. This topos was abundantly invoked in the Judean literature of Hellenistic times "as a paradigm of humiliation and exaltation" and is found in numerous works of the time.[40] In particular, the theme of the Suffering Servant was grafted onto the prototypical Qumran figure of the Teacher of Righteousness, known from the Commentaries on the Prophets (Pesharim) and the Hymns of the Teacher (Hodayot, 1QH cols. 10–16).[41] The theme appears in the persecution account of 1 Maccabees (1:56–57) and again in Daniel 12:3. Likewise, the similarity between this insistent reference to the Suffering Servant in Daniel and the key role assigned to the exemplary dead (the so-called martyrs) in 2 Maccabees is striking.

DANIEL 11:36

The king will do as he wishes. He shall exalt himself and consider himself greater than any god, and shall speak horrendous things against the God of gods. He shall prosper until the period of wrath is completed, for what is determined shall be done.

Commentary. This verse reads as the archetypal description of the sinful king. Collins has compared it to similar images in Daniel 7:8, 20; 8:4, 10, 11; and 11:2, 16.[42] Should we read an allusion to the royal cult into this verse?

DANIEL 11:37-38

[37] He shall pay no respect to the gods of his ancestors, or to the [god] beloved by women; he shall pay no respect to any other god, for he shall consider himself greater than all. [38] He shall honor the god of strongholds instead of these; a god whom his fathers did not know he shall honor with gold and silver, with precious stones and costly gifts.

Commentary. The coded allusion here has puzzled modern commentators. Three elements of interpretation may tentatively be suggested. First, the statements "he shall pay no respect to the gods of his ancestors" and "a god whom his fathers did not know he shall honor with gold and silver, with precious stones and costly gifts," must be read in the light of similar statements in biblical texts referring to sinful

Israelite kings. The ancient Judean definition of the devious cultic behavior (what modern scholars inappropriately call their "idolatry") of these kings stresses that the gods honored were "gods whom their fathers did not know," whereas for the Judeans, YHWH is the "god of their ancestors."[43] Second, "he shall pay no respect to any other god, for he shall consider himself greater than all," may tentatively be read as an allusion to the royal cult. Third, the mention of the "god of strongholds" needs to be compared with "the sanctuary of the stronghold" of 11:31. The stronghold must be identical in both cases. On the basis of this assumption, the clause "He shall honor the god of strongholds instead of these" is probably to be interpreted in the light of 2 Maccabees 6:2.[44] According to this reading, Daniel 11:37–38 stigmatizes Antiochos IV's sinful pretension to honor the god of Jerusalem instead of his own gods and in the place of the Judeans, who are the lawful worshippers of the god of Jerusalem, since He is the god of their ancestors. Moreover, the passage seems to allude to the institution of a sacrifice that was performed on the twenty-fifth day of each month (1 Macc. 1:59), the date of the king's birthday (2 Macc. 6:7).[45] The sacrifice must have been made in his name rather than to him, as in the Greek royal cult. However, given that this sacrifice was the explicit counterpart of the royal cult of the Greek poleis, the author of Daniel exploits this detail to indict Antiochos.

The allusion to "the [god] beloved by women" is as obscure as the reference to Dionysos in 2 Maccabees 6:7. In both cases, we probably have allusions to rites that were performed by the foreign military settlers. The god here may well be Dionysos, who was worshipped by *thiasoi* of women, the *Bacchai*.

DANIEL 11:39

He will act for those who fortify strongholds, the people of a strange god. Those who acknowledge him he will make more wealthy, and will make them rule over the common people and divide the land as their wages.

Commentary. The first sentence seems to allude to the building of the Akra and to the foreigners who honored the god of the stronghold (i.e., of the sanctuary of Jerusalem) under the name Zeus Olympios. The second sentence has famously been taken by Bickerman to refer to the confiscation of land for the benefit of the military settlers.[46]

6.2.2. *The Literary and Historical Value of Daniel's Account*

Altogether, the interpretation of Daniel 11:29–39 above ties in with the notion that the persecution accounts are basically descriptions of atrocities carried out in the context of military repression. The factual elements pinpointed to sustain this argument may be summarized as follows.

The account of Daniel treats the assaults of Antiochos IV and Apollonios (i.e., the Mysarch) as a single conceptual unit including the profanation of the temple, the interruption of the daily offering, and its replacement with a sacrifice hailed as impure, affirming a timeline that is notably different from that of 1 and 2 Maccabees. Following Bickerman's contention that the military repression and the religious persecution were two distinct episodes, modern scholars usually take it for granted that the correct chronological outline is that of the parallel Greek works, whereas Daniel is seen to lump the data together.[47] Yet, as we saw above (§6.1), Josephus's shrewd reordering of the events in 1 Maccabees suggests that Daniel's scenario actually makes much better sense.

The first of the three basic topics covered in Daniel 11:29–39 is the desecration of the temple. This theme includes the profanation of the temple, the interruption of the daily sacrifice, and its replacement with an "abomination of the appaller": that is, an impure sacrifice instituted by Antiochos, the rededication of the temple, the fact that the king honored the god of Jerusalem despite this not being his ancestral god, and last, a sacrifice in honor of the king's birthday(?). It is excluded that the impure sacrifice instituted by Antiochos involved swine, given that all ancient peoples of the Mediterranean and Near East area firmly believed that each god and goddess should be honored according to the specific cultic requirements they themselves had prescribed to men. Given that a sacrifice was a means of communication between men and gods, it was nonsense to choose any means of communication rejected by the divine addressee. That said, as 4QMMT shows, there were occasions on which the sacrifice of the ritually designated animal could result in an abomination through other violations: for instance, if the sacrifice were made by priests in a state of impurity or not wearing the appropriate garments. Likewise each sacrifice had its prescribed time of execution, and time limitations also applied to its consumption. Moreover, insofar as ritual regulations are never secluded from social and political considerations, it is plausible that a sacrifice that would have been subsidized by Antiochos and performed in his name by Menelaos, the wicked high priest, would have been automatically considered an abomination by the defeated rebels. According to modern commentators, the Qumran community held the Jerusalem temple as defiled precisely for this sort of mixed political and ritual quarrel. We might venture that the cited sacrifice in honor of the king's birthday and the "abomination of the appaller (or appallers)" are one and the same, although the accounts leave room for alternative suggestions. For Judean worshippers, the disruption of the daily burnt offering was a traumatic affair, just as the removal of cultic statues in Mesopotamian (and Egyptian) temples were.[48] Therefore it is not surprising that this event is given prominent attention in this passage. In truth, the discontinuation of the daily offering is a central topic in Daniel (8:11–14; 9:27; 12:11), to the point that it may be surmised that the whole book was written in response to this specific event. Its reference in 12:11 is part of the concluding verses of the book as a whole (12:9–13).

The second of the three basic topics covered is the persecution of the people, which is cast in the literary topos of the Persecuted Faithful Ones and the Suffering

Teacher (or Teachers). Last, various references target the soldiers of the Akra, including a direct mention of the land confiscations and the presence of the soldiers of the Akra. The detailed historical reconstruction of this situation will be explored later, in Chapter 11 (§§11.2–3).

One last remark is worth adding. The modern view that the author of Daniel is against armed struggle seems to derive from a literal (and modern) reading of the verses in this work that allegedly extol nonviolent resistance—for instance, that of the *maśkilim* or wise men (11:33).[49] The Persecution of the Righteous, or the Suffering Servant, is a topos that stems from the corpus of Isaiah's prophecies and was widely used in the Hebrew and Greek literature of Judea in Hellenistic times. When Daniel is compared against 1 and 2 Maccabees, it is tempting to see a connection between the Suffering Teacher of Daniel and the martyrs of 2 Maccabees. As Weitzman has pointed out, Eleazar, whose exemplary death is told in 2 Maccabees 6:18–31, is presented as a scribe (6:18).[50] Not only does the author of 2 Maccabees extol the heroism of the faithful who chose an exemplary death, but he claims that their self-sacrifice was instrumental in turning God's wrath to mercy (2 Macc. 8:2–5). However, it would be absurd to infer from the pointed attention given to the Suffering Righteous (the so-called martyrs) in 2 Maccabees that the author had reservations about armed struggle. It is unclear why the author of Daniel, contrary to those of 1 and 2 Maccabees, should consider that righteous action and armed struggle are incompatible. In the Judean conception of the world, sinners are always punished by God, but God always uses men as agents of His wrath. Similarly, the righteous are vindicated by God, who again uses human agents to carry out His divine purpose. Therefore the difference is not one of worldview but one of emphasis, possibly due to the differing literary genres.

6.3. THE ACCOUNT OF 1 MACCABEES 1:41–64

6.3.1. Linear Commentary

1 MACCABEES 1:41–42

[41] The king wrote to all his kingdom, for all to become one people [42] and for each to abandon his own customs. All the gentiles agreed to the terms of the king's proclamation.

Commentary. If we follow Weitzman's analysis, the sentence introducing the persecution account in 1 Maccabees casts Antiochos IV as the archetype of the wicked king who, instead of acting as the agent of cult restoration, disrupts the cultic order. The theme of the king sending letters to all his kingdom is found variously in Hebrew Judean literature (e.g., Esther 1:20, 22; 3:12–15; Daniel 3:2–7).[51] However, in the Judean cultural context, the king's writing to all the people of his kingdom invoking them to become one may have been the author's way of indicting the king with hybris. To quote Daniel 11:36: the wicked king "exalts himself and considers himself greater than any god," and, as in Daniel 8:11, "he grew great even up to the prince of the host [i.e., God]."[52] In this way, 1 Maccabees 1:41–42 seems an inversion of the theme of all the nations' knowing that YHWH restored His temple, characteristic of Ezekiel's prophecies (36:23, 36; 37:28; 39:7).[53] The theme of the universal kingdom of God, of which these verses of 1 Maccabees seem to be an inverted mirror, is found in the book of Daniel (7:13–14; cf. also the introduction to the "Epistle of Enoch," 1 Enoch 92:1).[54] In Daniel 7, Antiochos equates himself with God, and whereas this claim is plainly expressed in Daniel 11:39, in 1 Maccabees 1:41–42 it is given a novelized rendering.

Actually the two themes of the king as agent of cult restoration and of universal acknowledgment appear to be merged in other Judean texts of Hellenistic times, most remarkably in Qumran texts featuring the prototypical figure of the Teacher of Righteousness. As we saw above (§6.2.1, Daniel 11:32b–35, *Commentary*), the Teacher of Righteousness is shaped after the Servant of Isaiah 52–53. The earliest commentators of the Qumran literature pointed out that the Teacher-Servant of the Qumran community had the function of restoring the true covenant of Israel.[55] The following verse from the Hymns (Hodayot) refers to the Teacher (1QH 14:12):[56]

And all nations shall know your truth, and all peoples your glory.

In Ben Sira (46:6), this topic is applied to Joshua:

He overwhelmed that nation in battle,
and on the slope he destroyed his opponents, so that the nations might know his armament,
that he was fighting in the sight of the Lord,
for he was a devoted follower of the Mighty One.

The first two verses of the persecution account of 1 Maccabees are the inverted version of a theme found in contemporary literature.

In a historical perspective, the literary topos of the king's letter could have been called in by any royal decree ordering a punishing measure, like the installation of the military settlement and the confiscation of estate properties to the benefit of the soldiers, or conversely any edict concerning the temple of Jerusalem.

1 MACCABEES 1:43

Many Israelites, too, accepted his religion and sacrificed to idols and violated the Sabbath.

Commentary. The theme of the Israelites' adopting the gods of the gentiles is also found in the description of the *gymnasion* in 1 Maccabees 1:11–15. As we saw in

Chapter 5 (§5.1.3), it is stereotypical, borrowing from expressions used in various biblical passages to refer to those who followed gods other than YHWH. The topic is found in other texts from Hellenistic times—for instance, in Daniel 11:14, as well as in the Apocalypse of Weeks inserted in 1 Enoch 92–104.[57] In other texts, the motif of the Israelites' following other gods is reinterpreted to stigmatize Israelites' following distinct ritual traditions. Thus we read in the Nahum Pesher, from Qumran (frgs. 3–4, col. 1, ll. 1–2):

> [* * *] 'Where the lion went to enter, the lion's cub [* * *] [and no one to disturb.' Its interpretation concerns Deme]trios, king of Greece, who sought to enter Jerusalem on the advice of the Seekers-after-Smooth-Things.

In the specific context of 1 Maccabees, the theme of the unfaithful Israelites is associated with the zealous figures of Phineas, Joshua, and Caleb (1 Macc. 2:54, 56; cf. Ben Sira 45:23; 46:7). Both in the description of the *gymnasion* and in that of the persecution in 1 Maccabees, Jason and Menelaos (who are never named) are styled as typical Israelite idol worshippers. The historical reality that underpins the literary topos is Jason's personal allegiance to Antiochos IV, which was manifested in his coup against Onias III and the politicization of Jerusalem,[58] and Menelaos's political faithfulness to Antiochos IV at the time of the popular revolt.

1 MACCABEES 1:44–50

[44] The king sent letters by messengers to Jerusalem and the towns of Judah containing orders to follow customs foreign to the land, [45] to put a stop to burnt offerings and meal offering and libation in the temple, to violate Sabbaths and festivals, [46] to defile temple and holy things, [47] to build illicit altars and illicit temples and idolatrous shrines, to sacrifice swine and ritually unfit animals, [48] to leave their sons uncircumcised, and to draw abominations upon themselves by means of all kinds of uncleanness and profanations, [49] so as to forget the Torah and violate all the commandments. [50] Whoever disobeyed the work of the king was to be put to death.

Commentary. This sequence is a textbook inventory of wicked actions employed to transform Antiochos IV into an archetypical cult disrupter. In this case, the theme of the royal letter here and in 1 Maccabees 1:41 are doublets. The genesis of this catalogue of ills may be easily reconstructed. It hinges on the historical fact that atrocities were perpetrated, including genuine punishing measures, though none of the evildoings in this list can be reasonably identified as a genuinely historical measure. In other words, the historical events have been entirely reworked to fit a recognized literary pattern in order to make them meaningful. The items in the list may be sorted into two categories: measures that, albeit not intended as a punishment, undoubtedly shocked the vanquished rebels, such as the building of illicit altars; and stereotyped actions that have no historical basis but are called in as standard narrative elements of the set pattern. The order to profane the Sabbath and the festivals, along with the prohibition of circumcision and the Sabbath, are the most obvious instances. As the narrative pattern requires, the range of atrocities is presented as intentional action decreed by the wicked king to persecute the faithful. As we saw above (§6.2.1 at Daniel 11:32b–35), the Persecution of the Faithful is a widely popular theme in Judean literature of Hellenistic times. It is documented both in texts originating in Judea and in texts written in diaspora communities, like 3 Maccabees. The catalogue items may be briefly reviewed:

"To put a stop to burnt offerings and meal offering and libation in the temple, to violate Sabbaths and festivals, to defile temple and holy things" (1:45–46): A military assault on Jerusalem would likely occasion the profanation of the temple. In particular, the three primary sources concur that Antiochos IV plundered the temple when he returned from Egypt, and acts entailing the profanation of the temple and the altar could easily have occurred in the course of this episode, causing all sacrifices to be discontinued: not only the daily offerings and the libations but also the sacrifices of the Sabbaths and festivals.

"To build illicit altars and illicit temples and idolatrous shrines" (1:47a): Cf. 1 Maccabees 1:54–55, below. Logically, the military settlers would have built altars for their own use. The historical aspect of this topic will be discussed in full in Chapter 11 (§11.3).

"To sacrifice swine and ritually unfit animals" (1:47b): The topos seems to bracket two distinct deeds together—the sacrifices performed by the newcomers on their own altars and those performed in the Jerusalem temple. In the former case, these become sacrifices of swine, these being the ultimate signifier of what is deemed a "ritually unfit" sacrifice. In the latter case, any sacrifices performed at a defiled altar is automatically deemed unfit. As we saw above (§6.2.1 at Daniel 11:37–38), the sacrifices were resumed, which must mean that a new altar was built in replacement, although some of the Judeans did not consider this altar clean, because a sacrifice in honor of the king's birthday was performed on it. This contamination rendered all sacrifices performed on this altar abominations for those who continued the rebellion, even though they were ritually fit from Menelaos's viewpoint. Ritual quarrels of this sort are well known in this period. (Cf. 4QMMT.)

"To leave their sons uncircumcised, and to draw abominations upon themselves by means of all kinds of uncleanness and profanations, so as to forget the Torah and violate all the commandments" (1:48–49): According to Fredrik Barth's definition of ethnicity, circumcision may be defined as an identity marker of Judean society in Hellenistic times.[59] It is not surprising, therefore, that the prohibition of circumcision became emblematic for any form of pressure upon the community of the Judeans in this period. The cultural codes[60] of the Judean literati, furthermore, required the emblematic topic to refer to either the temple or the covenant in some way, and circumcision perfectly suited this need. Given that, in historical terms, the idea that Antiochos prohibited circumcision is totally implausible, the entire passage of 1 Maccabees 1:48–49 is certain to be a pure literary elaboration.

"Whoever disobeyed the work of the king was to be put to death" (1:50): Judeans who attempted to resist were certainly put to death during the repression. However, in line with the aforesaid cultural codes, the cause of their death is reworked, with the victims becoming the faithful ones who died for the Law—or, to use the terminology of 2 Maccabees, for *Ioudaïsmos*.

As we shall see, the persecution account of 1 Maccabees includes several topical doublets between the catalogue of 1 Maccabees 1:44–50 and the vignettes that precede and follow: the illicit altars (1:47a, 54b), the illicit offerings (1:47b, 55), the prohibition of circumcision (referred to twice: 1:48, 60–61), the Sabbath (1:43, 45).

1 MACCABEES 1:51–52

[51] Letters to the same effect he wrote to all his kingdom, and he appointed officers to watch over all the people and sent orders to the towns of Judah to offer sacrifices in every town. [52] Many from among the people gathered around the officers, every forsaker of the Torah, and they committed wicked acts in the land.

Commentary. Most of the topics included in these verses form doublets with the themes of 1 Maccabees 1:44–50, transposing the same wicked actions to a new arena, the "towns of Judah." This widening of the perspective from Jerusalem to the towns of Judea, however, may also be a literary elaboration, or a recasting of the atrocities perpetrated in the countryside in symbolically significant images. The most probable issue behind these verses is the wave of land confiscations. As will be argued in Chapter 7 (§7.4.3), the mention of illicit altars in the countryside in 1 Maccabees seems to be a coded reference to the land confiscations.

1 MACCABEES 1:53

And drove Israel into hiding places in all their places of refuge.

Commentary. These hiding places appear anew in 1 Maccabees 2:27–38. They are likely to be identical with the caves cited at 2 Maccabees 6:11a. See the relevant commentary.

1 MACCABEES 1:54A

On the fifteenth day of Kislev in 145 [S.E.] the king had a desolating abomination built upon the altar.

Commentary. Compare Daniel 11:31, with relevant commentary, as well as 1 Maccabees 1:59, below.

1 MACCABEES 1:54B–55

[54b] And in the outlying towns of Judah they built illicit altars, [55] and at the doors of the houses and in the squares they offered illicit sacrifices.

Commentary. Compare 1 Maccabees 1:47. The theme of the illicit altars is widened to the towns of Judah.

1 MACCABEES 1:56–57

[56] Whatever scrolls of the Torah they found, they tore up and burned; [57] and whoever was found with a scroll of the covenant in his possession or showed his love for the Torah, the king's decree put him to death.

Commentary. These verses appeal to the theme of the Suffering Teacher that is given prominence in the parallel account of Daniel. See in particular Daniel 11:33–34, with the commentary above. Compare further the character of Eleazar in 2 Maccabees 6:18. It may be assumed that the passage shapes the massacre of the Judeans who took part to the resistance to the military repression according to the appropriate cultural codes. The dimension of a broader armed struggle is erased.

The reference to the Torah scrolls gives a specifically Judean twist to 1 Maccabees' stereotyped catalogue of evildoings. As several scholars have argued, since Persian times Judean scribes imagined their society as a text-centered community, in which the book (i.e., a preset collection of written laws) was indispensable to the proper operation of the temple cult.[61] In this sense, the Torah scrolls played a similar role as statues did in Babylonian cult.[62] Moreover, as Christophe Nihan has argued, proper worship required priestly interpretation of the authoritative texts.[63] This tenet may explain the conflation of the reference to the scrolls with the theme of the Suffering Teacher in these two verses.

1 MACCABEES 1:58

Through their strength they acted against the Israelites who were found in the towns each month.

Commentary. Compare Daniel 11:32b ("but the people who know [i.e., are loyal to] their God shall stand firm and take action"). As in Daniel, the reference to the persecuted Judeans is narrowly associated with the theme of the Suffering Servant (or Teacher of Righteousness: Dan. 11:33–35, 1 Macc. 1:46–47) as a narrative device enabling the ancient authors to recount the suppression of the armed resistance—according to the ancient Judean cultural codes, this required yoking it to a symbolically meaningful image. Similarly, in 1 Maccabees the Israelites are transformed into defenseless victims throughout the persecution account. More specifically, in 1 Maccabees 2:27–38 the motif of defenselessness is recast into a pious abstention from warfare during the Sabbath. It is not excluded that these variations on the motifs of the Suffering Servant and Persecuted Faithful are exploited in 1 Maccabees as justification for armed struggle of the Maccabees. This would add a political twist to the author's use of these cultural codes.

> 1 MACCABEES 1:59
>
> As on the twenty-fifth day of the month they would offer sacrifices on the illicit altar, which was upon the temple altar.

Commentary. The "illicit altar, which was upon the temple altar," matches the "abomination" of 1 Maccabees 1:54a and Daniel 11:31. Whereas in Daniel the expression denotes a new sacrifice that allegedly replaces the daily offering, the present phrase in 1 Maccabees speaks of an "idol altar" (*bōmos*) built upon (*epi*) the temple altar (*thysiastērion*).[64] Realistically speaking, it is more probable that the incriminated altar was set up in the place of the existing temple altar. Its dubbing as an "idol altar" may be seen as invective aimed at the builder of the altar, not an objective description. The builder must be Menelaos, not the king, but the king may have been contacted in order to get his consent, and he may also have subsidized the replacement of the desecrated altar with a new one. Any form of royal involvement in the process would have resulted in the present literary transformation of the new altar into an idol altar. Alternatively, the invective may aim at otherizing Menelaos as the king's ally. In the same way, as we saw in Chapter 5 (§5.1.4), the semantic field of *Hellēnismos* in 2 Maccabees applies to Jason.[65]

The sacrifice performed "on the twenty-fifth day of the month" seems to match the sacrifice performed on the king's birthday of 2 Maccabees 6:7.[66] As we saw above, Daniel 11:37–38 may include one more allusion to this sacrifice.

> 1 MACCABEES 1:60–61
>
> [60] The women who had their sons circumcised they put to death according to the decree, [61] hanging the babes from their mother's necks and executing also their husbands and the men who had performed the circumcisions.

Commentary. On the theme of the prohibition of circumcision see the commentary above to 1 Maccabees 1:47, as well as 1:54b–55. The theme of circumcision plays a prominent role in 1 Maccabees. The image of the men persecuted because they had performed the circumcisions may be a variation of the theme of the Suffering Teacher (Daniel's *maśkilim* of 11:31). However, within 1 Maccabees it more specifically prepares the way to Mattathias's pious actions, since in 2:46 he is shown circumcising the uncircumcised babes. It may be worth noting that Mattathias is shown destroying the illicit altars as well in this passage (1 Macc. 2:45). The narrow association between the two topics evinces the conceptual link between faithfulness to the temple and to the laws.

The motif of mothers persecuted together with their sons may recall the story of the Mother and Her Seven Sons of 2 Maccabees 7.

1 MACCABEES 1:62–63

[62] Many Israelites strongly and steadfastly refused to eat forbidden food. [63] They chose death in order to escape defilement by foods and in order to keep from violating the holy covenant, and they were put to death.

Commentary. This last vignette is another variation on the motif of the Persecuted Faithful. This time it appeals to the topic of abstention from forbidden food. In light of its popularity in Judean literature of Hellenistic times both in Judea and the diaspora, it seems that the dietary laws had become as important an ethnic marker as circumcision for the Judeans of this period.[67] Cf. 2 Maccabees 5:27; Daniel 1:8, 12; Judith 12:1–2; and the Letter of Aristeas 139–71 and 181–86.

6.3.2. *The Literary and Historical Value of the Account of 1 Maccabees*

Although the interpretation above opts for a maximalist rationalization, associating almost every evildoing included in the persecution account with a possible historical deed, "maximalist" does not mean "literal." Antiochos did offer a sacrifice, and this sacrifice was rejected as impure by those in Judea who were his opponents, but Antiochos never sacrificed swine. Moreover, a few items clearly defy rationalization: no one forced the Judeans to eat forbidden foods. In the same way, Nabû-šuma-iškun never forced the priests of Nabu's Ezida temple of Borsippa to eat leeks, a food forbidden to them.[68] In the latter cases, the evildoing is a purely literary creation, based on the inversion of a fundamental value (swine as the emblematic impure animal in Judea; the prohibition for the priests of the Ezida temple to eat leeks).

As a result, the account may be read at two levels. One level consists in identifying the historical core. The interpretation offered above aims to vindicate our working hypothesis that the historical context of the persecution account is one of military repression and to substantiate the view that the accounts of Daniel and 1 Maccabees allude to the same topics, albeit each one in its own style. By this logic, the difference between the two accounts is one of literary genre rather than content: whereas Daniel's account tends to be more symbolic, and therefore its descriptions more allusive, 1 Maccabees is more novelistic. Generically, 1 Maccabees is closer to the books of Esther, Judith, and 3 Maccabees—as well as 2 Maccabees.

The account in 1 Maccabees may also be read at another level. It has been argued that the stories of persecution stemming from the Greek-speaking diasporas of Hellenistic and early Roman times (such as 3 Maccabees) and the court stories of Esther and Daniel did not reflect genuine persecutions but had the function of strengthening the identity of the community producing them.[69] The texts offered an occasion to articulate the values of the community, which its members should be ready to die for rather than relinquish. By this logic, the persecution account of 1 Maccabees lies midway between diaspora texts fulfilling this function and Mesopotamian priestly reflections detailing which actions are emblematic of the righteous king that generated the typified catalogues surveyed by Weitzman. The community values to be defended with one's life correspond to three identity markers contained in the account of 1 Maccabees, and these are circumcision (1:48, 61–61), the Sabbath (1:43, 45), and the dietary laws (1:62–63).

6.4. THE ACCOUNT OF 2 MACCABEES 6:1-11
6.4.1. Linear Commentary

2 MACCABEES 6:1

Not long thereafter the king sent Geron . . . to compel the Judeans to depart from their ancestral laws and to cease living by the laws of God.

Commentary. As in 1 Maccabees, the first verse of the persecution account of 2 Maccabees introduces the topic of the persecution and names the cult disrupter. In contrast with 1 Maccabees, however, an official replaces the king. The reason for this substitution has been suggested above (§6.1), where I argue that the author of 2 Maccabees creates a clear distinction between the three episodes of the temple plunder, the second massacre, which prompted Judas to withdraw from Jerusalem to organize the armed resistance, and the evildoings against the temple and the faithful Judeans by associating each one with a distinct character: Antiochos, Apollonios, and Geron the Athenian. If we leave this variation aside, the sentence is parallel to 1 Maccabees 1:41–42. As in 1 Maccabees, the account of 2 Maccabees is constructed in a way that turns traumatic memories into a catalogue of intentional evildoings assigned to the cult disrupter.

2 MACCABEES 6:2

He was also to defile both the temple in Jerusalem and the temple on Mount Gerizim and to proclaim the former to be the temple of Zeus Olympios and the latter to be the temple of Zeus Xenios according to the petition of the inhabitants of the place.

Commentary. The content of this vignette is unparalleled in 1 Maccabees. As suggested, Daniel 11:37–38 reads as an allusion to the fact that Antiochos IV honored the patron deity of Jerusalem, but the change of name could by no means be inferred from Daniel alone. Not only is the information that the Greek settlers identified the patron deity of Jerusalem as Zeus Olympios perfectly plausible from a historical point of view,[70] but the topic is hard to reduce to a set literary topos. The reason why the temple of Mount Gerizim is mentioned is obscure.

2 MACCABEES 6:3

The execution of the wicked project brought suffering and indignation to all.

Commentary. The topic of gentiles' sharing the same feelings of indignation as the faithful Judeans is found elsewhere in 2 Maccabees. (Cf. 4:35, 49.) It may perhaps be understood as an emplotted inversion of the theme found in Ezekiel, where the gentiles acknowledge that YHWH restored His temple.[71]

2 MACCABEES 6:4

The peoples filled the temple with debauchery and revelry, as they lolled with prostitutes and had intercourse with women in the sacred courts and also brought forbidden things inside.

Commentary. This verse has sometimes been read as evidence that the Seleukid soldiers were basically Syrians, who instituted in the Jerusalem temple the rite of sacred prostitution practiced in Syrian temples.[72] Leaving aside the vexed question of whether the rite of sacred prostitution genuinely existed or not,[73] the literary features of the persecution account of 2 Maccabees suggest an alternative interpretation. Several items in 2 Maccabees 6:1–11 seem to derive either from a ritual practice or from a ritual concept, which is inverted and emplotted. Thus the image of the Judeans forced to eat forbidden food emplots a forced transgression of the dietary laws. By this logic the vignette of the peoples having intercourse with prostitutes in the sacred courts emplots the transgression of the prohibition of fornication. Two topics from the Halachic literature of the time may underpin the fantasy of 2 Maccabees 6:4.[74] First, in the Halachic literature, the notion of fornication refers to forbidden marriages. The marriage regulations concerning the priests were particularly strict, precisely because the latter had access to the most sacred areas of the temple courts. This explains why they are explicitly referred to in the Testament of Levi (one of the Testaments of the Twelve Patriarchs), Levi, the third son of Jacob and Leah, being the ancestor of all the priests.[75] In the Prayer of Levi found in the Aramaic manuscript of Qumran, the prohibition of priestly fornication is recorded alongside unrighteous spirit and evil thought, evincing its importance.[76] Thus it is not surprising that the notion of fornication was most particularly associated with the priests and the area of the altar whose sacredness the laws aimed to protect. Another echo of this is found in the Psalms of Solomon (2:11, 13), of Hellenistic times.[77] In 2 Maccabees 6:4 the fantasy of people having intercourse with prostitutes in the area of the sacred courts dramatizes the theme of transgression in two ways: prostitutes are the most emblematic category of forbidden women, and having intercourse in the temple is a dramatic representation of forbidden marriage, leading to prohibited intercourse not only at home but also in the temple. Alternatively, the genesis of the episode may lie in a distinct exploitation of the notion of inappropriate sexual intercourse, which is illustrated in 4QMMT. The relevant passage reads as follows (4QMMT, Composite Text, ll. 3–9):[78]

> [And concerning the sowed gifts of the] new wheat grains of the [gentiles, which they * * *] and let their [* * *] touch it and de[file it, and no one should eat] any of the new wheat grain of t[he gen]tiles, [nor] should it be brought into the sanctuary. [And concerning the sacrifice of the purification offering] that they cook in a [copper] vessel [and that they * * *] in it the flesh of their sacrifices, and that they [* * *] in the temple court(?) [and that they * * *] it with the broth of their sacrifices. And concerning the sacrifice of the gentiles: [we are of the opinion that they] sacrifice to the [* * *] that it is like (a woman) who whored with him.

The passage tables particularly strict rulings for the offerings of the gentiles. Two of the notions mentioned may have been conflated in 2 Maccabees 6:4. One is the prohibition of bringing specific goods associated with gentiles into the sanctuary; the second is the equation between the sacrifice of the gentiles and having intercourse with a prostitute. In other words, the image of 2 Maccabees 6:4 may be a fanciful literary elaboration based on the sort of metaphorical representation of a Halachic concept such as "it is like (a woman) who whored with him," used in 4QMMT.

The picture of "the peoples ... [bringing] forbidden things inside the temple courts" in 2 Maccabees 6:4 was perhaps generated in a similar way. In *Antiquities* 12.145–46, for example, Josephus gives the text of a royal decree that he ascribes to Antiochos III, which enforces the view that the sacred area around the temple extended to the entire city of Jerusalem (*Ant.* 12.145–46):[79]

> It is unlawful for any foreigner to enter the enclosure of the temple, which is forbidden to the Judeans.... Nor shall anyone bring into the city the flesh of horses or of mules or of wild or tame asses, or of leopards, foxes or hares or, in general, of any animal forbidden to the Judeans. Nor is it lawful to bring in their skins or even to breed any of these animals in the city. But only the sacrificial animals known to their ancestors and necessary for the propitiation of God shall they be permitted to use.

A Halachic opinion reflected in 4QMMT offers an interesting cross-reference with the royal decree (4QMMT, Composite Text, ll. 29–31):

And we are of the opinion that the sanctuary [is the "tent of meeting"] and that Jerusalem is the "camp," and that "outside the camp" [is outside Jerusalem], that is, the encampment of their settlements.

The geographical delineation of the three areas (tent of meeting, camp, and outside the camp) was crucial for ritual practice, since different rules applied to each one. The issue was apparently a subject of controversy among the various circles that dealt with ritual law in Hellenistic times. As we saw in the quotation of 4QMMT, lines 3–9, the issue of what articles gentiles could bring into which area was another subject of Halachic discussion. The theme of the gentiles' insulting Jerusalem is also found in the Psalms of Solomon (2:2, 19; 17:13–14). The picture conveyed in 2 Maccabees 6:4 is indirect evidence of its high sensitivity in Judean society of the time.[80]

2 MACCABEES 6:5

The altar was filled with prohibited offerings excluded by the laws.

Commentary. This is the verse of 2 Maccabees that comes closest to the "abomination of the appaller" (or "desolation") of Daniel 11:31 and 1 Maccabees 1:54, 59. It is striking that the account of 2 Maccabees does not mention the daily offering's being discontinued.

2 MACCABEES 6:6

No one was allowed to observe the Sabbath or to keep the traditional festivals or even to confess he was a Judean.

Commentary. As Weitzman stressed, the wicked king "tampers with the structure of sacred time." Nabû-šuma-iškun "turned Festival Vigil and Festival Day into one Day," and according to the Verse Account Nabonidus suspended the New Year festival. The order to violate the Sabbath in 1 Maccabees 1:43 and 45 and 2 Maccabees 6:6 appeals to the same topos.[81] (Cf. also Daniel 7:23.) The recurrent theme of the king's officers' attacking the Judeans on the day of the Sabbath (2 Macc. 5:25 and 15:1–5; 1 Macc. 2:32–38) is partly related, although it serves other purposes as well.[82]

The "prohibition that anyone should confess that he was a Judean" is an idiosyncratic addition that cross-references with Antiochos IV's confession (2 Macc. 9:17).

2 MACCABEES 6:7A

On the monthly birthday of the king [the Judeans] were cruelly compelled to partake of the meat of pagan sacrifices.

Commentary. On the monthly birthday of the king, see the commentaries above to Daniel 11:31 and 1 Maccabees 1:54 and 59.

The image of the Judeans' being compelled to partake of the meat of pagan sacrifices has no historical basis whatsoever. Both for the Judeans and for the Greeks, partaking of a sacrifice defined membership in the community. Hence, no foreigner was allowed to share in the sacrifice, and the willing participation of a foreigner in the sacrifice—let alone his forced participation—was considered sacrilege. Such acts, however, are a literary topos commonly found in the descriptions of wicked kings. Similarly, Nabû-šuma-iškun allegedly compelled the priests of Nabu's Ezida temple of Borsippa to eat leeks, a food forbidden to them.[83] The vignette of 2 Maccabees 6:7 is a dramatic elaboration of the theme found in 1 Maccabees 1:62 ("Many Israelites strongly and steadfastly refused to eat forbidden food"). The fact that the forbidden food is the meat of an illicit sacrifice amplifies the misdeed and the suffering.

2 MACCABEES 6:7B

When a festival of Dionysos was celebrated, they were forced to put on a wreath of ivy and march in the procession in honor of the god.

Commentary. Historically speaking, the Judeans were never forced to participate in any procession celebrated by the Greek settlers; yet here the statement is remarkably specific, and it is tempting to surmise that the vignette encapsulates the memory of festivals celebrated by the Greek settlers in Jerusalem and witnessed by outraged and impotent Judeans. Alternatively, it may well be that processions in honor of Dionysos were witnessed by Judeans in neighboring Greek cities, in which case the vignette is purely a literary elaboration.

2 MACCABEES 6:8-9A

[8] A decree was published in the neighboring Greek cities, on the proposal of the citizens of Ptolemaïs, that they proceed against the Judeans in the same manner and compel them to partake of the meat of pagan sacrifices [9a] and that they butcher those Judeans who refused to go over to the Greek way of life.

Commentary. This reference to the neighboring Greek cities is unparalleled in 1 Maccabees. It is hard to tell whether it is a pure literary elaboration or an echo of some historical event. In the latter case it would suggest that the troubles extended to the whole satrapy of Koilē Syria and Phoinikē.[84] However, it is far from certain that the vignette has a historical core, since it notably emplots the same topics as 2 Maccabees 6:7, with a geographical variation.

2 MACCABEES 6:9B

It was clear that a time of trouble had come.

Commentary. Cf. 1 Maccabees 4:64.

2 MACCABEES 6:10

Two women were brought to trial for having circumcised their children. Their babies were hanged from their breasts, and the women were paraded publicly through the city and hurled down from the walls.

Commentary. Cf. 1 Maccabees 1:60–61.

2 MACCABEES 6:11

Other Judeans hastily assembled nearby in the caves to observe the Sabbath in secret. On being denounced to Philip they were all burned to death, because they refrained from defending themselves, out of respect for the holiest of days.

Commentary. Cf. 1 Maccabees 1:53, with the commentary to this verse above. As we shall see in Chapter 7 (§7.4.4), the claim that the Judeans fled to the caves in order to observe the Sabbath is a typical rereading of the historical reality deemphasizing mundane aspects of an episode (armed resistance to a royal general) to shift the focus onto the symbolically meaningful ones (the Suffering of the Faithful). The caves of the Judean desert repeatedly served as places of refuge, from where the resistance to invaders was organized;[85] therefore there can be little doubt that the Judeans attacked by Philip were fighters. Indeed, this is the claim of 1 Maccabees 2:27–38, which refers to the same topic but relocates it from the persecution account to the story of Mattathias's resistance. In the context of Mattathias's story, first the Judeans are massacred, because they refrain from fighting during the Sabbath. Therefore Mattathias and his partisans take the decision to fight on the Sabbath. This staging is apparently intended to justify the war of the Maccabees. It duplicates the pattern of the unprovoked attack used twice in the first chapter of 1 Maccabees to recount Antiochos's and the Mysarch's respective attacks of Jerusalem (1 Macc. 1:20, 29–30). As we shall see in Chapter 11 (§11.2.1A), the presentation of the attacks is deliberately distorted in order to hide the fact that the attacks were motivated by a popular rebellion.

6.4.2. Daniel and 1 Maccabees versus 2 Maccabees

If we consider the literary form of the three primary accounts of the persecution, 1 and 2 Maccabees display certain generic affinities with each other, whereas Daniel belongs to a distinct literary genre. From a topical point of view, however, the accounts of Daniel and 1 Maccabees are closer than are the accounts of 1 and 2 Maccabees. In fact, it may be argued that the main difference between the accounts of Daniel and 1 Maccabees is merely a question of genre. In contrast, the account of 2 Maccabees seems to belong to a distinct tradition. The comparison between 1 and 2 Maccabees is particularly telling. Not only does 2 Maccabees use distinct topics, but its literary construction is different, as evinced by the fact that the various vignettes are emplotted in a remarkably precise way. In particular, the personal and topographical names are notably precise, whereas the account of 1 Maccabees uses generic characters. Thus, in 1 Maccabees the agent of cultic disruption is "the king" (1:41–42), whereas in 2 Maccabees it is "Geron the Athenian" (6:1). The temple of Mount Gerizim is mentioned in 2 Maccabees 6:2, and the illicit names of the patron deities of the temples of Jerusalem and Gerizim, Zeus Olympios and Zeus Xenios, are spelled out in the same verse. In 6:7, the illicit ceremony becomes a "festival of Dionysos," a precision supported by an accurate reference to a specifically Dionysiac rite (the wreath of ivy). Similarly, the Greek word *kōmos* in 6:4 seems intended to stage the debauchery and revelry of the peoples in a Dionysiac context. Finally, the name of the capital of the satrapy, Ptolemaïs, arises in 2 Maccabees 6:8. The reference to the birthday of the king (2 Macc. 6:7) may belong to this greater precision as well. The technique of interspersing precise historical names in the account undeniably lends a certain historical authenticity, unlike 1 Maccabees. In the absence of external sources of evidence, modern historians are at a loss to distinguish between genuine information and literary embroidering. On a first impression, the change of the name of the Jerusalem god to Zeus Olympios is likely to be authentic. Even if we assume it is, however, we have no means to decide whether the claim that the temple of Mount Gerizim was renamed after Zeus Xenios is equally genuine or was added for the sake of dramatization. Similarly, it is impossible to assess the historical validity of the references to the events of Ptolemaïs and to the birthday of the king.

If we turn to content, some differences between 1 and 2 Maccabees may be explained simply by their respective intratextual references. Thus, the topic of circumcision recurs variously in 1 Maccabees 1–2. In 2 Maccabees, the indignation of the gentiles (6:3) cross-references with 2 Maccabees 4:49, and the confession of identity with Antiochos IV's confession in 2 Maccabees 9:17. Finally, the image of the Judeans living in the neighboring Greek cities being killed if they refused to go over to the Greek way of life echoes the description of the *gymnasion* in 2 Maccabees 4.

What is more interesting, whereas the ritual practices referred to in 1 Maccabees (circumcision, Sabbath, dietary laws) are prominent identity markers of the time, the topics composing the vignette of 2 Maccabees 6:4 seem to emplot Halachic concepts that did not necessarily have this status: fornication and the prohibition of gentiles' bringing things within the temple. That said, the cognitive process by which priestly normative values like those of 2 Maccabees 6:4 are summoned to compose a catalogue of evildoings is documented in Mesopotamia. As Steven Cole pointed out, the list of misdeeds ascribed to Nabû-šuma-iškun was inspired by the ritual of the king that took place during the New Year festival of Babylon. During the festival the king made a negative confession, ritually stating that during the past year he had not committed any of the misdeeds included in the confession.[86] Last, the fact that the account of 2 Maccabees fails to refer to the disruption of the daily offering is puzzling, but is this omission enough to cast doubt on the accounts of Daniel and 1 Maccabees?

. . .

What may be "unique" in the persecution accounts is the combination of two factors: we hear the voice of the victims, and the historical events are reshaped according to set narrative patterns. Whereas massacres were numerous in antiquity, history is usually told from the side of the winners. Two conditions are required for the voice of the victims to be preserved: the first is a reversal of fate, by which the victims eventually become the victors. Moreover, the victims need to be one of the rare peoples from antiquity whose literatures have been extensively preserved. Because these conditions are seldom fulfilled, only a handful of traumatic events are reported in the extant literature of antiquity: the sack of the Athenian Acropolis by the Persians, the sack of the Capitol by the Gauls, and, of course, the Hannibal's invasion of Italy.

In addition, the Judean accounts of Antiochos IV's military repression constitute a unique case within this meager corpus because of their unfamiliar literary codes. Although 1 and 2 Maccabees are written in Greek, they belong to a Near Eastern narrative tradition documented in both Mesopotamia and Judea by which historical events are reshaped to give them due cogency. The literary topoi and narrative patterns used to achieve this effect are basically what has prompted the myth of the religious persecution. As modern scholars develop greater awareness of the interplay between the direct reporting of historical events on the one hand and use of preset narrative patterns infusing the living experience with meaning on the other, the literary uniqueness of the Judean accounts is likely to become increasingly questioned. Accordingly, in a recent new analysis of the Delian Sarapis aretalogy, Ian Moyer has dissected the account of the trial, the main topic of the inscription, which states that "envious men" brought a lawsuit against Apollonios, the priest of Sarapis, and his newly built temple, but Apollonios won the lawsuit with the god's help. The story of the legal victory takes its pattern from the mythical struggle between Horus and Seth, which ends with the former's victory at a trial brought before Osiris. Moyer shows that the priest's opponents are depicted in terms that equate them with Seth: like him they are "rebellious, evil, envious, and filled with rage."[87]

For the purpose of our own inquiry, the Delian aretalogy is of additional interest, as it endorses my claim that events were recast according to a preset narrative pattern in the very generation who experienced them, and this restyling is not the outcome of a long tradition of transmission and piecemeal embroidery. That said, although Josephus's accounts (*Ant.* 12.248–56, *War* 1.1.32–35) are of no help in identifying the historical core of the "persecution," they nonetheless offer valuable testimony about the development of the tradition. Because it betrays a literal rereading of its source, Josephus's paraphrase of the primary account of 1 Maccabees in *Antiquities* 12.248–56 reveals how the original literary elaborations became hard facts at a very early stage of their transmission—as much "history" as Theseus's war of defense against the Amazons when they invaded the Acropolis was for Plutarch.[88]

As we shall see in Chapter 7, ancient Judean cultural codes not only shape the persecution accounts in 1 and 2 Maccabees but pervade the narrations. In particular, they shape the authors' respective accounts of the causes of the rebellion.

7

The Causes of the Rebellion according to 1 and 2 Maccabees

INTRODUCTION

At this point in our inquiry it has become clear that the modern view of the Judean political arena in the 170s and 160s as being dominated by a struggle between a party of Hellenizers on the one hand and a party of religious traditionalists on the other is the product of an uncritical rationalization of ancient Judean cultural codes, a misperception that arises from mistaking narrative form for content. The ancient authors' depiction of the factors disrupting the lawful order of things—or in modern terms the causes of the rebellion—is shaped by the culturally determined tenet that only matters affecting the fate of the temple, whether positively or negatively, are meaningful and therefore worth writing about.[1] The present chapter investigates in what ways and to what extent the authors of 1 and 2 Maccabees complied with this cultural code in phrasing their views on the causes and nature of the crisis. Irrespective of whether they did this intuitively—because this cultural code genuinely reflected their personal perception of reality as a symbolic universe—or reflexively, to continue the traditional way, an accurate inquiry into this matter is the only way to establish what they actually thought were the causes of the rebellion. Therefore it is a prerequisite to undertaking a proper historical reconstruction of the rebellion, using the Maccabees books as sources. As we shall see, not only are the authors' analyses of causality rational but they offer insights into matters whose central place in the crisis has been overlooked thus far in modern historical studies.

The discussion in Chapter 5 (§5.1.4) regarding the status of the *gymnasion* in 2 Maccabees as a synecdoche provided an important preliminary to our present inquiry by casting light on the fundamental narrative code that shaped the author's analysis of causes and effects. To summarize: although the creation of the *gymnasion* was only one aspect of Jason's reforms in Jerusalem—and from a modern historical perspective not the main one—owing to this use of synecdoche, this specific institution acquired a prominent role in the way these reforms were later remembered by ancient Judeans. As a visible landmark in the cityscape, the *gymnasion* came to represent a wide range of issues of a largely intangible nature, such as the inevitable economic consequences of the politicization of Jerusalem.[2] In this way, the *gymnasion* operated as the stock "sign" symbolizing the entire chain of reforms effected. Furthermore, as we shall presently see, insofar as the author wished to comment upon Jason's reforms, his main concern—in view of the aforesaid cultural code—was to show their impact upon the temple, either directly or obliquely, and the *gymnasion* naturally provided the emblem bridging the two places because of the ease with which the *gymnasion,* as an institution, could be construed as directly competing with the temple—not merely as a foil to it but actually as a form of antitemple. Thus, in addition to delineating a self-contained semantic field comprising the ramifications of Jason's politicization of Jerusalem, the synecdochic function of the *gymnasion* also mediates the conceptual incorporation of the reforms into the sphere of the temple, the core symbol of Judean life, enabling the author to both cite the reforms and pass judgment on them as well. However, I argue that the resulting description of the reforms in 2 Maccabees—indeed, the description of *all* the historical episodes in 1 and 2 Maccabees—exhibits as much awareness of political, social, and economic issues as modern, supposedly pragmatic accounts do. The main difference between the ancient and modern ways of presenting the reforms appears to lie in how causality is constructed: for the authors of the Maccabees books, the main purpose of investigating causality was to show precisely how the material issues affected the temple by revealing the relationship between them. In other words, their skill as historians consisted in correctly identifying the synecdochic items mediating between those issues and the temple:[3] hence the pivotal function of the mediating synecdoches in 1 and 2 Maccabees. The purpose of this chapter is to show how systematic is this process of semantic concatenation, wherein political, social, and economic matters are connected to the temple through the mediation of synecdochic signifiers in the causal analysis of the crisis presented by the two Maccabees authors. Although this perception of reality led them to map the causes of the rebellion onto the causes of disrupting the temple service, it is wrong to infer from this that their understanding of the world in which they lived was *essentially* simplistic—as modern scholars tend to imply when they refer to it as "theological." Nor was it naive: this culturally conditioned way of constructing causality could definitely be used disingenuously, to serve certain political ends. As we shall see here, it is not always easy to distinguish between the two processes of cultural conditioning and biased construct.[4]

As we saw briefly in the Methodological Introduction to Part II, the differing thematic emphases of 1 and 2 Maccabees resulted in the two works' emphasizing different chronological phases of the events. Because 1 Maccabees uses the Akra as its main synecdoche, this work is much more eloquent than 2 Maccabees regarding the "factors of disruption" that originated in the same circumstances as its creation, namely the installation of a garrison within its confines and the extensive land confiscations that were being carried out for the benefit of the military settlers. Conversely, having the *gymnasion* as its major mediating synecdoche, 2 Maccabees deals with the parallel problems that arose on the eve of the rebellion, in particular the Seleukid meddling with the appointment of the high priests and the correlated increase in the tribute rate. Despite these neat differences, there are enough cross-references between the two works to indicate that the authors shared the same ideological perspective on the revolt and objectively analyzed its roots and essence in much the same way. Thus, as 2 Maccabees also mentions the Akra and the land confiscations, albeit with minor relevance, 1 Maccabees likewise touches on fiscal issues and the appointment of the wicked high priests. Moreover, as we shall see, while the *gymnasion* and the Akra are by far the main mediating synecdoches in 1 and 2 Maccabees, respectively, additional items could occasionally be used to the same end.

Given that it refers to an earlier phase of events than does 1 Maccabees, and that its discursive logic has been so blatantly misinterpreted in modern scholarship, the evidence in 2 Maccabees will be examined first. To start, I will establish conclusively that the author of 2 Maccabees *was* interested in political and economic matters. Several issues pointedly recur in three passages, namely the account of Jason's establishment of the *gymnasion*, Antiochos IV's so-called confession (2 Macc. 9:14–17), and Lysias's utterance of his prospective vengeance (2 Macc. 11:1–3), all of which together suggest that the author deemed these as particularly worthy of interest. Accordingly, the three passages will be analyzed in detail below (§7.1). Next (§7.2) I will focus more specifically on the two issues of the royal appointment of the high priest and the increase of the tribute rate, with a view to showing that the author of 2 Maccabees identified them as interrelated and essentially the main cause of the crisis. Although these two matters are also cited in 1 Maccabees they remain secondary (§7.3). Indeed, all the causes of the crisis highlighted in this work point directly to the Akra and the devastating consequences of the establishment of a military settlement on the territory of the Judeans. The way these affairs are handled in the work will be investigated in the final section (§7.4) of this chapter.

7.1. THE POLITICAL AND ECONOMIC FACTORS OF THE REBELLION ACCORDING TO 2 MACCABEES

At first sight one might mistakenly assume that the author's understanding of the causes and nature of the rebellion can be best deduced from the royal letters cited en bloc in 2 Maccabees 11:16–33; actually, the most informative sections for this purpose are the description of the *gymnasion* (2 Macc. 4:7–15), Antiochos's so-called confession (2 Macc. 9:14–17), and Lysias's utterance of his prospective vengeance (2 Macc. 11:1–3)—that is, the very passage most frequently cited as proof of the author's "religious" perspective, plus two speeches that are patently fictitious. (Note that from Thucydides onward, the function of speeches was precisely to offer commentary on action.)[5] Given that I have already demonstrated the pivotal function of the *gymnasion* section, our inquiry will continue from there.

7.1.1. The "Pragmatic" Grievances Linked to the Gymnasion in 2 Maccabees 4:7–15

To learn which issues the authors of 1 and 2 Maccabees respectively identified as the main causes of the rebellion, we need to investigate how each one describes the threats that caused the regular service of the altar to be disrupted. In 2 Maccabees these are mentioned in conjunction with Jason's establishment of the *gymnasion* and its *palaistra*, whose activities, as we saw in Chapter 5 (§5.1), allegedly distracted the priests from their dutiful performance of the sacrifices (2 Macc. 4:7–15). Notwithstanding the moralizing tone of the authorial comments closing the passage (2 Macc. 4:16–17), the "peril" of the *gymnasion* is not conveyed through moral, "religious," and "cultural" arguments alone, but instead the description deliberately groups together a range of precise ritual, political, social, and economic issues, which we will proceed to disentangle.

The passage is composed of a factual description of the situation (4:7–10) followed by a string of authorial comments (4:11–17).[6] The former details four distinct issues: first, the eviction of Onias III, the ruling high priest (4:7), allegedly at Jason's initiative; second, the accession of Jason, Onias's brother, to the high priesthood in his stead (7), with the king's assent (10); third, the increase of the tribute to 360 silver talents, and an additional levy of 80 talents (8); and last, the payment of 150 talents for the royal authorization to establish a *gymnasion* and an *ephēbeion*, and to inscribe those in Jerusalem as Antiochenes: namely to institute a body of citizens (9) with the king's assent (10). Next the authorial comments of 4:11–17 raise three grievances and one claim: first, the grievance that the changes instituted by Jason with the king's consent amounted to the cancellation of the "royal concessions" (*philanthrōpa basilika*) that had been negotiated in earlier times (11); although the Greek phrase *philanthrōpa basilika* may refer to political concessions, in most cases it denotes fiscal privileges.[7] Second, the complaint that Jason abolished the lawful social order (*nomimoi politeiai*) and instituted a new one deemed illegitimate (*paranomoi ethismoi*: 11). Third, the complaint that the institution of the *ephēbeion* entailed the neglect of the sacrifices (12–14). Finally, in light of these alien novelties (*Hellēnismos*), it is claimed that Jason is impious and has no legitimate entitlement to the high priesthood (13).

Since Bickerman and Tcherikover, all modern historical commentaries on 2 Maccabees 4:7–15 have insisted on the political significance of creating the *gymnasion*, while at the same time lamenting that the author failed to provide an accurate description of the political reform owing to what they see as an overemphasis on the cultural and religious fallout that the establishment of the *gymnasion* entailed.[8] This idea of a skewed viewpoint is belied by the fact that the author used accurate technical terminology in this section, a clue that his omission of a comprehensive legal description of the transformation of Jerusalem into a polis is not through any disregard for legal matters but is the result of his way of presenting—and probably also perceiving—reality.[9] In keeping with the cultural values of his society, he pays only scant attention to matters that he deems to be of little relevance to the fate of the temple, while emphasizing those aspects that could be shown to have a negative impact on its functioning and that as such were culturally—and emotionally—reprehensible. At the same time, of course, the author's comments are not exempt from bias of an ideological nature, whereby claims of harm done to the temple are intertwined with censure against Jason's doings, such as the charge of introducing "novelty" (*ekainizen*, 4:11).[10] If we read beyond this cultural filter, as it were, we can see that the author is actually denouncing a comprehensive set of reforms: the eviction of the lawful high priest, the royal appointment of a new high priest, tax increases, the politicization of Jerusalem, and the weakening of the status of the temple.

Although this string of measures is presented as a coherent whole, upon closer analysis it appears that certain particularities were inappropriately dragged into the sphere of the *gymnasion*. From a strictly legal point of view, the institution of the *gymnasion* and its *ephēbeion* indeed was directly related to the politicization of Jerusalem, and the payment of 150 silver talents (4:9) is unquestionably the price for its establishment; whereas the eviction of Onias from the high priesthood, his replacement by Jason, and the increase of the tribute are quite a separate matter. However, legal technicalities aside, it is easy to understand how the author could, in comparatively good faith, perceive these various matters to be interrelated, since it was easy for him to "discover" semantic associations between them: the setting up of the *gymnasion* (the antitemple) is part of the legal transformation of Jerusalem; this is agreed to by the king as a counterpart to an additional tax payment (4:9). These 150 talents are coupled with the increase of the tribute (4:8), which in turn is linked to the change of high priest (4:7–8). On the one hand, it is clear that a political supporter of Jason would have never "discovered" this specific semantic concatenation, by which, according to the author of 2 Maccabees, the *gymnasion* and the allegedly ensuing neglect of the sacrifices stand as signs for the change of high priest and for the tribute increase: in the first place, he would not have seen any causal link between Jason's founding of the *gymnasion* and the alleged neglect of the sacrifices. In that regard, this specific concatenation is a manipulative construct, as most political arguments are. On the other hand, the way in which the author of 2 Maccabees establishes this link between the temple and the two reforms in question is not arbitrary but is conveyed through a semantic concatenation that, technically speaking, is perfectly acceptable. Thus, the section on the *gymnasion* in 2 Maccabees illustrates how culturally conditioned tools of describing reality—the semantic concatenation—could be used for factional attacks. At the same time, we can see how these cultural codes perfectly enable the author to address two issues of major political and economic importance—the advent of a wicked high priest in unlawful circumstances, and the increase in the tribute—by presenting them as detrimental to the temple. More precisely, the fact that these two issues are denounced in conjunction with the establishment of the *gymnasion*, the episode presented as the initial cause of the disruption of the sacrifices in 2 Maccabees, shows that the author considers them to be major factors in the turmoil that is to follow.

The fact that modern historians have repeatedly misinterpreted the author's claim that Jason's reform canceled the "royal privileges" (*philanthrōpa basilika*, 4:11) as referring either to the "religious" organization or to the political "constitution" of Jerusalem, and have in consequence consistently overlooked the prominence of the fiscal protest in the *gymnasion* section,[11] is a direct result of Bickerman's persistent influence. Actually the phrase *philanthrōpa basilika* regularly refers to tax concessions in the Seleukid and Ptolemaic evidence, and 2 Maccabees is no exception.

A. *Philanthrōpa Basilika.* The vocabulary of royal euergetism found in Hellenistic inscriptions evinces a marked inclination for pomp at the expense of technical accuracy, with transactions of a concrete nature—whether fiscal, economic, administrative, or legal—being consistently presented in abstract, high-flown ideological terms.[12] *Philanthrōpa* is a good case in point. Whereas the term formally means "benefactions,"[13] studies based on both the Ptolemaic and the Seleukid papyri and inscriptions have shown that, in the context of royal decisions, it invariably denotes the granting of extraordinary privileges and, more particularly, "benefactions" of an economic and fiscal nature. The most common use by far refers to either tax exemption or to the cancellation of a debt owed to the royal treasury.[14]

Most scholars have endorsed Bickerman's view that the settlement (*philanthrōpa basilika*)—negotiated by a certain Ioannes and made obsolete by Jason's changes—was the same one publicized in Antiochos III's decree of 200/198 B.C.E., reported in Josephus (*Ant.* 12:138–44).[15] Although this proposition is indeed the most likely, Bickerman's tremendously influential interpretation of the decree itself,[16] and hence of 2 Maccabees 4:11, is untenable, as I intend to show.

Bickerman's commentary on the settlement of 200/198 B.C.E. hinges on two premises that have been refuted by more recent historiography on the stately culture of the Hellenistic kingdoms. One is his "surrender and grant" theory predicated on the "legalistic approach,"[17] whereby both Greek poleis and *ethnē* automatically lost their political status by right of conquest and recovered it (or not) at the behest of the conqueror. Consequently, Bickerman interpreted the notion of royal *philanthrōpa* in a narrow political sense. Given that the first act of kindness bestowed by kings on conquered cities was to restore their previous status, the historian saw Antiochos III's decree for Jerusalem as a political charter, after the medieval model.[18] Bickerman's second error lies in his insistence that Greek poleis and non-Greek *ethnē* were treated differently, with the implication that whereas[19]

> for a Greek city, the clause [that the people should live "according to the laws of their fathers"] meant the retention of the democratic constitution, of self-rule, . . . for the Jews "the laws of the fathers" meant Torah. . . . In Jerusalem, [the ancestral constitution] prescribed the obligation to observe the Sabbath rest.

Contrary to Bickerman's view, it is now accepted that the status of local communities was always the outcome of a negotiation between king and local representatives. Kings refrained from meddling with local traditions—especially the traditional prerogatives of local deities[20]—and as a rule the modifications they imposed were limited to the political structures of the local communities and were aimed primarily at quashing potential sources of political hostility.[21] The bulk of the negotiations bore instead on the economic and fiscal settlement.

As a matter of fact the settlement of 200/198 B.C.E. *was* negotiated, and 2 Maccabees 4:11 even specifies the identity of the man who led the Judean embassy to Antiochos III. But while the Sabbath rest did not call for royal regulation, the Judeans, like any other political community, were governed by political institutions. These required confirmation from the conqueror, depending on the ambassadors' ability to convince him of the loyalty of the Judean leaders. The clause cited in *Antiquities* 12.142[22] indicates that the high priest and the *gerousia* were allowed to maintain their political prerogatives, since they were willing to cooperate. In exchange for their loyalty, their fiscal privileges were upheld, and it is no coincidence that the political and economic issues are dealt with in the same sentence in the royal decree. Similarly, the phrase *nomimoi politeiai* in 2 Maccabees 4:11 has a standard political (and not "religious") connotation.[23]

In view of the content of Antiochos III's decree, the objection in 2 Maccabees 4:11 that Jason abolished the *philanthrōpa basilika* negotiated by this Ioannes may allude to the fact that Antiochos III consented to the continued hereditary transmission of the office of high priest, without imposing any royal control over the incumbents. That said, the bulk of the clauses included in Antiochos III's decree pivots on economic and fiscal issues, as was usually the case with royal edicts stipulating settlements in the wake of military conquests.[24] Given that the denunciation of Jason's reforms in 2 Maccabees 4:7–15 systematically correlates their political and economic aspects—Jason's appointment as high priest was accompanied by his pledge to raise the tribute rate, and his request to establish a *gymnasion* and inscribe the Antiochenes was granted in return for his promise of an additional payment—the phrase *philanthrōpa basilika* in all likelihood alludes to both and not to the political side of the reforms alone.

7.1.2. The "Pragmatic" Causes in 2 Maccabees: The Corroboration of the Speeches

Altogether, the *gymnasion* section raises four concrete grievances: the king's meddling with the appointment of the high priest; the tribute increase; establishment of a *gymnasion* and an *ephēbeion;* and the change of Jerusalem's status (if indeed *nomimoi politeiai* in 4:11 refers to the politicization of the city and is not simply intended as a general comment on Jason's reforms). Before we return in section 7.2 to the author's pointed correlation between the royal appointment of wicked high priests and the increase of the tribute rate—which crops up again on the occasion of Menelaos's appointment (2 Macc. 4:24–25, 27–28)[25]—let us first survey the material issues tabled in 2 Maccabees. Precisely because Antiochos IV's "confession" (2 Macc. 9:14–17) and Lysias's avowal of revenge (2 Macc. 11:1–3) are purely literary constructs, these provide the proper starting point for understanding how our author perceived the causes of the revolt.

A. *Antiochos Epiphanes' "Confession," 2 Maccabees 9:14–17.* Turning to God when he finally understands that his end is nigh, Antiochos announces a fourfold repentance in his so-called confession. It cannot be mere chance that this repentance largely mirrors the grievances raised against Jason in the *gymnasion* section. This correspondence would suggest that, in the opinion of the ancient author, these four topics epitomized the king's crimes—and, to drive the point home, the author appends reminders of the king's evildoings as ironical counterpoints to each of the king's promises. The first sin acknowledged by Antiochos most probably alludes to his abolition of the laws (2 Macc. 9:14):

> "I shall proclaim Jerusalem a free city [*eleuthera*]"—the same holy city toward which he had been hastening with the intention of razing it to the ground upon his arrival and turning it into a mass grave.

In the political discourse of the Greek cities in Hellenistic times, the notion of freedom (*eleutheria*) basically indicates the absence (or removal) of all tokens of subjection, though the term's connotations vary. Used as an adjective (*eleutheroi*) referring to the collective civic body, the word is sometimes coupled with phrases specifying that the citizens are once again allowed to live by their own laws. In other cases, either an evacuation of the garrison or an exemption from tribute is mentioned in conjunction with the granting of freedom.[26] Taking into account the rule of literary variation, in the latter case the sense of "free of garrisoning" seems more probable, since Antiochos's second pledge in 9:15 pivots on a political issue, and the third (9:16) on an economic one. The overseers (and garrisons?) left in Jerusalem and Mount Gerizim are cited earlier in the narrative (2 Macc. 5:22–23), and the Seleukid garrison of the citadel is mentioned in passing in 4:28. Therefore we may accept that 9:14 refers to the Akra—but if anything this summary attention to the Akra in 2 Maccabees[27] endorses the contrast with 1 Maccabees. The second sin reads as follows (2 Macc. 9:15):

> "I shall make all Judeans equals [*isous*] to the Athenians"[28]—the same Judeans whom he had resolved to deny even the right of burial: he would have cast out their bodies, with those of their little children, to be devoured by birds and beasts!

This reference to the Athenians makes sense only as an ironic hyperbole to provide a counterpoint to the "Antiochenes" early in 4:9. Antiochos repents for what is now presented apparently as *his* politicization of Jerusalem. His specification that the new status he intends to grant to his former victims will concern "all" (*pantes*) Judeans is a tenable confirmation that the politicization of Jerusalem involved the disenfranchisement of part of the population.[29] Although the real cause of resentment against the polis is not disclosed, the text indicates two high symbolic issues: the division of the Judeans into two groups and the sin of *Hellēnismos*, for which Athens is the ultimate signifier. The third set of compensations promised by the king concerns the temple (2 Macc. 9:16):

> "I shall embellish the holy temple with the finest votive gifts, and I shall make manyfold restitution for the sacred vessels, and I shall provide from my own revenues the sums required for the sacrifices"—the same temple that he had previously plundered!

While all three of the matters mentioned in conjunction with the temple are economic in nature, from the author's cultural perspective the content of this sentence is perhaps best summarized in reverse: the economic issues are denounced expressly according to their impact on the temple and ordered in decreasing symbolic importance. First, Antiochos's promise to make votive gifts alludes to the royal practice most suited to showing that relations between him and the local community were harmonious.[30] The second matter is partly connected to the first, since the vessels plundered by Antiochos included gifts received from other kings (2 Macc. 5:16). His last pledge refers to the increase of the tribute—the most overtly economic grievance—but only in an indirect way.

Antiochos's sudden solicitude for the sacrifices is patently to compensate for the priestly omissions censured in 4:14, more particularly because the cause of their neglect was the lure of the *diskos* announcing the "unlawful distribution" (*paranomos chorēgia*)[31] of the *palaistra*. As numerous inscriptions attest, the supply of a source of income out of which a city could buy oil for its *gymnasion* was one of the most common forms of royal euergetism toward Greek cities.[32] Examples include Eumenes II's letter to the people of Tyriaion granting them the right to become a polis, which is followed by a second letter informing the newly constituted citizens of temporary measures to ensure the oil supply for their *gymnasion*.[33] On the face of it, Antiochos's promise exposes a contrast between two forms of royal subsidy: the one (unlawful) for the *gymnasion* and the other (lawful) for the sacrifices. This latter subsidy is the first topic of Antiochos III's decree for Jerusalem (*Ant.* 12.140), but his successor's promise adds ironic hyperbole to the customary procedure by stating that from now on those subsidies will be provided out of his private revenues (*idiai prosodoi*). The usual source of the royal generosity is, of course, the royal land.

However, lurking behind the ostensible emphasis on the temple in 2 Maccabees 9:16 is an implicit allusion to the contested increase of the tribute. As a rule, the royal seizure of the economic surpluses from subject communities through taxation was formulated as a reciprocal transaction between the king and the local community.[34] In non-Greek communities in which the temple was a central focus of communal life, the royal subsidies to the temple cult constituted the king's part in this exchange, legitimizing his claim to receive a part of the temple revenues in return. As noted earlier, in 2 Maccabees the institution of the *gymnasion* is ostensibly paired with the increase of the tribute (2 Macc. 4:8–9). Therefore, Antiochos's pledge to provide the sums required for the sacrifices suggests a return to the situation that prevailed before the *gymnasion* was set up. At that time, the king subsidized the sacrifices and not the unlawful distributions of the *palaistra*; and furthermore he demanded a (far?) lower tribute. Although the specific issue of the tribute is kept in the background (as too mundane) and is eclipsed by the overtly temple-related aspects, the original audience of 2 Maccabees would nonetheless have been aware of it.

In closing, Antiochos goes completely overboard (2 Macc. 9:17):

> "Furthermore, I shall become a *Ioudaios*[35] and shall make a tour of the entire inhabited world, telling of the might of God."

The reason for this overstatement is twofold. In 2 Maccabees, numerous Seleukid officers acknowledge the might of the god of Jerusalem, among them Heliodoros (3:35, 36–39), Nikanor son of Patroklos (8:36), and Lysias (11:13). In his role as supreme ruler Antiochos has to raise the ante for his promise and transform himself into a *Ioudaios*, no less. At the same time his closing statement seems to allude to the repression against the *people* that had accompanied the desecration of the temple, whereby "no one was allowed to observe the Sabbath or to keep the traditional festivals or even to confess he was a *Ioudaios*" (6:6).

If this analysis of Antiochos's confession is correct, the accompanying list of issues—military (14), political (15), economic (16), and ritual (17)—may reasonably be taken to reflect the author's understanding of the crisis and to disprove the modern view that he read the revolt through a "religious" lens, in the narrow, modern sense of this word. In his symbolic universe, all these issues were interconnected.

B. *Lysias's Threat of Revenge, 2 Maccabees 11:1–3.* The next passage with a catalogue of material issues is Lysias's vow of revenge prior to starting his military campaign against the *Ioudaioi* (2 Macc. 11:1–3):[36]

> Only a short time thereafter, Lysias, guardian and "kinsman" of the king and chief minister, very angry over the course of events, mustered about 80,000 men and the entire cavalry and marched against the Judeans, intending to *turn their city into a dwelling place for Greeks,* to make their *temple subject to a levy in money* like the shrines of the other nations, and to *turn the high priesthood into an office to be put up for sale annually.*

Since Lysias did not fulfill any of these declared intentions (*logizomenos,* 11:2), the list is clearly another instance of authorial comment on events, like Antiochos's confession. In this case, "Greeks" is most likely a synonym for "wicked men" rather than a straightforward ethnic label, like *Hellēnismos* in the context of the *gymnasion*[37] and "Athenians" in Antiochos's confession. As they stand, each of the three items couples a highly symbolic element with a mundane one, as if some sardonic take on the escalating havoc: first a *gymnasion* and now the whole city as a place for "Greeks";[38] first the increase of the tribute and an additional tax for the *gymnasion* and now a levy on the temple; first the king appointing the high priests (for life?) and now the annual sale of the high priesthood. Read in this way, the list is strikingly similar to the triad of grievances associated with the *gymnasion* in 2 Maccabees 4:7–15, namely the politicization of Jerusalem, the tax increase, and the royal interference with the appointment of the high priests. The parallels are hardly coincidental and offer further confirmation that our author's commentary on the rebellion recurrently picks out a set of distinctly rational issues. In this set, the issue of the tribute is particularly prominent. Thus Nikanor's reported intention to make up "the total of the tribute owed to the Romans, which amounted to 2,000 talents," out of the sale of Judean prisoners of war (2 Macc. 8:10) sounds like an inconsequential topos but nonetheless contributes to constantly keeping this matter present in the background.

7.2. THE SELEUKID APPOINTMENT OF HIGH PRIESTS AND THE TAX INCREASE IN 2 MACCABEES

Paradoxically, whereas the fictitious speeches present us with relatively straightforward lists of the main causes of the crisis identified by the author of 2 Maccabees, the cultural codes shaping the narrative itself considerably hamper its readability for a modern audience. Over time, numerous modern scholars have been misled into believing that the author was interested only in theological matters, because of his culturally conditioned shift of narrative emphasis that—from our modern, pragmatic standpoint—diverts attention away from the political and economic issues (such as those arising from the politicization of Jerusalem) toward the collateral damage caused to the temple (the neglect of the sacrifices by the priests hurrying to the distribution in the *gymnasion*'s *palaistra*).[39] In truth, not only does our author refer to mundane issues but the accuracy of his phrasing[40] is evidence that, far from merely paying lip service, he genuinely meant to *comment* on them.

The topic of imperial taxes is a striking illustration of the contribution of the literary approach proposed here. Whereas its prominence in 1 Maccabees has long since been noted, because it is dealt with in a straightforward way in the official documents inserted in this work, the even greater centrality of the tax theme in 2 Maccabees comes to light only through the analysis of what I have dubbed the "semantic concatenation" whereby the theme is systematically harnessed to the fate of the temple. Moreover, this approach allows us to pinpoint the type of nuance applied by the ancient authors and shows how the two detailed accounts of Jason's and Menelaos's being appointed high priests emphasize the correlation between the increase of the tribute and the imposition of new taxes, the interference of the Seleukid king with the appointment of the high priests, and the unworthiness of the appointees. Upon closer examination, there are grounds to think that in 2 Maccabees the two issues of Seleukid control of the high priesthood and the tax increase are perceived as converging and the main cause of the crisis. The present section analyzes how these two threads are entwined. Incidentally, a correct understanding of how the author construed the link between these correlated matters and the temple—as well as his possible political bias—is a prerequisite to determining to what extent the standpoint of the author may be endorsed for modern historical reconstruction.

7.2.1. Royal Appointment and Unworthy High Priests

As shown in Part I of this book (e.g., §1.2), in the political culture of Hellenistic Judea to hail a leader as either pious or impious was a factional statement, not an objective description of reality. While this practice is amply borne out in 2 Maccabees, the labeling of Jason, Menelaos, and Alkimos as wicked rulers is also intended as an attack on the Seleukid kings' interference with the appointment of the Jerusalem high priests.

Modern scholarship has tended to downplay the irregularity of the Seleukid control of the high priesthood by claiming that this was a standard royal prerogative.[41] As is typical of the legalistic approach, this view presupposes that ancient laws were defined objectively around abstract and unbending concepts of political thought and that kings enforced their decisions from above at will. The problem appears in a very different light if it is admitted that laws were continually reshaped by custom and tradition and that such changes entailed negotiations. According to Josephus, the dynasty of the Oniads ran for fifteen generations from Cyrus's time (*Ant.* 20.233–34). Even without accepting this claim at face value,[42] it would mean that according to Judean official memory no king had been outwardly involved in the appointment of the Judean high priests since the days of the Return. In historical terms, this can be taken to indicate that the high priesthood had enjoyed a smooth hereditary transmission—for the last few generations at least. At all events, Antiochos IV's interference was not backed by any recent precedent, let alone by custom, and could be legitimately contested by the leading Judean families who were not allied with the royal appointees. In 2 Maccabees this unprecedented imperial interference is turned into a contentious matter (in contrast with 1 Maccabees, where it is downplayed), and a rhetorical device employed to condemn it was to yoke the Seleukid appointment directly with the wicked priests.

For this reason, in 2 Maccabees the circumstances that led to the appointments of Jason and Menelaos by Antiochos IV, and of Alkimos by Demetrios I, are narrated in detail, and in a particularly unfavorable light (respectively, 4:7–15 and 23–29; 14:3–13). Conversely, the pious Onias III reached his position by hereditary right, and one may say that Judas's "appointment" by Onias III and Jeremiah (2 Macc. 15:12–16) is made to resemble a sort of divine election.[43] In contrast, while in 1 Maccabees the circumstances of Simon's appointment are likewise equated with a form of divine election, with the people collectively acting in the stead of a prophet (1 Macc. 14:41),[44] by continuing his account down to John Hyrkanos the author forfeits his chance to expose the wrongfulness of this Seleukid involvement, because both Jonathan and Simon effectively owe their initial nominations (and Jonathan also all his confirmations in the office) to kings and contenders.[45] Only after Demetrios II concedes the autonomy of the *ethnos* of the Judeans (1 Macc. 13:36–42) is Simon appointed anew by the people's assembly (1 Macc. 14:25–49); whereas in 2 Maccabees the author's focus on Judas allows for a more systematic reflection on what the legitimate source of the high priests' power is.

As one would expect, the underlying political reflection is emplotted and embodied within the narration rather than articulated in abstract concepts. The author's stance lies not in the moralizing authorial comments that modern scholars like to scrutinize (and on the basis of which they usually conclude that he had no interest in political matters)[46] but in his narration of how Jason, Menelaos, and Alkimos came to power. Moreover, he ensured that these episodes explored several complex issues at once, outlining not only what was intended by a "good" priest[47] but also what the legitimate source of authority in the appointment of high priests should be. Thanks to his multilayered construction of these episodes, the author could at once assert the legitimacy of the Hasmoneans over rival high priests and support their claim to autonomy vis-à-vis Seleukid imperial rule. To comment on these themes, the author employs a system of semantic concatenation whereby imperial domination is shown to be illegitimate because the kings appoint wicked high priests and by doing so harm the temple and all the Judeans, the temple's people. To be exact, the argument of illegitimacy rests on the double claim that the men appointed as high priests by the king are unsuitable to the office and that they are self-interested and eager to serve the interests of the king rather than devote themselves to their country and people. These two arguments will be examined in turn.

A. The Seleukid Selection of Unsuitable Priests. To believe the author of 2 Maccabees, all three high priests appointed by the Seleukid kings lacked the most basic requirements of legitimacy. Although the author notes that Jason is in fact an Oniad, this hardly works in his favor. Not only does Jason ignominiously overthrow his own brother to obtain the position (2 Macc. 4:7), but the author squarely states that Jason does not qualify as a high priest because of his impious behavior (4:13).[48]

The muddled manuscript tradition makes it impossible to know with certainty how the author presented Menelaos's genealogy. According to the Greek witnesses, Menelaos's brother Simon (2 Macc. 4:23) was "of the tribe of Benjamin" (2 Macc. 3:4): that is, an Israelite from one of the twelve tribes and hence not related to a priestly clan. The Vetus Latina states instead that he was "of the clan of Balgea," the latter identifiable as the priestly clan of Bilgah known from other texts (1 Chr 24:14; Neh. 12:5). Bickerman is probably correct in surmising that the Vetus Latina's version is a late emendation by a scribe who noticed the oddity of a nonpriest's holding an administrative function in the temple.[49] If this is the case, the eventual aim of 2 Maccabees' author must have been to try to delegitimize Menelaos's appointment as high priest by denigrating his genealogy, but such a claim was so implausibly slanderous that he opted for an oblique shot, specifying instead the genealogy of Simon, his (genuine? or alleged?) brother. The author's slanderous innuendo about the man's low social position is exposed in the description of his nomination by Antiochos (2 Macc. 4:23–25, emphases added):

> On being introduced to the king, *Menelaos magnified his own importance by giving the impression that he was a man of authority,* and by adding 300 talents of silver to Jason's bid, he gained for himself the high priesthood. He came home holding the royal decree *but with no qualifications for the high priesthood.*

Given that preliminary inquiries would have been made into the aspirant's social position, it is unlikely that Menelaos could have deceived the king as claimed (4:24).[50] Conversely, the author's disqualification of Menelaos (4:25) is suspiciously similar to his indicting Jason as being "no true high priest" in 2 Maccabees 4:13.

The issue of Seleukid interference with temple appointments arises yet again regarding Alkimos (2 Macc. 14:3–13).[51] This time our author is not able to associate him with a controversial increase in taxes and instead resorts to a ready-made argument, namely that the man *"voluntarily [hekousiōs] defiled himself"* when he was high priest a first time. Being deprived of "the distinction of [his] forefathers" (*progonikēn doxan*) by Judas and the *Asidaioi*, and with no hope of support from his fellow countrymen, Alkimos turns to King Demetrios to secure his reappointment to the office, and the latter complies with the outrageous request (2 Macc. 14:3–7a). Although we have no means to either corroborate or refute Alkimos's claim to hereditary entitlement to the high priesthood, the author's charge that Alkimos "voluntarily defiled himself" can only be a defamatory invention. Once again the story is clearly aimed to "demonstrate" that the men chosen by the Seleukids to be high priests are consistently unworthy of this office.

B. Seleukid Appointment and Self-Interested High Priests. Not only do the royal appointees fail to meet the basic requirements of legitimacy, but their grasping, self-interested behavior contrasts with the noble intentions of Onias III and Judas: the former acting for the sake of the city, the people, and the laws in trying to curb the consequences of Simon's treason (2 Macc. 4:2, 5), the latter fighting for *Ioudaïsmos*, with him and his men selling their possessions (8:14) and fighting for "city and the sanctuary," fearing less for their wives and children than for the temple (2 Macc. 14:17–18).[52] In blunt contrast, Menelaos had no apparent concern for *Ioudaïsmos* whatever: "His thought was not for the preservation of his country but for his own appointment to office" (2 Macc. 13:3). When, after storming Jerusalem, Antiochos IV leaves Menelaos in office, this step is presented as part of the string of repressive measures, alongside the installation of overseers in Jerusalem and at Mount Gerizim (5:22–23).

Alkimos fares no better in 2 Maccabees, as his speech to Demetrios shows (14:7b–10, emphases added):

> I have come here now for two reasons: *first*, because I have *the king's interests* truly at heart; and second, because I am seeking the welfare of my own fellow citizens [*politai*]. Please take note of all this, Your Majesty, and take thought for our country, and bring your provident intervention to bear upon the land and upon our sorely beset nation with the ready kindness you show to all, for as long as Judas survives, it is impossible for the commonwealth to have peace.

The irony in Alkimos's speech is unmistakable. First, if he genuinely cared for the interests of his fellow citizens (2 Macc. 14:8), he would not require the high priesthood, since—allegedly—he is defiled (14:3). Second, not only does he openly state that he holds the interests of his fellow citizens second to those of the king, but he treacherously insinuates that Judas's death is in the interest of the country, whereas of course it is in the interest of the king and of Alkimos himself. This insidious speech is immediately followed by the account of Alkimos's treason against his people and Judas, which as we saw in Chapter 4 mirrors Simon's treacherous maneuvers against Onias III.[53] Nikanor's campaign is intended both to reinstate Alkimos and to suppress Judas (14:13), two goals serving the interests of the impious settlers "who had fled Judas" (14:14) and not those of the faithful *Ioudaioi*. After peace is concluded, Alkimos is once again accused of inciting Demetrios to resume warfare (14:26–27).

The forceful case of illegitimacy mounted against all three rival high priests leaves no doubt about the author's intended message, which was that in overlooking the sources of legitimacy accepted by the forefathers of the *Ioudaioi*, the wicked high priests were seriously misguided in turning to the Seleukid kings for support.

7.2.2. Seleukid Appointment and Fiscal Issues: The Case of Menelaos

While such accusations of the high priests' unworthiness, self-interest, and general wickedness are fairly routine in a politically biased work, in 2 Maccabees they receive an extra twist by being associated with the issue of royal appointment, an association that means they can be used to vilify both the rival high priests and Seleukid imperial domination at once. Moreover, at the center of this collusion between kings and wicked high priests is the onerous question of the tax increase.

Much like the contentious topic of royal appointment, the tax issue in 2 Maccabees is used to contrast the portrayals of the high priests as good or wicked. By this means, Onias III is shown successfully preventing Heliodoros from laying his hands on the temple's money;[54] whereas Jason and Menelaos, allegedly of their own initiative, obtained the high priesthood from the king by promising to increase the tribute (2 Macc. 4:7–9, 24). That said, the fact that the tax theme is lacking from the account of Alkimos's appointment may indicate that the arguments, polemical though they may be, are always based on a kernel of historical truth.

Even if this should prove true, there remains an intriguing similarity between the account of Menelaos's accession to the office of high priest (2 Macc. 4:23–24) and that of Jason. In both cases, the villain evicts the ruling high priest by promising to pay a higher tribute to the king, thereby earning his appointment. It is likely that the two stories are actually doublets, in the sense that, whereas Menelaos may effectively have succeeded Jason within three years, the tribute itself was adjusted only once and not twice; the lack of reliable alternative evidence[55] prevents us from knowing which story is the "historical core." If so, the purpose of the narrative duplication would be to emphasize that the Seleukid appointment of the high priest and the rise of the tribute rate are closely interrelated.

7.2.3. Who Devised the Increase to the Tribute Rate?

As argued in Chapters 9 and 10 below (§§9.2, 9.4, and 10.2), there is a historical basis to the connection indicated in 2 Maccabees between the tax increase and Seleukid interference with the appointment of the high priests from Antiochos IV onward. But even if the author's account is not entirely fabricated, he seemingly took some liberties with his historical concatenation of events, imputing to Jason and Menelaos the tribute increase: on the basis of extratextual evidence, there are grounds for believing that an increase in the tribute rate was required by the king in the first place. Although the question of who was responsible for increasing the tribute cannot be conclusively settled by means of literary analysis alone, it largely exposes the distortions of 2 Maccabees' version of events, in that this version tallies with the work's tendency to show the unworthy high priests as taking the initiative and the Seleukid kings as reacting accordingly. However, in the case of Antiochos IV, this depiction of the king as strictly reactive does not match the man's known traits. The ancient Greek historians portrayed Antiochos IV as a vigorous albeit contested ruler, and modern scholars concur. This king took the initiative of invading Egypt twice and is known to have made economic and monetary reforms in Seleukis Syria.[56] If we add the fact that the author's device of imputing the initiative of Antiochos's wicked acts to the rival high priests neatly suits his political agenda of blackening the memory of the internal enemies while condemning Seleukid interference in the affairs of Judea, his version of events is decidedly suspect. Thus, while literary analysis cannot provide decisive arguments either way about how the fiscal crisis was generated, it certainly opens up the range of possible historical interpretations by establishing that 2 Maccabees' version is not necessarily reliable, to say the least.

To better illustrate the aforementioned literary pattern of action and reaction, we will now widen our inquiry as a first step toward reconstructing how, through semantic concatenation, the author shaped his claim that Jason and Menelaos devised the tribute increase themselves, even though this was a royal directive.

A. *Wicked Priests and Kings in 2 Maccabees.* Whereas above in Chapters 3 through 5 our literary analysis has shown the narrative's systematic binary contrast between the three wicked high priests and the pious heroes Onias and Judas, most episodes, especially those featuring Jason and Menelaos, comprise a third set of relations that involve the Seleukid kings and hinge on several distinct topics:[57]

> *The method of appointment:* Jason obtains the high priesthood from Antiochos IV by promising money, although the pious high priest Onias is currently in charge, and Jason himself is "no high priest at all"; in turn, Menelaos acquires the high priesthood from Antiochos, despite his being of unworthy extraction; Alkimos obtains it from Demetrios, despite having

defiled himself and being ritually unfit to be high priest.[58] In contrast, Judas is "appointed" by Onias and Jeremiah (2 Macc. 15:12–16). Told from a different angle, Jason evicts Onias III (4:7–10) and Menelaos subsequently assassinates him by means of an accomplice (4:32–34), whereas Judas is recognized by the pious Onias as his rightful heir (15:12).[59]

The sins of the wicked high priests against the temple prefigure those of the king: Jason builds the *gymnasion* and neglects the sacrifices (2 Macc. 4:9, 12–14); Menelaos's talion associates him with Jason's sin against the altar (13:8); Antiochos subsequently causes the total disruption of the sacrifices (6:1–7).[60] Menelaos steals the holy vessels (4:32, 39), and in turn Antiochos plunders the temple, also taking the gifts from previous kings (5:15–16, 21).[61] In contrast, the pious Judas refounds the temple (10:1–8).

The method of appointment and the sins of money are narrowly related: Jason deposes Onias and is appointed by the Seleukid king because he promises a tribute increase, along with additional taxes to build the *gymnasion* and thereby disrupt the temple sacrifices (2 Macc. 4:7–15). Menelaos ousts Jason by pledging an additional tribute increase to the Seleukid king and steals the holy vessels to pay the inflated sum (4:24–26, 32, 39). With the stolen vessels he further corrupts Seleukid officers into assassinating Onias and condemning the three elders to death (4:32–34, 43–50). In a complete antithesis, the virtuous Judas applies the spoils of war to provide for the widows and the orphans (8:28),[62] and for his righteous endeavors he is accordingly acknowledged as the legitimate high priest and "king" by Onias III and Jeremiah,[63] and hailed therefore as worthy rather than appointed by some Seleukid king.

Other, symbolically less significant sins perpetrated by the wicked high priests also prefigure similar sins by the king: Jason and Menelaos engage in a struggle for power (2 Macc. 5:5–7), and Jason does not hesitate to kill his fellow citizens to seize control (5:6, 8–10), foreshadowing the massacre committed by Antiochos (5:12–14). In turn, Alkimos stirs up conflict against Judas (14:3–30). For his part, Judas instead fights for *Ioudaïsmos*,[64] thereby emulating his forerunner Onias (whose "purpose was not to bring charges against his fellow Judeans but to look to the collective and individual interests of all the people," 4:5) unlike his rival high priests, whose wickedness is prefigured by Simon (who "acted against . . . his own country," 4:1). Likewise, the three elders who come before Antiochos IV to prosecute Menelaos and are unjustly executed (4:43–50) act as "the spokesmen for city and the people and the sacred vessels" (4:48).[65]

Most of these episodes have already been commented upon, but it is worth looking more closely at the allegation that the civil strife between Jason and Menelaos led

Antiochos to believe that Jerusalem was in revolt, prompting him to storm the city and ransack the temple,[66] since this story offers the best parallel to the question whether or not Jason and Menelaos of their own accord offered Antiochos IV an increased tribute in order to obtain the high priesthood.

B. A Comparison: Antiochos IV's Assault on Jerusalem. The account of the events that led to Antiochos's assault on Jerusalem provides a neat contrast between the dutiful manifestation of loyalty from the people on the one hand (2 Macc. 5:1–4) and on the other the reckless behavior of Jason and Menelaos, who by engaging in civil strife caused both the death of their fellow citizens and Antiochos's dire response (5:5–16). Allegedly, the king "believed" (*dielaben,* 5:11) that the Judeans were in revolt—as shown in Chapter 6 (§6.1), he was not mistaken; indeed, his harsh behavior can be explained only as a reaction to a wide-scale uprising. Moreover, there are indications that the unrest extended to other regions as well, since we learn that the king appointed overseers (*epistatai*) not only in Jerusalem (5:22) but also on Mount Gerizim (5:23). Finally, he perhaps also stormed the town of Arados.[67] As we saw earlier,[68] it is easy to see why the two Maccabees authors were eager to conceal the existence of this rebellion, since otherwise they would have acknowledged that Antiochos's crackdown was justified. But whereas the author of 1 Maccabees used a paratactic style to suppress causality altogether, thereby painting Antiochos's attack as unprovoked,[69] the other writer put the blame for Antiochos's dire suppression on the rival high priests, by alleging that their civil strife was what caused of Antiochos IV's misjudging the situation. To summarize: the wicked high priests act, and the kings react, all incurring the author's censure.

C. The Increase in the Tribute and the Deposition of Onias III. In 2 Maccabees 4:7–10, the deposition of Onias is identified outright as Jason's doing, with Antiochos IV allotted a strictly reactive part. Although this account is not implausible per se (admittedly, we could well imagine the king rejoicing at this impromptu arrival of money),[70] it is too obviously to be credible part of the scheme whereby Jason ousted Onias and Menelaos assassinated Jason (2 Macc. 4:32–34), whereas Judas was Onias's legitimate heir (2 Macc. 15:12).

Actually, to devise his version of the facts the author did not need to breach the rules of historical verisimilitude so much as reshape an existing memory. Thus his starting point was the establishment of the *gymnasion* and the correlated politicization of Jerusalem. To judge from the Tyriaion inscription,[71] it appears that kings granted the status of polis to non-Greek cities and military settlements at the request of embassies sent by local leading men. This must have been the case with Jerusalem, implying that Jason genuinely "promised to pay 150 [talents] if he should be granted by virtue of his office the power to establish a *gymnasion* and an *ephēbeion,* and to draw up the list of Antiochenes in Jerusalem" (2 Macc. 4:9).

Consequently, all our author needed to do was to couple the negotiation over the status of Jerusalem and its associated 150 talents with the royal demand for raising the tribute to "360 silver talents and an additional revenue of 80 talents" (4:8) and the deposition of the recalcitrant Onias III, which originally was a distinct matter.[72]

In conclusion, the literary device in 2 Maccabees that links the wicked high priests, pious high priests, and kings casts suspicion on the author's allegations about who was ultimately responsible for the twofold political and economic crisis—the toppling of the Oniad dynasty and the sharp rise in taxes.

7.3. TRIBUTE AND APPOINTMENT OF THE HIGH PRIESTS IN 1 MACCABEES

The insistence in 2 Maccabees of yoking the correlated themes of tax increase and royal appointment of the high priests to damages incurred by the temple shows that the author considered these as major issues. The theme of the tribute is also mentioned in 1 Maccabees, however, albeit with a quite different slant, and the same applies to the Seleukid pretension to control the nomination of the high priests. This section will now examine how the two principal issues of 2 Maccabees are tackled in the other work, prior to investigating which matters are considered of chief importance in 1 Maccabees in section 7.4.

7.3.1. Fiscal Issues in 1 Maccabees

Despite growing epigraphic evidence, 1 Maccabees continues to be one of the main sources of evidence regarding the imperial tax policy instituted by the Seleukids, thanks in particular to the royal decrees reproduced in 10:25–45, 11:29–37, and 13:36–40.[73] It should be noted, however, that these official documents are cited not merely to record them for posterity but as part of the author's argument. Several incidents in the narrative clearly serve to condemn the pretension of the Seleukid imperial administration to apply levies, and the fact that the issue of taxes is linked to the temple's fate confirms how important it was to the author's political argument, as we shall now see.

The first allusion to the tribute ties it to circumstances of considerable symbolic significance: readying his army for war against Judas, the king realized that "his treasury had run out of money and that the tribute from his territories was small because of the dissension and disorder that he caused in his land by abrogating the laws that had been in force from the earliest times" (1 Macc. 3:29); the king therefore set off for Persis in order to "gather a large sum of money by collecting the tribute of the territories" (3:31). Thus the king's decree "to all his kingdom for all to become one people and for each to abandon his own customs" (1:41–42), which precipitated the "persecution" against the recalcitrant Judeans, emptied the royal treasury.⁷⁴ From a strictly narrative point of view, the observation that the king's financial strictures were the result of the "persecution" is not indispensable, and hence it is mentioned to create a conceptual link with a symbolically significant matter; again, this is a case of semantic concatenation. Moreover, the text notes that once in Persis the wicked king indulges in looting temples (6:1–4) under the pretext of collecting the tribute (3:31).⁷⁵ Antiochos's impious way of applying his military force to the plunder of temples may be contrasted with Judas's glorious acquisition of booty from the battlefield after his defeat of the king's armies (6:6; see 4:23).

By the same logic, the author's insertion of an anecdote about Tryphon's treachery in the context of Simon's preliminary victories serves to denounce the illegitimate nature of the tribute: Tryphon, the contender to the Seleukid throne, demands a hundred talents of silver and two of Jonathan's sons as hostages for the release of Jonathan himself, who is being held "because of money [he] owed the royal treasury in connection with his official capacities" (1 Macc. 13:15). Whereas Antiochos's levy of taxes takes the form of temple plunder, Tryphon extorts funds through ransom, and eventually murders Jonathan instead of releasing him (13:23). Thereafter Simon purportedly justifies his request of tax exemption to King Demetrios II as compensation for Tryphon's theft (13:34).

The central issue of this episode is autonomy from the Seleukid imperial yoke. In both the Achaimenid and the Seleukid empires the imposition of tribute was the most conspicuous mark of imperial subjection, whereas not having to pay tribute to anyone was equated with autonomy.⁷⁶ In his reply to Simon's request, Demetrios II waives all taxes, including arrears, owed by the *ethnos* of the Judeans and concedes the right for them to man their own fortresses, effectively granting them self-rule (13:36–40). These Judean fortresses, of course, were strengthened by Simon and, as seen in Chapter 4 (§4.2), provide an element of the legitimizing theme of the fortifications in 1 Maccabees. Although the association between the revocation of the tribute and the concession of fortifications is not remarkable per se, in 1 Maccabees the fortifications also function as a mediating synecdoche by means of which the issue of the tribute is turned into a legitimate object of discussion.

Finally, the last allusion to the tribute links it to the Akra. This time the "unlawful" request comes from Antiochos VII, who demands from Simon the payment of "500 talents for the damage you have done and for the taxes due from the cities [of Joppe and Gazara and the Akra in Jerusalem]" (1 Macc. 15:31). Although Simon agrees to pay the compensation for Joppe and Gazara (15:35)—but not for the Akra—he reasserts his claim to autonomy, the author once again using his reply to color the Seleukid demand for the tribute as an unjust imposition.⁷⁷ By including the Akra in the list of places for which Antiochos demanded compensation, he creates a conceptual link between the territorial contest over Joppe and Gazara and the Seleukid's construction of the Akra: that is, with the desecration of the temple.

Thus the narrative handling of the tribute question leaves no doubt that the crux of the matter is the moral right of the Seleukid kings to levy taxes, which is systematically presented in a negative light and linked obliquely to an issue of symbolic resonance (here, the Akra). Although as in 2 Maccabees the arguments adopted here reflect as much political bias as the cultural need to associate the levying of the tribute with the temple, the two texts employ quite distinct mediating synecdoches to adapt the symbolic vehicle to the narrative context. Whereas in 2 Maccabees the emphasis is on the increased tribute rate—principally to denounce the rival high priests through the mediation of the *gymnasion* and the holy vessels, and only secondarily against the king—in 1 Maccabees the contention over the tribute is aimed at denouncing the Seleukid imperial yoke and therefore is accordingly linked to the Akra and territorial issues.

7.3.2. *The Seleukid Appointment of the High Priests in 1 Maccabees*

As seen above (§7.2.1), in 1 Maccabees Seleukid interference with the appointment of the high priest could not be granted prominent attention because of the sympathetic tone that the author used elsewhere in his narration of Jonathan's confirmation in the high priesthood by Demetrios II (1 Macc. 11:25–26). To compensate, the author shaped his account of the failed attempt of Ptolemaios son of Aboubos to eliminate Simon and his sons and seize the high priesthood for himself (1 Macc. 16:11–24), using the ignominious pattern of the competitor's pledge to increase the taxes in a bid to secure his appointment from the king.

A. Seleukid Appointment and Taxes: Ptolemy Son of Aboubos in 1 Maccabees 16:11–24. According to 1 Maccabees, Ptolemaios was the son-in-law of the high priest (i.e., Simon?) and affluent enough to hire murderers and bribe others to assist him in his coup (16:11–12). After having Simon and two of his sons murdered, Ptolemaios is said to have sent a messenger to ask the king "to send him troops to assist him, offering to deliver to the king the cities and the taxes" (1 Macc. 16:18). Ptolemaios's alleged offer would have greatly appealed to the king, given that previously Simon had managed to exact from Demetrios II a complete tax exemption and the removal of the garrison from Jerusalem (15:5–8). From the author's point of view, Ptolemaios was ready to put an end to the Judeans' hard-won "autonomy."

B. Alkimos's Appointment in 1 Maccabees: The Struggle Over Land Possession in 1 Maccabees 7:5–9. 1 Maccabees' account of Ptolemaios son of Aboubos notwithstanding, the respective depictions of the circumstances that brought Alkimos to power in 1 and 2 Maccabees are further evidence that the two authors lay the emphasis on different factors of disruption, although they paint this episode in equally hostile terms: in 1 Maccabees it is claimed that Ptolemaios gathered "all the sinful and wicked men of Israel" (1 Macc. 7:5) around him, brought charges against his own people (7:6), and in this way secured his appointment as high priest from Demetrios (7:9). However, while 2 Maccabees focuses on the contentious theme of royal appointment, 1 Maccabees fails to exploit the topic. Conversely, in 1 Maccabees the speech attributed to Alkimos and his supporters emphasizes the struggle over the land, which has no equivalent in its counterpart,[78] suggesting that land issues are of pivotal importance for the author of 1 Maccabees (1 Macc. 7:6–7). As we shall now see, he effectively treats land disputes as the main cause of the crisis, whereas the issue is downplayed—albeit by no means ignored—in 2 Maccabees.

7.4. THE AKRA, THE SELEUKID *KATOIKIA*, AND LAND CONFISCATIONS

If in 2 Maccabees the loci that really reveal how the author construed the causes of the crisis are the fictitious statements of intent—Antiochos's confession and Lysias's prospective vengeance—in 1 Maccabees the equivalent sections are the lamentations contained in the first three chapters (1 Macc. 1:36–40, 2:7–13, 3:45), which intimate that the true threat to the temple is the presence of the Akra and all it implies. The poem appearing in 1:36–40 immediately after the account of its fortification by Antiochos (1:33–35) underlines the dire consequences of garrisoning the fort, including its settlement by outsiders (*katoikoi*, 1:38).[79] The theme of the Akra's foreigners' (*huioi allogenōn*) supplanting the lawful inhabitants of Jerusalem recurs in 1 Maccabees 3:45,[80] while Mattathias's lamentation pivots on the foreigners' (*allotrioi, ethnē*) control of the temple (1 Macc. 2:7, 12).[81]

With their freight of prophetic themes,[82] these verses create a framework familiar to the original audience, in which the otherwise untraditional themes of the Akra and foreign settlement may be smoothly incorporated, and the insinuation of an *intrinsic* link between the foreign colony and the desecration of the temple infused. Thus, while the poems ostensibly focus on the temple (the meaningful element), they smuggle in several material issues that, precisely because they are presented as major threats to the temple, must be those that the author of 1 Maccabees saw as the main problems occurring in the second stage of the struggle against the Seleukids, namely the establishment of a military colony in Jerusalem, the ensuing confiscation of lands for the benefit of the settlers, and possibly also the privileged access of the latter to the temple.

The theme of land confiscation for military allotment appears again in prose when Antiochos imparts instructions to Lysias before departing for Persis (1 Macc. 3:34b–36, emphases added):

> As for the inhabitants of Judah and Jerusalem, [Lysias] was to send against them a force to wipe out and destroy the strength of Israel and the remnant of Jerusalem and

erase their memory from the area, settling foreigners throughout their territory and giving out their land in allotments.

As this passage shows, Antiochos IV's offensive against the rebelling Judeans is depicted in 1 Maccabees as a concerted effort to quell the revolt and repopulate Judea with new settlers, the installation of a foreign settlement being a well-documented means for Hellenistic kings to punish rebellious subjects.[83]

7.4.1. The Akra, the Settlers, and Land Confiscations in 1 Maccabees

Although from a historical point of view the establishment of the fortress dominating the City of David and the settling of "foreigners" throughout the territory are clearly interconnected, in 1 Maccabees they are treated separately. This split apparently stems from the author's decision to insert a section centered on Mattathias, which needed fleshing out either by duplicating his narrative material or by splitting narrative elements that originally belonged to Judas's time unit. As the narrative progresses, however, the two (or three) themes are joined up again, so that the land issue is given prominent emphasis in the grievances that the wicked Israelites allied with the men of the Akra against Judas's siege of the fortress lodged before the king (1 Macc. 6:21–27).[84]

Immediately before their speech, it is specified that Judas decided to besiege the Akra because "the men of the Akra had been besetting Israel in the neighborhood of the sanctuary as they continually sought to do evil and give aid to the gentiles" (1 Macc. 6:18). Here the author's primary aim is to justify Judas's siege of the Akra by symbolically linking it to the temple—by emphasizing that the garrison's very presence poses a vital threat to the temple. However, the phrasing also makes clear that those whose lands are wrecked are in fact wicked Judeans. It therefore seems that the various issues related to the land—the property of the wicked Judeans (6:24), the royal domains (6:25), and the military allotments[85]—conflate around the Akra. Indeed the wicked Israelites allegedly are the first to associate the fate of their own property with that of the royal domains (6:25; cf. 7:7).

When Simon finally ejects the garrison from the Akra, he reverses the wrongdoings of the kings and their supporters. First, the non-Judean inhabitants of Joppe are expelled, and the town is repopulated with Judeans (13:11); and later the same procedure is reiterated in Gazara (13:43–48).[86]

7.4.2. Garrisons in 2 Maccabees

Unlike his counterpart, the author of 2 Maccabees not only devotes scant attention to the Akra, but he tends, moreover, to underplay its part as a factor of the crisis. Modern scholars have been swift to surmise a close connection between Jason's Antiochenes (2 Macc. 4:9) and the garrison of the Akra, but in actual fact 2 Maccabees provides no positive evidence to support the link, as the author remains silent on this matter. Likewise, 2 Maccabees makes a casual reference to the Seleukid commander of the citadel and his Cypriot mercenaries (4:28–29), narrating merely that Antiochos left Philip as overseer after his first assault on Jerusalem, making no mention of a garrison (5:22). Ultimately, readers are left to wonder who were the "peoples" who had fled from Judas and who came to meet Nikanor, and why they were in Judea in the first place, and where (14:12–14). Insofar as the *gymnasion*, not the Akra, was indicated as the source of impurity threatening the temple, for the author of 2 Maccabees the Akra was not worth talking about, and its symbolic status is left unspecified. The only explicit allusion to the settlers is Lysias's talk of "turning their city into a Greek settlement" (11:2).[87]

7.4.3. The Altars of the Countryside as the Mediating Synecdoche of the Land Allotments

As we saw, far from being neutrally descriptive, the references to the Akra in 1 Maccabees serve to signify what the central issue of the crisis was, and yet these references do not exhaust the author's view of the matter. It seems that the theme of the illicit altars built throughout the land was intended as an additional synecdochic signifier to refer to the confiscation of agricultural estates and the allotment of land parcels to the settlers of the military *katoikia*. Because talking about the land confiscations per se did not carry any symbolic resonance, it failed to convey the sense that such confiscations were a major problem; whereas the building of illicit altars in the fields bore vast significance. The logic linking the two is simple enough: the confiscated lands were shared out among the military settlers, who naturally built altars for their own use on their allotments. By creating an equation between the building of the illicit altars in the countryside and the desecration of the temple altar, the author linked the economic issue of the land confiscations to the fate of the temple, by means of this system of semantic concatenation already observed in 2 Maccabees. In 1 Maccabees the settlers' altars function as the mediating synecdoche for the military allotments. It is perhaps no coincidence that the passage that most clearly bears this function out—an allusion to the *katoikoi* taking possession of their lands and housing lots—is part of the description of the "persecution" (1 Macc. 1:54–55).[88]

Thus, although in several instances in 1 Maccabees the issue of the agricultural allotments of the *katoikoi* is referred to in transparent, undiluted terms, it is also mediated by a synecdoche. The consequence of this discursive construction has been to blur the modern reader's perception of just how prominent the topic of the allotments is in this work.

7.4.4. The Mediating Synecdoches of Warfare in the Countryside

By this logic, the theme of the destruction of the unlawful altars (*bōmoi*) serves as the mediating vehicle for discussing warfare in the countryside. Thus in Mattathias's narrative unit the destruction of the *bōmoi* is coupled with forced circumcision (1 Macc. 2:45–46).[89] This pairing mounts a particularly malicious allegation against the wicked Judeans, whose property, as noted earlier (§7.4.1), is wrecked alongside the settlers' (1 Macc. 6:21–27, 7:5–7). Not only does the author reiterate the charge that the wicked Judeans had forgone circumcision—previously leveled in conjunction with their frequenting the *gymnasion* in 1 Maccabees 1:15—but the indictment of idolatry contained in the same episode is restated directly.[90] In contrast, we may assume that in historical terms those said to "flee the repression" to join the ranks of Mattathias's men and the *Asidaioi* (1 Macc. 2:43) were the victims of the aforesaid confiscations.

Curiously, in 2 Maccabees the theme of the destruction of the illicit altars is transposed to Jerusalem and inserted into the context of the temple's purification (2 Macc. 10:2).[91]

A. *The Sabbath as Mediating Synecdoche for Warfare in 1 and 2 Maccabees?*   Reference to the destruction of the forbidden altars suggests further possible mediating synecdoches adopted in 1 and 2 Maccabees to speak of the war. One that is easily identified is the recurrent use of the theme of the Sabbath. Thus in 2 Maccabees the Judeans allegedly take refuge in caves to ensure that they keep the Sabbath (2 Macc. 6:11);[92] but this account is suspect, given the abundant historical evidence that the caves of the desert of Judah were frequently used by the native population to mount guerilla operations against invaders.[93] Therefore, the first goal of the people fleeing the Seleukid soldiers to the caves was in all likelihood to offer armed resistance of some kind; certainly, once they were in the caves, they could also freely observe the Sabbath.

Elsewhere, the various evildoers of 1 and 2 Maccabees are often recorded as taking advantage of the Sabbath to attack the pious Judeans (e.g., 1 Macc. 2:32–38, 2 Macc. 5:24). Although attacks doubtless sometimes occurred on the Sabbath, such incidents are too frequently cited to be taken for factual reporting and are more a means of exploiting their symbolic potential.

As this overview shows, the apparent matter-of-fact style of 1 Maccabees is deceptive, as instead the details are carefully selected to satisfy an internal narrative function. Despite their differences in style, 1 Maccabees is far closer to 2 Maccabees in its narrative devices and principles of composition than it is to Polybius.[94]

. . .

From the examination above we can conclude that the system of semantic concatenation mediated by symbolically meaningful synecdoches provides an authorial comment on the causes of the rebellion (in 2 Maccabees) and on the matters of contention that emerged in the course of the military suppression[95] (in 1 Maccabees). The fact that a topic is harnessed to the temple's fate through the mediation of a symbolically loaded synecdochic signifier per se is evidence that this threat was identified as a major factor of disruption of the social and cosmic order, or in our words, a major cause of the rebellion. Having now established, however, that it was indispensable for the Maccabees authors to link with a major peril to the temple the political and economic matters that they wished to mention, we must query to what extent the foregoing "political and economic matters" were genuinely central in the days of the rebellion—or at least were remembered as such under the Hasmonean dynasty. In particular, doubts may arise because, as argued in the Methodological Introduction to Part II, our authors selected the topics they meant to emphasize according to literary parameters, primarily the principle of internal narrative coherence—the author of 2 Maccabees focusing on affairs that could in one way or another be connected to the *gymnasion,* whereas in 1 Maccabees the focus is on the Akra. Therefore it is appropriate to conclude this chapter with an evaluation of the relation between text and historical reality.

My working assumption that the use of mediating synecdoches is not a pure literary artifice of the Maccabees authors' but a reliable marker of what their contemporary audience construed as the main issues that emerged on the eve and in the course of the rebellion—that assumption is ultimately supported by the question how the works were received in their day: that is, by the argument of reception. Had the authors selected their material—the political, military, economic, and fiscal issues that they "showed" as affecting the temple—on a purely literary basis, disregarding the collective memory of their contemporaries, they would have irremediably jeopardized the verisimilitude of the events related, and hence the trustworthiness of their accounts.

In my view, the list of issues shown to be incorporated by concatenation into the sphere of the temple in either 1 or 2 Maccabees (or the two) in the foregoing analysis vindicates this standpoint. Once it is stripped of the more blatant elements of political bias and adapted to modern nomenclature, this list may be summarized thus: a fiscal crisis prompted by a seemingly sharp increase of the tribute; the political destabilization of the Judean leading circles resulting from the deposition of the Oniad dynasty and the Seleukid attempt to impose new rules for the appointment of the high priests; the politicization of Jerusalem, the practical implications of which are not absolutely clear to us. (And the same applies to the related establishment of the *gymnasion,* if at least it was an issue per se, which is not certain.) So much for the catalyzing factors. The predicaments that emerged in the course of the repression were the establishment of a military settlement with its fortress (the Akra); the accompanying land confiscations; the Judeans' dispossession of their temple to the benefit of the settlers as the ultimate punishment of their rebellion; and a Judean claim to autonomy. Not only could all these topics honorably feature in modern works of history under the same heading, "Main Causes," but some, in particular the initial fiscal crisis and the Seleukid attempt to control the high priests, are largely overlooked in modern studies of the rebellion. Conversely, we can safely ditch the modern myth that the author of 2 Maccabees construed the rebellion as a struggle of Judaism against Hellenism, not to mention the alleged prohibition of Jewish customs.[96] For these reasons I hold the literary analysis of the system of mediating synecdoches as an indispensable auxiliary to modern investigations of the Judean rebellion.

Part III of this book will present an historical reconstruction of the causes and nature of the Judean rebellion against Antiochos IV, drawing from what the two Maccabees authors themselves tell us about it. Although we need not subscribe to their understanding of its causes in every detail—in particular, we must rule out their political bias—my reconstruction treats the two literary works as reasonably reliable sources of evidence. In particular, this new analysis challenges the ongoing derogatory attitude of modern scholars toward the author of 2 Maccabees both before and after the historiographical shift of the 1970s.

CONCLUSION

To reach a full understanding of the extent to which the system of semantic concatenation by which pragmatic matters were incorporated into the symbolic sphere of the temple through the mediation of synecdochic items is a wider cultural trait, and not the fruit of a personal conservative attitude of a writer within a given culture, let us try to imagine how a supporter of Menelaos might have recounted the events of Judea in the days of Antiochos IV. In such a work the audience would expect to find much on Menelaos's piety and righteous concern for the welfare of his people. We would also certainly learn that Judas was the utter embodiment of evil-doing, a man so godless as to wage war on the Sabbath (quite an innovation indeed!) and relentlessly endeavor to destabilize Menelaos's rule as high priest, acting "not for the sake of his countrymen" (in contrast with Menelaos), "but for selfish and impious interests." If the work was written before Antiochos IV's assault on Jerusalem, we would have been convinced that this king was a new Cyrus.[1] After this event, we would have admired Menelaos's personal efforts to save his people and temple. Works of this period are the outcome of a specific interplay between culturally conditioned mindscape and political bias. A different political support would have provided a wholly different account. It would have taken another angle altogether, the mediating synecdoches would have been worked out differently, and as a result the account of events would have looked very different. However, this account would have been informed by the same cultural and narrative tools as 1 and 2 Maccabees.

The premise that the accounts of 1 and 2 Maccabees are shaped by culturally conditioned narrative codes encapsulates a twofold methodological claim concerning the use of these works for historical reconstruction. On the one hand, the texts cannot be read as transparent factual descriptions. Not only their ideological biases but also their cultural codes require attention. Ignoring them means misreading as objective facts—that is, what modern historians describe as such—elements belonging to the symbolic construction of the text. Cases of this misapprehension include the modern idea of Jason and Menelaos as Hellenizers and the Maccabees as religious conservatives, along with the current view that the author of 2 Maccabees read the Judean rebellion against Antiochos IV as a struggle between Judaism and Hellenism.

On the other hand, the fact that the accounts are informed by narrative patterns does not qualify them as fictitious. Such a hypercritical stance is based on the erroneous assumption that the normal procedure at the time was to tell a story in a dry and unembellished way. This is another way of mistaking style for content.[2] In fact, the use of discursive codes distinct from the modern Western canons of historiography does not preclude the presence of a historical core based on fact. On the contrary, insofar as it was standard procedure to inform a story with a set narrative pattern, using intertextuality with already known stories, and equating a living person with a prototype by shaping his biography upon that of the prototype, our working premise should acknowledge that the intrinsic literary construction of the tale related is never arbitrary. Not only the choice of a specific mode of literary elaboration is meaningful and therefore informative per se, but moreover we must take for granted that the story *has* a historical core of facts. The reconstruction of the story merely becomes a more intricate matter, especially because the relation between the historical core and its literary elaboration is more flexible than in a (purportedly) straightforward account, and it is not always easy to determine which particular parameters are at play in the redaction of a given passage.

There is a tendency in recent scholarship to treat 2 Maccabees with circumspection and consider it of limited use for historical reconstruction because deemed to offer a religious and cultural reading of the causes of the rebellion, whereas the real causes, so to speak, must surely have been political. But these real causes unfortunately remain obscure, because the early authors omitted them from their accounts. When the discourse in 1 and 2 Maccabees is analyzed not as a dry description of reality in the (supposed) style of Polybius, but as a synthesis of cultural codes and political bias, what the authors do say about the causes of the rebellion appears in a totally different light. Leaving aside the desecration of the temple and the killing of the population, the issues stigmatized with most insistence in 2 Maccabees are the increase in the tribute and the Seleukid meddling with the appointment of the high priests. In 1 Maccabees the issues most recurrently emphasized are the establishment of a garrison, the fortification of the Akra, the land issues, and the Seleukid demand of the tribute. Nothing in this list would shame a modern historiographical work. It will be the purpose of the last part of this book to show that the causes pointed out by the ancient literary sources may indeed serve as a basis for a modern historical reconstruction of the causes and nature of the Judean rebellion against Antiochos IV.

PART III

History

*The Judean Rebellion in Historical Perspective,
200–164 B.C.E.*

A SUMMARY OF THE CONCLUSIONS OF PARTS I AND II

From Literary Analysis to History

The literary analysis of Part II showed how the accounts of 1 and 2 Maccabees constructed their respective discourses about reality. It argued that their genesis resulted from two fundamental rhetorical elements: their culturally conditioned discursive codes and their political biases. According to the former, the narrative foci of 1 and 2 Maccabees systematically shift toward the aspects of both pious deeds and evildoings that have an impact on the temple, because the temple's fate was what was worth remembering, whereas discussing more mundane matters per se was not legitimate. However, this slant was applied differently in each work. Whereas either the account of 2 Maccabees focuses directly on the temple or else the link to the temple is mediated by the *gymnasion*, in 1 Maccabees the mediating vehicle is the Akra—which is presented as a constant threat of impurities upon the temple. This difference between the two books impinges on the concrete issues that are pointed at in each work through mediating synecdoches. In 2 Maccabees, the politicization of Jerusalem lurks behind the *gymnasion*, whose creation is treated as the cause for neglecting the sacrifices; the mention of the tax increase is delegitimized by the twofold allegation that it was associated with Jason's establishment of the *gymnasion* and was the cause of Menelaos's theft of the holy vessels. In 1 Maccabees, the outrage over the creation of the military settlement, by focal shift, centers on the construction of the Akra; opposition to the land seizures lurks behind the account of Mattathias's destruction of the illicit altars in the countryside—whose construction is associated with the desecration of the temple altar. Finally, when the process of focal shift is deconstructed and the reading is rationalized, the accounts of the "persecution" in 1 and 2 Maccabees appear to refer to a military repression following a popular uprising and to the establishment of a military garrison involving the expropriation of land and the new settlers' assuming control over the temple. Incidentally, this rationalized outline basically dovetails with the range of topics epitomized by the Akra in 1 Maccabees.

At the same time, the authors of 1 and 2 Maccabees had a political agenda. Their primary concern was to legitimize the Hasmoneans' rise to power and in particular their specific form of power, namely their unprecedented combination of highpriestly and royallike functions. The aim was to vindicate the Maccabees' actions on three fronts at once. One was to illustrate why they were the legitimate heirs of Onias III—which meant depicting the internecine struggle for power in a manner that magnified their piety, and hence their political legitimacy. The second was to show why their rival contenders were illegitimate, by presenting them as impious—thereby clearly drawing the line between good and wicked. Finally, it was necessary to reiterate why the uprising against the Seleukids—which ultimately led to the establishment of a semi-autonomous kingdom—was legitimate.

Each author embodied these political topics according to the subject matter of his second legitimizing account. Since 2 Maccabees focuses on Judas and the temple, the sins attributed to Jason and Menelaos relate to the temple: in building the *gymnasion* Jason induced the priests to neglect the sacrifices, and Menelaos was a temple looter. Conversely, 1 Maccabees focuses on Simon, the city walls, and the purification of the Akra; and therefore the wrongdoing that delegitimizes Alkimos, the wicked high priest in this work, is his alleged intention to demolish the walls. These divergent emphases also explain why each author emphasizes different contentious issues. The main factors of the crisis denounced in 2 Maccabees are interlaced around the issue of the *gymnasion:* the appointment of the high priests by the Seleukid king, the subsequent increased tribute demand, and the politicization of Jerusalem. In 1 Maccabees, the issue of land seizures was easier to tie to the Akra—which explains why these feature prominently in the work (although, as noted, this theme is further tied to the illicit altars and thereby to the desecration of the temple altar). In contrast to 2 Maccabees, where the issue of taxes is associated with the appointment of the high priests, in 1 Maccabees it is linked to the issue of autonomy.

To some extent, one may say that the main thrust of 2 Maccabees is to attack the rival high priests and to demonstrate why the Hasmoneans were the legitimate heirs to Onias III, whereas 1 Maccabees sets out more specifically to denounce Seleukid rule. Therefore the hostility of the author of 2 Maccabees is aimed primarily at the rival high priests—Jason, Menelaos, and Alkimos—and only secondarily at the kings. The Seleukid yoke is denounced indirectly, through a literary montage that systematically presents Antiochos IV's evildoings as an amplification of the evils allegedly perpetrated by the high priests—Jason's disruption of the sacrifices and Menelaos's theft of the sacred vessels. Conversely, in 1 Maccabees there is no mention of Jason and Menelaos, although Alkimos, the third rival high priest, is vehemently attacked, and the kings' greed and deceitfulness is more clearly highlighted in 1 Maccabees than in the other work.

Even more clearly, the topical distribution between the two parallel works corresponds to a chronological divide, 2 Maccabees more particularly dealing with the run-up to the rebellion, whereas 1 Maccabees covers the phase of military repression after the rebellion has begun. This explains why the authors' catalogues of material grievances are slightly different, in the sense of complementary. The problems emphasized in 2 Maccabees are the imperial appointment of the high priest; the increased tribute demand; the establishment of the polis of the Antiochenes and the *gymnasion*; and the tax paid for the new status. This list may be considered to reflect the author's own analysis of the causes of the rebellion. In contrast, the issues featuring in 1 Maccabees are the land seizures, the installation of the military garrison and the fortification of the Akra, the tribute, and autonomy from the Seleukids.

The aim of this final part of this book is to show that the material issues pointed at in the ancient sources can serve as the starting point of a plausible historical reconstruction of the two parallel dimensions of the crisis that eventually brought the Hasmoneans to power: the internal struggle for power and the causes and evolution of the Judean rebellion against the Seleukids. However, the version of events presented in those sources cannot be accepted at face value, because of the authors' political biases. These entailed three fundamental distortions, which should be restated before we turn to the detailed discussion of the last four chapters of this book, in order to justify why the historical reconstruction proposed here substantially departs from the accounts presented in the sources. The first distortion is due to the need to delegitimize the rival high priests on grounds of impiety, and it affects their portrayal and the description of their actions. The second is motivated by the need to legitimize the Maccabees as pious. Its effect may be pointed out in two related descriptions: the contrast alleged between Jason, Menelaos, and Alkimos on the one hand and the Maccabees on the other, and the claim that the Maccabees joined the struggle only after Antiochos IV's atrocities in Jerusalem. The latter distortion was driven by the need to prove that the rebellion was legitimate. In this perspective it was indispensable to pretend that Antiochos IV's assault was unjustified and to disguise all hints that his attack was in response to popular rebellion.

Although the two Maccabees authors are intent on absolving the people of any responsibility for the dire events narrated, the third issue is treated differently in the two works. In 1 Maccabees, the deliberately paratactic style obscures their logical concatenation, thereby suppressing causality. Antiochos IV's attack on the temple becomes an unprovoked aggression and therefore pure wickedness. The narrative construction of 2 Maccabees is more complex: it is the wicked high priests who are responsible for Antiochos IV's assault and brutality. Whereas

1 Maccabees uses omission, this declarative approach of 2 Maccabees has been particularly damaging for modern interpretations of the crisis. It must therefore be deconstructed before any alternative interpretation can be attempted. This may be done by compiling the impressive list of misdeeds imputed to Jason and Menelaos in this work.[1]

First, Jason: he deposes Onias III of his own accord; further, he takes the initiative in raising the tribute; he establishes the *gymnasion* and neglects the sacrifices. (Antiochos later discontinues them entirely.) Next, Menelaos: he ousts Jason, raising the tribute yet again; being unable to raise the amount required, he robs the temple of the holy vessels—a portent of Antiochos IV's future plundering of the temple—and thereupon with the stolen vessels he bribes Andronikos into assassinating Onias III (2 Macc. 4:32–34). It is further insinuated that he bribed Ptolemaios son of Dorymenes into intervening on his behalf when the elders accuse him in front of the king, leading to the execution of the elders themselves (2 Macc. 4:45–50). Finally, Jason and Menelaos together: while the people dutifully pray for the success of Antiochos IV's campaign in Egypt, Jason takes advantage of the royal campaign to attack Jerusalem and launch a civil war against Menelaos (2 Macc. 5:1–10). This attack on Jerusalem and Jason's killing of his fellow citizens is a harbinger of Antiochos's punitive assault shortly thereafter: the internal strife leads the king to believe that Jerusalem is revolting against his rule, prompting him to storm the city, massacre the population, and plunder the temple. Thus, Jason in particular, but Menelaos too, is portrayed as being ultimately responsible for Antiochos IV's actions.

The case against Jason and Menelaos is constructed carefully and systematically. One layer—the semantic field of wickedness and impiety—is an echo of the cultural and rhetorical conventions of the time and may be easily disposed of. Jason's alleged neglect of the sacrifices and Menelaos's alleged looting of the holy vessels unquestionably belong to this layer—as may their real or imputed transgressions against Onias (Jason by ousting him and Menelaos by having him assassinated). However, it is not sound methodology to dispose of these fabrications because they are of a "religious" nature while assuming that the rest is historical, because it suits our criteria of rationality. Even if we leave aside the misdeeds belonging to this layer of impiety, the list of charges imputed to Jason and Menelaos remains implausibly long, and there can be little doubt that their portrayals are politically motivated distortions. Deconstructing the list of their wrongdoings is essential to a more reliable historical understanding of the background of the uprising.

The chapters in this final part of this book propose a historical reconstruction based on the aforementioned premises. Its basic contention is that the nexus of tax increase and the political destabilization prompted by Antiochos's interference with the appointment of the high priest—which the author of 2 Maccabees focuses upon—was indeed a crucial factor in sparking off the Judean rebellion against the Seleukid king. The analysis of the ancient author is supported by extratextual evidence. To provide a proper account of the origins of the fiscal aspect, the inquiry must begin with the conquest of the region by Antiochos III, since this was when the status of Jerusalem and the *ethnos* of the Judeans as a whole was defined. The discussion will move on chronologically to cover the reigns of Antiochos III the Great (200/198–187 B.C.E.), Seleukos IV Philopator (187–175 B.C.E.), and Antiochos IV Epiphanes (175–164 B.C.E.) before and after the revolt—with particular attention to the elements likely to cast light on the uprising's dual nature, both political and fiscal.

8

*Judea and Koilē Syria and Phoinikē under
Antiochos III, 200–187 B.C.E.*

INTRODUCTION

Flourishing studies on Hellenistic statehood and statesmanship in recent years have considerably enhanced our understanding of what may be called the Hellenistic culture of empire. The term refers not merely to the motivations for conquering and controlling foreign lands but to the modus operandi of the interaction between kings and subject communities. The state of the question emerging in these matters calls for a reexamination of how the Judean polity was incorporated into the Seleukid empire and how the leading Judean families developed their strategies of power within the imperial setting. These issues form the structural backdrop against which the causes and nature of the Judean rebellion against Antiochos IV may be understood.

It is now well accepted that the administrative and imperial culture of the Ptolemies and the Seleukids—and the Attalids—cannot be treated as though the Hellenistic kingdoms were modern Western states.[1] In its ideal form, the modern Western state features a centralized government that implements its decisions through top-down processes of transmission, channeled through an administrative apparatus whose personnel are socially disembedded and act in accordance with predefined objective rules. By contrast, the current understanding of Hellenistic imperial states assumes a different state model,[2] one by which the Hellenistic king had neither the means nor the will to impose his policy unilaterally. Although recent studies acknowledge the existence of central governments aiming to subsume local diversity within imperial unity,[3] any notion of an all-powerful centralized government is misplaced. The stability of the dynasty was contingent upon the cooperation between the king and local elites: the king needed the local elites, because it was they who exerted social control over the local population and collected the taxes. In return, the elites enjoyed additional prestige by virtue of their privileged relationship with the king, which strengthened their power locally. Cooperation between the central power and the local elites was carried on through institutionalized channels of interaction. To take a few examples, the royal practice of euergetism—one fundamental difference between the Achaimenid and Hellenistic cultures of empire—was a major means of communication available to the kings.[4] The royal cult in Greek cities and in Egypt, and the sacrifices performed in the king's name in Babylon and Jerusalem, were one such means of communication available to subject communities. Another avenue open to non-Greek elites was the adoption of (some veneer of) the Greek way of life.[5] Finally, as we shall see in this chapter (§10.2.2), ceremonially welcoming conquerors was a major means for conquered cities to manifest their willful adherence to their new overlords.

Because of this vital need for cooperation, decisions were always negotiated between the king and the local elites, and not imposed by one side on the other. This principle of cooperation also explains why the king generally refrained from interfering with the local social and political structures of power, doing so only when it was imperative. Moreover, when such royal interventions did occur, they often took the form of a change of personnel rather than fundamental reforms imposed from above. As a rule, administrative reforms were introduced to address an immediate need. For the most part, they were reactive, and seldom prescriptive. This praxis, and practical limitations of personnel, explain why the concepts of administrative harmonization and efficient rationalization were foreign to the Hellenistic culture of empire, in which overlapping administrative structures were a deliberate means of distributing power among different groups and persons.

That said, Hellenistic kings were not averse to changes when such served their interests. Whereas in the 1980s and 1990s the generation of scholars identified with the Gröningen Workshop underlined the continuity between the Achaimenid empire and the Hellenistic kingdoms, more recent studies strike a more balanced view, highlighting substantial alterations as well as continuities—dictated both by local conditions and the Greek culture of the Ptolemaic and Seleukid dynasties.[6] Generally these were motivated by the need to secure or improve one or more of the aspects of government that most interested the king—namely the extraction of economic surpluses by taxation, the political loyalty of the local elites, and the political and military stability of the king and empire.

This new understanding of the Hellenistic administrative and imperial culture provides an interpretive framework for understanding how the local Judean community was incorporated within the Seleukid empire. This chapter will establish the premises for this revised approach, starting with the events associated with the reign of Antiochos III. The first section (§8.1) reviews Antiochos III's conquest of

Koilē Syria and Phoinikē from the Ptolemies in 200/198 B.C.E. That takeover was immediately followed by the settlement of the status of the conquered communities. Antiochos III's decree concerning Jerusalem, preserved in Josephus (*Ant.* 12.138–144), deserves a thorough discussion, since it documents both the conditions of the Jerusalemites' surrender and the political and fiscal settlement that was granted by the king. This will be the object of this chapter's second section (§8.2). Finally, that decree offers an opportunity to examine relations between the king and local prominent families. Since the domestic and imperial levels are intertwined to some degree, the social make-up of the leading families and the nature of the domestic tensions between them must also be examined. There are, as is well known, two dominant theories in modern research on the nature of these tensions: one sees them as being between a Hellenized urban elite and the rural conservative families, and the other—underlining the entanglement of domestic and geostrategic tensions—holds that they represented a feud between Ptolemaic and Seleukid factions. As we shall see in the final section of this chapter (§8.3), both these theories are questionable.

8.1. ANTIOCHOS III'S ORGANIZATION OF KOILĒ SYRIA AND PHOINIKĒ AFTER THE FIFTH SYRIAN WAR, 202–198 B.C.E.

Antiochos III conquered the southern part of Syria from the Ptolemies during the Fifth Syrian War (202–198 B.C.E.).[7] His policy in the region after the conquest is documented in several literary sources, in the Hefzibah inscription near Skythopolis, and in numismatic evidence. These attest the usual blend of standard Hellenistic behavior in situations of conquest and pragmatic adaptation to specific local conditions. The king's immediate goal after any conquest was to restore stability, and the most expedient way to achieve this was to retain existing administrative arrangements, insofar as they maintained the delicate balance between the new conqueror's interests and those of the local populations. The very notion of standardization was fundamentally alien to the political culture of the Hellenistic kingdoms, and no time was wasted on unnecessary reforms.

8.1.1. *The Territorial Scope of the Satrapy of Koilē Syria and Phoinikē*

The geographical boundaries of the Ptolemaic province appear to have been left unchanged—however, its name was changed from Syria and Phoinikē to Koilē Syria and Phoinikē. While the Ptolemaic term "Syria" reflected the Alexandrian court's territorial claim over the entire Levantine coast, the addition of the prefix "Koilē" after the Seleukid conquest was designed to distinguish this, the southern satrapy, from the northern core of Seleukid Syria, which was known as Seleukis Syria.[8] The satrapy extended from the Eleutheros River in the north (the modern

Nahr el-Kebir, on the border between Syria and Lebanon) to Gaza in the south, at the border with Egypt, and encompassed all territories west of the Jordan River and the Dead Sea, as well as some territories east of the Jordan. On the coast, most of the Phoenician cities were included, from Tripolis in the north to Tyre and Akē-Ptolemaïs, the provincial capital, in the south—although the territory of Arados, situated north of the Eleutheros River, fell outside it. Further to the south lay the *Paralia* (in which Akē-Ptolemaïs is sometimes included), followed by Philistia/Palaistinē, stretching from Ascalon to Gaza. In the hinterland, Galilee, Samaria, Judea, and Idumea were included. The status of Damascus in the northernmost part is uncertain. Farther to the south, the territories under Seleukid control stretched as far as the borders of northern Arabia. The Nabateans, whose capital, Petra, lay south of the Dead Sea, remained independent.[9] The satrapy's capital, Akē-Ptolemaïs, was renamed Antioch,[10] but 2 Maccabees attests that the name Ptolemaïs continued to be used well into the Seleukid period.

8.1.2. Stabilizing the Conquered Area

Ptolemaios son of Thraseas, who had been appointed governor and high priest of the province of Syria and Phoinikē by Ptolemy V and was in charge when Antiochos's troops attacked, switched allegiance in time and was rewarded by being kept in his dual function of governor and high priest—a position that he apparently continued to hold until his death shortly afterward, in 195 B.C.E.[11]

Antiochos III's most notable decision concerns his monetary policy, especially with regard to silver coinage.[12] Under Ptolemaic rule, the silver coinage issued in the southern Syrian satrapy observed the Ptolemaic standard. Between 310 and 295 B.C.E., Ptolemy I had instituted a closed monetary economy in the territories under his rule, and his successors in Alexandria followed suit. This monetary policy stipulated a lighter standard for the silver tetradrachm as compared with the Attic standard adopted by Alexander, which remained in use in the Antigonid, Seleukid, and Attalid provinces. The Ptolemaic weight was finally set in 295 B.C.E. at approximately 14.25 grams, whereas Alexander's Attic standard was about 17.32 grams. In addition, Ptolemy I prohibited the use of coins of other standards in his dominion: the coins of traders entering the Ptolemaic realm were exchanged at a rate of 1:1 at the border, resulting in a substantial loss of more than 3 grams of silver (over 15%) per coin, and nearly as much benefit for the royal treasury after deducting the cost of recasting the metal in coins of the Ptolemaic standard.[13]

Remarkably, after conquering southern Syria, Antiochos III maintained the exclusive use of Ptolemaic currency in the satrapy. Excepting the initial postconquest period—when bronze coins and low-denomination silver coins (hemiobols) were struck by traveling mints accompanying the army to pay the soldiers—there is no documented issue of silver by Antiochos III in the satrapy, and bronze coins were issued only at Tyre and Akē-Ptolemaïs.[14] Under Seleukos IV (187–175 B.C.E.), only a single issue of silver tetradrachms of the Attic weight standard, of unknown date, can be assigned to the Ptolemaïs mint, and a few more to Antiochos IV between 170 and 164. Under Antiochos V (164–161 B.C.E.) two distinct types were issued at Ptolemaïs: one of the Attic standard, displaying Zeus Nikephoros on the reverse (after the type minted at Antioch), and the other of the Ptolemaic standard, with the well-known Ptolemaic stamp of an eagle gripping lightning bolts in its talons on the reverse. This double silver currency system continued until the end of Seleukid rule in the region. The relative distribution of tetradrachms of the Ptolemaic and Attic standards in various monetary hordes led Georges Le Rider to conclude that the Ptolemaic standard by and large remained the sole currency in circulation in the satrapy of Koilē Syria and Phoinikē from 200 B.C.E. until the end of Seleukid domination, in the late second century B.C.E.[15] Furthermore, it remained exclusive to this satrapy, and Seleukid officials and soldiers paid in Attic-standard coinage were expected to spend it only outside the satrapy's borders. Thus, far from fiscally integrating the newly conquered province into the rest of his empire, Antiochos III kept it as a self-contained monetary area, as it was under the Ptolemies.

This policy has intrigued modern scholars, who have pointed to its negative repercussions for the Seleukids:[16] by refraining from introducing their own coins into the province, Antiochos III and his successors were relinquishing an important source of prestige, as well as the tax revenue that was levied on minting. However, these drawbacks must have been offset by important advantages. As Le Rider has pointed out, by upholding the Ptolemaic currency, Antiochos III was probably seeking to avoid destabilizing the local economy, since substituting the Ptolemaic standard, of 14.25 grams, for the Attic one, of 17.32 grams, would have meant de facto a devaluation; conversely, replacing the Ptolemaic coins with Seleukid ones would have entailed a huge cost for the royal treasury.[17] As noted above, the Ptolemies gained much from the creation of a closed monetary economy through the imposition of an exchange rate of 1:1 between the Attic and Ptolemaic currencies at the border, and Antiochos III may have found it to his advantage to continue this practice.[18]

By conquering the Ptolemaic province of Syria and Phoinikē, Antiochos III sought to make it part of his empire. This meant that a war economy—that is, plundering—was ruled out, in favor of converting the region quickly to royal economy. According to Book 2 of the treatise *Economics* attributed to Aristotle, a royal economy sought to strike a careful balance in subject territories between extracting the maximum possible revenue through taxation and preserving their resources in the long run.[19] To this end, the stabilization phase immediately following a conquest was particularly critical: the conqueror had to take into account the destruction brought on by war, and regular exploitation of the region was further contingent upon securing the population's loyalty. Therefore, any delay in launching the regular exploitation of a newly conquered territory was a transitional phase that the king sought to make as brief as possible, governing by strictly pragmatic considerations. Indeed, Arthur Houghton and Catherin Lorber's interpretation of Antiochos III's monetary policy in the province confirms that the primary purpose of his conquest was to extract surpluses.[20] Maintaining the Ptolemaic policy of a closed monetary economy was precisely such a pragmatic decision, as it provided an opportunity to draw lucrative benefits from the newly conquered satrapy from the outset.

8.2. ANTIOCHOS III'S SETTLEMENT FOR JERUSALEM: *ANTIQUITIES* 12.138–44

Pragmatism was the order of the day also in negotiating settlements concerning the political and economic status of each of the individual communities—poleis and *ethnē*—in the satrapy. Of these, only the settlement concerning Jerusalem is known, thanks to Josephus's quotation of the royal decree (*Ant.* 12.138–44).[21] Although each settlement was negotiated separately and its details were adapted to each situation, the underlying factors of the compromise reached in each case were similar: preexisting political and fiscal arrangements between the local community and the imperial power were retained, possibly with slight modifications to suit the specific Seleukid praxis; the king's wish to extract the greatest revenue as quickly as possible was reconciled with objective local conditions at the time of negotiations (such as destruction by war); the terms of surrender and immediate military and strategic considerations carried some weight; as did the negotiation skills of each side also.[22] In the case of Antiochos III's decree concerning Jerusalem, two considerations in particular are singled out as justifying the subsequent proclamation (*Ant.* 12.139). The first is the need to "to requite them for these acts." According to Josephus, the region was first invaded by Antiochos III in 202/1 B.C.E., reconquered by Skopas on behalf of Ptolemy V, probably during the winter of 201/0, and then invaded yet again by Antiochos after his decisive victory at Panion in the summer of 200.[23] In the final phase of the war, as recorded in the decree's preamble (*Ant.* 12.131–38), the Judeans provided active help in expelling the Ptolemaic garrison, which had withdrawn to the citadel in Jerusalem. Antiochos's first consideration therefore refers to the local population's peaceful surrender and cooperation. The second consideration refers to the material collateral damage of the war ("We have seen fit . . . to restore their city, which has been destroyed by the hazards of war," *Ant.* 12.139).

The king's emphasis on the local leadership's active cooperation deserves further comment. A detailed examination of the formal protocol of surrender casts doubt on both Bickerman's postulation of a "surrender and grant" procedure and the theory that the local population was divided between Ptolemaic and Seleukid factions. (Although this reconstruction will be discussed in greater detail in section 8.3 below, it is worth bearing in mind in the present discussion.) Finally, the content of the political and fiscal clauses of the decree must be reassessed, since the classic commentaries regarding them are misleading.[24]

8.2.1. "Surrender and Grant"—or Negotiated Surrender?

The status of conquered communities has been a hotly disputed topic among scholars of the Hellenistic world. In the first half of the twentieth century, the debate was founded on three premises: first, that Greek poleis and native communities were treated differently (native communities, in this context being either "cities" or *ethnē*—the term *poleis* being reserved for the Greek cities, whose model of government was thought to be distinctive);[25] second, that relations between kings and Greek poleis were founded on clearly defined legal principles, which can be inferred from the practice documented in the literary sources and inscriptions; finally, that both legal principles and practice were identical throughout the dominion of any given dynasty, and indeed throughout the entire Hellenistic world.

These premises underpin Bickerman's influential view on the effect of conquest, by which the political identity of both the Greek poleis and the native communities as autonomous polities was temporarily suspended and was reconferred by the conqueror—a two-stage scenario summed up in John Ma's phrase "surrender and grant."[26] Bickerman's commentary on Antiochos III's decree for Jerusalem is based on this notion.[27]

Our present understanding of the consequences of conquest on local communities is quite different. If we postulate that the relationship between local communities and rulers was defined by custom and modified by praxis, rather than by set legal principles, the notion that there was a clear distinction between Greek and non-Greek communities becomes irrelevant. Diverse regional customs and pragmatic adaptation to local circumstances meant that the agreed contract reached between king and community differed from one constituency to the next. Finally, any changes made to this relationship were negotiated, not imposed from above—as is evident from numerous case studies that dispute Bickerman's surrender-and-grant scenario in favor of flexible praxis.[28] Antiochos III's settlement for Jerusalem must be read in this light.

When a community was conquered, its fate depended first and foremost on its attitude toward the victors. Faced with the approach of an invading army, local inhabitants could choose between resisting—placing their hopes in their walls or in a successful counteroffensive by their current overlord—or initiating negotiations for their surrender. Betting on the correct side was, of course, crucial, and therefore local communities would often wait and watch until the very last moment. When the outcome of the war became a foregone conclusion, siding with the prevailing contestant was the wisest option[29]—and indeed, this seems to have been common practice, making the difference between lenient treatment or massacre, material destruction, and punitive measures. Moreover, the local community could hope to be in a more favorable bargaining position when it came to negotiate its final status if it had showed goodwill in time. Thus, the citizens of Herakleia-under-Latmos, in Asia Minor, sided with Zeuxis, Antiochos III's chief minister, after he had routed Philip V at Kynoskephaloi in 196 B.C.E., because—as Christophe Chandezon has pointed out—they had no real choice in the matter.[30] Similarly, the synopsis of events in the preamble to Antiochos's decree confirms that the Judean leadership delayed their move until Antiochos had already begun invading the territory of the *ethnos* (*Ant.* 12.138, emphasis added):[31]

> Inasmuch as the Judeans, *from the very moment when we entered their country,* showed their eagerness to serve us and, when we came to their city, gave us a splendid reception and met us with their *gerousia* and furnished an abundance of provisions to our soldiers and elephants, and also helped us to expel the Egyptian garrison in the citadel . . .

8.2.2. *The Welcome Ceremony*

The preamble mentioned above echoes a well-documented pattern of surrender, as analyzed by Pierre Briant based on the Greek descriptions of the surrenders of Sardeis, Babylon, and Susa to Alexander.[32] In each instance, the local leaders came out of the city to greet the invader at some distance from the city walls, signaling the city's readiness to yield to him without the threat of siege. In Sardeis, in 333, Alexander was welcomed by Mithrenes, the Achaimenid commander of the garrison quartered in the acropolis, and by the city's chief officials (Arr. 1.17.3)—the former yielding the citadel and the treasury, and the latter the city itself. A similar scene occurred when Alexander headed for Babylon after his victory at Gaugamela (330/29 B.C.E.).[33] The satrap Mazaios, who had fled back to the city after Gaugamela, came to meet Alexander in person with his grown children, offering the city (Curt. 5.1.17). When Alexander approached the city gates, the Babylonians emerged with a ceremonial welcome, the procession of priests and musicians being led by the so-called Magi and Chaldeans. Bagophanes, in charge of the citadel and the royal treasury, had the road covered with flowers and bordered with frankincense altars, cattle, horses, and wild beasts in cages as gifts (Curt. 5.1.19–23). This set ceremony was repeated at Susa. Josephus's description of Alexander's welcome at Jerusalem follows the same pattern (*Ant.* 11.329–40), although the historicity of Alexander's visit to these places after Issos is doubtful.[34] The welcome ceremony offered to Antiochos III by the Jerusalemites in 200/198 B.C.E. was certainly not so lavish as those offered to Alexander by the inhabitants of the opulent Babylon and Susa, but it was still impressive enough relative to its size to persuade the conqueror of their loyalty.

What was the purpose of the welcoming ceremony? After all, such a practice was alien to the diplomatic culture of Greek poleis—nor is it systematically documented in the case of cities of the ancient Near Eastern cultural tradition. Thus, although the Phoenician cities of Arados, Byblos, Sidon, and Tyre readily sent ambassadors to Alexander to signal their surrender, no lavish ceremonies are recorded; nor are any in Egypt.[35] A possible answer is that these extravagant welcome ceremonies fulfilled a function similar to the honors accorded to the kings in Greek cities. As John Ma has argued, these were designed first and foremost as a mark of "goodwill, loyalism or even submission" to the king.[36] In accordance with the cultural tradition of the local community, formal displays of goodwill were particularly necessary when the community had been late in declaring allegiance and its bargaining position was low. In contrast, the Phoenician cities, which had highly valuable assets to offer as tokens of goodwill, were able to dispense with expensive formalities. The kings of Arados, Byblos, and Sidon yielded their warships, for example (Arr. 2.20.1)—a strategic gift that clearly dwarfed any ceremonial manifestations of loyalty. Straton son of Gerostratos, king of Arados and regent of the city, went even further, offering Alexander a golden crown in the Greek tradition when Alexander reached the Aradian *peraia* (the city's territory on the mainland) and formally ceding the entire *peraia* to him (Arr. 2.13.8).

The Jerusalemites had no fleet to offer, so they expressed their goodwill by entertaining Antiochos III's troops and elephants with "abundant supplies" (*Ant.* 12.138), much as the Babylonians had done for Alexander's troops for no less than thirty days (D.S. 17.64.4). In addition, they helped Antiochos to expel the Ptolemaic garrison.

8.2.3. *The Immediate Decisions: The Garrison*

Alexander's historians describe how the first steps that Alexander took after conquering a city were to appoint officials in charge of military, fiscal, and administrative affairs, respectively. The local garrison's commanders (*stratēgoi*) were replaced with Macedonians whom the conqueror could trust. Nonmilitary officials were appointed to oversee tax collection, apparently for security reasons. Unlike the military and financial officials, who were Macedonians, the Achaimenid satraps who had surrendered in good time were allowed to keep their positions, "in order to induce others to surrender," as Curtius notes.[37] Thus, Antiochos III's reinstatement of Ptolemaios son of Thraseas, Ptolemy V's former *philos* and official, as governor and high priest of the satrapy of southern Syria, is not surprising.[38]

The Ptolemaic garrison of Jerusalem must have been replaced with a Seleukid one. The military stability of the region remained shaky—as is evident from the fact that Antiochos III's decree concerning Jerusalem does not include any exemption of a garrison. According to 2 Maccabees 4:28, the citadel's commander was also in charge of tax collection—as we noted earlier (§8.2.2), this claim contradicts Alexander's practice but may reflect a subsequent evolution.

This pattern of city surrender suggests that ideological considerations did not play a part. Nor can the massive rallying of officials and communities to Alexander's side[39] be plausibly explained on ideological grounds. Therefore, Bickerman's hypothesis of a struggle between Ptolemaic and Seleukid factions in southern Syria of the third and second centuries B.C.E. per se has no explanatory value in the context of Jerusalem's surrender to Antiochos III—if any at all.

8.2.4. The Political Settlement

The thrust of Chandezon's refutation of Bickerman's surrender-and-grant model concerns the latter's claim that poleis and *ethnē* automatically lost their political status upon being conquered.[40] In Jerusalem—as in Herakleia-under-Latmos a few years later—the community's status was established through negotiation, and not by the victor's unilateral decree. Moreover, these negotiations most probably involved two stages—the first being *prior to* the surrender, probably regarding the conditions of surrender and the king's pledge to preserve the existing status of the *ethnos* and possibly even to enhance it (for instance, by an exemption from billeting, as granted to the citizens of Herakleia-under-Latmos).[41] The precise details of the political and economic status of the community were worked out at the second stage, once the military phase of the conquest was complete.

Given the importance of this stage, the community took care to send its best negotiators: the Herakleians' delegation to Zeuxis, for example, comprised no fewer than twenty-two ambassadors—one for each dossier, according to John Ma.[42] The name of the man who either single-handedly negotiated the status of Jerusalem and Judea, or (more probably) led the Judean delegation that met with Antiochos III or with his representative, is recorded in 2 Maccabees 4:11 ("John the father of Eupolemos"). In Antiochos's decree for Jerusalem, the political status of the Judean community is summed up simply: "All those who are members of the community shall have a form of government in accordance with their ancestral laws" (*Ant.* 12.142).[43] The reason for this economy of language is easy to guess: Antiochos was simply reinstating the autonomy in all domestic affairs that the Judeans had enjoyed under the Ptolemies; therefore there was no need to go into details. However, Bickerman's assumption that Greek cities and non-Greek communities were treated differently led him to misinterpret this.[44] In *The God of the Maccabees*, he went as far as to conclude:[45]

> For a Greek city, the clause meant the retention of the democratic constitution, of self-rule. But for the Jews "the laws of the fathers" meant Torah. Only Torah and nothing but Torah. Every time Jewish texts and pagan rulers apply this Greek formula to the Jews, they mean the laws of Moses. In a Hellenic city, for example, the ancestral constitution determined the law for the election of officials. In Jerusalem, it prescribed the obligation to observe the sabbath rest.

However, Hellenistic kings were primarily concerned with their subjects' political loyalty. Although they could punish a rebel community by dispossessing it of its temple, there is no example that they cared for ancestral customs per se.[46]

The attitude of conquerors toward local leaders and political regimes was pragmatic, just as it was regarding the *philoi* of vanquished kings who were in office in the conquered area at the time of the conquest. In most instances, the community's political organization remained intact, even when the leaders were replaced. Thus, in Phoenicia, Alexander allowed the kings of Arados and Byblos, who had surrendered without resistance after the battle of Issos in the fall of 333 B.C.E. (Arr. 2.13.7–8, 15.6; D.S. 17.40.2; Curt. 4.1.15), to remain on their thrones. By contrast, the king of Sidon, a known pro-Persian appointee, was removed, but Alexander retained the Sidonian kingship, appointing a loyalist by name of Abdalonymos in his place (D.S. 17.47, Curt. 4.1.18–26).[47] In Karia, in 332 B.C.E., he did something similar. Ada daughter of Hekatamnos, wife of Hidrieus, the late satrap of Karia, had succeeded her late husband but was then evicted by a kinsman. Upon the latter's death, King Darius III had appointed another member of the satrap's family to succeed him, but when Alexander invaded Asia Minor, Ada sided with him in the hope of recovering her position, and Alexander rewarded her by granting her request (Arr. 1.123.7–8).

The situation in Greek cities was more complex, because of their particular political culture. According to Arrian's sweeping commentary, Alexander "ordered the oligarchies everywhere to be overthrown and democracies to be established; he restored its own laws to each city and remitted the tribute they used to pay to the barbarians [i.e., the Persians]" (Arr. 1.18.2). Alexander's policy was pragmatic: the tyrants and oligarchies of these cities were pro-Persian, whereas the supporters of democracy were hostile both to Persian rule and to the Persian allies within the city. By bringing the democratic leaders to power, Alexander exploited the internecine civic divisions to his benefit.[48] By contrast, the Sardeians were allowed to keep their political regime (*nomoi*) after their peaceful surrender (Arr. 1.17.4).[49]

In Jerusalem, the high priest, the rest of the leadership, and the population all pledged allegiance to Antiochos III, and thus the Judean political and social organization and leadership were left intact. The good relations between the king and the political elite were further strengthened by the king's grant of fiscal privileges to the priests and members of the *gerousia*. Notably, his political and fiscal decisions were proclaimed in the same sentence (*Ant.* 12.142), suggesting that the fiscal privileges he was granting were merely an affirmation of the preexisting situation. Ezra 7:24 confirms that the temple personnel enjoyed tax-exempt status in Persian times. Moreover, the priests and Levites received a regular stipend in kind, paid out of the temple's tax income. Both the Achaimenid and the Seleukid authorities were interested "in a well-organized political and fiscal administration," for which the cooperation of the ruling classes was essential;[50] fiscal concessions catering to their specific interests helped to secure this loyalty and cooperation. Insofar as the king's decision to uphold the status quo was the counterpart to the community's goodwill and the outcome of the negotiation, it needed to be duly uttered in the royal decree. This is the function of the political clause recorded in *Antiquities* 12.142.

8.2.5. The Economic and Fiscal Clauses of Antiochos III's Decree

Unsurprisingly, most of the clauses in Antiochos III's decree regarding Jerusalem relate to economic issues.[51] This emphasis on economic matters is indicative of the primary purpose of imperial domination—surplus extraction—and is a consistent feature of the agreements reached between kings and subject communities.[52] Antiochos's decree follows the usual hierarchical pattern. First were matters pertaining to the local deity—a royal subvention (*syntaxis*) for the temple sacrifices, as a mark of the king's piety (*Ant.* 12.140), followed by an exemption of toll charges on timber imported for the temple's restoration (12.141). Next came an announcement that the *ethnos*'s traditional form of government was preserved, coupled with an exemption of the privileged classes—the elders, the priests, and several categories of temple personnel—from the head tax (12.142). Next, the city's inhabitants were granted a three-year exemption from taxes and a permanent reduction of one-third of the tribute (12.143). Finally, all Jerusalem inhabitants who had been sold as slaves were declared freed (12.144).

In typical fashion, the fiscal clauses are presented as the community's share in the exchange of reciprocal gifts between two contractual—albeit unequal—partners. The king announces his own contribution—the royal subsidies to the temple cult—before declaring the obligations of the other party, a form of presentation that Véronique Chankowski dubs the "dialectics of exchange."[53] This preliminary gift, presented in the "language of euergetism,"[54] is what distinguished a royal economy from a predatory one. The word used for the royal subsidies of the temple sacrifices in Antiochos III's decree, *syntaxis* (*Ant.* 12.139), is often used in royal decrees to refer to the "contribution" incumbent upon the local community—taxes.[55] The granting of money and goods to subsidize temple cults both in Greek cities and in non-Greek communities was a regular feature of royal euergetism, although the closest parallel to our document is a decree by the citizens of a city in Asia Minor—possibly Apollonia-on-the-Rhyndakos—in honor of an Attalid governor who, "as the citizens were destitute because of the war, supplied at his own expense cattle and other victims for the public sacrifices."[56] The construction, decoration, and repair of temples—in the aftermath of war or otherwise—was similarly often financed by the royal treasury.[57] However, there was a difference between the royal gifts granted to Greek cities and those given to non-Greek communities. In the former, the royal grants covered various fields of activity—the supply of oil for the civic *gymnasion* being one of the most common. In non-Greek communities, however, the temples—which were the main focal points of the collective identity—naturally served as the main channel of political communication between the kings and local leaders; therefore they were deemed the most appropriate recipients of royal largesse. When read in this context, the gifts bestowed by Antiochos III upon Jerusalem appear to be standard practice.

Remarkably, the fiscal clauses are also presented as part of the king's patronage. The opening references to willing cooperation of Jerusalem's leaders in the final phase of the conquest and to the devastation brought on by war (12.139) set the tone to justify the economic settlement that follows. However, from Bickerman onward the king's generosity has not impressed modern commentators. Neither his gifts to the Jerusalem temple nor his concessions are thought to be particularly magnanimous when compared with those granted to other cities.[58] Recently George Aperghis has dismissed the notion that Antiochos III was generous at all:[59] rather, what is known about his fiscal settlements with Sardeis, Teos, and Herakleia-under-Latmos suggest that his prime concern was to adapt his fiscal demands to the cities' economic capabilities. This was true both in times of peace and in the aftermath of conquest.[60] Sardeis in particular is instructive in this regard: at first, the citizens were harshly punished for choosing the wrong side in the war of 216–214/3 B.C.E. between Antiochos III and Achaios. However, only a few months later, in March 213, they were able to negotiate a new, far more lenient fiscal settlement.[61] Antiochos III's pledge to restore the city of Jerusalem and repeople it (12.139) was in the king's interest as much as in that of the local inhabitants. Antiochos III took similar steps in favor of Sardeis in 213 B.C.E., Amyzon in 203, and Lysimacheia in the Chersonesos in 196 B.C.E.[62] Nevertheless, these concessions were granted not as matter of course but were the result of negotiations, as shown by Zeuxis's letter to the Herakleians.[63]

The fiscal clauses making up the remainder of Antiochos's decree for Jerusalem are presented as a series of tax exemptions. Fiscal concessions were a regular feature of bilateral settlements: situated as they were at the interface between economic and political relations, they were part of the long-term policy of surplus extraction.[64] Like other manifestations of royal euergetism, they were intended as much as a reward for past actions as a guarantee of the beneficiaries' continued support in future.[65] The concessions granted to the population of Jerusalem as a whole are limited to a period of three years—that is, the immediate period of economic recovery (12.143). Even the one-third reduction in the tribute is apparently granted to meet immediate needs ("We shall also relieve them in future from the third part of their tribute, so that their losses may be made good," *Ant.* 12.143). As Aperghis has pointed out, most of Antiochos III's tax requirements—in particular the taxes on agricultural produce—are not mentioned at all in the decree, suggesting that these taxes remained the same as before.

Antiochos's generosity seems decidedly modest when compared with the tax exemptions granted by Demetrios I Soter in 153 B.C.E. (1 Macc. 10:30–45) and Demetrios II in 145 B.C.E. (1 Macc. 11:29–37). The difference may be explained in part by the fact that those rulers were negotiating from a position of weakness, whereas Antiochos III had the upper hand. That said, the recent tendency of scholars to downplay Antiochos III's gifts must not be pursued too zealously. When the tribute was increased at the start of Antiochos IV's reign (2 Macc. 4:7–9), the author of 2 Maccabees looked back wistfully at the royal concessions (*philanthrōpa basilika*) negotiated by John, Eupolemos's father (2 Macc. 4:11)—a reference, according to virtually all modern commentators, to the settlement reached with Antiochos III. Many Judeans, it seems, also shared this sentiment—for while the text of his decree was preserved for posterity, those of Seleukos IV and Antiochos IV were forgotten. However modest Antiochos III's generosity may have seemed at first, with hindsight it became greatly magnified. However, before turning to Seleukos IV's fiscal policy in Chapter 9, we must examine the modern notion that domestic tensions dividing the leading Judean families under the Seleukids reflected geostrategic tensions between Ptolemies and Seleukids.

8.3. THE POLITICAL CULTURE OF THE LEADING JUDEAN FAMILIES

Writing in the heyday of the *Quellenforschung* and functionalist methodologies, Bickerman attributed the differences between the versions of 1 Maccabees, 2 Maccabees, Josephus, and Daniel to their respective sources. In the *Quellenforschung* perspective, 2 Maccabees and Josephus were "dependent upon the Seleucid tradition," whereas Daniel was the Jewish version, and 1 Maccabees "a Hasmonaean work, written at a time when the dynasty was at the zenith of its power."[66] The functionalist method ascribes such differences to the fact that their authors hailed from different social circles and held different political and "religious" opinions.

The literary perspective dismisses both these approaches. As we saw in Chapter 4, the Methodological Introduction to Part II, and Chapter 7, the discrepancies between the accounts of 1 and 2 Maccabees are due to literary reasons and by no means reflect different political and religious opinions. In particular, they stem from a different narrative focus in each case: the author of 1 Maccabees was writing primarily about Simon and the Akra, while his fellow writer was focused on Judas and the temple. A political explanation for their differences therefore is unwarranted.

The literary analysis of Chapters 1 to 4 likewise shows that the notion that the Maccabean rebellion reflected a struggle between religious conservatives and a Hellenizing party is unfounded. As we have seen, this erroneous modern interpretation[67] arose from a positivist rationalization of the rhetoric of piety versus impiety that dominates 1 and 2 Maccabees—a hallmark of the political culture of the Judean, Mesopotamian, and Egyptian societies in pre-Hellenistic and Hellenistic times. The vocabulary of piety versus impiety of the Greek-language texts (1 and 2 Maccabees) holds the same semantic connotations as the concepts of righteousness versus wickedness in the Hebrew and Akkadian sources: describing a king as "pious" (or "righteous") was a statement of political support, whereas attaching the label "impious" ("wicked") to a past king or a living opponent was a polemical statement.[68] When one reads the behavior of the Judean high priests through the polemical rhetoric of 1 and 2 Maccabees, the most reasonable inference is that Jason and Menelaos were no less pious than Judas, Jonathan, or Simon Maccabee[69]—and equally, that the latter were no less Hellenized than Jason and Menelaos.

The literary approach also casts doubt on the modern view that the political scene in Judea under the Seleukids was dominated by a struggle between Ptolemaic and Seleukid factions. This theory was first put forward by Bickerman in his *God of the Maccabees* and readily adopted in subsequent studies.[70] However, Dov Gera has at last systematically disproved this two-party theory on historical grounds.[71] His analysis may be corroborated both by a literary reappraisal of Josephus's *Antiquities* and Jerome's *Commentary on Daniel,* and by recent Hellenistic research into the political culture of the Hellenistic kingdoms, which by defining them as premodern states implies that the notion of political parties was thoroughly alien to it. The following sections will tackle each of these two issues in turn.

8.3.1. Party Politics versus Family Feuds

Bickerman cites four passages in the ancient sources in support of his theory that the Judean leading families were torn between two parties: Polybius 5.86.10; Josephus, *Antiquities* 12.239-40 and *War* 1.1.31-32; and Jerome, *Commentary on Daniel* 11:14.[72] None of them stands up to close scrutiny. The quotation from Polybius (5.86.8-11) is a disparaging comment about the unseemly haste of the cities of southern Syria to side with Ptolemy IV after the battle of Raphia in 217 B.C.E. (Polyb. 5.86.9-10):[73]

> Possibly all men at such times are more or less disposed to adapt themselves to the needs of the hour, and the natives of these parts are naturally more prone than others to bestow their affections at the bidding of circumstances. But at this juncture it was only to be expected that they should act so, as their affection for the Egyptian kings was of no recent growth; for the peoples of Koilē-Syria have always been more attached to that house than to the Seleukids.

Bickerman concluded from this quote that the throngs of Koilē Syria formed a pro-Ptolemaic party. However, Polybius does not actually speak of parties; merely of "affection" (*eunoia*), which could easily be explained by the close economic ties between the two regions. Moreover, leaving aside the contemptuous insinuations of Polybius's comment, it can be easily reconciled with the pattern of surrender to the victorious side described above (§§8.2.1–2).[74]

Bickerman's interpretation might be justified if supported by further evidence, but it was not. It is no coincidence that the two other authors that Bickerman cites—Josephus and Jerome—wrote in Roman times. They drew upon the Roman experience of the civil wars to make their respective sources more intelligible to their readers. In *Antiquities* 12.239–41, Josephus filled in the blanks of 1 Maccabees 11–15 with data found in 2 Maccabees 4 and 5 (especially names) and portrayed Jason and Menelaos as party leaders besides (*Ant.* 12.239–40):

> And when the former high priest Iesous rose against Menelaos, who was appointed after him, the populace was divided between the two, the Tobiads being on the side of Menelaos, while the majority of the people supported Jason.

It is easy to imagine how Josephus came to this conclusion. Since 2 Maccabees 5:5–7 provides no explanation as to why Jason attacked Menelaos, Josephus felt compelled to supply one of his own. Since Jason and Menelaos were both Judeans, Josephus concluded that their feud was a case of civil war. His knowledge of the history of the civil wars of the late Roman Republic and the early empire provided him with a plausible pattern of causality to cast upon his source. Josephus also refers to pro-Ptolemaic and pro-Seleukid parties elsewhere in his work[75]—but on each occasion this reading appears to be his own personal interpretation, anachronistically superimposing the experience of the Roman civil wars onto the very different world of the Hellenistic East.

Jerome's comment on Daniel 11:14 reads as follows:[76]

> When Antiochos the Great fought against the military leader Ptolemy [202–200], Judea, which lay right between the two warring parties, was torn by the struggle between two parties, one of which favored Antiochos, the other Ptolemy.

However, Daniel 11:14 offers no ground at all for Jerome's interpretation. Rather, Daniel 11:3–15 casts the Syrian wars of the third and second centuries B.C.E. in quasi-mythical terms of the age-old struggle between the Empire of the South and the Empire of the North. Like Josephus, Jerome is not using an independent source to cast light on Daniel but has devised a paraphrase of his own, drawing from his (and his readers') experience.

Party politics was part and parcel of the political culture of ancient Rome—however, it is highly questionable as a model of the politics of the Judean elite in the Hellenistic period. Party politics was utterly foreign to the political culture of the societies of the region, whose social and political organization centered on a royal court on the one hand and temples and priestly classes on the other.[77]

8.3.2. The Alleged Social Differences between the Maccabees and the "Hellenizers"

The political culture of Judea may be characterized as aristocratic politics: powerful families feuding with one another for prestige and power. This is not to say that there were no political differences: judging by the literary works produced in Hellenistic Judea, familial, regional, and social differences often resulted in divergent ritual traditions, calendars, and possibly also narrative traditions (such as different stories of Creation and different historical memories).[78] However, the once prevalent hypothesis that there was a conflict between a Hellenized, urban aristocracy (represented by Jason, Menelaos, and Alkimos) and a traditionalist, rural aristocracy (represented by the Hasmoneans) must be discarded. This functionalist representation of Judean society was based on the erroneous premise that the rebellion was led by religious and nationalist conservatives against Hellenizers (a term uncritically used as a synonym for modernizers). As previously noted (§8.3, opening paragraphs), this in turn was based on a misinterpretation of the vocabulary of piety and impiety in 2 Maccabees.

As Brent Nongbri has shown, the literary sources provide neither geographical nor sociological evidence for this depiction[79]—indeed, there is ample evidence to indicate that the Maccabees belonged to the same social class as Jason, Menelaos, and Alkimos. Nongbri's analysis begins with a commentary by Seth Schwartz comparing the Maccabees with what he calls the "village strongmen" of Judea and its neighboring regions, as documented in the Zenon papyri, 1 and 2 Maccabees, and Josephus.[80] These strongmen were well-to-do landowners of high social standing in their regions. In 1 Maccabees 2:17, Mattathias is hailed as the local leader by the royal officials arriving in the village of Modein, and Schwartz compares his hostile reaction to them (1 Macc. 2:19–26) with an incident recorded in the Zenon papyri in which two officials—Zenon's agent and the agent of a local official—were expelled from a village by one Ieddous when they came to collect a debt from him.[81] Similarly, Joseph the Tobiad encountered violent resistance on arriving in Ascalon to collect taxes (*Ant.* 12.181).[82]

To Schwartz's analysis Nongbri objected that the Maccabees should be seen as Jerusalem insiders much like Jason and Menelaos rather than as village strongmen.[83] According to 1 Maccabees 2:1, when Mattathias arrived in Modein he was coming from Jerusalem. Josephus saw no contradiction between Mattathias's living in "Modai" and his being a Jerusalemite (*Ant.* 12.265). Similarly, in 2 Maccabees 5:27 Judas Maccabee is shown withdrawing from Jerusalem to its uninhabited surroundings. However, the alleged contrast between the Jerusalemite aristocracy and village strongmen must not be pursued too far: high social status was inextricably bound up with material affluence, and landed property was the main source of wealth at this time, certainly in a hinterland country like Judea. The Tobiads are a case in point: Hyrkanos lived in Transjordan (*Ant.* 12.222) but kept his money at the Jerusalem temple (2 Macc. 3.11), and there is no reason to doubt that he was actively involved in the capital's politics. In other words, Schwartz's village strongmen and the Hellenized elites of Jerusalem were one and the same.

Moreover, the accounts of 1 and 2 Maccabees, showing either Judas (in 2 Maccabees) or Mattathias (in 1 Maccabees) joining the struggle following Antiochos IV's atrocities, are both chronologically confused and misleading.[84] If indeed Judas Maccabee withdrew from Jerusalem after Apollonios's assault, as 2 Maccabees 5:27 claims, there is little reason to doubt that he had taken part in armed resistance before that. In other words, not only were the Maccabees actively involved in the political life of Jerusalem, but they most likely were part of the struggle for power from the outset.

The functionalist premises that differences in external signs of Hellenization reflected distinct social and geographical lineages and that being Hellenized was incompatible with being faithful to one's ancestral tradition, and vice versa, are disproved by numerous case studies of the cultural strategies of Egyptian and Mesopotamian social elites in Hellenistic times. For example, Timothy Doty studied the families of two men of the priestly elite of Uruk in the mid- and late third century B.C.E. over five generations (two older and two younger than the two men).[85] Each of the two men bore a double—Greek and Akkadian—name. Anu-uballiṭ alias Nikarchos was city administrator in 244 B.C.E., and Anu-uballiṭ alias Kephalon was overseer of temple personnel of the city in 202 B.C.E.—the latter therefore ranking slightly lower than the former. In the family of Anu-uballiṭ alias Kephalon, many individuals over the five generations bore either a Greek or a double name, including one woman (Kephalon's wife). By contrast, Anu-uballiṭ alias Nikarchos was the only one in his family with a Greek name. Why this was so is unknown, but it is certainly not owing to different social backgrounds. To cite examples from Ptolemaic Egypt, the high priests of Ptah in Memphis, who entertained close relations with the Ptolemies, bore double names that were both Egyptian and never Greek, whereas an Egyptian priestly family from Edfu, in Upper Egypt—a region whose loyalty to the Ptolemies was shaky—erected two funerary steles for each one of three family members—one in hieroglyphs and one in Greek, the former displaying Egyptian names and the latter Greek ones.[86]

. . .

As Seth Schwartz has argued, the Maccabees ultimately owed their success to the fact that they were able to recruit wide circles of supporters beyond their regional sphere of influence.[87] Admittedly, the reasons for this success remain elusive, but the broad social, regional, economic, and Halachic diversity of the groups that rallied to their struggle belies the traditional view that the Maccabees were conservative, in the sense of small-town parochial. Their political strategy, if nothing else, was certainly innovative.

In summary, a literary analysis of the ancient sources highlights the shortcomings that invalidate the two most widely accepted readings of domestic tensions in Judea prior to the rebellion against Antiochos IV. The domestic tensions are not a story of piously conservative Maccabees rising up against Hellenizing high priests—nor were Jason and Menelaos "religiously" skeptical modernists. Similarly, the division was not between Ptolemaic and Seleukid camps. The next chapters will explore alternative factors to explain both the tensions within the priestly elite of Jerusalem and the rebellion against the Seleukids.

9

Seleukos IV Philopator and the Revision of Antiochos III's Settlement in Judea, 187–175 B.C.E.

INTRODUCTION

No financial settlement was guaranteed to endure indefinitely. As we saw in the previous chapter, Seleukid kings adapted their fiscal requirements to a realistic assessment of the cities' economic capabilities and granted temporary exemptions in times of hardship. For the same reason, they were equally quick to recognize improvements in the economic situation of subject communities and impose adjustments to their own benefit. A string of administrative, fiscal, and economic reforms appears to have been carried out in the satrapy of Koilē Syria and Phoinikē under Seleukos IV Philopator (187–175 B.C.E.) and in the early years of Antiochos IV Epiphanes (175–164 B.C.E.). Although a detailed picture remains elusive, clues from the literary, epigraphic, and archeological evidence may be pieced together into a coherent outline: while the Seleukid administration's interventions in the economic life of the satrapy of Koilē Syria and Phoinikē and its individual communities had been kept to a relatively low level following the conquest in order to facilitate its integration into the empire, reforms under Antiochos III's two successors led to a progressively much tougher regime of administrative control and fiscal and economic exploitation.

The claim that Seleukos IV and Antiochos IV implemented a tough fiscal policy is likely to strike a familiar chord among modern scholars. Textbooks on Seleukid (and Roman) history tell us that the reigns of Antiochos III's immediate successors were hamstrung by exceptional circumstances. The treaty of Apamea, of 188 B.C.E., marking the defeat of Antiochos III at the hands of Publius Cornelius Scipio at Magnesia-on-Maiandros the year before, included harsh financial penalties. This fiscal burden on the Seleukid kingdom allegedly explains why the actions of Seleukos IV pale in significance beside those of his illustrious father, and why Antiochos IV, Seleukos's brother, was restricted in his renewed ambitions. It was also universally cited by ancient historians as the single reason for their negative image of these two reigns—a judgment widely echoed by modern historians, with a few notable exceptions. Consequently, any economic and fiscal step taken by either Seleukos IV or Antiochos IV has been interpreted as a means of meeting the war-indemnity payments.

That the financial clauses of Apamea affected subsequent Seleukid policy is undeniable—indeed, one may reasonably assume that this was their original purpose. However, a more nuanced appreciation of the precise nature and mechanism of this impact is in order. The notion that the Seleukid empire fell into a period of prolonged decline from the mid-second century B.C.E. onward is increasingly called into question.[1] The Seleukids' relationship with their territory, like that of the Achaimenids before them, was flexible. Since the king's status was not founded on any territorial definition, territorial losses could be suffered without undermining his position to any substantive degree: they would be made up for either by subsequent reconquest of the lost regions or the conquest of new ones. Recently it has been argued that the Seleukid empire ultimately collapsed not because of the territorial losses incurred in the defeat of 189 B.C.E. or the economic impact of the treaty of Apamea, but because of the dynastic quarrels that began plaguing it immediately after the reign of Antiochos IV.[2]

The interaction between the financial penalties imposed at Apamea and subsequent Seleukid policy is therefore more complex than is usually assumed. The fiscal and economic reforms in the satrapy of Koilē Syria and Phoinikē under Seleukos IV and Antiochos Epiphanes need not necessarily be seen as emergency expedients in direct response to the financial burden of the war indemnity but may have possibly been simply the outcome of a regular policy aimed at exploiting available sources of income more efficiently and relaunching a policy of conquest.

In the satrapy of Koilē Syria and Phoinikē, two factors in particular are worth paying attention to. First, the conquest of the region had been recent—barely fifteen years before Seleukos IV's accession to the throne—and there was still room left for adjustment. The period immediately after the conquest must have been devoted to establishing and consolidating essential local allegiances. Reforms aimed at tightening the exploitation of surpluses in the region must have been implemented progressively.[3] As was usually the case, these must have been carried out as opportunities arose, rather than systematically.[4] Second, Antiochos IV invaded Egypt in 169 B.C.E. and again a year later, in a campaign that had apparently been planned a few years in advance and carefully prepared for. To rebuild Seleukid war capacity, Antiochos IV needed to rebuild his financial base. The economic and monetary reforms that he carried out in Seleukid Syria are now well known,[5] but it is quite likely that the invasion preparations also affected the satrapy of Koilē Syria and Phoinikē: besides being (comparatively) underexploited, as we have noted, it lay at the very border of Egypt, which may have served as an additional incentive to increase its contribution to the war.

Thus, a correct contextualization of the administrative, economic, and taxation reforms in Koilē Syria and Phoinikē under Seleukos IV and Antiochos IV may be more complex than may be assumed at first glance. They may have been conceived in response to the renewed economic prosperity of the region, as emergency measures to meet the payments of the war penalty, or as part of a general strategy of rebuilding the empire's economic and financial capacity in order to resume an offensive foreign policy. In the first case, the overall tax raise may have been moderate, whereas the latter two scenarios potentially imply a more onerous increase. Moreover, Seleukos IV and Antiochos IV may not have pursued the same goals in their respective policies—indeed, the notion that they did makes sense only if one assumes that their tax policies were motivated exclusively by the need to finance the war indemnity to the Romans. If, however, one allows that the successors of Antiochos III enjoyed a margin of discretion, the trend of tax increases may have been instigated by Seleukos IV as a routine policy of adjustment, rising sharply to meet the more pressing needs of Antiochos IV, to the point where they became a destabilizing factor. It is this scenario that I shall advocate in the present chapter and the next.

Given the central role accorded by modern scholars to the war-indemnity burden in all subsequent Seleukid initiatives, our first step is to review recent reassessments of its impact on Seleukid domestic and foreign policy. This question partly interlocks with recent debates on the degree of monetization of the Seleukid taxation system. Because the war indemnity to Rome was paid in minted coins, as were the Seleukid armies, the issue of the composition of the taxes (either in silver coinage or in bronze coinage and commodities) that were levied throughout the empire necessarily affects our appreciation of the part played by the war indemnity in Seleukid foreign policy (§9.1). Next, two episodes will be examined that occurred under Seleukos IV and that in all likelihood were related to the fiscal repercussions of an administrative reform in the satrapy of Koilē Syria and Phoinikē. The first concerns the appointment of a certain Olympiodoros as high priest of the satrapy in 178 B.C.E., as recently disclosed by the publication of a fragmentary inscription from Marisē in Idumea (§9.2). The second is the well-known story of Heliodoros's attempted plundering of the Jerusalem temple, featuring a subnarrative about a feud between Onias III and Simon, the temple *prostatēs*, in 2 Maccabees 3:4–4:6. After a preliminary literary analysis of the passage in question in the third section of this chapter (§9.3), we will delve more deeply into the probable relationship between the appointment of Olympiodoros and the events in 2 Maccabees (§9.4).

9.1. THE WAR INDEMNITY OF APAMEA AND THE DEGREE OF MONETIZATION OF THE SELEUKID ECONOMY

According to the treaty of Apamea, Antiochos had to pay three thousand silver talents to the Romans and fifty to Eumenes immediately. A further twelve thousand talents were to be paid to the Romans in twelve installments of a thousand per year over twelve years, and 350 talents to Eumenes at a rate of seventy talents annually over five years. The final installment to Eumenes was apparently due in 184/3, and that to the Romans in 177/6. This schedule would have covered all but the final year of Seleukos IV's reign.[6] However, the money paid by Antiochos IV to the Romans in 174/3 (Livy 42.6.6) appears to be an overdue installment of the Apamea fine and has been interpreted in modern scholarship as evidence that the king experienced severe financial hardship. This interpretation has been given further credence by the obscure claim in 2 Maccabees 8:10 that two thousand talents were still owing to the Romans in 165 B.C.E. and by ancient stories about temple-plundering expeditions led by Antiochos III, Seleukos IV (the Heliodoros story of 2 Maccabees 3), and Antiochos IV, which have been taken at face value and read as further evidence of the disastrous impact of the fine on Seleukid finances.[7]

The annual payment of a thousand silver talents does indeed appear to be particularly onerous when compared with the fine imposed upon the Carthaginians in 201 B.C.E. The Carthaginians were required to pay a war indemnity of ten thousand talents, in installments of two hundred talents a year over fifty years. However, Georges Le Rider, and more recently François de Callataÿ, have questioned the validity of this comparison by pointing out that the annual war indemnity imposed at Apamea was not disproportionate when measured against the Seleukids' annual revenues at the time. Le Rider added an analysis of Seleukos IV's minting policies as a further criterion of evaluation.[8] In the decades following Antiochos III's defeat by the Romans at Magnesia in 189 B.C.E., the Seleukids still possessed vast territories. The loss of cis-Tauric Asia Minor was compensated by the newly conquered satrapy of Koilē Syria and Phoinikē, and Antiochos III's anabasis of 212–204 B.C.E. resulted in the restoration of vast regions in the Upper Satrapies to firm Seleukid control. During his march on the Persian Gulf in 205 B.C.E., Antiochos III received five hundred talents of coined silver from the Gerrhaeans as a gift (Polyb. 13.9.5), and the annual tribute by the economically insignificant city of Jerusalem may have amounted to three hundred talents (1 Macc. 11:28) before the increase under Antiochos IV.[9] Compared with these sums, the annual remittance of a thousand talents to the Romans was likely an "irritating burden, but not as unbearable as is often thought."[10] This revised evaluation is further supported by an analysis of Seleukos IV's monetary policy. By comparing the number of mints in operation and the volume of tetradrachm issues produced by each mint under Antiochos III, Seleukos IV, and Antiochos IV, Le Rider has shown that there was no significant change from one king to the next. In other words, the available evidence bears no hint of emergency measures taken in Seleukos IV's time, suggesting that the war-indemnity payments were met from the royal treasury's regular income. The alternative—and far less plausible—option would be to speculate that the thousand talents were coined at these mints expressly and exclusively for the purpose of indemnity payments to Rome, leaving no hints in the archeological record.[11]

Nonetheless, the burden of the war indemnity on Seleukid finances also depends on the extent of the monetization of their tax income—a factor that Le Rider overlooks.[12] This question has been a point of contention between George Aperghis and de Callataÿ. Basing his argument on two documents—the well-known Mnesimachos inscription detailing the taxes paid by a group of villages on royal lands in Asia Minor and Demetrios's letter to the Judeans quoted in 1 Maccabees 10:25–45—Aperghis puts forward the claim that some of the taxes due to the royal treasury were paid in silver coins rather than in commodities and bronze coins, as the economic models accepted till the 1990s had assumed.[13] To this end, the villagers had to sell their agricultural produce in the regional urban market. However, de Callataÿ has criticized Aperghis's model by questioning his reading of these documents and pointing to alternative evidence that in his opinion supports the traditional view that taxes were for the most part paid in commodities.[14] The most expedient way to monetize tax collection was tax farming, but there is no evidence of this practice in the Seleukid empire.[15] However, Robert van der Spek has made the case for a relatively high level of silverization of the taxation system in Babylonia in Achaimenid and Seleukid times, citing also the case of Persian Judah and thereby bringing new arguments in support of the modernist view.[16]

If the modernist model is endorsed, Le Rider's contention that the financial clauses of Apamea had only a limited impact on the Seleukid economy would be fully justified. Conversely, if we follow de Callataÿ's conservative calculation that only a third of the tribute was in the form of coins—that is, three thousand out of some ten thousand talents of the Seleukid annual income—then the war indemnity of a thousand talents, which was entirely in the form of coined silver, had a greater impact on the Seleukid policy than Le Rider assumed, albeit not quite the crushing effect envisaged by the traditional view. Even if the overall economy of the Seleukid empire was unaffected, the war indemnity did significantly constrain the kings' military capacity, since military expenditures—in particular, the soldiers' wages—were the largest expense item of the Seleukid finances.[17] This conclusion casts a new light on the real thinking behind the Romans' policy in the region. Their immediate interest was to maintain a balance of power between the Seleukid empire and their Attalid and Rhodian allies, and so from the Roman point of view an excessive weakening of the Seleukids' economy would have been counterproductive. However, the financial clauses of Apamea, together with the banning of war elephants and the dismantling of the Seleukid fleet, was a simple but effective means of limiting Antiochos's ability to rebuild his warring capacity.[18]

In his pioneering paper of 1986, Michael Austin argued that the drive for new territorial conquests was a structural feature of Hellenistic kingdoms.[19] Antiochos IV's resumption of a policy of aggression is the best evidence that the financial settlement of Apamea fell short of preventing a vigorous Seleukid king from rebuilding his cash reserves. However, the extraction of surpluses from the provinces through taxation could not be increased at will, since in normal conditions taxes had been running at maximum capacity. Only two regions may have stood out as underexploited by the end of Antiochos III's reign: the province of Koilē Syria and Phoinikē, and the Upper Satrapies.

The situation in this region at the time is uncertain. Despite Antiochos III's eight-year anabasis of 212–204 B.C.E., his actual control of the Eastern satrapies appears to have remained shaky, especially in fringe regions. The success of his expedition to reestablish his suzerainty over the dynasts of Bactria is debatable, and Antiochos IV's campaign in Armenia in 165 was a genuine expedition of reconquest.[20] The stories of the plundering of various temples by Antiochos III and Antiochos IV during their anabases have been variously interpreted as acts of war and as the forced recovery of tax arrears.[21] If the latter interpretation is accepted, these stories of plunder originated from a historical context similar to the story of Heliodoros's attempted plundering of the Jerusalem temple in the time of Seleukos IV. As we shall see, the Heliodoros story of 2 Maccabees 3 must be read in the context of the Seleukid overhaul of the fiscal exploitation of southern Syria. What appears to have been a major administrative and fiscal reform of the satrapy of Koilē Syria and Phoinikē under Seleukos IV is now documented, thanks to a recently published fragmentary inscription from Marisē, the capital of Idumea. Before we turn to 2 Maccabees, the evidence provided by this inscription should be examined in detail.

9.2. THE APPOINTMENT OF A SELEUKID HIGH PRIEST IN THE SATRAPY OF KOILĒ SYRIA AND PHOINIKĒ IN 178 B.C.E.: AN ADMINISTRATIVE REFORM WITH FISCAL IMPLICATIONS

As a rule, reforms were implemented as opportunities arose. In the summer of 178 B.C.E., approximately nine years after acceding to the throne, Seleukos IV appointed a certain Olympiodoros "to take care" (*epimeleia: SEG* 57.1838, l. 25) of the sanctuaries in the satrapy of Koilē Syria and Phoinikē. The reason that the king cited was his desire to repair neglect: while his concern for the welfare of his subjects throughout his kingdom always prompted him to ensure that the sanctuaries in other satrapies received the traditional honors, those of Koilē Syria and Phoinikē had thus far lacked anyone to manage them in the manner they deserved.

The appointment of Olympiodoros must have been announced on several inscriptions throughout the satrapy. One copy, preserved in a fragmentary state, comes from Marisē, the capital of Idumea and the administrative capital of one of the four meridarchies that made up the province.[22] Four fragments so far published include two cover letters transmitting the royal decree down the ranks from Heliorodos, Seleukos IV's chief minister, through Dorymenes, the governor of the satrapy, and Diophanes, the official in charge of the district of Marisē (*SEG* 57.1838, ll. 1–12).[23] Moreover, most of the long preamble to the royal *prostagma* addressed to Heliodoros (ll. 13–39) has survived.[24] The letter predictably opens with the moral motivation for the king's initiative (ll.14–20), followed by the name of the new appointee, Olympiodoros, and a synopsis of his early career (ll. 27–35). However, the administrative definition of his new function falls outside the extant fragments, and as noted, all that is known is that Olympiodoros was appointed to take care of the sanctuaries of the satrapy (ll. 35–38). Olympiodoros was a *syntrophos* of Seleukos IV—a former chamberlain and one of the king's First Friends. Based on these data, Dov Gera has convincingly argued that Olympiodoros was appointed high priest (*archiereus*) of the satrapy, rather than overseer of its temples (*epi tōn hierōn*) as Hannah Cotton and Michael Wörrle surmised. Indeed, Olympiodoros's early career and high rank in the court hierarchy bears a striking resemblance to that of Nikanor, whom Antiochos III appointed high priest of all Seleukid satrapies in cis-Tauric Asia Minor in 210/9 B.C.E. In contrast, the temple overseers were not members of the court.[25]

As is usually the case in inscriptions of this sort, the king's motivation is cast in the "moralizing language" of euergetism to divert attention from the real purpose.[26] Nonetheless, our general knowledge of Seleukid administrative practices and of the rhetorical conventions of Seleukid official correspondence reasonably supports the premise that the appointment of a high priest was indicative of a major administrative reform, whose primary aim was to tighten control over the inner administration and revenues of the temples. This meant a more efficient fiscal extraction.

9.2.1. A Genuine Reform: The Chronological Gap

In his letter, Seleukos justifies his decision to appoint Olympiodoros by citing the situation elsewhere in the empire. This reference to other satrapies may indicate that the king had no local precedent to cite.[27] The last high priest before Olympiodoros must have been Ptolemaios son of Thraseas, who was appointed by Ptolemy V as governor of the Ptolemaic satrapy of Syria and Phoenicia and, in the Ptolemaic tradition, combined the function of high priest with that of governor (*stratēgos kai archiereus*). When the Fifth Syrian War broke out (202–198 B.C.E.), his rallying to Antiochos III was critical to the conquest of the region. As a reward, he was kept in his position after the Seleukid takeover.[28]

Combining the functions of governor and high priest appears to have been a regular practice in the Ptolemaic possessions outside Egypt and may be related to the royal cult. The same was true of the governor of Cyprus, "high priest of the sanctuaries of the island," which according to another inscription meant "the cults of Artemis D[*. *. *.], the gods, the king, and the other gods to whom sanctuaries are dedicated on the island."[29] However, this custom was alien to Seleukid administrative practice, and the fact that Ptolemaios retained his dual function under Antiochos III was clearly due to the exceptional circumstances of the conquest. Ptolemaios's official position under Antiochos III is known thanks to the Hefzibah inscription, which features eight (or nine) pieces of correspondence between Antiochos III and Ptolemaios. The purpose of the correspondence was to secure confirmation of various privileges, in particular the exemption from billeting granted to the villages owned by Ptolemaios in the region of Skythopolis, where the stele was found. Four dates are recorded in the dossier, ranging from late 201 to early 195 B.C.E.[30] Ptolemaios seems to have left his post shortly after—probably he died— and Cotton and Wörrle, followed by Gera, have reasonably suggested that the reform of the governor's competence, which brought the new satrapy in line with the other Seleukid provinces, coincided with the nomination of Ptolemaios's immediate successor.[31] Two governors in place under Seleukos IV—Apollonios son of Thraseas and Apollonios son of Menestheus—are indeed mentioned in 2 Maccabees with the sole title of governor (2 Macc. 3:5, 4.4), and Cotton and Wörrle take this as evidence for the reform's chronology.[32]

If this chronology is correct, over ten years elapsed between Ptolemaios's departure and the appointment of a new high priest in 178, and therefore Seleukos's step may be seen as a genuine reform. In his preamble, the king justifies Olympiodoros's appointment on the grounds that he wishes to show the same concern for the welfare of his subjects in the satrapy of Koilē Syria and Phoinikē as elsewhere in his kingdom. However, administrative standardization for its own sake was hardly a principle of government, either in the Seleukid realm or in any other Hellenistic kingdom.[33] The preamble of Seleukos's *prostagma* is a typical instance of what John Ma has called the "generalizing vocabularies" that "transformed individual acts into paradigmatic manifestations of character" and made "individual transactions into shows of character."[34] But this "language of euergetism" was also a means of "dissimulat[ing] or deproblematiz[ing] the fact of domination." The reasons for appointing a high priest after a lapse of ten years therefore clearly lay elsewhere.

9.2.2. *The Essence of the Reform*

To identify the purpose of the reform, the only possible starting point is to have a clear view of the role of provincial high priests. Despite the allusive nature of the "language of euergetism," the sphere of their authority may be reconstructed with some precision. The most explicit allusions found in Seleukos IV's *prostagma* refer to the king's concern that the sanctuaries of the satrapy "receive the traditional honors with the care befitting them," and his royal will to "in[crease] the honors of the gods" (ll. 20–22, 36). A similar royal concern for increasing "the sacrifices and the [other honors]" is expressed in Antiochos III's letter of appointment of Nikanor as high priest and overseer of the sanctuaries in cis-Tauric Asia Minor in 209 B.C.E. This time the phrasing makes it clear that "increasing the sacrifices" was precisely the task incumbent upon the high priest (*SEG* 37.1010 = Ma 2000a, no. 4, ll. 30–41, transl. p. 291):

> We have appointed him high-priest [*archiereus*] of the sanctuaries in the region beyond the Taurus, as he has asked himself, being convinced that because of his character, he will carry out both the business concerning the sacrifices and the rest in a manner worthy of the zeal which we have concerning these matters, making it our intention to increase them, as is appropriate. We thought necessary that he should also be in charge of the sanctuaries [*epi tōn hierōn*], and that their revenues and the other matters should be administered by him, just as was done under our grandfather by Dion.

The tenor of Antiochos III's decree for Jerusalem, and the references in the inscriptions and literary sources of Hellenistic times to royal gifts honoring temples, provide a more precise understanding of the meaning behind the elliptical wording of the decrees of Antiochos III and Seleukos IV.[35] As we saw in Chapter 8 (§8.2.5), the postconquest settlement negotiated between Antiochos III and the Judeans stipulated an annual allowance (*syntaxis*) from the king of "sacrificial animals, wine, oil and frankincense to the value of 20,000 silver [drachmas][36] and sacred artabae of fine flour in accordance with the law of the country, and 1,460 medimni of wheat and 375 medimni of salt" for the temple's needs (*Ant.* 12.140). The provision of regular subventions to temples to defray the costs of sacrifices was common royal policy. In concrete terms, the vague statements of the royal letters that the royally appointed *archiereis* were to increase the sacrifices of the gods mean that they were responsible for transmitting both the money and the goods allocated to the temple cults from the royal treasuries and granaries to the temples under their jurisdictions.[37]

That said, we may rule out that the royal subsidies to the temples were discontinued in the satrapy of Koilē Syria and Phoinikē when the high priesthood fell vacant following either the death or the departure of Ptolemaios son of Thraseas. It may be surmised that in the absence of a high priest, either the governor or a high-ranking financial official of the satrapy, such as the *dioiketēs*, supervised the transfer of money and goods and cared for the temples' other needs.[38] Therefore the motive for Olympiodoros's appointment is more likely to be found in two further clues provided by the Nikanor and Olympiodoros inscriptions. First, in both cases the sacrifices are said to be *increased* (*auxein*, Nikanor inscription, l. 36; *syn*[*auxein*], Olympiodoros inscription, l. 36).[39] Second, part of the description of Nikanor's position was to administer the sanctuaries' revenues—a task sometimes assumed by a subaltern officer referred to as the *epi tōn hierōn*.[40] The fragmentary state of the Marisē inscription prevents us from knowing whether Olympiodoros's competences were limited to channeling the increased royal subventions to the temples or extended to its attendant aim of a more rigorous oversight by the Seleukid administration of the temple revenues. In any event, the king's declaration of his "increased gift" to the temples can only imply that he expected something in return—if not higher taxes in a direct way, at least an increased control over the temples' revenues, which could easily lead to more efficient taxation. In the words of Véronique Chankowski, the tributary economy of the Seleukids was based on a "dialectics of exchange," and the principle of reciprocity colored both political and economic relations between kings and subject communities.[41] As Nikanor's dual function suggests, Antiochos III's announcement of increased royal subventions to the temples of Asia Minor was a prelude to a higher extraction of temple surpluses, and the administrative reform implemented by Seleukos IV in Koilē Syria and Phoinikē almost certainly was for a similar reason. Irrespective of whether Olympiodoros was appointed as both high priest and *epi tōn hierōn* or a subaltern official was to assist him in his task of supervision, the appointment of the high priest was the cornerstone of what must in essence have been an indirect fiscal reform targeting the temples' revenues.

At least some of the subaltern personnel who were to work with Olympiodoros[42] were already in place. The precise differences between the competences of the *epi tōn hierōn* and those of the *prostatēs tou hierou* are unknown, but both were involved with temple finances.[43] Heliodoros's visit to Jerusalem and the feud between Onias III and Simon, the *prostatēs tou hierou* of the Jerusalem temple cited in 2 Maccabees 3:4–4:6, are most likely directly related to the appointment of a provincial high priest.

9.3. THE HELIODOROS STORY, 2 MACCABEES 3:4–4:6: BETWEEN DISCURSIVE CONSTRUCT AND POLITICAL BIAS

The Heliodoros story has become part of the cultural heritage of the Christian West thanks to Raphael's Vatican fresco showing the Seleukid minister floored by God's angel. Heliodoros's angels have also been responsible for the protracted reluctance of academic scholarship to take the third chapter of 2 Maccabees seriously. Nevertheless, in recent years progress has been made in the literary analysis of the story. Two issues in particular need to be restated here, since they bear directly upon a possible connection between the appointment of a regional high priest and the story of 2 Maccabees 3. The motif of plundering the temple may be seen as a case of incorporating a historical event (a dispute about tax payment) into the symbolic universe of the temple;[44] and the author's chronological manipulation may be due to his political bias against Menelaos, to whom Simon was said to be a kinsman.

9.3.1. Stories of Temple Plunder in Times of Peace

Five instances of plunder and attempts at plunder are attributed to Antiochos III and Antiochos IV in the ancient literary sources. They concern the temples of "Anahita" in Ecbatana and Bel in Elymaïs (Antiochos III), and Hierapolis-Bambykē, Jerusalem, and one further temple of "Artemis" (Nanaia) in Elymaïs (Antiochos IV).[45] Analyzing four of the five stories, Peter Franz Mittag points out that all these temples were major religious centers,[46] making the imputation of sacrilegious behavior in the sources all the more startling. Temples were regularly looted as part of war expeditions or during punitive expeditions against rebellious communities.[47] However, the idea that kings could replenish their empty coffers anytime they chose by freely ransacking the temples of subject communities in times of peace is quite another matter.[48] Unprovoked aggression was seen as blatantly arbitrary, and the culprit would have immediately lost his legitimacy as king among both the local population and the ruling elite, possibly sparking a full-scale revolt. Such a risk was rarely if ever worthwhile. Ruling out the notion of temple plundering as a literary motif of the tyrant topos, therefore, Mittag put forward the alternative interpretation, based on 1 Maccabees 3:27–31, that Antiochos IV's assault on the temple of Elam/Elymaïs, which ancient authors presented as a plunder expedition, was in reality aimed at recovering tax arrears.[49] The Elamite priestly elite had taken advantage of the weakness of the Seleukid power in this remote region either not to pay the tribute or to pay only part of it.[50]

Mittag's suggestion is an instance of rereading four texts that repeat a well-attested literary motif (the tyrant topos) on the basis of a passage informed with another literary topos, internal to 1 Maccabees, whereby the author builds a case against the (legitimate) Seleukid claim to the tribute by presenting the kings' demands for payment as acts of sacred theft.[51] This topos ties in with the construction of mediating synecdoches shaping numerous episodes of 1 and 2 Maccabees.[52] This reasoning is circular. For his part, Niels Stokholm shows that the scene of Heliodoros trying to force his way into the temple treasury and being miraculously repulsed by divine intervention bears a striking similarity to a Babylonian story of the misfortunes of the king of Elam.[53] It is certainly no coincidence that the three further stories of temple plunder involving Antiochos III and Antiochos IV relate to their expeditions of 212–204 and 165–164 B.C.E., respectively, in the Upper Satrapies. While Epiphanes' plunder of Jerusalem was a lawful act of war in the course of putting down a rebellion,⁵⁴ the Heliodoros story and the four stories listed by Mittag are most likely shaped by the literary motif of contested payment demands disguised as attempted sacrileges.

That said, just because a literary motif can be discerned does not mean that the stories should be disregarded altogether. The hypothesis that the accusations of plunder are distorted echoes of contentious recoveries of tax arrears is indeed plausible. Alternative situations that may have generated story of temple plunder may also be thought of. For instance, as we know from a Babylonian astronomical diary, in February/March 187 B.C.E. Antiochos III visited Babylon for the second time in his reign. On this occasion the city's civil representatives—the high priest (*šatammu*) and temple council of the Esagila, Marduk's temple—offered the king a golden crown of a thousand shekels of gold. The royal governor of the city (the *pāḫāt Bābili*) also presented the king with either gold or golden objects. Although the astronomical diary describes the gifts as voluntary donations, one cannot rule out that some form of royal pressure had been involved. That same day, Antiochos III went to the Esagila and to the New Year temple located out of town. Valuables from the treasury house are mentioned in the context of his visit to the latter: although the context is now unfortunately lost, these items either may have been offered as a gift or were confiscated by the king, and it is possible that the priests were merely entertaining their guest by showing him prestigious curiosities. One of the items mentioned is a golden box of the goddess Bēltīya; another was a purple garment that had belonged to Nebuchadnezzar II.⁵⁵ Confiscating a golden box belonging to a goddess would have been an act of sacrilege, and Antiochos III probably knew better. However, even assuming that objects from the temple treasury were not simply expropriated, the king's request for an extraordinary tax in the form of a golden crown during his visit was likely to leave a bad impression. Given that the king was also in contact with sacred objects that day, the two memories may have subsequently merged into a story of plunder.

The Olympiodoros inscription invites us to reconstruct the context of Heliodoros's visit to Jerusalem in yet another way. The likely backdrop to the story was a contention about the attempt of the royal administration either to *increase* the taxes or to raise additional revenues, and not a demand for paying tax arrears. Moreover, Maurice Sartre's recent proposition that Josephus's story of the Tobiads must be situated in the days of the Seleukid domination of southern Syria, and not in the later part of the Ptolemaic period, opens the way to yet another interpretation, pointing to regional entanglements underpinning the Heliodoros story.⁵⁶

9.3.2. Further Literary Problems: The Chronology of the Feud and Heliodoros's Visit to Jerusalem

Before reading the Heliodoros story in the light of the new Olympiodoros inscription (and of the Tobiads story), a problem of chronology must be tackled. In 2

Maccabees, Simon reports twice to the governor of the satrapy. The first time the governor is Apollonios son of Thraseas (2 Macc. 3:5, 7); the second time, it is Apollonios son of Menestheus (2 Macc. 4:4). As Gera showed, although the two governors mentioned in 2 Maccabees are probably historical figures, the chronology of the text cannot be validated.[57] According to the Olympiodoros inscription, the governor of the satrapy at the time of the high priest's nomination—midsummer 178—was Dorymenes. Apollonios son of Menestheus left the satrapy by 175/4 B.C.E., since he is documented to have been somewhere else at that time, and must therefore have been appointed shortly after the date of the Olympiodoros inscription, either in late 178 or in early 177. Apollonios son of Thraseas cannot possibly have served between the two and must therefore have been governor before Dorymenes. Insofar as he was affiliated with—and perhaps the younger brother of—Ptolemaios son of Thraseas, who as we have said was governor of the region at the time of Antiochos III's conquest, Apollonios son of Thraseas may have been appointed immediately after Ptolemaios and administered the province in the late 190s and early 180s.

Gera has suggested that the chronology of 2 Maccabees was therefore the product of a deliberate literary montage. The two stories of Simon accusing Onias in front of the governor (2 Macc. 3:4–7 and 4:1–6) are narrative doublets. Based on his reconstruction of the list of governors, Gera concludes that the second episode, featuring Apollonios son of Menestheus, was probably a genuine incident, whereas the first one was contrived "to implicate another Apollonios, the son of Thraseas, with similar activity against Onias III."[58] Although it is unclear why the author of 2 Maccabees would have been interested in defaming Apollonios son of Thraseas, the doublet may have served to support his case against Simon. The latter is noted as impious (2 Macc. 3:11), and his portrayal as "an informer against the money and against the country" (4:1) is the antithesis of Onias, who protected the money and the country against Heliodoros's assault. Therefore, the purpose of the narrative doublet was apparently to illustrate Simon's two negative qualities separately: as an informer against the money when he appeals to Apollonios son of Thraseas in 2 Maccabees 3:4–7 and as an informer against Onias on the second occasion (4:2). Moreover, Simon is presented as Menelaos's brother (4:23), and maligning Simon was an indirect means of vilifying the latter, since a person's character was defined by his family affiliation, and not only by his individual conduct.

Gera's identification of the doublet, and the implication that only one true incident lies behind the text's literary montage, is plausible. Using two namesakes as governors was certainly a way for the author to suggest a similarity between the two episodes in his audience's mind, and chronological manipulations of this sort abound in 2 Maccabees.[59] The decision to date the episode of Simon's report to the governor at the time of the first or the second Apollonios may be more arbitrary,[60] but since the chronology of the text is muddled, there is no formal impediment to placing it *after* Olympiodoros's appointment, namely at the time of Apollonios son of Menestheus. Such a reading would allow a connection to be made between the recent appointment of a provincial high priest and the Heliodoros story—one that may be borne out in new translations of Daniel 11:20—the one verse understood by modern commentators to refer to Seleukos IV's time—that replace "official" with "tribute collector."[61] John Collins has suggested that this was an allusion to Heliodoros in 2 Maccabees 3 and must therefore be based on a genuine episode. As we shall see, the Olympiodoros inscription definitely justifies this translation.[62]

9.4. THE HELIODOROS STORY: READING THE FEUD BETWEEN SIMON AND ONIAS III IN THE LIGHT OF THE OLYMPIODOROS INSCRIPTION

The description of the first quarrel between Simon and Onias III appears to conflate two, if not three, distinct issues. The episode is formally ascribed to 2 Maccabees 3:4–7, but the preceding verse may be related to it (2 Macc. 3:3–7, emphasis added):

> In fact, Seleukos, king of Asia, provided for all the expenses of the sacrificial cult out of his own revenues. There was a certain Simon from the clan of Bilgah who held the office of *prostatēs* of the temple. This Simon had a dispute with the high priest over the *agoranomia* of the city. Unable to prevail over Onias, he went to Apollonios *son of Thraseas*, who was governor of Koilē Syria and Phoinikē at this time, and informed him concerning the indescribable sums of money with which the treasury of Jerusalem was replete, to such an extent that the amount of the surpluses was incalculable. These funds, he said, had not been brought to the account of the sacrifices, and therefore it was possible for them to fall under the control of the king.[63] In a conversation with the king, Apollonios son of Menestheus reported the disclosures concerning the money. The king summoned Heliodoros, the chief minister, and sent him with orders to collect the aforesaid money.

The tone of the quote is so contentious as to make unclear whether Simon appealed to Apollonios regarding the *agoranomia*, or about the money kept at the temple, or both, yet the two issues appear to be unrelated. Likewise, whether and how either matter is related to Simon's office as "*prostatēs* of the temple" on the one hand and to Heliodoros's visit to Jerusalem on the other is hard to discern.

In all, there are five questions about the Heliodoros story in general, and the above-quoted passage in particular, that need clarification; and these will be the subjects of the five subsections that will follow below. First, what is a temple *prostatēs*? Second, what was the object of Simon's report to the governor (2 Macc. 3:6)? Third, what does the "*agoranomia* of the city" have to do with the priestly administration of the temple? Fourth, why does Heliodoros, and not Olympiodoros, come to Jerusalem—or alternatively, should we read "Olympiodoros" and not "Heliodoros"?[64] And fifth, finally, why does Simon report to the governor and not to Olympiodoros? The first three questions require a detailed treatment, whereas the latter two may be addressed in passing. To make the course of the following discussion as clear as possible, it may be helpful to state in advance how the issues may be disentangled. To begin with, whereas Olympiodoros was responsible for transferring the royal subsidies to the temples of the satrapy, and probably also had the power to supervise their inner administrations, he was not in charge of levying the taxes that were raised on the temples. Apparently, the governor was. Second, Simon is a royal agent in the temple. Third, the feud about the *agoranomia* was due to Onias's opposition to tightened control of the temple revenues, which obviously opened the way to tightened taxation: that is, there is a close link between the affair of the *agoranomia* and Olympiodoros's new function in the satrapy. Fourth, likewise, the object of Simon's report was the money deposited in the temple as part of its banking activity, and apparently it specifically targeted sums deposited by Hyrkanos, which Heliodoros was sent to expropriate. Fifth, if, as is probable, there was a link between Olympiodoros's appointment and this affair as well, it is not paralleled by the discernible sphere of competence of the other known provincial high priests. Next, the manuscript tradition naming Heliodoros is correct, and should not be emended to "Olympiodoros." Last, we may surmise that the report also listed additional items of temple revenue as part of the administrative reform linked to Olympiodoros's appointment.

9.4.1. Simon's Position at the Temple: The Prostatēs tou Hierou

Prostatai are documented in Greek and native temples of Asia Minor. In the Asklepieion of Kos, they were in charge of the keys of the *thēsauroi*, the chambers where the in-kind temple revenues were kept, whereas *epistatai* were financial officials.[65] One Menestratos, *epistatēs* of the Artemision sanctuary of Amyzon in Karia, is documented around 203–201 B.C.E. (Ma 2000a, no. 10, ll. 6–7): he not only supervised the temple but also repeopled it (i.e., its lands) with citizens of Amyzon, apparently coercively. Although such coercive intervention was probably exceptional, and *epistatai* were not systematically appointed in all temples of Asia Minor,[66] Menestratos's case does show that the competences of temple administrators could be extensive and involve the use of force. In native temples of Ptolemaic Egypt, *prostatēs* was used to translate the Demotic *pA rd (n) Pr-aA*, "agent of the Pharaoh." Although this official was an Egyptian priest, in most cases he served as the representative of the royal administration in a temple in which he had no family ties rather than in his temple of origin; and he had authority over the *lesōnis*, who, albeit also a representative of the royal administration in the temple, belonged to a local priestly family. Whereas the Greek title *epistatēs* could be applied to various officials, including the *prostatēs* and the *lesōnis*, and seemingly referred to an activity of sorts rather than to a specific position. Given that in Egyptian it was translated as *pA rmT nty Sn*, "the man who draws up the inventory," his activity must have been that of a royal fiscal administrator.[67]

Finally Simon's position may be compared with that of the *paqdu/prostatēs*, as documented in the temples of Babylon and Uruk.[68] The word *paqdu* means "delegate" or "representative."[69] In Babylon, the *paqdu* was a member of the local priesthood who acted as the king's representative at the temple.[70] His high-ranking status is evident in the fact that he occasionally took part in meetings of the board comprising the *šatammu*—high priest and chief administrator of the temple—and the *kiništu*, the temple board of the Esagila, who together governed the city of Babylon.[71] Both in Babylon and in Uruk the *paqdu* is found overseeing the expenditure of temple incomes, such as the payment of wages and rations.[72] In Uruk he is also documented issuing regulations about the exploitation of temple land.[73] In other words, the Greek, Egyptian, and Mesopotamian sources consistently point to the *prostatēs* and *epistatēs* as financial administrators of temples. In Egypt and Mesopotamia, the two titles translate native titles denoting priests acting as the king's representatives in the temple administration. This definition suits the context of 2 Maccabees 3 perfectly: Simon may be seen as the king's representative within the priestly financial administration of the Jerusalem temple.

9.4.2. The Object of Simon's Report

The object of Simon's report to the Seleukid governor has notoriously confounded modern commentators, and not only because the author's literary presentation makes it difficult to get a clear idea of its historical backdrop. Part of the problem derives from modern misrepresentations about the economic and administrative structures of the Jerusalem temple. As a result, translations of 2 Maccabees 3:6 diverge substantially. This issue must be handled at the outset, with the discussion about the specific purpose of Simon's report postponed to the end of our inquiry.

A. Translating 2 Maccabees 3:6. The following sample is selected from the most recent and currently most authoritative translations, by Félix-Marie Abel, Christian Habicht, Jonathan Goldstein, Daniel Schwartz, and Robert Doran, after Elias Bickerman's commentary in each case. Italics highlight renderings that in my view are questionable:[74]

1. καὶ προσήγγειλεν . . .

    Abel: "il *dénonça* . . .
    Habicht: "Er teilt ihm mit, . . .
    Goldstein: "and divulged the information . . .
    Schwartz: "and informed him . . .
    Doran: "and declared . . .

2. ... περὶ τοῦ χρημάτων ἀμυθήτων γέμειν τὸ ἐν Ἱεροσολύμοις γαζοφυλάκιον ...

> Bickerman: "le trésor de Jérusalem est plein d'argent, en quantité inexprimable ...
>
> Abel: "... le trésor de Jérusalem pour regorger de richesses indicibles ...
>
> Habicht: "... die Schatzkammer in Jerusalem strotze von so unsäglichem Reichtum, ...
>
> Goldstein: "... that the treasury at Jerusalem was full of untold sums of money, ...
>
> Schwartz: "... concerning the indescribable sums of money with which the treasury of Jerusalem was replete ...
>
> Doran: "... that the temple in Jerusalem was full of immense funds ...

3. ... ὥστε *τὸ πλῆθος τῶν διαφόρων* ἀναρίθμητον εἶναι ...

> Bickerman: [... de telle sorte que le *montant des excédents* était inestimable ...]⁷⁵
>
> Abel: "... au point que la *quantité des sommes* en était incalculable ...
>
> Habicht: "... daß die *Menge* der Gelder unzählbar sei. ...
>
> Goldstein: "... such that *their total* was incalculable. ...
>
> Schwartz: "... to such an extent that it was impossible to calculate the *massive discrepancies* ...
>
> Doran: "... so that the *excess amount* could not be counted. ...

4. ... καὶ μὴ προσήκειν αὐτὰ πρὸς τὸν τῶν θυσιῶν λόγον ...

> Bickerman: "... et les *reliquats* [de la subvention royale, allouée pour les frais des sacrifices], *ne furent pas portés* au compte [spécial] des sacrifices, [comme il se devait]. ...
>
> Abel: "... et nullement en rapport *avec le compte exigé par* les sacrifices "...
>
> Habicht: "Sie würden jedoch nicht auf dem Konto für die Opfer gebucht, ...
>
> Goldstein: "These funds, he said, had not been brought *as offerings* to the account for sacrifices; ...
>
> Schwartz: "... and that since they had not been applied to the account of the sacrifices ...
>
> Doran: "This [excess] had no connection with the account for sacrifices, ...

5. ... εἶναι δὲ δυνατὸν ὑπὸ τὴν τοῦ βασιλέως ἐξουσίαν πεσεῖν ταῦτα.

> Abel: "... ajoutant qu'il était possible de les faire tomber en la possession du roi."
>
> Habicht: "... und es sei möglich, diese Mittel unter die Verfügungsgewalt des Königs fallen zu lassen."

Goldstein: "... rather, it was possible for them all to fall *under the provisions of the king's right to confiscate.*"

Schwartz: "... it was possible *for them to revert* to the royal authority."

Doran: "... but could fall under the authority of the king."

Bickerman's influential commentary on this passage was predicated on his belief that the Jerusalem temple had no revenues of its own—even to the extent of accepting at face value the claim of 2 Maccabees 3:3 that Seleukos underwrote the cult's entire expenditure. He concluded, therefore, that Simon was accusing the high priest of embezzlement: a surplus from the money provided by the king to subsidize the sacrifices[76] had been diverted into a separate account for the priests' own use rather than being kept in the sacrifices account as required. Hence his paraphrase of clause 4. Schwartz's translation of clause 5, that the sums should *revert* to the king's treasury, is in line with Bickerman's understanding.

B. Elements for an Alternative Interpretation of Simon's Report. If there is one thing that we may learn from the literary commentary in Parts I and II of the present book, it is that were Onias III indeed defrauding the king, we would not have learned about it from 2 Maccabees. This work is replete with criticism of Jason and Menelaos but unabashedly laudatory of Onias. Therefore Bickerman's interpretation is certainly wrong. Moreover, 2 Maccabees' account is suspiciously reminiscent of the pattern used to defame Jason and Menelaos, in that it presents Simon's report as being his own ill-intentioned initiative. There is something far too methodical in the manner in which the two wicked high priests are presented as hatching their wicked schemes in 2 Maccabees, and it is easy to see why, in the present text, this pattern was extended to Simon: not only is Simon Menelaos's brother; he also plays the part of the archvillain in the Heliodoros story.[77] In Chapter 7 (§7.2.2) it was suggested that although the author of 2 Maccabees claims that Jason deposed Onias III on his own initiative and offered to the king that he would increase the tribute in order to be appointed as high priest in his stead, there is room to believe that Jason was strongly encouraged by the king to depose Onias III because Onias III successfully resisted the king's demand to raise the tribute.[78] Similarly, it seems much more likely that Simon submitted a report *because, as temple prostatēs, he was ordered to do so.*

These literary considerations may be supplemented by further arguments that provide further reasons to reject Bickerman's commentary. First, as Bickerman clearly saw, clause 4 of 2 Maccabees 3:6 above implies that the revenues of the Jerusalem temple were divided between different accounts, one of which was dedicated to the sacrifices. Bickerman's premise that the temple had no independent revenues besides the royal subsidies compelled him to conclude that the other account was illegal, supplied with funds diverted from the sacrifices account.

However, diverting money from the sacrifices account would have meant defrauding not only the king but the divine patron of the temple, whom the monies belonged to in the first place. In other words, it was a sacrilege, and it takes considerable modern cynicism to suppose that priests would have yielded to this temptation lightly. Bickerman's premise, therefore, leads to an impasse.

Second, most modern commentaries, including Bickerman's, take at face value the claim of 2 Maccabees that Simon's alleged denunciation was motivated by his feud with Onias—leading to the conclusion that Simon was reporting a structural problem. Hence a common way to rationalize Heliodoros's failed attempt at plundering the temple is to read it as an attempt to recover tax arrears. Like Bickerman's secret funds, the tax-arrears hypothesis places the Judeans at the root of the tensions between them and the royal administration. These interpretations are questionable on two grounds. The first objection, again, is literary. As previously noted, the two issues—the report and the feud—are not necessarily related. Narrative conflations of this sort are not uncommon in 1 and 2 Maccabees,[79] the most relevant parallel being the conflation of two issues in the story of Jason's founding of the *gymnasion* in 2 Maccabees 4:7–15. As we saw in Chapter 7 (§7.1.1), this passage lumps together issues of the politicization of Jerusalem (the establishment of the *gymnasion*, the inscription of the Antiochenes, and the payment of a special tax) with those concerning Antiochos IV's pretension to meddle with the appointment of the high priest (Jason's eviction of Onias III and the increased tribute). Similarly, combining Simon's report of the temple's metal assets with his feud with Onias could be motivated by the author's desire to link Simon's hostility toward Onias III to an alleged misdemeanor affecting the temple. In other words, this literary montage was at least partly motivated by the codes of the semantic concatenation.[80]

The second objection is inspired by the Olympiodoros inscription. Reading Simon's report in light of the recent appointment of a provincial high priest suggests that the responsibility for the tensions lay with the royal administration. In presenting a report to the governor, Simon was not acting on his own initiative, and therefore was not denouncing either a structural problem (tax arrears) or a structural misconduct (Bickerman's secret funds), but merely was ordered to do so by the Seleukid officials to whom he was accountable. His report, in other words, may be understood as a detailed survey of the temple's revenues, or of the assets that were deposited in it as a bank, or both. In the first case, it was part of the tighter oversight of temple revenues throughout the satrapy, which was the counterpart to Olympiodoros's appointment. Whether the second was related to Olympiodoros is uncertain, albeit probable.

The argument that Simon's report was preparing the ground for a tax increase targeted specifically at the temple revenues runs counter to the current view that the Jerusalem temple's economic assets since its reconstruction under the Persians were limited as compared with other temples. In a way Bickerman's view that the temple had no independent revenues at all apart from the king's subsidies is only the extreme version of this tenet. Therefore the vexed issue of the economic structure of the Jerusalem temple in Persian and Hellenistic times must be reexamined.

9.4.3. The Revenues of the Jerusalem Temple: The Traditional View

The scholarly vulgate about the structure of the revenues of the Jerusalem temple in Persian and Hellenistic times relies mainly on the biblical texts of the Persian era—extrapolating both from what they say and from what they *don't* say. For example, no reference is ever made to land estates belonging to the temple. Despite a few unconvincing attempts to argue the opposite, the accepted view that the Jerusalem temple possessed no sacred lands may be endorsed.[81] Surveys of the temple revenues in Persian times typically include royal subsidies, voluntary offerings and gifts, and taxes levied on the Judean population.[82] However, this list is problematic. Although the Achaimenids' practice of gift offerings to temples is well documented, gifts by definition were not a regular source of income, whereas it is far from certain that the Persian kings made a regular allowance to the cult's costs. The two decrees of Darius and Artaxerxes inserted in the book of Ezra (Ezra 6:1–12, 7:11–28) are the only evidence we have of royal subsidies (Ezra 6:8–10 and 7:21–24), but their authenticity is widely contested.[83] Therefore the earliest substantive evidence we have of royal subsidies to the temple is Antiochos III's decree of 200/198 B.C.E. (*Ant.* 12.140), which is generally regarded as genuine.[84] The (supposedly) voluntary taxes are spelled out in the book of Nehemiah (10:32–39; 13:10–13, 31). Although they consist overwhelmingly of commodities, two types of metal taxes are listed. First, one-third of a shekel (Neh. 10:33), followed by the redemption prices for people's firstborn and for unclean animals (Neh. 10:36, with Num. 18:15–16).

This picture must be incomplete, given the known revenue sources of other temples in Greece, Asia Minor, Mesopotamia, and Egypt on the one hand, and on the regular expenditure of the Jerusalem cult on the other. The likelihood that the Achaimenids did not subsidize the temple on a regular basis means that in Persian times the operational deficits would have been simply unsustainable. However, basing the study of temple revenues exclusively on literary sources is about as reliable as basing a study of the Ptolemaic economy on Theokritos's *Idyll* 17[85] or studying the Athenian domestic economy on the basis of Athenian forensic oratory alone. It may be assumed that Judean literary sources would mention only the symbolically significant sources of income and omit the rest. According to the social and cultural values of the Judeans, there was no reason to give a comprehensive record of the temple economy.[86] Thus, the voluntary taxes paid by the Israelites to the temple and the priests are given prominent attention because they are the material expression of the bond between community and temple, and probably also because they were a mark of membership in the community, like the original participation in the rebuilding of the altar and the temple and the annual partaking of the Passover sacrifice.[87] Likewise, royal gifts were a matter of prestige. Besides their obvious—and admittedly far from negligible—financial function, they symbolized the good relations between the kings and local communities, and from the kings' point of view proclaimed their *eusebeia* (piety). For the same reason, Greek sanctuaries kept records of gifts from illustrious visitors.[88]

Royal allowances to the temples were similarly a matter of prestige as well as a financial asset. The pointed statement of 2 Maccabees 3:3 that "Seleukos, king of Asia, provided for all the expenses of the sacrificial cult out of his own revenues" is another way of saying that the Jerusalem temple was the greatest in the world (2 Macc. 2:19, 3:12). The claim that the subsidies were financed out of the king's own revenues is clearly an exaggeration, since they were undoubtedly taken from public revenues, if at all (compare Ezra 6:8 and 7:21), and suspiciously recalls Antiochos IV's hyperbolic pledge on the eve of his death (2 Macc. 9:16).[89] Recognizing the hyperbole in the idealized description of Seleukos's era casts further doubts on the additional claim that the king's subsidies covered all the cult's expenditures.

Accurate data about the extent of the royal subsidies provided by the Hellenistic dynasties—or even the proportion of the cult expenses that they covered—are lacking. However, a rough estimate may be attempted, based on Antiochos III's decree. According to the text extant in Josephus, Antiochos agreed to grant the following (*Ant.* 12.140):

> In the first place we have decided, because of our piety, to furnish them for their sacrifices an allowance [*syntaxis*] of sacrificial animals, wine, oil, and frankincense to the value of 20,000 silver [drachmas][90] and sacred artabae of fine flour in accordance with the law of the country, and 1,460 medimni of wheat and 375 medimni of salt.

The sum of twenty thousand silver drachmas, in the form of an annual gift, may be compared with the total cost of 7,850 drachmas that the city of Kos, the officials, and the priests of Asklepios spent on the sole festival of the Asklepieia in the third century B.C.E.[91] This sum would hardly support the claim that the royal subsidies covered a substantial proportion, let alone the whole, of the cult expenses of the Jerusalem temple.

Moreover, the Hellenistic dynasties willingly supported the cult expenses of the temples falling under their jurisdiction through the award of lands and allowances.[92] As we have seen (§9.2.2), the very function of the *archiereis* in the Seleukid realm seems to have been linked to the administration of the royal subsidies. When viewed in this wider context, Antiochos III's endowment to the Jerusalem temple does not seem to have been out of the ordinary. It is hard to imagine what conditions would have induced Seleukos IV to increase his subsidies to cover the whole of the cult expenditures of the Jerusalem temple specifically. Therefore, the claim of 2 Maccabees 3:3 clearly has no factual basis. However, there may be another way of viewing this hyperbolic statement.

Taken at face value, the notion that Seleukos IV's allowance covered *all* the cult's expenditures implies that the voluntary taxes paid by Judeans to their temple had been discontinued. This absurd implication is totally unwarranted[93]—however, that may precisely be the intention of the statement, and Antiochos IV's equally lofty pledge to finance the cult out of his private revenues in his confession (2 Macc. 9:16) should probably be understood in the same way. These statements take on a new resonance once it is understood that they were articulated in the context of a tax reform, as argued here, and even more clearly if this tax reform targeted the temple revenues. Accordingly, the intended message may be understood as follows: before Simon's alleged plot, not only did Seleukos IV not personally order his officials to plunder the temple—he covered all its costs out of his own pocket. In other words, these statements are part of a political argument, an ideological counter in 2 Maccabees to 1 Maccabees' repeatedly equating the Seleukid tax demand with (illegitimate) theft.[94] Since 2 Maccabees 3:3 cannot be taken at face value, the question of the Jerusalem temple's sources of income remains. The picture that may be adumbrated on the basis of the book of Ezra-Nehemiah is most likely incomplete.

9.4.4. The "Economy of the Sacred": The Agoranomia of the City in 2 Maccabees

Three passages in 1 and 2 Maccabees provide concrete grounds for suspecting that the information provided in the book of Ezra-Nehemiah about the temple revenues is selective. However, before examining this evidence, we should clarify the concept of "sacred economy" and its precise relationship with the royal administration.

A. The "economy of the Sacred": Categories of Lands, Revenues, and Officials. In her *Economy of the Sacred in Hellenistic and Roman Asia Minor*, Beate Dignas questions the view, entrenched among the proponents of the notion of "polis religion," that the Greek sanctuaries in cities had no identity of their own within the public space of the city.[95] According to that view, the finances of the civic sanctuaries were treated as merely another branch of public finance, and the civic magistrates freely tapped into temple treasuries whenever necessary, especially when it came to funding war efforts.[96] The ancient Greeks themselves, Dignas argues, took great pains to distinguish between public and sacred wealth. Not only do they bear different names—the distinction between *dēmosia* (public) or *hosia* (secular) and *hiera* (sacred) *chrēmata* (money) being strictly maintained throughout the history of ancient cities—but they were administered by different officials: the public funds by *tamiai* (treasurers), and the sacred ones by *hieropoioi* and, in fifth-century Athens, *Hellēnotamiai*.[97] When civic magistrates did use money from the sacred treasures, it was in the form of a loan, and the deity to whom the money belonged was paid back with interest. Although Dignas's demonstration that sacred and public funds were kept strictly separate may readily be endorsed, she pursues the implications of this separation too far, arguing the untenable view that the royal officials of the Seleukid and Attalid administrations serving in the temples merely *administered* the sacred economy and did not extract revenues from either the temple finances or its sacred lands.[98] She further assumes, but never demonstrates, that all sacred properties, including the sacred lands leased to peasants, were *inherently* exempt from royal taxation.[99]

Dignas's assertion that the ancient Greeks took the distinction between the categories of the sacred and the secular seriously, and that this attitude had a direct bearing upon their economic practice, is valid and may unquestionably be extended to all ancient Mediterranean societies. However, this cannot imply that the royal administrations—of whichever dynasty—refrained altogether from taxing the temples' economic activities. There is too much evidence against this: the presence of royal administrators in the temples—*paqdu, pA rd (n) Pr-aA, epi tōn hierōn, prostatēs, epistatēs*—the principle of reciprocity implicit in royal euergetism; and above all, the inscriptions explicitly granting tax exemptions to the temples, indicating that the opposite was the rule.[100]

The great sanctuaries of mainland Greece, Asia Minor, Syria, Mesopotamia, and Egypt were key economic players on both regional and interregional scales. Studies of the economy of the ancient world usually take into account two separate spheres—the civic and the royal. In recent years, the debate has revolved around the need to discard Moses Finley's tenet, which had dominated this field of research since its articulation in 1973, that these two spheres were incompatible systems that coexisted with no interaction whatsoever and could therefore be studied separately.[101] Dignas's study is a fitting reminder that "the economy of the sacred" constitutes a *third* category of its own, which must be studied as such, if only because the ancients themselves perceived it so.

However, Dignas's understanding of the sacred economy, especially the sacred finances, must be further refined. To this end, her classification of sacred lands may be taken as a starting point. As Dignas points out, "a god's land could be sacred in varying degrees."[102] The land immediately surrounding the temple and altar was walled off—this area was not necessarily identical with the *temenos*. These two spaces were particularly sacred, and as we know from various ritual systems of the ancient Mediterranean and Near East, access to them was usually strictly regulated. The status of the cultivated lands belonging to the gods—the "sacred land" (*hiera gē*)—was clearly different, and the rules of purity that applied to them were far less stringent, if they applied at all.

The surviving evidence about the spheres of competence of the *paqdu* in Babylonia (Uruk) and the *epi tōn hierōn* in Asia Minor (Apollonia Salbakē) suggests that their boundaries corresponded to this inner distinction within the sphere of the sacred. As the king's representatives in the temples, the *paqdu* administered the part of the sacred economy comprising the outer, inferior level of the sacred domain—namely the cultivated lands and the villages within them, and the temple's business activity. This was the part of the sacred properties and assets that the king could legitimately extract surpluses from through taxation. By contrast, the sacrifices portion of the economy, associated with the inner sphere of the sacred space and permeated with the presence of the temple and the altar, was intrinsically out of bounds for any royal interference, including the presence of the king's representatives. It is precisely this distinction that Simon is referring to in his report to the governor of the satrapy, as the following translation understands (2 Macc. 3:6):

> [Simon] informed [the governor] concerning the indescribable sums of money with which the treasury of Jerusalem was replete, to such an extent that the amount of the surpluses was incalculable. These funds, he said, had not been brought to the account of the sacrifices, and therefore it was possible for them to fall under the control of the king.

B. Hints at Additional Sources of Income. 1 and 2 Maccabees include three clues that the sacred economy of the Jerusalem temple had the same dual structure as any other temple, even if it possessed no sacred lands. The reliability of Demetrios I's letter to Jonathan is admittedly uncertain, because it may well be a forgery. It details a long list of tax exemptions for the Judeans and indirectly refers to the royal taxation of the temple revenues (1 Macc. 10:42):[103]

> I also remit the 5,000 silver shekels which were until now paid from the annual income of the temple, and declare that they should be paid to the priests in charge.

Bickerman understood this clause to mean that the priests were being taxed on their share of the sacrifices.[104] This is most unlikely, for two reasons. First, this allocation, being related to the sacrifices, was part of the sacred economy that lay beyond the king's reach. Second, the priests were regularly exempted from general taxation—Antiochos III granted them exemption from the poll tax, the crown tax, and the salt tax (*Ant.* 12.142)—and therefore the idea that the priests were subjected to *sacrifices-related* taxes is highly improbable. In short, this clause makes no sense unless the Jerusalem temple was subject to royal taxation, like any other temple.[105]

The Heliodoros story provides two important clues that this is indeed the correct interpretation. The first is in Onias III's words when he attempts to dissuade Heliodoros from seizing the temple monies. This, as he vainly protests (2 Macc. 3:10–12), contrary to the false report of the impious Simon, consisted partly of deposits of widows and orphans and partly of deposits of Hyrkanos the Tobiad, a man of very high position, and ... the total amounted to 400 talents of silver and 200 of gold. The depositors had put their trust in the sanctity of the place and in the dignity and inviolability of the temple venerated throughout the whole world; to violate their trust, he said, was inconceivable.

The argument from plausibility, again, is decisive. Although the conversation between Onias III and Heliodoros is fictitious, it had to sound plausible, especially given the assumption, as I argue in this book (General Introduction, §6; and Chapter 2, §2.2.4), that 2 Maccabees was written in Jerusalem. Therefore it is unlikely that the existence of private deposits in the Jerusalem temple was a mere invention.[106] If Onias's words are to be believed, they are important evidence. Elsewhere in the Hellenistic world the deposit of private monies was related to the temple's function as a bank, and Beate Dignas has recently restated the importance of banking as a source of income for ancient temples.[107] Banking activity could develop irrespective of whether the temple had any landed assets and was therefore an ideal option for the Jerusalem temple. However, banking could also be linked to and supported by commercial activity—which brings us to George Aperghis's interpretation of the passage in 2 Maccabees 3:4–5 regarding the *agoranomia*.

C. *The* Agoranomia *of the City: 2 Maccabees 3:4–5.*   An *agoranomos* was a market supervisor, a well-known position in the civic officialdom of Greek cities. Section 11 in Antigonos Monophthalmos's long letter of 303 B.C.E. addressed to Teos in Ionia, Asia Minor, regarding the projected *synoikismos* of its civic body with that of Lebedos, provides details of the *agoranomos* function that, as Aperghis has noted, may shed light on the question of the *agoranomia* in 2 Maccabees.[108] Antigonos's primary concern is with taxes and with the *agoranomos* as tax collector. Further confirmation that the *agoranomos* was first and foremost a tax collector may be found in the second letter of Eumenes II to the citizens of Tyriaion in Phrygia, Asia Minor, dating shortly after 188 B.C.E. (*SEG* 47.1745 = Austin, no. 236):[109]

> and we grant to you, for the present, the revenue accruing from the office of the *agoranomos* for the [purchase of] oil for the *gymnasion* until such time as Herodes ... investigates the matter and determines other sources of income.

In the region of Tyriaion the *agoranomia* was controlled by a royal official and bound to revert to the king's control after a while. Oil, as is well known, was expensive, and purchasing it posed a heavy burden on civic finances, which is why it was often the object of royal euergetism.[110] In this specific instance, the *agoranomia* revenues—which were clearly from the taxes levied on the market business—temporarily devolved upon the citizens of Tyriaion. Eumenes II's letter reminds us that the Hellenistic East witnessed many innovative adaptations of traditional civic institutions and that no single, rigid model of the *agoranomia* should be postulated. Nevertheless, Aperghis's suggestion that in Jerusalem, Teos, and perhaps also in Tyriaion the *agoranomia* was handled by a tax farmer acting on the king's behalf is questionable. Not only is tax farming not documented in Asia Minor under the Seleukids,[111] but there is positive evidence that the taxes due to the king were collected by the cities and the temples from the areas under their control.[112]

According to 2 Maccabees 3:4–5, Simon quarreled with Onias over the *agoranomia* of the city and, being unable to prevail over the high priest, turned to the governor.[113] The passage must be read while bearing in mind Dignas's remark that sacred and secular treasures were administered separately. The fact that the *agoranomia* "of the city" of Jerusalem was in the hands of the temple's priestly personnel is plausible evidence that commercial activity took place in the porticoes of the temple. While explicit mention of the temple's commercial activity appears only in the Synoptic Gospels at a much later period (Matthew 21:12; Mark 11:15–16; Luke 20:45), Zechariah 14:21—which is datable to early Hellenistic times—may well allude to such an activity, and as Aperghis suggested, the assumption that the market was located in the temple as early as Hellenistic times may explain why Antiochos III explicitly spoke of rebuilding the temple's porticoes in his letter of 200/198 B.C.E. (*Ant.* 12.141).[114] If the notion that the commercial portico was located within the temple precinct is not acceptable, there may be yet another explanation for the control of the city's *agoranomia* by the temple's priestly administration. The high priest's authority appears to have extended either to the whole city or at least to the area within the walls in Hellenistic times. A royal edict outlawing the introduction of the flesh of animals forbidden by the Law of the Judeans into the city, which Josephus attributes to Antiochos III (*Ant.* 12.146), may be evidence that the entire city was viewed as an extension of the sacred space of the *temenos*. This symbolic perception of space cannot be entirely disconnected from actual practice and therefore implies the extension of the high priest's jurisdiction beyond the temple precinct. In this sense, the city market could be said to fall under the purview of the priests even though it was held outside the temple precinct.[115] The portico offered by Antiochos—son of Seleukos I and crown prince—to the city of Miletos may serve as a point of comparison. There, the portico was to be built in the city, but its revenues were set aside to pay for construction in the Didyma sanctuary. Antiochos's gift is known from two decrees voted by the citizens of Miletos in 299/8 B.C.E. in honor of him and his mother, Apame (wife of Seleukos I).[116]

Major Greek and native Anatolian sanctuaries developed as regional commercial centers precisely because of the regional and interregional influence of their cultic activity.[117] Festivals were the occasion of fairs held within the temple precincts.[118] The sanctuary of Baitokaikē, in northern Syria, was granted the right to hold tax-exempt fairs twice a month; this exemption, as we have noted, implies that fairs held in temples were generally subject to royal taxation.[119] The Jerusalem temple was a center of major festivals attracting pilgrims from within Judea and beyond, and its major religious status must have stimulated its development as a commercial center. There is little reason to doubt that the *agoranomia* of the city was lucrative and was an important source of revenues for the temple—particularly, although not only, during the fairs—and the revenues of the *agoranomia* from levies on commercial activities and the fairs were, as discussed, subject to royal taxation.

One final point must be raised. Aperghis proposes that the feud between Onias and Simon regarding the *agoranomia* was over the position of a tax contractor,[120] but this inference is not compelling. To begin with, the author's version of events is suspect. Moreover, assuming that there were indeed tensions, these may have been due to Onias III's attempt to obstruct Simon's work. Once again, the events depicted in 2 Maccabees 3 must be read in light of the appointment of Olympiodoros and its likely corollary of a revamping of temple taxation throughout the satrapy. As the king's representative at the temple, Simon may have been asked to make a new assessment of the *agoranomia* revenues administered by the high priest in light of the new fiscal demands. However, Onias's protestation that the monies deposited in the temple that were the object of Simon's report belonged to Hyrkanos (2 Macc. 3:10–12)[121] hints at another possible interpretation of the conflict between Onias and Simon and Heliodoros—the two may be complementary rather than mutually exclusive.

9.4.5. Heliodoros and Hyrkanos

A recent paper by Maurice Sartre possibly casts additional light on the context of Seleukos IV's appointment of Olympiodoros in 178 B.C.E. precisely and by extension on the nature of the aforesaid dispute.[122] The starting point is Daniel Schwartz's argument, endorsed by Sartre, that Josephus's story of Joseph the Tobiad (Hyrkanos's father) relates to the period that followed the marriage of Ptolemy V Euergetes and Cleopatra Syra, Antiochos III's daughter, in 193 B.C.E., and should not be redated to the mid-third or late third century B.C.E., when the Ptolemies ruled the region.[123] Antiochos III gave the tribute (*phoroi*) of "Koilē Syria, Samaria, Judea, and Phoinikē" (that is, the former Ptolemaic satrapy of Syria and Phoinikē) to Ptolemy V Euergetes as a dowry on this occasion (*Ant.* 12.154–55). According to Josephus, Joseph the Tobiad secured for himself the right to field the revenues of the entire satrapy, although the original purpose was (allegedly) to sell those of each region separately (*Ant.* 12.155, 175, 201). Given that Joseph was succeeded by his son Hyrkanos (*Ant.* 12.229), Onias's claim that the monies deposited in the temple that Heliodoros attempted to seize during his visit to Jerusalem belonged to Hyrkanos is likely to be correct.

According to Sartre, it seems that at Cleopatra's death, in 176 B.C.E., a dispute arose between Ptolemy VI, who had succeeded his father in 180 B.C.E., and Seleukos IV. Taking the queen mother's death as a pretext, Seleukos, and after him Antiochos IV, contested the continued levy of the aforementioned revenues to the Ptolemaic court, whereas Ptolemy seemingly replied by claiming the territory together with its revenues.[124] It is tempting to date the beginning of this dispute to Ptolemy V's death in 180 B.C.E. and not to his wife's in 176, and to place in this context Seleukos's appointment of a provincial high priest in 178.[125] If we pursue this track further, we may propose that the primary goal of Heliodoros's visit to Jerusalem was to lay hold of the revenues levied by Hyrkanos and deposited in the Jerusalem temple before their dispatch to Alexandria. This may also explain why Onias put up such fierce opposition to the royal envoy despite his high-ranking status and how he could be successful—Hyrkanos may have been able to confront Heliodoros with a small (private?) military force, the sort of detail that the author of 2 Maccabees would have omitted.

. . .

TEMPLE REVENUES AND THE MONETIZATION OF THE ROYAL TAXES

The two proposed interpretations of the quarrel among Onias, Simon, and Heliodoros—either over the *agoranomia* or over the Ptolemaic revenues—are complementary rather than exclusive, given that the tribute that Heliodoros attempted to confiscate was one thing and the temple revenues were another. The revenue structure of the Jerusalem temple highlighted in the discussion above (§9.4.3–4) makes it abundantly clear why it must have attracted the keen interest of Seleukos IV. Deposits, money loans, and the commercial activities of the regular market and those of the fairs accompanying the festivals were all monetized sources of income. Therefore, the appointment of a high priest in the satrapy must have been part of a major administrative and tax reform independent of Seleukos's plausible scheme to reclaim the tribute revenues.

Seen in this context, the tensions between Onias III and the representatives of the Seleukid administration—Simon, the governor, and Heliodoros—are easier to understand. The high priest, who was in charge of the tribute, was resisting one tax reform, or possibly two tax reforms at once. Moreover, this reconstruction vindicates 2 Maccabees' account on the identity of the royal official who visited Jerusalem. Dov Gera has argued that on the basis of the Olympiodoros inscription the name Heliodoros should be emended to "Olympiodoros" in the literary source;[126] but this is most likely wrong. If the purpose of the visit was to seize the monies levied on Ptolemy VI's behalf, Seleukos's decision to dispatch the man who ranked second after him in the empire makes sense. Similarly, it may be explained even if Heliodoros was only touring the satrapy to enforce Seleukos's unpopular reforms. According to 2 Maccabees, Simon, the *prostatēs*, reported to the successive governors of the satrapy, and not to the high priest. This may mean that whereas Olympiodoros was appointed to supervise the distribution of the royal subsidies to the temples, the governor, who enjoyed military powers, remained in charge of the levy of the temple taxes. The fact that the king dispatched none other than his chief minister to the satrapy may suggest that the Judean leader was not alone in objecting to the Seleukid administration's policy, but that there was considerable unrest throughout the province over the planned tax reform.

Was Onias III ultimately successful in resisting the attempt to seize additional monies from the temple treasury, as 2 Maccabees' version of the Heliodoros story claims? Based on what was to follow, it seems that he was.

10

Judea under Antiochos IV Epiphanes

The Reforms, from 175 until circa 172 B.C.E.

INTRODUCTION

As we saw in the previous chapter, in the satrapy of Koilē Syria and Phoinikē, Seleukos IV's reign was marked by a comprehensive administrative and fiscal overhaul, of which the appointment in 178 B.C.E. of Olympiodoros, most probably as provincial high priest, must have been only one aspect. Although some of the reforms may have simply been a routine adjustment of the fiscal exploitation of the region two decades after its conquest, the main purpose of the move—as argued in the previous chapter—seemingly was to seize back the provincial tribute that Antiochos III had ceded to Ptolemy V in 193 B.C.E. The role of Olympiodoros in this scheme is unclear, because of the typical vagueness of Seleukos IV's decree of appointment and the deliberate bias of the 2 Maccabees account. The royal decree certainly betrayed the king's intention to tighten his grip on the revenues of the satrapy's temples, since this was the expectable counterpart to the king's proclaimed concern to increase his subsidies to the local gods and, as a consequence, harbingered a tougher tax levy. In all likelihood therefore the quarrel between Onias III and Simon over the *agoranomia*, the lucrative supervision of the market activity, was related to its prospective submission to royal taxation. Apart from this inference, it is unclear whether there is a relation between Olympiodoros's nomination and Heliodoros's failed attempt to expropriate Hyrkanos's monies—which by our interpretation were the tax revenues collected by Hyrkanos on behalf of Ptolemy VI and deposited in the temple pending dispatch to Alexandria. If, as we may presume, the two incidents are related, this means that Olympiodoros's prerogatives in the satrapy of Koilē Syria and Phoinikē were wider than those enjoyed by Nikanor, the Seleukid high priest of cis-Tauric Asia Minor, in order to meet royal objectives locally. Simon, the royal *prostatēs* in Jerusalem, was required to hand over to the *stratēgos* (the provincial governor) a report either listing the temple's sources of income that were liable to increased royal taxation or assessing the monies collected by Hyrkanos on behalf of Ptolemy VI—or both.[1] These steps were met with the fierce opposition of Onias III, the high priest, who quarreled with Simon about the *agoranomia* and successfully repelled Heliodoros's attempted intrusion in the temple chambers.

As this chapter will argue, the events marking the beginning of Antiochos IV's rule were a direct follow-up to the crisis generated by Seleukos's bold moves and Onias's effective resistance. Before a solution could be found, in September 175 B.C.E. Seleukos was murdered by Heliodoros. His successor did not exactly opt for conciliation: the recalcitrant high priest was deposed, and his office was handed down to the highest bidder—Antiochos IV making the most of the opportunity not only to secure the new incumbent's pledge to pay the tribute to him rather than to Ptolemy VI's tax farmer but also to impose a raise in the rate of the tribute to be paid to him, either by incorporating increased taxation of the temple revenues with the rest of the taxes making up the tribute or independently. These reforms, which took a particularly brutal turn after Antiochos IV's accession to the throne, constitute the immediate causes of the rebellion. As a way to contextualize Antiochos IV's vigorous policy in Judea, the first section of this chapter (§10.1) will summarize Antiochos IV's monetary policies in Seleukis Syria and Koilē Syria and Phoinikē, respectively, as well as his reputation as a city founder. The second section (§10.2) will examine the link between the deposition of Onias III and the king's demand for a larger tribute. As was seen in Chapter 7 (§7.2), this connection is repeatedly underscored by the author of 2 Maccabees. Comparative data suggest that the author's claim is not an arbitrary construct but is to be taken seriously. In his study of the relationship between the Ptolemies and the Egyptian priesthoods, Gilles Gorre has pointed to the interrelation between the Ptolemaic administrative and fiscal policy and the ever-heavier interventions of the royal administration in the social composition of the priestly personnel of the Egyptian temples. Because the evidence from Ptolemaic Egypt is exceptionally abundant, Gorre's analysis provides the most valuable comparative reference with which to understand how the destabilization of the high priesthood of Jerusalem and the fiscal policy of the Seleukids were similarly interrelated. The Ptolemaic data may be supplemented with some Seleukid material: alongside Antiochos III's appointment of Nikanor as high priest in cis-Tauric Asia Minor, the most intriguing material relates to administrative changes that affected the status of the high priests of Babylon and Uruk, the main cities of Babylonia, under Seleukid rule. Although the available evidence is not so informative as one might wish, students of Seleukid Babylonia have drawn parallels between Judea and these two cities, and therefore the data need to be reviewed here. The third section (§10.3) will deal with Jason's establishment of the *gymnasion* and the polis of the Antiochenes. New comparative material and, no less important, new theoretical approaches to the notion of Hellenization may be cited in a reexamination of Jason's reforms, offering new avenues for appreciating the impact of the reform both in political and in cultural terms. These data include not only the recently published inscription from Tyriaion in Asia Minor but also, possibly, the social evolution of the city of Babylon. Under either Antiochos III or Antiochos IV a community of *politai* was established in Babylon. Although its ethnic makeup is disputed and the evidence ultimately proves inconclusive, it is not excluded that as in Jerusalem these *politai* were members of the priestly elite of Babylon who assumed Greek customs, including Greek-style athletic and military training in their *gymnasion*. Given the potential importance of the Babylonian *politai* for the study of Jason's reforms, the relative evidence will be discussed in this chapter.

10.1. THE FISCAL AND ECONOMIC REFORMS OF ANTIOCHOS IV'S REIGN

The circumstances under which Antiochos, youngest son of Antiochos III and brother of Seleukos IV, came to power presaged an ambitious reign. Antiochos, who had been living as a hostage in Rome since 189 B.C.E., was exchanged for his nephew Demetrios, Seleukos IV's son, in 176 or 175 B.C.E. He was on his way back to Syria when he heard the news that Seleukos IV had been assassinated. According to the Babylonian astronomical diaries, Antiochos IV became king in September 175 B.C.E.[2] He spent the first months of his reign consolidating his position at court and in the empire.[3]

Although the notion that Antiochos IV carried out a coherent program according to a preconceived plan is anachronistic,[4] the range of initiatives that may be brought to his credit, in particular his economic and monetary reforms, and city foundations and refoundations, is impressive. Since this policy is likely to form the backdrop to the larger tribute demands in Judea—in fact, in the entire province of Koilē Syria and Phoinikē—and the deposition of Onias III and politicization of Jerusalem, a review of it will provide a useful introduction to discussion of the events in Judea during his reign.

The monetary reforms carried out by Antiochos IV in Seleukid Syria are now well known. However, while older studies presented Antiochos's monetary policy as a wide-scale, coherent reform,[5] recent reappraisals emphasize the pragmatic motivations behind them. Scholars distinguish between two levels of monetary policy in Antiochos's reign. Silver tetradrachms were used to pay the army and officials. In 173/2 B.C.E., the weight of tetradrachms minted in Antioch-on-the-Orontes was reduced, but recently analysis has found this to be a readjustment necessary to bring the royal tetradrachms in line with the other coins used throughout the Seleukid kingdom. Similarly, the first Seleukid issues of smaller denominations—especially hemidrachmas and diobols—are dated to the early part of Antiochos's reign.[6] In contrast, bronze coinage was used for local, regional, and interregional commerce. Issues of bronze coinage in Seleukid Syria are documented between 173/2 and 169/8 B.C.E. As with the silver coins, recent studies have downplayed the notion that this was the result of a coherent reform carried out according to a prescriptive plan.[7]

The numismatic evidence from Koilē Syria and Phoinikē does not document any extraordinary initiatives in this province under Antiochos IV. No change is noted at the provincial level. Antiochos III had maintained the Ptolemaic monetary standard in the province after his conquest of the region, and the Ptolemaic silver coins remained in use. Georges Le Rider has explained this policy by Antiochos III's desire to keep trade between Egypt and the region unaffected by the conquest.[8] Antiochos IV followed his father's policy with regard to the silver coinage, and in general the region was maintained as a "closed space," to quote Le Rider, down to the 120s.[9] The few Seleukid issues specifically tailored for the region pointedly used the Ptolemaic standard, which was lighter than the Attic-standard coinage used elsewhere in the Seleukid empire, supplied by mint of Akē-Ptolemaïs, the capital of the province of Koilē Syria and Phoinikē.[10]

As part of Antiochos IV's monetary reforms of 169/8, the five Phoenician cities, along with twelve other cities in core areas of the Seleukid empire, were granted the right to issue so-called quasi-municipal bronze coins for local use. These coins belonged to the king, as Antiochos IV's portraits on the obverse proclaimed—however, a local symbol was also displayed there, with the name of the city inscribed next to the king's name and occasionally even without it. Four of the five Phoenician cities also made use of Phoenician script besides the Greek one—a right granted to them exclusively in the entire empire and, according to Oliver Hoover, an exceptional concession, reflecting the strategic position enjoyed by Phoenician cities under Antiochos IV.[11] The treaty of Apamea (188 B.C.E.), following Antiochos III's defeat by the Romans at Magnesia in 189, had considerably restricted the Seleukid royal navy. Although recent appreciations of Antiochos IV's rule consider that he complied only loosely with the clauses of the treaty,[12] in this new international context the importance of the Phoenician fleets certainly increased—and they indeed played a crucial role in the brief occupation of Cyprus in 168 B.C.E.[13] As Hoover points out, besides the right to use the Phoenician script, the Phoenician cities must have extorted other privileges from the king in promotion of their civic identities.

Finally, Antiochos IV seems to have introduced a reform of weights and measurements in the satrapy circa 173/2 B.C.E.[14] This policy was certainly aimed at boosting the region's economic activities and thereby the royal revenues,[15] but it was by no means unique to Koilē Syria and Phoinikē: similar measures are documented elsewhere in the Seleukid empire.[16] An interesting question, which is unfortunately impossible to answer, is whether these measures complemented Seleukos IV's fiscal reform or were unrelated.

Antiochos IV is also well known for his numerous city refoundations. Virtually all the Seleukid refoundations of Phoenicia and southern Syria have been attributed either to Seleukos IV or to Antiochos IV, but in almost every case these are assumed rather than certain.[17] It is also difficult to assess to what extent this general context may be relevant to understanding Jason's redesignation of Jerusalem as a polis. In general, the changes documented in more remote cities, especially Babylon, appear to provide a far better point of reference than the refoundations of other cities in the southern satrapy.

10.2. THE EVICTION OF ONIAS III AND THE INCREASE IN THE TRIBUTE

If we are to believe the author of 2 Maccabees (4:7–10), Jason overthrew Onias III shortly after Antiochos IV became king. He usurped the high priesthood by promising the king an apparently substantial increase in the tribute paid by the *ethnos* of the Judeans, and the king agreed. This scenario was repeated three years later (2 Macc. 4:23–27),

> when Jason sent Menelaos, brother of the aforementioned Simon, as bearer of the money to the king and as his agent for executing royal decisions on pressing matters. [Menelaos] magnified his own importance by giving the impression that he was a man of authority [and persuaded the king to appoint him high priest in Jason's stead] by adding 300 talents of silver to Jason's bid. [However, Menelaos failed to deliver the promised money.] Hence Sostratos, the commander of the citadel, whose duty it was to collect the money, repeatedly demanded payment. As a result both men were summoned by the king.

This summary is easily disputed. On the one hand, if the commander of the citadel was responsible for collecting the tribute, it is hard to understand why Jason would send Menelaos to take the money to the king. Therefore the true purpose of Menelaos's journey, if indeed it took place, is no doubt being misrepresented. On the other hand, military commanders were not usually entrusted with the collection of the tribute. Therefore the reason for both the confrontation between Sostratos and Menelaos and their summons to Antioch, if it ever took place, is also lost. However, the main reasons for distrusting the version of 2 Maccabees are literary. First, in all likelihood the two accounts of the deposing of the incumbent high priest—first Onias then Jason—are doublets,[18] since it is hard to believe that the tribute was so sharply raised twice in three years. More important, Jason and Menelaos are systematically portrayed in 2 Maccabees as being responsible for every misfortune befalling the Judeans and for crimes depicted as foreshadowing Antiochos IV's misdemeanors. The author of 2 Maccabees had particularly good reason for singling out Jason as the one responsible for the toppling of Onias III. The nature of the relations between Onias III and the high priests who succeeded him was a marker of legitimacy, and 2 Maccabees is unequivocal in this regard: Jason overthrew Onias III and Menelaos assassinated him in his bid to avoid prosecution for stealing the holy vessels—whereas Judas Maccabee was acknowledged by Onias III to be his true heir (2 Macc. 15:12–16).[19] This portrayal of events serves the author's political purposes too well to be credible. If now we appeal to the extratextual evidence, the context of Seleukos IV's appointment of a provincial high priest, coupled with comparative evidence from Egypt, also leads one to question the account given in 2 Maccabees. Although the author argues that Jason offered to increase the tribute in order to persuade the king to appoint him high priest, it is far more likely that it was the king who instigated the tax increase and that this was the real trigger to the chain of events. Onias was deposed because he refused to comply with the increased demand, and he was replaced with a more cooperative incumbent. Alternatively, it may have been because Onias resisted Heliodoros's seizure of the tax revenues collected on behalf of Ptolemy VI that the king evicted Onias and obtained his replacer's agreement to a tribute increase in exchange for the office. To support either interpretation, we must first clarify the role of the temple as a fiscal center. This will be the purpose of the following section.

10.2.1. The Temple and Collection of Royal Taxes in Persian Times

The book of Ezra-Nehemiah is the main source of evidence that in Persian times the priestly personnel of the Jerusalem temple administered and perhaps collected the taxes that were imposed both by the temple and by the royal administration.[20] The Persian taxation system was organized at the level of the satrapy, but the collected tribute was stored at the main temples of the various regions constituting it—the Jerusalem temple being one of them—as well as in administrative complexes, such as the one excavated at Ramat Rachel.[21] The royal taxes were three: the tribute (Hebrew *middā*, cognate with the Akkadian *mandattu*), the poll tax (*belō*, Akk. *biltu*), and a land tax (*halāk*, Akk. *ilku*: e.g., Ezra 4:20). The population at large paid all three taxes (Ezra 5:4), whereas according to Ezra 7:24 the priests were exempt.[22] The taxes levied by the temple for its own benefit were known either as a "tithe" or under the general name *tərūmā* (Neh. 10:40).[23] The tribute was paid in metal or in kind, and so too was the tithe due to the temple. Whereas produce was probably used to pay the local salaries, especially those of the priests, the temple possessed a foundry where the metal was melted down and recast in standardized ingots. These were either stored at the temple treasury or used for payment, especially those corresponding to the temple *tərūmā*. The king's share was eventually forwarded to the central treasuries of the Achaimenid empire in Persepolis and Susa.[24]

The committee in charge of the treasure may have been reorganized by Nehemiah in his capacity as the king's representative in Jerusalem. The new committee comprised two priests and two Levites (Neh. 13:12–13; Ezra 8:33–34) and was in charge of the collection and distribution of the tithe and probably of the royal taxes as well. In addition it administered the temple treasures.[25] The "caster" or "founder" mentioned in Zechariah 11:13 probably refers to the high-ranking supervisor of the temple foundry, who held senior financial and administrative responsibilities, rather than to the craftsman who actually did the metal casting. When coined money was introduced in the satrapy, the founder may have acted as the head of the temple mint as well.[26] The office of the founder is documented in Babylonia also. There the founder was probably subordinated to and a close associate of the *rēš šarri bēl piqitti*, who according to the evidence from the temple of Eanna in Uruk was a royal commissioner and overseer over the temple property.[27] The biblical sources are silent about this official's counterpart at the temple of Jerusalem, but of course this is not proof that there was none.[28] Likewise, the relationship between Nehemiah's committee of two priests and two Levites and the founder is uncertain, and therefore the overall picture of the administrative structure of the temple treasury remains unclear.

A further reorganization may have been necessary when the high priest acquired his prominent position, apparently at the start of the Hellenistic era. However that may be, the system of tax collection that was in place when Antiochos IV became king shared two crucial principles with the Persian one: the supervision of the double system of taxation by the temple and the presence of at least one representative of the king in the temple's administration.[29] The association between the high priest and the collection of the royal taxes is presupposed by several literary anecdotes: the story of the meeting between Alexander and the high priest in Jerusalem (*Ant.* 11.338), the start of the story of Joseph the Tobiad (*Ant.* 12.158–66, 175–85), the Heliodoros story of 2 Maccabees 3, and the circumstances surrounding the appointment of Jason and Menelaos, respectively, as high priests (2 Macc. 4:7–8, 23–25). Likewise, the Heliodoros story features one Simon, who at this time (Seleukos IV's late reigning years) held the office of temple *prostatēs*—that is, of royal representative in the temple. However, there can have been no continuity between the imperial representatives of Persian times and this Simon, because the system of tax collection inherited from Persian times underwent several substantial reforms, first under the Ptolemies and again under the Seleukids down to Antiochos IV's accession. Moreover, given that these reforms were systematically aimed at weakening the high priest's economic position among the *ethnos* of the Judeans, in all likelihood Simon enjoyed wider powers than his Persian predecessors.[30]

10.2.2. The System of Tax Collection from the Ptolemies to Antiochos IV: The Story of Joseph the Tobiad, Antiquities *12.158–66 and 175–85*

An important source of evidence about the fiscal organization of the region in the third and early second centuries B.C.E. is Josephus's story of Joseph the Tobiad (*Ant.* 12.158–66, 175–85). According to the story's outline, the high priest Onias, son of Simon the Just, was small-minded and greedy, and thus refused to pay the tribute of twenty talents of silver that "his fathers had paid to the kings out of their own revenues; and he roused the anger of King Ptolemy" (*Ant.* 12.158). In response, Ptolemy threatened to turn Judea into a settlement for his soldiers if the tribute was not paid. Onias was persuaded to send Joseph the Tobiad to the king to settle the crisis, but while in Egypt Joseph secured for himself the tax-farming rights of the entire province of Syria and Phoinikē. Although Josephus purports to describe how a system of tax farming was instituted in the satrapy of Syria and Phoinikē under the Ptolemies, his account is marred by two sets of problems. On the one hand it displays easily recognizable distortions that are clearly designed to glorify its hero at the expense of the high priest, and on the other it conflates two historically distinct situations, namely the Ptolemaic period of domination and the early second century. While the system of tax farming was definitely introduced in the region by the Ptolemies, it was presumably abolished in the aftermath of the Seleukid conquest in 200/198 B.C.E., only to be at least partly resumed when Antiochos III ceded back the tribute of the province to Ptolemy V as a dowry for marrying his daughter in 193.[31] As Maurice Sartre has pointed out, Josephus, who did not understand how the tribute could be levied on behalf of the Ptolemies under Seleukid domination, erroneously transposed the story of Joseph's acquisition of the rights of farming the provincial tribute to the late third century B.C.E., whereas its correct setting is the matrimonial transaction of 193 B.C.E.

Tax farming was introduced in Egypt by Ptolemy II Philadelphos, most probably in the 270s or 260s. To understand what the rationale could be of extending this system to cover the satrapy of Syria and Phoinikē, it is necessary to look at how it was implemented in Egypt itself.[32] In contrast with the system of tax farming that had been known in Athens since the fourth century B.C.E., in which taxes were collected by the farmers themselves, in Ptolemaic Egypt tax collection was partly carried out by royal officials. Nevertheless it continued partly to rely on the preexisting administrative apparatus of the Egyptian temples, which in principle was distinct from the royal administration. Because of its apparent redundancy with the preexisting structures, the system set up by Ptolemy II has been deemed useless and absurd by modern scholars. However, as Joseph Manning has recently pointed out, this is true only when it is analyzed in strictly economic terms and measured against the yardstick of rational efficiency characterizing the modern Western state. When, instead, we compare the state culture of Ptolemaic Egypt with that of non-Western premodern states—especially early modern China and the Ottoman Empire—it becomes apparent that the reform also, and perhaps primarily, had a political dimension. By setting up an administrative apparatus of tax collection that partly competed with that of the Egyptian temples—even though for practical reasons it was not entirely independent of it—the king was able to increase his control over the country's tax revenues at the expense of the temples, thereby considerably weakening their economic power base. The institution of the tax-farming system was therefore a key part of the state centralization that Manning sees as characteristic of the Ptolemaic period.

Reading Josephus's story of Joseph the Tobiad in the light of Manning's analysis suggests an alternative scenario, which I put forward in two distinct steps. First, if we correct the personal bias of the account, the revised story may run as follows: at some point under Ptolemaic rule—either under Ptolemy II himself or under one of his two immediate successors—tensions over the payment of the Judean tribute arose, presumably because the king demanded that it be raised. As the political leader of the local community, the high priest assumed responsibility for negotiations with the king's representatives—even in Josephus's version, Joseph departs for Alexandria with Onias's agreement.[33] Moreover, as noted above, the story's details imply that the high priest had direct control over the revenues of the *ethnos*, and that therefore the temple was the center of tax collection.[34] Faced with resistance from the high priest, the Ptolemaic king bypassed him by setting up an alternative apparatus of tax collection. He appointed a *novus homo* at the head of the new system, and since the latter owed his new social and economic position exclusively to royal patronage, his loyalty to the king's interests was guaranteed.[35] Meanwhile, the high priest's own position was weakened to the same degree. Alternatively, the story of the tensions between the Ptolemaic king and Onias, which Josephus devised to explain how Joseph became tax farmer, may have been inspired in him by the story of Heliodoros's visit to Jerusalem, which stages the same Onias as resisting the (Seleukid) king's envoy. By this logic, the Ptolemaic king simply extended the system that had already been tried in Egypt to cover the neighboring province, in all likelihood with the same purpose in mind, namely weakening the temples' economic power base.

The revised scenario inspired by Manning's analysis also sorts out the elements belonging to two distinct historical settings, the period of Ptolemaic rule over Judea and the early second century. The system of tax farming, which was alien to Seleukid state culture, must have been abolished in the aftermath of Antiochos III's conquest,[36] and only the matrimonial transaction of 193 B.C.E. explains its entire or partial reestablishment, prompting Josephus to mix data from the two periods. Whereas the system of tax farming documents the Ptolemaic administration of the tribute, the position assigned to the high priest in the story reflects Seleukid conditions. The latter are documented by the Heliodoros story of 2 Maccabees 3, in which the part ascribed to Onias III presupposes that the high priest had control over the collected taxes, since he personally prevented Heliodoros from entering the temple chambers in which they were stored.[37]

However, unlike the Ptolemies', Antiochos IV's solution to bypass the high priest's resistance was not to institute tax farming but to replace the reluctant incumbent with an appointee of his own, in violation of local custom.[38] But although Antiochos's step hints that the Seleukids were decidedly uninterested in the Ptolemaic system of tax farming,[39] it is nonetheless strikingly reminiscent of yet another Ptolemaic state practice: the progressive change of the high-ranking administrative personnel of the temples beginning in the 270s or 260s B.C.E. dictated by the royal fiscal policy. This policy, as analyzed by Gorre, offers a useful comparative reference by which one may reconstruct the circumstances that brought Jason and Menelaos to the office of high priest. Therefore a summary is worthwhile.

10.2.3. The Fiscal Policy of the Ptolemies and the Egyptian Temples

Based on a prosopographical study of the Egyptian priests in late Achaimenid and Ptolemaic times, Gilles Gorre has demonstrated that whereas the old priestly families whose origins dated back to pre-Achaimenid times survived into the early years of Ptolemy II's reign, they were swept aside under his rule.[40] Their ouster, alongside other profound changes in the sociological profile of the Egyptian priesthood, was linked to Ptolemy II's implementation of a string of interconnected cultic, economic, and administrative reforms in the 270s and 260s B.C.E.[41]

Under the Achaimenids, the subsidies traditionally allocated to the temples by the royal administration had been considerably reduced, the temples being encouraged to be economically self-sufficient.[42] However, when Ptolemy son of Lagos was satrap (late fourth century B.C.E.), they were deprived of the revenues of the sacred lands, their main economic assets—evidence of the predatory economy that characterized the aftermath of the Macedonian conquest. As part of a string of reforms marking the switch from such predation to a regime of royal economy, Ptolemy II Philadelphos reintroduced a system of royal subsidies while taking advantage of the situation inherited from his father to keep the temples economically dependent and increase his grip on their inner administration. The occasion was the institution in 269/8 B.C.E. of the dynastic cult of Arsinoe, Ptolemy II's deceased wife, in the Egyptian temples, which was to be financed through royal allowances. To base these on a stable source of revenue, in 263 B.C.E. the king implemented a reform of the *apomoira*, the tax that was levied on vineyards and orchards. The reform particularly targeted the collection of the tax in the sacred lands. Whereas its levy in them used to be carried out by the temples themselves, the king transferred this task to tax farmers appointed by the royal administration.[43] As a consequence, the temples lost control of their own revenues, while a double economic and administrative system of royal supervision was created, at least as is documented in the region of Memphis. Besides the institution of tax farmers that allowed the centralization of collected revenues at the level of the *nomoi* (nomes, the largest territorial districts in Egypt) throughout the country, in Memphis Philadelphos instituted a new high priest of Ptah, whose dynasty was to enjoy a prominent hierarchical position among the Egyptian temples of the whole country.[44] Within the Memphite nome, the first high priest of Ptah seems to have played a major role in the establishment of the cult to Arsinoe, while according to Gorre his son and successor supervised the dispatch of the royal subsidies aimed at financing the royal cult in the temples of the district.[45]

In addition, rather than entrusting the task of establishing the dynastic cult and administering the royal subsidies *within* the temples to the old, high-ranking priestly families who had traditionally occupied the main positions of power in them, Ptolemy II appointed *novi homines* drawn from lower-ranking priestly families. As Gorre points out, the new appointees exclusively owed this newfound high status to their personal ties with the king, and therefore their loyalty to him was ensured.[46] Moreover, from Ptolemy II's time there appeared in Egyptian temples "agents of the Pharaoh" (in Greek, *prostatai*; sg. *prostatēs*), who were outsiders among the local priestly families and represented the royal administration within the temple. From now on the *lesōnis*, who in Persian times had acted as the local representative of the royal administration in the temple but was appointed by the local priests, was subordinated to the new royal official.[47] The royal administration's interference in the temples' financial affairs merely became heavier with time. From around 125 B.C.E. on, an increasing number of Egyptian temples were headed by high-ranking officials who had no family ties whatsoever with the local priesthood, such as the *stratēgoi*—the nomes' governors—themselves. In some cases it seems that the new incumbents were not even of priestly extraction and appear to have been incompetent to carry out the religious duties traditionally performed by the high priests, which were delegated to subordinate priests.[48] As Gorre shows, the Ptolemies' control over the appointment of priestly personnel was a key means for them to tighten their grip on the Egyptian temples' tax revenues.

Although the details are different, this pattern of royal intervention in the temples of Ptolemaic Egypt, combining the royal appointment of a new high priest of Ptah in Memphis, the institution of royal subsidies to the temples through the reform of the *apomoira*, and the increased grip of the Ptolemaic king on the inner temple administrations—first through the administrators of the royal subsidies and the "agents of the Pharaoh" (*prostatai*), and eventually through the new makeup of the high priests of individual temples[49]—is likely to shed light on the policy of Antiochos IV in Judea. Admittedly, at first glance the idea of drawing a comparison between the latter and Ptolemaic policy toward the Egyptian temples may seem incongruous, since scholars tend to refrain from comparative analyses between the Ptolemaic and Seleukid realms. However, recent studies by Philippe Clancier and Julien Monerie of the administrative changes that were carried out by the Seleukid administration in Babylon and Uruk show that the pattern linking royal control of the appointment of high priests and tighter royal grip on temple revenues that Gorre has adumbrated in Egypt was not alien to Seleukid practice. Moreover, Clancier and Monerie themselves both point to parallels between Jerusalem on the one hand and Babylon and Uruk, respectively, on the other. Yet given the state of the Mesopotamian evidence, their complementary conclusions at times rely on hints and scraps, and therefore the comparison with Jerusalem may seem speculative. Conversely, when the data concerning Judea and Babylonia, respectively, are read in the light of the Ptolemaic evidence, the three reinforce one another, and the comparison between the two Seleukid provinces gains weight.

10.2.4. The Tightening of Seleukid Control over the Babylonian Temples

In the early Seleukid period the cities of Babylon and Uruk, the main urban centers of northern and southern Babylonia, respectively, seem to have been organized in fairly similar ways. The two towns were dominated by chief sanctuaries, the Esagila—the temple complex of Marduk (Bēl)—in Babylon, and in Uruk, the Bīt Reš (the temple of Anu and Antu) and the Irigal (temple of Ištar and Nanaya). At the head of the Esagila and the Bīt Reš, respectively, there stood a *šatammu*, a title usually translated as either "high priest" or "chief administrator," and just below him the king's representative in the temple (*paqdu*) and a treasurer and accountant (*ganzabarri*).[50] In each city the *šatammu* was assisted in his administrative tasks by the temple board, the *kiništu*, which comprised "citizens" and occasionally the *paqdu* as well.[51] Both in Babylon and in Uruk the cultic and administrative responsibilities of the *šatammu* extended not only to all the other temples of the city but also to those of the neighboring cities—Borsippa and Kutha in the former and Larsa in the latter case.[52] Moreover, alongside the sanctuaries, the *šatammu* wielded administrative authority over the "citizens" and perhaps also the rest of the urban population and the population of the city's territory, as well as over the population of the neighboring cities.[53] The *kiništu* assemblies constituted the government of the cities and their citizens.

The procedure of succession of the *šatammu*, and in particular the question whether or not the position was hereditary, is debated,[54] and this slightly hampers our appreciation of whether the reforms imposed by Seleukos IV and Antiochos IV were as brutal as those in Jerusalem. Whatever the case, while the evidence from both Babylon and Uruk points to tighter royal control over the administration and revenues of the sanctuaries in early Seleukid times as compared with the Achaimenid situation,[55] the grip of the royal administration increased even further under these two kings. Given that the evolution was different in the two cities, they need to be surveyed separately. In Babylon, Antiochos IV found ways to undermine the *šatammu*'s position other than his brutal eviction. First, the *paqdu* (the king's representative in the temple) was made answerable to one Nikanor, who is documented between 265 and 258 B.C.E. (that is, under Antiochos IV). Even though Nikanor's precise competences are unclear, he apparently oversaw the finances of the temples at a regional level, and for this reason Clancier has compared him with the Seleukid high priest Nikanor who was appointed by Antiochos III in cis-Tauric Asia Minor.[56] Second, although the *šatammu* himself was left in place, Antiochos IV appointed the man's brother as *zazakku* and transferred to him some of the *šatammu*'s prerogatives, in particular his legal powers and control of the temple finances. The title *zazakku* is not otherwise attested in Hellenistic times, and although officials called *zazakku* are documented in the Neo-Babylonian period, their functions were quite distinct from and far more limited than those of Antiochos IV's appointee. Moreover, the *zazakku* was answerable to the king to such an extent as the *šatammu* had never been.[57] While the *zazakku*'s increased competences may compare with Simon, the Jerusalem *prostatēs*, the fact that Antiochos IV chose the *šatammu*'s brother as first incumbent is strikingly reminiscent of his replacing Onias III with Jason. In both cases, the rationale must have been that thanks to their family connections the royal appointees would be more easily accepted by the temple personnel of their respective cities.[58]

In Uruk, two instances of prominent officials' bearing untraditional titles are documented under the Seleukids. First, an inscription of 244 B.C.E. (that is, under Antiochos II) commemorates building works in the Bīt Reš, which were carried out in the name of Anu-uballiṭ, the *šaknu* (governor) of Uruk.[59] On the one hand, the building works meant nothing less than the appropriation by a leading local official of what according to Babylonian royal ideology was a royal prerogative. As Monerie stresses, the man's accrued prestige is evidence that by Antiochos II's time the Seleukid dynasty had stopped endorsing the local definition of kingship, promoting instead their own model.[60] On the other hand, Anu-uballiṭ prided himself on his personal ties with the king, ostentatiously recalling that Antiochos II himself had given him the Greek name Nikarchos.[61] The man's unusual title, the delegation of the royal competence of temple building to his benefit, and his personal ties with the king are reminiscent of the *novi homines* who in Egypt were appointed by Ptolemy II Philadelphos to new, prestigious positions on the basis of their personal allegiance to the king, entailing the social decline of once-prominent families.

In 221 B.C.E. (at the beginning of Antiochos III's reign), Anu-balassu-iqbi, the new prominent official of Uruk, who claimed the same ancestor (Aḫ'ûtu) as Anu-uballiṭ-Nikarchos, displayed two titles documented in two different texts: "overseer of the chief officials of Uruk" (*rab ša rēš āli ša Uruk*) and "manager of the temple [that is, the Bīt Reš]" (*paqdu ša bīt ilāni*).[62] Anu-balassu-iqbi transmitted his two functions separately to two sons of his, as a tablet of 209–208 (under Antiochos III) attests, and in turn the two men transmitted their respective functions to their own sons.[63] Like his namesake, the *šaknu* of 244 B.C.E., Anu-uballiṭ, who succeeded his father Anu-balassu-iqbi as "overseer of the chief officials," supervised rebuilding works, both in the Bīt Reš complex (in 202 B.C.E.) and in the Irigal.[64] Like his namesake, he bore a Greek name, Kephalon, and moreover married a Greek woman, the daughter either of a high-ranking Seleukid official or of a wealthy Greco-Macedonian settler of the region, undoubtedly as a means to strengthen his social position.[65]

Were it not for the split of the leading functions between two family lines, their hereditary transmission over three generations—combined once again with the endorsement of the royal function of temple builder by one of the family members—might have eventually led to the emergence of a dynasty not unlike that of the Oniads in Jerusalem.[66] But from the kings' standpoint, such an evolution was clearly undesirable. The son of Anu-uballiṭ-Kephalon, who succeeded him as *rab ša rēš āli ša Uruk*, was relieved of his function between 173 and 168 B.C.E. (that is, under Antiochos IV), in unknown circumstances. Thereafter, and possibly down to the Parthian takeover of 141, the title belonged to another family, the Ḫunzūs.[67] Moreover, this change roughly coincided with additional administrative and fiscal reforms under Seleukos IV (187–175) and Antiochos IV (175–164).[68] The parallel with the events of Judea—Seleukos IV's reforms, among them Olympiodoros's appointment as provincial high priest, and Antiochos IV's eviction of Onias III—is intriguing.[69]

What can we learn from the foregoing survey of the Ptolemaic and Seleukid policies toward the temples of Egypt, Babylonia, and Judea, respectively?[70] First, as part of a wide-ranging set of reforms, Ptolemy II Philadelphos promoted new priestly families to prominent positions, at the expense of the old, socially entrenched ones; in Babylon Antiochos IV appointed a *zazakku*, investing him with some of the functions—in particular, legal and financial—that hitherto had been wielded by the *šatammu*; in Uruk, the family that had been monopolizing the leading functions over three generations lost them (probably together with royal support) under Seleukos IV and Antiochos IV, while a new clan gained prominence; whereas in Jerusalem, Onias III's eviction put an end to the old, prestigious dynasty of the Oniads. Second, alongside various administrative and fiscal reforms that were carried out both at the provincial level of Babylonia and in the local temples of Babylon and Uruk under Seleukos IV and Antiochos IV, it seems that a regional overseer of the temples' administration and revenues was installed, in much the same way as the provincial high priests documented elsewhere in the Seleukid empire. At about the same time, Olympiodoros was appointed in Koilē Syria and Phoinikē. To some extent, the functions of the high priests of Ptah in Memphis, whose dynasty was started under Ptolemy II, may be compared with those of these Seleukid provincial high priests.⁷¹ Through these officials it appears that the royal administrations tightened their grip over the temples' inner administrations and finances to a far greater extent than had been the case both under earlier dynasties and in early Hellenistic times. Third, it appears that the lower-ranking officials who served the kings within the temples—the Mesopotamian *paqdu*, the Egyptian "agent of the Pharaoh," and Simon the *prostatēs* of Jerusalem—systematically enjoyed increased powers as compared with their counterparts of Achaimenid times. Taken together, these data suggest that, when faced with similar challenges—such as the need to improve administrative control of the territory and to tighten administrative and fiscal control over temple revenues—the two Greco-Macedonian dynasties adopted similar devices.⁷² By this logic, it appears that far from being an isolated incident, the removal of Onias III corresponded to a pattern of state praxis. To understand it, we need to see it as part of a more complex administrative move that also included the appointment of a provincial high priest and the use of a temple *prostatēs*. That said, the picture outlined above falls short of explaining why, if indeed the same pattern of administrative reforms was implemented in various regions of the Hellenistic East, in Judea specifically it led to a rebellion against the king. Clearly, the answer lies in the combination of two crucial institutional specificities of Judea. First, unlike the high priests of the Egyptian temples, the *šatammu* of Babylon and the high priest of Jerusalem were also political leaders. Second, the administrative structure of the Jerusalem temple was undoubtedly far less complex than that of the Egyptian and Babylonian temples, given that it did not possess sacred lands, and this may have contributed to the far greater centralization of power in Jerusalem. This may explain why the brutal deposition of the Jerusalem high priest prompted an unparalleled political and social destabilization. It is now time to explore this proposition in detail.

10.2.5. Antiochos IV's Appointment of Jason: Suggestion for a Revised Scenario

Up to and including Onias III, the high priesthood of Jerusalem was a hereditary function. The Oniad dynasty had apparently enjoyed a remarkably stable run for over two hundred years, surviving the Macedonian conquest of 332 B.C.E., the Ptolemaic takeover, and the Seleukid conquest of 200/198 B.C.E.⁷³ Ben Sira, writing in the third century B.C.E., reflects the tremendous political, social, and religious prestige that accrued to the high priests of the dynasty at this time.⁷⁴ This stability came to an abrupt end with the ousting of Onias III in or shortly after 175 B.C.E. A rapid turnover of high priests ensued: in a space of just over twenty years, no fewer than five individuals, from as many families, donned the high priest's vestment: Onias III was deposed by Jason, who apparently headed a minor branch of the Oniads; three years later he in his turn was ousted by Menelaos—who according to 2 Maccabees was kin to Simon and Lysimachos. After Menelaos was put to death, the position appears to have fallen vacant for a while, until Alkimos (whose family background is unknown) was eventually appointed high priest by Antiochos V.[75] Finally, Jonathan the Maccabee became high priest in 153 or 152 B.C.E., after yet another interval. This turnover is evidence of the acute political destabilization of Judean elite society after the fall of the Oniad dynasty.

A. *Antiochos IV's Reform.* This destabilization also coincided with an institutional shift. From Alkimos onward, both 1 and 2 Maccabees offer explicit evidence that the high priest was appointed by the king: Alkimos was appointed by Demetrios I (1 Macc. 7:9; 2 Macc. 14:3–4, 13); Jonathan was appointed by Alexander Balas (1 Macc. 10:20) and reappointed by Demetrios II (11:27) and again by Tryphon in the name of King Antiochos VI (11:57); and Simon was confirmed high priest by Demetrios II (1 Macc. 13:36; 14:38). How did this major break with the *patrioi nomoi* of the Judeans[76] come to be institutionalized under the Seleukids—and when? What about Jason and Menelaos? As we saw earlier, the claim by the author of 2 Maccabees that Jason overthrew Onias III of his own accord rather than at the bidding of Antiochos IV serves his ideological purpose a little too well. Accordingly, the most plausible scenario by far is that the institutional change coincided with Onias's removal and was in fact at Antiochos IV's instigation. Far from assenting to Jason's coup as a fait accompli, Antiochos IV actively encouraged it.

The initial selection of Jason, who after all was of the Oniad family, albeit of a minor branch, suggests that Antiochos IV was aware of local sensitivities. If this was the case, the reason why his intervention triggered a revolt may have been that too many controversial reforms were made at once: the institutional change, two violent removals of high priests within three years, the tax increase, and the politicization of Jerusalem.[77] However, the preliminary question remains: Why was Onias III deposed in the first place? The aforementioned Ptolemaic practice may help in this regard, all the more so since the account of 2 Maccabees suggests that the ousting of Onias III and the (sharp?) increase in the tribute were closely related.

B. *Antiochos IV's Motivation: A Hypothesis.* The problem facing Antiochos IV may have been lurking in the wings since the days of Seleukos IV. If the interpretation of the Heliodoros story put forward in Chapter 9 is correct (§9.4), Onias III successfully resisted the administrative and tax reform that was cued by the appointment of Olympiodoros as provincial high priest. At the very least, he seriously hampered the appraisal of temple assets that Simon, the king's representative at the temple, had been ordered to carry out.[78] Moreover, Onias III's confrontation with Simon and Heliodoros demonstrated all too well that in situations of tension with the royal administration, the high priest was able to exploit his cultic, social, and political prestige to galvanize popular resistance, rendering the king's reliance on his local representative (Simon the *prostatēs*) ineffective. Whereas the Ptolemies had successfully bypassed such high-priestly opposition by introducing the system of tax farming, this practice was alien to the Seleukids.[79] The only remaining option open to Antiochos IV, therefore, was to seize control of the high priesthood—which meant toppling the powerful Oniad dynasty and placing the position under royal appointment. Owing their new social position to the king alone, the new incumbents were expected to comply with the latter's fiscal demands.

The likelihood that the accounts of Jason's and Menelaos's coups in 2 Maccabees are narrative doublets[80] makes any detailed reconstruction uncertain. However, two points may be upheld: Menelaos succeeded Jason very quickly and Antiochos's fiscal demands eventually exceeded the community's economic capacity. If both these are correct, the volatile situation that followed Jason's coup must have had no time to stabilize when the crisis came to a head on both the political and the economic front. Menelaos was not an Oniad, and so his public standing was even weaker than Jason's and could easily be challenged by ambitious competitors, especially given the general instability brought on by the economic crisis and by the increasing regional tensions between the courts of Antioch and Alexandria. The social changes prompted by the politicization of Jerusalem would have made matters only worse.

The reason why Antiochos IV embarked on this dangerous policy in the first place must be related on the economic side to his preparations for his Egyptian operation and on the strategic one to his need to have a reliable ally at the head of the local constituency.[81] However, the fact that Antiochos IV must have played an active part in this episode need not imply that his local allies were not furthering their own interests. Whereas Antiochos was concerned with securing allies and increasing the tribute by any means possible, the politicization of Jerusalem must have been Jason's initiative.

10.3. THE *GYMNASION* AND THE POLITICIZATION OF JERUSALEM

Although it is now commonly accepted that Jason's creation of the *gymnasion* was, in essence, an act of political reform, the details and social implications of this reorganization are still disputed. The debate has long been dominated by the two diverging interpretations put forward by Bickerman and Tcherikover.[82] In recent years, a refinement of the theoretical tools used to understand what "Hellenization" precisely entailed, in particular the discarding of the essentialist conception of culture,[83] has allowed the fundamental issues to be restated in new terms. The process of politicization, by which a non-Greek urban community became a polis, Jason's motivations for undertaking his reforms, and those reforms' political and cultural implications can be examined on new grounds. In addition to these theoretical improvements, a systematic cross-referencing with comparative material—provided by the publication of new documents and the reappraisal of existing ones—has allowed substantial progress in understanding Jason's reforms. In particular, the publication in 1997 of an inscription documenting the joint politicization, shortly after 188 B.C.E., of a military settlement and the neighboring village of Tyriaion, in Phrygia, for the first time shed light on this procedure. Moreover, since the 1980s students of Seleukid Babylonia have been intrigued by the possible similarities between Jason's polis and the community of *politai* that was founded in Babylon under either Antiochos III or Antiochos IV.[84] Given the long history of modern comparison between these two cities, including, as we saw above (§10.2.4), their strikingly parallel administrative evolution under the Seleukids, establishing a parallel evolution also in this matter would offer a particularly precious means to situate Jason's reforms in a wider regional context. Unfortunately the comparison between the two cities is seriously hampered by ongoing debate about the ethnic makeup of Babylon's *politai*—whether Greek foreigners, or members of the local elite, or a mix of both. Despite the fact that the extant evidence is too elusive to support a conclusion either way, it is surveyed in detail below, because this episode of Babylon's history cannot be ignored when discussing Jason's polis. Finally, in the light of recent rephrasing of the old historiographical issues along with the new evidence, I will put forward new suggestions regarding Jason's motivations.

10.3.1. Jason's Reform according to Bickerman's and Tcherikover's Interpretations

Elias Bickerman was the first to insist that Jason's establishment of the *gymnasion* brought about a change in Jerusalem's political and social fabric. Citing a wide range of comparative material, he argued that the Antiochenes formed a *politeuma*—that is, a community living among the population of Jerusalem but with a distinct legal status.[85] His demonstration was questioned by Victor Tcherikover on philological grounds: in the description of the reform given in the crucial clause of 2 Maccabees 4:9,[86] *Antiocheis* is a predicate accusative, and thus the text should be translated as "Jason [was granted permission] to register the people of Jerusalem as Antiochenes." Tcherikover's philological analysis, which restated an older view, has been widely accepted against Bickerman's alternative interpretation.[87] However, Tcherikover qualified the practical implications of this translation by arguing that Jerusalem's new constitution must have been aristocratic by nature—that is, that not all its citizens were registered as Antiochenes.[88]

While Bickerman's and Tcherikover's commentaries helped definitely to establish that Jason's reform was essentially a political one, two basic questions continued to dog subsequent studies. One is the scope of the reform—an evaluation of which depends partly on the translation of 2 Maccabees 4:9 and partly on grounds of plausibility. Tcherikover's reluctance to believe that all Jerusalem's inhabitants were equally enfranchised is widely shared—which may explain why the debate over the scope of the reform persists, being regularly bolstered by new arguments.[89]

The second issue that remains in dispute is the effect that the reforms had on "religious" life in Jerusalem. Recent studies, especially by Robert Doran and Lester Grabbe, have argued that the *gymnasion*'s operation need not have entailed major breaches of tradition.[90] Addressing the impact of the reform on the running of the temple, Klaus Bringmann proposed the curiously rationalizing argument that Jason's primary motivation for preserving the traditional cult was economic, since the cult was a major source of revenues.[91] The new comparative material paves the way to a more refined understanding of both the political significance and the cultural and cultic impact of Jason's reforms.

10.3.2. New Insights from New Comparative Evidence: The Tyriaion Inscription

The Tyriaion (or Toriaion) inscription[92] contains two letters by Eumenes II addressed to the community of the "Toriaitoi" in response to their request to be granted civic status (*politeia*),[93] their own laws, and a *gymnasion* (ll. 10–11). The petition was jointly submitted by the members of the military settlement and the inhabitants of the neighboring village of Tyriaion, who wished to merge into a single civic body in an apparent attempt to exploit the favorable conditions of the hour. Phrygia had been offered to Eumenes II by the Romans after their victory over Antiochos III in 189 B.C.E. At the time of the petition, the region had been under Attalid control for only a short time, and the king was in dire need of support. As Eumenes records in his first letter (ll. 23–24), the Toriaitoi made their appeal at the right moment—knowing that he needed their continued goodwill too much to turn down their request. In his first letter, Eumenes grants them the right "to organize into a single citizen body [*politeuma*] and to use [their] own laws" (ll. 27–28). The new citizens are given the choice either to enact laws themselves subject to the king's approval or to receive from the king laws "suitable for establishing a council and other offices, and for dividing up and distributing the people into civic tribes, and for setting up a *gymnasion* and providing oil for the young men" (ll. 31–34).[94] The second letter grants the new citizens a provisional source of revenues with which to buy oil for their *gymnasion*.

The Tyriaion inscription documents the well-established procedure by which a local community was transformed into a polis for the first time, and its relevance for understanding the politicization of Jerusalem was soon noted.[95] A systematic rereading of the description of Jason's reforms in 2 Maccabees 4:7–15 in light of this inscription has now been offered by Nigel Kennell, who has pointed to numerous verbal parallels between the two texts. On the assumption that the Seleukid and Attalid administrations operated in similar ways, these verbal parallels are evidence that the author of 2 Maccabees was thoroughly acquainted with the practices of the Seleukid administration, since his description of Jason's reforms accurately reflects the same standard process.

Kennell's comparison of Eumenes II's letters with 2 Maccabees 4:7–15 represents a breakthrough in our understanding of Jason's reforms. However, the evidence of the Tyriaion inscription does not resolve all the controversies surrounding this episode. In particular, it is unclear to what extent the politicization of a military settlement and a neighboring village can be equated with that of a city like Jerusalem. This reservation notwithstanding, the similarities between Tyriaion and Jerusalem pointed out by Kennell may be taken as a starting point for restating the issues surrounding Jason's reform. This will be the purpose of the following review.

10.3.3. The Essence of Jason's Reform: Restating the Issues

The Tyriaion inscription sheds light on three main issues: whether there was a connection between the establishing of a *gymnasion* and the acquisition of civic status; who initiated the procedure, Jason or the king; and what the scope of the new legal entity was (a *politeuma,* the entire city). Whereas the evidence for the first two issues may be regarded as conclusive, the last one is more problematic, especially in view of Tcherikover's contention that enfranchisement was restricted by wealth criteria. Moreover, the new inscription is unhelpful with regard to the issue of the Hellenization of Jerusalem that allegedly resulted from the reform. To that end, we must call upon additional comparative material.

A. *The* Gymnasion *as Evidence for Civic Status and Military Training.* The Tyriaion inscription clearly confirms that there is a close association between the establishment of a *gymnasion* and the acquisition of civic status, disproving all previous doubts.[96] Moreover, pointing out recent studies demonstrating that the *gymnasion,* as a civic institution, fully retained its military function in Hellenistic times, Kennell convincingly concludes that 2 Maccabees 4:12 alludes to the military training undergone by the youth of the new civic body under Jason's personal command.[97] As he further points out, the public register in which the citizens' names were inscribed would serve as a basis for conscription.[98]

B. *The Politicization of Jerusalem as a Local Initiative.* The Tyriaion inscription offers incontrovertible evidence that the politicization process was instigated by the local community petitioning the king.[99] The use of a technical term for royal approval in 2 Maccabees 4:10[100] may be seen as a decisive clue that in the case of Jerusalem too the initiative for politicization came from the local leadership. The fact that Jason promised to pay an additional tax if the civic status were to be granted (2 Macc. 4:9) is yet another clue. Thus, the most plausible scenario appears to be as follows: Antiochos IV encouraged Jason to depose Onias III when the latter objected to the tax increase that the king demanded. Doubtless, the condition for the king's support was that Jason himself would agree to this increase. Jason, in turn, took advantage of his good relations with the king to request that Jerusalem be given civic status and the right to establish a *gymnasion*, which the king granted in return for yet another tax. From a literary point of view, the fact that Jason petitioned the king for the change in civic status and the *gymnasion* made it possible for the author to blur the distinction between the circumstances surrounding Onias's removal and those relating to "the list of Antiochenes" and the *gymnasion*—thereby portraying Jason as responsible for everything.[101]

Furthermore, the argument that it was Jason who initiated the politicization process may be supported on wider grounds. The old models, positing that the political, social, and cultural changes of the Hellenistic world perforce were the result of a planned royal policy pursued by the central administration of the Macedonian dynasties and imposed from above, have been replaced in recent years with models emphasizing that these changes were the product of negotiations between the king and local elites.[102] As part of this shift, researchers of the Hellenistic world have grown increasingly dissatisfied with the old view that the Hellenization of non-Greek communities—whether cities or sanctuaries—systematically was the result of an imperial fiat. Alternative models have proposed that local communities, including non-Greek ones, often actively sought to adopt the Greek civic model. Although explicit evidence such as is provided by the Tyriaion inscription is rare, the known instances of politicization of non-Greek communities, which hitherto had been seen as being the result of imperial fiat, are now being reappraised based on this revised premise. Thus, the revised models both support the argument that the politicization of Jerusalem was carried out at the behest of the local prominent men headed by Jason and provide besides a new framework for analyzing the cultural implications of the reform, which is our next focus.

C. Local Initiative and the "Hellenization" of Jerusalem. The common denominator of the new models is the premise that in processes of cultural transfer, the decisive role is played by the social agents of the borrowing society rather than by those of the source culture. This premise has figured in a departure from the essentialist view of culture that dominated the study of the Hellenization of the Hellenistic world until the 1970s if not later. The old perspective, coupled with a legalistic conception of political processes, is typically illustrated by Bickerman's and Tcherikover's shared view that the Torah—which Antiochos III had allegedly decreed as Jerusalem's legal constitution in what Bickerman calls his "charter" of 200/198 B.C.E.—was replaced with a Greek constitution when Antiochos IV came to the throne.[103] Bickerman took the adoption of a Greek *politeia* further, to mean that the Torah was abolished altogether—Tcherikover's refutation of this contention scarcely clarifies the matter, since it is based on the erroneous notion that a *politeia* is a political constitution with no bearing upon the realm of "religion."[104] The analytical tools now available allow for a more nuanced understanding of the cultural and cultic significance of Jason's reforms.

The outright adoption of a Greek *politeia* by a new civic community under royal control is attested in the royal new foundations peopled with Greco-Macedonian settlers. However, the politicization of non-Greek communities cannot be assimilated to this procedure. Cultural borrowing is selective and adaptive, and prone to misinterpretations and reinterpretations. Case studies of the adoption of the Greek civic model by non-Greek communities in Phoenicia and Asia Minor have shown that the borrowed model was adapted to local social structures and existing political traditions, which simply continued under the institutions' new Greek names.[105] Thus, it has been suggested that the title *dikastēs*—given to a Sidonian who won the chariot race in the Nemean Games and was commemorated in a Greek inscription of the late third or early second century B.C.E.—is a translation of the Phoenician title *šofet*, "judge." "Judges" were the chief officials of Phoenician cities in pre-Hellenistic times, and this inscription demonstrates that this function survived into the Hellenistic period.[106] In the cities of Lykia, the divisions of the civic body preserved traditional social structures. One particular category of population, known as the *perioikoi*, is cited in the inscriptions: although they were apparently considered part of the civic body, their status nevertheless gave them a certain distinction.[107] The city of Hanisa, in Cappadocia, adopted a Greek model of civic organization, as is reflected in its civic institutions (a *boulē*, an *ekklēsia*, a board of *prytaneis*, an eponymous *dēmiourgos*, and at least one *archōn*), a *gymnasion*, the publication on stone steles of honorific decrees written in excellent Greek, a Macedonian calendar, and the adoption of Greek proper names alongside Cappadocian and Semitic ones. However, there are a few discordant notes, revealing either a misinterpretation or a deliberate reinterpretation of a Greek institution to suit the needs of the local elite. Thus, a local benefactor was rewarded not only with an honorific inscription but also received the title *euergetēs* in his own city, whereas in the original Greek cultural context this title was awarded only to foreigners, never to citizens.[108]

It is debatable whether Tyriaion may be included in this list. In his letter to the Toriaitoi community, Eumenes II offers two options: that the Toriaitoi either make their own laws or accept laws from the king. In the latter case, the king would give them a constitution similar to that of another Greek city under his control. In the former case, it is far from certain that the laws would have been strictly Greek in character, since the new civic body merged the military settlers and local villagers into a single entity (ll. 26–27). Eumenes II's letter clarifies that the reason why he required laws to be submitted to him for approval was only to ensure that they did not include anything inimical to his interests: whether the laws were Greek or an amalgam of Greek and non-Greek influences made no difference to him.

It is striking that on occasion the Greek civic model was adopted by non-Greek communities well outside the dominion of a Macedonian dynasty. Hanisa, in Cappadocia, is a case in point. As Christoph Michels has pointed out, the theory of a top-down politicization process is particularly irrelevant in such cases.[109] Instead, he uses a modified version of the model of peer-polity interaction, originally developed as an alternative to core-periphery models to analyze processes of cultural transfer in early societies, which John Ma successfully applied to the Hellenistic world.[110] The model describes how autonomous and structurally similar polities would network together to form larger sociopolitical and economic units. To access their regional network or networks of Greek poleis, the local elite of Hanisa had to adopt the relevant discourse: this meant not only speaking Greek but acquiring a Greek education to master the Greek cultural codes—an essential prerequisite to gaining access to courtiers, since the Seleukid and Attalid courts mainly comprised citizens of Greek cities and non-Greeks fully conversant with Greek culture.[111]

A slightly different model, put forward by Rolf Strootman to explain the possible motivations for the prominent families of non-Greek cities and sanctuaries to adopt Greek civic institutions, is discussed below (§10.3.5). For our present purposes, it is the flexibility of the processes of cultural transfer involved in these models that should be underscored: elements from the source culture—in our case, the Greek civic model and the Greek *gymnasion*—that did not easily fit with local social structures and cultural and cultic traditions could be either ignored altogether or reinterpreted. It is inconceivable that the redesignation of Jerusalemites as Antiochenes and the founding of a *gymnasion* and an *ephēbeion* in Jerusalem by local prominent families in 175 B.C.E. involved changes offensive to local traditions.[112] The modern speculations regarding the allegedly mean schemes of the "Hellenizers" notwithstanding, one may safely surmise that Jason was personally as anxious as anyone else in Judea to preserve the integrity of the temple.[113] It is unlikely, therefore, that the politicization of Jerusalem per se caused such a turmoil, since it did not do so anywhere else.[114] Therefore, the problem may lie in the makeup of the new civic body and in the economic implications of the politicization.

D. *The Antiochenes: Implications of the Inclusive Interpretation.* Based on numerous epigraphical parallels, Kennell restated Tcherikover's conclusion that *Antiocheis* in 2 Maccabees 4:9 is a predicate accusative and therefore the clause should be translated as "to inscribe those in Jerusalem as Antiochenes." From a strictly philological point of view, the entire city became a polis.[115] However, as most commentators since Tcherikover have felt, the historical implications of this translation are problematic. Judean society was hierarchical, and it is hard to see why Jason would have been interested in giving equal rights to everyone, thereby undermining the social prestige of prominent families. Moreover, the account of 2 Maccabees appears to suggest that the politicization of Jerusalem triggered economic hardship.[116] It is a question whether this aspect can be reconciled with the hypothesis of truly inclusive enfranchisement.

According to a recent reconstruction by George Aperghis, it can. Pointing out that Antiochos III's decree established the city of Jerusalem as a distinct fiscal unit, separate from the rest of Judea, Aperghis argues that this different fiscal regime between city and countryside may explain how the reforms could generate economic resentment even if the whole urban population was enfranchised.[117] Even assuming that the additional tax that accompanied the grant of civic status was shouldered by the new citizens, the heavier tribute as a whole was imposed on the entire population or perhaps exclusively on the population who lived outside the fiscal unit of the city: that is, the noncitizens. Thus, not only was the rural population excluded from the potential economic benefits accruing from the city's new status, but they had to bear the negative economic consequences of the reforms, namely the added tribute. An additional question is whether all priestly families were enfranchised. If the Maccabees clan, for instance, was excluded, it is easy to see how their sudden social demotion could have incited great resentment. If we add to this the fact that Jason's political position was still insecure so shortly after toppling the legitimate high priest, social unrest could easily translate into political destabilization.

Irrespective of the original makeup of Jason's polis, the inclusive hypothesis becomes unsustainable in its second stage of development, marked by Antiochos IV's establishment of foreign settlers in the city and the construction of the Akra fortress, because the accounts of both 1 and 2 Maccabees seemingly imply that the impious Judeans and the foreigners formed a single community.[118] Be that true or not,[119] this claim could have come across as plausible to the books' original audience if—and only if—the politicization had been implemented in a manner that preserved the traditional social stratification. Indeed, this very model of politicization has been advocated about Babylon. Although in truth the evidence is inconclusive, the potential parallel cannot be ignored here. Let us review the data together with the relative debates.

10.3.4. The Politai of Babylon

In his monograph on late Achaimenid and Hellenistic Babylon published in 2004, Tom Boiy devoted several pages to a systematic comparison between Babylon and Jerusalem under the Seleukids.[120] Taking as granted that the two were "temple states with a certain degree of autonomy within a large world empire," he extended his comparison to three fields: their institutions during the Hellenistic period, both states being headed by a high priest having cultic, political, and administrative authority who was assisted by a temple council, the *kiništu* in Babylon and the *gerousia* in Jerusalem;[121] the increased royal control on temple property, with Seleukos IV appointing Simon as *prostatēs tou hierou* in the Jerusalem temple and Antiochos IV installing a *zazakku* to control the temple's income in Babylon;[122] and finally the foundations of poleis. Because the extant evidence does not unambiguously support the picture Boiy obviously has in mind—namely that like Jerusalem's "Antiochenes," the "*politai* who are in Babylon" were local families—in his explicit comments he remains cautious, noting that the Seleukid kings "probably support[ed] the Greek/Hellenised inhabitants of these cities in order to get a better control over the cities."[123]

Boiy's appendix stirred a debate about whether the *politai* community of Babylon was made up of Greek or Hellenized inhabitants of the city or a mix of both. His stance that the *politai* community was at least partly made up of local families, which he recently reiterated, was endorsed with far more detailed arguments by Rolf Strootman.[124] Conversely, other scholars maintained that the *politai* were ethnic Greeks who were brought to Babylon by either Antiochos III or Antiochos IV and enjoyed their own institutions. Robert van der Spek went so far as to talk of "a kind of 'apartheid' between the community of *politai* and the rest of the city's inhabitants."[125] Clancier struck a middle course by suggesting that whereas the labeling of the *politai* as "Greeks" in a text of 163 B.C.E. is evidence that originally their status was exclusive, with time some elite members who belonged to the "Babylonians" may have been incorporated among the *politai*, especially those who could handle Greek and enjoyed a double status.[126] If anything, this array of opinions proves how elusive the available evidence is. A detailed review is indispensable.

When Seleukos I founded Seleukeia-on-Tigris, he moved all the Greeks of Babylon, especially those descended from the settlers introduced by Alexander the Great, to the new city.[127] In the years that followed, there is no documentation of a Greek presence in Babylon until a community of *politai* appears in the reign of Antiochos IV. The word *politai* is found in the cuneiform documents in transcribed form (*pu-li-ṭe-e* and *pu-li-ṭa-nu*). Its earliest known instance to date is in a chronicle dated 140 S.E. (May–June 172 B.C.E.) known as the *Politai Chronicle* (*BCHP* 13).[128] Thereafter most of the evidence comes from the Babylonian astronomical diaries and chronicles, some dating to Parthian rule (beginning in 141 B.C.E.), with a few Greek inscriptions and other archeological data completing the picture.[129]

The fact that the *politai* formed a distinct community within the Babylonian society is beyond doubt, since they are regularly mentioned as a group, and in several documents are listed alongside other categories of population, in particular the "Babylonians."[130] They had their own institutions: they were headed by a *pāḫāt Bābili* (translating the Greek *epistatēs*, "governor") and may have had a *boulē* and a council of elders (*pe-li-ga-na-a-nu*: Greek *peliganes*?).[131]

The *politai* displayed their ostensibly Greek way of life in an extensive range of activities.[132] Two documents in particular deserve attention. The first is the *Greek Community Chronicle* (*BCHP* 14), dated 149 S.E. (163/2 B.C.E.).[133] It shows that the *politai* were also known as "the Greeks," had a *gymnasion*, in which they were said to "anoint with oil just like the *pol*[*itai*] who are in Seleukeia, the royal city, on the Tigris and the King's Canal,"[134] and could be drafted in military operations under the command of their *epistatēs* (*pāḫāt Bābili*), to back "the prefect [*šaknu*] and the people of the land who are in Babylon." The second text documenting the *politai*'s Greek way of life is the Diary of Month V 143 S.E. (= 17 August–15 September 169 B.C.E.), which notes that "the *politai* [(*pu-li-ṭe-e*) established] a Greek-style procession [*pu-up-pe-e*: Greek *pompē*] and a ritual in the Greek fashion" to mark Antiochos IV's victory in Egypt.[135] Moreover, they had a theater, which is documented archeologically, and in which, according to the astronomical diaries, they gathered to have the royal letters read to them.[136]

The issue on which the comparability between the Jerusalem "Antiochenes" and Babylon's *politai* depends is the latter's ethnic makeup. Few if any of the arguments that have been adduced either way are irrefutable. Scholars who believe they were foreigners point out that they are also referred to as "Greeks" in the tablets, taking this label as a genuine ethnic signifier.[137] However, this is hardly incontrovertible, in view of the parallel evidence. It has long since been noted that in Ptolemaic Egypt the ethnic label *Hellēnes* denoted either all persons of foreign descent as distinct from native Egyptians or else fiscally privileged categories comprising groups or individuals of various ethnic backgrounds, including people who in other contexts could qualify as Egyptians—at least according to modern classification.[138] On the basis of the interpretation of *Hellēnismos* proposed in Chapter 5 (§5.1.4), it may be reasonably presumed that after they constituted themselves as a polis, Jason and his fellow citizens described themselves as "Greeks."

Next, Greek names appear in the cuneiform documents from the reign of Antiochos IV onward—but contrary to Spek's claim,[139] this cannot count as definitive evidence that the *politai* were ethnic Greeks either: not only did three high priests of Jerusalem—Jason, Menelaos, and Alkimos—have Greek names, but Babylonians bearing double names are positively documented in the cuneiform tablets of the same period, and if the *politai* were local families, Greek names must have been fashionable among them.[140]

Likewise, the fact that the *politai* displayed a Greek way of life is no hint to their ethnicity. As in Jerusalem, these men "brought to the *Hellēnikos charaktēr*" could in fact be *homophyloi*: that is, native Babylonians.[141] Spek's claim that "admittance to the gymnasium was normally restricted to the citizens of Greek cities and was a hallmark of Greek citizenship" is correct if it refers to the status of citizens but patently wrong if it is meant to establish the Greek ethnicity of the *politai*—the Jerusalem evidence and the Tyriaion inscription clearly disprove this. Strikingly, the evidence concerning the *politai* of Babylon appears to support Kennell's assertion that the Jerusalem *gymnasion* served for military training: besides the *Greek Community Chronicle*, the expression "the *politai* and their army" (l. 7) also appears in a fragmentary chronicle.[142]

The expression that the *politai* "anoint with oil just like the *pol*[*itai*] who are in Seleukeia, the royal city," could be read as the community's statement about itself: in other words, a matter of self-representation. Michels's modified model of peer-polity interaction may be a helpful tool of interpretation in this context. As we saw above, Michels used this model to show that the elite of Hanisa, a Cappadocian city, acquired a Greek education and adopted a Greek model of civic institutions and practices, including the epigraphical habit, because doing so was a "prerequisite to find access to the networks of Greek *poleis*." The Greek language and culture formed the dominant discourse both of these city networks and of the courtiers of the Macedonian dynasties.[143] In similar fashion, it could be claimed that the *politai* of Babylon, as Hellenized Babylonians, not only established a *gymnasion* and began anointing themselves with oil in conscious imitation of the Greeks of Seleukeia but were eager to publicize their adoption of such shared customs as much as possible.

The fact that the ceremony held by the *politai* to mark the king's victory is referred to by the Greek word for "procession" transliterated into Akkadian may be evidence that it was deliberately conceived by the *politai*, and perceived by all Babylonians, as an alien ceremony. The ritual conducted "in the Greek fashion" had the same purpose and effect. However, the description of these two ceremonies is strikingly reminiscent of the terminology used in 2 Maccabees to describe the Antiochenes of Jerusalem: Jason "began to bring his people [*homophyloi*] over to the Greek style of life [*Hellēnikon charaktēra*]" (2 Macc. 4:10) and "there was in this way a pinnacle of *Hellēnismos* and an advance in the adoption of alien ways [*allophylismos*]" (4:13).[144] It could be argued that in both Jerusalem and Babylon the privileged "citizens" proudly and loudly proclaimed their "Greekness," referred to themselves as "Greeks," and liked to be dubbed "Greeks" by others. The "Greek" character of the *pompē* and the "ritual in the Greek fashion" may have been merely local reinterpretations of things "Greek": wearing something exotic—such as the *petasos* at the Jerusalem *gymnasion*[145]—holding the ceremony in Greek, and imitating the exotic gestures observed at similar ceremonies in Seleukeia may easily have qualified as a "Greek ritual" in Babylon, even if ethnic Greek visitors may have thought otherwise.[146]

Logically, if Babylon's *politai* were ethnic Babylonians anointing themselves in imitation of the (Greco-Macedonian) *politai* of Seleukeia-on-the-Tigris, they could have been as eager to model their institutions after those of the neighboring royal city. As Spek notes, *peliganes* are documented in Seleukeia, and therefore, despite the fact that this is a typically Macedonian word for "elders," the existence of *peliganes* in Babylon is no evidence that the *politai* were ethnic Macedonians.[147] Moreover, the fact that they described themselves as "Greeks" is hard to explain if they were ethnic Macedonians.[148] Therefore it may be plausibly argued that they borrowed their council of elders together with its name from Seleukeia and were unaware of the specifically Macedonian connotation this institution originally had. Other evidence cited by Spek in support of his contention that the *politai* were a community of foreigners may be rejected out of hand.[149]

Conversely, none of the arguments put forward by scholars advocating the view that Babylon's *politai* were Hellenized Babylonians are absolutely compelling. As Tom Boiy, Peter Mittag, and Rolf Strootman have noted, the fact that no Greek temple has been unearthed in Babylon is intriguing, but as Spek has already retorted, the area of Homera, in which the remains of various Greek buildings, in particular the theater, were found, is not fully excavated.[150] Therefore it is not excluded that remnants of a Greek cult may come to light in the future.

Next, the discovery of Greek inscriptions from the second century B.C.E. has been variously interpreted. Spek attributes them to the *politai*, but Strootman has pointed out that there are remarkably few of them if one assumes that a colony of Greek foreigners was settled in the city.[151] It may be added that the presence of Greek officials and a garrison in the city could explain the presence of these inscriptions.[152] However, in Babylonia stone steles were rarely used for inscriptions, and we cannot exclude that alternative, perishable materials were employed for publicizing official texts.[153]

In short, none of the extant factual details about the *politai* provides clear-cut evidence concerning their ethnicity. We need, therefore, to turn to circumstantial data. Two matters in particular, relating to urban space, are noteworthy. The first of these is the statement in the *Greek Community Chronicle* that the *politai* "in the past at the command of King Antiochos [III or IV?] ⟨had entered⟩ Baby⟨lon⟩"— which modern scholars understand to refer to the founding of the *politai* community. But although the inferred suppletion "had entered" (if we can assume that it is correct) suggests foreigners being brought into Babylon from outside, the *politai* also held a *pompē* to celebrate Antiochos IV's victory in Egypt in 169 B.C.E., and therefore we may surmise that they "entered" the city on a ceremonial occasion— for instance, as an honorary escort during the king's visit to the city—and not only when they first arrived in the city.[154] This hypothesis may be compatible with the view that the *politai* were Hellenized Babylonians.

The second spatial clue deserves more attention. Spek—and subsequently Clancier—has pointed to the different uses of urban space by the *politai* and the "Babylonians," respectively, in support of the view that the *politai* were foreigners. Whereas the *kiništu* (council) of the "Babylonians," headed by the *šatammu* (high priest), held its gatherings in the *bīt milki* (house of deliberation)—situated in the administrative area of the Esagila complex called the "Juniper Garden"—the *politai*, headed by the *pāḫāt Bābili* (*epistatēs*), held theirs in the theater (*bīt tamarti*, house of observation). The latter was located in the part of the city known as Homera, which in all likelihood was the center of the *politai* community, and which stood inside the city walls but outside the Esagila complex itself.[155] The establishment of the *politai* community appears therefore to have entailed a reshaping of the political space—but Spek and Clancier disagree about how to interpret this change. According to Spek, the *bīt milki* and the theater were the respective political centers of the two communities, as evidenced by the fact that official communications from the Seleukid and (after 141 B.C.E.) Parthian Arsakid kings were read aloud to either community at these respective locations, a distinction suggesting that the two communities coexisted in a state of ethnic segregation.[156]

Clancier, however, rejects the notion of ethnic segregation, arguing that this spatial reconfiguration was indicative of a shift in the location of power in the city instead: the *epistatēs* and the *politai* had become the king's chief addressees in Babylon, and the theater replaced the "house of deliberation" (*bīt milki*) as the city's main political and administrative center. In support of this interpretation, Clancier points to a clear difference in the content, and indeed a hierarchy, of royal correspondence to the two communities: whereas letters on military and administrative matters (such as the appointments of royal military officials and officials of the *politai* themselves) were sent to the *epistatēs* and the *politai* and read out at the theater,[157] the royal communiqué to the "*šatammu* of the Esagila and the Babylonians" that was "read at the house of deliberation in the Juniper Garden," as summarized by the astronomical diary of 94 B.C.E., announced the imposition upon the "Babylonians" of a corvée duty on a canal—a matter of interest to them alone.[158] Moreover, the evidence suggests that the relationship between the "Babylonians" and the *politai* was one of collaboration, not segregation: in two instances, we learn that the *šatammu* and the "Babylonians" of the *kiništu* of the Esagila provided a bull and several sheep as an offering to the king's messenger at the "Gate of the Son of the Prince of Esagila," sacrificing them to Bel and Beltia—although the messenger was delivering a communication to the *epistatēs* and the *politai*.[159] Similarly, there are hints that the *šatammu* and other delegates of the "Babylonians" were present at the theater when royal letters were read out there.[160]

A diary account of a legal procedure—the only one of Seleukid times involving the theater—lends additional support to Clancier's view that the shift in Babylon's political center involved cooperation between the officials of the two communities rather than segregation.[161] Although the tablet's fragmentary state makes reconstruction uncertain, it appears that the trial was conducted before the *epistatēs*, perhaps at the theater, and involved cooperation—and not, as Spek presumes, conflict[162]—between "the *epistatēs* of Babylon and the *politai* who are in Babylon" and "the *šatammu* of the Esagila and his brothers." The accused, who were "people of the land,"¹⁶³ appear to have faced charges of stealing sheep belonging to the Esagila. In former days, any legal proceedings involving temple property would have been handled by the *šatammu* and the *kiništu*. If Clancier's interpretation of this document is correct, it confirms, first, that the Seleukids tightened their control over the temples in the aftermath of Apamea.¹⁶⁴ Second, it shows that in Babylon this involved the appointment not only of new temple officials such as the *zazakku*—to whom the *šatammu* of the Esagila had indeed ceded most of his legal and financial privileges since Antiochos IV—but also of imperial officials outside the temple, in particular the *epistatēs*.¹⁶⁵ The identity of the first *zazakku*—the *šatammu*'s own brother—also raises a possibility that has been overlooked by modern commentators: that like Jason and Menelaos, who headed the Jerusalem *politai*, the first *epistatēs* of Babylon's *politai* was one of the *šatammu*'s local rivals, not a foreigner.¹⁶⁶ However, even if this is correct, there is one important difference between the two cities: whereas in Jerusalem the high priest himself originally headed the Antiochenes, thereby enjoying a dual status and identity, the *šatammu* and the "Babylonians of the *kiništu* of the Esagila" lost most of (if not all) their political and administrative powers to the *epistatēs* and the *politai*, and this institutional change makes it implausible that the *šatammu* himself instigated the reform.¹⁶⁷ Therefore, in all likelihood the *politai* community of Babylon was a royal foundation, in contrast to Jason's polis—a difference that makes the comparison between the two far less relevant. That said, a comparison of the *politai* of Babylon with Jerusalem's polis may be appropriate with regard to the aftermath of the Judean rebellion, when the latter was refounded by Antiochos IV.¹⁶⁸ As with Babylon's *politai*, this refounded polis was headed by an *epistatēs* (2 Macc. 5:22), and Menelaos himself appears to have retained only his cultic functions—although 2 Maccabees (5:23) is irretrievably vague in this regard.

As the outcome of this survey, it appears that, although Boiy's intuition that Jerusalem's and Babylon's poleis are parallel case studies cannot be vindicated in any indisputable way, it cannot be dismissed out of hand either. It is not excluded that, as in Jerusalem, Babylon's *politai* were members of local elite families who called themselves "Greeks," "playing Greeks" in Greek-style processions and in their *gymnasion*, in which they trained as Greco-Macedonian soldiers, their primary motivation being to strengthen their links with the king and local royal officials. Moreover, the example of Jerusalem's polis leaves open the possibility that at the time of its foundation, the *politai* community was ethnically and socially homogeneous, although from the start marriages with daughters of Seleukid officials must have been a highly sought-for asset. Intermarriages, and more simply the will of *politai* families to name their children after powerful Greek friends, could explain the profile of the Greek names listed in a Greek clay tablet recording the ephebes and *neoi* winners of athletic competitions of 111/0 B.C.E.—sixty years at least after the polis foundation. As Strootman pointed out, a high proportion of the Greek names recorded are theophoric and could be translations of Akkadian and Aramaic names.[169] However, some are genuinely Greek—but they hardly provide firm evidence either that the original *politai* were foreigners or that from the outset they were a mixed community: only that these Greek names were adopted by *politai* families at an early stage of the polis's existence—in any case in the days of Seleukid rule.

In spite of all, so long as the ethnic makeup of Babylon's *politai* community remains uncertain it cannot provide valuable comparative material for Jason's polis.[170] Therefore we must sideline it to proceed to our conclusions on Jason's reforms.

10.3.5. Jason's Motivations: New Suggestions

The growing awareness today that the politicization of non-Greek cities in Hellenistic times could be the result of local initiative rather than a royal policy of Hellenization offers a broad context in which the politicization of Jerusalem under Jason can be appreciated. Jason's reforms, Tyriaion, and Hanisa (and Babylon?) appear as particularly well-documented instances of a social and cultural development affecting various—possibly numerous—non-Greek communities in Phoenicia, Asia Minor, and other parts of the Hellenistic East. Moreover, the specific mechanisms of political and cultural change involved in local initiatives of politicization are now better understood. As noted above (§10.3.3C), the adoption of a Greek civic model by the social and political elites of non-Greek communities involved adapting it to the preexisting social structures and the political and religious traditions of each community. Viewing Jason's reforms as just one instance of a wider phenomenon invites us to reconsider his motivations and aims. Quite naturally, at a time when scholars understood Hellenization in strictly cultural terms, indulging in discourses about the intrinsic attractiveness, if not superiority, of Greek culture,[171] speculations about a "Hellenizing party" drawn by the intrinsic attraction of Greek culture were aired in modern studies of Jason's (and Menelaos's) reforms. Early reactions to this approach displayed an instrumentalist slant, whereby culture was seen as a mere tool to achieve economic goals.[172] Instead, given the current awareness that cultural behavior is a serious aspect of social strategy, explanations should take into account both the structural organization of the Hellenistic empires and the role of Greek culture within it.

Recent analyses of the cultural changes of the Hellenistic world are based on the notion that the Greek language and culture were the idiom of the Greco-Macedonian dynasties and their courts. The Hellenization of the non-Greek elites, like their Iranization under Achaimenid rule and their Romanization after that, is better understood as either a strategy of communication with the king, or as a strategy of power locally and at the imperial level, or both.[173] Michels's use of a modified version of the peer-polity interaction model to explain the adoption of a

Greek civic model in Hanisa and other non-Greek cities has been reviewed above (§10.3.3C). This model will certainly prove useful in analyzing aspects of the politicization of Jerusalem. However, Strootman has suggested a slightly different model, stressing specifically the relationship between the local elites and the king.[174] It undoubtedly provides a fundamental means of appreciating Jason's reforms.

Strootman's starting point is Mary Louise Pratt's concept of a "contact zone"—a term coined to define "social spaces where cultures meet, clash, and grapple, often in contexts of highly asymmetrical relations of power"[175]—which he uses to "identify the place, time and social context where negotiations between empire and city [took] place" in the Seleukid empire.[176] As he argues, in the Hellenistic world the interaction of cultures primarily involved the non-Greek urban prominent families and the imperial elite, and the contact zone where they met was what he calls the "outer court," namely "a temporary expansion of the stable but much smaller . . . dynastic household," which occurred on "the occasion of great events, such as inaugurations, wedding ceremonies or religious festivals, that attracted elite persons from all over the empire." At court, the visitors interacted with the royal *philoi,* who were essentially Greeks, and at their contact[177]

> would adopt what they believed to be the right manners of the court. They would take these prestigious manners home with them to signify their affiliation with the empire's central source of prestige, the king, and to distance themselves from rivals who did not enjoy royal favor.

Turning the city into a Greek polis and "playing Greek" in the *gymnasion* was part of this double strategy of power, which combined a local and an imperial level.

Strootman's analysis raises further considerations. Jason may have felt the need to establish Jerusalem as a polis because he was aware that his personal and political standing within the power networks centered on the Seleukid court was weak. Hence his politically wise decision to renovate his avenue of communication with the king and the court in a way that would be more attractive to the other side. Quite possibly, he sought also to improve his own chances of becoming a *philos* of the king. A few years later, Jonathan the Maccabee was luckier, since rivalry between two contenders to the Seleukid throne gave him the opportunity to get this prestigious title without the need for him to be as enterprising as Jason: first, Alexander Balas appointed him high priest as well as *philos* (1 Macc. 10:20), granting him the right to wear purple clothes (10:62), and finally he enrolled him in the list of Friends of the First Rank on appointing him *stratēgos* and *meridarchēs* (10:65). Demetrios II also confirmed Jonathan's position as high priest and his other privileges, reckoning him among the Friends of the First Rank (1 Macc. 11:27). Finally, Tryphon confirmed Jonathan as high priest in the name of King Antiochos VI (11:57). It would be interesting to know whether Menelaos also achieved the rank of *philos*. One suspects that if he did, 2 Maccabees would not be the place to learn about it.

. . .

The causes of the rebellion had nothing to do with an alleged cultural and religious reform or, by extension, any religious conservative backlash to it. Similarly, the politicization of Jerusalem per se cannot be regarded as a decisive factor. It is now clear to students of the Hellenistic East that the adoption of a Greek civic model by the elites of non-Greek communities was a common phenomenon: the fact that in Jerusalem it resulted in civil war and eventually a full-scale revolt against the Seleukids should be regarded as exceptional, suggesting exceptional circumstances. In view of 1 and 2 Maccabees, these may be results of a combination of three main factors: the social and economic consequences of politicization, the larger tribute requirement, and the ousting of the legitimate high priest, who enjoyed unusually centralized powers. The reforms, involving a radical social reorganization of Jerusalem as well as Judea as a whole, coupled with unpopular economic initiatives by a high priest of tenuous personal legitimacy (having assumed the role only recently, and by questionable means), created favorable conditions for unrest. Added to this is the possibility that some priestly families were excluded from the new civic framework. Their social demotion and, no less important, their loss of fiscal privileges that they had previously enjoyed, as attested by Antiochos III's decree (*Ant.* 12.142), would have created an explosive situation, provoking an all-out struggle for power. Opponents to Jason from within the priestly class were able to muster popular support because of the economic fallout of the reforms. On the ideological front too they could easily further their political ambitions by accusing Jason of violations of tradition.

One final word on the nature of the conflict between Jerusalem's priestly elite families. In the power struggle following Onias III's eviction from the high priesthood, families adopted divergent strategies from one another. Jason, Menelaos, and Alkimos sought, or won, the king's support. Judas chose to oppose the king, but his motivations for this choice forever escape us. Quite possibly, he too initially competed for the king's support but switched to an alternative strategy and a different ideological discourse only after finding himself outflanked by Jason, Menelaos, or Alkimos. When Jonathan was offered the honor of becoming a royal *philos*, his ideological discourse must have changed accordingly. However, Jonathan's strategy was the exception in his family: when Simon came to power, he adopted a discourse closer to Judas's. This is definitely not the scenario we read about in 1 and 2 Maccabees—however, since these works were written by supporters of the Hasmoneans in the days when this dynasty ruled, they are too heavily biased to be reliable.

11

Judea under Antiochos IV Epiphanes

The Suppression of the Rebellion, 169/8–164 B.C.E.

INTRODUCTION

As argued in Chapters 9 and 10, the outbreak of the Judean rebellion may be explained quite classically as a combination of economic (that is, fiscal), political, and geostrategic causes. The economic aspects started from the fiscal reforms initiated by Seleukos IV in 178 B.C.E. and pursued by Antiochos IV in the satrapy of Koilē Syria and Phoinikē. To some extent, these reforms were simply a matter of routine imperial policy. Two decades after the conquest of the region by the Seleukids, it was natural for the royal administration to impose changes to maximize its extraction of economic surpluses from the province. The Olympiodoros inscription documents a fiscal reform that targeted the temples of the satrapy under Seleukos IV. Archeological finds hint at a reform of weights and measures in the early years of Antiochos IV's rule (ca. 173/2 B.C.E.). However, as Maurice Sartre has contended, Seleukos IV and his successor may also have contested the right for the Ptolemies to levy the tribute of the province (or part of it), which was Antiochos III's dowry to Ptolemy V when he gave him his daughter Cleopatra in marriage in 193 B.C.E.[1] If the quarrel started at Ptolemy V's death in 180 B.C.E., and not at Cleopatra's death in 176 B.C.E. as Sartre surmises, it is tempting to link Seleukos's desire to enforce his appropriation of the tribute, his appointment of Olympiodoros as provincial high priest, and his sending Heliodoros to Jerusalem to the temple in which Hyrkanos the Ptolemaic tax farmer deposited the collected monies before their dispatch to Alexandria. As Sartre suggests, Hyrkanos's suicide in his estate of Iraq al-Emir shortly after Antiochos IV's accession to the Seleukid throne (*Ant.* 12.236) could be related to the tensions between the Seleukid and the

Ptolemaic courts about the revenues of the satrapy. Indeed, there is a striking chronological coincidence between the tax farmer's suicide and the ousting of Onias, who according to 2 Maccabees 3 successfully resisted Heliodoros's efforts to enter the temple treasure chambers. Moreover, Onias was murdered a few years later in Daphne-near-Antioch (2 Macc. 4:32–34) in unclear conditions—the Maccabees author's claim that he was assassinated on Menelaos's order to avoid being indicted for embezzlement is utterly unreliable.[2]

Whatever the precise details, there is no doubt that while Seleukos IV's and Antiochos IV's administrative and fiscal reforms per se concerned the whole satrapy, in Judea specifically they were entangled with political affairs. On the one hand, the political repercussions amplified the impact of the provincial reforms, first because Antiochos IV took advantage of his political coup against Onias to increase the rate of the tribute paid by the Judeans by selling the high priesthood to the highest bidder, and second because Jason exploited the fact that Antiochos was in dire need of securing his loyalty in order to obtain the right to turn Jerusalem into a polis, a request to which Antiochos consented in exchange for additional taxes. On the other hand, whereas these cumulative tax raises may explain the popular resentment and thus wide-ranging scope of the rebellion, the ousting of the legitimate representative of the Oniad dynasty and his replacement with an incumbent who owed his position exclusively to a foreign king destabilized the traditional local balance of power and sparked a power struggle among the leading priestly families. The civil strife could only be aggravated by the economic and social changes inevitably entailed by Antiochos IV's risky game and Jason's politicization of the city on the one hand and the regional tensions between the Seleukid and the Ptolemaic courts on the other. The Maccabees presumably joined in this struggle at an early stage (at least they were fighting in Jerusalem when Antiochos's officer Apollonios attacked: 2 Macc. 5:27). In this potentially explosive situation, Antiochos's war in Egypt—perhaps more specifically the rumor of his death (2 Macc. 5:5)—provided the trigger for the uprising.

All together, this summary is close to the analysis of the main causes of the rebellion offered in 2 Maccabees. As noted in Chapter 7 (§7.2), the author points to the nexus of the tax increase and royal meddling with the appointment of the high priest as the main factors of the disruption. The present chapter will pursue our historical reconstruction of events by surveying what happened in the wake of Antiochos IV's reaction to the revolt, the phase of events highlighted in 1 Maccabees.[3] That Antiochos's response was quick and violent is not surprising, given that it broke out in the midst of his campaign in Egypt, and moreover in the bordering region whose control was once again being disputed between the two dynasties.[4] But was the military repression deliberately followed by a phase of (in Bickerman's view), or inadvertently accompanied by (according to more recent studies),[5] the "prohibition of the Jewish customs"? The literary analysis of the three parallel accounts of the "persecution" found in 1 Maccabees 1:41–64, 2 Maccabees 6:1–11, and Daniel 11:29–39 in Chapter 6[6] has established that they do not describe a separate "religious persecution," as Josephus already understood (or rather, misunderstood) but simply overemphasize the cultic aspects of the military suppression, depicted through cultural and narrative codes and intertextual references that were familiar to the Judean literati of Hellenistic times. The present chapter offers a reconstruction of the various aspects of the Seleukid military suppression based on this revised reading of the literary sources, cross-checked with documentary evidence from across the Hellenistic world. Moreover, as just noted, the proposed reconstruction will take as a guide the list of the punishing measures that the author of 1 Maccabees—and secondarily that of 2 Maccabees too—stigmatizes as the main factors of distress, using mediating synecdoches to show how they harmed the temple.[7] As was argued in Chapter 7 (§7.4), 1 Maccabees' narration focuses on the construction of the Akra, the establishment of the military settlement, and the related wide-scale confiscation of land, obliquely referred to through its account of the edification and destruction of the illicit altars built in the countryside. In addition, of course, the disruption of the daily sacrifice ritual was a major cause of distress. These problems eventually rekindled the rebellion.

Insofar as the determination of the causes and nature of the rebellion is so narrowly connected with the analysis of its chronology, this issue will be tackled first. After examining the chronological and geographical frame of the rebellion in its regional context (§11.1.1 and 2), the first section of this chapter will restate the reasons to reject the accepted view that the military and political suppression was followed by a phase of "prohibition of the Jewish customs" (§11.1.3).[8] The second section (§11.2) proposes a linear outline of the events that is based primarily on 1 Maccabees 1:20–2:48 and 2 Maccabees 5:1–6:11. The relevant sections from the book of Daniel will supplement the analysis, but Josephus's *Wars* and *Antiquities* will be excluded from discussion since they are not seen as independent sources—except when it is necessary explicitly to demonstrate their dependency. The third section of the chapter (§11.3) tackles the fate of the temple. The analysis will be predicated on the assumption that the community of the Antiochenes and the military settlement did not merge into a single legal entity at any point, and therefore the temple depended exclusively on the Antiochenes throughout.

11.1. THE CHRONOLOGICAL AND GEOGRAPHICAL FRAME

The chronology of the Judean events is famously muddled. Two distinct issues are involved, which must be examined separately. One is the date of the outbreak of the rebellion—during either Antiochos's first or his second Egyptian campaign—and the second is the number of distinct episodes: in a nutshell, how many times

Antiochos attacked the temple. Given that it was argued in Chapters 9 (§9.4) and 10 (§10.2.5) that the starting point of the rebellion was a tax reform, the question of the possible extension of the unrest to other parts of the satrapy is also worth examining.

11.1.1. Antiochos's Egyptian Campaigns

It stands to reason that Antiochos IV's two campaigns in Egypt during the Sixth Syrian War had an impact on the neighboring region of Koilē Syria and Phoinikē. However, that impact need not have been overwhelmingly negative, and therefore it does not constitute a motive for any troubles per se.

A. *The Sixth Syrian War.* Antiochos's first campaign in Egypt began in the summer of 170 B.C.E. Antiochos was in Tyre in July and August 170, and in November 170 he reached Pelousion, where the first battle against the army of Ptolemy VI Philometor took place. After an initial victory, Antiochos negotiated a truce. Fighting resumed in March 169, when water levels in the Nile were low. Antiochos first marched against Memphis and from there made his way toward Alexandria, where he portrayed himself as the protector of the young Ptolemy VI. The Seleukid army also led a successful military campaign in southern Egypt; a hieroglyphic inscription attests that foreign troops—obviously the Seleukid army—were garrisoned in Thebes in October 169. Antiochos withdrew from Egypt in the autumn of 169, leaving a strong garrison at Pelousion, and was back in Antioch by the end of the year.[9] The winter of 169/8 saw the dispatch of diplomatic missions to Rome by Antiochos IV as well as Ptolemy VIII Euergetes and Cleopatra II.[10] The Seleukid navy resumed hostilities by attacking Ptolemaic Cyprus in the late winter of 168, probably with the purpose of tightening the blockade of Alexandria.[11] Land warfare also resumed in Egypt, and Antiochos IV's troops captured Memphis, where the invader may have been crowned as king of Lower and Upper Egypt. From Memphis Antiochos marched toward Alexandria. Upon reaching the suburb of Eleusis he was met by the Roman legate, Gaius Popillius Laenas, in July 168. On the conclusion of this meeting, which Polybius (24.27.4) describes as humiliating for the Seleukid king, Antiochos withdrew from Egypt.[12]

In Egypt, the power of the Ptolemies was thoroughly weakened by Antiochos's invasion, as well as by the conflict between Ptolemy VI and Ptolemy VIII. Between 168 and 164 B.C.E., Dionysios Petosarapis, a member of the court and a native Egyptian, tried to exploit the well-known animosity between the two brothers to incite the Alexandrian crowds against Philometor. Defeated in his coup attempt, Dionysios Petosarapis resorted to arms but was defeated near Eleusis. Surviving his defeat in the Delta, he continued to stir up rebellion among the Egyptian populations in Middle Egypt, in Memphis, and in the Fayum.[13] Meanwhile, another revolt broke out, in the Thebaid. Most of the rebels were defeated and their remaining forces holed up in Panopolis, which was eventually captured by the royal troops.[14]

B. *The Date of the Judean Rebellion and Antiochos's Assault on Jerusalem.* The chronology of the events in Judea is muddled by the fact that based on the literary sources (1 and 2 Maccabees and Daniel) it is impossible to ascertain whether the rebellion broke out during Antiochos IV's first or second campaign in Egypt, and therefore precisely when the king stormed Jerusalem.[15] While scholars usually handle the chronological issue by arguing for the reliability of this or that source against the others on the basis of a positivist reading, a properly literary approach shows that the three sources have equal chances of being historically unreliable constructs. The author of 1 Maccabees conflates the two Egyptian campaigns into a single one (1 Macc. 1:20), clearly because mentioning the two campaigns had no narrative relevance to his account. The author of 2 Maccabees explicitly places Antiochos's assault in the wake of the second campaign (2 Macc. 5:1). Although on the face of it no obvious reason for chronological manipulation can be discerned, such procedure cannot be ruled out altogether, since this author is accustomed to it. Daniel 11:28 and 30 are narrative doublets. The author knew about two Egyptian campaigns and therefore has the king return with hostile intentions on both occasions.[16] While Daniel 11:31 conflates the two successive assaults on Jerusalem, 1 and 2 Maccabees distinguish between Antiochos's assault (1 Macc. 1:20–24, 2 Macc. 5:11–16) and a second assault on Jerusalem by a royal officer (1 Macc. 1:29–35, 2 Macc. 5:24–26).[17] Clearly it was not the concern of the three respective authors of these works to write accurate chronicles, let alone to imitate the Babylonian astronomical diaries: the chronology of these works is simply useless.

Thus we are left with educated guesses. A rebellion in Judea is easier to place in the context of the second invasion of Egypt. First, Antiochos's initial campaign was victorious; he had left a strong garrison in Pelousion, at the border between Egypt and Sinai, when he left in the fall of 169 B.C.E., and the proximity of the garrison may have been dissuasive. Second, Antiochos may not have been able to launch his second campaign in 168 had a rebellion broken out so near the Egyptian border in the interim. Third, the author of 2 Maccabees specifies that Jason attacked Jerusalem ("a rebellion broke out in Judea") when a false rumor spread that Antiochos had been killed in Egypt (2 Macc. 5:5). When we try to identify an incident likely to have generated such a rumor, the king's humiliation by Popillius Laenas on "Eleusis Day" in July 168 is by far the most plausible option. Finally, Antiochos's second campaign tipped Egypt into a state of total instability.[18] Such a context was favorable to a rebellion in the neighboring area of Judea. However, these arguments remain shaky, and the detailed chronology of the Judean rebellion remains irreparably confused. The historical reconstruction in the present chapter will refrain from proposing a precise chronological framework. Before we turn to the events of Judea, however, the possibility that the rebellion extended to other parts of Koilē Syria and Phoinikē must be examined.

11.1.2. A Provincial Scope for the Rebellion?

As is well known, Bickerman argued that the Roman intervention that forced Antiochos out of Egypt in the summer of 168 B.C.E. encouraged pro-Ptolemaic elements throughout the cities of Koilē Syria and Phoinikē to resume their hostile activities. In support of this theory, Bickerman pointed to a late literary source claiming that Antiochos stormed Arados and devastated the territory along the Phoenician coast (Porphyry *ap.* Jerome, *Commentary on Daniel* 11:44).[19] Porphyry's evidence is most likely unreliable, and the basis for Bickerman's theory of the struggle between Ptolemaic and Seleukid parties is precarious, relying as it does on the testimony of Josephus and Jerome, and overlooking the fact that these two viewed the events of Judea through the lens of the Roman civil wars of Late Republican and imperial times.[20] In light of the current state of the evidence, the hypothesis that the Judean rebellion was part of a broader outbreak of unrest throughout the satrapy of Koilē Syria and Phoinikē is unsupported. However, various clues suggest that the entire issue may gain from fresh reexamination in future. Although a detailed discussion is presently unwarranted, it is worth spelling out those clues.

The main reason for revisiting the hypothesis of a wide-ranging rebellion within the province is the fiscal issue. As argued in Chapter 7 (§§7.2 and 7.3), the two Maccabees authors give this issue a prominent role. Moreover, as we saw in Chapter 9 (§§9.2 and 9.4), the recent publication of the Olympiodoros inscription offers evidence that throughout the province of Koilē Syria and Phoinikē Seleukos IV imposed a tighter control over the temples' administrations and revenues. The new inscription supports the conclusion that the tensions between the Seleukid administration and Onias III, as recounted in the Heliodoros story (2 Macc. 3:1–4:6), were sparked by the king's increased interest in acquiring the temples' wealth. The rumor of Antiochos IV's death in Egypt would have therefore provided an ideal context for a fiscal rebellion throughout the province.

Several passages of 1 and 2 Maccabees can easily be taken as evidence that the troubles extended beyond Judea. According to 2 Maccabees 3:8, Heliodoros, Seleukos IV's chief minister, arrived in Jerusalem during an inspection tour of the cities of the province. If this information is genuine, it may support the conclusion that Seleukos IV's fiscal policy induced unrest throughout the satrapy, not only in Judea. In 2 Maccabees 5:22–23, we are told that Antiochos IV left an overseer in Jerusalem after storming the city and another one at Mount Gerizim: why this official was deemed necessary at Mount Gerizim as well is left unexplained. What is more important, the accounts of 1 Maccabees 5 and 2 Maccabees 12 describe turmoil in several regions of the province. The two accounts focus on Judas

Maccabee's wars with the neighboring peoples, and the author of 1 Maccabees claims that these were caused by the rebuilding of the altar and the temple (1 Macc. 5:1). However, in all likelihood this claim aims to link a mundane matter to the temple, according to the process of semantic concatenation analyzed elsewhere in this book,[21] and therefore modern scholars are not obliged to accept it. Therefore the context of these generalized troubles is open to reexamination. Conversely, the fact that the Phoenician cities kept quiet may be explained by their peculiar status. After the treaty of Apamea deprived the Seleukids of their ships, the Phoenician fleets acquired a strategic importance; therefore we may surmise that the Phoenician cities were spared the tough fiscal treatment experienced by other regions of the satrapy.

That said, the currently available evidence of the numismatic and archeological data speak against a wide-scale rebellion, given that there is no apparent disruption in the issue of coinage in the region in the years 169–167 B.C.E. Similarly, a recent survey of the archeological data of the region offers nothing to substantiate the hypothesis of a provincewide rebellion.[22] Therefore, the causes of the Judean rebellion should be sought in the local conditions.

11.1.3. One Phase of Suppression, or Two?

A survey of the various historical reconstructions of the Judean rebellion proposed in modern times—starting with the seminal studies of Bickerman and Tcherikover[23]—confirms that identifying the main causes of the revolt, and thereby its nature, is inseparable from the issue of chronology.

The pioneering interpretation of the revolt put forward by Bickerman in his *God of the Maccabees* was based on a straightforward, typically positivist reading of 1 and 2 Maccabees, Josephus, and Daniel. The chronological outline Bickerman was able to establish, based on his factual reading, distinguishes three phases of events, the first two being separated by an interval of two years. The first phase is dominated by Antiochos's assault on Jerusalem and plundering of the temple on his return from his campaign in Egypt (1 Macc. 1:20–24, 2 Macc. 5:5–23). The second starts with the second assault on the city led by Apollonios, Antiochos IV's general, "two years later" (1 Macc. 1:29)—that is, according to Bickerman, in the fall of 168 B.C.E. It includes the pulling down of the city walls, the construction of the Akra citadel, the establishment of a military garrison there, and the wide-scale confiscation of lands assigned to the military settlers (1 Macc. 29–41, 2 Macc. 5:24–26, Daniel 11:39). The third phase is that of "religious persecution," which began in December 167 B.C.E. and ended de facto in December 164 with the Maccabees' reconquest of the temple and de iure in March 163 with the grant of amnesty (2 Macc. 11:27–33).[24] According to this outline,[25] the popular rebellion broke out in reaction to the persecution, and the Maccabees joined in as its leaders only at this stage. In the first phase, Antiochos IV's assault was triggered by the feud between

Jason and Menelaos. Bickerman's main departure from the version put forward by the sources was a slight extrapolation from Josephus. Drawing on the experience of the Roman civil wars in his accounts of the family feuds that plagued the Judean elite in Hellenistic times, Josephus divided the Judeans into two camps, one led by Hyrkanos and the elder son of Joseph the Tobiad (*Ant.* 12.228), the other by the Oniads and the rest of the Tobiads—a division that he subsequently characterized as pro-Seleukid party versus a pro-Ptolemaic one (*Ant.* 12.237–41). This Seleukid-versus-Ptolemaic division, which is also found in Jerome (*Commentary on Daniel* 11:14) for similar anachronistic reasons, was famously extended by Bickerman to present Jason's attempt at recapturing Jerusalem during Antiochos's campaign in Egypt (2 Macc. 5:5–10) as evidence for the revival of the Ptolemaic party in the context of the Sixth Syrian War.[26][note 27 becomes note 26] As is well known, Bickerman's theory of the Seleukid and Ptolemaic parties garnered tremendous popularity among subsequent scholars.[27]

Tcherikover was the first to express unease about the supposed causal link between Jason's failed coup and Antiochos's brutal repression.[28] Antiochos's wide-scale massacre of the population seems totally disproportionate if the king was merely reacting to a feud between Jason and Menelaos and a handful of their respective followers. This conclusion led Tcherikover to depart from the sources' versions on four crucial points, two of which affect the chronology. First, although Tcherikover did not question the sources' claim that the Maccabees became leaders of the revolt only after the persecution, he argued that the popular rising had started much earlier, shortly after Menelaos was appointed high priest. Its earliest manifestation was the riot in which Lysimachos, Menelaos's brother, was killed for stealing temple vessels on Menelaos's behalf (2 Macc. 4:39–42). Second, this revised chronology of the popular rebellion further led Tcherikover to conclude that "it was not the revolt that came as a response to the persecution, but the persecution which came as a response to the revolt. Only on this assumption can we understand Antiochus' decrees and their political purpose."[29] In other words, Tcherikover was the first to propose a rational interpretation of Antiochos's repression, although he did not question the contention that it was a religious persecution. He surmised that the initial popular rebellion was religiously motivated and featured religious leaders, the Hasidim. In Tcherikover's view, the religious character of this opposition explains why Antiochos specifically targeted the religious domain in his repression. Third, this rationalized interpretation of the persecution compelled Tcherikover to reject the theory of an interfamily feud. In his view, the tensions were between the Hellenizing aristocracy and the people. Fourth, apart from the religious emotions prompted by Menelaos's and Lysimachos's looting of the holy vessels, Tcherikover pointed to the political and economic aspects of the popular discontent, identifying the rebels as the *plebs urbana*—that is, the "poorer sections of the people," who had been left outside the citizen body of the new polis in 175

B.C.E.—"the agricultural population of the villages around the city," and the "lower priesthood."[30]

Since Bickerman's interpretation, no one has doubted that Antiochos's actions in Jerusalem were designed to "punish an insubordinate province and keep it in line."[31] However, this is as far as Bickerman's combined version of 1 and 2 Maccabees and Josephus should be followed. Tcherikover's realization that Antiochos's brutal military repression cannot be explained by the alleged interfamily feud is vindicated by the rereading of 2 Maccabees proposed in Parts I and II of this book.[32] As noted there, the author of 2 Maccabees systematically presents Jason and Menelaos as paving the way to Antiochos's sins by their own wrongdoings. The wicked high priests both foretell the king's misdemeanors and cause them to be. Thus, not only does Jason's massacre of his fellow citizens during his attack on Jerusalem (2 Macc. 5:6) foretell the one later perpetrated by Antiochos, but Jason's attack erroneously leads Antiochos to believe that Jerusalem is in full revolt and therefore has to be attacked and subdued. As the one portrayed as responsible for Antiochos's attack, Jason is also implicitly to blame for the king's plunder of the temple and wide-scale massacre. This version of 2 Maccabees is not reliable—nor is its counterpart in 1 Maccabees. The author of 1 Maccabees suppresses causality, and that narrative construction renders Antiochos's attack an act of pure wickedness.[33] The common denominator of these two versions is to present the rebellion of the Judeans against Antiochos IV, and therefore Judas's and Simon's actions, as legitimate: acknowledging that Antiochos IV's assault was intended to put down a rebellion might have suggested an embarrassing admission that Antiochos's repression was justified, casting doubt on the legitimacy of Judas's and Simon's actions. Once the ancient authors' motivations for presenting the events as they did are understood, the likelihood that their respective accounts distorted the true course of events appears to be very high. As Tcherikover observed, the nature of events motivating Antiochos's suppression should be deduced from the description of the suppression itself rather than from the description of the alleged feud between Jason and Menelaos. The suppression points to a popular rebellion, which initially broke out during Antiochos's Egyptian campaign, was severely but not entirely quashed, and broke out again following the land confiscations and what was perceived to be the desecration of the temple.[34]

However, Tcherikover's assumption that the popular rebellion was motivated by Menelaos's extreme Hellenizing policy must be dismissed. As we saw throughout Parts I and II of this book (e.g., §§I.2.3; 1.4.3, 1.4.4; 5.1, 5.2), modern scholars' characterization of Jason and Menelaos as Hellenizers is an uncritical rationalization of their portrayal in 1 and 2 Maccabees as impious individuals. This motif is questionable—intended to brand these rival high priests as illegitimate rulers—and cannot be accepted at face value. Therefore our interpretation of the nature of the rebellion must be based on entirely new grounds.

11.2. THE REBELLION AND ITS CONSEQUENCES: A PROPOSED OUTLINE

The manner in which the rebellion unfolded may now be examined. Although some details remain uncertain, an outline of the main events can be sketched out based on 1 Maccabees 1:20–2:48 and 2 Maccabees 5:1–6:11, which must be read bearing in mind the conclusions of the literary analysis presented in Parts I and II of this book.

The rebellion first broke out during Antiochos's campaign in Egypt. It is unclear whether that was during the first or the second invasion, although the second one seems more likely. On his way back from Egypt, Antiochos attacked Jerusalem— an immediate punitive expedition followed by a far-better-planned military suppression "two years later," according to 1 Maccabees 1:29. This is described in great detail in the literary sources: a new massacre was perpetrated (unless Apollonios's massacre is merely a narrative doublet); the temple altar was defiled;[35] the citadel of the Akra was erected; a military settlement was established; and lands were confiscated. However, for reasons that cannot be determined from the literary sources, this attempt at pacification ultimately failed; Antiochos IV eventually agreed to a peace treaty, and Menelaos negotiated an amnesty.[36] The emergence of rival contenders to the Seleukid throne around this time must have been instrumental in the eventual success of the revolt, which resumed shortly afterward and ultimately brought the Hasmoneans to power.

The hypothesis that wide-scale rebellion broke out during Antiochos's Egyptian campaign makes it possible to interpret the events in the literary sources as a military suppression of a popular insurgency. When read in this light, nothing in Antiochos IV's actions appears to depart from the ancient rules of warfare. Although some details remain obscure, there is no reason to think that Antiochos IV behaved in an extraordinary way in Judea. The suppression was undoubtedly harsh, but this was the usual praxis of war. It was not "unique"[37] either in scale or in its nature. In the following section (§11.2) we shall attempt to reconstruct the fate of the population, and the section after that (§11.3) will address the fate of the temple separately.

11.2.1. The Outbreak of Revolt during Antiochos's Campaign in Egypt: 1 Maccabees 1:20–24 and 2 Maccabees 5:5–23

A. *The Judean Uprising and its Suppression.* There is no explicit reference to the rebellion in the sources—so much so, it is as if the authors of 1 and 2 Maccabees did everything possible to conceal it. One telling episode, however, not only has survived but is dwelt upon at length: Antiochos IV's assault on Jerusalem, including his massacre of its inhabitants and plundering of the temple (1 Macc. 1:20–24; 2 Macc. 5:12–16, 21). As we saw earlier (§11.1.3), the cause of his attack is either omitted or distorted and must be inferred from the sheer ferocity of the assault. Nonetheless, the real significance of Antiochos's action is obliquely disclosed by the author of 2 Maccabees (2 Macc. 5:11):

> When the king received the news of the events, he concluded that Judea was in revolt. Accordingly he broke camp and set out from Egypt. With the fury of a wild beast he took the city, treating it as enemy territory captured in war.

Antiochos was not mistaken: Judea *was* in revolt. When understood in this context, his plundering of the temple and massacre of the population become legitimate punitive actions according to the ancient rules of warfare.[38]

The popular-uprising hypothesis casts into doubt the author's contention that the attack on Menelaos was led by Jason (2 Macc. 5:5–10). It is difficult to see how a feud between two rival contenders for the high priesthood could have precipitated a situation that incited Antiochos not only to storm the city but, more seriously, to plunder and desecrate the temple.[39] Furthermore, we must remember that the authors always made sure to keep their accounts within the bounds of plausibility: they knew they could not diverge too far from what their original audience remembered.[40] For this reason, it is unlikely that Jason's part in the assault was entirely fabricated by the author of 2 Maccabees. There are, however, several possible scenarios: Jason may have seized the opportunity to regain power when the popular rebellion broke out—or he himself may have led the rebellion (if the latter is true, Judas Maccabee was merely replacing him in the role a few months later). Alternatively, Jason may just have been involved in the attack without leading it— in which case, the author's claim that he instigated the attack on the city must be read as his taking one more opportunity to blame Jason for the disastrous consequences of the failed rebellion (Antiochos's onslaught).

B. *The Overseers Left by Antiochos: 2 Maccabees 5:22–23.* Moreover, before departing Antiochos left behind civil officials who were to administer both Jerusalem and Mount Gerizim on his behalf (2 Macc. 5:22–23):[41]

> He went so far as to leave overseers [*epistatai*] in charge of maltreating our race: at Jerusalem, Philip, . . . and at Mount Gerizim, Andronikos; and in addition, Menelaos, who was worse than the others because he lorded over his fellow citizens, being of hostile disposition toward the Judeans, his fellow citizens.

This administrative reform can be understood only as a punitive step, but two details make it hard to reconcile with the civil-strife hypothesis:[42] the fact that Philip, the royal overseer, coexisted with Menelaos and the fact that a second overseer was put in charge of Mount Gerizim. As opposed to the many occasions when the bias of the author of 2 Maccabees against Judas's opponents induced him to suppress data, this time he offered us a valuable piece of information, because he relished the opportunity to compare Menelaos with Philip and Andronikos.[43] That said, the division of powers between the royal official and Menelaos is unclear. Obviously Menelaos retained his cultic functions as high priest, but it is not excluded that he also retained some of his functions as leader of the "Antiochenes in Jerusalem," especially if those did not join the rebellion. We may even surmise, although this remains speculative, that the rebels' anger before Antiochos's intervention was directed against the Antiochenes because they saw the creation of the polis as the reason for their worsened economic plight.[44] This would explain why Menelaos felt personally threatened and had to take refuge in the citadel during the rebels' assault (2 Macc. 5:5). The indication that a royal overseer was left at Mount Gerizim as well comes as a surprise to modern readers. If there is any truth to this reference, it is evidence that the uprising was not limited to Judea alone, especially since in the text the reference to this *epistatēs* cannot be separated from the contention that the Mount Gerizim temple was renamed after Zeus Xenios, "as the inhabitants of the place requested" (2 Macc. 6:2). Unfortunately, the current state of the evidence prevents this line of inquiry from being pursued any further.

11.2.2. The Second Phase of the Suppression: 1 Maccabees 1:29–64 and 2 Maccabees 5:24–6:11

The hypothesis that Menelaos and the "Antiochenes" were the primary target of the rebellion may explain the main features of the suppressive steps that were to follow.

A. The Fate of Captured Cities in Ancient Times. When Alexander reached Gaza, the inhabitants of the city chose to resist rather than surrender. When Alexander captured the city after a protracted siege, all the armed men were killed, the women and children were enslaved, and the conqueror repopulated the city with inhabitants from the surrounding area (Arr. 2.27.7). When Alexander gave the final assault on Tyre after months of resistance, eight thousand Tyrians were killed. Those who had sought refuge at the sanctuary of Herakles—including the king, leading city officials, and Carthaginian delegates—were spared, whereas the rest were enslaved. In all, Alexander sold thirty thousand prisoners, both Tyrians and foreigners. He then offered a sacrifice to Herakles (Arr. 2.23.4–6). Arrian does not say what the surviving Tyrians thought of this pious deed.

Killing or expelling the entire population of a vanquished town and repopulating it with willing or unwilling new inhabitants from other parts was common wartime practice in the ancient world, and the history of both classical Greece and the Roman Republic offers many similar instances.[45] In the Greek world of the Balkans and the islands, conquered territory was usually either occupied by the victors themselves (if they were a civic community) or—in the case of a Hellenistic king or the Romans—handed over to a third party. Shortage of arable land explains why the destruction of entire communities was not uncommon. In Asia Minor and in the Levant, the conditions of agricultural occupation were different.[46] Although the demographic argument does not explain Alexander's comparative clemency toward the Tyrians, it may explain other instances. Thus, when the Pedieis—a population of non-Greek dependent cultivators of royal land whose territory was controlled by the city of Priene—rose up in revolt with the help of the neighboring city of Magnesia-on-Maiandros, killed many Prieneans, and ransacked their territory in about 187 B.C.E., King Lysimachos intervened to save the Prieneans. However, instead of massacring the defeated Pedieis he merely handed them back to Prienean control:[47] they were too valuable as a workforce and as taxpayers to be killed or expelled.

If we are to believe the author of 2 Maccabees, "80,000 were brought to ruin in the course of three days, of whom 40,000 fell by the sword and an equal number were sold as slaves" (2 Macc. 5:14). Leaving aside the exaggerated number of casualties (allegedly greater in Jerusalem than in Tyre!), the fate of Jerusalem at the hands of Antiochos appears to be more like the fashion in which Alexander treated Tyre than how he disposed of Gaza. Like the Tyrian king, Menelaos was spared and ordered to rebuild, and of course to swear political allegiance and pay the tribute. Antiochos may have had more pressing matters to deal with in this border region with Egypt at this time than to repopulate Judea, and he was probably loath to lose an entire year of tribute. Alternatively, Menelaos may have eloquently interceded on behalf of his own people—for whom he remained the high priest, despite the new legal distinction between the Antiochenes and the Judeans—and on behalf of his temple, which needed Judeans to serve it. However, 2 Maccabees is not where we would expect positive accounts of Menelaos to be given.[48]

B. The Assault of Apollonios the Mysarch: 1 Maccabees 1:29–40 and 2 Maccabees 5:4–2. 1 and 2 Maccabees give the impression that the second assault on Jerusalem, led by Apollonios, was unrelated to Antiochos's attack two years before. In a sense, this literary presentation ties in with the suppression of causality apparent in the description of Antiochos's assault. The authors must have been aware that the actions of Antiochos's general could easily be understood as aimed at quashing a rebellion and therefore felt the need to obscure causality for his actions too. To that end, the rhetorical devices used by the author of 1 Maccabees are particularly effective: the paratactic style characterizing the entire first chapter is capped by the chronological notation "two years later" in order to provide a clear narrative cut between Antiochos's onslaught and the new one (1 Macc. 1:29). In contrast 2 Maccabees is silent about the two-year interval (2 Macc. 23b–24).

In the parallel descriptions of Apollonios's assault in the two works, two elements stand out, albeit to opposite effect. On the one hand, the occurrence of two massacres within such a short space of time is puzzling, raising the question whether they are both genuine, or whether the second is a narrative doublet. Such a doublet may well have served as a convenient substitute for causality: by inducing familiarity through repetition, it renders questions about the reasons for the massacre—and thereby answers—nearly redundant. If on the other hand the second massacre did occur, the claim in both 1 and 2 Maccabees that Apollonios used deception and launched a surprise attack is hard to believe (1 Macc. 1:30, 2 Macc. 5:25). According to 2 Maccabees, the Seleukid general first pretended to come in peace, then attacked on the Sabbath. The choice of the author to focus his account on this impiety is a case of using a mediating synecdoche to incorporate the narration of the war atrocities in the symbolic universe centered on the temple.[49] Moreover, that choice furnished an opportunity to contrast Apollonios's impiety with Judas's piety (2 Macc. 5:24–27). Leaving these narrative codes aside, the report of Judas's withdrawal with a small group of men to the surrounding hills (2 Macc. 5:27) begs the question what they had been doing in the city until that time. Had they been fighting? If so, Apollonios's attack definitely did not catch anyone unprepared.

1 Maccabees is far more explicit than the parallel work about Apollonios's actions after capturing the city. The reason for this may be that these actions included fortifying the Akra.[50] The description suggests that the punitive measures taken were typical of the military suppression of an insurgency (1 Macc. 1:30–35):[51]

> He hit the city hard with a surprise attack, killing many Israelites. He plundered the city, set fire to it, and destroyed its buildings and the walls around it. He and his army took the women and the children captive and took possession of the cattle. Thereupon they fortified the City of David with a high strong wall and strong towers so as to have a citadel, the Akra. They stationed in it a breed of sinners, wicked men, who grew strong there. The garrison was provided with a store of arms and provisions.

The reason why our two authors tried as much as possible to hide the fact that the Judeans had been in revolt is obvious. According to the customary ancient rules of warfare, the benefits that the winning side drew from the war were legitimate only insofar as the war was just. No legitimate rights could be obtained from an unprovoked assault.[52] Providing an explanation (a cause) for Antiochos's attack would have undermined the Hasmoneans' case against the Seleukids. Their demands for autonomy from the Seleukid imperial power were legitimate only if Antiochos IV's actions could be construed as being genuinely wicked—that is, as merely arbitrary. Since the motivations of the authors of 1 and 2 Maccabees for presenting events as they did are readily apparent, their accounts need not be accepted at face value.

C. *The Punitive Measures: Establishing a Permanent Garrison.* The massacre (or pair of massacres) was not aimed at annihilating the population but was part of a decisive campaign aimed at stamping out the rebellion. The string of punitive steps is told in detail in the three primary sources (1 Macc. 1:41–64, 2 Macc. 6:1–11, Dan.

11:30–39), all through the lens of mediating synecdoches, and therefore most of what is told concerns the temple. This slant is obviously what elicited the eventual transformation of the military repression into a "religious persecution."[53] It may also explain why, in 1 Maccabees, other, non-temple-related aspects of the operation were relegated to a different narrative section—1 Maccabees 2—which must be included in our present review. In all, we are told of Judeans fleeing to the caves of the desert "to observe the Sabbath" (1 Macc. 2:32–38, 2 Macc. 6:11) and most likely to reorganize their military resistance as well. 1 Maccabees also harps on the theme of illicit altars built in the countryside (1:54, 2:45).[54] Finally, in one of the short hymns punctuating the early chapters of 1 Maccabees reference is made to a "colony of foreigners" (*katoikia allotriōn*) whose presence disrupted the proper operation of the temple (1 Macc. 1:38–39).[55]

While the account of 1 Maccabees, in tune with the cultural and narrative codes of the text,[56] focuses on the Akra, from our modern perspective the link between the various elements mentioned in the sources is the colony of foreign settlers. Apollonios's attempts at squashing the rebellion involved destroying the city walls to thwart further uprisings, creating a fortified citadel controlling the temple, and installing a permanent garrison. In peacetime, Jerusalem hosted a small garrison, since well before the revolt we witness the citadel commander pressuring Menelaos to pay the overdue tribute (2 Macc. 4:28)—moreover, Antiochos III's decree has no hint that the city was ever granted exemption from garrisoning.[57] We must infer therefore that the new garrison force was far larger than before—the sort that requires a full-scale military settlement.

Several hints in the literary sources allude to foreigners' being settled on confiscated land. Thus in the wake of Bickerman's analysis, Daniel 11:39 is understood to refer to a wide-scale seizure of lands in favor of the military colonists.[58] A citation from the historical recapitulation that forms the preamble of the people's decree in favor of Simon in 1 Maccabees 14:36 may be understood in a similar fashion.[59] Finally, as noted in Chapter 7 (§7.4.3), the illicit altars of the countryside that are mentioned several times in 1 Maccabees 1–2 function as a mediating synecdoche referring to the land allotted to the *katoikoi*.

Bickerman has described the process by which a community whose free status was acknowledged by the king becomes a subordinate population after a failed uprising.[60] However, his commentary is marred by a confusion over the respective statuses of the Antiochenes' community and that of the military settlers. This crucial issue must be addressed first, before the fate of the *ethnos* of the Judeans is explored any further.

11.2.3. The "Antiochenes of Jerusalem" and the "Men of the Akra"

What is known about the relationships between civic communities and garrisons throughout the Hellenistic world suggests from the outset that it is highly unlikely that the local community of the Antiochenes and the military garrison established in Judea after the uprising ever merged institutionally.

A. *Cities and Garrisons in the Hellenistic World.* Admittedly, garrisons were sometimes incorporated into the civic body of the cities where they were stationed. Two instances are particularly well known, thanks to the preservation of their enfranchisement decrees, giving precise details about the groups involved and the conditions of their incorporation into the civic body. In both cases, the granting of citizenship was due to exceptional circumstances. In the first, it was the war against Andronikos following the death of Attalos III in 133 B.C.E. The people of Pergamon granted citizenship to several groups who had actively helped them defend the territory during the war.[61] In the second, the context is that of the Third Syrian War of 246–241 B.C.E., when Ptolemy III invaded the Seleukid possessions of Asia Minor. Immediately afterward, the citizens of Smyrna, who had sided with Seleukos II, forged a treaty of friendship with the citizens of Magnesia-by-Sipylos, who had supported Ptolemy III, and incorporated them into their civic body. The grant of citizenship was also extended to the military groups who had either settled or were garrisoned in the Magnesian territory, on condition that they swear allegiance to Seleukos II.[62] The military and political motivation for offering the citizenship to these soldiers does not need elaboration.

Strikingly, in both these instances several military groups are cited as being awarded citizenship. In Pergamon, we learn about the mercenaries and auxiliary troops who served in the city in 133 B.C.E.: "Macedonians" (probably the descendants of the Seleukid military settlers whose presence in the city dated back to the third century), "Mysians" (indigenous military settlers), active soldiers in the citadel and the old town, and the military settlers in Masdye and mobile troops who protected the countryside (*paraphylakitai*).[63] In the case of Smyrna, the military contingents awarded citizenship included settlers (*katoikoi*), the cavalry and infantry in the city, and the soldiers in the camp (*hypathroi*).[64] A unit linked to the fort of Old Magnesia, which possessed two *klēroi* (lots, allotments of land) near the fort and had been excluded from the original treaty, was granted citizenship at a later period, under terms that guaranteed their continued exemption from taxation as before, again on condition of loyalty to Seleukos II.[65] Another enfranchised unit consisted of "Persians," commanded by one Omanes.[66]

However, the two inscriptions make clear not only that were the circumstances surrounding the enfranchisement of the military groups exceptional but that their members had been longtime local residents. If Angelos Chaniotis's comment is correct, the "Macedonians" of Pergamon had been stationed in the town's vicinity for well over a century and a half before their enfranchisement. Other forms of collision between the local civic body and military settlers may be worth recording: on some occasions the soldiers sided with the local population in disputes with the imperial authorities that had put them there—suggestive, as Chaniotis points out, of considerable social interaction between the foreign soldiers and local inhabitants.[67] That said, the more common theme in the inscriptions is of tensions between the garrison soldiers and the local inhabitants.[68] In 215 B.C.E., the citizens of Larisa in Thessaly objected to the collective enfranchisement of "Thessalians and other Greeks" (obviously soldiers) whom Philip V had stationed there to repopulate the city after the war[69]—so much so, that the names of the enfranchised soldiers were subsequently erased from the stele on which they had been inscribed. In other words, the enfranchisement of foreign soldiers was definitely not the rule, especially with regard to troops who had only recently arrived.

Another reason for doubting that the settlers involved with the citadel of the Akra were incorporated in the body of the Antiochenes of Jerusalem is that the two groups had more to lose than to gain from such a merger, given their different privileges. On the one hand, citizenship offered certain privileges that its current beneficiaries had no reason to share with newcomers, such as access to the local temple and to certain lands. On the other hand, citizens and soldiers were subject to distinct fiscal regimes. The cleruchs (*klērouchoi,* military settlers assigned landholdings by lot) of Old Magnesia clearly feared that their enfranchisement might result in the imposition of civic taxes on their landholdings; hence the treaty between them and Smyrna explicitly stipulated that their tax exemption would be preserved.[70] It is conceivable that tax exemption for landholdings was a common incentive to attract soldiers to a new settlement, which the new settlers in Jerusalem may have enjoyed. In contrast, the Antiochenes were certainly subject to taxation, since their enfranchisement had been granted at their request. (2 Maccabees 4:9 indeed mentions a special payment.) In short, neither party had an interest in merging—nor was it customary for kings to impose mergers of this sort.

Despite all this, most scholars examining the relationship between the Antiochenes and the military settlers have concluded that the two groups formed a single entity from the outset.[71] It is easy to see how such an interpretation can be drawn from the literary sources, which are purposely deceptive on this point. The author of 1 Maccabees deliberately and skillfully contrived this insinuation; and Josephus, in a misguided attempt to remove the ambiguity, helped to perpetuate it—but the notion of the two groups' unity is clearly false nonetheless, for reasons that are apparent upon reexamination of the literary evidence.

B. The Evidence of 1 Maccabees and Josephus. When read in isolation, the numerous passages of 1 Maccabees referring to "those of the Akra" are perfectly understandable as referring strictly to the military contingent.[72] However, other passages are deliberately ambiguous.[73] The very first mention of the Akra in the book (1 Macc. 1:34) sets the tone: "They stationed in it a bread of sinners, wicked men, who grew strong there."[74] The author's failure to specify the identity of the Akra's occupiers is probably intentional. Even if his original audience knew that they were foreigners, the vocabulary used here—"sinners," "wicked men"—would unavoidably have prompted the contentious association between these and the Israelite sinners, since the latter are far more prominent in the book—although the Seleukid kings, their officials, and their subordinates are occasionally dubbed "wicked men" as well. Similarly, the statement that "the men of the Akra served [Gorgias, the Seleukid commander,] as guides" during the first important Seleukid campaign against Judas (1 Macc. 4:1-2) is deliberately made to suggest that they knew the region very well; and in the absence of any further elaboration the audience is invited to amalgamate the men of the Akra with the wicked Israelites who sided with the king.

The likelihood that the author knowingly blurred the distinction between the "men of the Akra" and the "wicked Israelites" (the "Antiochenes" of 2 Maccabees) is supported by three key passages in which the wicked Israelites act as spokesmen for those in the Akra. Two of these passages concern Judas's and Jonathan's failed assaults on the citadel and may be regarded as narrative doublets (1 Macc. 6:18-28, 11:20-22). The third passage describes the circumstances of Alkimos's appointment as high priest by Demetrios I (1 Macc. 7:5-9). The issue of the lands, which is prominent in two of the three passages (1 Macc. 6:21-27, 7:5-7), provides the key to understanding how the author of 1 Maccabees was able to lump together Alkimos and the men of the Akra without overstepping the boundaries of verisimilitude. The "Antiochenes" community was made up of the prominent men of Judea: that is, the landowners, whose lands must have been impacted in the economic riots just as much as those of the foreign settlers.[75]

It is unsurprising that Josephus was fooled. As a self-esteemed historian, he saw it as his duty to remove the ambiguities of his source (1 Macc. 1:29-35) in his paraphrase, in *Antiquities* 12.248-52, for the sake of his readers (*Ant.* 12.248):

> Two years later, as it happened, in the hundred and forty-fifth year, on the twenty-fifth day of the month that by us is called Chasleu, and by the Macedonians Apellaios, in the hundred and fifty-third Olympiad, the king went up to Jerusalem, and by pretending to offer peace overcame the city by treachery.

The original expression "two years later" (1 Macc. 1:29) is both quoted and clarified by conscientiously noting the year and month by the Judean and Macedonian calendars, and rather than sending the obscure *archōn phorologias* of the source text, "the king" comes in person. Next, the statement in 1 Maccabees (1:31) that the *archōn phorologias* (the Mysarch) plundered the city is embellished for dramatic effect—by means of a detailed description of the king's plundering the temple and suspending the sacrifices (*Ant.* 12.249-50)—before Josephus returns to a more straightforward paraphrasing of his source, of how "the king" plundered the city, massacred people, and made many others prisoners (12.251). In the first half of

12.252 he continues to paraphrase 1 Maccabees when describing the construction of the Akra (1 Macc. 1:32–33). Finally, his reference to the garrison in the rest of 12.252 is a rewording of 1 Maccabees 1:34–35 (*Ant.* 12.252):

> ... and stationed a Macedonian garrison therein. Nonetheless there remained in the Akra those of the people who were impious and of bad character, and at their hands the citizens were destined to suffer many terrible things.

For Josephus, it was clear that these "impious men" could only be wicked Israelites—hence his distinction between them and the "Macedonian garrison."

In summary, the author of 1 Maccabees slyly encourages his audience to equate the "men of the Akra" with the "wicked Israelites"—a blurring of their distinct identities presumably designed to otherize the latter.[76] In actuality, however, none of the references to the "men of the Akra" supports the conclusion that the military settlers and the "Antiochenes" were one and the same in terms of their legal status. Inasmuch as he merely paraphrases 1 Maccabees, Josephus cannot be regarded as an independent source of evidence—either in *Antiquities* 12.252 or in the other passages where he explicitly contends that wicked Israelites were found at the Akra.[77]

11.2.4. The Fate of the Rebel Judeans

The new social order that emerged after the rebellion had been put down was comprised of three distinct communities: the polis of the Antiochenes, the Judeans, and the military settlers. The Judeans lost their free status and became a dependent population of the polis. The military settlers ensured their pacification.

The status of dependent peasantry cultivating royal land and placed under the control of a polis, a temple, or an individual holding the land as a *dōrea* is well documented in Asia Minor. These populations, known simply as *laoi*, "native populations," in the inscriptions, were free communities of villagers working royal land (*basilikē chōra*). Handing over *laoi* villages to the control of a town, a temple, or a *dōrea* holder was a convenient solution for the king, since it allowed him to use the civic and priestly administrations for his own purposes: in effect, these became collectors of both local and imperial taxes, handing over the latter portion to the king.[78] The status of the *paroikoi*, however, was apparently slightly different. The *paroikoi* were native populations who were subjects of a Greek polis. However, as with the *laoi*, their titles to their lands were acknowledged, and they were subject to a double taxation, to the city and the king. The phrase "those from the land" (*hoi apo tēs chōras*) is also used, although it is uncertain whether or not it denoted a distinct status.[79]

The current evidence suggests that privileged cities and their dependent populations in Asia Minor normally belonged to distinct ethnic groups (Greeks versus natives), whereas in Judea—according to Bickerman—the dividing line lay within the local community. Despite this difference the evidence from Asia Minor offers the most convincing frame of reference for reconstructing the fate of the rebel Judeans.[80] It suggests that although the Judean population remained free, their territory was redesignated royal land, and they were placed under the control of the Antiochenes—much as the Pedieis were handed back to the Prieneans after their revolt was quashed. (It remains undocumented, however, whether a military garrison was left in Priene to keep them in check, as was the case in Judea.) Bertrand has speculated that these tributary populations on royal land were under the control of either the Smyrnaeans or the Magnetes of Magnesia-by-Sipylos, although the stationing of a military contingent there may have had nothing to do with the subject population.[81]

Two points remain unresolved. The persecution accounts in 1 and 2 Maccabees suggest that the Judeans' access to the temple was severely limited, but the details are obscure. The second question concerns the extent of the land seizures. These certainly included the lands of rebels who had been killed[82]—however, the renewed outbreak of rebellion may be more easily explained if they further involved expulsions. The story of Mattathias's actions in 1 Maccabees tells how he was joined by *Asidaioi*—"warriors who all volunteered in defense of the Torah" and "all those who were fleeing the persecutions" (1 Macc. 2:42–43)—and how the growing troops put the "sinners" to flight and "went around destroying the illicit altars" (2:44–45). Beneath the symbolically oriented vocabulary portraying these men as faithful Judeans, one is tempted to identify the rebels as men dispossessed of their lands.

The argument that the Antiochene community and the military colony remained distinct entities throughout is relevant to our understanding of the fate of the temple in the settlement after the rebellion. Insofar as the polis coexisted with the military *katoikia*, and the king maintained in office the native high priest whom he had appointed, there is no reason to doubt that the Antiochenes, who were headed by that high priest, retained exclusive control of the temple.[83] However, it is possible that Menelaos—followed by Alkimos—was compelled to make certain concessions to accommodate the cultic needs of the foreign settlers.

11.3. THE FATE OF THE TEMPLE

It is not easy to ascertain the fate of the temple after the rebellion had been quelled. Not only did the cultural codes of the Maccabees authors lead them to overemphasize how the narrated events affected the temple, but emotions ran particularly high as soon as the temple became involved, and the sources must be approached with care.[84] It is nevertheless possible to establish a few guidelines for a *plausible* scenario. To this end, two currently prevailing premises must be discarded from the outset. The first is the notion of "renegade"—or "Hellenizing," "modernizing," "liberal"—Jews.[85] The cultural significance of the notions of piety and impiety in the ancient Judean literate culture, as well as their contentious use in 1 and 2 Maccabees, has been commented on repeatedly throughout the literary analysis of Parts I and II of this book.[86] As we saw, this rhetoric, which is typical of much of the Hebrew literature of the time, is also replete with defamatory insinuations—especially in 2 Maccabees. Thus, the slanderous claim that Menelaos stole holy vessels from the temple is most likely unfounded, as is the insinuation that Jason intended to sacrifice to Herakles in Tyre.[87] Religious skepticism was thoroughly alien to ancient Mediterranean and Near Eastern societies: rejecting a political leader meant denouncing not only his actions in the field of what modern Westerners call "pragmatic" politics but his cultic decisions as well: that is, it meant impugning his piety.[88] There is little reason to doubt that Menelaos's initiatives were mainly motivated by the context of crisis, and as such may be defined as political, but inevitably they also potentially impinged upon the cultic realm. For instance, political allegiance to a specific king or to his dynasty necessarily also meant performing sacrifices on his behalf. Political opponents were likely to question the propriety of such sacrifices and cite them as proof of impiety. The following outline assumes that Menelaos was moved by genuine faithfulness to the God of his ancestors—but the political context of his days was very different from what it had been, for example, under Antiochos III. After the rebellion, the *ethnos* of the Judeans lost its status as a free community, and although the Antiochenes were treated more favorably, the high priest's political position must have been severely weakened, and Menelaos may have been forced to make concessions that he would not have contemplated only a few months earlier. His opponents ignored such nuances and preferred instead to portray his compromises as acts of deliberate impiety.

The second premise that must be discarded is the notion of "prohibition of the Jewish customs." Even though Bickerman's belief in a deliberate, wide-scale religious persecution has few supporters today, there is still a broad consensus that the Jews were compelled to participate in "pagan" rites and that "Jewish customs" were prohibited. Several scholars have worked out scenarios in which this situation was generated by a misunderstanding or was the unintentional consequence of some administrative measure.[89] A fundamental shift of perspective is needed on our part regarding what could constitute sacrilege in the context of the military repression. If we accept the notion that a rite is apt performance,[90] ritual modifications that according to our modern sensibility are minor changes could have been experienced as sacrilegious by insiders. Moreover, the perception that an act is sacrilegious can be situational, precisely because ritual performance does not constitute a separate field of human activity. For instance, in the context of peaceful relations between the imperial king and the local community, the community will willingly support the institution of sacrifices performed on behalf of the king. In contrast, that Menelaos could perform the same sacrifice in honor of Antiochos IV in the years of the suppression would have been perceived only as provocation by the victims, and as an unlawful rite. Similarly, if the altar was desecrated during military operations, we may imagine that Menelaos took the steps necessary toward building a new altar. But accepting that the new altar was lawful was a way of acknowledging Menelaos's legitimacy as a high priest, and therefore also the legitimacy of the king who supported him. When the partisans of the Maccabees built their own altar sometime later, they could proclaim that the lawful sacrifices were resumed. But at some point other people disagreed—those living in Qumran, for instance, refrained from taking part in the temple ritual.[91] In the days of the "persecution," there were undoubtedly changes in the settlement of sacred matters that had been applying since the time of Antiochos III—changes that were imposed upon the high priest rather than of his making. In other circumstances, such changes might have been accepted by most people in Judea—however, coming as they did immediately after the brutal quashing of the rebellion, the slightest modification was likely to inflame the population that was being dispossessed of its temple. Together, these two premises form the backdrop against which the cultic issues raised in the sources will be read.

The elements in the literary sources that are likely to have a factual historical core and that therefore are worthy of comment boil down to the following:

The temple was renamed after Zeus Olympios (2 Macc. 6:2).

The altar was desecrated.

The daily sacrifices were discontinued, and the Sabbaths and festivals were interrupted (1 Macc. 1:45–46, 4:53–54; 2 Macc. 6:5–6, 10:3; Dan. 11:31).

An "abomination" replaced the daily sacrifice (Dan. 11:31), or alternatively "the king had an abomination built upon the altar" (1 Macc. 1:45). See also 2 Maccabees 6:5: "The altar was filled with prohibited offerings excluded by the laws"(?).

A monthly sacrifice was performed on the twenty-fifth day of the month, apparently in the king's honor (1 Macc. 1:59, 2 Macc. 6:7).

Illicit altars and shrines were built across the city (1 Macc. 1:47, 2 Macc. 10:2) and the countryside (1 Macc. 1:54–55).

People were killed, probably while resisting the land confiscations. However, this last issue is not directly related to the temple.

The rest, as we have argued in Chapter 6, is literary embellishment. Note, moreover, that some of the items in the list above may overlap.

11.3.1. *Zeus Olympios of Jerusalem: 2 Maccabees 6:2*

The Greeks' attitude toward foreign deities in their conquered dominions is documented by many sources.[92] As we may learn from them, the Greeks had no qualms about appropriating sanctuaries along with the lands on which they were sited, but they did respect the gods of the land.[93] Along with the territorial control of the local sanctuary (or sanctuaries), they also assumed control of the human side of the contract with the gods: providing the resident deity with the share of sacrifices that he or she was entitled to receive, scrupulously respecting the species and number of animals sacrificed, and no less scrupulously performing the rites prescribed by the sanctuary's sacred laws and abiding by its ritual prohibitions.

Antiochos's settlers naturally assimilated the local deity of Jerusalem with Zeus Olympios (2 Macc. 6:2). This practice is well known:[94] the local deities of Asia Minor and Syria were almost invariably referred to in Greek as "Zeus,"[95] and in several instances they were even renamed "Zeus Olympios," the dynastic deity of the Seleukids.[96] Thus, Zeus Koryphaios (of the Height) of the Pereia of Seleukeia, and Zeus Keraunios (of the Thunder) of Homs—corresponding with Hadad, the main deity of northern Syria—were also worshipped under the name Zeus Olympios—as was Baalshamîn, the Lord of Heaven of the Phoenician coast.[97] However, a deity's name was his or her essence.[98] From the point of view of YHWH's people, worshipping Him under another name was equivalent to revering a foreign god in a place "not his" (Dan. 11:39).[99]

11.3.2. *The Decree of Antiochos III as Reported in* Antiquities *12.145–46 and the Illicit Altars of the City and Countryside*

One can only speculate about the circumstances that prompted Antiochos III—if at least Josephus's attribution is correct—to issue his well-known decree on the rules of purity in Jerusalem (*Ant.* 12.145–46).[100] Its phrasing sounds like the outcome of an arbitration in favor of the high priest—similar to the outcome of Seleukos II's arbitration in a dispute between Korris, the priest of Zeus Labraundeus, and the city of Mylasa, in Karia, over the ownership of some sacred land circa 240 B.C.E. In his letter to Olympichos, his governor, the king, who has obviously been persuaded by the priest's arguments, ruled in favor of the sanctuary. However, in a subsequent letter he revoked this order, after hearing counterarguments from Mylasan envoys.[101] In the case of Jerusalem, the king's proclamation may have been in settlement of a dispute between the high priest and a community of foreign merchants, relating to the area in which the laws of purity applied. At the time, the high priest's jurisdiction—and by extension the laws of purity—covered either the entire city of Jerusalem or, more probably, the area within the walls. The foreigners, however, presumably argued that it should be restricted to the *temenos* of the temple. The royal decree, as Josephus presents it, appears to have supported the high priest's position.

The extension of the boundaries of the sacred area beyond the walled *temenos* of the temple during the second century B.C.E. is confirmed by contemporary literary sources (e.g., 4QMMT).[102] Extrapolating from Antiochos III's decree on the purity laws, one may tentatively argue that Antiochos IV for the benefit of the military settlers reversed his father's arbitration upholding the extension of the purity laws to the city. This too is more likely a sign of Menelaos's disadvantaged position in negotiations with the king rather than of his alleged apostasy.

What happened in the countryside is easily surmised: the military settlers naturally brought their gods with them and set up altars for their own private use.[103] As pointed out in Chapter 7 (§7.4.3), the references to the illicit altars of the countryside in 1 Maccabees 1:54 are a mediating synecdoche used by the author to talk about the land confiscations. Altars must have been erected by the settlers both within their dwellings and on their agricultural lands.[104]

1 and 2 Maccabees also allude to illicit altars built within the city (1 Macc. 1:47, 2 Macc. 10:2). If this account is reliable, it definitely confirms that the settlers were able to impose their will on Menelaos: clearly, the purity law's boundaries were now restricted to the *temenos* of the temple. It is conceivable that one of the altars set up by the settlers was dedicated to the local god under the name Zeus Olympios in what was genuinely intended as a mark of respect. However, as we may imagine, the dramatic contraction of the sacred area, in stark defiance of the recent history of Jerusalem, must have been perceived both as a sacrilege and a humiliation by the vanquished Judeans. Menelaos probably felt the same, especially if the revised arrangement had been forced upon him at the outcome of a new arbitration procedure in which he had personally defended the case of the temple.

11.3.3. *The Fate of the Altar*

However shocking the altars erected by the settlers in the city and the countryside were to the Judeans' sensibilities, the desecration of the temple altar was orders of magnitude worse. The circumstances in which this occurred are obscure—however, it may not have been a deliberate act of punitive retribution. The city had suffered either one or two successive assaults in a short span of time: the altar may have been inadvertently desecrated during the fighting, and this would have entailed the immediate suspension of daily sacrifices. The traumatic effect resulting from the interruption of the regular cultic rites is well documented both in the Judahite/Judean culture and in Mesopotamia, and it hardly needs elaboration.[105] Unsurprisingly, all three primary sources dwell on this issue at length (1 Macc. 1:45-46, 2 Macc. 6:5-6, Dan. 11:31). The account in Daniel, in particular, focuses on it almost exclusively as far as the temple is concerned, with the remaining description of wicked actions dwelling on the suffering of the wise (Dan. 11:31-35).

A. *The "Abomination."* The suspension of sacrifices also meant that no sacrifice could be performed in the king's honor either. Therefore, Antiochos IV must have had an added interest in restoring the altar. Generally the Seleukid kings took great care of the temples of their subject communities and were keen to proclaim their piety in official letters. There is little reason to doubt their sincerity, even if this care and concern never prevented them from coveting the temples' revenues. They must have had a particular interest in the sacrifices to them that were carried out in Greek cities and on their behalf in the temples of non-Greek communities like Babylonia and Judea, since these sacrifices were a mark of political loyalty. Temples of revolted communities could legitimately be destroyed[106]—however, once Antiochos IV restored the Antiochenes community and confirmed Menelaos as high priest, both the regular temple rituals and the sacrifices performed in his name had to resume.

Whose initiative was it to rebuild the altar? 1 Maccabees 1:45 points to the king, with the strong implication that this was an act of unspeakable sacrilege—however, given the persistent anti-Seleukid bias of all three primary sources, we need not take this at face value. A more likely scenario is that Menelaos petitioned the king on this matter and received his consent. There can be little doubt that the high priest was the only individual recognized by all concerned—the king, the Antiochenes, and the military settlers—as having the authority necessary to resume the sacrifices. Presumably Menelaos did precisely what Judas and his followers did two years later (1 Macc. 4:47, 2 Macc. 10:3): he built a new altar to replace the desecrated one. This must be the altar built on the altar alluded to in 1 Maccabees 1:54.

If the high priest and not royal officials built the new altar, why do the sources present this act as an outrage—and why was it necessary for Judas's men to cleanse the temple and remove the new altar (1 Macc. 4:43, 2 Macc. 10:3) after liberating the *temenos*? Hints of an answer may be found in 4QMMT.[107] As we learn from this polemical text, the temple could be regarded as defiled even if no foreigner had actually desecrated it. Disagreement over the rules of purity and rejection of the high priest's political (and hence cultic) legitimacy could have been interpreted the same way. In the eyes of the dispossessed Judeans, the sacrifices offered on the new altar were unlawful (2 Macc. 6:5).

The possibility that the "abomination" in question was an unlawful altar is supported by the context of its mention in the opening words of 1 Maccabees 1:54a, since the rest of the passage refers to other altars (1 Macc. 1:54b–55).[108] In Daniel 12:11, the same phrase appears to refer to a sacrifice replacing the daily sacrifice.[109]

B. The Monthly Sacrifice: 1 Maccabees 1:59 and 2 Maccabees 6:7? Menelaos's new altar was rendered all the more unacceptable by the fact that, according to 1 and 2 Maccabees, the "wicked" high priest instituted an innovative sacrifice on the twenty-fifth day of the month ("on the illicit altar, which was upon the temple altar": 1 Macc. 1:59). If, as 2 Maccabees 6:7 suggests,[110] this monthly sacrifice was made on behalf of the king, it may well have been performed by the native high priest at the temple's traditional altar. Sacrifices subsidized by the king—and later by the emperor—and performed in the ruler's name are well documented in

Jerusalem and need no elaboration. In normal times, they symbolized the local community's political allegiance to the imperial authority of the ruling king and were readily accepted by the local population. However, these were not normal times, and a sacrifice honoring the king who had dispossessed them of their lands would have only infuriated the disenfranchised Judeans. A cultic innovation that is not accepted is synonymous with an impiety.

. . .

This reconstruction of the cultic consequences of the presence of a foreign garrison in Jerusalem is based on three interrelated premises. First, the foreign settlers conducted themselves in Jerusalem exactly as they would have done elsewhere: they strove to accommodate their own cultic needs while displaying genuine respect for the local deity of the place where they were stationed. Second, Menelaos, the native high priest in charge of the temple, did the best he could to protect the interests of his sanctuary. Third, relations between the foreign settlers and the high priest must be understood in the context of the aftermath of the rebellion, when the high priest's political position was particularly weak. Whenever there was a conflict of interests between the settlers and the Antiochenes, his negotiating position was limited.

Together, these premises form what may be called as a minimalist view of the "religious persecution." The scenario we have just described is knowingly based on it—if only for the sake of illustration—even though many of its details are speculative. One question remains: To what extent is such a minimalist scenario reconcilable with the literary descriptions of the "persecution"? The answer—as we proposed in Chapter 6—is that if the literary descriptions are seen as an elaboration of reality shaped by the cultural codes of the Judean literati rather than as realistic eyewitness accounts shaped according to our own cultural codes, it is easy to see how they could have been produced from just such a minimalist scenario.[111]

The notion that events in Judea were "unique"[112] is the outcome of two combined factors. First, while massacres were numerous in antiquity, history is usually told from the side of the winners. Only a handful of traumatic events are reported in ancient literature, because of a reversal of fortune that turned the victims into the eventual victors, notably: the sack of the Acropolis by the Persians in 480 B.C.E., which is portrayed in the iconographic program of the Parthenon metopes; and the sack of the Capitol by the Gauls, and Hannibal's invasion of Italy, both events extensively covered in Roman literature. The second factor of the narrative and literary construction of the persecution accounts is the combined outcome of cultural and narrative codes, intertextual load, and political bias. When they are properly analyzed, the persecution accounts may be normalized, as in truth can all other aspects of the Judean rebellion against the Seleukids. At the start of the revised interpretation proposed in Part III of this book is the proposition that the supposed uniqueness of the ancient Judean "religion" is a modern construct unduly laying the stress on beliefs ("monotheism"). Once we accept normalizing the ancient Judean cultic system, it may be easier to accept the proposition that as with all other peoples in antiquity, the Judean rebellion against Antiochos IV was in essence caused by economic distress and political destabilization. In a sense, students of Hellenistic Judea have been persuaded that this was the case. The historical reconstruction proposed here, I believe, differs in two fundamental aspects: the identification of said economic and political problems is not based on an instrumentalist view of "religion," and conversely, it takes the ancient sources far more seriously than is usually the case—especially as far as 2 Maccabees is concerned.

APPENDIX A

The Literary Composition of 1 Maccabees

I. OUTLINE OF THE LITERARY UNITS COMPOSING 1 MACCABEES

The six narrative cycles composing 1 Maccabees are discrete time units, each one corresponding to a different character—except the first cycle, which corresponds to the time of disruption.

1:1–64: The time unit of *disruption:* The rise to power of the dynasty of Alexander and the disruption of the temple order.
2:1–70: The time unit of *Mattathias.*
3:1–9:22: The time unit of *Judas.*
9:23–12:53: The time unit of *Jonathan.*
13:1–16:22: The time unit of *Simon.*
    13:1–15:41: The time unit of Simon alone.
    16:1–22: The deeds and reign of Simon in association with his sons.
16:23–24: The time of *John.*

II. OUTLINE OF THE LITERARY COMPOSITION OF 1 MACCABEES ACCORDING TO THE TEMPLE-BUILDING PATTERN

The four main time units (2:1–16:22) are composed—albeit with uneven levels of completeness—according to the narrative pattern of temple building, comprising three steps: the preliminary phase, the entitling building, and the subsequent blessings. (See §2.1.2A.) The pattern is carefully crafted in the time units of Judas and Simon but loose in those of Mattathias and Jonathan, these latter being preliminary episodes in which the stress is laid on the causes of disorder (with the construction and reconstruction of the Akra a prominent theme in both).

2. Mattathias: 2:1–70

I. The *preliminary phase* consists of the introduction of Mattathias and his sons as well as the exposition of the causes of disruption.

2:1–5: Presentation of Mattathias and his sons.

2:6–14: Presentation of the disruption: The temple lies in ruins, and the presence of the foreigners of the Akra entails its defilement. (Compare 2:7–13 with 1:36–40.)

II. The *entitling building* is replaced by Mattathias's entitling imitation of Phineas.

2:15–26: Mattathias's entitling deed: He successfully opposes the enforcement of the unlawful sacrilege and murders the unfaithful Israelite.

III. The *subsequent blessings*.

2:27–48: Mattathias enrolls pious men to fight and wins the first victories.
2:49–70: Mattathias's last words.

3. Judas: 3:1–9:22

I. The *preliminary phase* (3:1–4:35) is centered on Judas's appointment, his entitling victories, and the demonstration of his piety. Two disruption themes are also included: the impiety of Judas's enemies and the building of the Akra.

Judas's appointment.
   3:1–9: Judas is appointed by his father and enrolls pious men.
Judas's entitling preliminary victories.
     3:10–26: Preliminary minor victories: Judas defeats Apollonios (3:10–11) and Seron (10–26).
     3:27–4:25: The entitling victory over Nikanor and Gorgias.
     4:26–35: The last preliminary campaign: Lysias against Judas and Israel.
Judas's piety.
        3:17–22: Theme of the few against the many winning with God's support because their war is just.
        3:45–54: Reconciliation (ceremony of Mitzpah).
        3:56: Restoration of social justice.
        4:30–33: Judas's just war: Judas invokes the Lord. Simile of David and Jonathan son of Saul.
Impiety of the enemies.
     3:28–29, 37: Antiochos's unlawful levying of the tribute.
     3:35–36, 39–41, 42: Nikanor and Gorgias's sinful campaign.
The Akra.
     4:2: Gorgias is helped by the men of the Akra who served him as guides.

II. The *entitling building* (4:36–61): The Rededication of the temple by Judas.

III. The *subsequent blessings* (5:1–9:22): Judas's victorious wars.

However, the restoration of order remains incomplete, since Judas fails to conquer the Akra (6:18–20, 32).

4. Jonathan: 9:23–12:53

The incomplete restoration of order allows a new cycle of disruption to resume (9:23–27). It is cued by the rebuilding of the Akra by Bacchides (9:52–53; compare Antiochos Epiphanes in 1:33–35). Jonathan's cycle is incomplete.

I. The *preliminary phase*.

The rebuilding of the Akra.
- 9:52–53: Bacchides strengthens the Akra.
- 10:11: Jonathan strengthens the city and temple fortifications. (Compare Judas in 4:60.)
- 11:20–24: Jonathan unsuccessfully besieges the Akra.
- 11:39–43, 53: Jonathan asks Demetrios to remove the garrison of the Akra, but Demetrios rejects his demand.
- 12:35–37: Jonathan circumvallates the Akra in order to starve its inhabitants, but he is taken prisoner and murdered by Tryphon before seeing his plan through.

5. Simon: 13:1–16:1–22 + 23–24

I. The *preliminary phase* (13:1–42) is centered on Simon's entitling victory and evidence of his piety.

Simon's appointment.
- 13:1–10: Simon's appointment ("election") as leader by the people in order to "take vengeance for my nation and our sanctuary and wives and children." In the absence of a true prophet the collective of the people acts as a surrogate (13:7; compare 14:41).

Simon's victories.
- 13:11: The preliminary minor victory: The conquest of Joppe.
- 13:12–33: The entitling victory over Tryphon.
- 13:34–42: End of war: Demetrios acknowledges Judean autonomy (exemption from tribute; right of the Judeans to have their fortresses). End of Seleukid domination in 170 S.E. and first year of Simon's rule as high priest, commander and chief of the Judeans (13:41–42).

Simon's restoration of social justice: He offers his murdered brother Jonathan a lavish burial (13:25–30).

Disruption themes.
- The Akra and the fortifications (13:10b). Simon strengthens the walls of Jerusalem.
- Impiety of the enemies: Tryphon sinfully levies tribute (13:15–19) and treacherously puts Jonathan to death (13:23).

II. *The entitling building* (13:43–53): The description of the conquests of Gazara and the Akra mixes temple-building and palace-building themes. Simon builds two palaces, one for himself (in the Akra) and one (in Gazara) for his son John, whom he thereby associates to his rule (13:43–53).

13:43–48, 53: Conquest of Gazara
- 13:47a: Expulsion of the inhabitants of Gazara and purification of the place.
- 13:47b: Simon enters Gazara singing hymns and praises.
- 13:48a: Resettlement of the city with Judeans faithful to the Law.

13:48b: Simon's improvement of fortifications and building of a residence for himself.
13:53: Gazara becomes a residence to John, Simon's son and coruler.
13:49–52: Conquest of the Akra
    13:50: Expulsion of the men of the Akra and purification of the place.
    13:51: Solemn ceremony: The date of the victory is specified
    13:52: Simon decrees an annual commemoration, as Judas and his men had decreed Nikanor's Day. He improves the fortifications of the temple mount and makes the Akra a residence for himself and his retinue.

III. The *subsequent blessings* are distributed among three passages separated by minor episodes. All three aim at confirming Simon's political legitimacy.

(14:1–3: Minor episode: Demetrios's anabasis to Media, where he is defeated and made prisoner by Arsakes, king of Persia and Media.)
14:4–15: Blessing section: Simon's Eulogy, which characterizes Simon's rule by bringing in the themes of peace (14:4, 8–13), justice (14:4, 14), might (14:12b), and piety (14:15).
(14:16–24: Minor episode: Simon's renewal of the alliances with the Romans and the Spartans.)
14:25–49: Blessing section: The people's decree in honor of Simon, appointing Simon high priest and *hēgemōn* for life, with the sovereign people acting as surrogate for a prophet (14:41).
(15:1–36: Minor episode: Simon's "victorious negotiation" with Antiochos son of Demetrios, which strengthens Simon's autonomous rule. The tax exemption and the right to have fortified cities are asserted anew. Moreover, the right to strike coinage is granted.)
16:1–24: Blessing section: Simon is succeeded by his son John.
    16:1–10: Simon associates his son John to his rule.
    16:11–22: Simon is treacherously assassinated.

6. John: 13:23–24

16:23–24: The work is rounded off with John's succeeding his father, marking the establishment of the dynastic principle. John inherits the title of high priest (16:24), wages victorious wars, and builds walls (16:23).

APPENDIX B

The Literary Composition of 2 Maccabees 3:1–15:37

I. OUTLINE OF THE LITERARY UNITS COMPOSING 2 MACCABEES

The five narrative cycles composing 2 Maccabees are also time units built around the pairing of an imperial king and a high priest—except the last one (15:37b), which corresponds to the time of the Hasmonean dynasty. According to this definition the Hanukkah story is in fact a double unit, since it is built around two kings (Antiochos IV and Antiochos V), and two high priests (Jason and Menelaos).

3:1–3: The initial time of bliss under Onias III (time unit of Seleukos IV and Onias III, beginning).
3:4–4:6: The Heliodoros story (time unit of Seleukos IV and Onias III, continued): First cycle of disruption and incomplete restoration of order.
4:7–13:26: The Hanukkah story (double time unit of Antiochos IV and Antiochos V; and Jason and Menelaos): Second cycle of disruption and incomplete restoration of order.
14:1–15:37a: The Nikanor's Day story (time unit of Demetrios I and Alkimos): Third cycle of disruption.
15:37b: The final restoration of order and return to the time of bliss.

II. OUTLINE OF THE LITERARY COMPOSITION OF 2 MACCABEES ACCORDING TO THE TEMPLE-BUILDING PATTERN

The Hanukkah story and the Nikanor's Day story are strictly composed according to the narrative pattern of temple building, comprising three steps: the preliminary phase, the entitling building, and the subsequent blessings. (See §2.1.2A.) In contrast, the narrative structure of the Heliodoros story is much looser, as topically it may be defined as a story of temple liberation rather than of temple foundation.

1. The Initial Time of Bliss under Onias III (3:1–3)

Time unit of Seleukos IV and Onias III (beginning). The narrative of 2 Maccabees opens on a period of ideal time guaranteed by legitimate rulers (a good king and good high priest).

2. The Heliodoros Story (3:4–4:6)

Time unit of Seleukos IV and Onias III (continued). This is the first cycle of disruption, ending with an incomplete restoration of order. The disruption is caused by Heliodoros, the king's agent, and Simon, Menelaos's brother.

I. The *preliminary phase.*

3:4–14, 23: The assault.
3:15–22 + 24–34: The assault is repelled thanks to the people's prayers and heavenly intervention.
   3:31–34: Onias's prayer is fulfilled.
4:1–6: Continued disruption, showing that the restoration of order is incomplete.

3. The Hanukkah Story (4:7–13:26)

Second cycle of disruption and incomplete restoration of order. This cycle is composed of a double time unit: first, the time unit of Antiochos IV Epiphanes and Jason and Menelaos (4:7–10:9), which structurally corresponds to the preliminary phase (I) and the phase of the entitling building (II); and second, the time unit of Antiochos V Eupator (Antiochos IV's son) and the apparent want of a high priest (10:10–13:26), which structurally coincides with the phase of the subsequent blessings (III). The disruption is caused by the wicked king (Antiochos IV) and the associated wicked high priests (Jason and Menelaos).

I. The *preliminary phase* is composed of two distinct phases.

4:7–5:26: Phase of disruption.
   Jason deposes Onias III in an illegitimate way and founds the *gymnasion* (the antitemple, 4:7–15), causing the partial disruption of the sacrifices (4:14). Menelaos succeeds Jason in the same illegitimate way (4:23–26), and steals the holy vessels (4:32).
5:27–9:29: Phase of reconciliation.
   5:27: First appearance of Judas, characterized as the new pious (i.e., legitimate) leader.
   6:1–7:42: The exemplary death of the faithful ones. The disruption caused by Antiochos IV is inserted here (6:1–11), since it is the cause of their deaths.
   8:1–36: Judas's initial legitimizing victory betokens the reconciliation and opens the way to the refoundation of the temple. Preliminary restoration of justice by Judas (8:28).
   9:1–18: The talionlike death of Antiochos Epiphanes, manifesting divine retribution against the wicked king and the preliminary restoration of justice.

II. The *entitling building.*

10:1–8: Temple refoundation.

Judas's refoundation of the temple and founding celebration of the Festival of Tabernacles of Kislev. The refoundation of the temple is the major turning point in the narrative. Judas's victories are the consequence of the temple's refoundation, and they manifest divine approval of the refoundation and the new leader.

III. The *subsequent blessings*.

10:10–13:26: First reversal following the refoundation of the temple, marked by Judas's victories against both the Seleukid armies and the neighboring peoples.

However, the restoration is incomplete, as is evidenced by the fact that this is a time of war.

4. The Nikanor's Day Story (14:1–15:37a)

Third cycle of disruption and time unit of Demetrios I and Alkimos. The disruption is caused by illegitimate rulers (a wicked king and a wicked high priest). This cycle is followed by the final restoration of order.

I. The *preliminary phase* is composed of four steps.

14:1–36: New disruption, by Nikanor, the wicked royal official.
14:37–46: Reconciliation through the martyrs (Razis).
15:1–29: The entitling victory of Judas against the wicked Nikanor.
    15:12–16: Judas is acknowledged as the legitimate high priest and legitimate king by Onias III and Jeremiah in a vision.

II. The *entitling building*.

15:30–37a: Second temple refoundation by Judas.

III. The *subsequent blessings*.

(This phase [15.37b] not only rounds off this narrative cycle but may also be considered a fifth time unit. See the following section.)

5. The Final Restoration of Order (15:37b)

The last verse of the cyclical composition proclaims the final restoration, which is manifested by peace, creating a ring composition with the opening verses of the narrative (1:1–3). The restoration of peace continues to "our" very days: that is, the days of the Hasmonean dynasty. (The authorial comment that rounds off the book at 15:37c–39 is not part of the cyclical composition.)

ABBREVIATIONS

With a few small and familiar variations, the titles of biblical books are abbreviated as in *NRSV* (*q.v.*). Likewise, the abbreviations of journal titles are those appearing in the annual issues of *L'Année Philologique*, and the names of ancient authors and the titles of their works are abbreviated according to the frontmatter list found in Simon Hornblower and Anthony Spawforth, eds., *The Oxford Classical Dictionary*, 4th edition (Oxford, 2012).

For corpora of inscriptions, the abbreviations used follow the *Guide de l'épigraphiste: Bibliographie choisie des épigraphies antiques et médiévales; Quatrième édition, entièrement refondue*, ed. F. Bérard, D. Feissel, N. Laubry, P. Petitmengin, D. Rousset, and M. Sève (Paris, 2010). For papyri, they follow the *Checklist of Editions of Greek, Latin, Demotic and Coptic Papyri, Ostraca and Tablets*: http://library.duke.edu/rubenstein/scriptorium/papyrus/texts/clist_papyri.html

§	Indicates a chapter section in this book
1 Enoch	G. W. E. Nickelsburg and J. C. VanderKam, *1 Enoch: A New Translation Based on the Hermeneia Commentary* (Minneapolis, 2004)
1QH	H. Stegemann and E. Schuller, eds., trans. C. Newsom, *1QHodayot^a, with Incorporation of 1QHodayot^b and 4QHodayot^{a-f}* (Oxford, 2009)
4QMMT	*Miqṣat Ma'aśe Ha-Torah* [Some Works of the Torah]. The Composite Text, ed. and trans. D. W. Parry and E. Tov. In *The Dead Sea Scrolls Reader*, Part 1, *Texts Concerned with Religious Law*, 326–37 (Leiden, 2004)
ABC	A. K. Grayson, *Texts from Cuneiform Sources*, vol. 5, *Assyrian and Babylonian Chronicles* (Locust Valley, 1975) [Online at http://www.livius.org ? Mesopotamia ? Babylonian chronicles.]

AfO	*Archiv für Orientforschung*
AfP	*Archiv für Papyrusforschung*
AncSoc	*Ancient Society*
Ant.	Flavius Josephus, *Jewish Antiquities*
Austin	M. M. Austin, ed., *The Hellenistic World from Alexander to the Roman Conquest: A Selection of Ancient Sources in Translation*, 2nd ed. (Cambridge, 2006)
BCH	*Bulletin de Correspondance Hellénique*
BCHP	I. Finkel and R. J. van der Spek, eds. and trans., *Babylonian Chronicles of the Hellenistic Period* [Online at http://www.livius.org ? Mesopotamia ? Babylonian chronicles.]
BMCR	*Bryn Mawr Classical Review*
Bull. Épig.	*Bulletin Épigraphique* [in *REG*]
Burstein	S. M. Burstein, ed., *The Hellenistic Age from the Battle of Ipsos to the Death of Kleopatra VII* (Cambridge, 1985)
BZ	*Biblische Zeitschrift*
CA	*Classical Antiquity*
CBR	*Currents in Biblical Research*
CE	*Chronique d'Égypte*
CP	*Classical Philology*
CQ	*Classical Quarterly*
CRBS	*Currents in Research: Biblical Studies*
CRIPEL	*Cahiers de Recherches de l'Institut de Papyrologie et d'Égyptologie de Lille*
EN	Ezra-Nehemiah
FGH	F. Jacoby, ed., *Die Fragmente der griechischen Historiker*, 4 vols. (Leiden, 1999) [Originally published 1957.]
Fornara	C. W. Fornara, ed., *Archaic Times to the End of the Peloponnesian War*, 2nd ed. (Cambridge, 1983)
Hanukkah story	2 Maccabees 4:7–13:26
Heliodoros story	2 Maccabees 3:1–4:6
HSCP	*Harvard Studies in Classical Philology*
HZ	Haggai-Zechariah 1–8
IEJ	*Israel Exploration Journal*
INJ	*Israel Numismatic Journal*
JANER	*Journal of Ancient Near Eastern Religions*
JANES	*Journal of Ancient Near Eastern Studies*
JBL	*Journal of Biblical Literature*
JCS	*Journal of Cuneiform Studies*
JHSc	*Journal of Hebrew Scriptures*
JHSt	*Journal of Hellenic Studies*
JJP	*Journal of Juristic Papyrology*
JJS	*Journal of Jewish Studies*
JSJ	*Journal for the Study of Judaism in the Persian, Hellenistic and Roman Period*

JSOT	*Journal for the Study of the Old Testament*
JThS	*Journal of Theological Studies*
LCL	The Loeb Classical Library (London; Portsmouth, N.H.; and Cambridge, Mass.)
LXX	Septuagint
MT	Massoretic Text
Nikanor's Day story	2 Maccabees 14:1–15:37a
NRSV	*Holy Bible, with the Apocryphal/Deuterocanonical Books: New Revised Standard Version* (New York, 2007)
PCPS	*Proceedings of the Cambridge Philological Society*
RBi	*Revue Biblique*
RC	C. B. Welles, *Royal Correspondence in the Hellenistic Period: A Study in Greek Epigraphy* (Rome, 1966) [Originally published 1934.]
REA	*Revue des Études Anciennes*
REG	*Revue des Études Grecques*
REJ	*Revue des Études Juives*
RHPhR	*Revue d'Histoire et de Philosophie Religieuses*
RHR	*Revue de l'Histoire des Religions*
RPh	*Revue de Philologie*
SCI	*Studia Classica Israelica*
S.E.	Seleukid Era
ST	*Studia Theologica*
Stern	M. Stern, *Greek and Latin Authors on Jews and Judaism*, vol. 1 (Jerusalem, 1974)
STU	H. Hunger, *Spätbabylonische Texte aus Uruk*, vol. 1 (Berlin, 1976)
TAD	B. Porten and A. Yardeni, eds., *Textbook of Aramaic Documents from Ancient Egypt*, 4 vols. (Jerusalem, 1986–99)
TAPA	*Transactions of the American Philological Association*
Vermes	G. Vermes, *The Complete Dead Sea Scrolls in English*, 4th ed. (Harmondworth, 1997)
VT	*Vetus Testamentum*
ZA	*Zeitschrift für Assyriologie*
ZAW	*Zeitschrift für die Alttestamentliche Wissenschaft*
ZDPV	*Zeitschrift des Deutschen Palästina-Vereins*
ZPE	*Zeitschrift für Papyrologie und Epigraphik*
Zutot	*Zutot: Perspectives on Jewish Culture*

GENERAL NOTES

GENERAL INTRODUCTION

1. This assertion will be justified in Chapter 6.
2. See Gafni 1989, and Chapter 6 in this book. The full section based on 1 Maccabees is *Antiquities* 12.241–13:212.
3. See below, §4.1.
4. For a historiographical survey, see Williams 2001, 173–74, and 2003, 73–74; Doran 2012, 14–15.
5. See Bartlett 1998, 17–19.
6. See below, §5.2.
7. This crucial discussion is explored in more detail below in §5.
8. See the survey by Doran 2012, 8–11. One of the most recent commentaries on 2 Maccabees, by D. R. Schwartz, reverts to full-fledged *Quellenforschung* analysis. See D. R. Schwartz 2008, 1–37.
9. Ibid., 8–9.
10. Ibid., 16–37.
11. Doran 1981, 23. For his review of the source-analysis theory, see ibid., 12–23.
12. See the historiographical survey in Tcherikover 1959, 386–87; and Doran 2012, 15–16.
13. The opinion that good Greek supposes rhetorical training in Alexandria is still propounded by Hengel 1974, 1.95, although he has our author write in Jerusalem after his training.
14. D. R. Schwartz 2008, 6–7 and 45–55. As just noted, Schwartz considers the section describing the rededication of the temple (2 Macc. 1:1–8) as an interpolation.
15. Doran 2012, 16.
16. Doran 1981, 107–8, stresses the "significant differences" between 2 and 3 Maccabees, despite their common fondness for epiphanies. In particular, "the temple does not occupy the central position in 3 Maccabees as it does in 2 Maccabees" (108). Henten 1997, 50, con-

curs by pointing to the literary content of the work, "most notably the content of the history of liberation and the headings of the festal letters (1:1, 10)." For additional references, see Doran 2012, 15–16. See below, §6.

17. D. R. Schwartz 2008, 48: "Indeed the focus on martyrdom is typically diasporan."

18. See Nickelsburg 2003 [1971], 668 ("throughout the book, the temple and its status are in focus"); Doran 1981 sees 2 Maccabees as "temple propaganda," and his view has been endorsed by Zsengellér 2007. Doran 2012, 3–4 and 13–14, maintains his original view—only substituting the concept of propaganda for "theomachy"—despite his locating the author in the diaspora. According to Ego 2007, 151, "the temple . . . stands directly under God's protection." See further ibid., 152.

19. D. R. Schwartz 2008, 7–8, contends that 2 Maccabees was originally meant to encourage the observance of the Nikanor's Day festival celebrating "the establishment of stable Jewish rule in the city [of Jerusalem]," whereas the Hanukkah theme is a secondary addition.

20. Nickelsburg 2003 [1971], 669–70, 672; Doran 1981, 114. Ego 2007 offers an analysis of the operation of God's righteousness in 2 Maccabees that highlights the role of the martyrs, whereas Judas Maccabee does not feature in her survey. Henten, 1997, 68, and 2003, 26–27.

21. Kampen 2007, 16: "The conflict between Judaism and Hellenism provides the ideological framework for the composition [of the epitome]." See also Habicht 2006a [1974].

22. Ego 2007, 154–55, argues that two different concepts of God's righteousness are at work: the measure-for-measure principle over the Greek oppressors and Hellenists like Jason and Menelaos and the "pedagogical punishment, a punishment whose aim is to turn Israel from their sinful ways."

23. I present my view below in §6.

24. Nickelsburg 2003 [1971]; Hengel 1974, 1:96–97 ("his theological views are stamped much more with the piety of the Palestinian Hasidim than with the Jewish Hellenism of Alexandria"); Doran 1981; Henten 1997 and 2003; Sartre 2001, 334 (the author's main purpose is edification and not history); Berthelot 2007, 48 (2 Maccabees' pious tone), 52 ("the religious fervor advocated by the book"; "the book has a clear theological agenda"); Ego 2007, 142 ("the theological context of [the measure-for-measure] motif in 2 Maccabees") and passim; Zsengellér 2007, 184 ("the thematic theological nature of 2 Maccabees"; "the author of the epitome was a skilled theologian"). Weitzman 2004, 221 with n. 13, endorses Doran 1981's definition of the rhetorical objectives of 2 Maccabees as "temple propaganda."

25. Orrieux and Will 1986, 126, 156 ("pieux auteur"); Habicht 2006a [1974], 94 ("devout Jew"); Aperghis 2011a, 69 and passim ("pious author"). It may be added that even scholars who do not explicitly dub the author as pious may still indulge in identifying Menelaos and his partisans as "Hellenizing Jews" (or "Reformers") and Judas Maccabee's partisans as "pious Jews." Thus Bringmann 1983, 98 and passim; Ma 2012, 74 ("le groupe maccabéen, qui rassemble les forces traditionalistes hasidiques"), 81–82 ("Juifs hellénisants," "Juifs pieux"). Wilker 2011, 225, 232, still endorses the old view that the "pious Hasidim" who initially supported the Maccabees broke away from them when a peace treaty was concluded with Antiochos V. All these views are predicated on the same flawed premises. See below, §§4.4 and 6.

26. Tcherikover 1959, 384; Nickelsburg 2003 [1971].

27. See Tcherikover 1959, 384, summarizing the older historiography on 2 Maccabees.

28. See D. R. Schwartz's summary and refutation (2008, 384).

29. Nickelsburg 2003 [1971].

30. Doran 1981, 114: 2 Maccabees "is primarily temple propaganda. . . . By downplaying the heroism of the Maccabean family, by upgrading the role of pious observers of the Law, and by placing God as the truly decisive actor in the divine drama, the author provides his readers with the proper religious perspective from which they can assess their present leaders."

31. See, for instance, Berthelot 2007; Zsengellér 2007. Out of habit: for instance, Wilker 2011, 216 n. 1. See also Kooij 2012, 29: "Since 1 Maccabees was written in order to legitimize the leadership claim of the Maccabean rulership, I will of course pay attention to this book." By implication, 2 Maccabees' purpose was different.

32. Grabbe 2000, 59: "Both works [1 and 2 Maccabees] represent a pro-Hasmonean bias"; Kampen 2007, 18: "The arguments advanced in 1 and 2 Maccabees support the legitimacy of the Hasmonaeans to arbitrate these issues (who has control of the temple, who has control of the sacred, who is able to define Jewish identity?) on behalf of the centre institution of Jewish society, the temple."

33. It is reviewed in more detail below in §5.1 and in Chapter 1. The fact that there are theological motives in the work, of course, was admitted much earlier. See Bickerman 1979 (originally published in 1937), 21, 22, and passim.

34. Kampen 2007, 16, 17. See further the studies cited below in n. 36.

35. On the argument of the supposed tragic misunderstanding, see below, §3.3. Gruen 1993, 257–59 is a remarkable—albeit to my knowledge isolated—attempt to argue against the view that the ancient author presents the rebellion as a conflict between "Judaism" and "Hellenism."

36. Hengel 1974, 1:98; Habicht 1976, 185; Himmelfarb 1998, 20; Collins 1999 and 2001, 46. (See also ibid., 42, where Collins upholds the notion of a conflict between "Hellenism" and "Judaism" in history and not only in the textual representation of the events.)

37. Bartlett 1998, 33.

38. Bickerman 1937. For its English translation, see Bickerman 1979.

39. In 1936 Bickerman had just completed the manuscript of his *Institutions des Séleucides*, a masterly survey of the organization and operation of the Seleukid empire as a state (see Bickerman 1938), and thus he was particularly well placed to take up this challenge. See Ma 2012, 70–71. For the early crystallization of Bickerman's pioneering conviction that Jewish history must be studied in context, see Baumgarten 2010, 221–26, and 2012, 76.

40. Bickerman 1979, 32–34; quotation from p. 33.

41. Ibid., 38–42.

42. For example, in his commentary on the civil strife between Jason and Menelaos, ibid., 44–46.

43. Apparently after 1 Maccabees 1:20–24.

44. Bickerman 1979, 46–53.

45. The description of the status of the Judeans as a subordinate community draws on comparative material, in particular the incorporation of the sanctuary of Zeus of Labraunda in Karia into the polis of Mylasa and that of the sanctuary of Zeus at Panamara in Karia into the polis of Stratonikeia. See ibid., 51–52.

46. Ibid., 45, 53–54, 60. Two chapters are devoted to the religious persecution, ibid., 61–92.

47. Ibid., 34. Compare Bickerman's commentary (1979, 48) on the phrase *ta Hellēnika* found in Antiochos V's letter confirming the restoration of the status quo ante granted by his late father to the Judeans (2 Macc. 11:24): "The Greek phrase *ta Hellēnika* when spoken by a Seleucid, does not at all mean the observance of a pagan cult.... In the decree of Antiochus V, the term, which is contrasted with the Jewish constitution, points to the form of public life peculiar to the Greeks.... This means that Antiochus IV had imposed upon the Jews a Hellenic constitution in place of the law of Moses."

48. Ibid., 41.

49. On Bickerman's idiosyncratic depiction of the Hellenizing reformers, see Baumgarten 2010, 240–70, and 2012.

50. Bickerman 1979, 55.

51. On Tcherikover, see further Grabbe 1992, 251–52.

52. Tcherikover 1959, 161–65, 404–8.

53. Ibid., 166.

54. Ibid., 167 for the two quotations.

55. Ibid., 167–69.

56. Ibid., 186–203.

57. Ibid., 190.

58. Ibid., 191.

59. Martin Hengel's *Judentum und Hellenismus*, published in 1973, was still extensively indebted to Bickerman's thesis. For the English translation, see Hengel 1974. On Hengel's thesis, see the critical reviews by Millar 1978 and Gruen 1993, 256–60. On Hengel's thesis about Hellenization and the Jews, see further Grabbe 1992, 148–50, and Hengel's own hindsight (2001).

60. For a recent example, see Aperghis's statement (2011a, 80–81): "The Jewish sources provide a picture of Antiochus IV and the Seleucid administration as openly hostile to the Jews and exerting undue force and compulsion in political, economic, religious and cultural matters. The discrepancies in the sources themselves, coupled with what is known of Seleucid practice generally, suggest that the truth might be quite different."

61. Grabbe 1992, 255. On Bringmann's thesis, see Grabbe's summary, ibid., 253–55; and Gruen's critical comments, 1993, 252–53.

62. Bringmann 1983, 111–20.

63. Ibid., 74–82.

64. Ibid., 93.

65. Ibid., 118.

66. Ibid., 126–32.

67. Ibid., 111, 129–33.

68. Ibid., 130–32.

69. Ibid., 133–37.

70. I borrow the concept of paradigm from surveys of the historiography of the classical Greek polis. Ultimately it derives from Thomas Kuhn's analysis of scientific knowledge. See Manville 1994, 21–22; Kuhn 1970.

71. I choose this denomination rather than "the Bringmann paradigm," because although Bringmann is its first proponent scholars happen to return to the two original works to refine details.

72. For its continued influence see, for instance, Orrieux and Will 1986, 113–75; Hyldahl 1990; Grabbe 1992, 255; Sartre 2001, 333–64; Mittag 2006, 225–81; Dąbrowa 2010, 13–41; Aperghis 2011a; Wilker 2011; Ma 2012, even though the latter pays homage to Bickerman.

73. For diverging views, see Bickerman 1979, 101–11, and 1984; Bringmann 1983, 15–28; Grabbe 1991. For an overview of the dating issues, see Hyldahl 1990, 194–97; Bartlett 1998, 35–53.

74. For a concise summary of the problem, see Hyldahl 1990, 199. The phrase "prohibition of the Jewish religion" is used, for instance, by Hyldahl 1990, 199; Ma 2012, 79.

75. See Sachs and Wiseman 1954; Boiy 2004, 162.

76. Habicht 2006c [1976], 115–16.

77. In part this uncertainty has to do with the question whether 1 Maccabees uses one or two calendar computations. See Hyldahl 1990, 196–97.

78. Habicht 2006c [1976], 116.

79. For a detailed overview of this issue, see Chapter 2, §2.1.2D.

80. Ma 2013 and 2014.

81. Antiochos's review of his troops at Daphne, near Antioch, dates to this time. On the Daphne festival, see Mittag 2006, 282–95. On the problems of its precise date (the fall of 166 B.C.E.?), ibid., 282 n. 1.

82. According to Yoel Bin-Nun (1991), an eight-day-long festival starting on 25 Kislev was celebrated long before the days of the Maccabees. Therefore the rededication ceremony led by Menelaos may indeed have taken place on its occasion. The memory of this ceremony was eventually appropriated by the Hasmoneans.

83. Although neither expressly refers to Tcherikover, Hyldahl 1990, 199, and Sartre 2001, 345–46, observe that the popular rebellion must have preceded, and explains, Antiochos's assault on the city (Sartre) and the "prohibition of the Jewish religion" (Hyldahl).

84. Bartlett 1998, 58. For a more cautious wording, Gruen 1993, 246.

85. Doran 2012, 18.

86. Bickerman 1979, 38.

87. Either Jason himself or his "party", the so-called Hellenists. For instance, Orrieux and Will 1986, 115–16; Gruen 1993, 242; Sartre 2001, 338; Mittag 2006, 235–37; Dąbrowa 2010, 16–17. See Millar 1978, 7.

88. See lastly the historiographical survey by Mittag 2006, 239–41. Mittag downplays the difference between the two options.

89. Tcherikover 1959, 161 and 404–9. Tcherikover's view is followed by Hengel 1974, 1:277; Bringmann 1983, 84–92; Hyldahl 1990, 192. Cohen 1994 endorses Bickerman's view.

90. Sartre 2001, 340. Ma 2012, 76, concurs, interpreting Jason's list as the constitution of a *politeuma* in the sense "civic body" and not in Bickerman's sense of a body with no civic status. In Ma's view Jason's reform does not consist in the refoundation of Jerusalem as a Greek city, since the temple-state continued existing alongside the newly founded Antiocheia.

91. Kennell 2005, 14–16, 23; Doran 2012, 98–101. Doran translates "to inscribe the Antiochenes in Jerusalem" (ibid., 94, justified pp. 99–100).

92. Sartre 2001, 340–41; Doran 2012, 98–99 (Apamea-Silhu and Seleukeia-Eulaeu); Ma 2012, 76 (Babylon; the coexistence of the city of Mylasa and the sanctuary of Zeus Labraundeus in Karia; and that of Antioch of Pisidia and the sanctuary of Men Askaianos); Stroot-

man 2013 (Babylon). On both the Tyriaion inscription and the parallel with Babylon, see further below, §4.5A.

93. Politicization means the transformation of a native city into a Greek polis.

94. Ma 2013 and 2014. See further below, §3.3A.

95. Doran 2012, 100–101. See already Doran 1990.

96. Sartre 2001, 340. See also Strootman 2013.

97. See already Hyldahl 1990, 190. However, in Hyldahl's view although the "Jews" enjoyed the "privilege to live according to the laws of their fathers" before Antiochos III, Antiochos III's decree introduced a threat that this privilege might be withdrawn, and this is what happened in 168 B.C.E.

98. See Orrieux and Will 1986, 152–54; Sartre 2001, 345; Mittag 2006, 278–80; Aperghis 2011a, 75.

99. Hengel 1974, 1:278, 299. Hengel's thesis is reviewed and fiercely refuted by Millar 1978. See also Collins 2001, 43–47, refuting the idea that Jason's and Menelaos's innovations reflected a Hellenized understanding of religion.

100. Aperghis 2011a, 68–69 (Jason), 79–80 (Menelaos).

101. Bringmann's instrumentalism is criticized by Gruen 1993, 252–53.

102. For instance, Sartre 2001, 341–45. Mittag 2006, 237–39, restates Bringmann's view that Jason's Hellenizing reform was geared toward stimulating the Judean economy through a better integration in the surrounding world, and consequently Mittag downplays the religious consequences of the reforms (ibid., 244–45).

103. Doran 2001; Grabbe 2002.

104. Kennell 2005. His view is endorsed by Doran 2012, 101–3.

105. Bartlett 1998, 57 deems it "scandalous." Scholars who emphasize Menelaos's economic motivations because of their instrumental view of religion downplay this aspect. See Bringmann 1983; Gruen 1993, 244.

106. See, for instance, Orrieux and Will 1986, 154–55; Gruen 1993, 248 (cautiously).

107. Ma 2012, 2013, and 2014.

108. Ethnic Syrians: Bringmann 1983 (see above, §2.3); Cohen 1994 argued they were Sidonians. See further the historiographical survey in Cohen 2006, 259–60. Greeks: Bar-Kochva 1989, 92–105 and 438–44, criticized by Cohen 2006, 260.

109. For earlier historiographical surveys, see Gruen 1993, 250–64; Bartlett 1998, 62–64.

110. Bringmann 1983, 130; Sartre 2001, 351–52; Mittag 2006, 258, with a detailed survey of the evidence on pp. 256–68. Bickerman's thesis is thoroughly criticized by Collins 2001, 47–52. Baumgarten has shown how Bickerman's interpretation of the Hellenizing reform was underpinned by his engagement in contemporary debates about Jewish assimilation. See Baumgarten 2010, 241–69, and 2012.

111. Momigliano 1975, 100; Millar 1978, 16. Hyldahl 1990, 199, exonerates Menelaos, seeing the prohibition as "a logical and consistent part of the suppression of the rebellious population."

112. As we saw, this thesis is found in Bringmann 1983. Tcherikover 1959, 175–203, seems to be the starting point for it. For recent endorsements, Aperghis 2011a; Doran 2011; Ma 2012, 2013, and 2014. See further below, n. 158. The surmise that Antiochos IV could be unaware that enforcing cultic changes in Jerusalem would unavoidably have devastating consequences is made implausible by recent studies of the operation of the Seleukid admin-

istration. Laurent Capdetrey and Jean-Marie Bertrand, in particular, have shown that, contrary to what modern scholars used to believe, the Seleukids had fairly good control over their immense territory. Although their studies are concerned with the circulation of orders from the central administration all the way down to toparchy officials in each province, the comparison with Ptolemaic Egypt, on which they rely, supports the idea that to the same extent regular reports and memoranda circulated from local officials to the central power. See Capdetrey 2006 and Bertrand 2006.

113. This notion goes back to Bickerman 1979, who talks of a "unique" event (61), "the sole enigma in the history of Seleucid Jerusalem" (62). It is reiterated in Momigliano 1975, 100 ("Such direct interference in the ancestral cults of a nation was unheard of in the Greek-speaking world from immemorial times"); Millar 1978, 16–17; and Weitzman 2004, 221–22, 234 (on whom see below, introduction to §5). A notable exception is Hydahl 1990, as cited above, n. 111.

114. Ma 2012 (77–82), 2013, and 2014. Ma subscribes to the misunderstanding thesis.

115. Aperghis 2011a, 76–77, 80.

116. For the older historiography on Antiochos's alleged Hellenizing policy, see Gruen 1993, 250 n. 34; Grabbe 1992, 248–49. On Antiochos's religious policy, Gruen 1993, 251 n. 42. Its historicity is refuted by Mørkholm 1966, 130–34; accepted by Millar 1978, 12–14; refuted by Gruen 1993, 251. Sartre 2001, 350, vehemently criticizes the old view that Antiochos promoted a cultural and religious unification of his kingdom. Mittag 2006, 139–45, examines anew the ancient sources and concludes that there is no evidence that Antiochos made any attempt to impose the cult of Zeus Olympios, although he utilized religious measures to stabilize his power.

117. Scholars accepting at face value the historicity of the decree and its content as described in 1 Maccabees: Orrieux and Will 1986, 144, 148; Sartre 2001, 346. Scholars expressing skepticism about either its content or its existence: Bringmann 1983, 103, 146; Grabbe 1992, 249; Gruen 1993, 251; Mittag 2006, 267–68.

118. Ma 2012, 82–83.

119. See in particular Ma 2000a (with Chandezon 2004), 2003a, 2012; Strootman 2006a and 2011b; Capdetrey 2007.

120. Several studies published in these years take due note of the new turn of Hellenistic studies to offer innovative interpretations of Judean events. See in particular Sartre 2001, 333–64; Kennell 2005; and aspects of Ma 2012, 2013, and 2014. Moreover, scholars working on Seleukid Babylonia are paying increasing attention to Judean events, and their "regard croisé" perspective is likely to contribute innovative insights to our understanding of the latter. See Strootman 2013; Clancier and Monerie forthcoming (1); Graslin forthcoming. Regev 2013 was published too late to be taken into account in this book.

121. The parties theory was finally deconstructed by Gera 1998 passim. See further Chapter 8, §8.3.

122. Josephus, *Antiquities* 12.237–38, and Jerome, *Commentary on Daniel* 11:14. Bickerman (1979, 44) further quotes Polybius 5.86.10, but Polybius does not speak of parties in Josephus's and Jerome's sense.

123. On Josephus himself, see Gafni 1989. More generally, Wiseman 1979, 12–26.

124. See Gera 1998 and further below Chapter 8, §8.3.1.

125. See the following appreciation of the author of 1 Maccabees: "His writing is on the whole factual and objective, and perhaps in spite of the author's Maccabaean sympathies, *owes something to Hellenistic historiography.*" (Emphasis added.) See Bartlett 1998, 33.

126. For inscriptions, see the pioneering work by Ma 2000a. For 2 Maccabees, see Ma 2000b; Doran 2011.

127. Moyer 2011, 142–207. For the text and translation of the aretalogy, see ibid., 282–86.

128. This is how John Ma dubbed it. For a summary of Bickerman's theory, see Ma 2000a, 150–74 (for the phrase, see, e.g., 152), 2003a, and 2012, 65. Bickerman put it forward in several studies: for instance, 1939a; 1980a [1935], 69; and 1979, 32. Further studies by Bickerman are quoted by Chandezon 2004, 132 n. 4.

129. Bickerman 1980a [1935] and 1979, 32–34.

130. See lastly D. R. Schwartz 2008, 220–21, and Doran 2012, 103–4, both at 2 Maccabees 4:11.

131. The model of the modern Western state underpins Mittag's monograph on Antiochos IV. See Mittag 2006 and the critical review by Strootman 2006a. The surrender-and-grant model is criticized by Chandezon 2004. See further Chapter 8, §8.2.1.

132. For an early criticism of the modernist, legalist model, see Austin 1986.

133. Manning 2010, 1–19, 55–73. Although Manning formerly deals with Ptolemaic Egypt, his analysis may be applied to the Achaimenid and Seleukid empires as well. He points to the Ottoman empire and early modern China as examples of premodern bureaucratic states. Useful surveys of the differences between the old legalistic and new views of the political culture of the Hellenistic kingdoms may be found in Austin 1986 and Strootman 2006a. Ma 2000a is one of the leading proponents of the notion of "empire as negotiation," despite the fact that he endorses (a moderate version of) Bickerman's surrender-and-grant theory. See in particular Ma 2000a, 179–214 and 243–53. Strootman has also adopted the premise of the Seleukid empire as a negotiated enterprise, on the basis of Charles Tilly's model of state formation. See Strootman 2011b and 2013; Tilly 1990 and 1994. Various formulations of the current perception of the Seleukid empire are also found in Kuhrt and Sherwin-White 1993, Austin 2003, Ma 2003b, Martinez-Sève 2003, Chankowski 2004, Capdetrey 2007.

134. See below, §4.3, and Chapter 10, §10.3.

135. The context of Alexander's conquest provides numerous examples. See Chapter 8, §8.2.

136. Doran 2011 advocates the opposite view. See below, n. 157.

137. For illuminating comparisons between the old and new models, see Manville 1994 and Scafuro 1994. For a recent overall discussion, see Vlassopoulos 2007.

138. See Michels 2013 and below, Chapter 10, §10.3.

139. Strootman 2013. I had no access to Strootman 2006b. Ma 2012, 76–77, points out that the polis that was founded in Babylon existed alongside the local community centered on its temples. This leads him to conclude that the civic community founded by Jason coexisted with and was distinct from the temple-state of Jerusalem. On the polis of Babylon and its implications for Jerusalem, see below, Chapters 10 and 11.

140. See, e.g., Parker 2005 and Scheid 2005. For a refined critic of instrumentalism in modern studies of Greek religion, see Kindt 2009. For theoretical anthropological studies, see in particular Bell 1992 and Asad 1993, 27–79.

141. See the Methodological Introduction to Part I below.

142. For recent endorsements of this picture inherited from Bickerman and Bringmann, see Aperghis 2011a and Ma 2012, 82.

143. See Bickerman 1979, 84–88. For the revised view, see below, Chapter 11, §11.3.

144. For a good overview, see Potter 2003; and see further the Methodological Introduction to Part I below.

145. See Potter 2003.

146. See Ma 2012, 70–71.

147. Bickerman also uses the comparative material to emphasize the specificity of the Jews. For instance, he dwells on the assumed different consequences of the presence of a *gymnasion* in the cities created in the former temple-states of Asia Minor and in Jerusalem: "Whereas athletic contests were merely strange to Cappadocian custom, they were objectionable according to Jewish law." See Bickerman 1979, 43.

148. Millar 1978, 3–6.

149. See Boiy 2004, 220–25, citing a few studies of the 1980s and 1990s on this matter (ibid., 220–21). Ma 2012, 76 and 77, appeals to Babylon to support Bickerman's view that Jason's Antiochenes formed a *politeuma* within the city of Jerusalem. See also Strootman 2013; I had no access to Strootman 2006b.

150. See in particular Gorre 2009 and 2013; and Gorre and Honigman 2013.

151. See Part III of this book.

152. See in particular Ma 2012, 74–75; Sartre forthcoming; and below, Chapter 9, esp. §§9.2–9.4.

153. See Ameling 2003; Kennel 2005; Sartre forthcoming. Ma 2012, 79, has argued that the new inscription casts light on the mission of "Geron the Athenian" (2 Macc. 6:1).

154. See Kennell 2005.

155. See Sartre forthcoming; see further below, Chapter 9, §9.1.

156. Doran 2011 and Ma 2012. Ma incorporates his overview of Judean events in an article devoted to a historiographical survey of Seleukid studies since Bickerman's *Institutions des Séleucides*.

157. Doran bases his revised analysis on the claim that in Greek poleis the phrase *patrioi nomoi* (ancestral laws) includes customs of worship. By analogy, he contends that the alleged prohibition of Judean rites was the automatic consequence of Antiochos IV's abolition of Antiochos III's charter at the creation of the polis of the Akra, that the king substituted one set of *patrioi nomoi* for another. Now, it may be objected that the meaning of this phrase changes according to context. Although it may refer to civic cultic traditions in domestic affairs, in the context of relations between kings and cities it refers to political institutions alone. There are no cases known in which changes that kings imposed on cities affected citizens' ritual practices, except in matters related to ruler cult. In Bickerman's wake John Ma (2012 [79–81], 2013, and 2014) compares the fate of the dispossessed Judeans after the creation of the polis of the Akra to that of *paroikoi*, subordinated communities that were dependent on Greek cities in Asia Minor, pointing out that the *paroikoi* took part in their cities' festivals. However, it may be objected that in the case of the *paroikoi* the element of compulsion is excluded, because it contradicts everything we know of Greek civic cultic practices. Therefore the participation of *paroikoi* in civic rites does not provide an appropriate comparison with the persecution accounts.

158. Doran 2011, 432–33; Ma 2012, 79–82. Ma (ibid., 83) puts the blame for the outstandingly cruel enforcement of the royal order on overzealous low-ranking Seleukid officials.

159. Lastly by Ma 2012, 78, 82.

160. See Chapter 11, §11.2.3.

161. Trans. Kennell 2005, 10.

162. Ma 2012, 66 with 77, has appealed to the now well-accepted view that Seleukid state culture combined central institutions and flexible forms of territorial control to claim that in Judea specifically, *politeia* meant Torah, a conclusion made possible because of his persistently legalistic conception of institutions. However, as we saw above, other scholars of the Seleukid empire understand local diversity in a totally different way. I subscribe to the latter view. See Kuhrt and Sherwin-White 1993 and Capdetrey 2007.

163. It is overlooked by Bringmann 1983.

164. The probable meaning of *philanthrōpa basilika* in 2 Maccabees 4:11 is discussed below in Chapter 7, §7.1.1A.

165. I use the phrase "Judean traditions" to lump together the categories of "biblical" texts and "pseudepigraphic" texts. Inasmuch as the biblical canon was established much later, this distinction may be misleading when we are concerned with the intertextuality of 1 and 2 Maccabees.

166. See, for instance, Ma 2012, 74–75. For the literary topos, see Stokholm 1968. For detailed discussion, see Chapter 9 below, esp. §§9.2–9.4.

167. Joshua's model: see Goldstein 1976 and 1983, and the bibliography cited in Berthelot 2007. Berthelot is the main proponent of the alternative view. Munnich forthcoming compares 1 Maccabees 3:55–56 with Deuteronomy 20:5–8.

168. See Bartlett 1998, 33.

169. Weitzman 2004, 222, citing Hayden White's works in n. 17. Weitzman appeals to the earlier, more moderate phase of White's works, during which White did "not deny the existence of historical 'facts'" (222).

170. Ibid., 234.

171. Nickelsburg 2003 [1971].

172. Doran 1981.

173. Henten 1997 and 2003. For a more detailed survey of their studies see below, Chapter 1, §1.3.

174. On the erroneous premises of this stance, see further the Methodological Introduction to Part I below.

175. *Pace* Ego 2007, 151: Thanks to the measure-for-measure motif "it is made clear that the temple itself stands directly under God's protection"; Zsengellér 2007, 184: "the main theme of the epitome is to proclaim the successful defence of the temple against foreign pagan aggression"; and Doran 2012, 3–4 (quoted below in Chapter 1, p. 67) and 13. See further below, Chapter 1, §1.2.

176. On this assertion, see the Methodological Introduction to Part I below.

177. Zsengellér 2007, 184 and 186.

178. Ego 2007, 151.

179. *Pace* Ego 2007, 153–54: "the 'measure for measure' principle . . . is seized upon in order to demonstrate God's definitive judgment over the Greek oppressors and prominent Hellenists like Jason or Menelaos."

180. My use of the terms "Judahite," "Yehudite," and "Judean" is clarified below in §8B, at the end of this General Introduction.

181. See further Part I of this book.

182. On his "theological" concerns, see Goldstein 1976, 3–36 and 62–89; Bartlett 1998, 28–33. The view that the author of 1 Maccabees was pro-Hasmonean is generally agreed upon. See the concise historiographical survey by Williams 1999, 98 n. 8. Williams points to only two discordant opinions.

183. See Williams 1999, 4.

184. See my alternative division under "Summary" at the beginning of this General Introduction.

185. For concise summaries of Martola 1984 and Williams 1999, see Williams 2001, 172–73. Bartlett 1998, 21–28, draws on Martola.

186. Martola 1984, 268–79. For a summary, see Williams 1999, 4–5 and 129–30.

187. Williams 1999, 57–58, 69, 108–27, 130–31.

188. Ibid., 98–107

189. Ibid., 97.

190. Ibid., 59.

191. Zsengellér 2007.

192. Ibid., 188. Although Zsengellér departs from Martola's and Williams's obsession with additions, he accepts that the last two chapters of the work (1 Macc. 15–16), which are omitted in Josephus's paraphrase, may possibly be one (ibid., 188).

193. See in particular Goldstein 1976 and 1983.

194. Zsengellér 2007, 194.

195. See also Regev 2008.

196. Zsengellér 2007, 195.

197. On the issue of religion and politics, see further the Methodological Introduction to Part I below.

198. On the notion of the emplotment of meaning through narrative archetypes, see White 1985.

199. On this issue, see further the Methodological Introduction to Part II below.

200. On this document, see above, §4.5.

201. For tentative answers, see the Methodological Introduction to Part I below.

202. The book of Daniel will be used mainly to analyze the so-called religious persecution; and Josephus's account in *Antiquities* 12.237–56, which is derivative, will be referred to mainly when we need to address modern interpretations making use of this work.

203. On Alexandrian poetry, in particular Callimachus and Theocritus, see Koenen 1993, 81–113; Selden 1998; Stephens 2003, 20–74. On the Delian Sarapis aretalogy, see above, §4.1; for Upper Egypt, see further Yoyotte 1969; for the Asoka inscription from Baktria, see Potter 1983, 420–21.

204. Goldstein 1976 and 1983.

METHODOLOGICAL INTRODUCTION TO PART I

1. On the former proposition, see Asad 1993, 27–54. On the latter, see Bell 1992, 13–29, and 1997, 3–22.

2. Geertz's influential paper "Religion as a Cultural System," in particular, contributed to its late propagation. See Geertz 1973 [1965]. On Geertz, see in particular Asad 1993, 27–54, and below in this chapter, §I.

3. On this notion, see the historiographical survey of the General Introduction, §§2 and 4.

4. This section is heavily indebted to Asad 1993, 27–54.

5. Geertz 1973 [1965], 91.

6. Geertz 1973 [1965], 98–99; see Asad 1993, 43.

7. Geertz 1973 [1965], 100; see Asad 1993, 45.

8. Geertz 1973 [1965], 93; see Asad 1993, 32.

9. See Asad 1993, 47.

10. For a different, historically more accurate classification, see Potter 2003, 424–26.

11. See the General Introduction, §5.1; and below, Chapter 1, §1.2.

12. Asad 1993, 31–33.

13. "It is not mere symbols that implant true Christian dispositions [in pre-Enlightenment Europe], but power—ranging all the way from laws (imperial and ecclesiastical) and other sanctions (hellfire, death, salvation, good repute, peace) to the disciplinary activities of social institutions (family, school, city, church) and of human bodies (fasting, prayer, obedience, penance). . . . It is not the mind that moved spontaneously to religious truth, but power that created the conditions for experiencing that truth" (ibid., 35). Quotation in text: ibid., 33.

14. Ibid., 47.

15. Ibid.

16. Ibid., 39. Asad (ibid., 40–42) argues that Geertz's definition of religion as a matter of symbolic meaning linked to ideas of general order (Geertz 1973 [1965], 98–108) is also the legacy of the philosophical speculations of the seventeenth century about Natural Religion. The latter were prompted by the combined impact of the Great Discoveries and the wars of religion.

17. This example is inspired by Scheid's (2005, 23–43) description of the complex sacrifice to Dea Dia that was performed every year by the Roman Arval Brethren. Scheid offers a meticulous and extraordinarily vivid reconstruction of the set of gestures that unfolded over three days and constituted the sacrifice.

18. Scheid, ibid. Kuhrt 1990b, 150–54, gives a similar description of the complementary functions carried out by a wide array of craftsmen in the service of the gods in Babylon. See below, §I.3.1.

19. See Potter 2003, 408–13.

20. See Schmidt 2001 [1994], 198–243, based on Mary Douglas's well-known theory (Douglas 1966).

21. See the General Introduction, §§2.2 and 2.3.

22. For a critical overview, see Nongbri 2005, and below, Chapter 8, §8.3.2.

23. On the conception of ritual as goal-oriented, see Parker's (2005, 158–59, with further bibliography) critical comments applied to ancient Greek ritual. I borrow my examples from Parker's p. 158.

24. On Bringmann's extreme instrumentalist view, see the General Introduction, §2.3.

25. My comments on the relationship between conceptions of ritual and the self in the premodern and modern eras are heavily indebted to Asad 1993, 55–79.

26. Ibid., 65.

27. Ibid., 67. Compare the following quotation from Deuteronomy 13:1–4, which takes for granted that deeds and feelings ("love") are one and the same: "If prophets or those who divine by dreams appear among you and promise you omens or portents, and the omens or the portents declared by them take place, and they say, 'Let us follow other gods' (whom you have not known) 'and let us serve them,' you must not heed the words of those prophets or those who divine by dreams; *for YHWH your God is testing you, to know whether you indeed love YHWH your God with all your heart and soul.* YHWH your God you shall follow, Him alone you shall fear, His commandments you shall keep, His voice you shall obey, Him you shall serve, and to Him you shall hold fast."

28. See for instance Bell 1992; Humphrey and Laidlaw 1994. Parker 2005, 155–91, applies these revised definitions to a case study of ancient Athenian festivals.

29. Hierarchy between gods and men: see Scheid 2005, 58–70; giving the gods their share of honor: Parker 2005, 158.

30. "In performing an act in ritualized form *as* a ritual act, you perform it as you do, and not some other way, just because it is so prescribed, and not because it makes sense to you to do so, or because you have reasons for doing so. You have reasons only for 'enacting the ritual,' and whatever those purposes may be, the way to 'get it right' as a physical act remains the same": Humphrey and Laidlaw 1994, 167. My quotation does not reproduce the original context exactly. See below, §I.2.2.

31. See further below, Chapter 6, commentary to Daniel 1:31 and 1 Maccabees 1:47b.

32. See, for instance, the Babylonian diary of Month V 143 S.E., quoted below in Chapter 10, §10.3.4, with the commentary there.

33. See Parker 2005, 158. On ancient Greek rituals as shared experience and memory, see further Chaniotis 2006.

34. Parker 2005, 159.

35. Asad 1993, 55–79, who analyzes the case of Christian discipline in medieval monasticism. See further Bell 1992.

36. On theories of ritual as performance, see Bell 1997, 72–76. The notion of apt performance is Asad's (1993, 62).

37. Smith 1987, 109–11, has stressed the importance of the ritual sequence.

38. On the notion of imitation as a way of learning virtue, see Asad 1993, 63. Jokiranta 2006 argues that the figure of the Righteous Teacher of the Qumran community was a social prototype: that is, an abstract model in which a given social group projects what its members construe as their typical traits. The prototype encapsulates the specific identity of the group, serving both to reinforce in-group cohesiveness and to stress its differences with outsiders. Individual members are encouraged to identify with the prototypical figure and to follow his model in everyday life.

39. Bell 1992, 70–74; quotation from p. 74. See further Smith 1987, 102–17; Humphrey and Laidlaw 1994, 167.

40. Kuhrt 1990b, 150–51; quotation from p. 151.

41. Ibid.

42. *IG* I³ 52; English translation in Fornara, no. 119, ll. 15–16. On the meaning of *hosios*, see Rudhardt 1992, 30–36.

43. *Miqṣat Ma'aśe Ha-Torah*, "Some Works of the Torah." See the list of abbreviations.

44. See Koenen 1993, 48–81.

45. *OGIS* 90 (the Rosetta Stone) = Austin, no. 283, l. 26.

46. Koenen 1993, 70. See further Koenen 1959, 110–12; Veïsse 2009.

47. See the historical survey in the General Introduction, §4.

48. The full argument will be presented below in §5.2.

49. Kuhrt 1990b, 153. Waerzeggers (2011, 735) objected to Amélie Kuhrt's view that the personnel serving in the Babylonian temples cannot be subsumed under a single category that we may call "priests," pointing out that the various professional categories involved were organized by a single system of prebends (*isqu*): that is, the allocation of a source of regular income against the regular performance of a specific task in the temple. By this logic, we may justifiably use a single term to designate them, provided that the word "priest" indicates "an active participant in the institutional, temple-based worship of the gods." In the present perspective, the key element of the priestly category lies in its economic contract with the temple—a person receiving an income from the temple for the performance of a skilled service in the temple, irrespective of the fact that said person could also exercise other activities outside the temple.

50. Ibid., 153 and 150. As she stresses, "it is a vexed question how the two [temple administrative officials and royal officials] were separated and what might have been their respective spheres of competence" (ibid., 150).

51. Ibid., 150–53.

52. Ibid., 153 and 154.

53. As Christophe Nihan points out to me, the royal and priestly functions were also linked to two institutions, the palace and the temple, albeit not in a one-to-one relationship, since there were priests serving in the palace, chapels for gods in the palace too, and conversely the king was actively involved in temple life. Moreover, in the Babylonian and Ugaritic myths of creation the temple is the god's palace. Actually, as we shall see in Chapter 2, §2.1, Near Eastern myths of creation, and the narrative pattern of temple building to which they are related, bring this four-part nexus—king, priest, palace, and temple—together into a coherent whole.

54. Kuhrt 1990b shows through a meticulous analysis that modern scholars who have studied Babylonian society with modern categories of religion and politics in mind have drawn a completely erroneous picture of the relations between kings and priests there.

55. See Cole 1994, 220–21, for the description of the text and 222 for its title. On this text and similar ones, see also Waerzeggers 2011, 738–40.

56. These examples are taken from cols. ii and iii of the text.

57. Kuhrt 1990b, 154. See further Waerzeggers 2011.

58. The respective duties of Neo-Babylonian and Judean kings toward the temples were roughly similar, especially since neither had the authority to officiate as cultic agents but needed the mediation and assistance of priests. This was in marked contrast to Assyrian kings, who held priestly titles and assumed priestly roles in ritual. On Neo-Babylonian kings, see Waerzeggers 2011, 733–38; on Assyrian kings, Machinist 2006. According to the Assyrian royal ideology the king was the representative of the gods on earth. As such the king was the mediator between the human world he governed and the divine world "that furnish[ed] the ultimate authority over the created order." See Machinist 2006, 152. I thank Christophe Nihan for pointing out this matter to me.

59. The Apocalypse of Animals is dated to Hellenistic times. Translation: Olson 2004, 201.

60. "We have indeed sent you some of the precepts of the Torah according to our decision, for your welfare and the welfare of your people. For we have seen [that] you have wisdom and knowledge of the Torah. Consider all these things and ask Him that He strengthen your will and remove from you the plans of evil and the device of Belial so that you may rejoice at the end of time, finding that some of our practices are correct. And this will be counted as a virtuous deed of yours, since you will be doing what is righteous and good in His eyes, for your own welfare and for the welfare of Israel" (4QMMT, Composite Text, e, ll. 26–32).

61. 4QMMT, Composite Text, e, ll. 25–26. Unfortunately it cannot be proved whether this text was genuinely intended for the ruler or is merely a staged dialogue.

62. This, indeed, may be one reason why this narrative pattern has not been identified in 1 and 2 Maccabees by biblical scholars thus far, although it is familiar to them.

63. The circumstances of this shift will be examined in Chapter 2. As Christophe Nihan points out to me, there was no alternative to kingship in the political thought of ancient Near Eastern societies.

64. On the Hebrew notion, see Chapter 2, n. 70.

65. Isaiah 24:16 (sg.); Proverbs 12:12 and Isaiah 26:7 (pl.). I am grateful to Katell Berthelot for help in this inquiry.

66. See the discussion of Tcherikover 1959, 46, with further bibliography. Parenthetically: the rabbinic tradition about Simeon the Just (*Šim'on ha-ṣadiq*) corroborates the transfer of royal virtues to the high priest.

67. It may be noted that in Greek too justice (*dikaoisynē*) may be associated with piety (*eusebeia*), whereas the two adjectives *dikaios* (just) and *hosios* (pious) are commonly paired. See Rudhardt 1992, 13, 32.

68. "Judas, also known as Maccabee, in a group of about ten, withdrew to the mountains, where he and his men eked out a living like beasts. There they stayed, eating herbs for food, in order to keep clear of defilement" (2 Macc. 5:27). On the importance of the dietary laws as an identity marker for Judeans of Hellenistic times, see my commentary to 1 Macc. 1:62–63 below in Chapter 6, §6.3.1 and in Honigman forthcoming.

69. Kaestli 2007; Perdue 2008. The clearest exposition of the old view is Collins 1997, 24–26. See also the studies critically reviewed by Seow 2008. For an alternative picture in which priests and scribes are closely associated, see B. G. Wright 2008, 147–63.

70. In Perdue's view (2008, 266), "the book of Ben Sira represents a conservative, although not reactionary, position of those Jews of Eretz Israel who did not wish to participate too dramatically in the new social and cultural metamorphosis of Judaism in the province, including Jerusalem, and yet were still open to engaging new insights and challenges." In contrast, "Qumran and Leontopolis became reactionary centers against the Hellenization of Jerusalem and Jewish religion."

71. For a summary, see the General Introduction, §4. Capdetrey 2007 and Manning 2010 are important proponents of the new comprehension of the Hellenistic states. A *status questionis* of the continuity-and-break issue between Persian and Hellenistic times is offered in Ma 2012.

72. Gauthier 1997. On the *gymnasia* of Ptolemaic Egypt, see Habermann 2004; Clarysse and Thompson 2006, 2:133–35.

73. Potter 2003 stresses the continued centrality of concerns about purity in Greek religious praxis of Hellenistic times.

74. See Capdetrey 2007; Manning 2010. See further Strootman 2013; Gorre and Honigman forthcoming; and Chapter 10, §10.2 below.

75. For Egypt, see Gorre 2009 and 2013. In Babylonia, the Persian and Seleukid kings could play one temple against another.

76. On the Greek education of Egyptian priests, see Clarysse and Thompson 2006, 2:125-33. On their coping with Greek culture, see Dieleman 2005; Moyer 2011, 84-141. On the priestly elites of Babylon, see Strootman 2013 and below, Chapter 10, §§10.2.4 and 10.3.4.

77. It will be tackled in Chapters 3 and 5, §§3.3 and 5.1, respectively.

CHAPTER 1. 2 MACCABEES AS DYNASTIC HISTORY

1. For the early historiography of 2 Maccabees, see the survey by Tcherikover 1959, 381-82; Doran 1981, 84 with n. 30; and 2012, 3. As noted by Doran (1981, 84), Niese's (1900) categorization of 2 Maccabees as tragic history is still accepted by Bickerman 1937 (and Bickerman 1979) and Habicht 1976.

2. The sequence is known to biblical scholars from Deuteronomy 28-39. Nickelsburg 2003 [1971], 668, tracks parallels with Deuteronomy 28, 30, 32. See further Nickelsburg 1981, 118; D.R. Schwartz 1998b, 228, argues that the four-part sequence is more specifically inspired by Deuteronomy 32. However, contrary to what the phrase "Deuteronomic view of history" implies, the pattern is well documented throughout the ancient Near East, and by no means specific to the Deuteronomist. On the state of the question among biblical scholars, see the collected papers in Pury, Macchi, and Römer 2000.

3. See the historiographical survey of the General Introduction, §5.1.

4. See in particular Goldstein 1976 and 1983.

5. Doran 1981; Henten 1997 and 2003.

6. Doran 1981.

7. See the historiographical survey of the General Introduction, nn. 24 and 25.

8. See the Methodological Introduction to Part I.

9. D.R. Schwartz 2008; Doran 2012.

10. D.R. Schwartz 2008, 7-8.

11. Ibid., 3 (emphasis added).

12. Ibid., 6.

13. On Schwartz's arguments to support this claim, see, for example, ibid., 46, 48-49.

14. Ibid., 46, 48.

15. Ibid., 48.

16. Doran 2012, 6.

17. Ibid., 1-17.

18. Ibid., 3-4. See further ibid., 13.

19. Henten (1997, 25-26), Williams (2003, 77-78), and Doran (2012, 12-13) note the division according to the four Seleukid reigns but neglect both its combination with the other two elements and the crucial fifth cycle.

20. The reason why Jason and Menelaos are paired together and associated with Antiochos IV, rather than being distributed between Antiochos IV's and Antiochos V's time units, will be examined below in this chapter, §§1.4.2 and 1.4.4.

21. By "local" I mean Judahite/Judean in the narrower sense, and ancient Near Eastern in the wider.

22. See the Methodological Introduction to Part I, §I.3.1.

23. In accordance with their concept of the individual, the ancients were convinced that a person's character traits were familial in nature (and hence clannish, dynastic) and not that individual's own. This fact would seem to invalidate the claim that the author of 2 Maccabees admired Judas Maccabee but did not support the Hasmonean dynasty of his time. (See in particular Goldstein 1976 and 1983.) Depicting the founder of the ruling dynasty in a favorable light is a fundamental signifier of political support for the ruler himself. Wiseman 1979, 12–26, showed how this tenet about the familial definition of character was essential to Roman historiography. Historians had no doubt they could reconstruct the early history of the Republic by extrapolating from contemporary experience. Munnich forthcoming argues that the author of 1 Maccabees lent to Alexander the Great (1 Macc. 1:2) features that in the book of Daniel are related to Antiochos IV (LXX and MT Dan. 8:24–25). Munnich's discussion points to a deliberate borrowing.

24. *Pace* Ego 2007, 151 ("it is made clear that the temple itself stands directly under God's protection"), and Zsengellér 2007, 184 ("the main theme of the epitome is to proclaim the successful defense of the temple against foreign pagan aggression.").

25. That is, it is not optional.

26. Doran 1981, 79–81. See further the detailed analysis of these passages in Henten 1997, 19–23, and 2003, 64–65.

27. Goldstein's translation is slightly modified here.

28. Henten 2003, 65, is probably correct in noting that *historia* in 2:24, 30, and 32 must be translated as "history" and not "inquiry": "i.e. a written account of certain events" (p. 65). However, the difference between the two meanings should not be pressed too hard. As Henten himself shows, 2 Maccabees does not merely relate events but provides a frame of interpretation.

29. Thus D. R. Schwartz 2008, 3–6.

30. D. R. Schwartz 2008, 5.

31. Doran 1981, 12–23, and 2012, 11. On 2 Maccabees 3 (the Heliodoros story), see Doran 1981, 20–21. In assessing the status of the Heliodoros story two issues need to be distinguished, namely the literary history of the passage itself and the moment when it was inserted in 2 Maccabees. There can be little doubt that the Heliodoros story began as an independent source, perhaps as a self-contained narrative unit. D. R. Schwartz 2008, 4–6, has made the cogent point that, unlike the rest of the work, the story uses generic rather than personal names (e.g., "the high priest" and not "Onias"). Moreover, he points out close literary similarities between the Heliodoros story and the one found in 3 Maccabees 1–2. However, the independent origin of this narrative unit leaves open the question whether it was inserted in the work by the author of 2 Maccabees himself or was interpolated at a later stage by other hands. The methodologically acceptable way to answer this question is to decide whether the Heliodoros story has a function in the overall balance of the literary composition of the work. Curiously, Schwartz (ibid., 6) concluded that the story of Heliodoros belonged to the original composition but was part of the prologue. Doran's conclusion (1981) that the Heliodoros narrative unit has its place in the body of the work is more convincing, since it is supported by a detailed analysis of the work's composition. The alter-

native analysis of the composition of the work proposed below in Chapters 3 and 4 will stay in line with Doran's conclusion.

32. D. R. Schwartz 2008, 6.

33. The capacity of one narrative component to stand for the whole sequence in a synecdochic relation (*pars pro toto*) is a well-documented mechanism. See for instance Clifford 1984, 186, and below in the Methodological Introduction to Part II, n. 6.

34. Doran 1981 and 2012; Henten 1997 and 2003. This is the pattern found in the festal letter of 2 Maccabees 1:10b–2:18.

35. On the Judean historiographical tradition, see Ben Zvi forthcoming.

36. The attention to causality shown by the author of 2 Maccabees is sometimes set against the alleged lack of interest in cause and effect that modern scholarship attributes to the author of 1 Maccabees. However, this verdict on 1 Maccabees, which is mainly inspired by the paratactic style used to narrate the events in the first chapter, is wrong. The two authors simply employed different rhetorical tools to express causality. The paratactic style is an elaborate rhetorical tool that allows him to knowingly suppress causality. For instance, it effectively generates the impression that Antiochos attacked the Judeans *unprovoked*. And if his attack was not legitimate, then implicitly the rebellion against him was. In subsequent chapters we find that causality is expressed through temporality. In particular, the purification and refoundation of the temple triggers a series of reactions from the neighboring peoples and the king (1 Macc. 5:1–2, 6:8).

37. The latter is Doran's phrase (1981, 94).

38. For an early Near Eastern example see, for instance, the bilingual (Sumerian and Akkadian) fragmentary historiographical text of middle Babylonian time known as The Seed of Kingship, which reflects on the removal of Marduk's statue by the Elamites. The departure of the god symbolized by the abduction of his statue is ascribed to divine wrath against the deeds of the king. See the edition and translation by Lambert 1967. (I owe this reference to Christophe Nihan.) For Hellenistic and Roman times, see the examples quoted by Doran 1981, 89–95.

39. Doran 1981, 47–48; Henten 2003, 79–82.

40. Plb. 23.10, 17; Livy 40.5–24. See Doran 1981, 89–90.

41. See further the list of instances gathered by Doran 1981, 95; Ego 2007, 146–48.

42. These digressions are 2 Maccabees 4:16–17, 5:17–20, and 6:12–17. See D. R. Schwartz 1998b, 227, adding 7:18 and 32 and 10:4. On the latter two, see further Doran 1981, 53–54; Henten 1997, 135–40.

43. For a discussion of this reverse mechanism in Roman religion, see Scheid 2001, 35–45.

44. The identification of the *gymnasion* as the trigger (the "cause") of the entire crisis, as well as the meaning of the semantic field of Greekness in 2 Maccabees, will be dealt with in Chapter 5, §5.1.

45. "He who had perpetrated many sins regarding the altar (the fire and ashes of which are holy) met his death in ashes."

46. It may be worth noting that Josephus is at odds with 2 Maccabees in ascribing the creation of the *gymnasion* to Menelaos and not to Jason (*Ant.* 12.240–41). Menelaos, moreover, is presented as Jason's brother. Traditions associating Menelaos with the *gymnasion* could only strengthen the credibility of the *talio* of the ashes, but the fact remains that the author of 2 Maccabees does not use them.

47. This discrepancy between Bickerman's view and Menelaos's literary portraiture has been underscored many times. See Goldstein 1976, 159; Millar 1978, 10–11 and 17; Gruen 1993, 259.

48. See Herodotus's distinction between pretexts and real intentions in his account of Darius's and Xerxes' expeditions against Greece (6.44 and 94 and 7.138), Thucydides' well-known methodological introduction (1.23), and Polybius 3.6–7.3 and 12.18.2–11.

49. Prosopographical studies confirm that some at least of the royal officials named in 2 Maccabees were historical figures. See Chapter 9 n. 32.

50. To quote Goldstein's apt paraphrase of *doryalōtos*.

51. For its function in the Bickerman-Tcherikover paradigm, see the historiographical survey of the General Introduction. For a different historical outline, see Chapter 6, §6.1, and Chapter 11, §11.1.3.

52. Bickerman 1979, 12 and 18, already pointed out the systematic removal of any Judean responsibility in initiating warfare in 1 and 2 Maccabees. Bickerman interprets this feature in the context of Judean politics, a far more convincing reading than Doran's. The latter (1981, 68–70) sees an apologetic purpose in it, aimed at addressing charges of misanthropy raised against Jews in the diaspora.

53. On the reason to speak of sin and retribution and not a Deuteronomic view of history, see above, n. 2. The original study was presented in Nickelsburg 2003 [1971], 668. A revised version of the table found there is included in Nickelsburg 1981, 118. That is the one reproduced here.

54. See the survey of the scholarship in Henten 2003 68, n. 13. Further surveys in Williams 2003, 76–78 (the prologue of 2 Maccabees [2:19–32] is of no help in determining the issue of the work's composition, *pace* Williams ibid., 76); Doran 2012, 11–12.

55. Doran 1981, 47–50. See further Henten 2003, 79–85, and now Doran 2012, 6–7. The two best-documented examples are the Festival of the Isiteria in honor of Artemis Leukophryene in Magnesia-on-Maiandros (Asia Minor) and the Festival of the Soteria at Delphi, refounded on a Panhellenic scale by the Aitolians.

56. Doran 1981, 47, and 2012, 6.

57. Doran 1981, 47 and 104.

58. Doran 1981, 49–50 and 103–4, and 2012, 6; Henten 2003, 79–82. The best-known catalogue of epiphanies is that of Lindos, which lists the apparitions of Athena Lindia. The inscription dates to 99 B.C.E.

59. Doran 2012, 6.

60. For the etiological account of the Isiteria festival in Magnesia-on-Maiandros, see Burstein, no. 30; Rigsby 1996, 185–90.

61. Henten 1997, 23–36, and 2003, 66–71.

62. Henten 1997, 26, and 2003, 68. Williams 2003, 77–78, similarly proposed a fourfold composition.

63. Henten, 2003, 68.

64. Doran 1981.

65. As noted above, D. R. Schwartz 2008 rejects the working hypothesis that 2 Maccabees is shaped by any narrative pattern and reverts to a linear analysis of its structure, including the interpolation theory. Doran 2012, 12, subscribes to Henten's (and Williams's) proposals that 2 Maccabees is composed of four parts corresponding to the four Seleukid

reigns, and moreover accepts Henten's correction that the narrative pattern of temple liberation (which he defines in four parts: "challenge to the deity; battle; victory of the deity; celebration concerning the temple") is repeated twice and not thrice in the narrative (ibid., 7). Curiously, however, he makes no attempt to combine these two principles in his own proposal of the book's compositional structure (ibid., 12–13). For additional proposals since Nickelsburg, see the survey by Doran ibid., 12.

66. See above, §1.2.1A, and below, §1.4.4.

67. It is analyzed in Chapter 4, §4.1.

68. The rationale for naming the high priests before the kings is explained below, in the opening of §1.4. For the definitive revised synopsis of the composition of 2 Maccabees, see Appendix B. The authorial comment of 2 Maccabees 15:37c–39 may be ignored.

69. Or, conversely, high priests and local kings in remote allegiance to the Seleukid king.

70. On commentators' bewildered responses to the fact that 2 Maccabees ends at this juncture, see the survey in Doran 2012, 9–10.

71. Doran 1981, 57–58 and 63–68, shows that the sections dealing with battles in 2 Maccabees were carefully constructed from a literary point of view. See further ibid., 1, and Doran 2012, 7–8 ("He did not want to have Antiochus repeal the harsh measures against the ancestral traditions of Judea or have Menelaus in any way try to ameliorate the situation": ibid., 7), and therefore inserted Antiochos IV's death before the temple liberation and postponed his account of the peace negotiation to Antiochos V's reign. Goldstein 1983, 66–67, argued that the chronological manipulations aimed at harmonizing the description of the battles with Daniel's prophecies.

72. See the historiographical survey of the General Introduction, §§2 and 3.3B.

73. For a theoretical overview, see Zerubavel 2003.

74. On the modern conception, see Anderson 1991, 22–31, quoting Benjamin 1973, 265. The malleability of experienced time has been extensively studied in Greek and Roman cultures as well as in ancient Judah. For Greece, see the collected papers in Darbo-Peschanski 2000; Clarke 2008 studies the relationship between the construction and use of temporal frameworks and the writing of history. For Rome, see in particular Beard 1987; Wallace-Hadrill 1987 and 2005, 58–62. For Yehudite/Judean texts relating to Persian times, see for example Japhet 2006b; Ross Bedford 1995. On cyclical time in LXX 1 Esdras, Honigman 2011. Rotstein forthcoming distinguishes between the denotational and connotational functions of time references. The former simply date events, whereas the latter add social and cultural significance to time.

75. An anecdote told by Herodotus about Egypt (2.143) illustrates a similar idea: when Hekataios of Abdera and Herodotus visited the priests of Thebes years apart, the latter counted the 345 statues of their successive high priests before their hosts. These statues represented all the intervening human generations since the last god and hero had been seen on Earth.

76. On the notion of the "four monarchies" in the Greco-Roman tradition, see Swain 1940; Momigliano 1983.

77. The idea of the succession of *politeiai* is most famously illustrated in Polybius 6.3–10.

78. See Massar 2000, 242. On this inscription, see further Higbie 2003.

79. Schmidt 2001 [1994], 38. However, it is not certain that Josephus referred to the temple in the absence of native political rulers, as Schmidt suggests.

80. For Babylon see Sommer 2000. See further Chapter 2, §2.1.

81. The complexities of multiple time-reckoning systems for synchronizing events occurring in different places spurred Greek historians to look for a Panhellenic system when an interest in universal history evolved in the late fifth century. The most popular solution was the four-year cycle of the Olympiads. See Fornara 1983. The best-documented example of a linear system is the Seleukid era (S.E.), which dissociated time from individual rulers. See Bickerman 1984, 61–62. In 262 B.C.E. Ptolemy II set up a new calendar based on a four-year cycle of three years of 365 days and one year of 366. This reform was linked to his institution of the Ptolemaieia, the penteteric festival in honor of his father, Ptolemy I, and its stated goal was to ensure that the festival would consistently be celebrated in winter. The new era was started between 1 January and 25 April 262 B.C.E. and was used for dating issues of coinage. See Le Rider 1995, 398, with further bibliography. The earliest examples of linear civic eras come from Seleukid Phoenicia—e.g., the era of Arados starting in October 259. See Rey-Coquais 1974, 149–61. Foundation eras became numerous after Pompey toppled the Seleukid empire in 63 B.C.E. However, objective and embedded systems of time reckoning still coexisted in the city of Rome under Augustus. Bowersock 1990 points out that the sundial that Augustus built in Rome marked his dates of conception and birth.

82. For the ideology of Hellenistic Greek kingship, see Walbank 1984; Ma 2003b. Manning's description of Ptolemaic Egypt as a state of the premodern, non-Western type now provides the conceptual background for situating this ideology in a definite material setting. See Manning 2010, 55–72, and further below, the opening section to Chapter 8.

83. On the Hellenistic court institution of the *philoi* see, for example, Le Bohec 1985; Strootman 2011a.

84. The same is true in 1 Maccabees.

85. Doran 1981, 57–58 and 63–68, shows that the sections dealing with battles in 2 Maccabees were carefully constructed from a literary point of view.

86. See, for instance, the career of Jonathan that emerges from 1 Maccabees. Jonathan is first acknowledged as high priest by Alexander Balas, and is also given the aulic rank of a *philos* of the king (1 Macc. 10:20). At a later stage, Balas grants him the right to wear purple clothes (10:62), enrolls him in the list of Friends of the First Rank, and appoints him as *stratēgos* and *meridarchēs* (10:65). In turn Demetrios confirms Jonathan in the high priesthood and in his other privileges, and has him reckoned among the Friends of the First Rank (11:27). Finally, Tryphon confirms him in the high priesthood in the name of King Antiochos (11:57). On Jonathan's career, see Bickerman 1938, 40–46.

87. On the latter, see the summary in Honigman 2003, 66–81.

88. The few references to Lysias in Polybius refer only to his regency under Antiochos V (Plb. 31.7.2–4 and 11.1–9).

89. For the details see Habicht 2006c [1976], 114–23, summarizing his view in Habicht 1976, 7; D. R. Schwartz 2008, 394–95; Doran 2012, 7.

90. These devices allow dissociation between the time of a given action and its account. Analepsis is "a narration of a story-event at a point in the text after later events have been told"; and a prolepsis, "a narration of a story-event at a point before earlier events have been mentioned." See Rimmon-Kenan 1983, 46; Prince 1987, 5 and 79. Thucydides' use of these narrative techniques has been studied by Rood 1998, from which the quotations from Rimmon-Kenan are borrowed (Rood 1998, 11).

91. On the evolution of the structures of power in Judah/Judea in Persian and Hellenistic times, see Chapter 2, §2.2.

92. See Honigman 2011, 190. That paper further analyzes the technical aspects of the literary montage and the symbolic function of the cyclical composition.

93. As in the Uruk Prophecy. See Beaulieu 1993.

94. Concerning Antiochos IV and Jason, this presentation is likely to be correct, since Antiochos IV became king in 175 B.C.E., and Menelaos had already overturned Jason when Antiochos IV led his (first? or second?) campaign in Egypt, in either 169 or 168 B.C.E. Moreover, Menelaos must have been in charge for at least one year, since he failed to deliver the promised payment (2 Macc. 4:27). Since the text claims that Menelaos overturned Jason "three years later" (2 Macc. 4:23)—i.e., two years later according to the modern reckoning—the modern dating of Jason's seizure of the high priesthood to 175 or 174 B.C.E. must be correct. In contrast all other montages are suspect.

95. D. R. Schwartz 2008, 8, takes it as evidence that 10:1–8 is an interpolation. See the response of Doran 2012, 7–8.

96. "There was a certain Alkimos, *who had previously been appointed high priest* but had voluntarily defiled himself during the times of purity" (2 Macc. 14:3; my emphasis). Goldstein 1983 translates *amixia* as "peace," but changing the usual connotation of the term to a temporal one is unnecessary in the present context. The literal connotation of the word, "purity," lends additional strength to the verb *molynō*, "to defile." Even though *chronoi* may have the meaning "periods," like *kairoi*, I understand it as referring here to ritual times (Sabbaths and festivals, *sabbata kai heortai* taken together). The use of the plural further accentuates the effect of *hekousiōs*, "voluntarily," to amplify the charge and suggests either a pure slander or a protracted ritual quarrel between rival schools of interpretation of the Law. Whatever the details, there can be no doubt that this proposition aims at delegitimizing Alkimos.

97. The evidence from 1 Maccabees and Josephus is inconclusive. 1 Maccabees 7:5 concurs with 2 Maccabees about chronology, but given that the characters of high priests are altogether erased before this point of the narrative, the fact that 1 Maccabees does not mention an earlier appointment of Alkimos does not mean anything. Josephus, *Antiquities* 12.387 and 20.235, claims that Iakimos, identified with Alkimos by modern commentators, was appointed high priest by Antiochos V Eupator and Lysias following Menelaos's execution. The reference to Lysias would suggest the time of Antiochos IV's anabasis to the eastern satrapies, during which Lysias was left in charge of the western part of the empire. In view of the analepsis of 2 Maccabees, Josephus's sequence may well be correct. It also makes sense unless we believe that Menelaos was executed a very short time before the king's assassination, therefore leaving him no time to institute a new appointment. However, we cannot exclude the possibility that Josephus just filled in a time gap with material of his own devising.

98. As we saw above (§1.3.4), the division between the rules of the kings denotes the division between the two subunits.

99. On the Uruk Prophecy, see Beaulieu 1993. The categorization of this text as a prophecy is modern, and Beaulieu (ibid., 50) noted its similarities with the genre of chronicles and chronographic texts.

100. The dissociation between the king and his wicked counselors is a well-known literary device. It is attested in Polybius (e.g., Ptolemy VI and Eulaios, 28.3.21) and 3 Maccabees.

101. Beaulieu 1993, 41.

102. In view of the author's use of ethnic labels in the work, it is highly possible that the term "Hebrews" excludes not only the Seleukids but also the wicked enemies from home. The mechanism of pseudoethnic otherization of internal rivals and equation of the social in-group with the boundaries of the ethnic group will be analyzed in depth below in Chapters 3 and 5, in §§3.3 (*Ioudaïsmos*) and 5.1 (*Hellēnismos*).

103. See above, n. 23.

104. "The king's thoughts had roused him to barbarous fury as he came intending to show the Judeans *far worse treatment than they had received under his father*" (my emphasis).

105. See the Methodological Introduction to Part II and below, Chapter 5, §5.1.

106. Bickerman 1979; Tcherikover 1959. Bringmann 1983 was more cautious.

107. Properly speaking the total disruption of the sacrifices is narrated together with the stories of the exemplary deaths and therefore is included in the subunit of the reconciliation process (2 Macc. 6). However, the final part of the disruption unit depicts Antiochos IV's plunder of the temple and the first atrocities (2 Macc. 5:11–26). As is argued below in Chapter 6 (§6.1), this narrative section does not refer to a distinct historical episode as compared to the persecution accounts, but it may be seen as a prolepsis.

108. Against D. R. Schwartz 2008, 8.

109. Habicht 2006c [1976]. On these letters, see also Mørkholm 1966, 155–57 and 162–65; and Bringmann 1983, 41–51. Habicht's reconstruction has been questioned by Ma (2013).

110. Habicht 2006c [1976], 112.

111. For 2 Maccabees, see above, §1.3.4, with note 71.

112. Mørkholm 1966, 156; Habicht 2006c [1976].

CHAPTER 2. TEMPLE FOUNDATION AND ROYAL LEGITIMACY

1. Doran 1981; for a summary, see Doran 2012, 6–7. Doran speaks of theomachy rather than temple propaganda. See Chapter 1 (§1.3.2).

2. See Doran 1981, 47, and 2012, 6: "The attackers approach, the defenders ask help of the deity, the deity responds, the attackers are repulsed, and the defenders rejoice."

3. For examples of divine epiphanies that are unrelated to the context of temple liberation in the Greek and Roman world, see Doran 1981, 97–98; in the biblical corpus, ibid., 99. For collections of epiphanies associated with the context of a military siege in the Hellenistic world, ibid., 103–10; for the book of Esther and 3 Maccabees, two texts emanating from Judean diasporan circles, ibid., 107–9.

4. My use of the names Judah, Yehud, Judea, Judah/Judea is explained in the General Introduction, §8.

5. Hurowitz 1992. See also Laato 1994, 56–62.

6. On Nehemiah, see Hurowitz 1992, 118–24. In the royal inscriptions of Neo-Babylonian kings, the fortification of Babylon's city wall "guaranteed the continuation of the offerings" in Marduk's Esagila temple, whereas the great East Wall erected at several miles from the city center of Babylon was meant to "strengthen the protection of the Esagila temple." (These examples are quoted from Waerzeggers 2011, 727.) The Assyrian inscriptions dealing

with the construction of temples and royal palaces down to Tiglath-Pileser III (747–727 B.C.E.) have been studied by Lackenbacher 1982. On the palaces, see also Lackenbacher 1990.

7. See 2 Samuel 7 (David) and 1 Kings 6:11–13 and 9:4–9 (Solomon). On sacral kingship see the overview by Albertz 1994 [1992], 114–22. See further Johnson 1967; Ishida 1977. This ideology is alluded to in the title of Hurowitz 1992 (*I Have Built You an Exalted House*): the king builds the house (temple) of his patron deity and the latter promises him a house (i.e., a dynastic continuity) in return. See further below, §2.1.2C.

8. On usurpers as restorers of order, see Kuhrt's remarks (1987, 41, 43–44). The legitimizing rhetoric based on the delegitimation of the former king is analyzed by Kuhrt and Sherwin-White in conjunction with the accounts of Alexander's reception by the Babylonians. Their analysis shows that this motive, which is attested over a very long period of time, was still part of the political culture of Babylonia at the fall of the Persian empire. See Kuhrt and Sherwin-White 1987.

9. This argument is also made by Regev 2008. However, Regev erroneously contends that the use of the temple for political legitimization was a Hasmonean innovation.

10. For a detailed exposition of this argument, see Chapter 1, §1.1–2.

11. For this typology see Hurowitz 1992, 27–28.

12. The Mesopotamian material is surveyed period by period in Hurowitz 1992, 32–92. For the mythical material, see ibid., 93–96. The Ugaritic material is studied ibid., 97–105.

13. For an overview, see ibid., 106–25.

14. Ibid., 131–310. The first references follow the Hebrew Bible and correspond to Hurowitz's references (1992). The references in square brackets follow *NRSV* wherever there are divergences.

15. Ibid., 106–10 and 135–36.

16. Psalms 47, 93, 96, 97, 98, and 99. The original study was Mowinckel 1921–24. For an English translation, see Mowinckel 1962. See further Eaton 1976, 87–134.

17. Hurowitz 1992, 111–13.

18. Whereas modern usage speaks of the Second Temple, the ancient Judean sources present the new building as the refoundation of Solomon's temple, obviously because they are primarily concerned with stressing the continuity between the new edifice and Solomon's temple. Insofar as the continuity motif will prove relevant to understanding the description of the temple rededication (refoundation) in 2 Maccabees, the edifice built in early Persian times will be referred to hereafter as a refoundation, not as the Second Temple. Nevertheless the term "Second-Temple era" will be retained for convenience when referring to periodization. On Ezra 1–6 and LXX 1 Esdras, see the bibliography quoted in Hurowitz 1992, 113 n. 1; add Edelman 2005, 151–208 (on the literary structure of Ezra 1–6), and Honigman 2011 (on 1 Esdras). On Haggai-Zechariah 1–8, see Edelman 2005, 131–47; Sérandour 1996.

19. On 2 Maccabees 1:18–2:18, see Honigman 2011, 199–200. On its thematic links with the narrative of 2 Maccabees, see Bergren 1997; Regev 2008. On Josephus, see Hurowitz 1992, 124–25.

20. Edelman 2005, 138, 159–62.

21. Edelman 2005, 151.

22. See Chapter 1, §1.3.4. As we saw in this chapter, §1.3, the status of the time unit of 2 Maccabees 10:10–13:26 is debated among modern scholars, some associating it with the preceding section (4:7–10:9) but others with the following one (14:1–15:37a).

23. The narrative units telling the Hanukkah story (2 Macc. 10:1–8, 1 Macc. 4:36–61, 2 Macc. 5:27–13:26) are analyzed in Chapter 3 (§§3.1 and 3.2, respectively) and the two last units of 1 and 2 Maccabees in Chapter 4 (§§4.2 and 4.1, respectively).

24. See the Methodological Introduction to Part I.

25. For a short survey of the cosmic symbolism of the temple and its role in uniting heaven and earth in Mesopotamia and Judea, see Cohn 1993, 137–38.

26. In Mesopotamian inscriptions the procession bringing the statues of the god and his consort into their proper place in the newly built temple was the climax of the dedication rites. See Hurowitz's (1992, 45) comment on the Gudea Cylinder B. On the rites of introduction of the gods to their houses in Assyrian inscriptions, see Lackenbacher 1982, 134–38. Solomon, likewise, had the ark carried into the temple (1 Kgs 8:1–9), and the glory of YHWH filled the edifice as He entered His house (1 Kgs 8:10–11).

27. Kapelrud 1963. On royal patronage of the temple, see Galling 1949–51.

28. See the Methodological Introduction to Part I.

29. On the distinction between the two types of myth, see Fisher 1965, 316.

30. The temple of the king-deity is equivalent to the palace of a human king. Moreover, the gods' houses have an ambivalent status, being palaces in the world of the gods depicted in the myths but temples in the cities of men. On this issue, see Clifford 1984, 198.

31. See Clifford 1984 and 1994. As he comments (1984, 186–87 and 201): "Ancient cosmogonies were primarily interested in the emergence of society, organized with patron gods and worship systems, divinely appointed kings or leaders, kinship and marriage systems"; "the 'world' which comes into being in the cosmogonies … is not simply the physical planet; it is the world of men and women living in a defined land, secure from enemies, with social and cultural systems well established. The order which the cosmogonies describe is the benign arrangement of the elemental forces to support human life."

32. An English translation of the myth of Enuma Eliš by Foster is found in Hallo and Lawson Younger 1997, 390–402. See Hurowitz's analysis of the myth (1992, 93–94). For English translations of the Baal cycle, see Gordon 1949; Gibson 1978. On this cycle, see Kapelrud 1952.

33. See the following note.

34. In Enuma Eliš the conflict opposes Marduk (whom the elder gods have acknowledged as their king) to Tiamat, the Sea Monster. In Ugarit, Baal fights either Yam, the Sea Monster, or Mot, Death. See Clifford 1984, 189–98, who argues that the battles of Baal against Yam and against Mot belong to two distinct myths whose narrative pattern is similar. In the Hebrew Psalms of Enthronement YHWH battles against either the Sea (Rahab, Leviathan) or the Desert (the place of infertility and death). On YHWH's taming of the Sea, see Psalms 74:12–17, 77:14–21, 89:9–12, 114; Exodus 15. His taming the desert: Psalm 78:41–55, Deuteronomy 32:7–14, Deutero-Isaiah 43:16–21. See Clifford 1984, 189 n. 17. On the similarities between YHWH's battle against the Sea and Baal's in the Ugaritic material, see Cohn 1993, 132–34, with additional bibliography ibid., 246 n. 7.

35. Clifford 1984.

36. References to texts articulating a similar notion are gathered by Kuhrt 1987, 30. On the palace as a concrete symbol standing for the abstract idea of kingship and rule over hostile forces, see Clifford 1984, 188 and 192. See further Fisher 1965, 318–20.

37. I follow Clifford's reconstruction of the myth (1984, 192).

38. Clifford 1984, 197.

39. Fisher 1965, 322. Gray 1979, 7–38.

40. The dating of Daniel 7–12 to the time of Antiochos IV is largely agreed upon. See, e.g., Collins 1993a, 61. The cosmogonic origin of the themes found in Daniel 7 has been recognized by many scholars, although it remains disputed. Collins 1993b offers a good historiographical survey that addresses the most common objections, in particular the chronological gap between the Ugaritic material and the time of redaction of the book of Daniel. He further proposes a slightly inflected restatement of the theory. More recently see Lacocque 2001, with earlier bibliography (116–17 n. 11). For Deutero-Isaiah, see Fisher 1965, 322–24; Clifford 1984, 189 n. 17; Lacocque 2001, 117 with n. 12.

41. Part of these texts was discovered at Qumran; others belong to the corpus of the Pseudepigrapha, which was transmitted through continued manuscript tradition. The book of the Watchers (1 Enoch 1–36) and the Astronomical Book (1 Enoch 72–82) preserve original myths of creation, whereas the Animal Apocalypse (1 Enoch 85–90) presupposes an historical outline of Israel's past that is not entirely compatible with the historical narrative of the biblical canon.

42. The pioneering study about the complex of Creation, temple building, and divine kingship in the Psalms of Enthronement and the identification of the Festival of Booths (Sukkoth) as their setting is Mowinckel 1921–24. See Eaton 1976, 87–134, which includes a survey of the rites of New Year and enthronement in the surrounding cultures.

43. The same continuity is demonstrated in Babylonia. The poem of Enuma Eliš was recited annually in Marduk's temple during the Akītu, the New Year festival, which was still celebrated in its traditional way in Seleukid times. In the days of native kingship, the temple was also the place where kings were first proclaimed and annually reinstated in their function during the same festival. On the complex ritual of the Akītu and its function, see Kuhrt 1987, 31–36; Sommer 2000.

44. Sérandour 2009, 92–93.

45. Sérandour 1996. See further below, §2.2.1.C.

46. The genre of royal building inscriptions is not documented in Ugarit.

47. For an overview of these six parts, see Hurowitz 1992, 64 and, further, 56 and 109–10. The present survey also makes use of the detailed summary found in Edelman 2005, 131–32.

48. As we see, the sin-retribution motif is embedded in the six-part pattern. On this motif, see the General Introduction, §5.1, and Chapter 1, §1.2.

49. For the fixing of norms as a topos of building accounts, see Kapelrud 1963. On destinies, see Lackenbacher 1982, 73, with the corresponding curse that kings who damage the edifice will either lose their kingship or be deprived of descendants (ibid., 163–64).

50. This inquiry will be pursued in the next chapter.

51. For temple building as the privilege of victorious gods and kings, see Kapelrud 1963; Hurowitz 1992, 82–83. For the link between victory and kingship, see Ishida 1977, 6–26.

52. Kapelrud 1963, 56–57; Hurowitz 1992, 93–94.

53. Ibid., 82–83, 93. See Hurowitz's inscription synopses, ibid., 74, 75 (drafting of captives to work in construction by Assyrian kings), 82, 83 (Nabopolassar). On Assyrian inscriptions, see also Lackenbacher 1982, 151–54.

54. On David and Solomon, see 2 Samuel 7 and 1 Kings 5:3–5 [4:23–25] (with 1 Kgs 4:20–5:1 [4:20–21]), with Hurowitz 1992, 93. The same motif is used about Moses as well. See

Kapelrud 1963, 61. On HZ, Zechariah 1:15, 18–21 [2:1–4], and 2:7–9, 13 [2:3–5, 9]. See Edelman 2005, 134. Sérandour 1996, 14, points out that Darius is explicitly referred to as king in Haggai 1:1 and 2:1 and Zechariah 7:1, the title indicating he is acknowledged as God's representative on earth in these texts.

55. See Edelman 2005, 160. Sérandour 1996, 14, understands that the victory vindicating the refoundation of the temple was Cyrus's.

56. On the Cyrus Cylinder, see Kuhrt 1983, 85–87. English translation by Michalowski in Chavalas 2006, 428–29.

57. Arrian 3.16.3–4, with 7.17.2–4; compare Curtius 5.1.19–23.

58. Arrian 3.16.5. On Alexander's acts in Babylon see Kuhrt 1990a. On the motif of the reconstruction of the temples neglected by the usurper's predecessor, Kuhrt and Sherwin-White 1987.

59. 2 Samuel 7, 1 Kings 9:3–9.

60. See above, n. 7. Sérandour 1996, 19, points to the different quality of the two promises: unconditional to David, conditional to Solomon—i.e., coupled with YHWH's threat to withdraw his support from Solomon's house should the king's sons depart from YHWH's way.

61. 1 Kings 9:3, Haggai 2:9. See Sérandour 1996, 16.

62. 2 Samuel 7:1, 1 Kings 5:4–5 [4:24–25]. See Kapelrud 1963, 60; Edelman 2005, 142.

63. Ibid., 134.

64. Zechariah 6:1–6, together with 2:6–13 [2:2–9]. See Edelman 2005, 136.

65. Gudea Cylinder A, cols. XIII.3–XIV.6. See Hurowitz 1992, 39. English translation of Gudea Cylinders A and B in Jacobsen 1987, 386–444.

66. See the Weld-Blundell Cylinder of Nabonidus, quoted by Hurowitz 1992, 39 n. 6.

67. Edelman 2005, 136.

68. See again Gudea Cylinder B, col. IV.15–21. See Hurowitz 1992, 43.

69. Ezra 1–6. See Edelman 2005, 151–208.

70. Smith 1993, 129–46 and 147–71, dubbed the social ideal in which the king and everyone in society strive to conform to the divine order a "locative world-view." His description is still suggestive, provided Geertz's concept of the worldview is discarded. The concept of social justice was expressed in Mesopotamia, Ugarit, and Judah by means of an hendiadys. In Hebrew, the most common pair of words was ṣedeq and mišpaṭ, "justice and righteousness." To follow Cohn's concise definitions (1993, 139), mišpaṭ denotes "the regular rule or government of Yahweh as king, and so the divinely appointed order itself." Ṣedeq "was the principle underlying the divinely appointed order." Ṣedeq is usually translated "righteousness," but as Cohn points out, it is better rendered "rightness," since "righteousness" introduces an anachronistic hint of morality. In Ugarit it is the "beneficent manifestation of the sun god . . ., who watched over the world as judge, bringing hidden crimes to light and righting wrongs done to the innocent." The visible manifestation of YHWH's activity was called ṣedaqah, a word derived from the same root as ṣedeq. "Everything that was right and proper, from Yahweh's bestowal of the right amount of rain at the right season to his furious smiting of the foes of Israel, was included in [z]edaqah." In turn, šalom, "peace," is the result of ṣedeq. (Cohn, ibid.) On the meaning of "ṣedeq and mishpaṭ," see Weinfeld 1995, 25–44. For "justice and righteousness" as a divine ideal, see ibid., 27–28; as the king's task, ibid., 45–56. For divine concern for justice in the Pentateuch, see Epztein 1986, 113–15. The link between the divine order and

social justice may be illustrated by the following verse: "So that they keep the way of YHWH by dealing with righteousness and justice" (Gen. 18:19), quoted by Weinfeld 1995, 30.

71. Or alternatively the plan of the edifice is revealed to them in a dream.

72. See the inscription synopses in Hurowitz 1992, 40 and 56 (Gudea Cylinder), 73, 76. On royal wisdom, see Kalugila 1980, who surveys Egypt, Mesopotamia, and the western Semitic area. On royal wisdom in Assyrian inscriptions, see Lackenbacher 1982, 67. Compare YHWH's promise to Joshua, Zechariah 3:7, Sérandour 1996, 19; on Solomon's wisdom, 1 Kings 3:9–12 (to govern); 1 Kings 5:12 [4:32] (to build the temple).

73. See also below, §2.2.1.

74. The present discussion combines the historical outlines proposed by Lipschits 2006, Sérandour 2009, 83–98, Nihan 2010, and a personal communication by the latter. Any inaccuracies are mine.

75. Sérandour 1996. However, Sérandour's depiction of the constellation of power that prevailed in Yehud under the Achaimenids as a dyarchy needs to be corrected. For the updated view, see Sérandour 2009, 83–98, and Nihan 2010, 94–100. In the present discussion the notion of dyarchy will be replaced with that of a division of power, after Christophe Nihan's suggestion to me. On the traditions about the temple refoundation preserved in HZ, see further Edelman 2005, 131–47.

76. On the myth of empty land, see Becking 2006; Ben Zvi 2010. Ben Zvi uses the theoretical concept of social memory to explain the genesis of the traditions as we now have them. On social memory, see Connerton 1989.

77. For the historical side, see the overviews by Lipschits 2006 and Sérandour 2009, 83–98.

78. See Lipschits 2006, 34–35, who dismisses the view that Judah was part of the province of Samaria until the days of Nehemiah.

79. *TAD* A4.1. Chronological reconstructions vary in detail, one point of contention being whether the reconstruction of the temple was the cause or a consequence of transferring the administrative capital back to Jerusalem. Edelman 2005, 332–51, advocates the view that it was its consequence, while dating the administrative reform to the reign of Artaxerxes I (565–525 B.C.E.); the opposite view is defended by Lipschits 2006, 30–40, who argues that Jerusalem became the capital of Yehud because of "internal Judean (or Jerusalemite) social, economic, political and demographic processes" and not as the result of a Persian planned policy. In his view, the decisive factor was that the temple had already been rebuilt. Lipschits dates the change in the city's status to Nehemiah's mission (ca. 445 B.C.E.) because of the latter's reconstruction of the city wall, pointing out that provincial capitals were fortified cities. The temple was rebuilt about two generations earlier, during Darius I's reign (522–486 B.C.E.), a date also endorsed by Nihan 2010, 92.

80. As the Passover papyrus (*TAD* A4.1) attests.

81. See Nihan 2010, 94.

82. Sérandour 2009, 87 (governor), 88–91 (high priest). For a more conservative study of the high priests of Judah/Judea in Persian and Hellenistic times, see VanderKam 2004; Brutti 2006.

83. Haggai 1:1, 12, 14.

84. Ibid., 2:2–9.

85. Ibid., 2:20–23. These verses are part of the editorial framing. Similarly Zerubbabel is singled out as the sole receiver of YHWH's conditional dynastic promise in the vision of

Zechariah 4. See Sérandour 1996, 16–19 and 23–27. Although the imagery used in the promise inserted at the end of the very book of Haggai is definitely royal, Sérandour (ibid., 17) insists that this passage does not allude to an attempt to reinstate the native kingship. Zerubbabel is nowhere hailed as king, the signet ring simply referring to his position as governor (Sérandour, ibid., 23). Conversely, Joshua rather than Zerubbabel is the one who is promised access to the divine council: i.e., wisdom and knowledge about the divine plans of Creation (Zech. 3:7), an honor that had been granted to Solomon (1 Kgs 3:9–12 and 5:9–14 [4:29–34]). See Sérandour, ibid., 19–20.

86. Haggai 1:1; 2:1.
87. Ibid., 1:1, 12, 14, and 2:2, 4–5, respectively.
88. This is why I prefer to speak of a collectivization of the royal prerogative to build rather than follow Edelman 2005, 133, 137, 139, who labels it a democratization. See also Chapter 3, §3.1.5A, and the Methodological Introduction to Part I.
89. Sérandour 1996, 16–17.
90. "For thus says YHWH of hosts: 'Once again, in a little while, I will shake the heavens and the earth and the sea and the dry land, and I will shake all the nations, so that the treasure of all nations shall come, and I will fill this house with splendor,' says YHWH of hosts. 'The silver is mine, and the gold is mine,' says YHWH of hosts. 'The latter splendor of this house shall be greater than the former,' says YHWH of hosts; 'and in this place I will give prosperity,' says YHWH of hosts" (Haggai 2:6–9).
91. Compare Hurowitz's (1992) step 2. On the gathering of material from the ends of the earth in view of the reconstruction of YHWH's temple in Ezra 1–6, see Halpern 1990, 90; Edelman 2005, 160. Tournay 1991 offers a detailed study of the representation of theophanies through the visual and aural images of lightning and thunder in the Psalms. The divine title "Lord of Hosts" (*YHWH Ṣeba'ot*) refers to YHWH's majesty as the dweller of the temple of Jerusalem under the native monarchy. It is related to the Ark of the Covenant—that is, the throne of the divine king (Num. 10:35–36). See the bibliography in Sérandour 1996, 13 n. 17, to which add Tournay 1991, 113.
92. Sérandour 1996, 15.
93. "The word of YHWH came a second time to Haggai on the twenty-fourth day of the month: 'Speak to Zerubbabel, governor of Judah, saying, "I am about to shake the heavens and the earth, and to overthrow the throne of kingdoms; I am about to destroy the strength of the kingdoms of the nations, and overthrow the chariots and their riders; and the horses and their riders shall fall, every one by the sword of a comrade. On that day, says YHWH of hosts, I will take you, O Zerubbabel my servant, son of Shealtiel, says YHWH, and make you like a signet ring, for I have chosen you, says YHWH of hosts'" (Haggai 2:20–23).
94. 2 Samuel 7 and 1 Kings 2:1–9.
95. Compare with 2 Samuel 7:1, 9, 11.
96. See also Haggai 2:18–19. Sérandour 1996, 17–18, explains the mention of Zerubbabel alone by Haggai's lack of competence to legitimize Joshua's rule, since the prophet is not a priest.
97. The ritual of the Sukkoth festival included music and hymn singing, which were conceived as representing visual and aural theophanies. See Tournay 1991, 112–30, and above, n. 91. On the overall passage see Sérandour 1996, 16–18.

98. 1 Esdras 1:40–41, 45, 54–56.

99. Catalogues of holy vessels: Ezra 1:9–11 = 1 Esdras 2:13–14; 1 Esdras 8:55–57. Catalogues of Returnees: Ezra 2:1–67 = Nehemiah 7:6–69 = 1 Esdras 5:7–46; Ezra 8:1–20 = 1 Esdras 8:28–49. On these catalogues as epitomes of the restored society see Honigman 2011, 204–7.

100. For a detailed discussion, see the Methodological Introduction to Part I.

101. Merchants: Nehemiah 13:15–22. On the foreign wives see Sérandour 2008.

102. In the second epistle prefacing 2 Maccabees, Nehemiah is identified as the builder of the temple and the altar (2 Macc. 1:18, 21–30). See Chapter 3, §3.1.5D.

103. "Solomon made a marriage alliance with Pharaoh king of Egypt; he took Pharaoh's daughter and brought her into the city of David, until he had finished building his own house and the house of YHWH and the wall around Jerusalem." (1 Kgs 3:1). I am grateful to Ehud Ben Zvi for drawing my attention to this parallel. Kuhrt 1987, 37, underscores a similar conceptual relationship between walls protecting cities and walls protecting temples.

104. Chronological issues are muddled, because the extant texts underwent a thorough editorial process. Lipschits 2006, 34–35, dates Nehemiah's mission to Jerusalem to 445 B.C.E.; Sérandour 2009, 91, situates it either in the mid-fifth or in the second half of the fifth century B.C.E. On the activities of Ezra and Nehemiah in Jerusalem, see Sérandour 2009, 91–98. Finkelstein 2008 argues against the historicity of Nehemiah's repair of the wall. On the ideological construction of time in EN, see Japhet 2006a [1994] and 2006c.

105. This is indeed Sérandour's reading (2009, 96–97). See Japhet 2006a [1994].

106. Hurowitz 1992, 118–24.

107. The following synopsis reproduces Hurowitz's numbering. See above, §2.1.2A.

108. On the catalogues, see above, §2.2.1D. Bodi 2008 has emphasized that the list of Nehemiah 3 refers to professional skills. While this aspect of the list makes sense in the context of the building works, the genealogical and geographical specifications show that the list had an additional, symbolic function similar to the catalogues of Returnees. In turn, the catalogue of Returnees inserted in Nehemiah 7:5–73 is presented as a catalogue of those who contributed to the work according to their ancestral houses (7:70).

109. Sérandour 2008, 160–62, argues that the verb "to separate," which is usually understood to refer to the repudiation of the foreign women, in fact refers to a ritual separation during the Sabbaths and festivals. See further Sérandour, 2009, 93–94, 97.

110. "From the days of Joshua son of Nun to that day the people of Israel had not done so [i.e., lived in booths]" (Neh. 8:17).

111. See Honigman 2011, 201–2. The context of the Festival of the Booths is emphasized by Sérandour 2009, 93.

112. Compare Ezra 3:10–13; 1 Esdras 5:58–62.

113. Ezra's precise status is unclear. What seems clear is that he was not the high priest. His reforms suggest that he enjoyed powers superior to the latter's, probably as the king's envoy. (See Sérandour 2009, 94.) If this was the case, the division of power as it is depicted in EN is an editorial construct.

114. According to 1 Chronicles 3:17–19, Zerubbabel and his sons were affiliated to David's line through Solomon and Jeconiah. The issue whether or not this genealogy is genuine need not detain us, since we are concerned with representations, not with factual accuracy.

115. Sérandour 2009, 93–94. About the date of the final edition of EN, see the historiographical survey by Grabbe 1992, 32.

116. Sérandour 2009, 93–94.

117. "The word of YHWH came to me: 'Collect silver and gold from the exiles.... Take the silver and gold and make a crown, and set it *on the head of the high priest* Joshua son of Jehozadak; say to him: "Thus says YHWH of hosts: 'Here is a man whose name is Branch: for he shall branch out in his place, and he shall build the temple of YHWH. *It is he that shall build the temple of YHWH;* he shall bear royal honor, and shall sit upon his throne and rule. *There shall be a priest by his throne, with peaceful understanding between the two of them*'"'" (Zech. 8:9–13; emphases added). See Sérandour 2009, 90. The dynastic alliance—i.e., the promise to found a dynasty—is symbolized by the image of the branch in the vision. Compare 2 Samuel 7 (David); 1 Kings 6:11–13 and 9:4–9 (Solomon).

118. Sérandour 2009, 90. It may have coincided with the disappearance of the Persian governor and his replacement with Greco-Macedonian governors, either in the wake of Alexander's conquest or under the Ptolemies, although this reconstruction is speculative. On the prestige and the sources of power of the high priest in Hellenistic times, see Watts 2007.

119. "Phineas son of Eleazar ranks third in glory, / For being zealous in the fear of the Lord.... / Therefore a covenant of friendship was established with him, / That he should be leader of the sanctuary and of his people, / That he and his descendants should have / The dignity of the priesthood forever. / Just as a covenant was established with David / Son of Jesse of the tribe of Judah, / That the king's heritage passes only from son to son, / So the heritage of Aaron is for his descendants alone" (Ben Sira 45:23–25). On the depiction of the high priests in Ben Sira, see Watts 2007, 325.

120. "The leader of his brothers and the pride of his people / Was the high priest, Simon son of Onias, / *Who in his life repaired the house* [of YHWH] / And in his time *fortified the temple.* / He *laid the foundations for the high double wall,* / The *high retaining wall for the temple enclosure.* / In his days a *water cistern* was dug, / A *reservoir* like the sea in circumference. / He *considered how to save his people from ruin,* / And *fortified the city against siege*" (Ben Sira 50:1–4, emphases added).

121. See also *Antiquities* 11:317–19.

122. On Hekataios, see Bar-Kochva 1996 and 2010, 90–135, to be read together with Wyrick 2011. The excerpt from Hekataios is quoted and translated in Stern, no. 11.

123. Although the date of the Letter of Aristeas is disputed, it is certainly later. Honigman (2003, 128–30) and Rajak (2009, 34) argue that it is datable to the second century B.C.E. on philological and literary grounds.

124. On the description of Jerusalem and Judea in the Letter of Aristeas, see Honigman 2004.

125. Honigman 2004 includes a survey of the specificities of the genre of the *politeia* in Hellenistic times, when it was appropriated by utopian geographers.

126. Johansen (2004, 7–23) has noted the close connection between Plato's *Republic* (*Politeia* in Greek) and the cosmogony and anthropogony of the *Timaeus*. But the topics of *politeia* and of cosmogony and anthropogony were, precisely, treated separately by Plato.

127. Herodotus, *Histories* 3.80–82.

128. Polybius, *Histories* 6.11–18. On the mixed constitution, see Hahm 2009.

129. "These are the words that Moses heard from God and declares unto the Jews" (trans. Stern, no. 1).

130. Whereas the term *theokratia* is first documented in Josephus's *Against Apion* 2.165, a text from the first century C.E., the excerpt on Judea from Hekataios and, even more clearly, the Letter of Aristeas 100-104 (together with 41) already call for it and leave no doubt that the concept, if not the term itself, went back much earlier. See Honigman 2004, 82-85.

131. For this date see now Winiarczyk 2002, 1-7. The main source for the travelogue is Diodorus Siculus 5.41-46.

132. Euhemeros's depiction of the *politeia* of his fictitious island drew inspiration from the Greek literary tradition about the Egyptian priesthood, in particular Plato's story of Atlantis (*Tim.* 17a-27b6 and *Critias*), and it is difficult to discern whether his knowledge about Egyptian priests was influenced by contemporary reports in addition to this bookish heritage. See Honigman 2009.

133. Aristotle, *Politics* 7.11.5, 1330b17-21.

134. See Honigman 2004, 82-85.

CHAPTER 3. *IOUDAÏSMOS* AS THE LEGITIMATE SOCIAL ORDER FOUNDED BY JUDAS MACCABEE

1. See Chapter 2 (§2.1.2A).

2. On this genre see, for instance, Beaulieu 1993; Weitzman 2004.

3. See the theoretical discussion of this issue in the Methodological Introduction to Part I.

4. The opinion that the author of 2 Maccabees invented the term is generally agreed upon in modern scholarship, and I endorse it in my analysis. See last D. R. Schwartz 2008, 173 at 2:21; Doran 2012, 67.

5. The notion of the divine order of the cosmos is equivalent to divine will and divine law. The prescriptions regulating food consumption, for instance, are part of divine law, because they reflect the divine order of the cosmos. On these notions, see the Methodological Introduction to Part I.

6. Metaphors: four great beasts (Dan. 7:3, 17, 23); ten horns and the additional horn (Dan. 7:7-8, 20, 24); ram and the male goat (Dan. 8:3, 5, 7-8, 20-21); the King of the North and the King of the South (Dan. 11:5-6, 11, and passim). The *pars pro toto* (the part stands for the whole) mode of quotation. On these two forms of synecdoche, see Clifford 1984, 187-88, quoted in the Methodological Introduction to Part II, n. 6. For the relevance of cosmogonies to our concerns, see Chapter 2 (§2.1). The notion of concentration upon one element without explicit reference to the whole explains why cosmogonies are relevant to the study of 1 and 2 Maccabees, even though this is counterintuitive to us (on which see further the Methodological Introduction to Part I). The reason why 1 and 2 Maccabees do not include any explicit cosmogony has to do with their literary genre, historiography.

7. Other possible objections are addressed elsewhere in this book. First, the possible impression of a forbidding time gap between classical Hebrew tradition and the time of 2 Maccabees' redaction is refuted by the diachronic survey of Chapter 2 (§2.2), which traces

the ongoing resurgence of the symbolic and political significance of the theme of temple building down to Hellenistic times (Ben Sira and the editorial framework of EN). Furthermore, Hurowitz 1992, 124-25, identifies the traditional narrative pattern in Josephus's description of Herod's works in *Antiquities* 15, which was written two centuries after the two Maccabees books. Second, in the Methodological Introduction to Part I (§I.3.2A) I advocate a conceptual equivalence between the Greek *eusebeia* (piety) in 1 and 2 Maccabees and the Hebrew notion of *ṣedeq* (righteousness). Third, the lack of a full-fledged cosmogony in 1 and 2 Maccabees is not a hindrance. As Clifford 1984, 188, points out, specific narratives frequently depict only one aspect of a complete narrative sequence, the rest being present by implication thanks to a deeply rooted cultural use of synecdoche. As we saw in Chapter 2 (§§2.1.1 and 2.2.1C), the cosmogonic elements that genuinely belong to the semantic field of temple building are usually dealt with in creation myths in Mesopotamia and in Ugarit, whereas in the Hebrew tradition they appear in the Psalms of Enthronement, prophetic texts (like HZ), and specific passages of the Pentateuch. In contrast, they are absent from historiographical works, such as EN and 1 Esdras. By their genre, 1 and 2 Maccabees are naturally closer to the latter. (Parenthetically: the cosmological background lurks in several authorial notations in 2 Maccabees, in particular in 2 Macc. 9:8.)

8. Regev 2008 also opines that the topical similarities between these texts have an ideological significance, although he misses the parallel in narrative pattern.

9. See further my summary in the introductory section of Chapter 2.

10. Hurowitz 1992, 106-10 and 135-36.

11. Ibid., 118. A similar narrative split is found in 1 Esdras. See Honigman 2011.

12. See Edelman 2005, 160.

13. The two texts 2 Maccabees 10:1-8 and 1 Maccabees 4:36-61 are presented as in Jonathan Goldstein's translations (1976 and 1983), slightly modified.

14. Josephus's account in *Antiquities* 12.316-26 is an embroidered paraphrase of 1 Maccabees and can be left aside.

15. See Chapter 2 (§2.1.2A).

16. Thus Zechariah 5:1-4 proclaims the establishment of justice prior to the beginning of the building works. War was the reason for David's incapability to build the temple, whereas peace allowed Solomon to carry out his father's intention (1 Kgs 5:3-4). See further 2 Samuel 7:15 and 1 Kings 5:18. On victory and temple building, see Chapter 2 (§2.1.2B).

17. Likewise the building of the temples of Marduk in Babylon and Baal in Ugarit are the climactic points of the creation in Enuma Eliš and the mythical cycle of Baal. See Chapter 2 (§2.1.1).

18. The second refoundation of 2 Maccabees 14:1-15:37a similarly includes unconventional and moreover totally implausible elements, in particular Judas's display of parts of Nikanor's body near the altar. These unconventional variants will be examined in detail in Chapter 4 (§4.1).

19. Hurowitz 1992, 131-34. See also Lackenbacher 1982, 57-64.

20. In 1 Maccabees the theme of the illicit altars and shrines appears in a different context. We first meet them when they are set up as part of a wave of atrocities that are perpetrated by Antiochos's men (1 Macc. 1:47; altars built outside Jerusalem in Judea: 1:54, 55). After that, their destruction throughout the land is attributed to Mattathias (2:45).

21. On the date formulas in temple-building accounts, see Hurowitz 1992, 224–33. In the Hebrew tradition, compare Ezra 7:15; 1 Esdras 1:22, 5:56, and 7:5. Also Haggai 1:1, 2:2, 10. Note the insistence in 1 Esdras that the ceremony of laying the foundation stone marks a new beginning: "In the second year after their coming to the temple of God in Jerusalem, in the second month, *Zerubbabel the son of Shealtiel and Joshua the son of Jozadak made a beginning,* together with their brethren and the Levitical priests and all who had come to Jerusalem from the captivity; and they laid the foundation of the temple of God on the new moon of the second month in the second year after they came to Judea and Jerusalem" (1 Esd. 5:56–57, emphasis added).

22. See Chapter 2 (§2.1.1). See further Regev 2008, 93–97.

23. On Solomon's ceremony, see 1 Kings 8:1–2. On Persian times, see 1 Esdras 5:48–51. In EN the celebration of Sukkoth (Neh. 9:1–3) follows the completion of Nehemiah's rebuilding of the city wall (Neh. 6:15) and the public reading of the Law (Neh. 8:1, 3). In contrast the ceremony of the dedication of the temple was followed by the celebration of Passover (Ezra 7:15–18, 1 Esd. 7:4–15).

24. Sérandour 1996, 15, pointing out that the editorial date found in Haggai 2:1 ("in the seventh month, on the twenty-first day of the month") corresponds to the last day of the festival. Moreover, the editorial verses framing HZ refer to "this house" and "this place" (Zech. 8:7, 9), and the use of demonstrative adjectives in his view suggests that the temple is already rebuilt when the account is told. However, see Edelman's (2005, 141) distinct albeit not necessarily incompatible interpretation of the date.

25. Emphasis added. The rite of lamentation mentioned in 1 Maccabees 4:39–40 does not seem to be an exact counterpart.

26. "When the builders laid the foundation of the temple of the Lord, the priests in their vestments were stationed to praise the Lord with trumpets, and the Levites, the sons of Asaph, with cymbals, according to the directions of King David of Israel.... And all the people responded with a great shout when they praised the Lord, because the foundation of the house of the Lord was laid. *But many of the priests and Levites and heads of families, old people who had seen the first house on its foundations, wept with a loud voice when they saw this house, though many shouted aloud for joy, so that the people could not distinguish the sound of the joyful shout from the sound of the people's weeping,* for the people shouted so loudly that the sound was heard far away" (Ezra 3:10–13; emphasis added). See also 1 Esdras 5:63–65.

27. Μακκαβαῖος δὲ καὶ οἱ σὺν αὐτῷ.

28. "And the people of Israel who came from the captivity ate [the Passover sacrifice], *all those who had separated themselves from the abominations of the peoples of the land and sought the Lord*" (1 Esd. 7:13; my emphasis).

29. On the continuity motif, see Ackroyd 1987; Hurowitz 1992, 264–65. On the similar function of the catalogues of the holy vessels and the catalogues of people in EN and 1 Esdras see Honigman 2011. In 1 Esdras, Nebuchadnezzar's removal of the holy vessels is mentioned three times in association with three successive Judean kings, Jehoiakim (1:39–42), Jehoiachin (1:43–46a), and Zedekiah (1:46b–57); and the vessels are likewise returned three times, each time together with Returnees: under Sheshbazzar's lead in King Cyrus's time; under Zerubbabel's lead in Darius's time; and under Ezra's lead in Artaxerxes' days.

30. On this notion of "sign," see Honigman 2011.

31. Note the pleonasm in 2 Maccabees 10:3: καὶ *πυρώσαντες* λίθους καὶ *πῦρ* ἐκ τούτων λαβόντες.

32. The reason for the narrative strategy of the author of 1 Maccabees in this matter will become clear when we turn to the analysis of Simon's unit in Chapter 4 (§4.2).

33. Although these epistles are secondary additions, the thematic relationship between the second one and the main account of 2 Maccabees is unmistakable, as shown by Bergren 1997. See also Regev 2008. Against D. R. Schwartz 2008, 8–9, I do not take this thematic connection to mean that the passage 2 Maccabees 10:1–8 was a late interpolation that is due to the redactors of the epistle, for two sets of reasons. First, because 10:1–8 is the keystone of the narrative pattern of temple building and interconnects with the longer section 2 Maccabees 5:27–13:26, and further with the last narrative unit, 2 Maccabees 14:1–15:37a, as this chapter and the next aim to demonstrate. Second, D. R. Schwartz's opinion overlooks the usual interplay between written text and the oral circulation of traditions. 2 Maccabees 10:3c and the content of the epistle undoubtedly echo each other, but a common redactor is not the only possible explanation why. The mention of the fire in 2 Maccabees 10:3c may perfectly antedate the redaction of the letter if we admit that both texts hinge on the same tradition that was circulated orally (or alternatively in written works that are no longer extant).

34. As Christophe Nihan indicates to me, the traditions narrated in the epistle may have been generated by the institution of the Hanukkah festival in Hasmonean times in order to provide the festival with the indispensable chain of tradition that it needed. Insofar as they draw on the same stock of traditions, to my mind the epistle casts light on the intention of the author of the main account.

35. For the fixing of norms as a topos of building accounts, see Kapelrud 1963. The imposition of social justice and the fixing of norms are set components of the narrative pattern of temple building. See Chapter 2 (§2.1.2A).

36. For my use of this phrase, see the diachronic survey of Chapter 2 (§2.2) and the Methodological Introduction to Part I (§I.3.1).

37. Edelman 2005, 133, 137, and 139.

38. On this practice, see Chapter 1, §1.4.1.

39. On the motif of reconciliation, see Hurowitz 1992, 140–43; Lackenbacher 1982, 71–72; Edelman 2005, 133, 134. See further Chapter 2, §2.1.2A.

40. "If [your people Israel] sin against you . . . and you are angry with them and give them to an enemy, so that they are carried away captive to the land of the enemy, far off or near; yet if they come to their senses in the land to which they have been taken captive, and repent, and plead with you in the land of their captors, saying, 'We have sinned, and have done wrong; we have acted wickedly'; if they repent . . . and pray to you toward their land, which you gave to their ancestors, the city that you have chosen, and the house that I have built for your name; then hear in heaven your dwelling place their prayer and their plea . . . and forgive your people who have sinned against you" (1 Kgs 8:46–50).

41. This section may be a secondary interpolation, since it has no structural function in the economy of the narrative, in contrast with the description of the atrocities perpetrated by Antiochos's men in 2 Maccabees 6:1–11. In the extant version, the original section, together with the author's exhortation to his readers in 6:12–17, may be seen as the necessary prelude to the account of the redemptory deaths.

42. Judas's time unit extends through 3:1–9:22.

43. Against Apollonios (1 Macc. 3:10–12), against Seron (3:13–26), against Gorgias (4:1–25), and against Lysias (4:26–35). In contrast, although 2 Maccabees 8:5–8 also alludes to more warfare antedating the temple's rededication, these events are succinctly summarized.

44. As pointed out by Zsengellér 2007, 192 with n. 35.

45. The story of the covenant at Mizpah is not found in 2 Maccabees.

46. S. Schwartz 1991, 25, has pointed out the echo with EN.

47. See further below, §3.3.2.

48. The parallel account in 1 Maccabees is 3:1–4:25.

49. The equivalence between *eusebeia* (piety) and *ṣedeq* (righteousness) is examined in the Methodological Introduction to Part I (§I.3.2).

50. See Weinfeld 1995, 44 (God) and 49 (Jeremiah's address to the kings of Judah, Jer. 22:3). For the protection of widows and orphans as a divine concern in the Pentateuch, see Epztein 1986, 113–15, who further quotes the Code of Hammurabi §§137, 173, 180–82 (Epztein 1986, 113). The addition of the murdered faithful to the widows and orphans in 2 Maccabees underscores the new importance of this theme in Judean society of the second century B.C.E.

51. As we saw in the Methodological Introduction to Part I (§I.2), true dispositions are manifested in deeds.

52. Goldstein 1983, 321, points out that the preparations for war follow the commandments of Deuteronomy 20:1–9.

53. I.e., unmediated by any leader.

54. The theme of the few against the many is found in 1 Maccabees also. See, e.g., 1 Maccabees 3:17–19 and 4:6–11, both in the account that is parallel to 2 Maccabees 8.

55. Cf. 1 Maccabees 4:8–11.

56. "Judas, also known as Maccabee, in a group of about ten, withdrew to the mountains, where he and his men eked out a living like beasts. There they stayed, eating herbs for food, in order to keep clear of defilement" (2 Macc. 5:27).

57. "Judas . . . and his men . . . enlisted the aid of their kinsmen and gained also the adherence of those who had remained faithful to *Ioudaïsmos*" (2 Macc. 8:1).

58. "Jason of Cyrene narrated the history of Judas Maccabee and his brothers, of the purification of the *greatest of temples* and the dedication of the *altar*, and also of the wars against Antiochos Epiphanes and his son Eupator, and of the epiphanies from heaven in favor of those who vied with one another in fighting bravely and gloriously for the sake of *Ioudaïsmos*; though they were a few, they took the spoils of the whole *land* and expelled the numerous Barbarians, recovered the *temple* famous in the whole world, freed the *city* and restored the *laws* which were on the point of being abolished. All this they accomplished because the Lord in the fullness of His grace became merciful of them" (2:19–22, emphases added).

59. Strictly speaking, the Hasmoneans were descended from Simon, and not from Judas. However, the figure of Judas is obviously exploited by them as their ancestor—exactly as Alexander was deceptively turned into the ancestor of their dynasties by the Ptolemies and the Seleukids.

60. In contrast to the traditional device of the synecdoche. See above, n. 6, and n. 6 of the Methodological Introduction to Part II.

61. These events, or at least the way that they were shaped by social memory, are told in EN and 1 Esdras.

62. For this assimilation of the in-group to the whole of the ethnic group and the ethnic "otherizing" of out-groups in the Yehudite/Judean political tradition, see Ben Zvi 1995. On the myth of "empty land," which is directly connected to this construction of in-groups and out-groups, see further Becking 2006; Ben Zvi 2010.

63. See, for example, Jokiranta 2006, 256: "On the theological level, group membership is described in terms of the law and the covenant: the members are those who keep the law (4QpPs^a II, 15; 4QFlor IV, 1–3; 1QpHab VIII, 1); they shall have the covenant blessings (4QpPs^a III, 1–5). Turning to the law and belonging to the covenant community seem to be criteria for the in-group membership."

64. See the discussion of *Hellēnismos* in Chapter 5 (§5.1).

65. See, e.g., Goldstein 1983, 479, and further Goldstein 1976, 64–65; D.R. Schwartz 2008, 471 at 14.6.

66. See note 62 above.

67. Detailed discussion may be found in Chapter 1, §§1.3.4 and 1.4.4.

68. The semantic fields of *Hellēnismos* and *allophylismos* will be examined in Chapter 5 (§§5.1.1A and 5.1.5, respectively).

69. On the Cyrus Cylinder, see Kuhrt 1983, 85–87. English translation by Michalowski in Chavalas 2006, 428–29. On the slanderous image of Nabonidus in the "Persian Verse Account" and the Cyrus Cylinder, see Kuhrt 1990b, 141–44. On the image of the Persians in the Greek historians of Alexander, see Kuhrt and Sherwin-White 1987.

70. See D.R. Schwartz 2008, 173 at 2:21.

71. E.g., 1 Maccabees 2:21, 27, 42, 50, 64, 67, 68; 3:21, 49–51, 58–59; 13:3–6; and passim.

CHAPTER 4. ROYAL HIGH PRIESTS AND TEMPLE FOUNDATION

1. As explained in the Methodological Introduction to Part I (§I.3), I use "priestly" and "royal" as alternative semantic categories to the modern "religious" and "political."

2. Funke 2011. This paper is part of Funke's Ph.D. dissertation, quoted here with his permission.

3. Translation modified.

4. Thus Carney 2000 has claimed that Alexander the Great consciously imitated Achilles' wrath. On the *imitatio Alexandri* of Roman generals of the Late Republic, see Spencer 2002, 165–203. Koenen 1993, 57–61, has shown how the persona of the Ptolemaic kings, like that of pharaohs before them, was assimilated to that of various Egyptian deities in the priestly decree of Memphis of 196 B.C.E. (*OGIS* 90 = Austin, no. 283). Moyer 2011, 142–207, has shown how the priest of Sarapis on Delos shaped the account of his trial according to the mythical struggle between Osiris and Seth. Jokiranta 2006 argues that the Teacher of Righteousness was a prototypical figure for all members of the Qumran community.

5. In the decree of the people voted in his honor according to 1 Maccabees, Simon is variously called *stratēgos*, *hēgemōn*, and *ethnarchēs* (1 Macc. 14:35, 41–42, 47). Aristoboulos was the first member of the dynasty to assume the royal title during his short reign, 104–103 B.C.E. Insofar as kingship in the two Maccabees books is a signifier denoting military power, the analysis put forward in this chapter is not evidence that the works were written after 104 B.C.E.

6. As the historical survey of Chapter 2 has shown, temple foundation originally was the preserve of the king but in Hellenistic times had come to be identified as part of the prerogatives of the high priest (e.g., Ben Sira 50:1).

7. Ben Sira (50:1–4) opted for yet another solution, assigning the prerogative of building all urban monuments, including the city fortifications, to the high priest.

8. See Chapter 3 (§3.1.6), and below (§4.3.1).

9. "Rescue us. . . . If not for our own sakes, act for the sake of Your covenants with our forefathers and for the sake of Your awesome and glorious names by which we are called."

10. On piety and impiety as virtues defining legitimate and illegitimate rulers, see Chapter 1 (§1.2). For the theoretical background, see the Methodological Introduction to Part I.

11. The term *Ioudaioi* is used subjectively to designate Judas's followers, while "Judeans" is used objectively, to refer to all the members of the *ethnos*. The reason for this denomination is argued in Chapter 3, §3.3.2B.

12. See also Chapter 3, §3.3.1.

13. Heavenly apparitions in support of Onias III: 2 Maccabees 3:25–34. They reappear as a favorable portent to Antiochos's expedition to Egypt (5:1–4) but change sides because of Antiochos's impious behavior (his so-called persecution). Judas, God's new champion, is bestowed personal protection by supernatural riders in the battle against Timotheos (10:29–30). A rider appears again at the call of Judas's men and that of the inhabitants of Beth-Zur (11:8).

14. Although Judas's protection of the widows and orphans in 8:28 is a traditional royal topic, Aperghis has argued that in 2 Maccabees it more specifically creates an intratextual link between Onias III (3:10) and Judas. See Aperghis 2011b, 32.

15. Cf. Jonathan acting as a judge in 1 Maccabees 9:73.

16. The purpose is to erase Menelaos's memory. See Chapter 1, §1.4.4A.

17. The parallel passage in 1 Maccabees 7:26–29 has a very different interpretation of Nikanor's exclusive attention to Judas, since Nikanor is said to have pretended to invite Judas to a friendly meeting with the aim of kidnapping him. Therefore the version of 1 Maccabees shows no change in Nikanor's mood from friendly feelings to hostility to comply with Demetrios I's own change of attitude (2 Macc. 14:15–30; cf. 1 Macc. 7:26–31). In 2 Maccabees the instigator of Demetrios I's change and therefore the culprit for the ensuing war, which put the temple in jeopardy, is Alkimos, whose wickedness is implicitly equated with that of Jason, who had put the temple in jeopardy by setting up the *gymnasion*.

18. Goldstein 1983, 476, introduction to linear commentary; D. R. Schwartz 2008, 498–515 and passim.

19. The thematic structure of the battle of 8:10–36 is analyzed in Chapter 3, §3.2.2.

20. D. R. Schwartz's translation (2008).

21. On purported intentions as a recurrent literary device in 2 Maccabees, see Chapter 5, §5.4.

22. See Woodman 1988, 70–83.

23. On Hezekiah and Sennacherib, see 2 Kings 18:13–19:35 and Isaiah 36–37. See Goldstein 1983, 500–501 at 15:22–24. The Galatians had moved from the Balkans to Asia Minor in the winter of 278/7 B.C.E. after being defeated by the Aitolians in the region of Delphi one year earlier. Between 275 and 268 Antiochos I put an end to their threat to the populations of Asia Minor by crushing them at the so-called "Battle of the Elephants." See S. Mitchell 2003, 283. Whereas the Galatians' incursions did not reach as far as Babylonia (Goldstein

1983, 331), we know of at least one contingent of Judean mercenaries stemming from Babylonia that was settled in Asia Minor by Zeuxis, Antiochos III's governor of the region (*Ant.* 12.148–53), and our author could have confused a battle won by Judeans from Babylonia with a battle won by Judeans in Babylonia.

24. As pointed out by D. R. Schwartz 2008, 427. See also Goldstein 1983, 439.

25. See Berthelot 2007, 48–49.

26. See the introductory paragraph to this section, above.

27. The victory against Sennacherib is referred to in the second locus alone in 1 Maccabees 7:41–42 (= 2 Macc. 15:22–23). See Goldstein 1983, 500 at 15:22–24. In 1 Maccabees 4:8–9 (= 2 Macc. 8:19–20) the simile selected is the onslaught of the Egyptians at the Red Sea.

28. See Chapter 3, §3.1.6A.

29. Antigonos Gonatas took the title *Sōtēr* (Savior) after vanquishing the Galatians in 277, and Antiochos I was first called *Sōtēr* after his own victory over Galatians in 275/268. Ptolemy I exploited a victory over the Gauls to enhance his royal prestige, and the incident received wide echoes in the court poetry of his day. A generation later Attalos I assumed the royal title in the wake of his defeating the Galatians. See S. Mitchell 2003, 283–84. On his commemorating monument, see Pollitt 1986, 79–97. The *koinon* of the Aitolians capitalized on their own victory politically and diplomatically by instituting a Festival of *Sōtēria* (Festival of the Rescue) at Delphi. See Nachtergael 1977.

30. *Contra* Henten (1999, 53), who argues that the references to the ancestral language of the Judeans that may be spotted in 2 Maccabees are to be read in the context of the "patriotic-political views of the Jewish people in the second century B.C.E." Language is also an issue in the book of Ezra-Nehemiah, in which it appears in conjunction with the prohibition against marrying foreign women. But whereas Nehemiah 13:23–24 deplores how the children of mixed marriages could not speak the language of Judah, Ezra 9:1–2 and 10–14 emphasize the issue of ritual purity as key, not language. Language and purity seem related, since Ezra had just instituted the public reading of the Law, and one needed to understand its reading in order to obey it and therefore refrain from impurities. In 4QMMT, the case of "the deaf who have not heard the laws and the judgments and the purity regulations, and have not heard the ordinances of Israel," is specifically addressed. See 4QMMT, Composite Text, a, ll. 52–54. It may also be noted that in the aretalogies of Isis of Hellenistic and Roman times the goddess is referred to as bearing many names. She was honored differently and by different rites under each one of these. This is most probably the meaning of Judas's addressing God "in the language of his forefathers." For an example of aretalogy, see Chapter 11 n. 98.

31. Goldstein's translation modified.

32. See Goldstein 1983, 476, introduction to his linear commentary.

33. In the parallel section of 1 Maccabees 7:5–18 the intrigue is more complex and involves many characters, both diluting Alkimos's responsibility and blurring the target of the treachery.

34. On Doran's paradigm of temple liberation, see Chapter 1, §1.3.2.

35. Goldstein 1983, 499 at 15:12, quotes a possible biblical model for the portrayal of Onias III in this verse.

36. Josephus alone preserves some information about Onias IV, in contrast with both 1 and 2 Maccabees. See in particular *Antiquities* 12.387.

37. Ben Zvi 2012.
38. Goldstein 1983, 499 at 15:14–17.
39. On heavenly apparitions to Onias and Judas, see above, n. 13.
40. Henten 2004 [2006].
41. The earlier text is the Canopos decree of 238 B.C.E. in honor of Ptolemy III Euergetes; and the last one, the second Philae decree of 185/4 B.C.E. in honor of Ptolemy V. Iconographic sources include the relief of the stele of Pithom, under which the Raphia decree of 217 B.C.E. is engraved; the stele of Damanhur, which contains one of the copies of the Rosetta decree. Two more reliefs adorn a pylon of the temple of Edfu, and the exterior eastern wall of the Isis temple at Philae, both of Ptolemaic times. All these references are quoted after Henten 2004 [2006].
42. Henten 2004 [2006], 15, takes the use of the sword motif in 2 Maccabees as evidence that the work circulated in Judean circles living in Egypt "during at least one stage of its transmission process," but his surmise overlooks the intense circulation of peoples and ideas between Jerusalem and Alexandria.
43. Henten 2004 [2006], 14–15, holds the use of the medium of the dream in 2 Maccabees as one further instance of Ptolemaic influence, pointing to the mention of the dream announcing to Ptolemy IV that he will be victorious against Antiochos III in the Demotic version of the Raphia decree in honor of Ptolemy IV. Pre-Hellenistic antecedents are recorded in Moyer 2011, 172, with nn. 93 (pre-Hellenistic texts) and 95 (the Raphia decree of 217 B.C.E.). The two interpretations are not incompatible. Another dream foretelling a victory, albeit in a lawsuit, is recorded in the Delian Sarapis aretalogy of the late third or early second century B.C.E. (*IG* XI.4.1299, ll. 26 and 76–80). As Moyer points out, the narrative pattern of dream commands originally emphasized the privileged relationship between the Ptolemaic king and either all the gods or the divine couple of Sarapis and Isis. The Delian aretalogy, which records no less than three dreams sent by Sarapis to his priest, is important evidence that outside Egypt the narrative pattern was taken over by priests and private worshippers. In the Delian aretalogy, the scheme of repeated dreams is used to legitimate a lineage of priests. For the text and a new translation, see Moyer 2011, 282–86; for Moyer's comments, see ibid., 165, 172–75.
44. This statement has no parallel in 1 Maccabees 7:49.
45. See below in this section for an interpretation of this literary construction.
46. See Chapter 2, §2.1.2A.
47. Henten 2004 [2006], 13–14. Henten holds the festival commemorating Judas's victory as one further Ptolemaic influence (p. 14). Interestingly, this is the significance of the festival in 1 Maccabees alone, since in 2 Maccabees it is (apparently in an overstated way) reinterpreted as commemorating the temple's salvation—i.e., as a festival of *Sōtēria*, to use a Hellenistic Greek term.
48. From a structural viewpoint, 2 Maccabees 15:37b, which refers to the blessings that follow from the ceremony of refoundation, is parallel to the section on Judas's victories (10:10–13:26) in the Hanukkah story.
49. See, for example, Goldstein 1976, 258–66 and passim, and 1983, 402–3.
50. See Chapter 2 n. 103. See also 1 Kings 7:1–12.
51. 1 Maccabees 4:36–61 at 41 and 60–61. See Chapter 3, §3.1.2.
52. For an overview of the compositional structure of 1 Maccabees, see Appendix A. Goldstein 1976, *ad loc.*, advocates relocating the Roman episode of 1 Maccabees 15:15–24

(according to the extant manuscript tradition) together with the Spartan episode of 1 Maccabees 14:16–24. This definitely increases the narrative coherence of the text. The suggestion is endorsed here on the basis of the assumption that the text of 1 Maccabees is a literary montage and not a linear chronicle of events.

53. The present discussion is unconcerned with the issues of the historical authenticity of the military actions or of the genuineness or not of the purportedly official documents inserted in Simon's time unit.

54. τὸ πνεῦμα τοῦ λαοῦ, 13:7.

55. See below, §4.2.3B.

56. 1 Kings 9:15–17. I owe this reference to Ehud Ben Zvi.

57. See its detailed analysis in Chapter 3, §3.1.

58. See Chapter 2, §2.2.3.

59. Compare "The temple was trampled, as foreigners were in the Akra" (1 Macc. 3:45b).

60. Compare "[Simon] succeeded in . . . expelling the inhabitants of the City of David in Jerusalem, *who had built themselves a citadel from which they used to go out and commit acts of defilement in the vicinity of the sanctuary and gravely impair its purity*" (1 Macc. 14.36; emphasis added).

61. Judas's attack on the Akra is narrated in 1 Maccabees 6:18–20 and 32. The story of the Akra in Jonathan's time opens a new cycle, which begins with Bacchides reinforcing the Akra anew (9:52–53; cf. Antiochos Epiphanes in 1:33–35) while Jonathan strengthens the city and temple fortifications (10:11; cf. Judas in 4:60). Thereafter, Jonathan mounts two assaults against the Akra (11:20–24; 11:39–43, 53) and eventually erects a wall in order to cut the Akra off from the city and starve its inhabitants out of the citadel (12:35–37), but he is made prisoner and murdered by Tryphon before seeing his plan through. His strategy is eventually carried out by Simon.

62. This issue will be treated in depth in the Methodological Introduction to Part II and in Chapters 6 and 7.

63. Henten 2001, referring to Hengel 1974 [1973].

64. Collins 1981, 238.

65. If we envisage the decree together with the hymn, we should not exclude the possibility that the ancient author was equally able to write a Greek decree of his own devising and to compose a hymn from piecemeal quotations from the Hebrew literature of his day. However, the issue of the authenticity of the decree as a "document" is of secondary concern in our present perspective. On this issue, see Henten 2001, 119, with further bibliography.

66. Collins 2000, 40, from which the quotation is borrowed. The intertextual allusions in the Hymns of the Teacher are collected in Carmignac 1959–60.

67. On the portrayal of the Teacher of Righteousness as a prototypical figure in the Commentaries on the Prophets (*Pesharim*) in Qumran, see Jokiranta 2006.

68. The following linear analysis is largely indebted to a list of intertextual references to biblical passages collected by Ehud Ben Zvi. See also Munnich forthcoming. Any errors are mine alone.

69. Verse 7bb may be a generic reference but may also allude to the specific narrative context of 1 Maccabees.

70. See the summary of Hurowitz's pattern in Chapter 2, §2.1.2A.

71. See above, n. 52.

72. Compare Ben Sira 50:1–4.

73. For the reappointment of officials at every new era see Chapter 1, §1.4.1.

74. On the technical aspects of the decree see Henten 2001.

75. "*Hēgemōn* and high priest," 14:35; "*hēgemōn* and high priest in perpetuity till a true prophet comes, as well as *stratēgos*," 14:41–42; high priest and *stratēgos* and *ethnarchēs* of the Judeans and the priests and president over all [*tou prostatēsai pantōn*]," 14:47; "priest and *ethnarchēs* of the Judeans," 15:1. Add 13:42: "high priest and *stratēgos* and *hēgemōn* of the Judeans."

76. According to ancient historians Alexander the Great was careful to keep the military and administrative functions distinct when he reorganized the local administrations of successive conquered satrapies. See Briant 1993, 17. Nonetheless, Capdetrey 2007, 287, notes that in the Seleukid empire the fundamental ambiguity of the word *stratēgos*, either civil governor or military commander, was concretely preserved in the prerogative of governors to command local military operations.

77. As stated in the introductory section of this chapter (n. 5), references to the semantic field of kingship do not necessarily date the redaction of the book to the period after Aristoboulos's assumption of the royal title in 104 B.C.E. In the two Maccabees books, kingship is a signifier denoting military power and therefore may cover various titles equivalent to "governor" (*hēgemōn, stratēgos,* and *ethnarchēs*) alongside kingship itself.

78. We may add 1 Maccabees 13:3. See above, §4.2.1.

79. On 1 Maccabees 15:15–24, see above, n. 52.

80. On Solomon, see above, n. 50; on Nehemiah, see Chapter 2, §2.2.2.

81. My attention was drawn to this intertextual allusion by Ehud Ben Zvi. See 1 Kings 11:41; 14:19, 29; and passim; 2 Kings 1:18, 8:23, 10:34, and passim; 2 Chronicles 13:22, 20:34, 25:26, and passim.

82. As pointed out to me by Ehud Ben Zvi. See 2 Kings 20:20: "The rest of the deeds of Hezekiah, all his power, how he made the pool and the conduit and brought water into the city, are they not written in the Book of the Annals of the Kings of Judah?"

83. "From that time on, the city has been held by the Hebrews" (2 Macc. 15:37b).

84. See Chapter 1, §§1.2, 1.4, and Chapter 3, §3.3.2C. The portrait of the rivals in 1 and 2 Maccabees is tackled in detail in Chapter 5 below.

85. See Chapter 1, §1.3.4.

86. On this alternative narrative pattern, see the General Introduction, §§5.1 and 6, and Chapter 1, §1.3.2.

87. See above, §4.1.2.

88. In 1 Maccabees Judas's genealogy is mentioned twice: in Mattathias's time unit (1 Macc. 2:1 and 54) and in the people's decree (1 Macc. 14:29). See Goldstein 1976, 330 at 8:16–23.

89. Hieke 2007 offers a line-by-line analysis of the intertextual connotations evoked by each of the names listed in Mattathias's Praise, and in particular points out the contrast between Mattathias's Last Words preserved in 1 Maccabees 2:49–70 and those lent to him by Josephus, *Antiquities* 12.279–84 (Hieke 2007, 61–62). In the two texts, Mattathias's Last Words "articulate a political message," but Josephus's program is composed in accordance with the cultural codes of the Greco-Roman social elite and nowhere uses intertextuality with exempla from Israel's past. See also Goldstein's linear commentary (1976, 6–8). On Ben Sira's Praise of the Fathers (44—50) see Chapter 2, §2.2.3. Hieke's observation (2007, 63) that

"there are completely different intentions behind" Ben Sira's and Mattathias's Praises may require closer examination.

90. For the details see Goldstein 1976, 6–7.
91. Funke 2011.
92. Goldstein 1976, 7–8.
93. Cf. the slightly different categorizing proposed by Hieke 2007, 74.
94. On Abraham, see ibid., 65–66.
95. On Joseph, see ibid., 66: "Joseph's reward for keeping the commandment is the power over Egypt ... or in other words, the justification of the exertion of political power through obedience to God's commandments."
96. Hieke (2007, 74) has similar conclusions.
97. Goldstein 1976, 7.
98. From a narrative viewpoint, Mattathias's zealous killing of the Judean man fulfills the same function as the faithful dying an exemplary death. Phineas's prototypical killing of the Israelite and the Midianite woman turned YHWH's wrath into mercy and put an end to the plague (Num. 25:11–13).
99. See Chapter 3, §3.1.5D.
100. Positing an interplay between a tradition crystallizing and being transmitted orally and its written transcription and reworking necessarily remains speculative when all that is extant is the written product. As a comparison, Ben Zvi has explained the formation and operation of the traditions reflected by Hebrew literature of Persian and early Hellenistic times about the Israelite past using the concept of social memory, which describes the reworking of past events into living traditions. See Ben Zvi 2011a and 2012. A similar process has been posited by Rajak 2009 to explain the genesis of the traditions about the translation of the Hebrew Pentateuch into Greek that underpin the account of the Letter of Aristeas. See Honigman 2003. On social memory, see Connerton 1989.

CONCLUSION TO PART I

1. For a detailed outline of the literary composition of the two works, see Appendixes A and B.
2. See the studies by Berthelot 2007; S. Schwartz 1991; Goldstein 1976 and 1983.
3. Doran 1981.
4. For a recent criticism of the notion of propaganda, or mission, see Moyer's (2011) commentary on the Delian Sarapis aretalogy, especially 144, 179, 181, and 194–207. Instead, Moyer argues for a strategy of self-representation.
5. Ben Zvi 2012. The emphasis is mine. Further, Ben Zvi 2011b. On social memory, see Connerton 1989.
6. Zerubavel 1997, 53–67.

METHODOLOGICAL INTRODUCTION TO PART II

1. For the notion of priestly and royal powers, see the Methodological Introduction to Part I (§I.3).
2. See in particular the analysis of 2 Maccabees 14:1–15:37a in Chapter 4 (§4.1).

3. In the two works, the desecration of the temple by Antiochos IV's men constitutes the final stage of the disruption, whereas the initial cause is imputed to the wicked high priests. See Chapter 1 (§1.4) and below, Chapter 7 (§7.2.3A).

4. The detailed analysis is presented below in Chapter 5 (§§5.1, 5.2). On the relation between Jason's and Menelaos's sins and Antiochos's subsequent total disruption of the temple service, see further Chapter 7 (§7.2.3A).

5. Berthelot 2006 argues that each work promotes a distinct "ideology of resistance," armed struggle and martyrdom, respectively. Given that Berthelot acknowledges that these two ideologies have a "religious" flavor, they may be seen as another token of complementarity rather than opposed backgrounds.

6. The term "synecdoche" denotes a single element that is chosen to represent either a complex narrative sequence or an abstract notion. The phrase *pars pro toto* (the part stands for the whole) is sometimes used to describe this synecdochic relation between the single element and the sequence it stands for. Thus as we saw in Chapter 2 (§2.1), the various components of the narrative pattern of temple building form so tight a semantic network that the mention of a single element is enough to evoke both the entire pattern and the abstract concept it emplots by synecdochic association. Here is how Clifford (1984, 187–88) illustrates the two forms of synecdoche in commenting upon the ancient myths of cosmogony: as examples of the "concentration upon one element without explicit reference to the whole," he points to the contrast between the Akkadian myths of Enuma Eliš, in which the story concentrates "on divine kingship and temple," and of Atraḥasis, in which it focuses "on the requisite qualities needed for a stable human society." As examples of "the expression of abstract ideas by concrete symbols," he points to the following: "The palace can stand for the idea of rule over hostile forces. Thunder can stand for mastery over humans and their habitat"; and Clifford concludes that "the cosmogonies proceed by way of allusion, summarizing complex realities in concrete symbols." The phenomenon of material objects' being taken to signify abstract notions was not restricted to set narrative patterns. For a compelling analysis of the function of objects as signs in Herodotus, see Dewald 1993; Hollmann 2011, 176–207. Zeitlin, 1996, 19–52, analyzes how in the scene of recognition between Ulysses and Penelope (Odyssey 23.153–240), Ulysses' bed operates as the "sign" of Penelope's fidelity. Extensive study has been made of the Greek relation to objects deposited in sanctuaries as signs, whose function was to remind the god or goddess as well as the visitors both of their owners and of the past stories to which they were connected. For a Hellenistic example, see the catalogue of ex-votos dedicated to Athena Lindia that was proudly displayed on a stele erected in the goddess's sanctuary at Lindos, on Rhodes, in 96 B.C.E. The prestigious names gathered in the catalogue were signs that outstanding heroes, kings, and cities paid visits to the sanctuary in order to honor the goddess, and their cumulative list was in turn a sign of the fame and importance of the sanctuary. See Higbie 2003; Massar 2000. Finally, the anchor symbol on Seleukid coinage was a "sign" reminding of Seleukos I's descent from Apollo and the god's status as the founder of the Seleukid dynasty. See Kuhrt and Sherwin-White 1993, 27.

7. On the concept of social mindscape, see the Conclusion to Part I. I owe the concept of symbolic universe to Frank Polak, whom I thank.

8. For the detailed argument, see Chapter 2 (§2.1.2D).

9. As argued in examining the semantic field of *Ioudaïsmos* in 2 Maccabees. See Chapter 3 (§3.3).

10. Another message underpinned by the aforementioned Judean cultural code, for instance, is that piety and impiety connote political legitimacy and illegitimacy. More specifically, in 1 and 2 Maccabees this cultural code informs the message that the Maccabees/Hasmoneans, being pious, are the legitimate leaders, whereas Jason and Menelaos (and Antiochos IV) are depicted in the opposite way, as impious men, and therefore illegitimate.

11. Culler 1975, 202. The notion of codes (or narrative codes) was forged by Roland Barthes (1974 [1970]). As Culler continues (1975, 202–3), "the codes enable one to identify elements and class them together under particular functions. Each code is 'one of the voices of which the text is woven,' . . . the marks of an implied movement towards the other members of a catalogue (a kidnapping refers one to all the kidnappings already written). . . . Codes are determined by their homogeneity—they group together items of a single kind—and by their explanatory function."

12. Prince 1987, 14, noting further that "the opposition between code and message is analogous to but more general than the famous Saussurean opposition between *langue* (language system) and *parole* (individual utterance): just as the language system governs the production (and reception) of the individual utterance, the code governs the production (and reception) of the message."

13. Culler 1975, 203; Hawkes 1977, 118.

14. The detailed analysis is found in Chapter 7.

15. To take a comparison that is only partially correct, in a modern work of economic history only facts having a bearing on the field of economy will be dealt with, and moreover the economic aspect of a fact alone will be tackled, while other aspects will be either recorded briefly or go unmentioned.

16. See further the Methodological Introduction to Part I. The implicit assumption that there is an alternative is the main flaw of Dov Gera's hypercriticism of the literary material. In Gera's view, demonstrating that a story told in the ancient historical sources is informed by a narrative pattern is enough to prove that the passage is useless for historical reconstruction. See in particular his analysis of the story of Joseph the Tobiad and of Onias's eviction (1998, 49–52 and 106, respectively). This stance supposes that the normal procedure was to tell a story as modern Westerners do. In contrast, by admitting the play of cultural conditioning we may posit that the normal procedure was precisely to inform a story with a set narrative pattern, to use intertextuality with a story already known, and to equate one person with a prototype by shaping his biography upon the prototype's.

CHAPTER 5. *HELLĒNISMOS*

1. Cicero, *Ad Familiares* 5.12. See Woodman 1988, 70–83.

2. See Chapter 3 n. 69.

3. For an overview of the literary structure of 2 Maccabees, see Appendix B. The detailed analysis is found in Chapter 1 (§1.3.4). On the contrast between 2 Maccabees 4:7–5:26 and 5:27–13:26, see Chapter 1 (§1.4) and Chapter 3 passim.

4. See Clifford 1984, 187–88, quoted in the Methodological Introduction to Part II, n. 6.

5. See Ben Zvi 1995 and above, Chapter 3 (§3.3.2).

6. Josephus's account is derivative and therefore will be left aside.

7. See Chapter 1 (§1.2.1A).

8. Kennell 2005, 10–11. Kennell's translation is slightly modified.

9. The translation and meaning of this phrase are discussed in Chapter 10 (§10.3). See Kennell's detailed commentary (2005, 14–16).

10. For the meaning of this phrase, see the General Introduction (§4.6) and Chapter 7 (§7.1.1A).

11. The *palaistra* is the wrestling yard.

12. I offer an explanation for this in Chapter 3 (§3.3.2C). Two further references to *Hellēnika* are found in 2 Maccabees 6:9 and 11:24.

13. The observation that *Ioudaïsmos* and *Hellēnismos* are never used together has led Gruen to doubt that the author genuinely sought to create such an opposition. See Gruen 1993, 256–59. Gruen's purpose is to insist that the author of 2 Maccabees is not hostile to Hellenism.

14. This term recurs twice in the context of the rededication of the temple (2 Macc. 10:2, 5).

15. They are fully vindicated by Doran's thorough study (1981, 24–46).

16. See, last, Mason 2007, 463–64.

17. *Allophylismos* may be reckoned as an additional semantic neologism.

18. Himmelfarb 1998, 19. Emphases added.

19. The Hebrew word *'abodah zarah,* usually held to correspond to our "idolatry," actually means "foreign service" and therefore insists on the rites performed and not on the "idol" as such. On the notion of apt performance, see the Methodological Introduction to Part I (§I.2.2).

20. Bickerman 1979, 41–42.

21. Grabbe 1992, 279: "Although it was also normal for the Greek gymnasia to be dedicated to Hermes, we have no indication that this was the case in Jerusalem. We have to keep in mind that the author of 2 Maccabees is looking for any possible indication of scandal, and he is able to give none. His silence on both issues is a strong indication that neither nude exercise nor any pagan ceremonies were connected with Jason's gymnasium." Grabbe 2002 restates his conclusion that the institution of the *gymnasion* did not entail any breach of the law. A similar conclusion is defended by Doran 1990 and 2001, albeit based on distinct arguments.

22. Grabbe 1992, 278–79; quotation p. 278.

23. Himmelfarb 1998, 24–25, with additional bibliography to authors sharing this view.

24. Ibid., 25.

25. The notion of slander points to a gap between the text and historical reality.

26. See the Methodological Introduction to Part I (§§I.1 and I.3).

27. See in particular the Methodological Introduction to Part I and Chapter 1 (§1.2).

28. The scheme turning the impious acts of the wicked high priests into forerunners of Antiochos's attacks on the temple recurs in the case of Menelaos's theft of the holy vessels. See below (§5.2.2).

29. For my use of *Ioudaioi*, see Chapter 3 (§3.3.2B).

30. Grabbe 1992, 278–79.

31. On the Uruk Prophecy, see Beaulieu 1993, 43 (king 2). Compare this excerpt from the long list of sins perpetrated by Nabû-šuma-iškun: "He detained Nabû in Babylon; and he turned Festival Vigil and Festival Day into one day. He covered the fine garment of Nabû

with the fine garment of Bēl of the month Šabāṭu.... Unshaven, he mutilated [the fingers of] his apprentice scribes; and wearing fine gold, he entered the cella of Bēl offering.... Leek—a thing forbidden in Ezida—he brought to the temple of Nabû and gave to the *ērib bīti* personnel to eat" (col. ii, ll. 9–18). See Cole 1994, 234.

32. Compare Deuteronomy 13:1–4: "If prophets or those who divine by dreams appear among you and ... say, 'Let us follow other gods,' whom you have not known, 'and let us serve them,' you must not heed the words of those prophets ...; for YHWH, your God, *is testing you, to know whether you indeed love YHWH your God with all your heart and soul.* YHWH, your God, you shall follow; Him alone you shall fear; His commandments you shall keep; His voice you shall obey; Him you shall serve; and to Him you shall hold fast" (emphasis added). See also Exodus 23:23–33; Jeremiah 44:25. I owe these references to Ehud Ben Zvi.

33. And also the welfare of the people in its land. As we saw in the Methodological Introduction to Part I (§I.3.2) and in Chapter 2 (§2.1.2D), the notion of royal righteousness interlaced the double aspect of implementing social justice and caring for the temple.

34. Compare further Jeremiah 44:1–19.

35. Schmidt 2001 [1994], 86–88. Schmidt also quotes 2 Baruch 10:17.

36. "'You expected much, but see, it turned out to be little. What you brought home I blew away. Why?' declares YHWH, the Almighty. 'Because of my house, which remains a ruin, while each of you is busy with his own house. Therefore, because of you the heavens have withheld their dew; and the earth, its crops'" (Hag. 1:9–10).

37. Note already the comments by Doran 1990, with a slightly different perspective.

38. Intertextuality explains why the author of 2 Maccabees is silent about the sinners' attempts to undo their circumcision, in contrast with 1 Maccabees (1:15; Josephus, *Ant.* 12.241, follows 1 Maccabees). The other author appeals to different intertextual and cultural references.

39. See Chapter 2 (§2.1.1).

40. The texts are 1 Esdras 1:1–22, esp. 20–21; 1 Esdras 5:47–55 = Ezra 3:1–6; 1 Esdras 5:54–65 = Ezra 3:8–13; and 1 Esdras 7:7–9 = Ezra 7:15–18.

41. "And they [i.e., Joshua with his fellow priests and Zerubbabel with his kinsmen] erected the altar in its place, ... and they offered sacrifices at the proper times and burnt offerings to YHWH morning and evening. They kept the Feast of Booths, as it is commanded in the Law, and offered the proper sacrifices every day, and thereafter the continual offerings and sacrifices on Sabbaths and at new moons and at all the consecrated feasts" (1 Esd. 5:50–52).

42. See the Letter of Aristeas 92.

43. Cicero, *De Oratore* 2.5.21, quoted by Kennell 2005, 18 with n. 31. For a short commentary about the meaning of *diskos* and additional examples, see there.

44. The importance of music in the ceremony of refoundation of the temple is strikingly illustrated in the texts depicting the ceremony of laying the foundation stone: priests play trumpets; Levites play cymbals and sing hymns. See 1 Esdras 5:58–62; also Ezra 3:10–13. Tournay 1991 is a detailed study of the representation of theophanies through visual and aural images in the Bible.

45. For this translation see Kennell 2005, 18–19, with additional commentary on the practice of the distributions in the *gymnasion*.

46. On the priestly share of these sacrifices see, e.g., Numbers 18:9. A survey with full references is found in Albertz 1994 [1992], 461.

47. See 1 Esdras 5:58.

48. The biblical sources for the garments of the priests are Exodus 28 and 39 and Leviticus 8:6-9. In addition to Ben Sira the most important sources of the Second Temple period are the Letter of Aristeas 96-99; Philo, *Moses* 2.109-35 and *Special Laws* 1.82-97; Josephus, *Antiquities* 3.151-78 and *War* 5.227-36. See Watts 2007, 325 and n. 12.

49. In 1 Maccabees, priestly vestments (although not those of the high priest) are displayed in the crucial prayer ceremony performed at Mizpah before the battle against Gorgias and Nikanor (1 Macc. 3:44, 46-54, esp. 49).

50. Josephus alludes to the garment of the high priest Jaddua in his account of Alexander's visit to Jerusalem (*Ant.* 11:331). See also the description of Simon the Just putting on his priestly vestments to welcome Alexander the Great found in Megillat Ta'anit, quoted by Tcherikover 1959, 46.

51. For the political potency of the garments of the high priest see further Swartz 2002. On the priestly garments, see more generally Sanders 1992, 92-102.

52. See above, n. 48.

53. This commentary follows Kennell 2005, 19-22. Kennell convincingly argues that the passage 2 Maccabees 4:12 has a military connotation, and therefore *kratistoi* refers to the "strongest" and not the "noblest" ephebes.

54. Compare 1 Esdras 1:10 and 7:9.

55. For a detailed treatment, see Honigman 2011, 207-8.

56. "And *the people of Israel, the priests, the Levites, and the rest of those who returned from exile who joined them,* did according to what was written in the book of Moses. They offered at the dedication of the temple of YHWH 100 bulls, 200 rams, 400 lambs, and *twelve male goats for the sin of all Israel, according to the number of the twelve leaders of the tribes of Israel*" (1 Esd. 7:6-8; emphases added).

57. On this issue, see the General Introduction (§3.2D), and see further Chapter 10 (§10.3).

58. This concept is borrowed from Swartz's (2002, 61) analysis of the ritual and political meaning of the priestly vestments in ancient Judaism. Drawing on recent works stressing the communicative function of clothing, Swartz emphasized "the ability of clothes to signal identity, convey power, and confer to the wearer new properties" (ibid., 59). The other items that compose the "counterritual" of the *gymnasion* in 2 Maccabees 4, like music and order, may of course be analyzed in a similar way. I am also thinking of the catalogues of evildoings that invert the ideal of the righteous king in the Mesopotamian tradition and, as we shall see in Chapter 6, in 1 and 2 Maccabees as well. On the Mesopotamian tradition, see Beaulieu 1993; Weitzman 2004.

59. In the General Introduction (§4.4), I underscored the disjunction between 1 Maccabees' claim that those who attended the *gymnasion* "concealed their circumcision" and 2 Maccabees' insistence that they were priests. By concealing their circumcision, priests would have debarred themselves from officiating as priests altogether. If this were the case, 2 Maccabees' charge that they "neglected the sacrifices" seems unexpectedly mild. The two allegations primarily aim to secure an emotional impact and are unlikely to be factual.

60. See in particular Deuteronomy 13: 12-15: "If you hear it said about one of the towns that YHWH, your God, is giving you to live in, that scoundrels from among you have gone

out and led the inhabitants of the town astray, saying, 'Let us go and worship other gods,' whom you have not known, then you shall inquire and make a thorough investigation. If the charge is established that such an abhorrent thing has been done among you, you shall put the inhabitants of that town to the sword, utterly destroying it and everything in it—even putting its livestock to the sword" (emphasis added). Compare also Exodus 23: 31–33 ("You shall make no covenant with them and their gods. They shall not live in your land") and Deuteronomy 7:1–2. I owe these biblical references to Ehud Ben Zvi.

61. On this detail, see below, Chapter 7 (§7.4.4).

62. See the Methodological Introduction to Part I.

63. On the Hellenistic *gymnasion* as a military institution, see Gauthier 1997. On 2 Maccabees 4, see Kennell 2005. On the Tyriaion inscription, see the General Introduction (§4.5) and Chapter 10 (§10.3.2).

64. Tcherikover 1959, 161–70.

65. Kennell 2005 offers a detailed inquiry into the institutional nomenclature contained in 2 Maccabees through comparisons with the Tyriaion inscription and related epigraphical material, and discusses the possible implications of the newfound inscription on our understanding of Jason's reform in Jerusalem. His conclusions are nuanced in the discussion about the historical dimension of Jason's reform below in Chapter 10 (§10.3). Further bibliography about the Tyriaion inscription is provided there.

66. On this notion, see the Methodological Introduction to Part II.

67. See also the Methodological Introduction to Part II. As noted above (opening section of §5.1, with n. 6), Josephus's account in *Antiquities* is derivative.

68. See the concluding section of Chapter 4.

69. See above (§5.1.2 and n. 36).

70. On the concept of symbolic universe, see the Methodological Introduction to Part II.

71. The description of 2 Maccabees suggests that the *gymnasion* is to be understood as an institution rather than a building. As Kennell 2005, 22–23, stresses, the construction of a *gymnasion* was expensive and took time. Jason may have converted an existing facility for use as a *palaistra*. This procedure may further explain the absence of archeological evidence for the latter.

72. In embarking on his campaign against the *Ioudaioi*, Lysias hoped "*to turn their city into a dwelling place for Greeks*, to make their *temple subject to a levy in money* like the shrines of the other nations, and to turn the high priesthood into an office to be put up for sale annually" (2 Macc. 11:2–3: Goldstein's translation, modified; emphases added). It is not excluded that the "Greeks" referred to here are the otherized Judeans, who have become Antiochenes.

73. On the association between Jason and Menelaos in the sin of the *gymnasion*, see Chapter 1 (§1.2.2).

74. See Ma 2003b, 179–86; Strootman (2013). Strootman (2013: 72–73) argues that the *politai* of Babylon (and probably also Jason's partisans in Jerusalem) referred to themselves as "Greeks" as a tribute to the culture of the Seleukid court.

75. On the equivalence between the Hebrew *ṣedeq* (righteousness) and the Greek *eusebeia* (piety), see the Methodological Introduction to Part I (§3.2A).

76. The external enemies are characterized as impious in 1 Maccabees as well. See, e.g., 1 Maccabees 3:15.

77. See Chapter 4 (§4.2).

78. See further 2 Maccabees 13:9 with 11.
79. See in particular 2 Maccabees 3:1-3, 13:23.
80. In Babylonia, a cuneiform cylinder records Antiochos I's performing a foundation rite in the temples of Esagila and Borsippa. See now Erickson 2011; Strootman 2013; Clancier and Monerie forthcoming (1). An Akkadian text (*ABC* no. 13b) shows Seleukos II celebrating the Akitu ritual of the New Year. See Sherwin-White 1983. In Judea, Antiochos III's decree for Jerusalem mentions the royal subsidies to the temple (*Ant.* 12.140). In Egypt, the trilingual priestly decree of Canopos (*OGIS* 56 for the Greek version alone, = Austin, no. 271) refers to the piety of Ptolemy III in traditional terms, since the king is said to have returned the statues of the gods to their temples. In the Memphis decree of 196 B.C.E. (the Rosetta stone, *OGIS* 90 = Austin, no. 283) the rebels against the king are dubbed "impious." On this concept see Koenen 1959, 110–12; and Veïsse 2009.
81. "On the very same date on which the temple was profaned by foreigners [*allophyloi*] occurred the purification of the temple, on the twenty-fifth of the ninth month [Kislev]" (2 Macc. 10:5); "They destroyed the illicit altars which the foreigners [*allophyloi*] had built around the marketplace and also the illicit shrines" (2 Macc. 10:2).
82. On this notion, see Chapter 2 (§2.1).
83. 1 Esdras 5:7–46 = Ezra 2 = Nehemiah 7; 1 Esdras 8:28–49 = Ezra 8:1–20. For a detailed analysis of the catalogues of people and vessels, see Honigman 2011, 202–7.
84. 1 Esdras 2:13–14, 8:55–57.
85. On this symbolic function of the vessels see Ackroyd 1987.
86. As is well known, Hellenistic kings repeatedly boast about increasing the revenues of the temples as a token of their piety toward the gods, as well as their goodwill toward either the local polities or specific high priests. See, e.g., the royal letter to the sanctuary of Zeus Baitokaike, in Syria: *RC* 70 = *IGLS* VII, 4028; English transl. Austin, no. 172. Compare the Canopos and the Memphis decrees in Egypt. (See the references above, n. 80.)
87. "With polluted hands he [Antiochos IV] seized the sacred vessels and swept up the gifts deposited by many other kings to magnify and glorify and honor the place, and he handed them over to his unclean hands."
88. See Cole 1994, 236: "In the sixth year, he set his hand to restoring Esagila, the palace of 'Enlil of the gods.' The possessions of Esagila, *all that the kings who preceded him had brought into it*, he took out, gathered in his palace, and made his own. Silver, gold, precious gems of exceedingly high value, and every divine appurtenance that there was—with them, he made offerings as he wished to the gods of the Sealand, Chaldea, and Aram. (With them) he adorns the women of his palace; (and) he offers them to Syria and Elam as gifts" (col. iii, ll. 34–45).
89. See Chapter 4 (§4.2.2).
90. Compare 1 Esdras 1:41, 45, 54.
91. Doran 1981, 68–70, has argued that Alkimos is depicted as a new Haman.
92. See below, §5.3.1A.
93. See below, §5.4, on the category of "intentional sins."
94. The Mysarch "plundered the city, set fire to it, and destroyed its buildings and the walls around it. He and his army took the women and the children captive and took possession of the cattle. Thereupon they fortified the City of David with a high, strong wall and strong towers so as to have a citadel, the Akra."

95. My attention was drawn to Alkimos's depiction as an "other" in 1 Maccabees by Ehud Ben Zvi. For the motif of the otherization of rival subgroups within the social (ethnic) group see Ben Zvi 1995.

96. On the notion of exempla see Chapter 4 (§4.4).

97. Compare 1 Maccabees 7:6: "They brought charges against their people, telling the king, 'Judas and his brothers have killed all your friends, and he has driven us from our land.'"

98. As pointed out to me by Ehud Ben Zvi.

99. Schürer 1973, 167. On the split between the *Asidaioi* and the Maccabees see also Bringmann 1983, 46–47. Bringmann dates the break shortly after 15 Xandichos 148 S.E. (= March 164 B.C.E.), the date of the third letter of 2 Maccabees 11:27–33 proclaiming the amnesty.

100. Schürer 1973, 169.

101. Wilker 2011, 225 and 232.

102. See Chapter 4 (§4.3.2).

103. "He sought to fulfill the Law and wiped out all the impious and wicked."

104. On Simon's Eulogy, see Chapter 4 (§4.2.3A).

105. "The king's thoughts had roused him to barbarous fury as he came intending to show the Judeans far worse treatment than they had received under his father," and he is denounced as blasphemous for these evil intentions.

106. See Chapter 1 (§1.4.4).

107. For derogatory appreciations of Menelaos, see Orrieux and Will 1986, 137–38; Hyldahl 1990, 199–200. For a striking rehabilitation, see Ma 2013.

108. Himmelfarb 1998, 32–33.

109. "These then, and the others, all took wives for themselves from whomever they chose.... They began teaching them sorcery and spell casting, and they showed them the cutting of roots and herbs" (1 Enoch 7:1); "Asael taught men to make swords of iron and breastplates of bronze. He revealed to them the metals of the earth and how to fashion gold into jewelry and silver into bracelets for women. He taught them about antimony and about making eye shadow, and about all kinds of precious stones, and about colored dyes. And the world was changed. [2] The result was great wickedness on the earth. Men committed fornication and went astray, becoming corrupt in all their ways. Shemihazah taught spell casting and the cutting of roots. Hermoni taught the release from spells, magic, sorcery, and craftiness. [*Other angels taught other things.*] And they all began revealing secrets to their wives" (1 Enoch 8:1–3). Translation: Olson 2004, 35. I owe these references to Loren Stuckenbruck.

CHAPTER 6. THE "RELIGIOUS PERSECUTION"

1. Bickerman 1979, 61–62.

2. Weitzman 2004. The new phrase is inspired by Millar 1978, 16. See the historiographical survey in the General Introduction (§3.3).

3. Weitzman speaks of the stereotyped image of the king. While the image is certainly stereotyped, the notion of archetype may be more appropriate. See further Beaulieu 1993. Analyzing the figure of the Teacher of Righteousness in Qumran, Jokiranta 2006 used the notion of prototype.

4. See also my comments on Weitzman's study in the General Introduction (§5). My comments here are also based on conversations with several scholars.

5. Weitzman 2004, 228–30.

6. On the texts relating to these traditions, which are in Aramaic, see now Lemaire 2010. The explanation retained by Lemaire (ibid., 138–39) to cast light on the inclusion of these Babylonian traditions in the Qumran library is that either the community of Qumran or at least its founder, the Teacher of Righteousness, came from Babylonia. As always with functionalism, this answer is far too mechanical. In particular it takes for granted that the Teacher of Righteousness was an historical character, whereas this assumption is being increasingly questioned by Qumran scholars. See, last, Jokiranta 2006. Generally speaking, although ideas travel with men, they are usually acclimated by circles much wider than those of the newcomers. The diffusion of Christianity in antiquity and Protestantism in early modern Europe could not be understood otherwise.

7. Mendels 1981. On the "Prayer of Nabonidus" (4QPrNab), see the bibliography quoted by Lemaire 2010, 126–27 nn. 3–5.

8. Lemaire 2010, 127, with the bibliography quoted in n. 4.

9. Hurowitz 1992. See above, Chapter 2.

10. See in particular Weitzman's concluding remarks (2004, 234): "The real Antiochus almost certainly acted in ways that justified his reputation, and to the extent that he did so, he made it easier for his memory to be framed within this plot line. But that Antiochus remains inaccessible."

11. As we shall see below (§7.1), Josephus's accounts are derivative and need not be dealt with in detail.

12. See further Chapter 7.

13. The novelistic character of the story of Eleazar's death in 2 Maccabees 6:18–31 and that of the Mother and Her Seven Sons of 2 Maccabees 7 does not need demonstration. These passages may be omitted from the present discussion, because they do not make any contribution to the analysis of the relation between historical core and literary rendering that is our concern in this chapter. Moreover their literary construction has already been analyzed in a convincing way by earlier studies, and it is enough to refer to these here. On the Mother and Her Seven Sons, see in particular Nickelsburg 2006 [1972], 119–38; Doran 1980 and 2012, 155–66; Henten 1997. On the relations between 2 Maccabees 7 and the rest of the work, see the historiographical overview by Himmelfarb 1998, 31–32. For further bibliography, see now D. R. Schwartz 2008, 294–95 and 319.

14. More synthetic comments are offered in Honigman forthcoming.

15. Whereas Persian kings used to remove the cult statues of the gods (in Jerusalem, the holy vessels replace the statue), it is unclear whether the Greco-Macedonian kings did the same, although some Ptolemaic inscriptions suggest that they may have. See, for instance, the Canopos decree, *OGIS* 56 = Austin, no. 271, l. 10 (238 B.C.E.).

16. See Bertrand 1987; Chaniotis 2005a; and the examples surveyed in Chapter 11 (§11.2.2A).

17. Bickerman 1979, 45–53.

18. Or perhaps "a chief collector of tribute."

19. See above, n. 2. Ma 2012, 74–84, is a recent attempt to interpret the "prohibition of the Jewish rites" as the unintended consequence of political measures.

20. See Bringmann 1983, 29.

21. See Bickerman 1979, 45, 53, and 60.

22. Ma 2012, 77.

23. On the basis of 1 and 2 Maccabees, the account of Daniel 11:29–39 is usually read as mistakenly bracketing together the military repression and the religious persecution. This reading is endorsed in Collins 1993a. See, for example, his commentary to Daniel 11:31 (1993a, 384–85).

24. See, for instance, [Aristotle], *Constitution of the Athenians* 20–21. In chapter 20, the author surveys the events explaining the reforms of Kleisthenes, whereas the reforms per se are described in chapter 21. Because of this narrative organization, it is uncertain whether they were carried out before or after Kleisthenes was expelled from Athens by Kleomenes. See Rhodes 1981, 244, *ad* 20.1.

25. Doran 2011 and, as noted above, Ma 2012 have explored innovative ways of reconstructing the events, the main thrust being that the "prohibition of the Jewish rites" was the consequence of Antiochos IV's political measures and not a separate matter. The reasons why I do not endorse their propositions are specified in the General Introduction, n. 157. See further the introductory section of Chapter 11.

26. The translation of Daniel 11:29–39 follows *NRSV*, modified after Collins 1993a, 381–90.

27. On this translation, see below, §6.2.1, Daniel 11:31, Commentary.

28. On the version of 1 Maccabees, see further Chapter 1 n. 36. The author of 2 Maccabees claims that the cause of Antiochos's assault was the civil strife between Jason and Menelaos. See Chapter 7 (§7.2.3A).

29. On the theme of the Akra in 1 Maccabees, see Chapter 4 (§4.2.2). On its symbolic value according to the cultural and narrative codes of the Maccabees authors, see the Methodological Introduction to Part II, and Chapter 7 (§7.4).

30. On this aspect, see Chapter 1 n. 36.

31. On this notion and the status of 2 Maccabees 5:27 as a prolepsis, see Chapter 1 (§§1.4.2 and 1.4.3A).

32. For the sake of clarity the citations introducing new sections in the Linear Commentary are italicized.

33. The Linear Commentary is partly indebted to Collins 1993a, 384–88.

34. On the daily offering, see Collins 1993a, 333–34, *ad* Daniel 8:11, as well as Lust 2001, 672–73.

35. Lust 2001. On Daniel, see ibid., 682–83. This interpretation is particularly fitting in Daniel 11:31 and 12:11. The precise meaning is more obscure in Daniel 8:11–13 and 9:27 but does not contradict this interpretation. On 1 Maccabees, see Lust 2001, 683–84.

36. Ibid., 684–87. The quotation is from p. 685.

37. The makeup of the various social groups that coexisted in Judea in the aftermath of the rebellion is investigated in Chapter 11 (§11.2.3). On Menelaos, see there (§11.2.1B). On swine, see Lust 2001, 682, and below (§6.2.2), as well as the Commentary to 1 Maccabees 1:47.

38. See Collins 1993a *ad* Daniel 11:32.

39. On the Antiochenes during the days following the repression, see further Chapter 11 (§11.2.3).

40. Collins 2000, 41. Collins quotes the Wisdom of Solomon, the Similitudes of Enoch, the "teachers" of Daniel 11–12, and the Teacher of Righteousness referred to in the Qumran literature. See further the sources collected and analyzed by Nickelsburg 2006 [1972]. On the *maśkilim* of the book of Daniel, see further Collins 1993a, 66–67.

41. See Jokiranta 2006, 257–59.

42. Collins 1993a, 386, *ad locum*.

43. See Exodus 23:23–33 and Deuteronomy 13:1–4. See further Chapter 5 (§5.1.1C).

44. As quoted below, §6.4.1.

45. On festivals celebrating royal birthdays in Greek cities, see Austin, nos. 169 (decree of the *koinon* of the Ionians for Antiochos I, ca. 267–261 B.C.E.); 252, l. 35 (festival in honor of an Attalid); 265 (decree of Itanos in Crete in honor of Ptolemy III, ca. 246 B.C.E.). In Ptolemaic Egypt the king's birthday was an important occasion for celebration throughout the country. Prisoners could apparently hope to be released on this date. (See Austin, no. 163.) According to the Canopos decree, feasts in honor of the Philadelphoi gods (Ptolemy II and Arsinoe) were celebrated on the first, ninth, and twenty-fifth days of each month in the Egyptian temples, the twenty-fifth being the day when Ptolemy Philadelphos received the monarchy from his father. See Austin, no. 271, ll. 6–7. A festival of Zeus celebrated in Alexandria was founded to commemorate Ptolemy II's birthday. See Austin, no. 294, n. 3.

46. Bickerman 1979, 47.

47. See Collins 1993a, *ad locum*.

48. See Lust 2001, 673. On the Babylonian theme of the removal of the cult statue and the disruption of the regular offering, see Beaulieu 1993, 44; and Weitzman 2004, 224. On the Ptolemaic kings' carrying off and bringing home the statues of the (Egyptian) gods, see Winnicki 1994.

49. See, for instance, Collins 1993a, 385–86, *ad* Daniel 11:32 and 11:33.

50. See Weitzman 2004, 238.

51. For a documentary source from outside the Judean cultural realm, cf. the Demotic version of the priestly trilingual inscription in honor of Ptolemy V to celebrate the victory of Raphia (217 B.C.E.): "As soon as he [i.e., the king] heard that much injury had been done to the images of the Egyptian gods, he issued a splendid order to the regions over which he ruled outside Egypt, that no further injury should be done to them, as he wished all foreign peoples to understand the greatness of the care that was in his heart for the gods of Egypt" (Austin, no. 276, ll. 19–20).

52. On this verse, see Collins 1993a, 333.

53. These references are quoted after Carmignac1959–60, 386.

54. "As I watched in the night visions, / I saw one like a human being / coming with the clouds of heaven. / And he came to the Ancient One / and was presented before him. *To him was given dominion / and glory and kingship, / that all peoples, nations, and languages should serve him.* / His dominion is an everlasting dominion / that shall not pass away, / and his kingship is one / that shall never be destroyed" (Dan. 7:13–14; emphasis added); "Written by Enoch the scribe (this complete sign of wisdom) (who is) praised by all people and a leader of the whole earth, to all my sons who will dwell on the earth, and to the last generations who will observe truth and peace" (1 Enoch 92:1).

55. See Collins 2000, 44.

56. Quoted ibid. The verse belongs to the Teacher Hymns (1QH cols. 10–16).

57. For instance: "Hold fast the thought of your heart, and do not erase my word from your heart. For I know that sinners will tempt people to do harm to wisdom, and no place will be found for her, and none of the temptation will diminish" (1 Enoch 94:5).

58. On the transformation of Jerusalem into a Greek polis, see Chapter 10 (§10.3).

59. Barth 1969, 14. As Barth writes, "although ethnic categories take cultural differences into account, we can assume no simple one-to-one relationship between ethnic units and cultural similarities and differences. The features that are taken into account are not the sum of 'objective' differences, but only those which the actors themselves regard as significant. . . . Some cultural features are used by the actors as symbols and emblems of differences, others are ignored."

60. On this notion, see the Methodological Introduction to Part II.

61. See Ben Zvi 2008.

62. As argued by Toorn 1997.

63. Nihan 2007, *ad* Leviticus 10. I thank Ehud Ben Zvi for drawing my attention to the status of the Torah scrolls in Persian and Hellenistic times. I am indebted to him for the bibliographical references relating to this issue.

64. Lust 2001, 683–84. See above (§6.2.1), Commentary to Daniel 11:31.

65. For full discussion of the historical interpretation, see Chapter 11 (§§11.2–3). See further the recapitulative Commentary to Daniel above (§6.2.2).

66. See above, n. 45.

67. I owe this observation to Susan Weingarten.

68. Cole 1994, 234, col. II, ll. 17–18. The text is quoted in Weitzman 2004, 224.

69. Rajak 2009, 204–9. On the court stories of Esther and Daniel, see P. Davies 1991, 163.

70. See Chapter 11 (§11.3.1).

71. See above (§6.2.1), Commentary to 1 Maccabees 1:41–42.

72. The Syrian track was famously promoted by Bickerman 1979, 61–75 passim. On the sacred prostitution, see ibid., 74.

73. Arnaud 1973 and Budin 2008 argued that it is a myth. An echo of the practice is found in Hebrew literature in the description of Josiah's cultic reforms (2 Kgs 23:7). Therefore the quotation of 2 Maccabees could be interpreted as a case of intertextuality used for the sake of fleshing out the catalogue of evildoings, with no historical basis.

74. I am indebted to Jonathan Ben Dov for the present discussion of the Halachic concept of fornication. Any errors are my own.

75. "Be on guard against the spirit of promiscuity [or "fornication"], for it is constantly active, and through your descendants it is about to defile the sanctuary. Therefore take for yourself a wife while you are still young, a wife who is free of blame or profanation, who is not from the race of alien nations" (Testament of Levi 9:9–10). Translation: Kee, in Charlesworth 1983, 791–92.

76. "Make far from me, O Lord, the unrighteous spirit, the evil thought and fornication, and turn pride away from me" (4QTLevi[a] 1:13). See Stone and Greenfield 1993, 250.

77. For an English translation of the Psalms of Solomon, see Wright in Charlesworth 1983, 651–70.

78. Translation by Qimron and Strugnell, in Parry and Tov 2004, 327.

79. For this interpretation, see the discussion in Chapter 11 (§11.3.2).

80. For the possible precise historical context of this image, see the discussion in Chapter 11 (§11.3.2).

81. "He shall speak words against the Most High, shall wear out the holy ones of the Most High, and shall attempt to change the sacred seasons and the Law." On this topos in Babylonian texts, see Weitzman 2004, 227.

82. See further the Commentary to 1 Maccabees 1:58 above, §6.3.1.

83. See above, §6.3.2. The text is quoted by Weitzman 2004, 224.

84. For a more detailed discussion, see Chapter 11 (§11.1.2).

85. See the references to the sources and bibliography given in D. R. Schwartz 2008, 283, *ad* 2 Maccabees 6:11.

86. See Cole 1994, 246. For the text of the confession, see Kuhrt 1987, 33.

87. Moyer 2011, 176–77.

88. Plutarch, *Life of Theseus* 26–28.

CHAPTER 7. THE CAUSES OF THE REBELLION ACCORDING TO 1 AND 2 MACCABEES

1. As argued in the Methodological Introduction to Part II.

2. That is, its legal reorganization as a polis of Greek type. I write "inevitable," because as a result of the cultural (or discursive) slant of the author described here, the precise consequences of the politicization for the local population are ill known to us, although it makes sense that they included economic aspects.

3. By referring to the authors' literary skill I do not insinuate that their presentation of events is in essence manipulative, but I mean that they gave a meaningful shape to these events. Only meaningful events are "facts," and the way all historians create their facts is culturally conditioned. See further the Methodological Introduction to Part II. However, as argued there, it may be justified to speak of manipulation when the primary purpose of the concatenation is to support the claim that a rival high priest is impious. What makes the argument manipulative is its *political* intention.

4. In addition to political bias, the literary constraints of topical integration—due to the different thematic emphases of 1 and 2 Maccabees, as described in the Methodological Introduction to Part II—also influenced the narrative construction of these two works.

5. See Walbank 1985, 242–61. Cf. the speech of the wicked Israelites allied to the men of the Akra in 1 Maccabees 6:21–27, as commented upon below (§7.4.1).

6. The passage is quoted in full in Chapter 5 (§5.1, opening paragraph).

7. See below, §7.1.1A.

8. The reforms per se are dealt with in Chapter 10 (§10.3). Here we are concerned with the author's writing.

9. On the technical terminology of 2 Maccabees, see Kennell 2005. Compare Ian Moyer's analysis of the strategy used by Apollonios, the head priest of the Sarapieion of Delos, to report the lawsuit brought against him and the newly built sanctuary in the Delian Sarapis aretalogy. While the type of lawsuit is described with accurate legal nomenclature, the nature of the accusation is omitted. Instead, Apollonios "chose to embed his allusive account of the legal conflict in a longer narrative that is shaped by three prominent features: his priestly lineage, the repeated motif of dream commands, and the trial itself.... Each of

these makes mutually supporting claims about the legitimate status of the priests and their sanctuary on the basis of Egyptian religious traditions and narrative patterns." See Moyer 2011, 159–61; quotation from p. 161. The narrative pattern is studied ibid., 161–79.

10. In traditional societies, the ideal social system to imitate is always one in the past, the ideal state being one of immutability. For this reason, proponents of reform will present it as the *restoration* of an original order, whereas opponents will condemn it as *innovation*. This rhetoric was commonplace not only in Judea and the ancient Near East but also in classical Athens. In the religious sphere, see, for example, Lysias 30.18, quoted in Price 1999, 79; and in the political arena, see ibid., 78.

11. Although Tcherikover and Bringmann were particularly intent on the economic side of Jason's reforms, albeit each with his own distinct emphasis, they paid no particular attention to this passage. See Tcherikover 1959, 117–51; Bringmann 1983, 74–82 and 111–20. Aperghis 2011a discusses the economic issues as though they were only tangential to the circumstances of the rebellion.

12. Perhaps a better way to describe the problem would be to put it the other way round, and deplore "the tendency of modern scholars to make pallid and abstract a whole set of very concrete words." The quotation just cited is taken from Kurke 1992, 91, and refers to scholars working on Greek archaic poetry. On the Hellenistic "language of euergetism" as "deproblematizing" power, see Ma 2000a, 182–201. To quote other examples, in Diodorus Siculus 19.91 *eunoia* means "political support" (of a city for a king), not "goodwill," and *euergesia* means "(royal) patronage." See Kuhrt and Sherwin-White 1993, 10. Likewise in the Tyriaion inscription (*SEG* 47.1745, ll. 9, 24–25), *eunoia* is "(political and military) support," whereas *charis* (l. 23) denotes a material concession (the grant of civic status). See Kennell 2005, 13.

13. See the bibliography quoted by D. R. Schwartz 2008, 220, *ad* 2 Maccabees 4:11.

14. On the Ptolemaic papyri, see Lenger 1953. Berthelot 2003, 20–27, surveys inscriptions and papyri from the Seleukid and Ptolemaic realms.

15. Bickerman 1979, 42, followed by Abel 1949; Habicht 1976; Goldstein 1983, 228–29; D. R. Schwartz 2008, 220; Doran 2012, 103–104; all *ad* 2 Maccabees 4:11.

16. Bickerman 1979, 34, and 1980a [1935]. On the historiographical aspect, see the General Introduction (§4.6).

17. The legalistic approach posits that, like modern Western states, the Hellenistic kingdoms were governed by a framework of objective administrative structures and rules prescriptively defined by law. Within this framework the relations between imperial ruler and local communities were unilaterally defined by the central government in an exclusively top-down stream of decision making. See further the discussion in the General Introduction (§4.2).

18. On Bickerman's "surrender and grant" theory in general, and his interpretation of Antiochos III's decree as a charter in particular, see further the General Introduction (§4.2).

19. Bickerman 1979, 34, and 1980a [1935], 69–71. His comment refers to the clause settling the political status of the *ethnos* of the Judeans in Antiochos III's decree (Josephus, *Ant.* 12.142). See below, n. 22.

20. Known cases of interference bear on a limited number of issues that were of direct concern to the king, namely the institution of the dynastic cult in local sanctuaries; economic matters, such as the royal subsidies to the sacrifices and the appropriation of surplus resources of the temples through taxation; and the delineation of the space under temple control (an issue with fiscal implications).

21. In practice, most of the documented cases date from Alexander's time. The pro-Persian tyrannies of the cities of Asia Minor were replaced by democracies governed by parties hostile to the Persians. Similarly, kings who had manifested their hostility toward the conqueror were removed, but the remedy was to appoint aspirants ready to cooperate as kings rather than abolishing kingship. See Briant 1993 and 2002, 852–64. Antigonos Monophthalmos adopted a similar policy pattern during his short domination of Babylonia in 315–308 B.C.E. See Kuhrt and Sherwin-White 1993, 12. On these issues, see further Chapter 8 (§8.2).

22. "All those who are members of the political community [of the Judeans] shall have a form of government in accordance with their ancestral laws" (πολιτευέσθωσαν δὲ πάντες οἱ ἐκ τοῦ ἔθνους κατὰ τοὺς πατρίους νόμους). Translation LCL, modified.

23. Kennell 2005 takes this for granted. See further Ameling 2003.

24. Typically, only the economic clauses that could be presented as royal benefactions (*philanthrōpa*) are detailed, starting with the king's pledge to subsidize the temple (*Ant.* 12.140–41) and followed by his purportedly generous grant of a handful of (partial) fiscal concessions (*Ant.* 12.142–44), whereas the list of taxes to be paid is omitted. See the detailed commentary of this decree in Chapter 8 (§.8.2.5).

25. Since the fiscal matters involved in the story of the conflict between Onias III and Simon as well as between Onias III and Heliodoros (2 Macc. 3:4–7, 9, 13, 40) are blurred in the literary construction of Heliodoros's story and can be detected only through cross-checking the text with external evidence, they will be dealt with only in Part III, Chapter 9 (§§ 9.3–4).

26. For the right to use their own laws, see for example Polybius 4.25.7, 18.44.2; for the exemption from garrison and the autonomy, see Diodorus Siculus 19.61.3. Ma 2000a, 154–55, suggests that *eleutheria* could refer to the exemption from the tribute ("royal taxation was synonymous with royal domination, to the point that the settlement of Asia by the Romans in 188 would define free cities as those exempt from paying tribute to anyone," ibid., 155). See further ibid., 282–83.

27. In particular it is omitted from the *gymnasion* section.

28. Goldstein's translation, modified.

29. In this perspective the scholarly controversy over whether the civic body included the elite alone or all the inhabitants of the city may be seen as secondary. See Chapter 5 (§5.1.2E).

30. On the royal gifts to the temple, see Chapter 5 (§5.2.2).

31. For this translation of *chorēgia*, see Kennell 2005, 18–19.

32. See Bringmann 2001, 206. See further Chapter 9 (§9.4.4C).

33. *SEG* 47.1745, ll. 41–47. The text and an English translation of the inscription may be found in Kennell 2005, 12–14.

34. On this issue, see below, Chapter 9 (§9.2.2).

35. *Ioudaios* is used here as in Chapter 3 (§3.3.2B), to denote a pious Judean. See the explanation in Chapter 3 (§3.3). On Antiochos's statement, see further Chapter 5 (§5.1.5B).

36. Goldstein's translation, modified; emphases added.

37. See Chapter 5 n. 72.

38. If the suggestion of an ironic inflation is correct, it may bolster the view that the polis of the Antiochenes did not encompass the whole city of Jerusalem. On this vexed issue, see Chapter 10 (§10.3).

39. For modern opinions about how the author of 2 Maccabees understood the causes and nature of the rebellion, see the historiographical survey of the General Introduction (in particular §§1 and 5) and the opening section of Chapter 1. The most common views are either that, as the writer of theological history, he was uninterested in mundane issues, or that he perceived the rebellion as a struggle between "Hellenism" and "Judaism."

40. See the analysis of the nomenclature used in the *gymnasion* section by Kennell 2005.

41. This view was first put forward by Bickerman (1979, 38), whose argument is strictly deductive and speculative. Bickerman is followed by Millar 1978, 7. See also Doran 2012, 96, *ad* 2 Maccabees 4:7-8. While admitting that Jason's usurpation was a breach of tradition, Grabbe (2002, 19) downplays the impact of the affair.

42. The ancient sources on the basis of which the succession of the high priests may be reconstructed are muddled. On modern tentative reconstructions, see VanderKam 1991 and 2004, 85–99; Fried 2003. On the history of the Oniads, see further Cross 1998, 151–52, with the cautionary remarks of Grabbe 1992, 112–14.

43. See Chapter 4 (§4.1.2).

44. See Chapter 4 (§4.2.3).

45. Jonathan is appointed by Alexander Balas (1 Macc. 10:20), and his appointment is confirmed first by Demetrios II (11:27) and later by Tryphon in the name of King Antiochos VI (11:57). Simon's original appointment is alluded to indirectly, when Demetrios hails him as the high priest in an official letter (1 Macc. 13:36).

46. According to the cultural conventions that the Maccabees authors were raised with, we cannot expect straightforward authorial comments to bear on issues of such secondary symbolic value as the tribute and the royal appointment of high priests.

47. This topic is analyzed in Part I.

48. The details are analyzed in Chapter 5 (§5.1.1–2).

49. Bickerman 1980b [1939–44], 162 n. 22, followed by D. R. Schwartz 2008, 95–96 and 189. (Contrast Doran 2012, 79, *ad* 3:4–6.) On this family see further Tcherikover 1959, 403–4. Josephus, *Antiquities* 12.238–39, claims that Onias III, Jason, and Menelaos were brothers, the three sons of Simon. However, the data provided in this sentence is confused, and one suspects one more instance of scribal intervention aimed to emend the same anomaly.

50. In Chapter 10 (§10.2), it will be argued that Antiochos deliberately sought to appoint a *novus homo*. To this effect, however, it sufficed that Menelaos was not an Oniad; that the king went so far as appointing a nonpriest seems unnecessarily provocative.

51. All data about his family line are suppressed in 1 and 2 Maccabees. Josephus's notation (*Ant.* 20.235) that Iakimos (Alkimos) "was of Aaron's line but not of the same family as Onias" could be a mere paraphrase of 1 Maccabees.

52. For a detailed analysis of the motif of Judas fighting for *Ioudaïsmos*, see Chapter 3 (§3.3.1).

53. See Chapter 4 (§4.1.2C).

54. For detailed argument that the coveted monies were claimed as taxes, see Chapter 9 (§§9.3, 9.4).

55. Gera 1998, 106, accepts Josephus's notation (*Ant.* 12.237) that Onias III died at the beginning of the reign of Antiochos IV and therefore rejects as fictitious both the story of Jason's overthrowing his brother and that of Menelaos's having him murdered. However, Josephus's chronology itself is suspect, as are all instances of high priests whose deaths and

accessions to power coincide with the deaths and enthronements of kings. On this system of patterning time, see Chapter 1 (§1.4). Moreover, if the story of Onias III's fleeing Menelaos is altogether forged, as Gera opines, it is unclear why the author has him seek refuge in Daphne—whose very name was associated with the temple of Apollo—and therefore introduce an insinuation of idolatry.

56. On Antiochos IV's policy, see Chapter 10 (§10.1).

57. This paragraph summarizes the previous discussions of Chapters 2 through 5.

58. This theme of the unworthy high priests has been commented upon in detail above (§7.2.1A).

59. See Chapter 4 (§4.1).

60. See Chapter 1 (§1.2).

61. See Chapter 5 (§5.2.2).

62. See Chapter 3 (§3.2.2).

63. See Chapter 4 (§4.1.2).

64. See above, n. 52.

65. This translation endorses D. R. Schwartz's arguments (2008, 245, *ad* 4:48) for reading *dēmos* (people), not *dēmoi* (villages).

66. See Chapter 6 (§6.1).

67. The historicity of this episode, which is known only from Porphyry *ap*. Jerome, *Commentary on Daniel* 11.44–45, is debated. On Porphyry's notice, see Chapter 11 (§11.1.2).

68. In Chapter 6 (§6.1).

69. See Chapter 1 n. 36.

70. Endorsing the version of 2 Maccabees, Bringmann 1983, 66, justifies Antiochos IV's attitude by the latter's will to see the protracted instability resulting from the tensions between Onias III and Simon come to an end.

71. *SEG* 47.1745 = Austin, no. 236. See now the new translation in Kennell 2005, 13–15. On the bearing of this inscription on the institution of the *gymnasion* in Jerusalem, see Chapter 10 (§10.3.2).

72. This reconstruction is advocated in detail in Chapter 10 (§10.2).

73. Aperghis 2004, 169–71 and 330–31 (Aperghis quotes Demetrios I's letter to Jonathan according to *Antiquities* 13.49–53, not 1 Maccabees 10:25–45); Capdetrey 2007, 398–407, esp. 401–2.

74. This claim plays on a logical argument that was common wisdom in ancient times and therefore is perfectly rational: peace brings prosperity and therefore revenues to the king. Cf. the words of a Ptolemaic governor to the Arsinoeans: "You will do well to work and sow all of it [i.e. your land], so that you yourselves may live in prosperity and so that the revenues that you provide to the king may be greater than those that were produced originally." See C. P. Jones and Habicht 1989, 319, ll. 6–9, quoted in Ma 2000a, 134–35. Similarly, the Samaritans pleaded before Antiochos IV to be spared during the anti-Judean repression, pointing out that "applying ourselves in security to our work, the revenues which we provide to you will be greater" (*Ant.* 12.261), quoted and translated by Ma 2000a, 135.

75. The story of Antiochos's plunder of the temple is regarded as unhistorical by Mittag, 2006, 307–10. For a literary analysis of the passage, see Stokholm 1968 and Weitzman 2004, 229.

76. See Ma 2000a, 154–55.

77. "We have not taken land that is not ours, nor have we conquered anything that belongs to others. Rather, we have taken our ancestral heritage, which had been unjustly conquered by our enemies using one opportunity or another. Now we, seizing our opportunity, lay claim to our ancestral heritage" (1 Macc. 15:33–34). Ma 2000a, 29–33, offers an illuminating analysis of the rhetoric misrepresenting conquests as the rightful recovery of the conqueror's ancestral territories, which he shows was abundantly used by Antiochos III in his reconquest of Asia Minor.

78. "Judas and his brothers have ... driven us from our land. Now, therefore, send a man whom you trust and have him go view all the havoc Judas has wreaked upon us and upon the king's domains." (1 Macc. 7:6–7)

79. "The (rightful) settlers [*katoikoi*] of Jerusalem were put to flight by them, and it became a settlement of foreigners [*katoikia allotriōn*]."

80. "Jerusalem was uninhabited like a desert; none of her offspring went in or out. The temple was trampled, as foreigners [*huioi allogenōn*] were in the Akra, lodging place of the gentiles."

81. "As the city fell into the hands of enemies, the sanctuary into the hands of foreigners [*allotrioi*].... Behold, our sanctuary ... has been laid waste, and the gentiles [*ethnē*] have profaned it."

82. Compare, for example, 1 Maccabees 1:39 and 3:45 with Amos 8:10–12: "I will turn your feasts into mourning and all your songs into lamentation; I will bring sackcloth on all loins and baldness on every head; I will make it like the mourning for an only son and the end of it like a bitter day. The time is surely coming, says YHWH, when I will send a famine on the land: not a famine of bread or a thirst for water but of hearing the words of YHWH. They shall wander from sea to sea and from north to east; they shall run to and fro, seeking the word of YHWH, but they shall not find it." I owe this reference to Ehud Ben Zvi.

83. Thus the celebrated siege of Gaza by Alexander ended in the wholesale massacre of the inhabitants and the subsequent repopulation of the city with inhabitants from the region (Arrian, *Anabasis* 2.27.7).

84. "They [Judas's men] have killed as many of us as they could find and have been plundering our property. Not only against us have they raised their hands but also against all your domains. And now at this very moment they are holding the Akra in Jerusalem under siege and mean to take it. They have also fortified the temple and Beth-Zur." See also 1 Maccabees 7:6–7, quoted above, n. 78.

85. If these last two are distinct.

86. For the details, see Chapter 4 (§4.2.2).

87. Antiochos's confession may include a reference to the garrison if *eleuthera* in 2 Maccabees 9:14 is interpreted as meaning "free of garrison." However, as was explained above (§7.1.2A), this interpretation does not seem the most plausible.

88. "On the fifteenth day of Kislev in the year 145 the king had an abomination of the desolation built upon the altar, and in the outlying towns of Judah they built illicit altars [*bōmoi*], and at the doors of the houses and in the squares they offered illicit sacrifices [*ethumiōn*]."

89. "Mattathias and his friends went around destroying the illicit altars [*bōmoi*] and forcibly circumcising all the uncircumcised babies they found within the boundaries of Israel."

90. For the charge of idolatry in relation to the *gymnasion* in 1 Maccabees, see Chapter 5 (§5.1.3).

91. "They destroyed the illicit altars [*bōmoi*] that the foreigners [*allophuloi*] had built around the marketplace and also the illicit shrines [*temenē*]."

92. "Other Judeans hastily assembled nearby in the caves to observe the Sabbath in secret. On being denounced to Philip they were all burned to death, because they refrained from defending themselves out of respect for the holiest of days."

93. On the caves as refuge in wartime, see the references to sources and bibliography in D. R. Schwartz 2008, 283, *ad* 2 Maccabees 6:11.

94. See further the chapters of Part I.

95. See Chapter 6 (§6.1).

96. See Chapters 5 and 6, respectively.

CONCLUSION TO PART II

1. This is an extrapolation from the reign of Nabonidus, who was king of Babylon in 556–539 B.C.E. and generated two opposite traditions of remembering in the subsequent scribal tradition. The Verse Account of Nabonidus evinces a hostile tradition that depicts him as the inverted type of the cultic restorer. In contrast, Nabonidus presents himself as a restorer of cults in his own texts. On Nabonidus, see Beaulieu 1989 and Kuhrt 1990b.

2. This stance of hypercriticism is illustrated by Gera 1998. See in particular his analysis of Josephus's story of Joseph the Tobiad (1998, 49–52) and, albeit with less clear-cut conclusions, the account of Onias's eviction in 2 Maccabees and Josephus (1998, 106–7).

A SUMMARY OF THE CONCLUSIONS OF PARTS I AND II

1. For the detailed analysis, see in particular Chapters 5 and 7.

CHAPTER 8. JUDEA AND KOILÊ SYRIA AND PHOINIKÊ UNDER ANTIOCHOS III

1. For a thorough criticism of the old view, see Austin 1986. The present survey of the current state of Hellenistic studies is succinct, since it is discussed at greater length in the General Introduction (§4).

2. Joseph Manning argues that the administrative and political culture of Ptolemaic Egypt should be compared with non-European premodern states, such as the Ottoman Empire. Manning also endorses the model of the state proposed by Mann 1986–94. See Manning 2001, 873–75, and 2010, esp. 1–18, 55–72. Rolf Strootman (2013) relies on Charles Tilly's model of state formation, which was formulated to analyze the dynamics of state formation in the early modern era, to define the Seleukid empire "as basically a negotiated enterprise." See Tilly 1990 and 1994.

3. See in particular Ma 2003b, 179–86; 2012, 59–70; and 2012.

4. On the different attitudes of the Achaimenid and Hellenistic dynasties toward subsidizing the temple cults, see Chapter 9 (§9.4.3) and also Gorre and Honigman 2013 and forthcoming.

5. See Chapter 10 (§§10.3.3C and 10.3.4).

6. See the works cited above in nn. 2 and 3.

7. On the chronology of the Fifth Syrian War, see Walbank 1967, 2:523–25, 546–47; Gera 1987 and 1998, 20–34.

8. On the Ptolemaic use of the wider geographical denomination "Syria" and its revision under Antiochos III to "Koilē Syria," see Will 1979–82, 1:83, 2:119. The Ptolemaic name is still found in the second petition engraved on the Hefzibah stele, dated 114 S.E. = 199/8 B.C.E. (For the date, see Cotton and Wörrle 2007, 194.) The text of the Hefzibah inscription with an English translation is found in Aperghis 2004, 318–20. On the use of the name Koilē Syria in the ancient sources, see Sartre 1988, 15–16, 21–26, with the bibliography listed at p. 28 n. 1.

9. On the geographical boundaries of the province, see Bickerman 1947, Schalit 1954, and Sartre 1988. Sartre points out that the precise boundaries between the various geographical regions of southern Syria vary from one ancient author to another. (On Phoenicia in particular, see ibid., 18–19.) The administrative unity of the former Ptolemaic satrapy was maintained for only a few decades. According to Strabo (16.2.4–5), the region was eventually subdivided into four smaller satrapies—a change usually dated to the second century B.C.E., although the main reason for this date appears to be historiographical. Earlier studies interpreted this subdivision as a deliberate administrative reform and speculated that it coincided with a similar subdivision of Seleukis Syria into four smaller satrapies as described by Strabo. See in particular Bengston 1944, 2:159–81, who dates the reform to ca. 162 B.C.E. Recently, Capdetrey has argued that this development was an evolutionary process in response to practical needs. In particular, the unrest in the region during the 160s and 150s B.C.E. led to the increased importance of the officials in charge of the four meridarchies (administrative subdivisions) at the expense of the governor (*stratēgos*) of the satrapy, given that they led the military operations, as evidenced in 1 and 2 Maccabees. See Capdetrey 2007, 248–50. Scholars disagree about the location of the four meridarchies. For a recent review, see Aperghis 2011b, 22–23.

10. On Akē-Ptolemaïs-Antioch, see Cohen 2006, 213–21.

11. On Ptolemaios son of Thraseas, see Chapter 9 (§9.2.1).

12. The following summary of the Seleukid monetary policy in Koilē Syria and Phoinikē is heavily indebted to Le Rider 1995 and Houghton and Lorber 2000–2002.

13. On the Ptolemaic standard and Ptolemaic monetary policy, see most recently Callataÿ 2005; Le Rider and de Callataÿ 2006, 36–37, 101–3, 131–68. The notion of a "closed monetary economy" is not to be confused with a "closed economy:" whereas the latter means economic autarchy, the former is a form of monetary policy.

14. Houghton and Lorber 2000–2002, 45–52.

15. Le Rider's conclusion is endorsed by Houghton and Lorber 2000–2002, 54–55.

16. The earlier interpretations are reviewed by Le Rider 1995, 396–97, and Houghton and Lorber 2000–2002, 54 n. 40. For Le Rider's view, see Le Rider 1995, 402–4, and Houghton and Lorber 2000–2002, 54–56.

17. Le Rider 1995, 403, followed by Houghton and Lorber 2000–2002, 56.

18. Houghton and Lorber 2000–2002, 56–57.
19. On the definition of the "royal economy," see for instance Descat 2003.
20. Houghton and Lorber 2000–2002. On the economic causes of war in the ancient classical world, see the important comments in Austin 1993.
21. The text of the decree and its LCL translation are quoted in Aperghis 2004, 328–29, document no. 12. Bickerman's detailed commentary to what he called Antiochos III's "charter for Jerusalem" remains the indispensable starting point. See Bickerman 1980a [1935] and 1938, 106–32 passim. However, Bickerman's commentary must now be supplemented by more recent works, in particular Aperghis 2004, 166–68, and 2011b, 24–26.
22. On the notion that the various local traditions were respected as far as possible, see Descat 2003. Compare the settlements negotiated between Antiochos III and Sardeis, Teos, and Herakleia-under-Latmos, respectively, in the context of Antiochos's reconquest of cis-Tauric Asia Minor between 226 and 192 B.C.E. (Ma 2000a, documents nos. 1, 3, 17, 31). See Ma's commentary, as well as the important observations by Chandezon 2004. On Sardeis, see also Gauthier 1989, 13–45 and 81–111. See also Martinez-Sève 2004, 86–87, emphasizing the king's concern for adapting his requirements to the temporary hardships experienced by the cities in the aftermath of conquest.
23. On the Fifth Syrian War, see the aforementioned bibliography (n. 7).
24. The classic commentaries are those of Bickerman 1979, 33–34, 49; and Tcherikover 1959, 82–84. For more recent work influenced by their approach, see (e.g.) Himmelfarb 1998, 23–24. While pointing to the correct interpretation of *patrioi nomoi* in Antiochos III's decree, Nonbgri's discussion is also evidence that these classical commentaries continue to frame the debate. See Nongbri 2005, 93–94.
25. One of the earliest studies to challenge the rigid distinction between Greek poleis and native "cities" was Briant 1993. For a methodical if somewhat overstated refutation of the old view, see now Vlassopoulos 2007.
26. See in particular Bickerman 1939a. Further studies on this issue by Bickerman are cited by Chandezon 2004, whose brief and useful review of earlier historiography on the subject (2004, 132) I follow here. Bickerman's outline of the "surrender and grant" procedure is followed by Ma 2000a, 150–74 (for the phrase, see, e.g., p. 152), and 2003a. However, Ma (2000a, 243–53) also insisted that the relations between kings and cities were decided through negotiation and interaction, not by royal fiat. Most students of the Hellenistic world now subscribe to the latter view. On the "surrender and grant" model, see also the General Introduction (§4.2) and Chapter 7 (§7.1.1A).
27. Bickerman 1980a [1935], 69, with comments on the political consequences of military conquest for cities as illustrated by inscriptions in Asia Minor, pp. 67–72 and 81–84. See also, more succinctly, Bickerman 1979, 32.
28. Chandezon 2004.
29. Compare the attitude of the Greek cities during the Persian Wars. According to Herodotus, most cities offered "earth and water"—i.e., submitted without resistance—to the Persian heralds (Hdt. 6.48–49; 7.132, 138).
30. Chandezon 2004, 134. The Herakleia-under-Latmos inscription is *SEG* 37.859 = Ma 2000a, 340–45, no. 31. See Wörrle 1988, 428–44; Ma 2000a, passim; Chandezon 2004, 134–35. Chandezon (ibid., 135–36) reviews further instances of anticipated negotiations involving Attalid and Ptolemaic kings. Both Ma and Chandezon provide important analyses of

the subtle power game between kings and cities as implicit in the settlement negotiations. They go on to assert that the same game applied in situations of voluntary surrender and violent conquest.

31. Josephus's own review in *Antiquities* 12.133 is most likely a paraphrase of the decree inserted in his summary based on Polybius (cf. 12.135) and not a genuinely independent source of evidence based on Polybius, as Gera (1987, 70 n. 38) believes.

32. Sardeis: Arrian 1.17.3–4. Babylon: Arrian 3.16.3–5, Curtius 5.1.17–23, and Diodorus 17.64.3–4. Susa: Arrian 3.16.6–9, Curtius 5.2.8–16, and Diodorus 17.65.5. See Briant 1993. On Alexander's conquest of the cities of the Persian empire, see the overview by Briant 2002, 842–50. Alexander's entrance into Egypt may be added: see Arrian 3.1.1–4, Curtius 4.7.1–5, and Diodorus 17.48.2–4, 49.1–2. This pattern of surrender was an old tradition, well documented in pre-Hellenistic Babylon. See Kuhrt 1990a.

33. "The Babylonians came to meet him *en masse*, with their priests and chief men, each section of the inhabitants bringing gifts and offering surrender of the city, the citadel, and the treasury" (Arr. 3.16.3). Transl. LCL.

34. See Tcherikover 1959, 42–48.

35. Arados: Arrian 2.13.7–8. Byblos, Sidon and Tyre: Arrian 2.15.6–7, Curtius 4.1.16, and Diodorus 17.40.2. See further Verkinderen 1987. The peaceful surrender of the Phoenician cities, except Tyre, has been interpreted as the result of the thorough Hellenization of Phoenicia at the time of Alexander's conquest, as well as the Phoenicians' desire to preserve their maritime and commercial interests. See Rey-Coquais 1974, 151. However, the attitude of the Phoenician cities was far from uniform, and cultural affinities are rarely a decisive factor when vital interests are at stake. A perusal of ancient sources suggests that the cities based their individual decisions on their analysis of their immediate strategic situation. Arados, the northernmost city, had virtually no choice when it surrendered. Darius was in flight, and prospects of a military intervention by pro-Achaimenid forces were very low. Moreover, according to Frédérique Duyrat (2005, 209–10), Alexander had probably already set up camp in Marathos, within Arados's *peraia,* and thereby already controlled the greater part of Arados's continental territory when the regent came out to meet him. The case of Sidon is noteworthy: after putting down the Sidonian-led revolt of the Phoenician cities against their rule in 350 B.C.E., the Persians had installed a pro-Persian king in Sidon. Since that time, the city had been politically plagued by tensions between the king and the representative institutions hostile to the Persians. The Sidonian prominent men were therefore only too willing to surrender their city to Alexander. See Briant 2002, 857–58. By contrast, the Tyrians tried to remain neutral by turning down Alexander's request to enter the city, allegedly to perform a sacrifice to Herakles. They were besieged and eventually forcibly conquered (Arr. 2.15.7–27). On Egypt, see above, n. 32.

36. Ma 2000a, 201–6; quotation p. 202.

37. Curtius 5.1.18, referring to Alexander's reappointment of Mazaios in Babylon. On Alexander's settlement at Babylon, see also Arrian 3.16.4 and Diodorus 17.64.5. Sardeis: Arrian 1.17.7. Susa: Curtius 5.2.16–17.

38. Austin 1986 offers a now-classic analysis of the structural versatility of the *philoi* of the Hellenistic kings.

39. See Briant 2002, 842–71.

40. Chandezon 2004, 134–35. See above, n. 26.

41. See Ma's comments on the inscription of Herakleia-under-Latmos (2000a, 113).
42. *SEG* 37.859 = Ma 2000a, p. 341, no. 31, BII, ll. 4–8. Commentary: ibid., 113.
43. Transl. LCL, modified.
44. Bickerman 1980a [1935], 69–71.
45. Bickerman 1979, 34. A similar confusion is repeated in his commentary on the phrase *ta Hellēnika* in Antiochos V's letter (2 Macc. 11:24). See Bickerman 1979, 48. Bickerman's extreme position is endorsed by John Ma (2012, 2013, and 2014).
46. Against Doran 2011 and Ma 2012. See the General Introduction, n. 157.
47. See above, n. 35. Briant 2002, 857, compares King Straton, the pro-Persian king of the Sidonians, with Syrphax, the pro-Persian tyrant of Ephesos. Both were removed in similar fashion. Verkinderen 1987 argues that after Alexander's conquest the Phoenician cities continued to enjoy a political and fiscal status very similar to that under the Achaimenids.
48. Alexander's exploitation of the tensions between democrats and oligarchs is well illustrated by events in Ephesos and Mytilene and on Chios. On Ephesos, see Arrian 1.17.10–12; on Mytilene, see Arrian 2.1.4–5 and 3.2.6; on Chios, Arrian 3.2.3–7.
49. "[Alexander] permitted the Sardians and the other Lydians to follow the old Lydian customs [*nomoi*], and he sent them away, allowing them to be free [*eleutheroi*]"; transl. LCL. The persons "sent away" were clearly ambassadors from Lydian cities who had come to meet Alexander at Sardeis when he took control of the satrapy's capital.
50. Schaper 1995, 337, where the quotation is found. The archives of the Esagila, the temple of Marduk in Babylon, show that rations for temple personnel were a major component of the temple economy in both Persian and Hellenistic times. For an overview, see Boiy 2004, 240–41.
51. On fiscal issues Bickerman 1980a [1935] is now to be complemented by Aperghis 2004, 164–69, and 2011b, 24–26. Gauthier 1989, 19–33, draws close parallels between Antiochos III's fiscal concessions to Sardeis in 213 and his concessions to Jerusalem in 200/198 B.C.E.
52. On the Seleukids' economic exploitation of their dominions and Seleukid tax policy in general, see Descat 2003; Aperghis 2004; the papers collected in Chankowski and Duyrat 2004; Capdetrey 2007; and see further Chapter 9 (§9.1). See also Ma 2000a on Antiochos III's settlements with cities of Asia Minor following his reconquest of the region in 197. On the inscriptions documenting the fiscal aspects of these agreements, see above, n. 22.
53. Chankowski 2004, 15–16. Capdetrey 2007, 422–25, offers an overview of the regional redistribution of goods (especially wheat and oil) through the royal treasury. On euergetism as a form of economic redistribution, see also Ma 2003b, 181–83.
54. Ma's phrase. Ma 2000a, 179–242, analyzes its vocabulary and operation.
55. See Bickerman 1980a [1935], 53.
56. *SEG* 2.663, ll. 13–15; transl. Austin no. 235. On royal euergetism, see Bringmann 2001. See further Chapter 9 (§9.2.2).
57. Bringmann 2001, 206.
58. Bickerman 1980a [1935], 57 and passim. Comparing between Antiochos's decrees for Jerusalem and Sardeis, Gauthier 1989, 26, agrees with Bickerman's assessment.
59. Aperghis 2004, 166–68, and 2011a, 26–28.
60. See further Martinez-Sève 2004, 86–87, and Descat 2003, 160–65.

61. On Sardeis, see Gauthier 1989, 13–39, esp. 38–39.

62. See Gauthier 1989, 22–23. Gauthier (ibid., 24–25) gathers further evidence of Hellenistic kings supplying timber to autonomous cities.

63. "Your ambassadors . . . have handed over the decree according to which you thought it necessary . . . to elect ambassadors who should speak concerning the poverty which has befallen the city from preceding times, on account of the wars and the destructions, and who should ask that the measures granted by the kings be preserved" (transl. Ma 2000a, pp. 341–43, no. 31, BI, ll. 4, 8, 11–15.).

64. Chankowski 2004, 15–16. A good overview of the economic and political functions of tax exemptions and royal subsidies may be found in Capdetrey 2007, 418–25.

65. This feature has been well analyzed in Ma 2000a, 179–214.

66. Bickerman 1979, 9–23. The quotations are from pp. 10, 14, and 18.

67. References to modern studies endorsing it are listed in the General Introduction, n. 25. See further there, §§2 and 3.3.

68. See the Methodological Introduction to Part I (§I.3), and Chapter 1 (§1.2).

69. See the Conclusion to Part II.

70. See Bickerman 1979, 44–45. For a recent endorsement, see (e.g.) Nongbri 2005.

71. Gera 1998, 18–20, 25–35, 105–8, 158–59, and passim. However, Gera basically follows Tcherikover's criticism of Bickerman, endorsing the old theory that Menelaos was a more extreme Hellenizer than Jason. Gera uses this theory to surmise that most people joined Jason in his attempted coup—and it was this broad popular support that precipitated the severity of Antiochos IV's military repression. See ibid., 159–61.

72. Bickerman 1979, 44–45.

73. Paton's LCL transl., revised by F. W. Walbank and C. Habicht.

74. Herodotus and Arrian give telling examples of cities of mainland Greece and Asia Minor that, faced with a threat of invasion—the Persian invasion in the former case, and Alexander's invasion in the latter—based their decisions either to surrender or resist on strictly local considerations. Thus, the Thessalians opted to side with the Persians for the strictly pragmatic purpose of settling an old quarrel with the Phocidians (Hdt. 7.172–74 and 8.27–31). For their part, the Phocidians—alone in their region—chose to resist the Persians out of hatred for the Thessalians (Hdt. 8.30). See also Herodotus 6.49 about the Athenians and the Aiginetans. On Selge and Termessos in Pisidia, see Arrian 1.28.1.

75. *Antiquities* 12.229; *War* 1.1.31–32.

76. Bickerman's translation (1979, 44), with spelling alterations. Josephus's *War* 1.1.31–32 does not add anything new as compared with the three main sources quoted by Bickerman.

77. To some extent Lynette Mitchell's comments on the notion of "political parties" in late fifth-century and fourth-century Athens are pertinent to the political culture of Hellenistic times. According to her, parties primarily clustered around persons, not programs. See L. Mitchell 1997, 42–46.

78. On ritual traditions, see, for example, 4QMMT; on calendars, see for example the book of Jubilees and the sectarian calendar of Qumran; on stories of Creation, see, for example, the traditions compiled in the book of Enoch; on historical memories, compare the different traditions about Ezra and Nehemiah in Ezra-Nehemiah, 1 Esdras, and 2 Maccabees 1:19–35.

79. See Nongbri 2005.

80. S. Schwartz 1993, 305–7. A more detailed review of this evidence may be found in Grabbe 2011.

81. *CPJ* I, no. 6, of 258 B.C.E. = Durand 1997, no. 23, pp. 157–60. See S. Schwartz 1993, 306–7.

82. In recent years various scholars have claimed that the village of Modein was located in Samaria, and that this location must be taken into account when analyzing the social status of the Maccabean family. See, e.g., Scolnic 2010, with earlier bibliography. This call for a functionalist analysis of society not only is questionable but is based on an anachronistic conception of territorial boundaries and ethnic affiliation. This conception is refuted by J. W. Wright (2006), who stresses that the territory settled by a social group was not continuous. Affiliation with a specific social group was a matter of lineage as well as, one may add, cultic affiliation with a specific temple, whereas the notion of affiliation based on a clearly delineated geographical border was fundamentally alien to ancient ethnic and territorial representations.

83. See Nongbri 2005, 99. Nongbri (ibid., 99–102) offers a good review of the social and geographical origins of the Maccabees.

84. Notably, the two narratives differ in the timing of Mattathias's departure from Jerusalem: in 2 Maccabees Judas leaves Jerusalem following Apollonios's assault and massacre (2 Macc. 5.24–26)—i.e., *before* the "religious persecution" launched with the arrival of "Geron the Athenian" (6.1). In 1 Maccabees the "persecution" is described in chapter 1, whereas Mattathias's withdrawal is mentioned in 1 Maccabees 2.1—i.e., *after* it. The chronological problems involved in these passages is analyzed in detail in Chapter 6 (§6.1).

85. Doty 1988.

86. On Memphis, see Thompson 2012, 134–35; on Edfu, see Yoyotte 1969.

87. See S. Schwartz 1993, 307–8, offering a review of the various groups that supported the Maccabees according to the literary sources.

CHAPTER 9. SELEUKOS IV PHILOPATOR AND THE REVISION OF ANTIOCHOS III'S SETTLEMENT IN JUDEA

1. See Erickson and Ramsey 2011a.

2. This insight was the main object of Laurent Capdetrey's lecture "Le royaume séleucide: La décadence permanente?" presented at the Fifth Table-Ronde of the *Aigyptos* Research Group held in Paris on 25 June 2011, quoted with permission. To illustrate the principle of territorial flexibility Capdetrey pointed to the loss and reconquest of Egypt by the Achaimenids: the Persians lost Egypt in 404 B.C.E. and reconquered it in 343. During the second Persian period (343–332), a short-lived rebellion led by Khababash deprived the Persians of their control of part of the country, but the whole country was eventually reconquered.

3. Even though, as pointed out in Chapter 8 (§8.2.5), Aperghis 2004, 166–68, has argued that from the outset Antiochos III's decree for Jerusalem made no particularly generous concessions. See also Aperghis 2011b, 24–26.

4. Capdetrey 2007, 329. See also below, n. 33.

5. See Le Rider 1994 (on the silver and bronze coinage minted in Antioch between 173/2 and 169/8 B.C.E.); Mittag 2006, 118–27 (on the tetradrachms coined in Antioch-on-the-Orontes in 173/2 B.C.E.).

6. The financial clause of Apamea is detailed in Polybius 21.17.4–6 and Livy 37.45.14–15. The present discussion closely follows Le Rider 1999 [1993].

7. On these stories, see below, §9.3.1.

8. Le Rider 1999 [1993]; Callataÿ 2004.

9. According to 2 Maccabees 4:8–9, the tribute was raised to 360 silver talents and 80 talents of other revenue, and Jason added 150 talents for the establishment of the *gymnasion*—i.e., the politicization of Jerusalem.

10. Le Rider 1999 [1993], 1278 for a review of the data and the quotation (my translation).

11. Le Rider 1999 [1993], 1270–76.

12. Callataÿ 2004, 43.

13. Aperghis 2001 and 2004, 137–79 and 247–62. For the text and an English translation of the Mnesimachos inscription, see idem 2004, 320–23. According to the accepted model that Aperghis questions, silver coinage was restricted to interregional trade and the payment of soldiers and officials.

14. See Callataÿ 2004; and Le Rider and Callataÿ 2006, 261–66. Accepting the proposition that the yearly tax paid by the Judeans to the temple was delivered in coin, Callataÿ (in Le Rider and Callataÿ 2006, 264) points out that, on the basis of a population of two hundred thousand, that meant 32 talents, whereas the annual tribute to the king was 300 talents. Callataÿ also cites studies on royal euergetism showing that royal donations to cities were often in the form of grain rather than coin, even if the grain was meant to be sold rather than for local consumption. See Callataÿ 2004.

15. Callataÿ 2004, 42, further quoting Bickerman 1938, 127–28; Le Rider and Callataÿ 2006, 261.

16. See Spek 2011.

17. Callataÿ 2004, 43. On military expenses, see Aperghis 2004, 189–205.

18. Callataÿ 2004, 43–44.

19. Austin 1986 and 1993 on the economic function of conquest.

20. On Antiochos III's campaign in Bactria, see opposing assessments by Kuhrt and Sherwin-White 1993, 197–202, and Bernard 1994.

21. See below, §9.3.1.

22. See Gera 2009, 145, 149, and Aperghis 2011b, 22, pointing out that Judea was probably incorporated in this meridarchy.

23. For the identification of the positions of Dorymenes and Diophanes, see Gera 2009, 140–46 and 149.

24. *SEG* 57.1838. The original publications are Cotton and Wörrle 2007 and Gera 2009. Emendations by C. P. Jones 2009 and Bencivenni 2011 are incorporated in the *SEG* republication.

25. Gera 2009, 131–36, refuting the arguments of Cotton and Wörrle 2007, 197–98, 201–3. As Maurice Sartre pointed out to me (personal communication) the formal titles borne by royal officials in different times and satrapies were not necessarily identical, and therefore the precise title of Olympiodoros remains uncertain. See further below, n. 33. For convenience, I will refer to him as an *archiereus,* to endorse Gera's comparison of his early career with Nikanor's. On Nikanor see *SEG* 37.1010 (*SEG* 54.1237) with Gauthier, *Bull. Épig.* 1989.276 = Ma 2000a, 288–92, no. 4 (inscription from Mysia), and *SEG* 54.1353 (inscription

from Phrygia). Further references in Cotton and Wörrle 2007, 195, nn. 17–18. Nikanor was appointed by Antiochos III, who invokes the precedent of his grandfather Seleukos II. Besides Nikanor one man whose name is not preserved was appointed by Antiochos III in 189 B.C.E. as high priest of Apollo and Artemis Daittai as well as of the other temples whose precincts are located in Daphne (*OGIS* 244 = *RC* 44 = *IGLS* III.2, 992). Some of these high priests and high priestesses were appointed in direct connection with the dynastic cult, and Capdetrey (2007, 322–27) has suggested that they all may eventually have been entrusted with its organization. This view is questioned by Ma (2000a, 26). On the Seleukid high priests, see also Müller 2000 and Dignas 2002, 45–54 passim. Nikanor was both high priest and "overseer of the sanctuaries," but elsewhere the office of overseer is documented as an independent function discharged by a lower-ranking official. One Demetrios *tetagmenos epi tōn hierōn* is mentioned in a decree of Apollonia Salbakē in Karia dating between 213 and 190 B.C.E. See Robert and Robert 1954, 285–302, no. 166 = Ma 2000a, 364–66, no. 44, l. 14. Further, Debord 1982, 147 and 261–62; Dignas 2002, 49–50, 67–68. The function of *epi tōn hierōn* was taken over by the Attalid administration under a slightly modified title (*epi tōn hierōn prosodōn*). See Robert and Robert 1982, 361–67 = *SEG* 32.1237, with Müller 2000, 523–24. Debord 1982, 440 n. 54, points to a letter that was addressed in the name of one Antiochos, probably Antiochos III, to the army in the area of Mylasa by Zeuxis, the *stratēgos* of Lykia (whose name is not mentioned in the extant fragment). Zeuxis had been ordered by the king to "take care [*epimeleia*] of the sanctuaries." See *Labraunda* III.1, 134–35, and *Labraunda* III.2, no. 46.

26. On the moralizing vocabulary of the royal inscriptions, see Ma 2000a, 188–92. On its function as communicating a "deproblematizing image of power," ibid., 193–201. For the phrase itself, see ibid., 199; "moralizing language of motivation," ibid., 196.

27. Contrast Antiochos III's reference to Dion, the high priest in charge of the cis-Tauric satrapies under his grandfather, Ma 2000a, no. 4, ll. 41–42.

28. Cotton and Wörrle 2007, 198–99. On Ptolemaios, see further ibid., 193–94; Gera 1987 and 1998, 28–34.

29. Bagnall 1976, 48, and Debord 1982, 440 n. 48. On Cyprus the double title of *stratēgos* and *archiereus* is attested for two governors of the late third and the early second century B.C.E. See Bagnall 1976, 46, 48–49, 253–56.

30. *SEG* 29.1613, 1808; 41.1574 = Aperghis 2004, 318–20, no. 4. For the dates of the dossier, see Cotton and Wörrle 2007, 194.

31. Cotton and Wörrle 2007, 198. Gera 2009, 138–42, tentatively reconstructs the list of governors operating under Seleukos IV. According to him, Apollonios son of Thraseas (2 Macc. 3:5), perhaps a younger brother of Ptolemaios, may have been his immediate successor in the late 190s and early 180s. Apollonios may still have been appointed by Antiochos III before 187 B.C.E. and remained in charge for some time into Seleukos IV's reign, in which case the reform of the governor's competence could have been carried out by Antiochos III and not Seleukos IV. At the time of Olympiodoros's appointment, in midsummer 178 B.C.E., the governor was Dorymenes. There may have been one more person in charge between Apollonios son of Thraseas and Dorymenes, or alternatively between Ptolemaios son of Thraseas and his younger brother. See further below, §9.3.2.

32. Contrary to all opposing claims, including Gera's, the reliability of the prosopographical data of 2 Maccabees are vindicated by the epigraphic evidence. Gera 2009, 148–

49, argues that "the Seleukid official who confronted the Jerusalem authorities [as told in 2 Maccabees 3:4–4:6] was in fact Olympiodoros and not Heliodoros, for it was Olympiodoros who was appointed as high priest of the satrapy." In his view the author of 2 Maccabees suppressed the figure of Olympiodoros and replaced him with Heliodoros, whose name was phonetically close, because the office of high priest was "unacceptable" to the Judeans. (Incidentally, if this argument were correct, the same author might have also suppressed the titles of high priest that were held by the two governors.) However, it is doubtful that Olympiodoros, as a high priest, enjoyed military powers, whereas 2 Maccabees explicitly states that "Heliodoros" was at the head of an armed force, and therefore Gera's suggestion must be rejected. Apollonios (presumably) son of Thraseas and Apollonios son of Menestheus are historical figures; the latter is documented in epigraphic evidence. Beside Gera 2009, 140–42, see Fischer 1980, 205; Savalli-Lestrade, 1998, 41–42; D. R. Schwartz 2008, 190–91.

33. Capdetrey's (2007) monograph on the Seleukid conception of space, territory, and state is a long and detailed demonstration that the organization and government of the territories under Seleukid dominion was underpinned by general principles, such as a general conception of the territory and a certain representation of space. The concern for extracting surpluses while preserving the long-term economic capacity of the exploited territories, which characterizes the tributary economy, may be added. See, e.g., Chankowski 2004. In contrast, as Capdetrey repeatedly emphasizes, the administrative means deployed to organize and govern the subject territories were adapted to the local conditions and traditions on pragmatic grounds, and therefore no standardization was ever sought. Thus, even though the Seleukids actively sought to tighten the control of their territory through a network of Greek settlements, no systematic model was applied to them. Both the poleis and the *katoikiai* display a range of models and statuses. See Capdetrey 2007, 158–66 (on *katoikiai*) and 191–224 (on cities). Even those kings who engaged in vast reforms, like Antiochos III and Antiochos IV, never proceeded according to a preconceived design. See ibid. (e.g.) 329: "Si l'action réformatrice d'Antiochos III fut très importante, nous aurions tort de la lire comme l'application d'un projet cohérent dont la mise en œuvre aurait été immédiate." Manning's (2010) recent handbook on Ptolemaic Egypt has defended a similar view about the stately culture of the Ptolemies. See also Manning 2001. Contrary to what Cotton and Wörrle 2007 claim, Seleukos IV's appointment of Olympiodoros cannot have been motivated by his concern for administrative standardization alone, nor can the pretext presented in the royal letter be taken at face value.

34. Ma 2000a, 190.

35. See already Gera 2009, 146–47. Gera's attempt to discern what concerned Ptolemaios as a *stratēgos* and as an *archiereus*, respectively (p. 147), is overstated. The premise that the competences accruing to each title were clearly delineated is typical of the "legalistic approach" and misrepresents the working of the Hellenistic administrations. For a critique of the "legalistic approach," see the General Introduction, §4.2. The practice of the royal giving of gifts to temples is amply documented in temple inventories. See Dignas 2002, 18–19. See also Bringmann 2001.

36. See Bickerman 1980a [1935], 45; transl. LCL.

37. The mechanism of intraregional and interregional redistribution is well documented in Asia Minor. Seleukid and Attalid kings regularly supplied cities with wheat and oil pro-

duced on royal lands. A useful overview is found in Capdetrey 2007, 422–25. See further Bringmann 2001.

38. In the decrees of Darius and Artaxerxes inserted into the book of Ezra, which in all likelihood are Hellenistic forgeries, the royal subsidies are supplied by the governor of the satrapy and the officials under his orders out of the satrapy's tribute (Ezra 6:6, 8) and by its treasurers (Ezra 7:21–22), respectively. On these decrees, see below, n. 83.

39. The notion of "increases" always has the connotation of a material benefit, in the form of either a grant or a tax exemption. See, for example, the inscription announcing the economic steps taken by one Seleukid king in favor of the sanctuary of Baitokaikē in the satrapy of Apamea in Seleukid Syria (*RC* 70, B and C = *IGLS* 7.4028 = Aperghis 2004, no. 15, p. 331 = Dignas 2002, 75–76 = Austin, no. 172). These benefactions, consisting of granting the village of Baitokaikē to the sanctuary and its revenues for one year, the right to hold tax-exempt fairs twice a month, the right of *asylia,* and an exemption from billeting, are bestowed "for the prosperity[literally, the "increase," *pros auxēsin*] of the sanctuary" (Dignas 2002, 75–76; *IGLS* 7.4028, C, ll. 24–25). In another dossier, King Eumenes II responded favorably to a delegation from the settlers of the village of Tyriaion, in Phrygia, Asia Minor, who asked for the right to organize as a polis and set up a *gymnasion*. In his second letter—this time addressed to the *citizens* of Tyriaion—Eumenes granted financial concessions to help the citizens buy oil for their *gymnasion.* Here too the economic concessions are presented as an "enhancement" (*synauxontes tauta*) of the privileges already granted: i.e., the right to become a polis and have a *gymnasion* (*SEG* 47.1745, l. 42 = Austin, no. 236; improved text and translation in Kennell 2005, 13–15). The dossier seems to date shortly after 188 B.C.E.

40. See above, n. 25.

41. Chankowski 2004, 15–16: "L'analyse des rouages de la fiscalité séleucide . . . n'en montre pas moins une réelle capacité des rois séleucides à concevoir dans la durée une fiscalité globale. . . . Il s'agit pour les rois d'organiser des moyens de drainer vers les caisses royales d'importants revenus, ce qui peut prendre aussi la forme d'une politique de concessions de la part du pouvoir royal. Ainsi, le renoncement royal à une partie des prélèvements crée une dialectique d'échanges avec les cités. . . . En même temps, la politique d'évergétisme royal, qui va souvent de pair avec la politique fiscale, assure une certaine redistribution des richesses prélevées." See also the similar observations about euergetism as a means of redistribution of the taxes by Ma 2003a, 182–83. The principle of reciprocal transaction is a basic trait of the Greek interaction both with the gods and with other men. On reciprocity in Greek worship, see Bremer 1998 and Parker 1998; on the social institutions of *philia* and *xenia,* see L. Mitchell 1997.

42. Compare the Nikanor inscription, *SEG* 37.1010, ll. 41–43: "Do therefore give orders for your subordinates to cooperate with him in the matters appropriate to what has been previously explained."

43. One Demetrios *ho tetagmenos epi tōn hierōn* appears alongside an *epistatēs* in the same region, Karia at about the same time, albeit in two different sanctuaries: the former in the temple of Apollonia Salbakē in a period between 213 and 190 B.C.E. (Ma 2000a, no. 44, l. 13) and the latter in the Artemision of Amyzon in 201 B.C.E. (Ma 2000a, no. 10, ll. 6–7). On the coexistence of the two functions, see Debord's bemused comment (1982, 261–62).

44. On this notion, see the Methodological Introduction to Part II and Chapter 7.

45. On the temple of "Anahita" in Ecbatana (Antiochos III), see Polybius 10.27. On Bel of Elymaïs, see Diodorus Siculus 28.3, 29.15. On the temple of Hierapolis-Bambykē (Antiochos IV), see Granius Licinianus 28.6. On the temple of Artemis-Nanaia in Elymaïs (Antiochos IV), the sources are 1 Maccabees 6:1–4, 2 Maccabees 1:13–16, Polybius 31.9; and Appian, *Syriaka* 66. On Jerusalem, see 1 Maccabees 1:21–23, 2 Maccabees 5:15–16. On Antiochos III's dubious exploits, see Schmitt 1964, 101 (Ecbatana); Capdetrey 2007, 186–87 (Elymaïs). On Antiochos IV, see Mittag 2006, 149–51 and 307–10.

46. Mittag 2006, 150.

47. References are gathered by Tozzi 1977; Le Rider 1999 [1993], 1276–77. The sacking of the Babylonian territory, including towns and temples, by Antigonos Monophthalmos during his invasion of the region in 315–308 B.C.E. is documented by the Akkadian *Chronicle of the Diadochoi* (*ABC*, no. 10). See Kuhrt and Sherwin-White 1993, 10.

48. Le Rider 1999 [1993], 1276–77, sought to downplay the significance of the alleged attacks on temples by Antiochos III and Antiochos IV by lumping the two situations together.

49. Mittag 2006, 310. A similar suggestion was made independently by Martinez-Sève (2004, 98), who rationalizes the story of Antiochos IV's plunder of the Jerusalem temple in similar fashion. So does Aperghis (2011b, 33) in commenting 2 Maccabees 4:32–42. Aperghis points out that Menelaos had just been summoned to Antioch because of his delay in paying the tribute. On the motif of the tyrant topos, see Mittag 2006, 149.

50. Mittag (2006, 309–10 with n. 52) quotes a similar situation featuring Antiochos III and one Xerxes, the young king of the city of Armosata in Mesopotamia, ca. 212 B.C.E. (Polyb. 8.23). After Antiochos III laid siege to the city, Xerxes negotiated a settlement with him. Antiochos confirmed him as king and "remitting the greater part of the sum which his father had still owed for tribute" (8.23.4, Paton's transl., rev. F. W. Walbank and C. Habicht, LCL 2011, p. 595.). Antiochos III further restored all Xerxes' dominions and gave him his daughter in marriage after receiving lavish gifts (8.23.5).

51. See Chapter 5 (§5.2.3).

52. On this concept, see the Methodological Introduction to Part II and Chapter 7. Either the author of 1 Maccabees exploited the distinct tyrant topos documented in the four texts that Mittag reviews (see above, nn. 45 and 46) or, more probably, all five are cases of mediating synecdoches, implying that this system was actually common to the literate traditions of Judea and other neighboring cultures.

53. Stokholm 1968, followed by Weitzman 2004, 229. Weitzman further quotes a story found in Herodotus (1.183) about Xerxes' plundering a statue from the temple of Esagila in Babylon.

54. See Chapter 6 (§6.1) and Chapter 11 (§11.2.1A).

55. Boiy 2004, 156–57.

56. Sartre forthcoming. See below, §9.4.5.

57. See Gera's (2009, 138–42) reconstruction of the list of the governors serving under Seleukos IV. See also above, n. 31. The career of Apollonios son of Menestheus is epigraphically documented. See above, n. 32.

58. Gera 2009, 141–42; quotation from p. 142.

59. See Chapter 1 (§1.4). Similarly, the battles waged against the two Nikanors in 2 Maccabees 8:10–36 and 15:1–29 are doublets, where the use of namesakes fulfills a similar cautionary purpose. See Chapter 4 (§4.1.1).

60. Gera's reasons for preferring Apollonios son of Menestheus over his namesake (2009, 141) are not necessarily compelling.

61. "In his place will arise one [Seleukos IV] who will make *a tribute collector* of royal splendor pass through." See Collins 1993a, 381. Compare "[Quelqu'un] se lèvera à sa place [i.e., of Antiochos III] et enverra dans la gloire du royaume [i.e., in the Jerusalem temple] *un collecteur [d'impôts]*," translation by Michaéli in Dhorme 1959, 2:671, quoted by Le Rider 1999 [1993], 1277. Contrast the *NRSV* translation: "Then shall arise in his place one who shall send an official for the glory of the kingdom."

62. Collins 1993a, 381–82.

63. The translation of this verse has been modified, for reasons cited below. Other modifications have also been made to Goldstein's translation.

64. As argued by Gera 2009, 148–49.

65. Dignas 2002, 21–22, 31, and 34.

66. Capdetrey 2007, 327. See also Aperghis 2004, 284.

67. See Gorre and Honigman 2013, 113–14. Bickerman (1980b [1939–44], 161 with n. 17) less convincingly compared Simon's function to that of the temple *epistatēs* of Ptolemaic Egypt, whom he defined as a "supervisor" representing the king within the temple. This title is documented in a papyrus of 165 B.C.E. concerning the Sarapieion of Memphis (*UPZ* I, 42), whose incumbent is also *oikonomos* (i.e., an official in the royal financial administration: *UPZ* I, 56) and bears the Egyptian title of "the king's scribe accountant." See also Gorre 2009, 246, no. 49, and 639.

68. Bickerman 1980b [1939–44], 161 n. 17, notes that the Hebrew *paqid* was translated *prostatēs* in the Septuagint (2 Chr 24:11). The *paqid*—being the Hebrew equivalent to the Akkadian *paqdu*—was the supervisor of the Jerusalem temple. His function seems to be similar to that of the *paqdu* of Babylon and Uruk.

69. Boiy 2004, 209.

70. Aperghis 2004, 286–87, and 2011b, 23; Capdetrey 2007, 183–84 and 327–28. Both scholars treat Simon and the Mesopotamian *paqdu* as one and the same.

71. Boiy 2004, 195, 209–10.

72. Spek 1987, 63; Boiy 2004, 195–96, 209–10. The office of *paqdu* appears to have persisted until well into the Parthian period. Two temple officials who seem to have been royal nominees bear the Iranian title *uppudētu*. The latter was the equivalent of the Greek *prostatēs*, which appears in a transliterated form in a letter addressed to the same person. This official supervised the temple's property, like Simon in Jerusalem and the *prostatai* of Egypt. His Iranian name may derive from the substantive *utru*, "surplus," "extra income." See Spek 1987, 64 with n. 13. Bickerman 1980b [1939–44], 164, translates *diaphora* (2 Macc. 3:6) as "surpluses" ("excédents").

73. Spek 2000, 31.

74. Abel 1949, Habicht 1976, Goldstein 1983, D. R. Schwartz 2008, Doran 2012. See Bickerman 1980b [1939–44], 162–64.

75. Here and below the translation is reconstructed from Bickerman's periphrastic commentary.

76. See Bickerman's commentary on *diaphoron*, 1980b [1939–44], 164.

77. On Jason and Menelaos, see in particular Chapters 1 (§1.4), 5 (§5.1–2), and 7 (§7.2), and the summary in the Introduction to Part III. On Onias, see Chapter 4 (§4.1.2 and 4.3.1).

78. See Chapter 7 (§7.2.3C). As we shall see below (§9.4.5), the reasons for Antiochos's ousting of Onias may be more complex.

79. Thus, the story of Alkimos's wrongful condemnation of the *Asidaioi* in 1 Maccabees 7:12–18 appears to conflate two originally distinct episodes. See Chapter 5 (§5.3.2).

80. For more on this notion, see the Methodological Introduction to Part II and Chapter 7.

81. Albertz 1994 [1992], 461. Weinberg 1976 [1974] went so far as to argue that not only was the temple deprived of land but the *ethnos* of the Judeans lacked a temple-based economy. This latter contention has been sharply disputed, and Albertz's contention (1994 [1992], 462) that "the temple developed into the most important economic factor in the community of Judah" represents the accepted view. For the view that the temple had lands, see, for instance, Blenkinsopp 2001.

82. See Albertz 1994 [1992], 460–62.

83. The arguments are mostly philological. See in particular Grabbe 2006 and Schwiderski 2000. Schwiderski (ibid., 381) shows that the redaction of the royal letters was not inspired by genuine Achaimenid documents and concludes the letters were written in early Hellenistic times. See further the historiographical survey in Grabbe 2006, 531. For a literary approach, see Edelman 2005, 151–206, who contends that the entire section Ezra 1–6 is a skillful literary montage fleshed out from information found in the books of Chronicles and various prophetic books. On Darius's decree, see Edelman 2005, 188–90. The existence of a regular royal stipend to the Jerusalem temple in Persian times is all the more improbable in light of the findings of recent studies that the Achaimenids were far less generous than their predecessors toward the temples of Egypt and Babylonia. With regard to the temples of Egypt, see Agut-Labordère and Gorre forthcoming. In Babylonia, although Cyrus continued the generous policy of the Neo-Babylonian kings, the Persian attitude toward the Babylonian temples changed for the worse after two rebellions successively suppressed by Darius the Great and by Xerxes. See Jursa 2007 and Waerzeggers 2004. On the Neo-Babylonian kings and Babylonian temples, see Waerzeggers 2011. For a general survey, see Gorre and Honigman forthcoming.

84. Bickerman 1938, 106–32 passim, and 1980a [1935]. In particular, the decree is implicitly deemed genuine by Aperghis 2004, 164–69, and 2011b, 24–26; Gauthier 1989, 19–33. On this decree, see further Chapter 8 (§8.2).

85. In praise of Ptolemy II.

86. The considerations underpinning this statement are detailed in the Methodological Introduction to Part II. See also Chapter 7.

87. From an economic point of view, they apparently replaced the rents paid by peasants to temples possessing sacred lands.

88. See, in particular, the catalogue of ex-votos dedicated to Athena Lindia, published on a stele in the sanctuary of the goddess at Lindos, Rhodes, listing the names of prestigious heroes, kings, and city representatives who had visited the sanctuary to honor the goddess. See above, n. 35; and further Massar 2000; Higbie 2003.

89. On Antiochos IV's confession, see Chapter 7 (§7.1.2A).

90. After Bickerman 1980a [1935], 45. The translation follows LCL.

91. Debord 1982, 192, based on the inscription *LSCG* 159 of the Asklepieion of Kos, third century B.C.E. On the cost of the sacrifices, see also his comments ibid., 192–93 with nn. 57–70; 402–5.

92. Bringmann 2001; Aperghis 2004, 107–12. In Egypt, a system of regular allowances was instituted by Ptolemy II to compensate for the confiscation of the sacred lands, the temples' main economic assets under the founder of the Ptolemaic dynasty. It was based on the revenues from the *apomoira*, the tax that was levied on vineyards and orchards and was partly monetized, and that was allocated to the temples, ostensibly to finance the cult of Arsinoe, Ptolemy II's deceased wife. On the *apomoira*, see Clarysse and Vandorpe 1998; Thompson 2008 and 2012, 119.

93. Double taxation of the temple (or the polis) and the king was the custom in Achaimenid times. For Yehud, see Schaper 1995 and 1997. On Greek cities, see Corsaro 1985.

94. See Chapter 5, (§5.2.3).

95. Dignas 2002, 1–12.

96. Ibid., 16.

97. Ibid., 15–16. On the *hieropoioi* see, e.g., J. K. Davies 2001b.

98. Dignas's (2002, 46–56) discussion of the functions of Nikanor, whom Antiochos III appointed as high priest of all temples in cis-Tauric Asia (*SEG* 37.1010 = Ma 2000a, no. 4; see above, §9.2), is an extreme illustration of her position. Ruling out in advance the notion that a royal official could transfer funds back and forth between the royal and the sacred treasures, she fails to provide any precise evidence for her assessment that the high priest "was generally in charge of the sacred funds" (53): "Will Nikanor 'safeguard' the sacred revenues or 'process' them? My inclination is that Nikanor would not lay hands on sacred revenues in order to fill the royal treasury" (49–50). Caught in an impasse of her own making, she then proposes the following: "We can infer that the chief-priest was going to supervise sacrifices and probably oversee festivals and everyday cult-activities" (48). This overlooks the fact that protecting and processing sacred revenues, like supervising sacrifices, were tasks incumbent upon the priestly personnel of the individual temples. Thus, to avoid the obvious conclusion that the Seleukid officials in charge of temples were intermediaries handling all the cultic, political, and, above all, economic relations between the two sides, Dignas suggests the activities of the royal officials bordered on sacrilege, meddling with the temples' internal affairs, even to the extent of supervising sacrifices. Her position that the temple economy was left outside royal taxation is best epitomized in her repeated suggestions that the only instances of kings appropriating temple revenues are the cases of plunder recorded in the sources—as in the above-cited comment ("Nikanor would not lay hands on sacred revenues in order to fill the royal treasury") and even more explicitly on p. 43 ("Occasional aggressive behavior by Hellenistic kings towards the wealth of famous cults *is* attested") with nn. 37 and 38.

99. See, e.g., ibid., 29, 74.

100. Despite Dignas's claim to the contrary. In all the instances documented, the tax exemptions were granted in response to a petition, and their scope was limited to specific items. Thus, in 185 B.C.E., Attalos, brother of Eumenes II, exempted the *katoikoi* of Apollo Tarsenos from the tax on sheep (*RC* 47, quoted and commented on by Dignas 2002, 44). On the tax concessions granted by a king of the late Seleukid period to the sanctuary of Baitokaikē, in the satrapy of Apamea, in Seleukid Syria, contrast Dignas 2002, 74–84, and Aperghis 2004, 110–11. For a general statement to the effect that temples paid taxes, see Aperghis 2004, 108. On the specific case of Baitokaikē, see ibid., 111. Generally, Dignas's approach is decisively at odds with that of Aperghis, whose book was published shortly after

hers. On the activities of the royal officials in temples, see also Debord's (1982) view, which differs very much from that of Dignas.

101. J. K. Davies 2001a. The point of reference of recent discussions is Finley 1973.
102. Dignas 2002, 29.
103. Translation by Bringmann 2001, 208.
104. Bickerman 1938, 114. Goldstein 1976 omits this sentence in his translation.
105. Schaper 1995 and 1997 do not address the issue of the Achaimenid taxation of the temple, because the evidence Schaper reviews is ambiguous. The temple was the center of collection of both temple and royal taxes, and therefore it is impossible to know precisely which taxes were rendered by the temple to the royal treasury. Schaper postulates that the taxes forwarded to the royal treasury were those collected from the population, but although Darius's forged decree grants a tax exemption to the priests (Ezra 7:24), thereby documenting the existence of this exemption (and perhaps a claim against an attempt to suppress it), we have no way of knowing whether the temple itself paid taxes or not.
106. For the suggestion that Onias III's claim that the monies Heliodoros tried to seize belonged to Hyrkanos, see Sartre forthcoming, and below, §9.4.5.
107. Dignas 2002, 21, 24–25, 70–74 (on the Artemision of Sardeis), and 146–49 (on Ephesos). See further Bogaert 1968, 279–304.
108. "The movements in and out [of the city] of all grain should be declared ‹in the portico of the ago›ra so that, if it is not profitable for someone to bring ‹his produce› to the a‹gora in order to s›end it out from there, he should have the right to send it out, having paid the dues on what was de‹clared in the agora.› And with regard to those villages and farms that are outside ‹your city,› we think it right that each person is required to reg‹ister the amount of produce› he wishes to send out of his farm, so that he might send it out, having informed ‹the market commissioner [*agoranomos*] and› paid the dues" (*RC* 3–4 = *SEG* 15.717 = Aperghis 2004, 311–12, appendix 2, doc. 1; Aperghis's translation, slightly modified.) "Sending out" may be understood as "exporting." For an alternative English rendition, see Austin, no. 48. For the commentary, see Aperghis 2004, 285, and 2011b, 23.
109. See above, n. 39. Translation by Aperghis 2004, 285, and Austin.
110. Bringmann 2001, 206; Gauthier 1989, 91–96.
111. See Callataÿ 2004, 42; and Le Rider and Callataÿ 2006, 261. See also Bickerman 1938, 127–28. Brixhe, *Bull. Épig.* 1999.509, p. 682, understands that Eumenes II conceded to the citizens of Tyriaion the tax revenues that were levied by the *agoranomos*. Granting to a city or a temple a tax revenue that was normally destined for the royal coffers was a common euergetical gesture. The fact that Antigonos Monophthalmos refers to the *agoranomos* (a civic official) as a tax collector in his letter to Teos is no evidence that the latter was a tax farmer on the king's behalf. The revenues of the *agoranomia* may have been subject to direct royal taxation, or alternatively Antigonos may have been aware that the *agoranomia* constituted the main source of revenue from which the civic community paid its tribute to him, justifying his concern about the correct payment of the taxes to the *agoranomos*.
112. This was the system prevailing under the Achaimenids. On the cities, see Corsaro 1985. On the Jerusalem temple, see Schaper 1995 and 1997. Bertrand 2005 offers a convincing reconstruction of the part played by two Greek cities, Smyrna and Magnesia-on-Sipylos, in the collection of the taxes levied on the native villagers in their respective territories. Although the land cultivated by the villagers was royal land, subject to royal taxation, the

taxes were levied by the cities. The latter must have received a certain percentage of the harvest (probably a tithe) and handed over a fixed amount to the royal administration, retaining the difference between the two.

113. For the text quotation, see above, at the start of §9.4.

114. See Aperghis 2011b, 26. I owe the reference to Zechariah 14:21 to Hervé Gonzalez.

115. The book of Nehemiah 13:16–22 describes Nehemiah, who was the royal governor, as forbidding merchants' access to the city on the Sabbath.

116. "And since now seeing the great interest his father also shows to the sanctuary of Didyma, judging it good to follow the policy of his father, he announces that he will build * * * in the city a stoa, of which the resources will give the people funds to pay for the building judged to be useful to carry out in the sanctuary of Didyma * * *" (*I.Didyma* 479, ll. 5–12); "And Antiochos her [i.e., Apame's] son has announced, honoring the policy of his father, Seleukos, ‹about the sanctuary of Didyma,› that he would build ‹as quickly as possible in the city a stoa› * * * to the god, in order that the revenues ‹from it might regularly accrue› and the sanctuary to be established * * *" (*I.Didyma* 480, ll. 10–14). Translations by Kuhrt and Sherwin-White 1993, 26. I thank Gilles Gorre for drawing my attention to these inscriptions.

117. See Debord 1982, 11–17; on Delos, Linders 1992.

118. Dignas 2002, 14.

119. Aperghis 2004, 111. On the Baitokaikē inscription, see above, nn. 39 and 100.

120. Aperghis 2004, 285, and 2011b, 23.

121. As quoted above, §9.4.4B.

122. See Sartre forthcoming. I thank the author for allowing me to cite his paper extensively before publication.

123. See D. R. Schwartz 1998b.

124. Sartre's (forthcoming) argument is based on an incident narrated by Polybius (28.20.6–10) in which Antiochos IV denied before Greek envoys after the conclusion of his first campaign in Egypt in 170/69 B.C.E. that Antiochos III had given the satrapy as his daughter's dowry. In Sartre's view, Antiochos Epiphanes was responding to an allegation contentiously raised by the Ptolemaic court. See also D. R. Schwartz 1998a, 51–52, for the refutation that Ptolemy V's territorial claim had grounds.

125. Renewed tensions between the two dynasties may explain Antiochos IV's eagerness to depose Onias III and appoint a trustworthy ally in his stead. On this episode, see below, Chapter 10 (§10.2).

126. Gera 2009, 148–49.

CHAPTER 10. JUDEA UNDER ANTIOCHOS IV EPIPHANES

1. Assuming the transfer of royal subsidies to the temples and the collection of the taxes on their revenues were separate, the former being supervised by the high priest and the latter by the governor.

2. Sachs and Wiseman 1954, 208.

3. On Antiochos IV's accession to the Seleukid throne, see Mørkholm 1966, 38–50; Gera 1998, 109–17; Mittag 2006, 41–48. Besides the monographs of Mørkholm and Mittag, a shorter review of Antiochos IV's biography and reign is found in Gera 1998, 109–222.

4. See Capdetrey 2007, 329. See also Strootman 2006a.

5. This interpretation was defended by Mørkholm 1982, 301–5. See also Mørkholm 1966.
6. On Antiochos's reform of the tetradrachms, see Le Rider and Callataÿ 2006, 29–30, 124–25; Mittag 2006, 118–27.
7. On the bronze coinage, see Le Rider 1994; Mittag 2006, 182–98; Le Rider and Callataÿ 2006, 31–35.
8. Le Rider 1995.
9. Ibid., 393–94 and 401–3.
10. Houghton 2004, 55.
11. Hoover 2004.
12. This opinion is supported by several scholars. See Le Rider 1999 [1993], 1277; Mittag 2006, 224.
13. Hoover 2004, 488–89.
14. Finkielsztejn 2004, 258. The archeological evidence is reviewed in full in Finkielsztejn 2007. Finkielsztejn's suggestion that a reform was carried out in 173/2 BCE is derived from the complete absence of lead weights in the region dating to earlier years. Ruling out the possibility that this is merely due to the random distribution of archeological finds, Finkielsztejn defends the view that the best explanation is that the weights were re-cast when the standards were changed.
15. Finkielsztejn 2004, 255–58.
16. See, e.g., Houghton 2004; Mittag 2006.
17. See the recapitulative table in Cohen 2006, 402. Detailed discussions are found ibid., s.vv. Add the refoundation of Beth-Shean-Skythopolis as Nysa after the name of Antiochos IV's eldest daughter. See Rigsby 1980, 241, and Finkielsztejn's (2004, 256–57) discussion of the evidence based on amphora stamps. Mørkholm 1966, 116–18, already downplayed Antiochos IV's activity as a city founder.
18. See Chapter 7 (§7.2.2).
19. See the summary in Chapter 7 (§7.2.3A). For the detailed argument, see Chapters 1 to 5.
20. The present paragraph is heavily indebted to Schaper 1995 and 1997.
21. On Ramat Rachel (Rahel), see Lipschits et al. 2011.
22. Schaper 1995, 535, and 1997, 204. It should be noted, however, that Ezra 7:24 relates to a decree of Artaxerxes that is of doubtful authenticity. See Chapter 9 n. 83.
23. Schaper 1997, 203.
24. Schaper 1995, 536–37.
25. Schaper 1997, 201–3.
26. Schaper 1995, 532, 533.
27. Ibid., 531. The *rēš šarri bēl piqitti* was instituted by Nabonidus in 553 B.C.E. On his origins and early functions, see further Dandamaev 1979, 590. It appears that this official, who is documented only in Neo-Babylonian and Persian times, was replaced by the *paqdu* in Hellenistic times. On the *paqdu*, see Chapter 9 (§9.4.1).
28. One possibility is that this function was fulfilled by Nehemiah himself.
29. According to Oded Lipschits, the administrative structures of the tax levy remained unchanged from the last quarter of the eighth century B.C.E. through the Neo-Babylonian conquest in 586 B.C.E. and the subsequent Persian, Ptolemaic, and Seleukid provincial systems to the aftermath of the Hasmonean revolt. See Lipschits 2012. Moreover,

whereas in the Hasmonean period the center of Ramat Rachel declined, there is no evidence that the reforms affected the temple administration. See Bocher and Lipschits 2011–12.

30. On the *prostatēs*, see Chapter 9 (§9.4.1). The evidence from Egypt and Babylonia suggests that in both the Seleukid and the Ptolemaic realms the representatives of the central administration in the temples enjoyed wider control powers than in Persian times. For Egypt, see Gorre and Honigman 2013; and for Babylonia, Clancier and Monerie forthcoming (1). See further Gorre and Honigman forthcoming.

31. See Sartre forthcoming. For the claim that the story of Joseph the Tobiad is genuinely to be dated to the early second century B.C.E., see Chapter 9 (§9.4.5).

32. This paragraph is heavily indebted to Manning 2010, 152–57.

33. Compare the role of the high priest during Alexander's (alleged) visit to Jerusalem (*Ant.* 11.138).

34. Or *one* major center, alongside the administrative palace of Ramat Rachel, whose existence is never recorded in the literary sources.

35. This argument is inspired by Gille Gorre's analysis of Ptolemy II's motivations for imposing changes of priestly personnel in the Egyptian temples in connection with his cultic, fiscal, and economic reforms. See Gorre 2009, and below, §10.2.3.

36. It is not impossible that the real significance of the political clause incorporated in Antiochos III's decree of 200/198 B.C.E. was the full restoration of the high priest's powers thanks to the abolition of the tax farming system (*Ant.* 12.142). On this clause, see Chapter 7 (§7.1.1A), with n. 22 there.

37. On the Heliodoros story, see Chapter 9 (§§9.3, 9.4).

38. The proposition that the royal appointment of the high priest was untraditional is justified in Chapter 7 (§7.2.1).

39. See Chapter 9, n. 15.

40. This section is heavily indebted to Gilles Gorre, whom I thank for discussing these matters at length with me. On the drastic decline of the old priestly families, see Gorre 2009, 495–99.

41. On Ptolemy II's reforms, see Thompson 2008; Gorre and Honigman 2013; Agut-Labordère and Gorre forthcoming.

42. See Agut-Labordère 2003.

43. See Vandorpe 2000 and 2005.

44. His prominent hierarchic status in the network of Egyptian local priesthood is related to the narrow connection between Apis, the animal hypostasis of Ptah, and Serapis, who was emerging as the patron of the Ptolemaic dynasty. As Gorre points out, since they owed their position to the kings, the high priests of Ptah were particularly loyal to them. On the dynasty of the high priests of Ptah, see Gorre 2009, 285–309 and 605–22; Thompson 2012, 128–36; Gorre and Honigman 2013, 108–13.

45. See Gorre 2009; Gorre and Honigman 2013, 111–13. Gorre (2009) bases his reconstruction on the administrative title of the second high priest of Ptah, "accountable scribe of Pharaoh for all things in the temple of [X]." In contrast his father did not enjoy any scribal title, implying that he exercised no function in the financial administration of the temples. See Gorre 2009, 294 and 304, respectively. On the titles of Esisout I–Petobastis I, the first high priest of Ptah, related to the dynastic cult, ibid., 287–88; also Thompson 2012, 119, 122; on the

cultic and administrative titles of Annōs, his son and successor, Gorre 2009, 298, 299. In each nome (district) the temple of the god or goddess who was the local chief deity enjoyed hierarchic primacy over the others, like that of Ptah in Memphis. However, the administrative procedure of the distribution of the royal subsidies based on the *apomoira* tax to the temples in other nomes than the Memphite is unknown, and we do not know whether it was supervised by the nome's chief high priest, as in the Memphite district, or by royal officials.

46. See Gorre 2009, 579–86.

47. See further Gorre and Honigman 2013, 113–14. On the *lesōnis* in Persian times, see Agut-Labordère and Gorre forthcoming (section 2.1).

48. Gorre 2009, 586–600. The delegation of cultic duties to lower-ranking priests is a common feature of the Egyptian cultic praxis. See also Gorre and Honigman 2013, 107–8.

49. This last evolution, though, started some five decades after the eviction of Onias III in Jerusalem.

50. See, for instance, Monerie 2012, 335. On the *šatammu* of Esagila in general, see Boiy 2004, 196–202. Because of the nature of the sources, the *šatammu*'s administrative powers are much better documented than their cultic functions, the latter being deduced mainly from what is known of their responsibilities in the Neo-Assyrian period.

51. On the *kiništu* of the Esagila, see Boiy 2004, 202–4. In Uruk a "*kiništu* of free men in Uruk" (*kiništu mar banî*), which was comprised of twelve members, is documented in one text. See Boiy and Mittag 2011, 109. The "citizens," also referred to as the "Babylonians" in this city, by no means encompassed the whole urban population, but only its elite members, who both governed the city and enjoyed functions and prebends in the temple, and as such are also known as "temple enterers" (*ērib bīti*, sometimes translated as "priests"). On the prebend system and the "temple enterers," see Kuhrt 1990b, 150–54, and Waerzeggers 2011, 734–35, 742–44. Other documented population categories in Hellenistic times are the "people of the land," the *politai* (see below, §10.3.4), and various slave categories. See Spek 2009, 108.

52. See Boiy and Mittag 2011, 108; Clancier 2012, 307–8; Monerie 2012, 327–28.

53. Boiy 2004, 145, 150, 197–98, 216–17; Spek 1987, 62.

54. On Babylon, Clancier (2012, 24) opines that transmission was in general hereditary. In contrast, while admitting that there are two documented cases of succession from father to son in the third century B.C.E., Boiy (2004, 201) refrains from any generalization. More likely, in his view, the function of *šatammu* was available to a small circle of influential families, and the succession from father to son may have been the exception to the rule. On the one hand, the "Babylonians" may have had a say in the appointment of a new incumbent, through the members of the *kiništu*. On the other, the Seleukid king may have sought to "use his influence to appoint a supporter of the royal dynasty" at the head of the city (ibid., 201–2).

55. See Clancier 2012, 314; Monerie 2012, 329–30, 333.

56. See Clancier 2012, 315. On the Seleukid high priests, see Chapter 9 (§9.2).

57. See Clancier 2012, 316–17. This *zazakku* appears in a single text dated 169 B.C.E.

58. Ibid. Clancier explicitly makes the comparison between the *zazakku*'s financial powers and Antiochos's interference with the finances of the Jerusalem temple, quoting 1 Maccabees 1:7–28.

59. An English translation of the text is quoted in Kuhrt and Sherwin-White 1993, 150. For the translation of *šaknu*, see also Doty 1988, 96.

60. See Monerie 2012, 332; Clancier and Monerie forthcoming (1).

61. Monerie 2012, 331, 333, pointing out that the grant of a Greek name by the king was probably a rare and highly honorific privilege (ibid., 331 n. 12).

62. For the translation of these two titles, see Doty 1988, 97–98. Monerie 2012, 334–39, discusses the functions that were associated with each title. The status of the *rab ša rēš āli ša Uruk*, in particular, is debated. As Doty points out (1988, 97), the "chief officials" he oversaw were "either a class of service personnel attached to the temple or a household." According to Boiy and Mittag (2011, 107), the *rab ša rēš āli* replaced the *šatammu*.

63. See Monerie 2012, 333–34, 339–40.

64. See Monerie 2012, 336–37; Doty 1988, 97.

65. Monerie 2012, 336–37, 340; Doty 1988, 97. Despite their common ancestor, Doty treats Anu-uballiṭ-Nikarchos and Anu-uballiṭ-Kephalon as belonging to two distinct families, apparently because Greek names were common among the latter's kin, whereas the former's genealogical tree has only one Greek name. See ibid., 100–101.

66. The claim that the Jerusalem high priests appropriated the royal prerogative of temple building is made in Chapter 2 (§2.2.3).

67. See Monerie 2012, 347.

68. Ibid., 346–49.

69. Although he had not yet taken notice of the Olympiodoros inscription, Monerie (2012, 347) explicitly compares the apparent eviction of Diophantos-Anu-balassu-iqbi and that of Onias III. See further Clancier and Monerie forthcoming (1).

70. The conclusions put forward here draw heavily on my joint research with Gilles Gorre. See Gorre and Honigman 2013 and forthcoming.

71. One crucial difference is that, as Egyptian priests, the high priests of Ptah could have enjoyed prominent cultic functions, such as the coronation of the Ptolemaic kings as pharaohs and the primacy in the priestly hierarchy of the country, as well as their administrative functions. Moreover, whereas the Egyptian high priests were actively involved in the establishment of the dynastic cult, the link between the Seleukid provincial high priests and the state cult was looser. On the comparison between the Ptolemaic and the Seleukid high priests and its limits, see Gorre and Honigman 2013, 108–13. On the relation between the Seleukid high priests and royal cult, see in particular Ma 2000a, 26–27.

72. Bringing together the various parallels between Seleukos IV's and Antiochos IV's policies in Babylon and Uruk on the one hand and Jerusalem on the other, Clancier and Monerie forthcoming (1) interpret them as hints that in reaction to the defeat of Apamea, Antiochos III's successors undertook an administrative overhaul that aimed at improving their control over the imperial territory. In light of their analysis, Gorre and Honigman forthcoming argue that in many ways this post-Apamean reorganization recalls the wide-ranging set of reforms that had been carried on in Egypt by Ptolemy II, one century earlier. On Egypt and Judea, see also Gorre and Honigman 2013.

73. On the history of the Oniads, see Cross 1998, 151–72; with the cautionary remarks of Grabbe 1992, 112–14, and in this book, Chapter 7 (§7.2.1). On the high priests of Judea in Persian and Hellenistic times, see VanderKam 2004; Brutti 2006.

74. On the prestige of the high priest in early Hellenistic times, see Watts's cogent remarks (2007).

75. It was argued in Chapter 7 (§7.2.1A) that the genealogical data about Menelaos and Alkimos provided in 2 Maccabees are unreliable.

76. For this claim, see Chapter 7 (§7.2.1).

77. In the context of increasing tensions between the Seleukids and the Ptolemies. See Sartre forthcoming and above, Chapter 9 (§9.4.5).

78. Moreover, if we follow Maurice Sartre's hypothesis, Onias III may have prevented Seleukos IV's official from seizing the monies levied by Hyrkanos on behalf of the Ptolemaic king. See Chapter 9 (§9.4.5).

79. Contrast Aperghis 2011b, 27. For a criticism of Aperghis's assumption (ibid., 23) that the *agoranomos* of Jerusalem was a tax contractor, see Chapter 9 (§9.4.4C).

80. See Chapter 7 (§7.2.2).

81. Sartre forthcoming emphasizes Antiochos's political motivation, pointing out that a hostile Judean leadership could have easily turned to the Ptolemies for backing, thereby providing the latter with the desired pretext for launching a campaign of reconquest in the region. However, if Antiochos IV had been exclusively concerned with securing political alliances to prevent a possible Ptolemaic attack, it is hard to understand why he imposed a tribute raise—or alternatively why Jason and Menelaos needed to offer such a tribute raise to secure their appointment—since such an economic step could only alienate the local population. For another, more structural (and perfectly compatible), line of interpretation, see Clancier and Monerie forthcoming (1) as summarized above, n. 72.

82. Bickerman 1979, 38–40; Tcherikover 1959, 161–69 and 404–9. See the General Introduction, §3.2. The literary questions raised by the two Maccabees accounts about the *gymnasion* are tackled in Chapter 5 (§5.1).

83. See the General Introduction, §4.3.

84. See in particular Boiy 2004, 220–25, with earlier bibliography; Clancier 2012; Clancier and Monerie forthcoming (1); Strootman 2006b and 2013; Graslin-Thomé forthcoming. According to Spek (1987, 65–70, and 2009, 108), the *politai* community of Babylon was founded by Antiochos IV ca. 173/2 B.C.E., whereas on the basis of a fragmentary astronomical diary, Boiy (2004, 207–9) argues that the *politai* were already present in the city when Antiochos III visited it in 187 B.C.E.

85. Bickerman 1979, 39–40. "The community of the gymnasium, which was named after its royal patron, thus also became a legal entity and was constituted [as] a corporation within Jerusalem. Such Greek or otherwise alien communities in the midst of a foreign population are frequently found in other places of the Hellenistic Orient. They were mostly called '*politeumata*', 'bodies of citizens'" (ibid., 39–40).

86. τοὺς ἐν Ἱεροσολύμοις Ἀντιοχεῖς ἀναγράψαι.

87. See Tcherikover 1959, 404–9, now corroborated by Kennell 2005, 14–16, 23, adducing new epigraphic parallels, in particular the Tyriaion inscription (see below, §10.3.2). However, while endorsing the view that Jason turned the whole city into a polis, Doran (2012, 94) translates "to inscribe the Antiochenes in Jerusalem" (with discussion ibid., 99–100).

88. Tcherikover 1959, 161: Jason "had to draw up a list of those people who were in his estimation worthy of being citizens of the city of Antioch. It is not to be imagined that all the inhabitants of Jerusalem became Antiochenes automatically." The "nobles and wealthy men of the city" alone were enrolled, and "the establishment of the *gymnasion* and *ephebeion* was also in harmony with the city's aristocratic character" (ibid., 161–62). Tcherikover (ibid.) cites the *politeia* of Rhodes as a comparison.

89. See the historiographical survey in the General Introduction, §3.2.

90. See Doran 2001 and 2012, 105; Grabbe 2002.
91. Bringmann 1983, 74–82.
92. L. Jones and Ricl 1997 = *SEG* 47.1745 = Austin no. 236. A revised edition together with a new English translation may be found in Kennell 2005, 12–14. "Toriaion" is the spelling found in the inscription, but the place is known as "Tyriaion" in Xenophon, *Anabasis* 1.2.14, and Strabo 14.2.29. See L. Jones and Ricl 1997, 8. For further references, see Brixhe, *Bull. Épig.* 1999.509, p. 680.
93. This translation adopts a suggestion by Brixhe, ibid.
94. The translation follows Kennell 2005, 13.
95. See in particular Ameling 2003; Savalli-Lestrade 2005, 10–12; and Kennell 2005.
96. Ibid., 14–15.
97. Ibid., 19–22. The claim that civic *gymnasia* retained their military function in Hellenistic times is cogently made by Gauthier 1997. See also the historiographical reviews by Doran 2001, 95–96, and 2012, 101–2.
98. Kennell 2005, 15–16. According to Josephus, *Antiquities* 11.339, Alexander recruited Judeans into his army during his visit to Jerusalem. This anecdote need not be taken at face value but casts light on the context in which the raison d'être of the *gymnasia* documented in non-Greek cities may be understood. See also 1 Maccabees 10:36. On the nexus between polis, *gymnasion*, and military training in Babylon, see below, §10.3.4.
99. On the vocabulary of royal approval, see Kennell's commentary (2005, 17).
100. Kennell 2005, 17.
101. For the detailed discussion, see Chapter 7 (§§7.1.1, 7.2.3B).
102. See the General Introduction, §4.2. Capdetrey 2007, 175–77, restates the old view that the redesignation of three major sanctuaries as cities named "Hierapolis" in Hellenistic times was the result of a royal initiative. However, on closer examination, this is a modern speculation, with no formal support in the ancient evidence. For a more critical stance, see Debord 1997, 415–16.
103. Bickerman 1979, 33–34, 48–49; Tcherikover 1959, 164. The term "charter" is Bickerman's (1980a [1935]). In a slightly modified version, Bickerman's view is now endorsed by Ma (2012, 2013, and 2014).
104. Tcherikover 1959, 165–68. The historiographical issues are reviewed in detail in the General Introduction, §§3 and 4.
105. See Doran's succinct survey of the evidence (2012, 98–99).
106. Bickerman 1939b, 97–98. See further Millar 1983, 62, 67.
107. Marek 2013, 241–42.
108. Michels 2013, 299.
109. Michels 2013, 294.
110. The model was first proposed by Renfrew and Cherry. See Renfrew 1986; Ma 2003c; and Michels 2013, 294–302.
111. As restated in Strootman 2011a.
112. See the well-founded remarks of S. Schwartz 1998. For nuanced reassessments of the cultural and cultic implications of the institution of the *gymnasion*, see above, n. 90. As is well known, Bringmann (1983, 82–97) argued against earlier interpretations that Jason's reform had an adverse effect on the temple, claiming that it was in Jason's economic interest to preserve the temple, whereas Menelaos put an end to the entire temple experience. The

new models render Bringmann's arguments unnecessary. In addition, his assertion that Jerusalem's polis status was abolished by Menelaos rests on slim evidence (ibid., 93)—namely that the royal letter preserved in 2 Maccabees 11:27–33, dated in late 165 B.C.E., is addressed to the "*gerousia* of the Judeans and the other Judeans," rather than to "the *boulē* and the *dēmos* of the Antiochenes of Jerusalem," as it should have been had the polis existed at this date. This argument is weak, in particular because it is based on at least three questionable assumptions: first, that the rest of Judea had no independent institutions, and therefore all official letters were addressed to the institutions of the polis; second, that we know what the polis institutions were; and third, that the address of the letter is correct.

113. This argument rests on the theoretical premises put forward in the Methodological Introduction to Part I.

114. In a series of recent articles John Ma (2012, 2013, and 2014) argues that the polis originally founded by Jason was refounded by Antiochos IV as part of the punishing measures that followed his assault on the city. In this repressive context, the king imposed a purely Greek *politeia*, designed by a special lawgiver, Geron the Athenian (2 Macc. 6:1). For a discussion of Ma's view, see the General Introduction, §3.5 and n. 157.

115. S. Schwartz 1998, 15–16. Kennell's translation of 2 Maccabees 4:7–15 is reproduced in Chapter 5 (§5.1 at note 8). As remarked above (n. 87), Doran's renewed objections show that the philological controversy may resurface, although he subscribes to the view that Jerusalem as a whole was turned into a polis.

116. This aspect is noted in Orrieux and Will 1986, 152–54; Sartre 2001, 345; Mittag 2006, 278–80; and Aperghis 2011a, 75.

117. Aperghis 2011b, 24–26.

118. According to John Ma, this phase marks a refoundation of Jason's polis through *synoikismos*: that is, the merging of two or more groups of people of distinct status into a single community. See above, n. 114.

119. This issue is tackled in Chapter 11 (§11.2.3).

120. Boiy 2004, 220–25.

121. On the *gerousia* (or *synedrion*, Sanhedrin) of Jerusalem, see Grabbe 1992, 74, 191–92; and Boiy 2004, 222–24. Its members enjoyed the same fiscal privileges as the priests (*Ant.* 12.142).

122. On this topic, see above, §10.2.4.

123. Boiy 2004, 224.

124. See Boiy and Mittag 2011, 124; Strootman 2013, 84–86.

125. Spek 2005 and 2009, 107. See already Spek 1987.

126. See Clancier 2012, 320, 323.

127. See the *Babylonian Chronicle* (*BCHP* 5), quoted by Spek 2009, 107.

128. See Clancier 2012, 319.

129. The evidence is conveniently reviewed by Spek 2009, 107–10.

130. See the astronomical diary about a census held in 145 B.C.E., quoted in Spek 2009, 108.

131. 2009, 107—11, offers a detailed survey of the evidence. For summaries see, for instance, Boiy and Mittag 2011, 124, and Clancier 2012, 320. The reading *boulē* in BCHP 14 is uncertain. On the reading *peliganes* in BCHP 18, l. 3, see Spek 2009, 109.

132. See Strootman 2013, 84.

133. English translation is available in Spek 2009, 108. See also his online edition and translation (*BCHP* 14).

134. "Anoint with oil:" Spek plausibly interprets the Akkadian phrase as a rendering of the Greek *aleiphomenoi*—a reference to youths undergoing physical training at the *gymnasion*. See *BCHP* 14 online (the *Greek Community Chronicle*), Commentary, note 4. A building excavated at the southern end of the theater has been interpreted as a *palaistra*, but this has been called into question. Spek 2009, 110, with n. 41. More interesting, a *gymnasiarchos* is mentioned in a Greek inscription, and a Greek clay tablet of 111/0 B.C.E. (Arsakid period, *SEG* 7.39) gives a list of ephebes and *neoi* winners of athletic competitions that year. See Spek 2009, 110, with nn. 40–42. For more on the *SEG* 7.39 inscription, see Kuhrt and Sherwin-White 1993, 157.

135. Quoted only online, *BCHP* 13 (the *Politai Chronicle*), Commentary.

136. On the theater, see below in this section.

137. See, apparently, Spek 2009, 108, despite his introductory cautions (ibid., 101–3); and Clancier 2012, 320.

138. On *Hellēnes* as foreigners, see Mélèze-Modrzejewki 1983. On *Hellēnes* as a tax status, see Clarysse and Thompson 2006, 2: 138–47.

139. Spek 2009, 107–8.

140. This conclusion is fully supported by the evidence from Uruk, where Doty has studied the family tree of two prominent men who bore double names, Akkadian and Greek, over five generations. In the family of Anu-uballiṭ alias Kephalon a high proportion of individuals, including at least one woman, had either Greek or double names. See Doty 1988. On the Greek names documented in Babylon, see also Strootman 2013, 83, 85.

141. I am, of course, paraphrasing the description of Jason's followers in 2 Maccabees 4:10. Here I use the term "Babylonian" as an ethnic label, and not, as elsewhere in this chapter, as a status.

142. Spek 2009, 109 with n. 37.

143. Michels 2013, 297–99; quotation p. 298.

144. Translation by Kennel (2005, 10–11).

145. 2 Maccabees 4:12.

146. In contrast *BCHP* 6 (*The Ruin of Esagila Chronicle*) documents a genuine Greek ritual, but the performer is the "son of the king," probably Antiochos, the son of Seleukos I, when he was crown prince. See Spek's online commentary. On this text, see also Strootman 2013, 82.

147. See Spek 2009, 109. The *peliganes* of Seleukeia are documented in Polybius 5.54.10, in the corrupt form *Adeiganes*.

148. In Antiochos I's well-known foundation inscription from Borsippa, the king is described as "Macedonian." See M. Stol and R. van der Spek's online English translation at www.livius.org., "the Antiochus Cylinder," col.1, l. 5.

149. See Spek 2009, 107–8. First, The Greek inscription *OGIS* 253, dated 166 B.C.E. and honoring Antiochos IV as *ktistēs*, is of unknown origin. As Sherwin-White 1982 underlines, the stone could originate from either Seleukeia-on-Tigris or any other Greek settlement in the region. See also Kuhrt and Sherwin-White 1993, 157. Second, the Lehmann text documents a petition of the Babylonian citizens aimed at securing their claim to a certain donation of land. The donation was made under Antiochos II, but the petition is dated 139

S.E. (= 173/2 B.C.E.). Spek's inference (2009, 107) that the citizens were protesting against land expropriation in favor of the Greek settlers is speculative. On this text see also Spek 1987, 62.

150. See Boiy and Mittag 2011, 124; Strootman 2013, 85–86; Spek 2009, 110–11. On the Homera area, see below, n. 155.

151. Spek 2009, 108; Strootman 2013, 85.

152. For the detail, see Spek 2009, 110 with n. 40. A garrison commander seems to be mentioned in the astronomical diary of Month V 149 S.E. = Aug–Sept 163 B.C.E., quoted in Spek 2009, 111 n. 50.

153. This point was made to me by Christophe Feyel (personal communication). One final objection that Strootman makes to the *politai*'s being foreigners is examined below, n. 160.

154. We know from the descriptions of Alexander's entries that the city officials and population welcomed him outside the city gates. See Chapter 8 (§8.2.2). I owe this interpretation of the *Greek Community Chronicle* to Philippe Clancier (personal communication).

155. Spek 2001, summarized in 2009, 109. Clancier 2012, 309–11 and 320–21, offers a detailed discussion of the spatial indicators, based on Spek's conclusions. On the theater, see Spek 2001, 445–46, and 2009, 107, 109, and 110. On the Homera area—where several buildings in the Greek style were unearthed—see Kuhrt and Sherwin-White 1993, 155–56. The theater was rebuilt in the mid-second century B.C.E. The phrase *bīt tamarti*, "house of observation," as used in the Akkadian diaries, is a literal translation of the Greek (Spek 2009, 109).

156. Spek 2001 and 2009.

157. Clancier 2012, 321. References to the theater in the astronomical diaries are translated and commented on in Spek 2001, 448–55. The texts are selected from Del Monte 1997. Military matters: Spek 2001, nos. 5 (pp. 451–53 = Del Monte 1997, 137; 124 B.C.E.), 6 (pp. 453–54 = Del Monte 1997, 149–50; 119 B.C.E.), 8 (p. 455 = Del Monte 1997, 172; 87 B.C.E.), and 9 (p. 455 = Del Monte 1997, 176; 82 B.C.E.). Appointment of officials: nos. 2 (pp. 449–50 = Del Monte 1997, 102–3; June/July 141 B.C.E., a few months after the Parthian takeover), 3 (pp. 450–51 = Del Monte 1997, 127–28; 132 B.C.E.), and 4 (p. 451 = Del Monte 1997, 141–43; April/May 125 B.C.E.).

158. Spek 2001, 454 no. 7 (= Del Monte 1997, 167–68).

159. Spek 2001, nos. 3 (pp. 450–51 = Del Monte 1997, 127–28; 132 B.C.E.) and 5 (pp. 451–53 = Del Monte 1997, 141–43; 124 B.C.E.). Royal officials and messengers delivering missives to either community were not allowed into the sacred enclosure of the sanctuary; they were ceremoniously received at the precinct gate, known as the "Gate of the Son of the Prince of Esagila," which thus fulfilled a clear political function. See Clancier 2012, 311–13.

160. Clancier (2012, 322–23) stresses that the evidence we have about the royal letters being read at the theater is drawn from the astronomical diaries written by the temple's astronomer-astrologers. Moreover, these diaries contain detailed accounts of the content of the letters, suggesting firsthand knowledge. Incidentally, Clancier's suggestion is a rejoinder to Strootman's last argument that the *politai* were Hellenized members of the local elite. In Strootman's view (2013, 85), the fact that our evidence about the *politai* comes exclusively from cuneiform tablets is a strong hint of this identification, since old Akkadian and cuneiform writings were distinctive hallmarks of the "Babylonians."

161. Spek 2001, no. 1 (pp. 448–49 = Del Monte 1997, 84–85; 162 B.C.E.).

162. See Spek 2001, 449.

163. That is, of a lower social status than the "Babylonians."

164. See above, §10.2.4 with n. 72.

165. On the *zazakku*, see above, §10.2.4.

166. In most cases we do not know the names of these *epistatai*. Moreover, as previously noted (see above at n. 140), even Greek names may be inconclusive as far as the ethnicity of their bearers is concerned.

167. As pointed out to me by Clancier (personal communication).

168. On the view that Jason's polis was refounded by Antiochos IV, see now Ma 2013 and 2014. See further the General Introduction (§3.3A) and Chapter 11 (§11.2.3A). In my view, however, it is highly unlikely that this refoundation involved the merger of the military settlers with Jason's Antiochenes, given the huge difference in social status between the two groups.

169. As noted by Strootman 2013, 85. On this list, see above, n. 134.

170. Comparisons between Jerusalem and Babylon in Seleukid times are further complicated by recent questionings, in particular by Clancier, Graslin-Thomé, and Monerie, about the characterization of Babylon and Uruk as temple states. Whereas this label denotes a constituency dominated by a central temple, headed by a high priest, and enjoying internal administrative autonomy from royal power, in the great Babylonian cities only the urban elites who are called the "Babylonians" and "Urukeans" were organically linked to the great temple complexes for social, economic, and cultic purposes. Other segments of the population (on which see above, n. 51) were not. Moreover, given that the activities and persons linked to the old sanctuaries are overrepresented in the evidence, we have no means of knowing whether the "citizens" genuinely constituted the prominent families of their respective cities in Hellenistic times or what the weight of the temples was in the overall economic activity. See Monerie 2012, 328, 351; Graslin-Thomé 2012. These matters were forcefully pointed out to me by Philippe Clancier and Laetitia Graslin-Thomé in personal communications. Any errors are mine. Studies comparing Jerusalem and Babylon as temple states are quoted in Boiy 2004, 220.

171. See the General Introduction (§§4.3 and 4.4) and the Methodological Introduction to Part I (§I.3) and Chapter 8 (§8.3).

172. See Bringmann 1983, 74–82, followed by Mittag 2006, 237–39.

173. On the use of Greek names by Urukean elite families as a local power strategy displaying the bearers' personal ties with the king and local high-ranking Seleukid officials, see Monerie 2012, 331, 341. Monerie describes their Hellenization as a veneer, as evidenced by the fact that clay inscriptions commemorating Anu-uballiṭ-Nikarchos's building works in the Bīt Rēš sanctuary were written in Aramaic. Contrast Doty's interpretation (1988)—endorsed in Kuhrt and Sherwin-White 1993, 149–55—emphasizing cultural aspects ("name-giving is an indicator of cultural integration," Doty p. 111) and overlooking games of power strategy.

174. Strootman 2013, 70, supporting his theoretical discussion with the case studies of Babylon and Jerusalem.

175. See Pratt 1991, 33.

176. Strootman 2013, 70.

177. Ibid., 72. Monerie 2012 offers a similar analysis applied to Urukean leading families.

CHAPTER 11. JUDEA UNDER ANTIOCHOS IV EPIPHANES

1. See Chapter 9 (§9.4.5).
2. The literary arguments supporting this conclusion are summarized in Chapter 7 (§7.2.1B).
3. On the chronological and topical divide between 1 and 2 Maccabees, see the Methodological Introduction to Part II.
4. On this point, see Sartre forthcoming.
5. Last, Ma 2012, 70–84; 2013; and 2014.
6. As argued there, Josephus's accounts in *Antiquities* 12.248–56 and *War* 1.1.32–35 are derivative. On the ancient literary sources, see further Honigman forthcoming.
7. On the notion of mediating synecdoche, see the Methodological Introduction to Part II and Chapter 7.
8. The alternative view that the "prohibition of the Jewish customs" was the unintended consequence of the administrative changes imposed by Antiochos IV to squash the unrest (see, e.g., Ma 2012, 81) is refuted above in the General Introduction, n. 157. It is also implicitly refuted by the alternative historical interpretation offered in the present chapter.
9. Gera 1998, 131–41.
10. Ibid., 161–62.
11. Ibid., 166–67.
12. Ibid., 168–73.
13. Ibid., 177–78. On Petosiris, see also Hölbl 2001, 181–83. The main source is Diodorus Siculus 31.15a = Austin no. 286a.
14. Gera 1998, 178. The source is Diodorus 31.17b = Austin no. 286b.
15. Josephus's accounts are derivative and therefore may be set aside.
16. "He shall return to his land with great wealth, but his heart shall be set against the holy covenant. He shall work his will, and return to his own land. . . . For ships of Kittim shall come against him, and he shall lose heart and withdraw. He shall be enraged and take action against the holy covenant. He shall turn back and pay heed to those who forsake the holy covenant."
17. See Chapter 6 (§6.1.2). See further Honigman forthcoming.
18. On the dispirited mood that prevailed in Egypt in these days, see Hölbl 2001, 181–83, and Thompson 1987, 106.
19. Bickerman 1979, 44–45. Porphyry's fragment is also quoted in Jacoby, *FGH* IIB, no. 260, F56, pp. 1227–28.
20. See the General Introduction (§§2.1 and 4.1) and Chapter 8 (§8.3). See also the detailed discussion by Duyrat 2005, 251–52.
21. On this notion, see the Methodological Introduction to Part II and Chapter 7.
22. See Hannestad 2011.
23. Bickerman 1979, 42–58; Tcherikover 1959, 154–205, for the events ranging from the eviction of Onias III in 175 B.C.E. to the point when the Maccabees became the leaders of the revolt. On the influence of Bickerman's and Tcherikover's reconstructions on subsequent scholarship, see the General Introduction to this book, §§2–4.
24. Bickerman 1979, 42–57.
25. On which see further Chapter 6 (§6.1).
26. Bickerman 1979, 44–46.

27. Tcherikover 1959, 186–203. Tcherikover's view is summarized in the General Introduction, §2.2.

28. It was, however, thoroughly criticized by Gera 1998. On the pro-Ptolemaic and pro-Seleukid parties, see the General Introduction (§§2.1 and 4.1) and Chapter 8 (§8.3).

29. Tcherikover 1959, 191.

30. Tcherikover 1959, 192. In his view, the interests of the urban plebs and those of the rural population of the villages were linked: "for both classes had a common enemy, the large estate owners permanently resident in the town, although their livelihood was derived from the villages of the Judean countryside" (ibid.).

31. Bickerman 1979, 46–53. The quotation is from p. 47.

32. See Chapter 1 (§1.4, introductory paragraph); Chapter 5 (§§5.1.1B and 5.2); and Chapter 7 (§7.2.1A).

33. See Chapter 1 n. 36 and Chapter 7 (§7.2.3B).

34. Tcherikover 1959, 187–88. See, however, John Ma's alternative reconstruction, as summarized below, n. 111.

35. Unless it was defiled during the first assault.

36. 2 Maccabees 11:16–33. On the chronology of the royal letters, see Habicht 2006c [1976]; Bringmann 1983, 42–43. See the summary of John Ma's alternative reconstruction below, n. 111.

37. This was Bickerman's term (1979, 61).

38. That the massacred population would have thought otherwise goes without saying—we must keep in mind that 1 and 2 Maccabees and Daniel narrate these events from the viewpoint of the victims turned victors.

39. Bickerman's opposite view (1979, 46) is predicated on the assumption that the Hellenistic king was an absolute monarch who laid waste to conquered territories at will. This view was in line with an understanding of Hellenistic statehood culture that prevailed in his days but today is doubtful.

40. For this contention, see the conclusion to Chapter 7.

41. Goldstein's translation has been modified.

42. On *epistatai* see D. R. Schwartz 2012, 263–64, and Doran 2012, 132.

43. On the author's suppression of information potentially favorable to Menelaos, see Chapter 1 (§1.4.4).

44. Daniel 11:30 is worth noting in this context: "He will return and rage against the holy covenant. He shall turn back and *attend to those who abandon the holy covenant*. Forces from him will arise and profane the sanctuary of the stronghold." The translation is from Collins 1993a, 384, based on *NRSV*. Emphasis added.

45. See the impressive dossier of sources collected by Bertrand 1987, 97–100.

46. Instances of mass expulsions are nevertheless documented. See, e.g., *SEG* 39.1426, quoted by Chaniotis 2005a, 461.

47. *I.Priene* 14, ll. 5–7. See Sherwin-White 1985, 78–80. The inscription *I.Priene* 14 is republished ibid., 87.

48. Christian Habicht's careful study of the dates of the official letters gathered in 2 Maccabees 11 supports the conclusion that it was Menelaos who negotiated the amnesty treaty with Antiochos IV. Their presentation within 2 Maccabees is designed to suppress his role. See Chapter 1 (§1.4.4) and Habicht 2006c [1976]. See also below, n. 111.

49. As we saw in Chapter 7 (§7.4.4A), the Sabbath serves as a mediating synecdoche for warfare in the two Maccabees books.

50. For a detailed discussion, see the Methodological Introduction to Part II, and Chapter 7 (§7.4).

51. This translation has been questioned by Cohen 2006, 257 (at ii), with earlier bibliography. However, the precise physical boundaries of the Akra within the city need not concern us at this point. For a review of this topic, see Cohen 2006, 256–59 nn. 1 and 2.

52. On this point, see also Chaniotis 2005a, 462–63.

53. The detailed literary analysis is found in Chapter 6. See further Honigman forthcoming.

54. See Chapter 7 (§7.4.3).

55. On this passage, see Chapter 4 (§4.2.2C) and Chapter 7 (§7.4, introductory paragraphs).

56. That is, the need to focus the narration on the fate of the temple. See the Methodological Introduction to Part II and Chapter 7.

57. See chapters 7 (§7.1.2A) and 8 (§8.2.3).

58. "He will act for those who fortify strongholds, the people of a strange god. Those who acknowledge him he will make more wealthy, and he will make them rule over the common people and divide the land as their wages" (*NRSV* translation, modified after Collins 1993a, 388). See Bickerman 1979, 47. Bar-Kochva 1989, 438–44, sought to refute Bickerman's and Tcherikover's view that a military colony had been established in Jerusalem by questioning their interpretation of 1 Maccabees 1:38 and Daniel 11:39. In his view the expression *katoikia allotriōn* in 1 Maccabees cannot have the technical meaning of a military colony, because it is merely a translation of the Hebrew for "dwelling." Moreover, the word *katoikoi* appears in the same verse to denote the inhabitants of Jerusalem (ibid., 438–39). This philological argument overlooks the fact that the Greek *katoikia* is a *terminus technicus* only in modern literature and in ancient times was merely a common term. See Capdetrey 2007, 158–59. It is difficult to see why the fact that the author stressed the contrast between the legitimate inhabitants of Jerusalem and the foreigners by twice using cognates of *katoikeō* (*katoikoi* and *katoikia*) is an argument against identifying the foreigners as a military settlement. Bar-Kochva's interpretation of Daniel rests on a chronological argument that assumes that the prophetic text provides an objective eyewitness account of the events (ibid., 439–40)—which of course is not the case. Therefore these objections should be dismissed.

59. "Thereafter during his time of leadership, *he succeeded in expelling the gentiles from his people's land*" (emphasis added). The quote continues with a reference to Simon's expelling the inhabitants of the Akra.

60. Bickerman 1979, 47–53. His study must now be completed with Ma 2012, 77–82; 2013; and 2014.

61. *I.Pergamon* 249 = *OGIS* 338 = Burstein no. 91. See Bertrand 2005, 43–45.

62. *OGIS* 229 = *Staatsv.* III.492 = Austin no. 174.

63. *I.Pergamon* 249, ll. 12–17. See Chaniotis 2005b, 89.

64. *Staatsv.* III.492, decree (b), ll. 35–37. The *hypathroi* were soldiers who lived in the countryside. See Chaniotis, ibid.

65. *Staatsv.* III.492, decree (c), ll. 93–104.

66. Ibid., ll. 104-7.
67. Chaniotis 2005b, 91.
68. Ibid., 88-93.
69. *IG* IX.2.517 = Austin no. 75.
70. See Bertrand 2005, 44.
71. See Bickerman 1979, 47-58 passim; Tcherikover 1959, 193-94 and passim. See lastly Cohen 2006, 256, 259 at n. 3, 260-61 at n. 8, with survey of the sources and earlier bibliography. Ma (2012, 78; 2013; and 2014) argues that Antiochos IV refounded Jason's polis through synoecism, merging the newcomers and some of the Judean elites. However, to my knowledge no documented synoecism provides an accurate parallel to the case of Jerusalem.
72. 1 Maccabees 4:2, 41; 6:18; 10:7; 11:41; 13:21; 14:36. See Cohen 2006, 260 n. 8.
73. Cohen's list (2006, 260 n. 8) of the "numerous citations that could be construed as referring to Jews who were also resident in the Akra" in 1 Maccabees includes 1:34; 4:2, 60; 6:18, 21; 11:21. Bickerman (1979, 47) thought the Akra "also housed renegade Jews" based on 1 Maccabees 1:34, 6:22-27, and 11:21.
74. The wider section (1 Macc. 1:30-35) is quoted above in §11.2.2B.
75. As Judas's men were besieging the Akra, "some of the men of the Akra slipped through the siege lines. Joined by some wicked Israelites, they went to the king and said '. . . We were willing to serve your father. . . . As a result, our own countrymen have become our enemies. Indeed, they have killed as many of us as they could find and have been plundering our property. Not only against us have they raised their hands but also against all your domains'" (1 Macc. 6:21-25); "Then all the sinful and wicked men of Israel came before [Demetrios I] led by Alkimos, who wanted to be high priest. They brought charges against their people before the king, saying, 'Judas and his brothers have killed all your friends, and he has driven us from our land. Now, therefore, send a man whom you trust and have him go view all the havoc Judas has wreaked upon us and upon the king's domains.'" (1 Macc. 7:5-7).
76. On the otherizing of Alkimos in 1 Maccabees, see Chapter 5 (§5.3.1A). See also Chapter 3 (§3.3.2) and Chapter 5 passim on the process of otherizing the wicked Judeans in 2 Maccabees.
77. *Antiquities* 12.305, 362, and 364. For this list of references, see Cohen 2006, 256, 260. In *Antiquities* 12.305 Josephus was fooled by 1 Maccabees 4:1-2, and in *Antiquities* 12.362 and 364 by 1 Maccabees 6:18-28 and 11:20-22.
78. Bertrand 2005, 45-46, suggested that the cities levied a proportional rate of the harvest as taxes, handing over a fixed sum to the king. The difference between the two was kept by the city.
79. See, e.g., *I.Priene* 17, l. 20. See also Bertrand 2005, 47. On the status of the *laoi* and *paroikoi*, see Papazoglou 1997. On the system of tax collection through the cities, see Bertrand 2005, 45-46.
80. Ma (2012, 79; 2013; and 2014) also compares the legal status of the Judeans with that of *paroikoi*, albeit to give a rationalized explanation of the alleged forced participation of the Judeans to "pagan" rites. This view is refuted above in the General Introduction, n. 157.
81. See Bertrand 2005, 44.
82. Compare the land confiscations following the revolt of the Judeans of Egypt in 115-117 C.E. See Mélèze Modrzejewski 1989.

83. Contrast Bickerman 1979, 47–58, and Tcherikover 1959, 195 ("the Syrian cults prevailed on Temple mount because the population of the *polis* of Antioch-at-Jerusalem was now partly Syrian").

84. See the Methodological Introduction to Part II and Chapter 7.

85. This phrase is Bickerman's, but his reading is shared by many. See Bickerman 1979, 47 and passim.

86. For the theoretical premises, see the Methodological Introductions to Parts I and II.

87. On Jason and on Menelaos, see Chapter 5 (§§5.1.1C and 5.2.2, respectively).

88. For the theoretical premises on which this proposition rests, see the Methodological Introduction to Part I.

89. Hyldahl 1990; Doran 2011; Ma 2012. See further the historiographical survey offered above in the General Introduction, §§3.1 and 3.3.

90. See the Methodological Introduction to Part I (§I.2.2).

91. See further Chapter 6 (§6.2.1; *Commentary on Daniel* 11:31) and Honigman forthcoming.

92. The following citation from Thucydides, for instance, is instructive: "The Greeks have a law [*nomos*] that whoever has under his power a piece of land, whether big or small, also owns the sanctuaries, managing them in the same manner as before to the best of his ability. For the Boiotians, as well as most other men, have used violence to expel another group of people and now hold their land, having as their own those sanctuaries, which belonged to others when they first came upon them" (4.98.2–3). I borrow this quotation from Chaniotis 2005a, 457.

93. See also Bickerman 1979, 61–62.

94. There is, therefore, no reason whatsoever to claim, as Hengel does, that the "Jewish apostates"—i.e., Menelaos and the Judeans of the Antiochenes community—were responsible for this equation. See Hengel 1974 [1973], 1: 283–84.

95. On the Anatolian deities, see Debord 2001. The author reviews the instances of Zeus Labraundeus and Zeus Osogo, both sanctuaries of the city of the Mylasans (Strabo 14.2.23), and that of Zeus Karios of Panamara. See also Capdetrey 2007, 168–69, who also lists Zeus Olbios of Olba in Cilicia (Strabo 14.5.10) and Zeus Abrettenos in Mysia (Strabo 12.8.9). On the Semitic deities of northern Syria, see Teixidor 1989, 83. Add Zeus of the sanctuary of Baitokaikē, in the satrapy of Apamea, in Seleukis Syria (*RC* 70 = *IGLS* 7.4028 = Aperghis 2004, no. 15, p. 331 = Austin no. 172).

96. Ma 2012, 82–83, contends that the cult of Zeus Olympios was genuinely imposed by Antiochos IV as a means to create a homogeneous imperial culture. See the critique of this view above in the General Introduction, §3.3.

97. Teixidor 1989, 83. Besides Zeus of Seleukeia of the Pereia and Zeus of Homs, Zeus of Heliopolis-Baalbek and Zeus Kyrios of Dura-Europos referred to Hadad.

98. To demonstrate that the Egyptians were the first to discover the twelve gods, Herodotus tells us that they adopted twelve *names* for their gods, which the Greeks then borrowed (*Histories* 2.4). Likewise the equation of a god's name and his or her essence is illustrated in a hymn (aretalogy) in honor of Isis that probably dates to the first century B.C.E., inscribed on a temple wall in Hermouthis in Egypt. The relevant passage reads as follows: "All mortals who live on the boundless earth, / Thracians, Greeks and Barbarians, / Express Your fair Name, a Name greatly honored among all, [but] / Each [speaks] in his own lan-

guage, in his own land. / The Syrians call You: Astarte, Artemis, Nanaia, / The Lycian tribes call You: Leto, the Lady, / The Thracians also name you as Mother of the gods, / And the Greeks [call You] Hera of the Great Throne, Aphrodite, / Hestia the goodly, Rheia, and Demeter. / But the Egyptians call You 'Thiouis' [because they know] that You, being One, are all / Other goddesses invoked by the races of men" (Hymn 1, ll. 14–24). In Hymn 4, the speaker, one Isidoros, priest of the temple, reveals both the power of the god Porramanres and the name by which the Egyptians call him, and who gave him his name (ll. 29–34, 39–40). See Vanderlip 1972: translations, pp. 18 and 65. Isidoros's way of demonstrating that his goddess is universal is to claim that she is the one revered under different names by different peoples. At the same time Isidoros knew perfectly well that she was differently honored by different rites under each one of these "names."

99. It has been speculated that the "god of the fortress" of Daniel 11:39 may have been Zeus Akraios. See Hengel 1974 [1973], 1: 284. See also Collins 1981, 386 n. 150.

100. "It is unlawful for any foreigner to enter the enclosure of the temple which is forbidden to the Judeans, except to those of them who are accustomed to enter after purifying themselves in accordance with the law of the country. Nor shall anyone bring into the city the flesh of horses or of mules or of wild or tame asses, or of leopards, foxes or hares or, in general, of any animals forbidden to the Judeans. Nor is it lawful to bring in their skins or even to breed any of these animals in the city. But only the sacrificial animals known to their ancestors and necessary for the propitiation of God shall they be permitted to use. And the person who violates any of these statutes shall pay to the priests a fine of 3,000 drachmas of silver."

101. On this well-known dossier, see (e.g.) Dignas 2002, 59–66.

102. See 4QMMT: "And we are of the opinion that the sanctuary [is the 'tent of meeting'] and that Jerusalem is the 'camp,' and that 'outside the camp' [is outside Jerusalem], that is, the encampment of their settlements" (Composite Text, a, ll. 29–31) and "And one must not let dogs enter the holy camp, since they may eat some of the bones of the sanctuary while the flesh is [still] on them" (a, ll. 58–59).

103. Leriche 1997 offers an interesting description of how the network of shrines became increasingly dense in Dura-Europos as newcomer communities brought along their own deities and set up shrines to worship them.

104. If the soldiers were billeted with the population, their houses were also those of Judeans. However, they were more likely accommodated in confiscated houses and lived separately from the locals.

105. On the cultic importance of the daily sacrifice (the *Tamid*) and the traumatic effect of its suspension in Judean culture, see Lust 2001, 673. Mesopotamian sources also refer to the removal of cult statues by enemy kings as traumatic. See, e.g., Beaulieu 1993, 45, 47.

106. On the Achaimenid practice, see Tozzi 1977.

107. Alternatively, see John Ma's hypothesis below, n. 111.

108. "On the fifteenth day of Kislev in 145 S.E. the king had a desolating abomination built upon the altar, and in the outlying towns of Judah they built illicit altars, and at the doors of the houses and in the squares they offered illicit sacrifices."

109. On Daniel 12:11, see Lust 2001, 682. On 1 Maccabees 1:54, ibid., 683–84.

110. 2 Maccabees 6:7 speaks of the king's monthly birthday. On the celebration of royal birthdays, see Chapter 6, n. 45.

111. Despite its speculative tendency, the alternative scenario sketched out by John Ma in two articles (2013 and 2014) is worth summarizing here, because it potentially solves most of the problems that the reconstruction outlined in this chapter leaves open. John Ma has contended that the temple was retrieved not through reconquest by the Maccabees but through peaceful negotiation between Antiochos V and Menelaos. His proposal is based on two observations. First, the alleged time of Judas Maccabee's victories coincided with Antiochos IV's major military demonstration at Daphne, and although there may have been some unrest in the neighboring satrapy of Koilē Syria and Phoinikē during the period in question, the idea is implausible that rebels could have waged a successful war of liberation. (On the Daphne festival, see Mittag 2006, 282–95.) Second, Ma draws on a pattern of punishment followed by the restoration of former rights through negotiation, which is well documented in inscriptions. Arguing (against Habicht 2006c [1976]) that the four official letters gathered in 2 Maccabees 11:16–38 are to be read in their present order and that the second and third letters are addressed to the Judeans who were headed by Menelaos (and not to the rebels, as Habicht averred), Ma contends that shortly after Antiochos IV's death, Menelaos presented a petition to the governor, Lysias, asking for the restoration of the temple to the Judeans. In response, Antiochos V restored the temple and reinstated the Judeans' laws and customs. Moreover, Menelaos also negotiated an amnesty for all the Judeans—the continued unrest after the date set for this may explain why Menelaos was eventually put to death. Although the historical reality of Ma's scenario is indemonstrable, it cannot be dismissed out of hand. Given the ideological importance of temple refoundation for establishing the legitimacy of a ruling dynasty in the Judean political tradition, the Hasmoneans could have appropriated the memory of the temple rededication even if in actuality it had been performed by Menelaos. The possibility that Judas Maccabee's refoundation of the temple is manipulated memory is made plausible by Yoel Bin-Nun's (1991) cogent demonstration that the Hanukkah festival commemorating this event was grafted onto a preexisting festival, altering its original raison d'être (to mark the end of the olive harvest and the astronomical shift from the shortest day of the year). Moreover, the Hasmoneans could have redated to the days of Antiochos IV victories that were actually won at a later time, when the Maccabees took advantage of the Seleukid dynastic quarrels to rise to power.

112. Bickerman 1979, 61.

BIBLIOGRAPHY

Sourcebooks cited by document number are included in the list of abbreviations; those cited by page number are listed below. In cases of double dating (e.g., 1974 [1973]), page references in the notes correspond with the first date. Dates in square brackets refer either (for books) to an original publication in a language other than English or (for articles) to either an original publication or a republication, depending on which one was used for the page references.

Abel, P.-M. 1949. *Les Livres des Maccabées.* Paris.

Ackroyd, P. R. 1987. "The Temple Vessels: A Continuity Motif." In *Studies in the Religious Tradition of the Old Testament*, 45–60. London.

Agut-Labordère, D. 2003. "Le sens du Décret de Cambyse." In *Transeuphratène* 29: 9–15.

Agut-Labordère, D., and G. Gorre. Forthcoming. "De l'autonomie à l'intégration: les temples d'Égypte face à la couronne des Saïtes aux Ptolémées (VIe–IIIe siècles av. J.-C.)." In Clancier and Monerie forthcoming (2), 000–00.

Albertz, R. 1994 [1992]. *A History of Israelite Religion in the Old Testament Period.* 2 vols. Louisville.

Ameling, W. 2003. "Jerusalem als hellenistische Polis: 2 Makk 4,9–12 und eine neue Inschrift." *BZ* 47: 105–11.

Anderson, B. 1991. *Imagined Communities: Reflections on the Origin and Spread of Nationalism.* London.

Aperghis, G. G. 2001. "Population—Taxation—Coinage: A Model for the Seleukid Economy." In Archibald, Davies, Gabrielsen, and Oliver 2001, 69–102.

———. 2004. *The Seleukid Royal Economy: The Finances and Financial Administration of the Seleukid Empire.* Cambridge.

———. 2011a. "Antiochus IV and His Jewish Subjects: Political, Cultural and Religious Interaction." In Erickson and Ramsey 2011, 67–84.

———. 2011b. "Jewish Subjects and Seleukid Kings: A Case Study of Economic Interaction." In Archibald, Davies, and Gabrielsen 2011, 19–41.
Archibald, Z. H., J. K. Davies, and V. Gabrielsen, eds. 2011. *The Economies of Hellenistic Societies, Third to First Centuries BC*. Oxford.
Archibald, Z. H., J. K. Davies, V. Gabrielsen, and G. J. Oliver, eds. 2001. *Hellenistic Economies*. London and New York.
Arnaud, D. 1973. "La prostitution sacrée en Mésopotamie: un mythe historiographique?" *RHR* 183: 111–15.
Asad, T. 1993. *Genealogies of Religion: Discipline and Reasons of Power in Christianity and Islam*. Baltimore.
Austin, M. M. 1986. "Hellenistic Kings, War and the Economy." *CQ* 36: 450–66.
———. 1993. "Alexander and the Macedonian Invasion of Asia." In *War and Society in the Greek World*, ed. J. Rich and G. Shipley, 197–223. London.
———. 2003. "The Seleukids and Asia." In Erskine 2003, 121–33.
Bagnall, R. S. 1976. *The Administration of the Ptolemaic Possessions outside Egypt*. Leiden.
Bar-Kochva, B. 1989. *Judah Maccabaeus: The Jewish Struggle against the Seleucids*. Cambridge.
———. 1996. *Pseudo-Hecataeus, "On the Jews": Legitimizing the Jewish Diaspora*. Berkeley and Los Angeles.
———. 2010. *The Image of the Jews in Greek Literature: The Hellenistic Period*. Berkeley and Los Angeles.
Barth, F. 1969. "Introduction." In *Ethnic Groups and Boundaries: The Social Organization of Culture Differences*, ed. F. Barth, 9–38. Boston.
Barthes, R. 1974 [1970]. *S/Z*. New York.
Bartlett, J. R. 1998. *1 Maccabees*. Sheffield.
Baslez, M.-F., and O. Munnich, eds. Forthcoming. *Autour des livres des Maccabées. La mémoire des persécutions*. Paris.
Baumgarten, A. I. 2010. *Elias Bickerman as a Historian of the Jews: A Twentieth-Century Tale*. Tübingen.
———. 2012. "Russian-Jewish Ideas in German Dress: Elias Bickerman on the Hellenizing Reformers of Jewish Antiquity." In *The Russian Jewish Diaspora and European Culture, 1917–1937*, ed. J. Schulte, O. Tabachnikova, and P. Wagstaff, 73–107. Leiden and Boston.
Beard, M. 1987. "A Complex of Times: No More Sheep on Romulus's Birthday." *PCPS* 33: 1–15.
Beaulieu, P.-A. 1989. *The Reign of Nabonidus, King of Babylon, 556–539 B.C.* New Haven.
———. 1993. "The Historical Background of the Uruk Prophecy." In *The Tablet and the Scroll: Near Eastern Studies in Honor of William W. Hallo*, ed. M. E. Cohen, D. C. Snell, and D. B. Weisberg, 41–52. Bethesda.
Becking, B. 2006. "'We All Returned as One!': Critical Notes on the Myth of the Mass Return." In Lipschits and Oeming 2006, 3–18.
Bell, C. 1992. *Ritual Theory, Ritual Practice*. New York and Oxford.
———. 1997. *Ritual: Perspectives and Dimensions*. New York and Oxford.
Bencivenni, A. 2011. "'Massima considerazione': forma dell'ordine e immagini del potere nella corrispondenza di Seleuco IV." *ZPE* 176: 139–53.
Bengston, H. 1944. *Die Strategie in der hellenistischen Zeit. Ein Beitrag zum antiken Staatsrecht*. 2 vols. Munich.

Benjamin, W. 1973. *Illuminations*. London.
Ben Zvi, E. 1995. "Inclusion in and Exclusion from Israel as Conveyed by the Use of the Term 'Israel' in Post-Monarchic Biblical Texts." In *The Pitcher Is Broken: Memorial Essays for Gösta W. Ahlström*, ed. S. W. Holloway, 95–149. Sheffield.

———. 2008. "Imagining Josiah's Book and the Implications of Imagining It in Early Persian Yehud." In *Studien zur Sozial- und Religionsgeschichte Israels und seiner Umwelt*, ed. R. Schmitt, 193–212. Münster.

———. 2010. "Total Exile, Empty Land and the General Intellectual Discourse in Yehud." In *The Concept of Exile in Ancient Israel and Its Historical Contexts*, ed. E. Ben Zvi and C. Levin, 155–68. Berlin.

———. 2011a. "The Memory of Abraham in Late Persian/Early Hellenistic Yehud/Judah." In *The Reception and Remembrance of Abraham*, ed. P. Carstens and N.-P. Lemche, 000–00. Piscataway.

———. 2011b. "On Social Memory and Identity Formation in Late Persian Yehud: A Historian's Viewpoint with a Focus on Prophetic Literature, Chronicles and the Dtr. Historical Collection." In *Texts, Contexts and Readings: Reflections on Historiography and Identity in Persian Period Yehud*, ed. L. Jonker, 000–00. Tübingen.

———. 2012. "Remembering the Prophets through the Reading and Rereading of a Collection of Written Prophetic Books in Yehud: Methodological Considerations and Explorations." In *Remembering and Forgetting in Early Second Temple Judah*, ed. E. Ben Zvi and C. Levin, 000–00. Tübingen.

———. Forthcoming. "Late Historical Books and Rewritten History." In *The Cambridge Companion to the Hebrew Bible: Old Testament*, ed. S. B. Chapman and M. A. Sweeney, 000–00. Cambridge.

Bergren, T. A. 1997. "Nehemiah in 2 Maccabees 1:10–2:18." *JSJ* 28: 249–70.
Bernard, P. 1994. "L'Asie centrale et l'Empire séleucide." *Topoi* 4: 473–511.
Berthelot, K. 2003. *Philanthropia Judaica. Le débat autour de la 'misanthropie' des lois juives dans l'Antiquité*. Leiden and Boston.

———. 2006. "L'idéologie maccabéenne: entre idéologie de la résistance et armée et idéologie du martyre." *REJ* 165: 99–122.

———. 2007. "The Biblical Conquest of the Promised Land and the Hasmonaean Wars according to 1 and 2 Maccabees." In Xeravits and Zsengellér 2007, 45–60.

Bertrand, J.-M. 1987. "Le statut du territoire attribué dans le monde grec des Romains." In *Sociétés urbaines, sociétés rurales dans l'Asie Mineure et la Syrie hellénistiques et romaines. Actes du colloque organisé à Strasbourg (novembre 1985)*, ed. E. Frézouls, 95–106. Strasbourg.

———. 2005. "À propos des πάροικοι dans les cités d'Asie Mineure." In Fröhlich and Müller 2005, 39–49.

———. 2006. "Réflexions sur les modalités de la correspondance dans les administrations hellénistiques: la réponse donnée par Antiochos IV Épiphane à une requête des Samaritains—Flavius Josèphe, *Antiquités juives*, 12.258–264." In Capdetrey and Nelis-Clément 2006, 89–104.

Bickerman, E. J. 1937. *Der Gott der Makkabäer. Untersuchungen über Sinn und Ursprung der makkabäischen Erhebung*. Berlin.

———. 1938. *Institutions des Séleucides*. Paris.

———.1939a. "Notes et discussions: la cité grecque dans les monarchies hellénistiques." *RPh* 13: 335–49.
———. 1939b. "Sur une inscription grecque de Sidon." In *Mélanges syriens offerts à Monsieur René Dussaud par ses amis et élèves*, vol. 1: 91–99. Paris.
———. 1947. "La Coelé-Syrie: notes de géographie historique." *RBi* 54: 256–68.
———. 1979. *The God of the Maccabees: Studies on the Meaning and Origin of the Maccabean Revolt*. Trans. H. R. Moehring. Leiden. [Originally published in German as *Der Gott der Makkabäer* (1937).]
———. 1980a [1935]. "La charte séleucide de Jérusalem." In *Studies in Jewish and Christian History*, part 1: 44–85. Leiden.
———. 1980b [1939–44]. "Héliodore au temple de Jérusalem." In *Studies in Jewish and Christian History*, part 1: 159–91. Leiden.
———. 1984. "Calendars and Chronology." In *The Cambridge History of Judaism*, vol. 1, *Introduction: The Persian Period*, ed. W. D. Davies and L. Finkelstein, 60–69. Cambridge.
Bin-Nun, Y. 1991. "The Day of the Foundation of God's Sanctuary according to Haggai's and Zechariah's Prophecies." *Megadim* 12: 49–97. [In Hebrew.]
Blenkinsopp, J. 2001. "Did the Second Jerusalemite Temple Possess Land?" *Transeuphratène* 21: 61–69.
Bocher, E., and O. Lipschits. 2011–12. "Initial Conclusions from the Study of the YRŠLM Stamp Impressions on Jar Handles." In *New Studies on Jerusalem*, vol. 17, ed. E. Baruch, A. Levy-Reifer, and A. Faust, 199–217. Ramat-Gan. [In Hebrew.]
Bodi, D. 2008. "Néhémie ch. 3 et la charte des bâtisseurs d'une tablette néo-babylonienne de l'époque perse." *Transeuphratène* 35: 55–70.
Boegehold, A. L., and A. C. Scafuro, eds. 1994. *Athenian Identity and Civic Ideology*. Baltimore.
Bogaert, R. 1968. *Banques et banquiers dans les cités grecques*. Leiden.
Boiy, T. 2004. *Late Achaemenid and Hellenistic Babylon*. Leuven.
Boiy, T., and P. F. Mittag. 2011. "Die lokalen Eliten in Babylonien." In Dreyer and Mittag 2011, 105–31.
Bowersock, G. W. 1990. "The Pontificate of Augustus." In *Between Republic and Empire: Interpretations of Augustus and His Principate*, ed. K. A. Raaflaub and M. Toher, 380–94. Berkeley and Los Angeles.
Bremer, J. M. 1998. "The Reciprocity of Giving and Thanksgiving in Greek Worship." In Gill, Postlethwaite, and Seaford 1998, 127–39.
Briant, P. 1993. "Alexandre à Sardes." In *Alexander the Great: Myth and Reality*, ed. J. Carlsen et al., 13–27. Rome.
———. 2002. *From Cyrus to Alexander: A History of the Persian Empire*. Winona Lake.
Bringmann, K. 1983. *Hellenistische Reform und Religionsverfolgung in Judäa. Eine Untersuchung zur jüdisch-hellenistischen Geschichte (175–163 v.Chr.)*. Göttingen.
———. 2001. "Grain, Timber and Money: Hellenistic Kings, Finance, Buildings and Foundations in Greek Cities." In Archibald, Davies, Gabrielsen, and Oliver 2001, 205–14.
Brutti, M. 2006. *The Development of the High Priesthood during the Pre-Hasmonean Period: History, Ideology, Theology*. Leiden and Boston.
Budin, S. 2008. *The Myth of Sacred Prostitution in Antiquity*. New York.
Callataÿ, F. de. 2004. "La richesse des rois séleucides et le problème de la taxation en nature." In Chankowski and Duyrat 2004, 23–47.

———. 2005. "L'instauration par Ptolémée Ier Sôter d'une économie monétaire fermée." In *L'Exception égyptienne? Production et échanges monétaires en Égypte hellénistique et romaine. Actes du colloque d'Alexandrie, 13–15 avril 2002*, ed. F. Duyrat and O. Picard, 117–33. Cairo.

Capdetrey, L. 2006. "Pouvoir et écrit: production, reproduction et circulation des documents dans l'administration séleucide." In Capdetrey and Nelis-Clément 2006, 105–25.

———. 2007. *Le Pouvoir séleucide. Territoire, administration, finances d'un royaume hellénistique (312–129 avant J.-C.)*. Rennes.

Capdetrey, L., and J. Nelis-Clément, eds. 2006. *La Circulation de l'information dans les États antiques*. Bordeaux.

Carmignac, J. 1959–60. "Les citations de l'Ancien Testament et spécialement des poèmes du Serviteur dans les hymnes de Qumran." *Revue de Qumrân* 2: 357–94.

Carney, E. 2000. "Artifice and Alexander's History." In *Alexander the Great in Fact and Fiction*, ed. A. B. Bosworth and E. J. Baynham, 263–85. Oxford.

Chandezon, C. 2004. "Prélèvements royaux et fiscalité civique dans le royaume séleucide." In Chankowski and Duyrat 2004, 131–48.

Chaniotis, A. 2005a. "Victory's Verdict: The Violent Occupation of Territory in Hellenistic Interstate Relations." In *La Violence dans les mondes grec et romain. Actes du colloque international (Paris, 2–4 mai 2002)*, ed. J.-M. Bertrand, 455–64. Paris.

———. 2005b. *War in the Hellenistic World: A Social and Cultural History*. Oxford.

———. 2006. "Rituals between Norms and Emotions: Rituals as Shared Experience and Memory." In *Ritual and Communication in the Graeco-Roman World*, ed. E. Stavrianopoulou, 211–38. Liège.

Chankowski, V. 2004. "Introduction." In Chankowski and Duyrat 2004, 9–21.

Chankowski, V., and F. Duyrat, eds. 2004. *Le Roi et l'économie. Autonomies locales et structures royales dans l'économie de l'empire séleucide*. Lyons.

Charlesworth, J. H., ed. 1983. *The Old Testament Pseudepigrapha*. 2 vols. London.

Chavalas, M. W. 2006. *The Ancient Near East: Historical Sources in Translation*. Oxford.

Clancier, P. 2007. "La Babylonie hellénistique: aperçu d'histoire politique et culturelle." *Topoi* 15: 21–74.

———. 2012. "'Le *satammu*, l'assemblée de l'Esagil et les Babyloniens': les notables de Babylone—du relais local à la marginalisation." In Feyel, Fournier, Graslin-Thomé, and Kirbihler 2012, 297–325.

Clancier, P., and J. Monerie. Forthcoming (1). "Les sanctuaires babyloniens à l'époque hellénistique: évolution d'un relais de pouvoir." In Clancier and Monerie forthcoming (2), 000–00.

———. Forthcoming (2). *Les Sanctuaires autochtones et le roi dans le Proche-Orient hellénistique. Entre autonomie et soumission*. Paris.

Clarke, K. 2008. *Making Time for the Past: Local History and the Polis*. Oxford.

Clarysse, W., and K. Vandorpe. 1998. "The Ptolemaic Apomoira." In *Le Culte du souverain dans l'Égypte ptolémaïque au IIIème siècle avant notre ère*, ed. H. Melaerts, 5–42. Leuven.

Clarysse, W., and D. J. Thompson. 2006. *Counting the People in Hellenistic Egypt*. 2 vols. Cambridge.

Clifford, R. J. 1984. "Cosmogonies, in the Ugarit Texts and in the Bible." *Orientalia* 53: 183–201.

———. 1994. *Creation Accounts in the Ancient Near East and in the Bible*. Washington.
Cohen, G. M. 1994. "The 'Antiochenes in Jerusalem' Again." In *Pursuing the Text: Studies in Honor of Ben Zion Wacholder on the Occasion of His Seventieth Birthday*, ed. J. C. Reeves and J. Kampen, 243–59. Sheffield.
———. 2006. *The Hellenistic Settlements in Syria, the Red Sea Basin, and North Africa*. Berkeley and Los Angeles.
Cohn, N. 1993. *Cosmos, Chaos & the World to Come: The Ancient Roots of Apocalyptic Faith*. New Haven.
Cole, S. W. 1994. "The Crimes and Sacrileges of Nabû-šuma-iškun." *ZA* 84: 220–52.
Collins, J. J. 1981. *Daniel, First Maccabees, Second Maccabees, with an Excursus on the Apocalyptic Genre*. Wilmington.
———. 1993a. *Daniel: A Commentary on the Book of Daniel*. Minneapolis.
———. 1993b. "Stirring Up the Great Sea: The Religio-Historical Background of Daniel 7." In *The Book of Daniel in the Light of New Findings*, ed. A. S. van der Woulde, 121–36. Leuven.
———. 1997. *Jewish Wisdom in the Hellenistic Age*. Louisville.
———. 1999. *The Hellenization of Jerusalem in the Pre-Maccabean Era*. Ramat Gan.
———. 2000. "Teacher and Servant." *RHPhR* 80: 37–50.
———. 2001. "Cult and Culture: The Limits of Hellenization in Judea." In Collins and Sterling 2001, 38–61.
Collins, J. J., and G. E. Sterling, eds. 2001. *Hellenism in the Land of Israel*. Notre Dame.
Connerton, P. 1989. *How Societies Remember*. Cambridge.
Corsaro, M. 1985. "Tassazione regia e tassazione cittadina dagli Achemenidi ai re ellenistici: alcune osservazioni." *REA* 87: 73–95.
Cotton, H., and M. Wörrle. 2007. "Seleukos IV to Heliodoros: A New Dossier of Royal Correspondence from Israel." *ZPE* 159: 191–205.
Cross, F. M. 1998. *From Epic to Canon: History and Literature in Ancient Israel*. Baltimore.
Culler, J. 1975. *Structuralist Poetics: Structuralism, Linguistics and the Study of Literature*. Ithaca and New York.
Dąbrowa, E. 2010. *The Hasmoneans and Their State: A Study in History, Ideology, and the Institutions*. Cracow.
Dandamaev, M. A. 1979. "State and Temple in Babylonia in the First Millennium B.C." In *State and Temple Economy in the Ancient Near East: Proceedings of the International Conference Organized by the Katholieke Universiteit Leuven from the 10th to the 14th of April 1978*, ed. E. Lipiński, vol. 2: 589–96. Leuven.
Darbo-Peschanski, C., ed. 2000. *Constructions du temps dans le monde grec ancien*. Paris.
Davies, J. K. 2001a. "Hellenistic Economies in the Post-Finley Era." In Archibald, Davies, Gabrielsen, and Oliver, 11–62.
———. 2001b. "Temples, Credit, and the Circulation of Money." In *Money and Its Uses in the Ancient Greek World*, ed. A. Meadows and K. Shipton, 117–28. Oxford.
Davies, P. 1991. "Daniel in the Lion's Den." In *Images of Empire*, ed. L. Alexander, 160–78. Sheffield.
Debord, P. 1982. *Aspects sociaux et économiques de la vie religieuse dans l'Anatolie gréco-romaine*. Leiden.
———. 1997. "Hiérapolis: du sanctuaire-État à la cité." *REA* 99: 415–26.

———. 2001. "Sur quelques Zeus cariens: religion et politique." In *Studi ellenistici* 13, ed. B. Virgilio, 19–37. Pisa.
Descat, R. 2003. "Qu'est-ce que l'économie royale?" In Prost 2003, 149–68.
Del Monte, G. F. 1997. *Testi dalla Babilonia ellenistica.* Vol. 1, *Testi cronografici.* Pisa and Rome.
Dewald, C. 1993. "Significant Objects in Herodotus." In *Nomodeiktes: Greek Studies in Honor of Martin Ostwald,* ed. R. Rosen and J. Farrell, 55–70. Ann Arbor.
Dhorme, E. 1959. *La Bible. L'Ancien Testament.* 2 vols. Paris.
Dieleman, J. 2005. *Priests, Tongues, and Rites: The London-Leiden Magical Manuscripts and Translation in Egyptian Ritual (100–300 CE).* Leiden and Boston.
Dignas, B. 2002. *Economy of the Sacred in Hellenistic and Roman Asia Minor.* Oxford.
Doran, R. 1980. "The Martyr: A Synoptic View of the Mother and Her Seven Sons." In *Ideal Figures in Ancient Judaism: Profiles and Paradigms,* ed. J. J. Collins and G. W. E. Nickelsburg, 189–221. Chico.
———. 1981. *Temple Propaganda: The Purpose and Character of 2 Maccabees.* Washington.
———. 1990. "Jason's Gymnasion." In *Of Scribes and Scrolls: Studies on the Hebrew Bible, Intertestamental Judaism, and Christian Origins,* ed. H. W. Attridge, J. J. Collins, and T. H. Tobin, 99–109. Lanham.
———. 2001. "The High Cost of a Good Education." In Collins and Sterling 2001, 94–115.
———. 2011. "The Persecution of Judeans by Antiochus IV: The Significance of 'Ancestral Laws.'" In *The Other in Second Temple Judaism: Essays in Honor of John J. Collins,* ed. D. C. Harlow, M. Goff, K. M. Hogan, and J. S. Kaminsky, 423–33. Grand Rapids.
———. 2012. *2 Maccabees: A Critical Commentary.* Minneapolis.
Doty, L. T. 1988. "Nikarchos and Kephalon." In *A Scientific Humanist: Studies in Memory of Abraham Sachs,* ed. E. Leichty, M. deJ. Ellis, and P. Gerardi, 95–118. Philadelphia.
Douglas, M. 1966. *Danger and Purity: An Analysis of the Concepts of Pollution and Taboo.* London.
Dreyer, B., and P. F. Mittag, eds. 2011. *Lokale Eliten und hellenistische Könige. Zwischen Konfrontation und Kooperation.* Mainz.
Durand, X. 1997. *Des Grecs en Palestine au IIIe siècle avant Jésus-Christ. Le dossier syrien des archives de Zénon de Caunos (261–252).* Paris.
Duyrat, F. 2005. *Arados hellénistique. Étude historique et monétaire.* Beirut.
Eaton, J. H. 1976. *Kingship and the Psalms.* London.
Edelman, D. 2005. *The Origins of the 'Second' Temple: Persian Imperial Policy and the Rebuilding of Jerusalem.* London and Oakville.
Ego, B. 2007. "God's Justice: The 'Measure for Measure' Principle in 2 Maccabees." In Xeravits and Zsengellér 2007, 141–54.
Epztein, L. 1986. *Social Justice in the Ancient Near East and the People of the Bible.* London.
Erickson, K. 2011. "Apollo-Nabû: The Babylonian Policy of Antiochus I." In Erickson and Ramsey 2011b, 51–65.
Erickson, K., and G. Ramsey, eds. 2011a. "Introduction: The Sinking of the Anchor?" In Erickson and Ramsey 2011b, 13–18.
———. 2011b. *Seleucid Dissolution: The Sinking of the Anchor.* Wiesbaden.
Erskine, A., ed. 2003. *A Companion to the Hellenistic World.* Malden.

Eshel, H. 2008. *The Dead Sea Scrolls and the Hasmonean State.* Grand Rapids and Jerusalem.
Feyel, C., J. Fournier, L. Graslin-Thomé, and F. Kirbihler, eds. 2012. *Communautés locales et pouvoir central dans l'Orient hellénistique et romain.* Nancy and Paris.
Finkelstein, I. 2008. "Jerusalem in the Persian (and Early Hellenistic) Period and the Wall of Nehemiah." *JSOT* 32: 501–20.
Finkielsztejn, G. 2004. "L'économie et le roi au Levant sud d'après les sources archéologiques et textuelles." In Chankowski and Duyrat 2004, 241–65.
———. 2007. "Poids de plomb inscrits du Levant sud: une réforme d'Antiochos IV?" In *Productions et échanges en Syrie hellénistique et romaine. Actes du colloque de Tours, juin 2003*, ed. M. Sartre, *Topoi*, Suppl. 8: 35–60. Paris.
Finley, M. I. 1971. *The Ancestral Constitution: An Inaugural Lecture.* Cambridge.
———. 1973. *The Ancient Economy.* Berkeley and Los Angeles.
Fischer, T. 1980. *Seleukiden und Makkabäer.* Bochum.
Fisher, L. R. 1965. "Creation at Ugarit and in the Old Testament." *VT* 15: 313–24.
Fornara, C. W. 1983. *The Nature of History in Ancient Greece and Rome.* Berkeley and Los Angeles.
Fried, L. S. 2003. "A Silver Coin of Yohanan Hakkôhen." *Transeuphratène* 26: 65–85.
Fröhlich, P., and C. Müller, eds. *Citoyenneté et participation à la basse époque hellénistique. Actes de la table ronde des 22 et 23 mai 2004, Paris, BNF.* Geneva.
Funke, T. 2011. "The Relation between Samaria and Jerusalem in the Early Maccabean Period Revisited: A Case Study about the Reception of Phineas." Paper presented at the session of the European Seminar in Historical Methodology held at the Annual Conference of the European Association of Biblical Studies, Thessaloniki, 8–11 August 2011.
Gafni, I. 1989. "Josephus and I Maccabees." In *Josephus, the Bible and History*, ed. L. H. Feldman and G. Hata, 116–31. Detroit.
Galling, K. 1949–51. "Königliche und nicht-königliche Stifter beim Temple von Jerusalem." *ZDPV* 68: 134–42.
Gauthier, P. 1989. *Nouvelles inscriptions de Sardes.* Vol. 2. Geneva.
———. 1997. "Notes sur le rôle du gymnase dans les cités hellénistiques." In *Stadtbild und Burgerbild im Hellenismus*, ed. M. Wörrle and P. Zanker, 1–11. Munich.
Geertz, C. 1973 [1965]. "Religion as a Cultural System." In *The Interpretation of Cultures: Selected Essays*, 87–125. New York.
Genette, G. 1972. *Figures III.* Paris.
———. 1983. *Nouveau discours du récit.* Paris.
Gera, D. 1987. "Ptolemy Son of Thraseas and the Fifth Syrian War." *AncSoc* 18: 63–73.
———. 1998. *Judea and Mediterranean Politics, 219 to 161 B.C.E.* Leiden.
———. 2009. "Olympiodoros, Heliodoros, and the Temples of Koilē Syria and Phoinikē." *ZPE* 169: 125–55.
Gibson, J. C. L. 1978. *Canaanite Myths and Legends.* Edinburgh.
Gill, C., N. Postlethwaite, and R. Seaford, eds. 1998. *Reciprocity in Ancient Greece.* Oxford.
Goldstein, J. A. 1976. *I Maccabees: A New Translation, with Introduction and Commentary.* Garden City.
———. 1983. *II Maccabees: A New Translation, with Introduction and Commentary.* Garden City.

Gordon, C. H. 1949. *Ugaritic Literature*. Rome.

Gorre, G. 2009. *Les Relations du clergé égyptien et des Lagides d'après les sources privées*. Leuven.

———. 2013. "A Religious Continuity between the Dynastic and Ptolemaic Periods? Self-Representation and Identity of Egyptian Priests in the Ptolemaic Period (332–30 BCE)." In Stavrianopoulou 2013, 99–114.

Gorre, G., and S. Honigman. 2013. "Kings, Taxes and High Priests: Comparing the Ptolemaic and Seleukid Policies." In *Egitto dai Faraoni agli Arabi. Atti del convegno: amministrazione, economia, società, cultura dai Faraoni agli Arabi, Milano, Università degli Studi, 7–9 gennaio 2013*, ed. S. Bussi, 105–19. Milan.

———. Forthcoming (1). "La politique d'Antiochos IV à Jérusalem à la lumière des relations entre rois et temples aux époques perse et hellénistique (Babylonie, Judée et Égypte)." In *Le projet politique d'Antiochos IV*, ed. C. Feyel, L. Graslin, C. Mileta, and P. F. Mittag, 000–00. Nancy.

Grabbe, L. L. 1991. "Maccabean Chronology: 167–164 or 168–165 BCE." *JBL* 110: 59–74.

———. 1992. *Judaism from Cyrus to Hadrian*. Vol. 1, *The Persian and Greek Periods*. Minneapolis.

———. 2000. *Judaic Religion in the Second Temple Period: Belief and Practice from the Exile to Yavneh*. London and New York.

———. 2002. "The Hellenistic City of Jerusalem." In *Jews in the Hellenistic and Roman Cities*, ed. J. R. Bartlett, 6–21. London and New York.

———. 2006. "The 'Persian Documents' in the Book of Ezra: Are They Authentic?" In Lipschits and Oeming 2006, 531–70.

———. 2011. "Hyparchs, *Oikonomoi* and Mafiosi: The Governance of Judah in the Ptolemaic Period." In *Judah between East and West: The Transition from Persian to Greek Rule (ca. 400–200 BCE)—A Conference Held at Tel Aviv University, 17–19 April 2007*, ed. L. L. Grabbe and O. Lipschits, 70–90. London.

Graslin-Thomé, L. 2012. "La Babylonie hellénistique: le point de vue des dominés." In Feyel, Fournier, Graslin-Thomé, and Kirbihler 2012, 237–58.

———. Forthcoming. "De Jérusalem à Babylone: les relations entre le temple de Jérusalem et les souverains achéménides et hellénistiques à la lumière des sources mésopotamiennes." In Clancier and Monerie forthcoming (2), 000–00.

Gray, J. 1979. *The Biblical Doctrine of the Kingdom of God*. Edinburgh.

Grayson, A. K., and W. G. Lambert. 1964. "Akkadian Prophecies." *JCS* 18: 7–30.

Gruen, E. S. 1993. "Hellenism and Persecution: Antiochus IV and the Jews." In *Hellenistic History and Culture*, ed. P. Green, 238–64. Berkeley and Los Angeles.

Habermann, W. 2004. "Gymnasien im ptolemäischen Ägypten." In *Das hellenistische Gymnasion*, ed. D. Kah and P. Scholz, 335–48. Berlin.

Habicht, C. 1976. *2. Makkabäerbuch*. Gütersloh.

———. 2006a [1974]. "Hellenism and Judaism in the Age of Judas Maccabaeus." In Habicht 2006b, 91–105.

———. 2006b. *The Hellenistic Monarchies: Selected Papers*. Ann Arbor.

———. 2006c [1976]. "Royal Documents in Maccabees II." In Habicht 2006b, 106–24.

Hahm, D. E. 2009. "The Mixed Constitution in Greek Thought." In *A Companion to Greek and Roman Political Thought*, ed. R. K. Balot, 178–98. Malden.

Hallo, W. W., and K. Lawson Younger, Jr., eds. 1997. *The Context of Scripture: Canonical Compositions from the Biblical World*. Vol. 1. Leiden.

Halpern, B. 1990. "A Historiographic Commentary on Ezra 1–6: A Chronological Narrative and Dual Chronology in Israelite Historiography." In *The Hebrew Bible and Its Interpreters*, ed. W. H. Propp, B. Halpern, and D. N. Freedman, 81–142. Winona Lake.

Hannestad, L. 2011. "The Economy of Koile-Syria after the Seleukid Conquest: An Archaeological Contribution." In Archibald, Davies, and Gabrielsen 2011, 251–79.

Hawkes, T. 1977. *Structuralism and Semiotics*. London.

Hengel, M. 1974. *Judaism and Hellenism: Studies in Their Encounter in Palestine during the Early Hellenistic Period*. 2 vols. London.

———. 2001. "Judaism and Hellenism Revisited." In Collins and Sterling 2001, 6–37.

Henten, J. W. van. 1997. *The Maccabean Martyrs as Saviours of the Jewish People: A Study of 2 and 4 Maccabees*. Leiden.

———. 1999. "The Ancestral Language of the Jews in 2 Maccabees." In *Hebrew Study from Ezra to Ben Yehuda*, ed. W. Horbury, 53–68. Edinburgh.

———. 2001. "The Honorary Decree for Simon the Maccabee (1 Macc 14:25–49) in Its Hellenistic Context." In Collins and Sterling 2001, 116–45.

———. 2003. "2 Maccabees as a History of Liberation." In *Jews and Gentiles in the Holy Land in the Days of the Second Temple, the Mishnah and the Talmud*, ed. M. Mor et al., 63–86. Jerusalem.

———. 2004 [2006]. "Judas the Maccabee's Dream (2 Macc. 15:11–16) and the Egyptian King's Sickle Sword." *Zutot* 4: 8–15.

Hieke, T. 2007. "The Role of 'Scripture' in the Last Words of Mattathias (1 Macc 2:49–70)." In Xeravits and Zsengellér 2007, 61–74.

Higbie, C. 2003. *The Lindian Chronicle and the Greek Creation of Their Past*. Oxford.

Himmelfarb, M. 1998. "Judaism and Hellenism in 2 Maccabees." *Poetics Today* 19: 19–40.

Hölbl, G. 2001. *A History of the Ptolemaic Empire*. London and New York.

Hollmann, A. 2011. *The Master of Signs: Signs and the Interpretation of Signs in Herodotus' Histories*. Washington, Cambridge, Mass., and London.

Honigman, S. 2003. *The Septuagint and Homeric Scholarship in Alexandria: A Study in the Narrative of the* Letter of Aristeas. London and New York.

———. 2004. "La description de Jérusalem et de la Judée dans la *Lettre d'Aristée*." *Athenaeum* 92: 73–101.

———. 2009. "Euhemerus of Messene and Plato's Atlantis." *Historia* 58: 1–35.

———. 2011. "Cyclical Time and Catalogues: The Construction of Meaning in 1 Esdras." In *Was 1 Esdras First? An Investigation into the Nature and Priority of First Esdras*, ed. L. S. Fried, 191–208. Atlanta.

———. Forthcoming. "The Religious Persecution as a Narrative Elaboration of a Military Suppression." In Baslez and Munnich forthcoming.

Hoover, O. D. 2004. "Ceci n'est pas l'autonomie: The Coinage of Seleucid Phoenicia as Royal and Civic Power Discourse." In Chankowski and Duyrat 2004, 485–507.

Houghton, A. 2004. "Seleucid Coinage and Monetary Policy of the 2nd century BCE." *Topoi* 6: 49–79.

Houghton, A., and C. Lorber. 2000–2002. "Antiochus III in Coele-Syria and Phoenicia." *INJ* 14: 44–58.

Humphrey, C., and J. Laidlaw. 1994. *The Archetypal Actions of Ritual: A Theory of Ritual Illustrated by the Jain Rite of Worship*. Oxford.
Hurowitz, V. 1992. *I Have Built You an Exalted House: Temple Building in the Bible in Light of Mesopotamian and Northwest Semitic Writings*. Sheffield.
Hyldahl, N. 1990. "The Maccabean Rebellion and the Question of 'Hellenization.'" In *Religion and Religious Practice in the Seleucid Kingdom*, ed. P. Bilde, L. Hannestad, and J. Zahle, 188–203. Aarhus.
Ishida, T. 1977. *The Royal Dynasties in Ancient Israel*. Berlin.
Jacobsen, T. 1987. *The Harps That Once . . .: Sumerian Poetry in Translation*. New Haven.
Japhet, S. 2006a [1994]. "Composition and Chronology in the Book of Ezra-Nehemiah." In Japhet 2006b, 245–67.
———. 2006b. *From the Rivers of Babylon to the Highlands of Judah: Collected Studies on the Restoration Period*. Winona Lake.
———. 2006c. "Periodization between History and Ideology, II: Chronology and Ideology in Ezra-Nehemiah." In Japhet 2006b, 353–66.
Johansen, T. K. 2004. *Plato's Natural Philosophy: A Study of the Timaeus-Critias*. Oxford.
Johnson, A. R. 1967. *Sacral Kingship in Ancient Israel*. Cardiff.
Jokiranta, J. 2006. "Qumran—The Prototypical Teacher in the Qumran Pesharim: A Social Identity Approach." In *Ancient Israel: The Old Testament in Its Social Context*, ed. P. F. Esler, 254–63. Minneapolis.
Jones, C. P. 2009. "The Inscription from Tel Maresha for Olympiodoros." *ZPE* 171: 100–104.
Jones, C. P., and C. Habicht. 1989. "A Hellenistic Inscription from Arsinoe in Cilicia." *Phoenix* 43: 317–45.
Jones, L., and M. Ricl. 1997. "A New Royal Inscription from Phrygia Paroreios: Eumenes II Grants Tyriaion the Status of a *Polis*." *Epigraphica Anatolica* 29: 2–29.
Jursa, M. 2007. "The Transition of Babylonia from the Neo-Babylonian Empire to Achaemenid Rule." In *Regime Change in the Ancient Near East and Egypt: From Sargon of Agade to Saddam Hussein*, ed. H. Crawford, 73–94. Oxford.
Kaestli, J.-D. 2007. "Les rapports entre apocalyptique et historiographie: réflexions à partir du livre de Daniel." In *Ancient and Modern Scriptural Historiography / L'Historiographie biblique, ancienne et moderne*, ed. G. J. Brooke and T. Römer, 191–201. Leuven and Dudley.
Kalugila, L. 1980. *The Wise King: Studies in Royal Wisdom as Divine Revelation in the Old Testament and Its Environment*. Lund.
Kampen, J. 2007. "The Books of the Maccabees and Sectarianism in Second Temple Judaism." In Xeravits and Zsengellér 2007, 11–30.
Kapelrud, A. S. 1952. *Baal in the Ras Shamra Texts*. Copenhagen.
———. 1963. "Temple Building, a Task for Gods and Kings." *Orientalia* 32: 56–62.
Kennell, N. M. 2005. "New Light on 2 Maccabees 4:7–15." *JJS* 56: 10–25.
Kindt, L. 2009. "On Tyrant Property Turned Ritual Object: Political Power and Sacred Symbols in Ancient Greece and in Social Anthropology." *Arethusa* 42: 211–50.
Koenen, L. 1959. "*Theoisin echthros*: ein einheimischer Gegenkönig in Ägypten (132/1^a)." *CE* 34: 103–19.
———. 1993. "The Ptolemaic King as a Religious Figure." In *Images and Ideologies: Self-Definition in the Hellenistic World*, ed. A. Bulloch, E. S. Gruen, A. A. Long, and A. Stewart, 25–115. Berkeley and Los Angeles.

Kooij, A. van der. 2012. "The Claim of Maccabean Leadership and the Use of Scripture." In *Jewish Identity and Politics between the Maccabees and Bar Kokhba: Groups, Normativity, and Rituals*, ed. B. Eckhardt, 29–49. Leiden and Boston.
Kuhn, T. S. 1970. *The Structure of Scientific Revolutions.* 2nd ed. Chicago.
Kuhrt, A. 1983. "The Cyrus Cylinder and Achaemenid Imperial Policy." *JSOT* 25: 83–97.
———. 1987. "Usurpation, Conquest and Ceremonial: From Babylon to Persia." In *Rituals of Royalty: Power and Ceremonial in Traditional Societies*, ed. D. Cannadine and S. R. F. Price, 20–55. Cambridge.
———. 1990a. "Alexander in Babylon." In *Achaemenid History*, vol. 5, *The Roots of the European Tradition: Proceedings of the 1987 Groningen Achaemenid History Workshop*, ed. H. Sancisi-Weerdenburg and J. W. Drijvers, 121–30. Leiden.
———. 1990b. "Nabonidus and the Babylonian Priesthood." In *Pagan Priests: Religion and Power in the Ancient World*, ed. M. Beard and J. North, 119–55. Ithaca.
Kuhrt, A., and S. M. Sherwin-White. 1987. "Xerxes' Destruction of Babylonian Temples." In *Achaemenid History*, vol. 2, *The Greek Sources: Proceedings of the Groningen 1984 Achaemenid History Workshop*, ed. H. Sancisi-Weerdenburg and A. Kuhrt, 69–78. Leiden.
———. 1993. *From Samarkhand to Sardis: A New Approach to the Seleucid Empire.* London.
Kurke, L. 1992. "The Politics of *Habrosyne* in Archaic Greece." *CA* 11: 91–120.
Laato, A. 1994. "Zechariah 4,6b–10a and the Akkadian Royal Building Inscription." *ZAW* 106: 53–69.
Lackenbacher, S. 1982. *Le Roi bâtisseur. Les récits de construction assyriens des origines à Teglatphalasar III.* Paris.
———. 1990. *Le Palais sans rival. Le récit de construction en Assyrie.* Paris.
Lacocque, A. 2001. "Allusions to Creation in Daniel 7." In *The Book of Daniel: Composition and Reception*, ed. J. J. Collins and P. W. Flint, vol. 1: 113–31. Leiden.
Lambert, W. G. 1967. "Enmeduranki and Related Matters." *JCS* 21: 128–31.
Le Bohec, S. 1985. "Les *philoi* des rois antigonides." *REG* 98: 93–124.
Le Rider, G. 1994. "Antiochos IV (175–164) et le monnayage de bronze séleucide." *BCH* 118: 17–34.
———. 1995. "Politique monétaire séleucide en Syrie et Phénicie après 200." *BCH* 119: 391–404.
———. 1999 [1993]. "Les ressources financières de Séleukos IV (187–175) et le paiement de l'indemnité aux Romains." In *Études d'histoire monétaire et financière du monde grec. Écrits 1958–1998*, vol. 3: 1265–79. Athens.
Le Rider, G., and F. de Callataÿ. 2006. *Les Séleucides et les Ptolémées. L'héritage monétaire et financier d'Alexandre le Grand.* Paris.
Lemaire, A. 2010. "Nabonide et Gilgamesh: l'araméen en Mésopotamie et à Qoumrân." In *Aramaica Qumranica: Proceedings of the Conference on the Aramaic Texts from Qumran in Aix-en-Provence, 30 June–2 July 2008*, ed. K. Berthelot and D. Stökl Ben Ezra, 125–39. Leiden and Boston.
Lenger, M.-T. 1953. "La notion de 'bienfait' (*philanthropon*) royal et les ordonnances des rois lagides." In *Studi in onore di Vincenzo Arangio Ruiz*, vol. 1: 483–89. Naples.
Lenzi, A. 2008. "The Uruk List of Kings and Sages and Late Mesopotamian Scholarship." *JANES* 8: 137–69.

Leriche, P. 1997. "Matériaux pour une réflexion renouvelée sur les sanctuaires de Doura-Europos." *Topoi* 7: 889–913.
Linders, T. 1992. "Sacred Finances: Some Observations." In *Economics of Cult in the Ancient Greek World: Proceedings of the Uppsala Symposium 1990*, ed. T. Linders and B. Alroth, 12–18. Uppsala.
Lipschits, O. 2006. "Achaemenid Imperial Policy, Settlement Processes in Palestine, and the Status of Jerusalem in the Middle of the Fifth Century B.C.E." In Lipschits and Oeming 2006, 19–52.
———. 2012. "Archaeological Facts, Historical Speculations and the Date of the LMLK Storage Jars: A Rejoinder to David Ussishkin." *JHSc* 12, article 4. [Electronic version.]
Lipschits, O., Y. Gadot, B. Arubas, and M. Oeming. 2011. "Palace and Village, Paradise and Oblivion: Unravelling the Riddles of Ramat Rahel." *Near Eastern Archaeology* 74: 2–49.
Lipschits, O., and M. Oeming, eds. 2006. *Judah and the Judeans in the Persian Period*. Winona Lake.
Lust, J. 2001. "Cult and Sacrifice in Daniel: The Tamid and the Abomination of Desolation." In *The Book of Daniel: Composition and Reception*, ed. J. J. Collins and P. W. Flint, vol. 2: 671–88. Leiden.
Ma, J. 2000a. *Antiochos III and the Cities of Western Asia Minor*. Oxford.
———. 2000b. "Seleukids and Speech-Acts: Performative Utterances, Legitimacy and Negotiation in the World of Maccabees." *SCI* 19: 71–112.
———. 2003a. "Dans les pas d'Antiochos III: l'Asie Mineure entre pouvoir et discours." In Prost 2003, 243–59.
———. 2003b. "Kings." In Erskine 2003, 177–95.
———. 2003c. "Peer Polity Interaction in the Hellenistic Age." *Past and Present* 180: 9–39.
———. 2012. "Relire les *Institutions des Séleucides* de Bikerman." In *Rome, a City and Its Empire in Perspective: The Impact of the Roman World through Fergus Millar's Research*, ed. S. Benoist, 59–84. Leiden.
———. 2013. "Re-examining Hanukkah." *Marginalia*: http://themarginaliareview.com/archives/3083.
———. 2014. "Notes on the Restoration of the Temple." In *Seleukeia: Studies in Seleucid History, Archaeology and Numismatics in Honor of Getzel M. Cohen*, ed. R. Oetjen and F. X. Ryan, 000–00. Berlin and New York.
Machinist, P. 2006. "Kingship and Divinity in Imperial Assyria." In *Text, Artifact, and Image: Revealing Ancient Israelite Religion*, ed. G. Beckman and T. J. Lewis, 152–88. Providence.
Mann, M. 1986–94. *The Sources of Social Power*. 2 vols. Cambridge.
Manning, J. G. 2001. "Twilight of the Gods: Economic Power and the Land Tenure Regime in Ptolemaic Egypt." In *Atti del XXII congresso internazionale di papirologia, Firenze 1998*, 861–78. Florence.
———. 2010. *The Last Pharaohs: Egypt under the Ptolemies, 305–30 BC*. Princeton.
Manville, P. B. 1994. "Toward a New Paradigm of Athenian Citizenship." In Boegehold and Scafuro 1994, 21–33.
Marek, C. 2013. "Political Institutions and the Lykian and Karian Language in the Process of Hellenization between the Achaemenids and the Early Diadochi." In Stavrianopoulou 2013, 233–52.
Martinez-Sève, L. 2003. "Quoi de neuf sur le royaume séleucide?" In Prost 2003, 221–42.

———. 2004. "La fiscalité séleucide: bilan et perspectives de recherche." In Chankowski and Duyrat 2004, 81–104.
Martola, N. 1984. *Capture and Liberation: A Study in the Composition of the First Book of Maccabees*. Åbo.
Mason, S. 2007. "Jews, Judaeans, Judaizing, Judaism: Problems of Categorization in Ancient History." *JSJ* 38: 457–512.
Massar, N. 2000. "La 'Chronique de Lindos': un catalogue à la gloire du sanctuaire d'Athéna Lindia." *Kernos* 19: 239–43.
Mélèze-Modrzejewki, J. 1983. "Le statut des Hellènes dans l'Egypte lagide: bilan et perspectives de recherches." *REG* 96: 241–68.
Mendels, D. 1981. "A Note on the Tradition of Antiochos IV's Death." *IEJ* 31: 53–56.
Michels, C. 2013. "The Spread of Greek *Polis* Institutions in Hellenistic Cappadocia and the Peer Polity Interaction Model." In Stavrianopoulou 2013, 283–307.
Millar, F. 1978. "The Background to the Maccabean Revolution: Reflections on Martin Hengel's 'Judaism and Hellenism.'" *JJS* 29: 1–21. [Reprinted in *The Greek World, the Jews and the East* (Ann Arbor, 2006), 67–90.]
———. 1983. "The Phoenician Cities: A Case-Study of Hellenisation." *PCPS* 209: 55–71.
Mitchell, L. 1997. *Greeks Bearing Gifts: The Public Use of Private Relationships in the Greek World, 435–323 B.C.* Cambridge.
Mitchell, S. 2003. "The Galatians: Representation and Reality." In Erskine 2003, 280–93.
Mittag, P. F. 2006. *Antiochos IV. Epiphanes. Eine politische Biographie*. Berlin.
Modrzejewski, J. M. 1989. "*Ioudaioi apheiremenoi*: la fin de la communauté juive en Égypte (115–117 de n.è.)." In *Symposion 1985. Actes du VIe colloque international d'histoire du droit grec et hellénistique (Ringberg, May 1985)*, 337–61. Cologne.
Momigliano, A. 1975. *Alien Wisdom: The Limits of Hellenization*. Cambridge.
———. 1983. "The Origins of Universal History." In *The Poet and the Historian: Essays in Literary and Historical Biblical Criticism*, ed. R. E. Friedman, 133–54. Chico.
Monerie, J. 2012. "Notabilité urbaine et administration locale en Babylonie du sud aux époques séleucide et parthe." In Feyel, Fournier, Graslin-Thomé, and Kirbihler 2012, 327–52.
Mørkholm, O. 1966. *Antiochos IV of Syria*. Copenhagen.
———. 1982. "Some Reflections on the Production and Use of Coinage in Ancient Greece." *Historia* 31: 290–305.
Mowinckel, S. 1921–24. *Psalmenstudien*. 6 vols. Kristiania.
———. 1962. *The Psalms in Israel's Worship*. 2 vols. Oxford.
Moyer, I. 2011. *Egypt and the Limits of Hellenism*. Cambridge.
Müller, H. 2000. "Der hellenistische Archiereus." *Chiron* 30: 519–42.
Munnich, O. Forthcoming. "Substrat hébreu et réminiscences scripturaires dans le premier livre des Maccabées." In Baslez and Munnich forthcoming, 000–00.
Nachtergael, G. 1977. *Les Galates en Grèce et les Sôtéria de Delphes. Recherches d'histoire et d'épigraphie hellénistiques*. Brussels.
Nickelsburg, G. W. E. 1981. *Jewish Literature between the Bible and the Mishnah: A Historical and Literary Introduction*. Philadelphia.
———. 2003 [1971]. "1 and 2 Maccabees—Same Story, Different Meaning." In *George W. E. Nickelsburg in Perspective: An Ongoing Dialogue of Learning*, ed. J. Neusner and A. J. Avery-Peck, vol. 2: 659–74. Leiden.

———. 2006 [1972]. *Resurrection, Immortality, and Eternal Life in Intertestamental Judaism and Early Christianity*. Expanded ed. Cambridge, Mass.
Niese, B. 1900. *Kritik der beiden Makkabäerbücher nebst Beiträgen der makkabäischen Erhebung*. Berlin.
Nihan, C. 2007. *From Priestly Torah to Pentateuch: A Study in the Composition of the Book of Leviticus*. Tübingen.
———. 2010. "Groupes et partis à Jérusalem et en Samarie à l'époque achéménide." In *Samaritains, juifs, temples*, ed. É. Nodet, 81–104. Paris.
Nongbri, B. 2005. "The Motivations of the Maccabees and Judean Rhetoric of Ancestral Traditions." In *Ancient Judaism in Its Hellenistic Context*, ed. C. Bakhos, 85–112. Leiden and Boston.
Olson, D. 2004. *Enoch: A New Translation*. Richlands Hills.
Orrieux, C., and E. Will. 1986. *Ioudaïsmos—Hellènismos. Essai sur le judaïsme judéen à l'époque hellénistique*. Nancy.
Papazoglou, F. 1997. *Laoi et paroikoi. Recherches sur la structure de la société hellénistique*. Belgrade.
Parker, R. 1998. "Pleasing Thighs: Reciprocity in Greek Religion." In Gill, Postlethwaite, and Seaford 1998, 105–25.
———. 2005. *Polytheism and Society at Athens*. Oxford.
Parry, D. W., and E. Tov. 2004. *The Dead Sea Scrolls Reader*. Part 1, *Texts Concerned with Religious Law*. Leiden.
Perdue, L. G. 2008. *The Sword and the Stylus: An Introduction to Wisdom in the Age of Empires*. Grand Rapids.
Polak, F. H. 2006. "Sociolinguistics and the Judean Speech Community in the Achaemenid Empire." In Lipschits and Oeming 2006, 589–628.
Pollitt, J. J. 1986. *Art in the Hellenistic Age*. Cambridge.
Potter, D. 2003. "Hellenistic Religion." In Erskine 2003, 407–30.
Pratt, M. L. 1991. "Arts of the Contact Zone." *Profession* 91: 33–40.
Price, S. 1999. *Religions of the Ancient Greeks*. Cambridge.
Prince, J. 1987. *A Dictionary of Narratology*. Lincoln and London.
Prost, F., ed. 2003. *L'Orient méditerranéen de la mort d'Alexandre aux campagnes de Pompée. Cités et royaumes à l'époque hellénistique: actes du colloque international de la SOPHAU, Rennes, avril 2003*. Toulouse.
Pury, A. de, J.-D. Macchi, and T. Römer, eds. 2000. *Israel Constructs Its History: Deuteronomistic Historiography in Recent Research*. Sheffield.
Rajak, T. 2009. *Translation and Survival: The Greek Bible of the Ancient Jewish Diaspora*. Oxford.
Regev, E. 2008. "Hanukkah and the Temple of the Maccabees: Ritual and Ideology from Judas Maccabeus to Simon." *Jewish Studies Quarterly* 15: 87–114.
———. 2013. *The Hasmoneans: Ideology, Archaeology, Identity*. Göttingen.
Renfrew, C. 1986. "Introduction: Peer Polity Interaction and Socio-Political Change." In *Peer Polity Interaction and Socio-Political Change*, ed. C. Renfrew and J. F. Cherry, 1–18. Cambridge.
Rey-Coquais, J.-P. 1974. *Arados et sa pérée aux époques grecque, romaine et byzantine. Recueil des témoignages littéraires anciens, suivi de recherches sur les sites, l'histoire, la civilisation*. Paris.

Rhodes, P. J. 1981. *A Commentary on the Aristotelian* Athenaion Politeia. Oxford.
Rigsby, K. J. 1980. "Seleucid Notes." *TAPA* 110: 233–54.
———. 1996. *Asylia: Territorial Inviolability in the Hellenistic World*. Berkeley and Los Angeles.
Rimmon-Kenan, S. 1983. *Narrative Fiction: Contemporary Poetics*. London and New York.
Robert, L., and J. Robert. 1954. *La Carie. Histoire et géographie historique.* Vol. 2, *Le Plateau de Tabai et ses environs*. Paris.
———. 1982. "Documents d'Asie Mineure." *BCH* 106: 309–78.
Rood, T. 1998. *Thucydides: Narrative and Explanation*. Oxford.
Ross Bedford, P. 1995. "Discerning the Time: Haggai, Zechariah, and the 'Delay' in the Rebuilding of the Jerusalem Temple." In *The Pitcher Is Broken: Memorial Essays for Gösta W. Ahlström*, ed. S. W. Holloway and L. K. Handy, 71–94. Sheffield.
Rotstein, A. 2014. *Literary History in the Parian Marble*. Cambridge, Mass.
Rudhardt, J. 1992. *Notions fondamentales de la pensée religieuse et actes constitutifs du culte dans la Grèce classique*. Paris.
Sachs, A. J., and D. J. Wiseman. 1954. "A Babylonian King List of the Hellenistic Period." *Iraq* 16: 202–12.
Sanders, E. P. 1992. *Judaism: Practice and Beliefs, 63 B.C.E.–66 C.E.* London.
Sartre, M. 1988. "La Syrie creuse n'existe pas." In *Géographie historique au Proche-Orient. Syrie, Phénicie, Arabie grecques, romaines, byzantines: actes de la table ronde de Valbonne, 16–18 septembre 1985*, ed. P.-L. Gatier, B. Helly, and J.-P. Rey-Coquais, 15–40. Paris.
———. 2001. *D'Alexandre à Zénobie. Histoire du Levant antique, IVe siècle av. J.-C.–IIIe siècle ap. J.-C.* Paris.
———. Forthcoming. "Histoire et mémoire(s) des Maccabées." In Baslez and Munnich forthcoming, 000–00.
Savalli-Lestrade, I. 1998. *Les Philoi royaux dans l'Asie hellénistique*. Geneva.
———. 2005. "Devenir une cité: *poleis* nouvelles et aspirations civiques en Asie Mineure à la basse époque hellénistique." In Fröhlich and Müller 2005, 9–37.
Scafuro, A. D. 1994. "Introduction: Bifurcations and Intersections." In Boegehold and Scafuro 1994, 1–20.
Schalit, A. 1954. "Κοίλη Συρία from the Mid-Fourth Century to the Beginning of the Third Century BC." *Scripta Hierosolymitana* 1: 64–77.
Schaper, J. 1995. "The Jerusalem Temple as an Instrument of the Achaemenid Fiscal Administration." *VT* 45: 528–39.
———. 1997. "The Temple Treasury Committee in the Times of Nehemiah and Ezra." *VT* 47: 200–206.
Scheid, J. 2001. *Religion et piété à Rome*. 2nd ed. Paris.
———. 2005. *Quand faire, c'est croire. Les rites sacrificiels des Romains*. Paris.
Schmidt, F. 2001 [1994]. *How the Temple Thinks: Identity and Social Cohesion in Ancient Judaism*. Sheffield.
Schmitt, H. H. 1964. *Untersuchungen zur Geschichte Antiochos' des Grossen und seiner Zeit*. Wiesbaden.
Schürer, E. 1973. *The History of the Jewish People in the Age of Jesus Christ (175 B.C.–A.D. 135)*. Ed. G. Vermes and F. Millar. Rev. ed. 3 vols. Edinburgh.

Schwartz, D. R. 1998a. "Josephus' Tobiads: Back to the Second Century?" In *Jews in a Graeco-Roman World*, ed. M. Goodman, 47–61. Oxford.

———. 1998b. "On Something Biblical about 2 Maccabees." In *Biblical Perspectives: Early Use and Interpretation of the Bible in Light of the Dead Sea Scrolls*, ed. M. E. Stone and E. G. Chazon, 223–32. Leiden.

———. 2008. *2 Maccabees*. Berlin and New York.

Schwartz, S. 1991. "Israel and the Nations Roundabout: 1 Maccabees and the Hasmonean Expansion." *JJS* 42: 16–39.

———. 1993. "A Note on the Social Type and Political Ideology of the Hasmonean Family." *JBL* 112: 305–17.

———. 1998. "The Hellenization of Jerusalem and Shechem." In *Jews in a Graeco-Roman World*, ed. M. Goodman, 37–45. Oxford.

———. 2001. *Imperialism and Jewish Society, 200 B.C.E. to 640 C.E.* Princeton.

Schwiderski, D. 2000. *Handbuch des nordwestsemitischen Briefformulars. Ein Beitrag zur Echtheitsfrage der aramäischen Briefe des Esrabuches*. Berlin.

Scolnic, B. E. 2010. "Mattathias and the Jewish Man of Modein." *JBL* 129: 463–83.

Selden, D. L. 1998. "Alibis." *CA* 17: 289–412.

Seow, C.-L. 2008. "The Social World of Ecclesiastes." In *Scribes, Sages, and Seers: The Sage in the Eastern Mediterranean World*, ed. L. G. Perdue, 189–217. Göttingen.

Sérandour, A. 1996. "Les récits bibliques de la construction du second temple: leurs enjeux." *Transeuphratène* 11: 9–32.

———. 2008. "Les femmes étrangères dans les livres grec et hébraïque d'Esdras: répudiation ou exclusion du culte?" *Transeuphratène* 36: 155–63.

———. 2009. "Histoire du judaïsme aux époques perse, hellénistique et romaine: de Cyrus à Bar Kokhba." In *Introduction à l'Ancien Testament*, ed. T. Römer, J.-D. Macchi, and C. Nihan, 83–121. Geneva.

Sherwin-White, S. M. 1982. "A Greek Ostrakon from Babylon of the Early Third Century B.C." *ZPE* 47: 51–70.

———. 1983. "Ritual for a Seleucid King at Babylon." *JHSt* 103: 156–59.

———. 1985. "Ancient Archives: The Edict of Alexander to Priene—A Reappraisal." *JHSt* 105: 69–89.

———. 1991. "Aspects of Seleucid Royal Ideology: The Cylinder of Antiochus I from Borsippa." *JHSt* 111: 71–86.

Smith, J. Z. 1987. *To Take Place: Toward Theory in Ritual*. Chicago and London.

———. 1993. *Map Is Not Territory: Studies in the History of Religions*. Chicago.

Sommer, B. D. 2000. "The Babylonian Akitu Festival: Rectifying the King or Renewing the Cosmos?" *JANES* 27: 81–95.

Spek, R. J. van der. 1987. "The Babylonian City." In *Hellenism in the East: The Interaction of Greek and Non-Greek Civilizations from Syria to Central Asia after Alexander*, ed. A. Kuhrt and S. M. Sherwin-White, 57–74. London.

———. 2000. "The Seleukid State and the Economy." In *Production and Public Powers in Classical Antiquity*, ed. E. Lo Cascio and D. W. Rathbone, 27–36. Cambridge.

———. 2001. "The Theatre of Babylon in Cuneiform." In *Veenhof Anniversary Volume: Studies Presented to Klaas R. Veenhof on the Occasion of His Sixty-Fifth Birthday*, ed. W. H. van Soldt, 445–56. Leiden.

———. 2005. "Ethnic Segregation in Hellenistic Babylon." In *Ethnicity in Ancient Mesopotamia: Proceedings of the 48th Rencontre assyriologique internationale, Leiden 2002*, ed. W. H. van Soldt, 393–408. Leiden.

———. 2009. "Multi-Ethnicity and Ethnic Segregation in Hellenistic Babylon." In *Ethnic Constructs in Antiquity: The Role of Power and Tradition*, ed. T. Derks and N. Roymans, 101–15. Amsterdam.

———. 2011. "The 'Silverization' of the Economy of the Achaemenid and Seleukid Empires and Early Modern China." In Archibald, Davies, and Gabrielsen 2011, 402–20.

Spencer, D. 2002. *The Roman Alexander: Reading a Cultural Myth*. Exeter.

Stavrianopoulou, E., ed. 2013. *Shifting Social Imaginaries in the Hellenistic Period: Narrations, Practices, and Images*. Leiden and Boston.

Stephens, S. 2003. *Seeing Double: Intercultural Poetics in Ptolemaic Alexandria*. Berkeley and Los Angeles.

Stokholm, N. 1968. "Zur Überlieferung von Heliodor, Kuturnaḫḫunte, und anderen missglückten Tempelräubern." *ST* 22: 1–28.

Stone, M. E., and J. C. Greenfield. 1993. "The Prayer of Levi." *JBL* 112: 247–66.

Strootman, R. 2006a. Review of Mittag 2006. *BMCR*: http://bmcr.brynmawr.edu/2008/2008-09-28.html.

———. 2006b. "Van wetsgetrouwen en afvalligen: religieus geweld en culturele verandering in de tijd der Makkabaeen." In *Religies in interactie. Jodendom en Christendom in de Oudheid*, ed. B. Becking and G. Rouwhorst, 79–97. Zoetermeer and Utrecht.

———. 2011a. "Hellenistic Court Society: The Seleukid Imperial Court under Antiochos the Great, 223–187 BCE." In *Royal Courts in Dynastic States and Empires: A Global Perspective*, ed. J. Duindam, T. Artan, and M. Kunt, 63–89. Leiden and Boston.

———. 2011b. "Kings and Cities in the Hellenistic Age." In *Political Culture in the Greek City after the Classical Age*, ed. R. Alston, O. van Nijf, and C. Williamson, 141–53. Leuven.

———. 2013. "Babylonian, Macedonian, King of the World: The Antiochos Cylinder from Borsippa and Seleukid Imperial Integration." In Stavrianopoulou 2013, 67–98.

Swain, J. W. 1940. "The Theory of the Four Monarchies: Opposition History under the Roman Empire." *CP* 35: 1–21.

Swartz, M. D. 2002. "The Semiotics of the Priestly Vestments in Ancient Judaism." In *Sacrifice in Religious Experience*, ed. A. I. Baumgarten, 57–80. Leiden.

Tcherikover, V. 1959. *Hellenistic Civilization and the Jews*. Philadelphia and Jerusalem.

Teixidor, J. 1989. "Sur quelques aspects de la vie religieuse de la Syrie à l'époque hellénistique et romaine." In *Archéologie et histoire de la Syrie*, vol. 2, *La Syrie de l'époque achéménide à l'avènement de l'Islam*, ed. J.-M. Dentzer, W. Orthmann, C. Augé, et al., 81–95. Saarbrücken.

Thompson, D. J. 1987. "Ptolemaios and 'The Lighthouse': Greek Culture in the Memphite Serapeum." *PCPS* 213: 105–21.

———. 2008. "Economic Reforms in the Mid-Reign of Ptolemy Philadelphus." In *Ptolemy II Philadelphus and His World*, ed. P. McKechnie and P. Guillaume, 27–38. Leiden and Boston.

———. 2012. *Memphis under the Ptolemies*. 2nd ed. Princeton and Oxford.

Tilly, C. 1990. *Coercion, Capital, and European States, AD 900–1990*. Cambridge and Oxford.

———. 1994. "Entanglements of European Cities and States." In *Cities and the Rise of States in Europe, A.D. 1000 to 1800*, ed. C. Tilly and W. P. Blockmans, 1–27. Boulder, San Francisco, and Oxford.

Toorn, K. van der. 1997. "The Iconic Book: Analogies between the Babylonian Cult of Images and the Veneration of the Torah." In *The Image and the Book: Iconic Cults, Aniconism, and the Rise of Book Religion in Israel and in the Ancient Near East*, ed. K. van der Toorn, 229–48. Leuven.

Tournay, R. J. 1991. *Seeing and Hearing God with the Psalms*. Sheffield.

Tozzi, P. 1977. "Per la storia della politica religiosa degli Achemenidi: distruzioni persiane di templi greci agli inizi del V secolo." *Rivista Storica Italiana* 89: 18–32.

VanderKam, J. C. 1991. "Jewish High Priests of the Persian Period: Is the List Complete?" In *Priesthood and Cult in Ancient Israel*, ed. G. A. Anderson and S. M. Olyan, 67–91. Sheffield.

———. 2004. *From Joshua to Caiaphas: High Priests after the Exile*. Minneapolis.

Vanderlip, V. F. 1972. *The Four Greek Hymns of Isidorus and the Cult of Isis*. Toronto.

Vandorpe, K. 2000. "The Ptolemaic *Epigraphe* or Harvest Tax (*shemu*)." *AfP* 46: 169–232.

———. 2005. "Agriculture, Temples and Tax Law in Ptolemaic Egypt." *CRIPEL* 25: 165–71.

Veïsse, A.-E. 2009. "L'expression 'ennemi des dieux': *theoisin echthros*." In *Faces of Hellenism: Studies in the History of the Eastern Mediterranean (4th century B.C.–5th Century A.D.)*, ed. P. van Nuffelen, 169–78. Leuven.

Verkinderen, F. 1987. "Les cités phéniciennes dans l'empire d'Alexandre le Grand." In *Studia Phoenicia*, vol. 5, *Phoenicia and the East Mediterranean in the First Millennium B.C.: Proceedings of the Conference Held in Leuven from the 14th to the 16th of November 1985*, ed. E. Lipiński, 297–308. Leuven.

Vlassopoulos, K. 2007. *Unthinking the Greek Polis: Ancient Greek History beyond Eurocentrism*. Cambridge.

Waerzeggers, C. 2004. "The Babylonian Revolts against Xerxes and the 'End of Archives.'" *AfO* 50: 150–73.

———. 2011. "The Pious King: Royal Patronage of Temples." In *Oxford Handbook of Cuneiform Civilizations*, ed. K. Radner and E. Robson, 725–51. Oxford.

Walbank, F. W. 1967. *A Historical Commentary on Polybius*. Vol. 2. Oxford.

———. 1984. "Monarchies and Monarchic Ideas." In *The Cambridge Ancient History*, vol. 7, part 1, *The Hellenistic World*, ed. F. W. Walbank, A. E. Astin, M. W. Frederiksen, and R. M. Ogilvie, 2nd ed., 62–100. Cambridge.

———. 1985. *Selected Papers: Studies in Greek and Roman History and Historiography*. Cambridge.

Wallace-Hadrill, A. 1987. "Time for Augustus: Ovid, Augustus and the *Fasti*." In *Homo Viator: Classical Essays for John Bramble*, ed. M. Whitby and P. Hardie, 221–30. Bristol.

———. 2005. "*Mutatas Formas*: The Augustan Transformation of Roman Knowledge." In *The Cambridge Companion to the Age of Augustus*, ed. K. Galinsky, 55–84. Cambridge.

Watts, J. W. 2007. "The Torah as the Rhetoric of Priesthood." In *The Pentateuch as Torah: New Models for Understanding Its Promulgation and Acceptance*, ed. G. N. Knoppers and B. M. Levinson, 319–31. Winona Lake.

Weinberg, J. P. 1976 [1974]. "Die Agrarverhältnisse in der Bürger-Tempel-Gemeinde der Achämenidenzeit." In *Wirtschaft und Gesellschaft im alten Vorderasien*, ed. J. Harmatta and G. Komoróczy, 473–86. Budapest.

Weinfeld, M. 1995. *Social Justice in Ancient Israel and in the Ancient Near East*. Jerusalem and Minneapolis.

Weitzman, S. 2004. "Plotting Antiochus's Persecution." *JBL* 123: 219–34.
White, H. 1985. "The Historical Text as Literary Artifact." In *Tropics of Discourse: Essays in Cultural Criticism,* 81–100. Baltimore.
Wilker, J. 2011. "Von Aufstandsführern zur lokalen Elite: der Aufstieg der Makkabäer." In Dreyer and Mittag 2011, 216–52.
Will, E. 1979–82. *Histoire politique du monde hellénistique (323–30 av. J.-C.).* 2 vols. 2nd ed. Nancy.
Williams, D. S. 1999. *The Structure of 1 Maccabees.* Washington.
———. 2001. "Recent Research in 1 Maccabees." *CRBS* 9: 169–84.
———. 2003. "Recent Research in 2 Maccabees." *CBR* 2: 69–83.
Williamson, H. G. M. 2008. "The Aramaic Documents in Ezra Revisited." *JThS* 59: 41–62.
Winiarczyk, M. 2002. *Euhemeros von Messene. Leben, Werk und Nachwirkung.* Munich and Leipzig.
Winnicki, J. K. 1994. "Carrying Off and Bringing Home the Statues of the Gods: On an Aspect of the Religious Policy of the Ptolemies towards the Egyptians." *JJP* 24: 149–90.
Wiseman, T. P. 1979. *Clio's Cosmetics: Three Studies in Greco-Roman Literature.* Leicester.
Woodman, A. J. 1988. *Rhetoric in Classical Historiography: Four Studies.* London.
Wörrle, M. 1988. "Inschriften von Herakleia am Latmos: Antiochos III, Zeuxis und Herakleia." *Chiron* 18: 421–71.
Woude, A. S. van der. 1982. "Wicked Priest or Wicked Priests? Reflections on the Identification of the Wicked Priest in the Habakkuk Commentary." *JJS* 33: 349–59.
Wright, B. G. III. 2008. *Praise Israel for Wisdom and Instruction: Essays on Ben Sira and Wisdom, the Letter of Aristeas and the Septuagint.* Leiden and Boston.
Wright, J. W. 2006. "Remapping Yehud: The Borders of Yehud and the Genealogies of Chronicles." In Lipschits and Oeming 2006, 67–89.
Wyrick, J. 2011. Review of Bar-Kochva 2010. *BMCR:* http://bmcr.brynmawr.edu/2011/2011-03-51.html.
Xeravits, G., and J. Zsengellér, eds. 2007. *The Books of the Maccabees: History, Theology, Ideology—Papers of the Second International Conference on the Deuteronomical Books, Pápa, Hungary, 9–11 June 2005.* Leiden.
Yoyotte, J. 1969. "Bakhthis: religion égyptienne et culture grecque à Edfou." In *Religions en Égypte hellénistique et romaine. Colloque de Strasbourg 1967,* ed. P. Derchain, 127–41. Paris.
Zeitlin, F. I. 1996. *Playing the Other: Gender and Society in Classical Greek Literature.* Chicago.
Zerubavel, E. 1997. *Social Mindscapes: An Invitation to Cognitive Sociology.* Cambridge, Mass.
———. 2003. *Time Maps: Collective Memory and the Social Shape of the Past.* Chicago.
Zsengellér, J. 2007. "1 Maccabees and Temple Propaganda." In Xeravits and Zsengellér 2007, 183–95.

INDEX LOCORUM

1 MACCABEES

1:1–6:17, 36
1:1–10, 35
1:11–64, 35, 199
1:11–15, 199, 210–11, 212, 237, 243
1:11, 5, 6, 65, 200
1:15, 203, 284, 463n38
1:20–2:48, 47, 380, 387
1:20–64, 231, 233
1:20–24, 18, 199, 220, 233, 235, 237, 382, 384, 387–89
1:20, 255, 382
1:21–23, 220, 489n45
1:24, 220
1:29–64, 389–92
1:29–40, 238, 390
1:29–35, 221, 233, 235, 291, 382, 391, 395–96
1:29–30, 255
1:29, 233, 235, 384, 387, 390, 395
1:30, 235, 236, 391
1:33–40, 167–68
1:33–35, 170, 172, 281, 457n61
1:36–40, 235, 281
1:38, 281, 392, 507n58
1:39, 168
1:41–64, 6, 229, 231, 234, 235, 242–50, 380, 391
1:41–42, 242–43, 250, 256, 278
1:41, 22, 172, 244
1:45–46, 245, 399, 401, 402
1:47, 238, 245–48, 399, 401
1:54–55, 238, 245, 247–48, 253, 283, 392, 399, 401, 402
1:59, 240, 247–48, 399, 402

2:1–14:15, 36
2:1–70, 6, 405–6
2:1, 313
2:7–13, 170–72, 281
2:15–26, 147, 179, 313
2:17, 313
2:18, 238
2:27–38, 179, 246, 248, 255
2:32–38, 253, 284, 392
2:39–48, 171, 179, 397
2:43, 284, 397
2:45–46, 211, 284
2:45, 249, 392, 449
2:49–62, 178–80
2:54, 147, 179, 244
2:66, 163–64

3:1–9:22, 6, 35, 119, 121, 136–41
3:1–4:35, 162–63
3:1–37, 138, 139
3:10–12, 138
3:13–26, 138
3:27–31, 326
3:27, 139
3:29, 278

3:31–37, 87
3:31, 278, 279
3:34–36, 138, 281
3:45, 281
3:46–54, 138, 139, 207
3:55, 139, 426n167
3:56, 138

4:1–36, 139
4:8–11, 163–64, 452n55
4:23, 163, 279
4:24, 163–64
4:26–35, 86, 406, 452n43
4:36–61, 36, 98, 119, 121, 122–36, 166–67
4:41, 166–67, 168
4:44–46, 164
4:45–47, 175
4:53–54, 399
4:54, 208
4:55, 126, 133–34, 136, 163
4:64, 254
4:8–11, 164, 452n11

5:1–68, 383
5:1, 139

6:1–17, 161, 164, 169, 220
6:1–4, 162, 279
6:5–6, 87
6:6–8, 139
6:6, 163, 279
6:8–13, 220
6:12, 220–21
6:18–14:15, 36
6:18–63, 87
6:18–28, 395
6:18, 280, 282
6:21–27, 282, 284, 395
6:28–63, 86

7:1–50, 150, 160
7:5–25, 220–25
7:5–9, 280–81, 284, 395
7:7, 282
7:8–26, 150
7:41–42, 157
7:47–50, 157, 158–59, 166, 168

9:1–22, 220–22, 224
9:1, 220–22, 224
9:22, 176
9:23–12:53, 6, 35, 221

9:50–56, 221
9:54–56, 190, 220, 221
9:54–57, 220–22
9:54, 221, 226

10:20, 209, 360, 376
10:21, 209
10:25–45, 278, 310, 320
10:42, 339
10:62, 376
10:65, 376

11:1–15:41, 312
11:20–22, 396
11:25–26, 280
11:27, 376
11:29–37, 278, 310
11:28, 319
11:57, 360, 376

13:1–16:24, 98, 114, 119, 128, 129, 149, 160–77
13:1–16:22, 148
13:1–15:41, 6
13:1–42, 162–63
13:11, 282
13:15–19, 164, 279
13:23, 279
13:36–42, 134, 161, 163, 271
13:36–40, 134, 164, 174, 278, 279
13:36, 360
13:42, 174, 175, 458n75
13:43–53, 161, 164–69
13:43–48, 166
13:49–52, 36, 128, 164–69

14:1–36, 183
14:1–3, 161, 169
14:4–15, 161, 169, 169–74, 176, 224
14:16–24 with 15:15–24, 36, 161, 170, 174, 456n52
14:25–49, 161, 169, 174–76, 176, 271
14:36, 360
14:38, 360, 392
14:41–42, 134, 174
14:41, 129, 134, 164, 175, 271

15:1–41, 161, 176–77
15:15–24. See 14:16–24 with 15:15–24
15:31, 279
15:35, 279

16:1–24, 161, 176–77
16:1–22, 6

16:2–3, 176
16:11–24, 280
16:11–22, 161
16:23–24, 6, 161, 164, 176

2 MACCABEES

1:1–2:18, 79
1:1–10a, 7, 81, 132
1:10b–2:18, 7
1:18–2:18, 97, 132
1:18–36, 132

2:9–13, 132
2:19–32, 7, 70–72
2:21, 141
2:23, 185

3:1–15:36, 34
3:1–10:9, 34, 80
3:1–4:6, 68, 71, 80, 81, 82, 83, 89, 95, 149, 177–78, 183, 383
3:1–40, 34, 78, 79
3:1–3, 62, 88, 89, 219
3:3, 333, 336, 337
3:4–7, 329
3:4–5, 340, 341
3:4, 272
3:5, 323, 328, 486n31
3:6, 329, 331, 333, 339
3:7, 328
3:8, 76, 383
3:10–12, 339–40, 342
3:11, 62, 328
3:31–32, 77
3:32, 215
3:35–39

4:1–10:9, 34, 79
4:1–7:42, 79
4:1–5:10, 78
4:1–6, 273, 276, 328
4:4, 323, 328
4:5–6, 77
4:7–13:26, 68, 71, 82, 83, 90, 95, 98, 119, 121, 136–41, 148, 183, 204
4:7–10:9, 7, 68, 71, 80–83, 98, 440n22
4:7–5:26, 83, 91, 134, 137, 141, 183, 198
4:7–50, 7
4:7–15, 12, 20, 32, 91, 199, 200–1, 212, 262–66, 269, 271, 276, 334, 363–64

4:7–10, 18, 91, 276, 277, 349
4:7–9, 32, 200, 263, 268, 274, 276, 310
4:7–8, 351
4:7, 88, 272
4:8, 263, 278
4:8–9, 268
4:9, 19, 32, 201, 210, 263, 267, 276, 277, 282, 362, 364, 367, 394
4:10, 201, 210, 364, 371
4:11, 31, 263–66, 306, 310
4:12–14, 276
4:12, 209, 364, 464n53
4:13, 202, 204, 216, 272, 273, 371
4:13–15, 121, 202, 204
4:14, 91, 206, 207, 208, 267
4:15, 201
4:16–17, 75, 262, 434n42
4:17, 210
4:19–20, 226
4:23–29, 219, 266, 271, 272–73, 274, 276, 349–50, 351
4:23, 229, 328, 438n94
4:26, 75
4:27–28, 12, 215, 266, 438n94
4:28–29, 267, 305, 283, 392
4:32–34, 219, 225, 276, 277, 294, 379
4:32, 218, 225, 276
4:35, 251
4:39, 58, 62, 218, 266, 276, 385
4:42, 62, 74
4:43–50, 225, 276, 294
4:49, 251, 256

5–6:11, 231, 233
5:1–27, 231, 233, 234, 312
5:1–11, 12, 77, 277, 294
5:1, 382
5:5–27, 235
5:5–23, 384, 387–89
5:5–10, 235, 276, 385, 388
5:5–7, 276, 312
5:5, 379, 389
5:10, 75, 78
5:11–6:17, 78
5:11–16, 129, 233, 237, 382
5:11, 77, 215, 277, 388
5:12–16, 387
5:14, 390
5:15–16, 12, 218, 276, 489n45
5:15, 63
5:16, 219, 267

5:18, 71
5:21, 276, 387
5:22–23, 237, 267, 273, 277, 283, 374, 383, 388–89
5:24–6:11, 389–92
5:24–26, 151, 233, 235, 238, 382, 384, 391
5:25, 236, 253, 391
5:27–13:26, 123, 141, 149
5:27–10:9, 83, 91
5:27–9:29, 124, 137–38
5:27, 62, 83, 91, 134, 137, 139, 141, 142, 145, 149, 198, 235, 249, 313, 314, 379, 391

6:1–7:42
6:1–11, 77, 227, 229, 231, 234, 235, 237, 250–57, 380, 391, 399, 401–3, 451n41
6:1–7, 129, 276
6:1–4, 162
6:1, 21, 91, 233, 235, 250, 256, 425n153, 501n114
6:4–7, 204
6:5, 75
6:6, 268
6:11, 246, 284, 392
6:18–8:4, 78
6:18–7:42, 7, 8, 137, 159
6:18–31, 242, 468n13
6:18, 242, 247

8:1–10:9, 79
8:1–36, 7, 71, 91, 127, 137, 139–44, 151, 152
8:2–5, 135, 242
8:2–4, 140, 142
8:4, 216
8:5–15:36, 78
8:9–11, 74
8:10–36, 140, 150–51, 160, 489n59
8:10, 226, 269, 319
8:14–16, 214, 273
8:15, 142, 149, 153
8:16–20, 140
8:18–20, 149
8:19–20, 151, 152
8:28, 139, 140, 142, 149, 276, 454n14
8:33, 74
8:34, 150
8:34–36, 74
8:36, 141, 268

9:1–18, 7
9:5–27, 230
9:5–6, 74
9:5–10, 151

9:8, 74, 151, 216, 449n7
9:14–17, 261, 262, 266–69
9:14, 266, 267, 477n87
9:16, 219, 267, 268, 336, 337
9:17, 216, 253, 256, 268
9:19–27, 134
9:19, 135

10:1–8, 7, 66, 82, 88, 91, 92, 95, 98, 101, 119, 121, 122–36, 137, 156, 157, 208, 276, 438n95, 451n33
10:1, 125, 131, 135
10:2, 128–29, 131, 216, 284, 399, 401
10:3, 125–26, 128–29, 131–32, 136, 204, 399, 402, 451n33
10:4–5, 134
10:4, 126, 133, 135
10:5–8, 81
10:5, 216
10:6, 101, 130
10:8, 127, 130, 133, 166
10:9, 78, 88
10:10–15:36, 34, 78, 79, 80
10:10–13:26, 7, 68, 71, 79, 81, 82, 83, 98, 124, 140, 149, 440
10:10, 90, 91, 214
10:11, 87
10:16, 140
10:21–22, 149, 152
10:23, 141, 149
10:25–26, 140
10:26, 140
10:28, 113, 140
10:31, 113
10:34–35, 214
10:36, 142, 214
10:38, 141

11:1–13, 86
11:1–3, 261, 262, 266, 269
11:2–3, 226
11:2, 239, 269, 283
11:6, 140
11:13, 141, 268
11:16–33, 135, 149, 262
11:16–38, 17, 92, 511n111
11:16, 135
11:23–26, 17
11:24, 135, 420n47, 462n12, 482n45
11:27–33, 17, 93, 384, 501n112
11:27, 135, 360
11:29, 134

12:6, 140
12:13–15, 152
12:26, 142, 214
12:31–32, 141
12:39–40, 205
12:40, 149
12:43–44, 142

13:3–8, 88, 134
13:3, 273
13:4, 215
13:6, 63
13:8, 75, 276
13:9–26, 86
13:9–11, 226
13:9, 90
13:10, 140, 142
13:12, 140
13:14, 141
13:20–24, 74
13:23–24, 150
13:23, 219
13:24, 93

14:1–15:36, 79, 81
14:1–15:37a, 7, 68, 71, 82, 83, 88, 90, 98, 119, 121, 123, 148, 149, 157, 161, 177, 183, 440n22, 449n18, 451n33
14:1–36, 183
14:1, 88, 90
14:3–30, 276
14:3–13, 154, 271, 273–74, 360
14:3, 63, 88, 91, 273
14:6, 144
14:12–14, 283
14:15–30, 454n17
14:15, 140
14:17–18, 273
14:19–26, 150
14:33–34, 154, 156
14:36, 154, 156
14:37–46, 142, 150
14:38, 142

15:1–29, 140, 150, 160
15:1–5, 151, 226, 253
15:3, 150
15:5, 151
15:7, 151
15:9, 151
15:12–16, 135, 151, 152–56, 157, 175, 219, 271, 276, 350

15:12, 154, 204, 276–77, 455n35
15:17–18, 151
15:22–23, 151–52
15:27, 141, 149
15:28–37, 158–59
15:29, 153
15:30–37a, 124, 135, 156–59
15:30, 151, 157
15:32–33, 74
15:33, 151
15:34, 154, 156
15:36, 81, 166
15:37–39, 70, 90, 436n68
15:37b, 68, 82, 83, 90, 157, 456n48, 458n83

DANIEL 11

11:3–15, 312
11:14, 244
11:20, 329
11:21–39, 229
11:21–35, 5, 401
11:28–31, 382
11:29–39, 229, 231, 234, 237–43, 380, 391–92, 469n26
11:30, 235, 506n44
11:31, 235, 399, 401
11:31–35, 401
11:39, 384, 392, 400, 507n58, 510n99

JEROME, *COMMENTARY ON DANIEL*

11.14, 5, 311, 312, 385
11.44–45, 383, 476n67

JOSEPHUS, *ANTIQUITIES*

11.138, 496n33
11.325–39, 115
11.329–40, 304
11.331, 464n50
11.338, 351
12.133, 481n31
12.138–44, 12, 25, 264, 299, 302–10
12.140–44, 474n24
12.140, 268, 324, 335, 336, 466n80
12.141, 341
12.142, 265, 308, 339, 377
12.142, 496n36, 501n121
12.145–46, 252, 400–1

12.146, 341
12.154–55, 342
12:156–222, 115, 342–43, 351, 352–54
12.181, 313
12.222, 313
12.228–36, 115, 342–43
12.228, 385
12.235, 475n51
12.236, 378
12.237–56, 5, 427n202
12.237–41, 385
12.237–40, 5
12.237–38, 18–19, 423n122
12.237, 475n55
12.238–39, 475n49
12.239–40, 311, 312
12.239–41, 312
12.240–41, 199, 200, 212, 434n46
12.241, 5, 463n38
12.242–45, 5
12.246–56, 236

12.248–56, 229, 257–58
12.248–52, 395
12.249–52, 395–96
12.265, 313
12.279–84, 458n89
12.305, 508n77
12.316–26, 449n14
12.362, 508n77
12.364, 508n77
12.387, 438n97, 455n36
15.380–425, 97
20.233–34, 271
20.235, 88, 438n14

JOSEPHUS, *WAR*

1.31–40
1.1.31–32
1.1.32–35, 229, 257

SUBJECT INDEX

1 and 2 Maccabees, 6, 33, 37, 38–40, 65–66, 86, 87, 94, 119–41, 147–81, 197–98, 210–11, 255–57, 259–88, 292–94; diverging, 10, 24, 44, 51–52, 65–66, 189–91, 222, 256–57, 280, 292–93, 310, 460n5; parallel, 35, 119–29, 183–85, 284

1 and 2 Maccabees, their value for historical reconstruction: 1 Maccabees, 11, 23, 32–33, 39, 41, 51, 65, 168–69, 194, 249–50, 257–58, 259–86, 287–88, 293, 314, 377, 383–84, 388, 457n53; 2 Maccabees, 10–12, 15, 16, 23, 31, 32–33, 39, 40, 41, 51, 65, 70, 76–77, 92–93, 169, 184, 194, 219, 220–21, 255–58, 259–86, 275, 287–88, 293–95, 314, 340, 345, 346, 350, 363–64, 377, 379, 383–84, 386, 388–89, 391, 394–95, 436n71, 472n3, 474n25, 486n32, 511n111; compositional montages in 2 Maccabees, 44, 75–76, 77, 82, 84–94, 141, 150–51, 156–57, 169, 225–26, 227, 236–37, 273–74, 277–78, 293–94, 328–29, 334, 349, 361, 382, 387, 390–91, 395, 436n71, 438n94, 438n97, 439n107, 457n52, 489n59; and modern rationalizing interpretations of, 11, 14–16, 20, 25, 26, 31, 40, 63–64, 223, 232, 233, 236, 249, 259, 263, 291, 294, 310–11, 334, 363, 385, 386, 489n49, 508n80; paratactic style in 1 Maccabees, 199, 211, 236, 277, 293, 390, 434n36. *See also* Bickerman-Tcherikover paradigm; causality; chronology of events; code; high priests, paired with kings; measure-for-measure; rebellion, causes of; religion; semantic concatenation; sin-retribution; state culture; synecdoche; temple (as a literary motif), accounts of 1 and 2 Maccabees centered on; time, construction of; war

1 Enoch, book of, 60–61, 101, 194, 227, 243, 244, 442n41, 467n109, 470n40, 470n54, 471n57, 483n78

1 Esdras, book of, 72, 87, 97, 106, 108, 110, 112, 122–23, 129, 130, 131, 207, 208, 209, 210, 217, 218, 220, 436n74, 440n18, 446n98, 446n99, 446n112, 449n7, 449n11, 450n21, 450n23, 450n26, 450n29, 452n61, 463n40, 463n44, 464n47, 464n54, 466n83, 466n84, 466n90, 483n78

1 Maccabees (selected): compositional structure, 7, 33–37, 39, 97–98, 119–21, 123–31, 133–34, 136–39, 161–77, 178–81, 183, 189–91, 282, 405–8; date of composition, 6, 310, 453n5, 458n77; literary genre, 6–7, 10, 11, 35–37, 51, 65, 146, 194, 388 place of composition, 43; purpose, 35–37, 42, 65, 68, 84, 119–20, 180, 184–85, 195–96, 197–99, 216, 292–93; subject matter, 6, 10, 11, 38, 40, 42, 44, 65–66, 84, 183–84, 189–91, 291–93. *See also* 1 and 2 Maccabees; chronology of events; John Hyrkanos; Jonathan's time unit; Josephus, derivative; Judas's time unit; Mattathias's time unit; Simon's time unit; temple building, narrative pattern of

540 SUBJECT INDEX

1 Maccabees, author of (selected), 6–7, 35–37, 47, 97, 168, 181, 184, 185, 195, 197, 216, 220, 278, 285, 292–93, 320, 326, 394–96, 427n182

2 Maccabees (selected), 68, 84, 94, 185; compositional structure, 7–9, 10, 32, 33–37, 39, 43, 51, 65, 66, 67–68, 70, 77–84, 87–88, 93, 97–98, 119–21, 122–29, 133–34, 136–41, 149–61, 177–78, 180–81, 183, 189–91, 194, 328, 409–11, 418n19, 436n71; date of composition, 6, 111, 212, 377, 453n5, 458n77; literary genre, 7–8, 10, 15, 32, 34, 35, 43, 51, 65, 66, 67–69, 70, 75, 81–84, 93, 117, 130, 146, 194, 277, 388, 475n39; place of composition, 8–9, 38, 43, 66–67, 68, 184–85, 418n17, 418n18; purpose, 8–10, 34–35, 37, 42, 51, 53, 65, 66–67, 68–69, 71, 72, 81, 84, 89–90, 93–94, 119–20, 135–36, 180, 184–85, 193–95, 197–99, 216, 292, 418n19; style, 11, 65, 68, 222, 288; subject matter, 7–10, 11, 27, 34–35, 38, 39–40, 42, 44, 66–67, 68–72, 84, 94, 142, 183–84, 189–95, 291–93, 418n17, 418nn20–21. *See also* 1 and 2 Maccabees; Hanukkah story; Heliodoros story; high priests, paired with kings; interpolations; measure-for-measure; Nikanor's Day story; sin-retribution; temple building, narrative pattern of; temple liberation accounts; temple propaganda; war

2 Maccabees, author of (selected), 8–11, 185, 193–95; disingenuous, 69–70, 74–77, 84, 85, 89–93, 156, 157, 159, 200, 207, 219, 226, 227, 237, 292, 326, 327–29, 472n3; his authorial comments, 71, 76–77, 93, 137, 157, 201, 227, 262, 263, 269, 271, 284; his literary and intellectual skills, 44, 70, 84, 93, 120, 121, 159, 194, 200, 201–2, 203, 205–7, 225–26, 227–28, 272–73, 277–78, 285, 326, 328, 343, 436n71; his pro-Hasmonean bias, 28, 35, 36, 38–39, 47, 66, 67, 69–70, 74–78, 82, 84, 85, 90, 91–93, 94, 97, 120, 128, 137–38, 144, 157, 181, 184, 185, 189, 195, 197, 204–5, 216, 217–20, 225–26, 227, 263, 271, 272–74, 275, 292–93, 326, 328, 350, 360, 377, 386, 388–89, 433n23; his religiousness, 8–11, 34–35, 36, 38–39, 66–67, 73, 74, 80, 193–95, 201, 262, 269, 270, 418nn24–25; slanderous and defamatory, 20–21, 58, 145, 195, 197, 203, 204, 205, 221, 224, 273, 294, 328, 333, 349–50, 379, 388, 390, 398, 428n96, 462n25. *See also* causality; codes; measure-for-measure; rebellion, causes of; semantic concatenation

2 Samuel, book of, 97, 123, 447n117

3 Maccabees, 95, 245, 250, 417n16, 433n31, 438n100, 439n3

4QMMT, 58, 61, 241, 245, 252–53, 400, 402, 431nn60–61, 455n30, 483n78

abomination, 20, 132–33, 144, 150, 235, 238, 241, 244–46, 247, 248, 253, 399, 401–2
agoranomia, agoranomos, 329–30, 337, 340–42, 343, 345–46, 493n108, 493n111, 499n79
Akra (fortress), 13, 20–21, 25, 31, 36, 40, 90, 125, 161, 162, 163, 164, 170, 171, 176, 183, 199, 221, 235, 237, 240, 261, 267, 279–80, 281, 282–83, 288, 293, 368, 380, 384, 387, 391, 392–93, 394–96, 457n61, 507n51; garrison of, 21, 31, 127, 128, 164, 198, 242, 282, 384; men of, 21, 31, 125, 281, 282, 392–93, 394–96; palace of, 44, 160, 161, 164–67; polis of, 13, 25, 31, 425n157; Simon's liberation and purification of, 44, 45, 114, 127, 128, 160, 164–69, 170, 171, 189, 190, 198, 282, 292, 310; mediating synecdoche, 190–94, 196, 213, 261, 280, 282, 283, 285, 291, 292
Alexander the Great, 6, 104, 115, 145, 197, 232, 305–6, 351, 369, 433n23, 443n58, 452n59, 453n4, 464n50, 496n33, 500n98; and civic welcome ceremonies, 304–5, 440n8, 481n35, 503n154; and conquered cities and regions, 305, 307, 389–90, 424n135, 447n118, 458n76, 474n21, 477n83, 481n32, 481n35, 481n37, 482n47, 482n49, 483n74
Alexander Balas, 209, 360, 376, 437n86, 475n45
Alkimos, 42, 45, 63, 68, 75, 81, 88, 91, 92, 121, 144, 150, 154, 177, 190, 195, 197–98, 216, 220–25, 227, 276, 292–93, 313, 370, 377, 395, 397, 438n96, 454n17, 455n33, 466n91, 475n51, 491n79, 498n75; and destruction of the city wall, 190, 217, 220–22, 226, 292; his appointment, 220, 270, 271, 273–74, 275, 280–81, 360, 395, 438n97; paired with Demetrios I, 68, 82–83, 84–88, 183, 271, 273. *See also* otherization, ethnic
Alkimos's time unit, 83, 88
allophylismos, 121, 144–45, 199, 200, 201, 214, 216–17, 221–22, 227–28, 371, 462n17
allophyloi, 131, 144, 216, 466n81
altar (of the temple), 75, 93, 132, 140, 141, 142, 192, 204, 207, 209, 251, 276, 338, 339, 401–3, 449n18; dismantled a., 133, 164, 175, 402; its dedication, inauguration, 7, 70–71, 72, 80, 92, 93, 113, 123–24, 125, 126, 128, 129, 130–33, 142, 143, 175, 208–10, 218, 245, 336, 384, 399, 446n102; its desecration, 75, 92, 124, 125, 129, 133, 154, 164, 175, 236, 238, 245, 248, 253, 262, 276, 283, 291, 292, 387, 399, 401, 402.

SUBJECT INDEX 541

altar, unlawful (in the temple), 238, 244, 245, 246, 247, 248, 249, 253, 399, 401–3, 449n20. See also *bōmos*

altars, unlawful (of the countryside), 179, 192, 244, 246, 247, 249, 283, 284, 291, 380, 392, 397, 399, 401, 449n20; mediating synecdoche, 262, 276, 283, 292, 384, 392, 401. *See also* Mattathias

amnesty, 17–18, 92, 93, 384, 387, 506n48, 511n111. *See also* decree, decrees, of amnesty

Antiocheia, 14, 19, 27, 421n90

Antiochenes, 12, 14, 19, 201, 205, 209, 210, 238, 262, 266, 267, 282, 293, 334, 347, 362, 365, 367–68, 369, 370, 371, 374, 380, 389, 390, 392–93, 394, 395, 396, 397, 398, 402, 403, 421n91, 425n149, 465n72, 474n38, 499n87, 501n112, 504n168, 509n94. *See also* settlers, military

Antiochos III, 12, 29, 46, 89, 297–315, 319–21, 322, 323–25, 326–27, 342, 357–58, 477n77, 479n8, 480n22, 482n52, 486n25, 486n27, 486n31, 487n33, 489n45, 489n48, 489n50, 490n61; and Babylon, 19, 357–58, 362, 369, 372, 499n84; his concession of the provincial tribute to the Ptolemies, 46, 342–43, 345, 352–54, 378, 494n124; his conquest of Koilē Syria and Phoinikē, 12, 45, 295, 299–302, 328; his settlement for Jerusalem, 12, 45, 265, 302–10, 324, 341–42, 368; his subsidies to the Jerusalem temple, 268, 335–37, 466n80. *See also* Apamea, treaty of; Nikanor (Seleukid high priest); *philanthropa basilika*; Sartre, Maurice; state culture; temple, of Jerusalem, royal subsidies to; temple plundering, stories of; war indemnity

Antiochos III's decree, 19–20, 31–32, 45, 264, 265–66, 268, 306–10, 324, 335, 336, 422n97, 474n24, 480n21, 496n36; charter, 13, 19–20, 25–26, 28–29, 30–31, 265, 365, 425n157, 503n103; economic and fiscal clauses in, 32, 45, 46, 265–66, 308–10, 339, 368, 377, 482n51, 484n3. See also *philanthropa basilika*; state culture

Antiochos III's second decree, 252, 341, 400–401

Antiochos IV Epiphanes (selected), 5, 12, 17, 18, 19, 22, 46, 71, 88, 91, 92–93, 215–16, 227, 275, 277, 287, 310, 317–18, 346–77, 378–404, 421n81, 423n116, 424n131, 433n23, 438n94, 476n74, 487n33, 495n17; and Antiochos III's and Seleukos IV's settlements in Koilē Syria and Phoinikē, 316, 319–21, 343, 346, 354, 360, 378, 494n124; and Antiochos V, 68, 82, 90, 98, 214; and Babylon, 19, 356–59, 362, 369, 372, 374, 498n72, 499n84, 502n149; cult disrupter, 85, 204, 211, 217, 229, 236, 267, 276, 294; and cultic changes in Jerusalem, 132, 150, 153, 238, 241, 251, 397–400, 401–4, 423n116, 509n96; his anabasis, 18, 87, 138, 169, 321; his assault on Jerusalem, 5, 7, 12, 13, 14, 15, 16–17, 18, 46–47, 77, 83, 138–39, 199, 220, 231, 233, 235–36, 237, 240, 250, 255, 277, 283, 293, 294, 384–86, 387–88, 421n83, 434n36, 469n28; his campaigns in Egypt, 5, 7, 13, 15, 16–17, 18, 46–47, 77, 199, 234, 235, 237, 275, 294, 317, 361, 370, 372, 379, 380–82, 387; his confession, 216, 253, 256, 261, 262, 266–69, 281, 336–37; his death, 7, 8, 17–18, 36, 46, 74, 87, 88, 92, 127, 137, 139, 151, 161, 169, 216, 219, 220–21, 230, 379, 382, 383, 436n71; his desecration of the temple, 9, 72, 74–75, 79, 83, 91, 92, 94, 96–97, 132, 198, 211, 236, 240, 245; his financial strictures, 12, 15, 30, 46, 162, 316–17, 319–21, 326; his military and political repression, 13, 17, 231, 233–37, 257, 267–68, 273, 283, 379, 383, 384–86, 387–97, 483n71; his plunder of the Jerusalem temple, 5, 7, 12, 13, 17, 18, 30, 62–63, 198, 199, 214, 218–20, 233–37, 245, 250, 267, 276, 277, 279, 292, 294, 319, 321, 384–86, 387–88, 395, 439n107, 476n75, 489n49; his prohibition of the Jewish customs, 5, 13, 14–15, 17, 21, 23, 25, 30–31, 78, 229–31, 233–37, 246, 421n83; his prohibition of the Jewish customs as unintended, 11, 16, 20, 21, 27, 30–31, 234, 422n111, 422n112, 425n157, 425n158, 469n25, 505n8; his reforms in Koilē Syria and Phoinikē and Syria, 275, 316, 317–18, 321, 347–49, 378–79, 498n72; his refoundation of the polis in Jerusalem, 13, 21–22, 25, 365–66, 374, 388–90, 425n157, 501n168, 508n71; his setting up of a military settlement in Jerusalem, 46, 138, 168, 190, 199, 281, 282, 368, 391–96, 403; impious and wicked, 90, 93, 127, 138, 142, 145, 151, 198, 214, 215–16, 219, 220, 229, 233, 240, 242, 243, 244, 275, 279, 287, 461n10; and Jason and Menelaos, 244, 273, 354, 355, 359–61, 449n81, 494n125, 497n58, 506n48; and Jason's politicization, 20, 212, 244, 267, 361, 365, 379, 425n157; and Onias III, 18–19, 40, 346, 349–50, 358, 364–65, 379, 476n70, 494n125; paired with Jason and Menelaos, 68, 82, 83, 88, 91, 142, 145, 183, 198; portrayed as merely reactive (in 2 Maccabees), 12, 17, 18–19, 46, 63, 138–39, 162, 235, 236, 275–76, 277, 292, 294, 386; and tribute increase, 40, 277–78,

Antiochos IV Epiphanes *(continued)* 279, 310, 318, 319, 346, 349–50, 360–61, 379, 499n81; and the wicked high priests, 12, 15, 85, 91–92, 93, 204, 217, 218, 219, 220–21, 237, 271–72, 275–76, 278, 294–95, 324. *See also* Akra, garrison of & men of; *allophylismos*; Apamea, treaty of; chronology of events; decree, decrees, of amnesty & of persecution; Hanukkah story; high priests, and kings; high priests, appointment of; Jason, paired with Antiochos IV; *katoikoi*; Menelaos; *paroikoi*; prohibition of the Jewish customs; rebellion, causes of; persecution, religious; rebellion, Judean; repression, military; state culture; settlers, military; temple desecration; temple plundering, stories of; tribute increase; war indemnity

Antiochos IV's time unit, 68, 80, 82, 83, 88, 91–92, 98, 198, 199, 438n94

Antiochos V Eupator, 7, 25, 68, 70–71, 74, 81, 82–83, 86–87, 88, 98, 150, 215, 360, 438n97; and the end of the crisis, 13, 17, 18, 92–93, 134, 219, 223, 418n25, 436n71, 511n111; impious, 90, 91, 145, 214, 226

Antiochos V's time unit, 7, 81, 82, 83, 87, 88, 91, 92–93, 98, 183. *See also* decree, decrees, of amnesty; letter, letters, royal; war

Antiochos VI, 161, 169, 360, 376, 437n86, 475n45

Antiochos VII, 176, 279

Apamea, treaty of, 12, 46, 316–17, 319–21, 348, 374, 384, 485n6, 498n72. *See also* war indemnity

Apollonios (Antiochos IV's general), 151, 162, 233, 235, 240, 250, 314, 379, 384, 387, 390–91, 392, 452n43, 484n84

Apollonios, son of Menetheus, 323, 328–29, 487n32

Apollonios, son of Thraseas, 323, 328, 329, 486n31, 487n32

Artaxerxes, 87, 111–12, 217, 335, 444n79, 450n29, 488n38, 495n22

Asidaioi, 144, 179, 222–25, 273, 284, 397, 467n99, 491n79. *See also* Hasidim

autonomous, autonomy, 40, 116, 134, 149, 160, 161, 164, 174, 175, 176, 271, 272, 279, 280, 285, 292, 293, 303, 306, 367, 368, 392, 474n26, 483n62, 504n170

battle, battles, 92, 150, 152, 155, 184, 436n65, 436n71, 454n13, 454n23, 464n49; inaugural, entitling, and legitimizing, 71, 127–28, 135, 137, 138–41, 150–51, 152–53, 155, 157, 160, 162–63, 452n43, 489n59. *See also* victory; war

Ben Sira, 63, 106, 114–15, 117, 133, 146, 147, 178, 209, 243, 244, 359, 431n70, 447n119, 447n120, 449n7, 454n6, 458n72, 458n89, 464n48. *See also* Praise of the Fathers

Bickerman, Elias J., 11–16, 17, 18, 19–20, 21–22, 24, 25, 26, 27, 28, 30–31, 41, 45–46, 56, 77, 85, 92, 94, 202–4, 226, 229, 233–35, 240, 241, 263, 264–65, 272, 302–3, 306, 309, 310, 311–12, 331–35, 339, 361, 362, 365–66, 379, 383, 384–85, 386, 392, 396–97, 398, 419n33, 419n39, 420n47, 420n49, 420n59, 421nn72–73, 421nn89–90, 422n110, 423n113, 423n122, 424n128, 424n133, 424n142, 425n147, 425n149, 425nn156–57, 432n1, 435n47, 435n52, 471n72, 473nn18–19, 475n41, 479n9, 480n21, 480n24, 480nn26–27, 482n45, 482n51, 482n58, 483n71, 483n76, 490n67, 490nn67–68, 499n85, 500n103, 505n23, 506n37, 506n39, 507n58, 508n73, 509n83, 509n85

Bickerman-Tcherikover paradigm, 16, 20, 22–32, 41, 51, 55, 63, 420nn70–71, 435n51

bōmos, bōmoi (unlawful altar), 238, 248, 283–84, 477n88, 477n89, 478n91

Bringmann, 15–16, 20, 21, 22, 27, 41, 54, 363, 418n25, 420n61, 420n71, 422n101, 422n102, 422n105, 422n108, 422n112, 423n117, 424n142, 426n163, 428n24, 439n106, 467n99, 473n11, 476n70, 482n56, 500n112

causality, 34, 36, 39, 69, 70, 72–73, 74–75, 139, 205, 211, 259, 260, 293, 312, 391, 434n36; suppressed, 139, 199, 235–36, 255, 277, 293, 326, 386, 387–88, 390, 434n36. *See also* code; measure-for-measure; rebellion, causes of; semantic concatenation; synecdoche

charter. *See* Antiochos III's decree

Chronicles, books of, 72, 97, 172–73, 238, 446n114, 491n83

chronology of events, 12–18, 20, 39, 44, 46–47, 84, 87, 112, 129, 138–39, 189–90, 231, 233–37, 240–41, 293, 314, 327–29, 378–83, 384–86, 387–88, 390–91, 421n82, 421n83, 436n71, 438n94, 438n97, 439n107, 467n99, 475n55, 484n84, 505n23, 511n111; in 2 Maccabees, 8, 71, 75, 82, 84–93, 127, 134, 136, 199, 250, 452n43. *See also* 1 and 2 Maccabees, their value, compositional montages; high priests, paired with kings; Judas Maccabee, his first appearance; Ma, John

circumcision, 27–28, 203, 211, 245–46, 248–50, 256, 284, 463n38, 464n59

code, codes, 44, 192, 461n11, 461n12; cultural and narrative, in 1 and 2 Maccabees, 39–40, 41,

44–45, 147, 189, 191–94, 207, 227–28, 230, 246, 247, 248, 257, 258, 259, 260, 264, 270, 287, 288, 291, 334, 380, 391, 392, 397, 403, 461n10; cultural, Greek and Greco-Roman, 367, 458n89. *See also* semantic concatenation; synecdoche
colonists. *See katoikoi*; settlers, military
colony, military. *See katoikia*; settlement, military
Crimes and Sacrileges of Nabû-šuma-iškun, 60, 219, 249, 253, 254, 256, 462n31
Cyrus, 87, 103–4, 108, 110, 123, 131, 146, 213, 217–18, 287, 443n55, 450n29, 491n83
Cyrus Cylinder, 145, 197, 443n56, 453n69

Daniel, book of, 3, 5, 16, 24, 45, 85, 101, 121, 194, 228, 229, 230–31, 234, 235, 236, 237–44, 245, 247–50, 251, 253, 255–57, 310, 312, 329, 380, 382, 384, 392, 401, 402, 427n202, 429n31, 433n23, 436n71, 442n40, 469n23, 469n26, 469n27, 469n34, 469n35, 469n38, 470n40, 470n49, 471n64, 471n65, 471n69, 506n38, 506n44, 507n58, 510n99, 510n109
Darius, 6, 87, 108, 123, 197, 209, 217, 335, 435n48, 443n54, 444n79, 450n29, 488n38, 491n83, 493n105
David (King), 32, 61, 103, 104, 108, 109, 114, 115, 123, 133, 146, 154–55, 156, 157, 159, 163, 178, 179, 206, 440n7, 442n54, 443n60, 446n114, 447n117, 447n119, 449n16, 450n26
decree, decrees: of amnesty (of Antiochos IV or Antiochos V), 17, 92, 93, 420n47; of commemoration (in 1 and 2 Maccabees), 127, 130, 131, 133, 165, 166; of Egyptian priests, 58, 155, 453n4, 456n41, 456n43, 466n80, 466n86, 468n15, 470n45; of Greek cities, 57, 308, 341, 366, 393, 470n45, 483n63, 486n25, 507nn61–69; people's d. in honor of Simon, 129, 134, 164, 169, 174–75, 179, 392, 453n5, 457n65; of persecution, 13, 14, 17, 21–23, 25, 30, 199, 223, 234, 235, 242–43, 244, 245, 246, 247, 248, 278, 423n117; of Persian kings, 213, 335, 488n38, 491n83, 493n105, 495n22; of Ptolemaïs, 254; royal decrees, in 1 Maccabees, 134, 176, 278, 320, 339, 475n45; royal Hellenistic decrees, 86, 92, 243, 265, 272, 306, 308, 310, 482n58. *See also* Antiochos III's decree; Antiochos III's second decree; Olympiodoros, O. inscription; Tyriaion inscription
Delian Sarapis aretalogy, 24, 257, 427n203, 456n43, 459n4, 472n9
Demetrios I, 71, 81, 82, 90, 144, 223, 271, 273–74, 275–76, 310, 320, 339, 347, 360, 395, 454n17,

476n73, 508n75; paired with Alkimos, 68, 83, 88, 183
Demetrios II, 134, 161, 163, 164, 168–69, 174, 279, 280–81, 310, 360, 376, 437n86, 475n45
Deuteronomic view of history, 34, 65, 432n2. *See also* measure-for-measure; sin-retribution
Deuteronomy, book of, 34, 426n167, 429n27, 432n2, 452n52, 464n60
disruption, 104, 129, 256; causes of, and factors of, 42, 91, 92, 183, 189–91, 192, 193, 195, 204, 227, 236, 261, 264, 276, 280–81, 285, 379; cycles of, and time of, 6, 42, 82, 83, 89, 90, 91–92, 121–22, 129, 132, 137, 141, 145, 183–84, 189–90, 195, 198, 199, 204, 211, 221, 439n107, 460n3. *See also* Antiochos IV, cult disrupter; *Hellēnismos*; high priests, their sins as forerunners of Antiochos IV's; rebellion, causes of; sacrifices, disruption of
Doran, Robert, 8, 9, 10, 19, 20, 30, 31, 34, 37, 66, 67–68, 70–74, 77, 78–80, 81, 82, 84, 95–96, 154, 185, 331–33, 363, 417n16, 418n18, 422n112, 425n157, 432n19, 433n31, 435n52, 435n65, 439n1, 469n25, 499n87, 501n115

Enuma Eliš, 97, 100–101, 103, 110, 441n32, 441n34, 442n43, 449n17, 460n6
ephebes, *ephebēion*, 20, 200–201, 209, 210, 212, 262, 263, 266, 277, 367, 374–75, 464n53, 499n88, 502n134
epistatēs: of cities, including Jerusalem, 235, 369, 370, 373–74, 389; of temples, 330, 331, 338, 488n43, 490n67. *See also* overseer
epi tōn hierōn (temple overseer), 322, 324, 325, 338, 339, 486n25, 488n43
Esther, book of, 95, 242, 250, 439n3, 471n69
ethnicization, 121, 143–45, 146, 198, 199, 216–17, 221–22. *See also Hellēnismos*; *Ioudaïsmos*; otherization
Euhemeros of Messene, 116–17, 448n132
Ezekiel, 97, 243, 251
Ezra, 113–14, 133–34, 87, 149, 210, 217–18, 446n104, 446n113, 450n29, 483n70; his reforms, 87, 105, 106, 111–13, 455n308
Ezra, book of, 72, 97, 105, 123, 130, 131, 173, 207, 335, 336, 488n38, 491n83
Ezra-Nehemiah, book of, 106, 108, 110–14, 123, 217, 218–19, 337, 350, 450n23, 446n104, 455n30, 483n78

few against the many, 141, 149, 152, 162, 163, 164, 452n54

544　SUBJECT INDEX

fortifications, 176, 279; of the Akra, 21, 162, 166, 167, 190, 198, 281, 288, 293, 457n61; legitimizing theme, 128, 160, 162–63, 164, 165, 166, 198, 221, 279, 439n6, 454n7, 457n61. *See also* Simon Maccabee

garrison, garrisons: of the Akra, 21, 127, 167, 168, 190, 198, 261, 267, 281, 282, 288, 292, 293, 384, 391–93, 396, 403, 477n87; exemption from, 176, 266–67, 280, 305, 474n26; in Jerusalem and Judea, 221, 283, 302, 304, 305–6; in other places, 266, 304, 305, 372, 381–82, 392, 393–94, 397, 503n152. *See also* Akra, men of
Gerizim (Mount, temple), 235, 250–51, 256, 267, 273, 277, 383, 388–89
Geron the Athenian, 21, 22, 235, 250, 256, 425n153, 484n84, 501n114
gerousia, 20, 225, 265, 304, 307, 369, 501n112, 501n121
Greek, Greeks (non-ethnic Greeks described as), 56, 144, 146, 199, 210, 214, 223, 269, 370–72, 374–75, 376, 465n72. *See also* ethnicization; *Hellēnes*; otherization; *politai*
Greek way of life (of non-Greek elites), 56, 75, 201, 202, 215, 256, 298, 347, 367, 370, 371, 374
gymnasion, gymnasia (in the Hellenistic world), 9, 12, 20, 30, 63–64, 202–3, 268, 309, 340, 347, 363–64, 370, 371, 374, 376, 425n147, 488n39, 502n134. *See also* Tyriaion inscription
gymnasion (in Jerusalem), 5, 6, 7, 12, 14, 20, 23, 27, 30, 53, 74–76, 85, 135, 193, 194, 196, 199–214, 217, 223, 256, 262–64, 266, 268, 269, 270, 277, 291, 293, 294, 334, 361–68, 371, 434n46, 462n21, 465n71, 500n98; antitemple, 45, 91–92, 190, 192, 193, 198, 199, 199–210, 211, 216, 260, 268, 276, 277–78, 280, 283, 291, 292, 454n17, 464n58; in 1 Maccabees, 20, 210–11, 237, 243–44, 284; mediating synecdoche of Jason's reforms, 190–91, 192, 193, 196, 211–14, 227, 228, 229, 259–60, 268, 276, 285, 291, 292. *See also Hellēnismos;* politicization

Haggai (prophet), 133–34
Haggai-Zechariah, book of, 97, 101–2, 103, 106–7, 108–10, 113–14, 123, 130, 440n18, 443n54, 444n75, 449n7, 450n24
Hanukkah festival, 7, 9, 17, 38, 53, 66, 67, 72, 78, 79–80, 79–80, 81, 88, 94, 95, 113, 126, 130–31, 132, 133, 183–84, 185, 229, 418n19, 421n82, 451n34, 511n111. *See also* Sukkoth festival
Hanukkah story, 7, 38, 67, 68, 82, 91, 94, 95–96, 97–98, 103, 121, 122–41, 149, 154, 156, 159, 180, 198, 204, 456n48. *See also* Hasmoneans, the Hanukkah story as founding myth of; temple foundation, narrative pattern of
Hasidim, 10, 14, 62, 385, 418n24, 418n25. *See also Asidaioi*
Hasmonean dynasty, Hasmoneans, 6, 36–37, 45, 47, 61, 65–66, 68, 69, 84, 85, 98, 101, 111, 118, 119–20, 121, 132, 143, 144–45, 146, 148, 159, 176, 177, 180, 181, 190, 193, 198, 212, 213, 214, 285, 293, 313, 387, 391, 440n9, 451n34, 461n10, 511n111; the Hanukkah story as founding myth of, 38, 82, 84, 85, 92, 94, 96–97, 98, 119, 148, 159, 180, 184, 185, 421n82; its legitimacy as subject matter of 2 Maccabees, 38, 42, 43, 44, 45, 68, 69, 84, 90, 97, 119–20, 135, 143, 148, 177–80, 184, 185, 189, 195, 213, 216, 272, 292, 391, 461n10; Judas as founder of, 83, 92, 94, 97, 135, 143, 189, 452n59; and narrative pattern of temple foundation, 101, 111, 118, 119, 146, 185, 189, 195, 213, 440n9; Onias III's legitimate heirs, 83, 84, 89–90, 93–94, 154, 177, 178, 179–80, 292; simultaneously high priests and kinglike rulers, 44, 68, 82, 119–20, 134, 146, 147, 148, 149–77, 179, 180, 184, 189, 276, 292. *See also* 1 Maccabees, purpose of; 2 Maccabees, purpose of; *Ioudaïsmos;* Judas Maccabee, and Hasmoneans & his second refoundation; Phineas; Simon, his legitimizing deeds; temple foundation, narrative pattern of, and Hasmoneans & its duplication; usurpers
Hasmoneans, time unit of, 44, 68, 82, 83
Hefzibah inscription, 299, 323, 479n8
Hekataios of Abdera, 106, 115–17, 447n122, 448n130
Heliodoros (Seleukos IV's chief minister), 12, 29, 32, 76–77, 79, 82–83, 89, 149, 154, 155, 177, 209, 215, 268, 274, 318, 321, 322, 325–30, 334, 339–40, 342–46, 350, 354, 360, 378, 379, 383, 487n32
Heliodoros stele. *See* Olympiodoros inscription
Heliodoros story, 7–8, 9, 46, 68, 71, 72, 76–77, 79, 80, 81, 82–83, 88, 89, 95, 149, 155, 177–78, 319, 321, 325–30, 333, 339, 344, 351, 353–54, 360, 383, 433n31
Hellenism, 11, 28, 462n13; as modernism, 23, 27, 63, 64, 195, 202, 313, 315, 375, 397–98, 422n99; struggle between H. and Judaism, 2, 9, 10, 27–28, 32–33, 194, 201–2, 286, 288, 419nn35–36. *See also* religion
Hellēnismos, 28, 32, 42, 45, 51, 64, 121–22, 135, 144–45, 195, 199, 201–4, 213, 214, 216, 217, 221,

227, 228, 248, 262, 267, 269, 370, 371, 462n12.
  See also ethnicization; *gymnasion*; Jason;
  order, social; otherization
Hellenization, 11, 20, 22, 25, 26, 29, 41, 56, 63–64,
  66–67, 75, 169, 347, 361, 365, 375, 481n35,
  503n160, 504n173; of Jerusalem, 23, 66, 78,
  364, 365–67
Hellenizers, 13, 14–15, 21–22, 23, 27, 30, 31, 38,
  45–46, 54, 63–64, 76, 85, 92, 94, 195, 217, 226,
  227, 259, 288, 299, 310, 311, 313–15, 375, 385,
  386, 397, 418n22, 418n25, 422n110, 483n71
Henten, Jan Willem van, 9, 34, 66, 70–75, 77,
  78, 80–82, 155–56, 157, 169, 432n19, 433n28,
  435n65, 455n30, 456nn42–43, 456n47
Herod, 97, 449n7
Herodotus, 11, 76, 85, 116, 435n48, 436n75, 460n6,
  480n29, 483n74, 489n53, 509n98
high priests, appointment of (in Jerusalem),
  39, 86, 88, 209, 278–81, 360; by kings, innovation, 18, 107, 265, 270–71, 285, 359–60,
  475n41; Seleukid interference with, 261, 263,
  266, 269–78, 280–81, 285, 286, 288, 292, 293,
  294–95, 334, 360, 376–77, 379, 397, 437n86,
  438n97, 475n5, 475nn45–46, 494n125; synecdoche of Jason's reforms, 190–91, 192, 193,
  196, 211–14, 227, 228, 229, 259–60, 268, 276,
  285, 291, 292. *See also* Alkimos; Jason; Judas,
  heir to Onias III; Menelaos; rebellion, causes
  of, political destabilization; Simon, his titles;
  tribute increase, and Seleukid interference
high priests, of Jerusalem, 20, 28, 38, 45, 68,
  134–35, 145, 174, 206, 209–10, 215, 217, 241,
  265, 271–74, 307–8, 311, 333, 351, 352, 353,
  359–60, 368, 372, 376–77, 388, 397, 433n31,
  438n97, 446n113, 464nn49–50, 475n42,
  496n33; acquired royal prerogatives, 43,
  61–62, 96–97, 98, 106, 107–8, 114–15, 116, 146,
  148, 174, 179, 180, 265, 351, 353, 359, 360–61;
  paired with kings, 68, 75, 83–85, 87–91, 142,
  145, 183, 278, 475n55; and priestly vs. royal
  functions, 42–43, 59–63, 106–11, 118, 119, 134,
  146, 147, 148, 155, 156–57, 167, 174, 177, 180, 189,
  430n53, 430n58; their sins as forerunners of
  Antiochos IV's, 12, 75, 85, 91–92, 204, 211, 217,
  218–19, 227, 235, 236, 275–76, 277, 292, 293–94,
  350, 386, 388, 460n3, 462n28; their sphere
  of powers, 106, 107–8, 148, 155, 180, 206,
  207, 341, 342, 346, 351, 377, 389, 390, 397–99,
  400–1, 402–3, 496n36. *See also* high priests,
  appointment of; Phineas; temple foundation,
  narrative pattern of, its adaptation; tribute,
  high priests responsible; *individual names*

high priests, other, 400, 436n75, 466n86; Babylonian, 327, 331, 346, 347, 356–59, 368–69, 372,
  374, 497n54, 497nn57–58, 504n170; Ptolemaic
  and Seleukid, 300, 305, 322–23, 486n25,
  486n27, 494n1m 498n71; in Ptolemaic Egypt,
  314, 355, 358–59, 496nn44–45, 498n71. *See
  also* Nikanor (Seleukid high priest); Olympiodoros (Seleukid high priest); Ptolemaios,
  son of Thraseas; *šatammu*
holy vessels, 12, 14, 15, 18, 20–21, 30, 45, 62–63,
  74, 110, 124, 125–26, 131, 190, 195, 198, 217–20,
  223, 225, 226, 267, 276, 280, 291, 292, 294, 350,
  385, 398, 446n99, 450n29, 462n28, 466n83,
  466n85, 466n87, 468n15
Hyrkanos the Tobiad, 313, 330, 342–43, 345–46,
  378–79, 385, 499n78

idolatry, 34, 142, 149, 165, 202, 203, 205–6, 211,
  238, 240, 243–45, 248, 284, 462n19, 476n55,
  478n90
impious. *See* Alkimos; Antiochos IV; Antiochos
  V; Apollonios (Antiochos IV's general); Heliodoros; Jason; Menelaos; Nikanor (Demetrios I's general); Simon (temple *prostatēs*)
interpolations, 6, 7–8, 35–36, 71, 72, 76, 78, 92,
  438n95, 451n33
Ioudaioi, 143–44, 146, 149, 150, 151, 153, 156, 158,
  204, 214, 216, 269, 274, 454n11; Antiochos IV
  as *Ioudaios*, 216, 268
Ioudaïsmos, 28, 32, 42, 44, 45, 51, 64, 70–71, 72,
  103, 105, 110–11, 120–22, 139, 141–46, 151, 153,
  195, 198, 201–4, 208, 213–14, 216, 221, 227, 228,
  246, 273, 276, 462n13. *See also* ethnicization
Isaiah, 101, 242
Isaiah, book of, 233, 239, 243, 431n65, 441n34,
  442n40, 454n23

Jamnia, 142, 149, 205
Jason, 6, 15, 27, 42, 51, 78, 81, 88, 144, 13, 55, 190,
  198, 214, 215, 220, 223, 244, 248, 266, 292, 312,
  334, 365, 386, 457n49; civil strife between J.
  and Menelaos, 7, 12, 15, 18, 51, 12–13, 17, 215,
  234–35, 276, 276–77, 294, 312, 382, 384–85,
  386, 388, 483n71; disrupter, 85, 45, 42, 83, 91,
  92, 121, 135, 190, 195, 199–206, 211, 214, 216,
  217, 221, 228, 26, 270, 276, 292, 294, 349–50,
  454n17; founded the *gymnasion*, 7, 12, 14, 91,
  434n46; Hellenizer, 64, 92, 14, 27, 38, 55, 56,
  63, 217, 227, 288, 311, 313–14, 367, 370, 371, 386,
  398, 422n99, 465n74, 483n71; his appointment, 5, 12, 262, 270–71, 275–76, 351, 354, 357,
  359–61, 438n94; his delegitimization, 45, 70,

546　SUBJECT INDEX

Jason *(continued)*
　92, 197–98, 206, 207, 216, 226–27, 262, 272–73, 292–94, 333, 350, 365, 461n10; his impiety, 28, 45, 54, 68, 75, 134–35, 145, 70, 218, 225–26, 262, 294, 311, 398; his measure-for-measure retribution 70, 75–76, 83, 91, 92, 94, 120, 134, 145, 154, 177, 195, 244, 418n22; his reform, 15, 19–20, 23, 25, 30, 38, 46, 21, 13, 31, 200–1, 210, 212–14, 244, 260, 261, 262–66, 347, 349, 361–68, 374–75, 375–77, 379, 421n90, 422n102, 424n139, 425n149, 465n65, 499nn87–88, 500n112, 501n114, 501n118, 504n168, 508n71; and tribute increase, 46, 32, 55, 262–66, 270, 274, 275, 291, 294, 333, 334, 349–50, 364–65, 499n81; and Onias III's deposition, 46, 91, 7, 12, 18–19, 40, 46, 91, 219, 262–63, 272, 276, 277, 294, 333, 349–50, 361, 364–65, 475n55; paired with Antiochos IV, 68, 82, 83, 88, 183, 275–76, 438n94. See also *gymnasion*; Hellenism, as modernism; *Hellēnismos*; high priests, their sins as forerunners of Antiochos IV's; Menelaos, his appointment & paired with Jason; otherization; politicization; religion, modern conceptions of, and impact
Jason of Cyrene, 7, 8, 70–71, 117, 452n58
Jason's time unit, 83
Jeremiah, 132, 148, 153–55, 157–58, 166, 175, 271, 276, 452n50, 463n32, 462n34
Jerome, 5, 12, 24, 311–12, 383, 385, 423n122, 476n67
Jerusalem. *See* temple, of Jerusalem; wall
John Hyrkanos, 6, 10, 66, 84, 161, 164, 165, 169, 176–77, 271
Jonathan Maccabee, 6, 66, 134, 164, 168, 174, 175, 209, 221, 271, 279, 280, 311, 339, 360, 377, 395, 437n86, 454n15, 457n61, 475n45
Jonathan's time unit, 6, 35, 161, 183, 186, 221, 457n61
Joseph the Tobiad, 63, 313, 352–54; story of, 46, 115, 327, 342–43, 351, 352–54, 461n16
Josephus, 24, 40, 46, 86, 115, 199–200, 236, 241, 257–58, 310, 313, 352–54, 380, 386, 394–96, 436n79, 438n97, 458n89, 475n49, 475n55; derivative, 5, 45, 380, 395–96, 427n202, 449n14, 461n6, 461n38, 468n11, 475n51, 481n31, 505n15, 508n77; *Jewish Antiquities*, 5, 12–13, 12–13, 18–19, 18–19, 45, 97, 236, 427n202, 438n97, 449n7, 461n6, 465n67, 468n11, 505n6; *Jewish Wars*, 5, 483n76; and parties, 24, 311–12, 383, 384–85, 423n122
Joshua, son of Jehozadak. *See* Zerubbabel and Joshua

Joshua, son of Nun, 32, 152, 170, 179, 243, 244
Judaism, 44, 52–53, 64, 111, 181, 203. *See also* Hellenism; religion
Judas Maccabee, 6, 28, 70–71, 72, 81, 94, 119–47, 148–59, 164, 168, 177, 185, 186, 314, 377, 386, 395, 455n30, 458n88; and the Akra, 160, 164, 168, 282–83; and Alkimos, 220–24, 273–74; fights for *Ioudaïsmos*, 72, 141–42, 144, 151, 152, 273, 376, 418n25, 454n13; and Hasmoneans, 66, 84, 90, 92, 94, 120–21, 143, 144–45, 148, 154, 177, 178, 189, 195, 198, 213, 214, 433n23, 452n59; heir to Onias III, 82–83, 90, 93–94, 148, 149, 150, 153–54, 155, 175, 177–78, 179–80, 204, 219, 271, 273, 275, 276, 277, 350, 454nn13–14; his death, 7, 10, 66, 221, 224, 274; his dream, 135, 151, 152–56, 175, 177, 178, 456n43; his first appearance, 62, 83, 91, 92, 134, 137, 139, 141, 198, 235, 237, 250, 313–14, 391, 454n13; his first temple refoundation, 45, 72, 83, 92, 101, 119–46, 148, 166, 167, 168, 189, 208, 221, 402; his harangues and prayers, 135–36, 140–41, 142, 151, 152–53, 155, 164, 178; his legitimation, 72, 92, 142, 148, 150, 159, 169, 178, 189, 195, 204, 218, 221, 271, 276, 386; his legitimizing victories, 7, 91, 124–27, 137, 138–41, 146, 150–53, 154, 161, 164, 456n48; his partisans, 54, 72, 91, 130–31, 137, 138, 139–40, 141–42, 144, 146, 149, 151, 153, 204, 222–23, 418n25, 454n11; his piety and righteousness, 28, 38, 39, 45, 54, 62, 70, 83, 91, 92, 140, 141–42, 143, 150–51, 153, 161, 177, 275, 276, 287, 311, 391, 418n25; his second refoundation, 7, 44, 83, 135, 148, 149–59, 161–64, 190, 292; his subsequent victories, 78, 92, 139, 146, 149, 279, 511n111; his wars, 9, 70, 91, 92, 127, 138–41, 142–43, 149, 152–53, 164, 166, 214, 278, 279, 282, 383–84; and imperial rule, 135–36, 150; kinglike leader, 92, 124, 133, 134–35, 138, 140, 141, 143, 144–45, 146, 148–51, 152–56, 157–59, 162, 167, 169, 178, 454n14; king of divine election, 149, 150, 151, 153, 154–56, 157, 158–59, 169–74, 178; and martyrs, 9, 66, 138, 142, 150, 159, 227, 418n20; and Menelaos, 91–93, 94, 134–35, 138, 148, 151, 157, 159, 218, 226, 287; and Nikanor (Demetrios I's general), 74, 150, 151, 154, 155, 156–57, 283, 454n17; and rival high priests, 85, 121, 122, 145, 185, 198, 204, 218, 219, 221, 275–76, 292, 314, 377, 388; and Simon, 45, 162–64, 167–69, 175, 178, 179, 183, 185, 186, 190, 195, 221, 227, 310, 386; and temple, subject-matter of 2 Maccabees, 9, 69, 70, 71–72, 189–90, 195, 271, 292, 310.

See also Hanukkah story; *Ioudaïsmos*; king (representation of); kingship; Nikanor's Day story; temple foundation, narrative pattern of; widows and orphans

Judas's time unit (in 1 Maccabees), 35, 119, 138–39, 145, 161, 169, 176, 183, 186, 221, 282

just. *See* righteous

justice, social, 99, 102–3, 104–5, 111, 112, 114, 117, 124, 132–33, 135, 136, 137–39, 140, 142–43, 224–25. *See also* righteousness

katoikia (military settlement), 487n33, 507n58; in Jerusalem, 44, 232, 283, 392, 397, 477n79, 507n58

katoikoi, 492n100; in Jerusalem, 281, 283, 392, 393, 477n79, 507n58

king, kings (historical, selected): and foreign gods, 229, 232–33, 237, 239, 241, 250–51, 253–54, 308, 399–400, 403, 468n15, 470n48, 470n51; and local communities, 12, 16, 25–26, 28–29, 31, 39, 77, 80, 86, 215, 229, 232–33, 238, 164–66, 264–66, 268, 300–10, 316, 319–23, 342–43, 345–49, 352–54, 363–77, 378–97, 458n76, 482n48; in Seleukid kingdom, 23, 25, 85, 86–87; and temples, 29, 104, 215–16, 218–19, 229, 321–25, 326–27, 329–37, 339, 340, 341–42, 343–44, 349–51, 354–61, 397–404, 443n58. *See also* high priests, appointment of; tax; state culture; temple, temples (in historical view); tribute increase; *individual names*

king (representation of), 121, 136, 145, 214–15, 216–19, 237, 443n60, 453n4, 456n43; and deity, 35, 38, 61, 68, 73, 83, 96, 103, 104, 110, 113, 117, 133, 135, 137, 138, 139, 153, 156, 239–41, 247, 267, 440n7; his sphere of powers, 42–43, 52, 59–62, 108, 114, 139, 146, 148, 149, 155, 156, 157, 167, 175, 224, 430n53, 430n54, 430n58, 443n70, 453n5; narrative morpheme, 98, 101, 114, 117, 121, 137; and narrative pattern of temple foundation, 43, 82, 96–97, 135, 180, 430n53, 460n6; pious or righteous and wicked, 38, 58, 60–62, 89–90, 96, 120, 142, 143, 145, 197, 206, 215, 216–17, 219, 220, 224, 226–27, 229–30, 231, 233, 237, 238, 239, 240, 242–43, 244–45, 246, 247, 250, 253–54, 256, 266, 434n38, 438n100, 443n70, 453n69, 462n31, 464n58, 466n80, 467n3, 470n48, 470n51, 478n1; and social justice, and social order, 98, 99, 100–1, 103, 104–6, 117, 133, 135, 140, 142, 143, 224–25, 228, 440n8; and temple, 68, 83, 100, 103, 107, 206, 215–19,

442n43, 430n53, 430n54, 430n58, 460n6, 466n80; and temple foundation, 68, 98, 99, 100, 102–6, 109, 117, 442n42, 442n49, 454n6. *See also allophylismos;* Hasmonean dynasty, simultaneously high priests and kinglike rulers; high priests, acquired royal prerogatives & paired with kings & and priestly vs. royal functions; Judas Maccabee; piety; religion, revised delineation; Simon Maccabee; temple foundation, narrative pattern of; usurpers; victory; war

Kings, books of, 72, 97, 101, 105, 111, 123, 128, 131, 132, 133, 156, 171–72, 174, 205, 206, 458n82

kingship (representation of, selected), 453n5; of divine election, 96, 104, 107–8, 109, 122, 133; metaphor for all forms of power, 99–100, 105–6, 108–9, 111, 114–15, 117–18, 119, 133–34, 135, 152, 431n63, 445n88; myths of, 97, 100–2, 103, 104, 108–10, 441n30, 441n31, 441n34, 442n42; native k., 68, 93, 94, 96, 99, 104–7, 111, 148, 149, 215, 442n43, 445n85, 460n6; native k., consequences of its demise, 43, 61, 96, 98, 99, 100, 106–7, 108, 114, 119, 133, 442n43. *See also* Judas Maccabee, kinglike leader; Judas Maccabee, king of divine election; Simon Maccabee, his titles and kinglike status; Sukkoth festival

land confiscations, 40, 142, 193, 232, 240, 242, 244, 246, 261, 280–82, 283, 285, 288, 291–92, 293, 380, 384, 386, 387, 392, 393, 394–95, 397, 399, 400, 401, 403, 508n82. *See also* altars, unlawful

laws, ancestral, 13, 14, 21–22, 23, 25, 26, 27, 28, 30–31, 70–71, 89, 142, 250, 306, 425n157, 474n22. See also *nomos*

Letter of Aristeas, 43, 106, 115–17, 249, 447n123, 448n130, 459n100, 463n42, 464n48

letter, letters, 58, 107, 112, 197; festal letters, 6, 7, 8, 9, 66, 79, 80, 81, 132, 180, 185, 418n16, 434n34, 446n102, 451nn33–34, 482n45; royal Hellenistic l., 309, 324, 340, 370, 373, 400–1, 446n86, 486n25, 490n72, 493n111, 503n160; royal l. (in 2 Maccabees), 17–18, 92–93, 134–35, 149, 261–62, 420n47, 467n99, 501n112, 506n36, 506n48, 511n111; 420n47, 467n99, 501n112. *See also* decree, decrees

lex talionis. See measure-for-measure

Lysias, 86–87, 93, 141, 163, 215, 223, 226, 261–62, 266, 268, 269, 281–82, 283, 437n88, 438n97, 452n43, 465n72, 473n10, 511n111

Lysimachos, 14, 58, 62, 74, 218, 225, 359–60, 385

548   SUBJECT INDEX

Ma, John, 18, 20, 21, 22, 30–31, 234, 303, 421n90, 425n157, 501n114, 501n118, 511n111
Maccabees, family, clan, Maccabees, family, clan, 18, 32, 35, 36, 37, 44, 45, 47, 65, 71, 102, 147, 178, 183, 248, 255, 292, 293, 419n30, 511n111; chronology of their joining the rebellion, 14, 293, 314, 379, 384, 385, 484n84, 505n23; and parties, 14, 51, 62, 222–23, 225, 310, 418n25, 467n99, 484n87; pious, 198, 227, 293, 461n110; their affiliation, 178–79, 184, 185; and their political rivals, 42, 45, 76, 197, 198, 199, 227; their reconquest and rededication of the temple, 108, 113, 122, 132, 148, 183, 198, 384, 511n111; their social milieu, 46, 288, 293, 313–15, 368, 484n82
martyrdom, 34, 66, 67, 80, 181, 418n17, 460n5
martyrs. *See* persecuted faithful Judeans
Mattathias, 6, 10, 66, 147, 163, 170, 171–73, 178–80, 185, 211, 249, 255, 281, 282, 284, 291, 313, 314, 397, 449n20, 458n89, 459n98, 484n84; his Eulogy of the Fathers, 147, 178
Mattathias's time unit, 35, 66, 149, 177, 183–84, 186, 283–84, 458n88
measure-for-measure, 9, 10, 34, 43, 69–70, 72–77, 83, 93, 136, 418n22, 418n24, 426n175; in Polybius, 73. *See also* sin-retribution
Menelaos, 6, 14, 15, 18, 27, 38, 42, 51, 55, 63, 70, 78, 81, 82–83, 84, 91–92, 93, 94, 120, 134, 144; assassinated Onias III, 225, 276, 277, 294, 350, 379, 385; Hellenizer, 13, 14, 15, 27–28, 30, 41, 54, 58, 64, 78, 92, 94, 226, 227, 288, 311, 313, 315, 386, 418n25, 422n99, 483n71; his actions as statesman, 18, 92–93, 134–35, 151, 226, 235, 237, 241, 244, 245, 248, 273, 287, 312, 313, 326, 374, 376–77, 387–90, 392, 397–99, 401–3, 421n82, 422n111, 454n16, 467n107, 489n49, 501n111, 506n48, 511n111.; his appointment, 12, 14, 88, 266, 270, 271, 272–73, 274, 275, 276, 294, 349–50, 351, 354, 359–60, 360–61, 397, 438n94, 475n50, 494n125, 499n81; his death, 88, 360, 438n97; his delegitimization, 45, 92, 120, 134–35, 177, 195–98, 225, 292, 293, 328, 333, 389; his genealogy and family ties, 14, 62, 272–73, 275, 328, 333, 360, 361, 434n66, 475nn49–50; his impiety, 28, 54, 62–63, 68, 75, 134–35, 142, 145, 154, 215, 227, 244, 270, 294, 311, 398; his measure-for-measure retribution, 62–63, 70, 75–76, 91, 92, 134, 276, 418n22; his religious reform, 15–16, 20, 23, 25, 38, 55, 85, 375, 500n112; paired with Antiochos IV, 68, 82, 83, 84, 91, 92, 142, 183, 198, 275–76; paired with Jason, 68, 75–76, 83, 88, 91–92, 183, 275–76; stole temple vessels, 12, 14, 15, 18, 20–21, 30, 45, 58, 62–63, 190, 195, 198, 217–20, 225, 276, 291, 292, 294, 385, 398. *See also* Greek, Greeks; Hellenizers; Jason, civil strife; otherization; Hellenism, as modernism; religion, modern conceptions of, and impact; tribute increase
Mizpah, 107, 138–39, 452n45, 464n49

Nabonidus, 59, 105, 197, 230, 253, 443n66, 453n69, 468n7, 478n1, 495n27
Nahum Pesher, 244
Nathan's prophecy, 97, 123, 154–55, 156, 157, 159
Nebuchadnezzar, 107, 110, 131, 217–18, 220, 327, 450n29
Nehemiah, 7, 111–12, 113–14, 129, 131–32, 133, 351, 446n102, 446n104, 446n108, 494n111, 495n28; his restoration of Jerusalem's wall, 97, 101, 106, 111–14, 128, 148, 160, 167, 168, 171, 176, 180, 222, 444n79, 446n102, 446n104, 450n23
Nehemiah, book of, 96, 106, 112–14, 134, 208, 235, 446n108, 455n30, 494n115
Nikanor (Demetrios I's general), 7, 71, 74, 79, 140, 150–51, 154–55, 156–58, 160, 162, 177, 214, 226, 274, 283, 449n18, 454n17, 489n59. *See also* Nikanor's Day festival; Nikanor's Day story
Nikanor (Seleukid high-priest), 322, 324–25, 346, 357, 485n25, 492n98; N. inscription, 324–25
Nikanor (son of Patroklos, Antiochos IV's general), 74, 140, 141, 150–51, 214, 226, 268, 269, 464n49, 489n59
Nikanor's Day festival, 7–8, 66, 71, 79, 81, 166, 168, 189, 418n19
Nikanor's Day story, 7, 68, 79, 80, 82–83, 90, 98, 119, 121, 140, 143, 149–59, 177, 214, 449n18. *See also* Heliodoros story
nomos, nomoi (law, customs), 142, 307, 509n92; *patrioi nomoi* (ancestral laws), 360, 425n157, 480n24, 482n49; *anomoi, paranomoi* (unlawful), 200, 207, 214, 223, 262, 267. *See also* laws, ancestral

Olympiodoros (Seleukid high priest), 29, 39, 46, 318, 321–25, 326, 328–29, 330, 334, 342–44, 345–46, 350, 358–59, 360, 378, 485n25, 487n32, 492n98; O. inscription, 18, 20, 29–30, 40, 46, 322, 324–25, 327–29, 334, 343, 378, 383, 498n69
Oniads, 40, 119, 271, 358, 359, 475n42; and Tobiads, 5, 12–13, 384–85. *See also* party
Onias, son of Simon the Just, 352–53

SUBJECT INDEX 549

Onias III, 77, 78, 155, 156, 180, 227, 271, 333, 346, 353–54, 433n31, 475n49, 475n55; and Heliodoros, 7, 77, 82–83, 89, 149, 154, 155, 177, 215, 274, 328, 339–40, 341, 342, 343–44, 346, 350, 354, 360, 379, 383; his assassination, 219, 225, 276, 277, 294, 350, 379; his deposition, 7, 12, 18–19, 39, 40, 44, 46, 91, 219, 244, 262, 263, 276, 277–78, 294, 333, 334, 346, 347, 349–50, 357–59, 360, 364–65, 377, 379, 461n16, 478n2, 498n69; his piety, 62, 68, 83, 89–90, 154, 215, 271, 275; and increase of tribute rate, 46, 262, 263, 277–78, 333, 334, 346, 347, 349–50, 359–61, 379, 383; and Jeremiah, 148, 153–55, 175, 271, 276; and Mattathias, 177, 178, 184; paired with Seleukos IV, 68, 82, 83, 88, 89, 183; and Simon the temple *prostatēs*, 15, 46, 89, 274, 275, 318, 325, 328, 329–30, 333–34, 341–42, 343–44, 345, 346, 360, 383, 474n25, 476n70. *See also* Antiochos IV; Hasmonean dynasty; high priests, appointment of, Seleukid interference with; Jason; Judas Maccabee; Menelaos; rebellion, causes of, political destabilization; tribute increase
Onias III's time unit, 83, 89–90, 184, 219
Onias IV, 84, 154, 455n36
order, 26, 42, 98–99, 473n10; cosmic, 43, 98–99, 100, 103, 104–5, 107–8, 109–10, 117, 121, 135, 143; divine, 45; political, 105, 110–11, 121, 132–33, 145; social, 43, 45, 86, 96, 98–99, 100, 103, 104–5, 107–8, 109–11, 112, 113, 114, 117, 120–22, 133–34, 135, 140, 142, 143, 145, 195, 198, 199, 204, 213, 214, 216, 228, 238, 440n8. *See also allophylismos; Ezra; Hellēnismos; Ioudaïsmos;* Judas Maccabee
otherization, 121, 144, 248, 396; ethnic, 199, 214, 215, 221–22, 439n102, 453n62, 457n95, 465n72. *See also* ethnicization; *Hellēnismos*
overseer, royal: of cities, including Jerusalem, 235, 267, 273, 277, 283, 383, 388–89; of temples, 314, 322, 324, 351, 357, 358, 486. *See also epistatēs; epi tōn hierōn; paqdu*

palace, 60, 104, 166, 430n53, 441n30, 466n88, 496n34; narrative morpheme, 198, 430n53, 441n36, 460n6; Simon Maccabee's, 44, 148, 161, 164–66, 167, 168, 169, 174, 175, 176, 440n6; Solomon's, 111, 160, 166, 180
palace building account, 44, 96, 97, 98, 100–1, 103, 104, 108, 148, 160, 176, 180, 224, 441n30. *See also* temple foundation, narrative pattern of

paqdu (royal official in Babylonian temples), 331, 338–39, 356–57, 359, 490n68, 490n70, 490n72, 495n27
paroikoi (status of the Judeans as part of Antiochos IV's repression), 396, 425n157, 508n79, 508n80
party, parties, 14, 222–23, 259, 310, 311–12, 375, 377, 483n77; pro-Ptolemaic and pro-Seleukid, 5, 12–13, 24, 45–46, 299, 302–3, 306, 311–12, 315, 383, 385, 423nn121–22. *See also Asidaioi,* Hasidim
Passover papyrus, 107, 444n80
persecuted faithful Judeans, 1, 5, 6, 7, 8, 9, 66, 69, 70, 78, 81, 83, 91, 137–38, 140, 142, 149, 150, 159, 179, 181, 205, 224, 227, 231, 233–35, 237, 239, 241–42, 245, 246, 247–49, 250, 251, 255, 397, 418n20, 452n50, 452n57, 459n98
persecution, religious, 6, 7, 13, 14, 17, 18, 26, 31, 40–41, 83, 229–30, 279, 384–86, 392, 396–404, 423n116, 427n202; p. accounts, 5, 32–33, 45, 74–75, 78, 196, 199, 227, 228, 229–58, 283, 291, 379–80, 397. *See also* decree, of persecution; prohibition of the Jewish customs; repression, military
Persian Verse Account, 197, 453n69
philanthropa basilika (royal concession), 31–32, 33, 34, 200, 262, 264, 265–66, 310, 426n164
Phineas (Phinehas), 37, 115, 133, 147–48, 179–80, 244, 447n119, 459n98
piety: and cognate notions, 54, 56–57, 60–63; and impiety, 57–58, 62–63, 214–15, 216, 223, 391, 403; political significance of p. and impiety, 28, 38, 39, 42, 52, 58, 70, 93, 204, 237, 287–88, 293, 294, 311, 313, 398, 461n10; royal p., 60, 308, 336, 401–2, 466n80, 466n86. *See also* impious; pious; religion; righteousness
pious. *See* 2 Maccabees, author of; few against the many; *Ioudaioi;* Judas Maccabee; Mattathias; Onias III; Seleukos IV; Simon Maccabee; war, warfare; warriors
politai (in Babylon), 46, 347, 362, 368–75, 465n74, 499n84, 503n160
politeia, 13, 14, 20, 25, 26, 85, 116, 142, 143, 262, 363, 365, 366, 499n88; of Jerusalem, 19, 25, 28, 365–66, 426n162, 501n114; literary genre, 115–17, 448n132
politeuma, 12, 13, 14, 19, 25, 362, 363, 364, 421n90, 425n149, 499n85
politicization, 19, 20, 26, 29, 30, 46, 212, 268, 277, 368–75, 376, 472n2, 488n397; of Jerusalem, 12–14, 19–20, 21–22, 25, 26, 27, 29, 44, 46, 191, 212, 214, 244, 260, 263, 266, 267, 269, 270, 277,

politicization *(continued)*
    285, 291, 292, 293, 334, 347, 349, 360, 361–68, 375–77, 379, 385–86, 389, 396, 421n90, 422n93, 424n139, 425n157, 472n2, 474n38, 499n87, 501n112, 501n118, 501nn114–15, 504n165, 504n168, 508n71. *See also* Akra; Antiocheia; Antiochenes; Antiochos IV; *gymnasion*; Jason; *paroikoi*; *politai*; tax; Tyriaion inscription
Polybius, 12, 39, 69–70, 73, 89, 116, 143, 284, 288, 311–12, 381, 423n122, 435n48, 436n77, 437n88, 438n100, 447n128, 474n26, 481n31, 485n6, 489n45, 494n124, 502n147
Praise of the Fathers, 106, 114–15, 133, 146, 147, 178, 458n89
proem (of 2 Maccabees), 7, 69, 70–72, 79, 90, 141, 142, 144, 184–85
prohibition of the Jewish customs, 15, 17, 21–22, 25, 30–31, 40, 196, 229, 234, 236, 286, 379, 380, 398, 421n74, 421n83, 422n111, 425n157, 468n19, 469n25; specific prohibitions, 245, 246, 248, 249, 251, 252, 253, 256, 400, 455n30. *See also* 1 and 2 Maccabees, their value, and modern rationalizing interpretations
prophet, 108, 115, 125, 129, 153, 154, 175, 221, 445n96; absence of, 125, 131, 133, 164, 175; people acting in lieu of, 161, 164, 175, 271
prostatēs tou hierou, prostatai (royal officials in temples), 46, 174–75, 318, 325, 330–31, 333, 338, 344, 346, 351, 355, 357, 359, 360–61, 369, 458n75, 490n68, 490n72, 496n30
Psalms of Enthronement, 97, 100–101, 108, 441n34, 442n42, 449n7
Ptolemaios, son of Aboubos, 280–81
Ptolemaios, son of Thraseas (provincial governor), 300, 305, 322–23, 324, 328, 479n11, 486n31, 487n35
Ptolemy II, 46, 352–53, 354–56, 357, 358–59, 437n81, 470n45, 492n92, 496n35, 498n72
Ptolemy V, 58, 300, 302, 305, 312, 322, 342–43, 345, 352, 378, 456n41, 470n51, 494n124
Ptolemy VI, 343, 345, 346, 350, 381, 438n100

Razis, 81, 142, 411
rebellion, causes of, 5, 10–12, 28, 40–41, 42, 44, 45, 46–47, 195–96, 294–95, 297, 321–26, 327, 329–30, 331–35, 337, 340–44, 345–47, 349–50, 359–68, 375–77, 379–81, 385, 404; cultural and religious, 11–32, 193, 201, 212, 227, 269, 288, 310–11, 311; economic and political, 65, 190–94, 199, 212, 227, 259–86, 287–88, 293–95; nexus of tribute increase and political destabilization as, 20, 39, 40, 270, 278, 280, 285, 292–95, 346, 359–61, 368, 377, 379, 381, 383; rational understanding of, by Maccabees authors, 31–32, 38–40, 41, 45, 190, 193, 194, 259, 269; suppressed memory of, 77. *See also* Akra; causality; codes; disruption, causes of; *gymnasion*; Hellenism, struggle; high priests, appointment of; persecution, religious; prohibition of the Jewish customs; repression, military; sacrifices, disruption of; semantic concatenation; synecdoche
rebellion, Judean, 5, 20, 43, 44, 46–47, 58, 70–71, 77, 92, 195–96, 294–95, 297, 387–404; historiography of, 10–11, 11–32, 194, 196; its chronology, 13, 14–15, 16–18, 40–41, 46–47, 92–93, 293, 380–83, 384–86, 387–88, 389, 395, 506n48, 511n111; its scope, 383–84; suppressed memory of, in 1 and 2 Maccabees, 215, 220, 235, 237, 255, 276–77, 293–94, 386, 387–88, 391, 393, 434n36. *See also* chronology of events; rebellion, causes of
rebels, 14, 17, 232, 241, 244, 385, 389, 390, 396–97, 398–99, 511n111. *See also paroikoi*
reconciliation (between deity and people), 34, 65, 66, 69, 73, 77, 78, 83, 91, 92, 102, 112, 124, 127, 135–36, 137–39, 141, 181, 205, 439n107
religion, religious, 51–63, 460n5, 473n10; as a discrete semantic category, 20, 23, 26, 27–28, 33, 34, 36–37, 39, 51–56, 66, 67, 100, 110, 120, 190, 195, 201–2, 203, 207, 211, 223, 229, 366; instrumentalist conception of, 15–16, 23, 27–28, 31, 55–56, 57–58, 310, 404, 422n102, 422n105; modern conceptions of, and impact on historical interpretation, 10–11, 12–16, 18, 20–21, 34–35, 226–27, 234, 235, 241, 262, 264, 265, 269, 288, 294, 310–11, 363, 377, 385, 431n70; revised delineation of its semantic field, 28, 34–35, 38–39, 41, 42–43, 44, 47, 55, 56–63, 67, 110–11, 185, 213, 226–27, 428nn17–18, 453n1. *See also* 1 and 2 Maccabees, their value; 2 Maccabees, author of; Bickerman-Tcherikover paradigm; codes; *gymnasion*; Hellenism; high priests, and priestly vs. royal functions; idolatry; *Ioudaïsmos*; Jason; king (representation of), his sphere of powers; Menelaos; party; persecution, religious; piety; prohibition of the Jewish customs; temple (as a literary motif), semantic sphere of
repression, military, 13, 18, 21–23, 40–41, 44, 45, 46, 92, 228, 231–37, 238, 240, 241, 246, 247, 248, 249, 257, 268, 277, 284, 285, 291, 293, 326–27, 379–80, 384–403

Returnees, 108, 110, 112, 113, 120, 130, 131, 143–44, 218, 446n99, 446n108, 450n29; Judas's partisans as new R., 130–31, 144
revolt. *See* rebellion
righteousness, 57–58, 60–62, 63, 311, 443n70, 449n7; God's, 9, 35, 69, 418n20, 418n22; royal, 96, 105, 117, 120, 133, 143, 144, 170, 174, 214, 228–29, 233, 250, 311, 463n33, 464n58. *See also* piety; Teacher of Righteousness
royal concessions. See *philanthropa basilika*
royal ideology, 35, 38, 41, 43, 61–62, 82, 96–100, 102–6, 109, 120, 133, 140, 142, 143, 146, 215, 224, 430n58, 437n82; and victory, 139, 146, 155, 156, 257, 267, 224. *See also* kingship; piety; righteousness; temple foundation, royal prerogative; temple foundation, narrative pattern of

Sabbath, 111, 140, 141, 167, 168, 208, 245, 246, 250, 253, 256, 265, 284, 306, 392, 399, 438n96, 446n109, 494n115; attacks on, 151, 226, 253, 284, 391; mediating synecdoche, 192, 255, 284, 391–92, 507n49; war on, 179, 194, 248, 255, 287
sacrifices, 7, 34, 56, 77, 85, 89, 91, 92, 104, 113, 132, 207–10, 213, 217, 232–33, 241, 252, 254, 298, 325–26, 333–34, 336, 339, 389, 398, 400, 402, 428n17, 473n20, 481n35, 492n98; disruption of, 5, 6, 7, 75, 85, 91, 92, 189, 204, 206–7, 217, 236, 238, 241, 245, 257, 276, 380, 395, 399, 401, 439n107, 510n105; disruption of, and *gymnasion*, 75, 91, 92, 190, 204–5, 208, 211, 217, 221, 262, 264, 276, 292; neglect of, 60, 75, 201, 204, 206, 207, 211, 217, 219, 249, 253–54, 256, 262, 263–64, 267, 270, 276, 291, 292, 294, 462n31, 464n59; resumption of, 92, 93, 103, 125–26, 129–30, 132, 136, 137, 139, 168, 181, 204, 245, 399, 402; royal subsidies for, 99, 267–68, 308, 324–25, 333–34, 336, 402–3, 473n20; unlawful, 56, 147, 179, 205, 213, 226, 232–33, 238, 240, 241, 243–44, 245, 246, 247, 248, 249, 252, 253–54, 398–403
Sartre, Maurice, 19, 20, 327, 342–43, 352, 378, 421n83, 423n116, 479n9, 485n25, 493n106, 494n124, 499n78, 499n81
Šatammu (in Babylon), 327, 331, 356–57, 358–59, 372–74, 497n50, 497n54, 498n62
Schwartz, Daniel R., 8, 9, 66–67, 71–72, 331–33, 342, 417n8, 417n14, 418n19, 432n2, 433n31, 435n65, 438n95, 451n33
Seleukos IV, 12, 30, 46, 68, 71, 90, 295, 301, 310, 316–44, 345, 346, 347, 349, 350, 351, 358, 486n31, 487n33, 498n72; his administrative and fiscal reform, 12, 29, 40, 46, 310, 316–18, 321–25, 327–29, 329–35, 339–40, 340–44, 345, 349, 350, 356, 358, 360–61, 369, 378, 379, 383, 487n33, 490n61, 498n72, 499n78; paired with Onias III, 80, 83, 88, 89, 183, 326–27. *See also agoranomia*; Antiochos IV; Heliodoros; Olympiodoros; Onias III; Simon (temple *prostatēs*); state culture; war indemnity
semantic concatenation, 192–93, 196, 212, 231, 260, 263–64, 270, 272, 275, 279, 283, 284–85, 287, 334, 384, 472n3. *See also* Akra; *gymnasion*; synecdoche
settlement, military, 29–30, 277, 282, 352, 362, 363–64, 394, 400, 487n33, 502n149; in Jerusalem, 16, 40, 44, 138, 164, 167, 226, 232, 243, 261, 281–82, 283, 285, 291, 380, 387, 392, 372, 392, 507n58. *See also* Akra; *katoikia*, land confiscations
settlers, military, 107, 358, 366–67, 369, 393–94, 397, 488n39, 503n149; in Jerusalem, 16, 21–22, 31, 56, 231, 232, 240, 245, 251, 254, 261, 274, 281–86, 291–92, 366, 368–69, 384, 392, 393–97, 400–2, 477n79; in Jerusalem, and Antiochenes, 380, 392–93, 394, 396, 397, 504n168. *See also* altars, unlawful; *katoikoi*; land confiscations
Sheshbazzar, 87, 217, 450n29
Simon (Simeon) the Just (high priest), 62, 115, 133, 209, 447n120, 464n50
Simon (temple *prostatēs*), 15, 46, 89, 272, 318, 326, 329–31, 341–46, 351, 357, 359, 360, 361, 369, 490n67, 490n70, 490n72; his denunciation, 76, 154, 273, 276, 328, 337; his report, 328, 329–30, 331–35, 339, 341–42; impious, 62, 328. *See also* Onias III
Simon Maccabee, 6, 10, 36, 66, 134, 160–77, 178, 179, 185, 195, 224, 227, 272, 290, 292, 310, 377; and dynastic transmission of power, 66, 84, 134, 161, 164, 165–66, 169, 175–77, 452n59; his Eulogy, 36, 161, 169–74, 175, 224; his legitimizing deeds, 45, 114, 128, 160, 161–63, 164–68, 180, 189–90, 198, 221, 222, 227, 279–80, 282, 386, 457n61; his justice and piety, 28, 38, 62, 160, 161, 163, 164, 190, 224, 311; his titles and kinglike status, 36, 134, 160, 161, 163–64, 169–76, 271, 360, 475n45; king of divine election, 166, 169, 176–77, 224; and palace-building account, 44, 148, 160, 161, 164–68, 175; people's decree in S.'s honor, 129, 161, 164, 174–76, 179, 271, 392, 453n5. *See also* Akra, Simon's liberation and purification of;

Simon Maccabee *(continued)*
  high priests, appointment of; king (representation of); palace building account; temple foundation, narrative pattern of
Simon's time unit, 35, 98, 119, 121, 149, 160–77, 183, 186
sin-retribution, 9, 10, 34, 65–66, 69, 72–76, 77–78, 80, 442n48. *See also* measure-for-measure
Solomon, 103, 104, 105, 109, 123, 128, 129, 132, 133, 136, 146
state culture of Hellenistic kingdoms, modern views of, 16, 25–28, 30, 41, 63–64, 86, 264–66, 270–71, 297–99, 310–12, 352–53, 365–66, 424n133, 426n162, 437n32, 473n17, 478n2, 480n26, 480n30, 487n33, 487n35. *See also* Alexander the Great; Antiochos III's decree; Bickerman-Tcherikover paradigm; *philanthropa basilika*; tax; tribute; tribute increase
Suffering Servant, Suffering Teacher, 231, 239, 241–42, 247–49
Sukkoth festival, 101–2, 109, 113, 126, 130, 132, 166, 207, 442n42, 445n97, 446n111, 450n23, 463n41. *See also* Hanukkah festival
swine, 56, 238, 241, 244–45, 249, 469n37
synecdoche, 44, 121, 190–94, 196, 198, 211–14, 217, 227, 233, 259, 260, 261, 279, 283–84, 285, 286, 287, 291, 292, 326, 380, 391, 392, 401, 434n33, 448n6, 449n7, 460n6, 489n52. *See also* Akra; altars, unlawful; *gymnasion*; high priests, appointment of; Sabbath; temple (as a literary motif)
synoikismos, 21, 340, 501n118

tax, taxation, taxes, 40, 46, 164, 209, 232, 269, 279–80, 298, 301, 308–10, 318, 321–25, 326–27, 329–35, 338–39, 340–42, 343, 345–61, 390, 394, 488n41, 493n111, 502n138; and Jason's politicization, 262–66, 269, 270, 293, 364–65, 368, 379, 394; t. concessions and exemptions, 31, 32, 262, 264, 307, 308–10, 342, 393–94, 474n26, 488n39, 492n100, 493n105; ways of tax collection, 63, 298, 305–6, 313, 318, 319–21, 329, 340, 342–44, 350–51, 352–54, 361, 378, 396, 492n93, 493nn111–12, 495n29, 496n36, 497n45, 508n78. *See also* Antiochos III's decree; Antiochos IV; *philanthropa basilika*; decree, decrees, royal; Seleukos IV; temple, of Jerusalem; temple, temples; temple plundering, stories of; war indemnity
Tcherikover, Victor A., 11, 13–16, 18, 19, 20, 54, 92, 212, 263, 361, 362–63, 364, 365–66, 367–68, 384, 385–86, 421n83, 421n89, 422n112, 431n66, 432n1, 473n11, 483n71, 499n87, 499n88, 505n23, 506n30, 507n58, 509n83. *See also* Bickerman-Tcherikover paradigm
Teacher of Righteousness, 58, 170, 239, 243, 248, 429n38, 453n4, 457n67, 467n3, 468n6, 470n40
Teacher of Righteousness, Hymn of, 170, 239, 243, 457n66, 470n56
temple (as a literary motif, selected): accounts of 1 and 2 Maccabees centered on, 39, 45, 191–96, 230–31, 234, 236, 237, 250, 259–60, 263, 268, 270, 272, 276, 278, 281–85, 287, 291–92, 380, 384, 391–92; conceptual status of, 18, 43, 247, 249; narrative morpheme, 98, 117, 121, 198, 430n53, 460n6; semantic sphere of, 43, 64, 68, 85–86, 107, 110, 191–92, 196, 260, 285, 287; synecdoche, 191, 211–14, 227. *See also* 1 Maccabees, subject matter; 2 Maccabees, subject matter; Antiochos IV; *Ioudaïsmos*; Judas Maccabee; palace; semantic concatenation; synecdoche
temple dedication (rededication), 7, 8, 17–18, 44, 96, 97, 104, 141, 241, 421n82, 511n111; its date in Maccabean times, 8, 17–18, 129, 421n82, 511n111; in the Judahite/Judean tradition, 129–33, 148, 156–57, 158, 206, 207–11, 440n18, 450n23; by Judas Maccabee, 122, 128, 129–33, 168, 175, 183–84, 189, 213, 241; rites of, 103, 104, 113–14, 125–26, 127, 441n26. *See also* Hanukkah festival; Nehemiah; Simon Maccabee, his legitimizing deeds; Solomon; Sukkoth festival; Zerubbabel and Joshua
temple dedication by the Maccabees, account of: 9, 92, 97, 98, 122, 123–24, 125–27, 128, 129, 131, 136, 141, 148, 159, 160, 166–67, 216; its location in the narratives of 1 and 2 Maccabees, 8, 92, 93, 98, 122–23, 139, 146, 417n14, 434n36, 452n43
temple desecration: accounts of, 9, 37, 72, 79, 85, 92, 96, 156, 168, 190. 211, 235, 236, 240, 241, 245, 268, 280, 281, 288, 460n3; by Antiochos IV, 7, 74, 122, 127, 386
temple foundation (refoundation), 37, 68–69, 84, 91, 93, 100–106, 107, 108, 109–15, 117–18, 122, 124, 125, 127–28, 133, 134, 135–36, 137, 138–39, 145, 146, 441n26, 466n80, 502n148; of Jerusalem temple, 83, 88, 91, 96–97, 98, 106, 108, 114–15, 130, 143–44, 146, 207, 211, 221, 434n36, 440n18, 443n55, 463n44, 511n111; royal prerogative, 38, 68, 93, 96, 103–4, 108, 114, 115, 132, 139, 146, 174, 357, 445n88, 454n6
temple foundation (refoundation) accounts, 37, 38, 41, 67–68, 79, 82, 83, 91, 96, 97, 98, 105, 111,

115, 117, 119, 121, 123, 128–29, 177, 207–10, 211, 216, 218, 434n36, 440n18, 449n18, 450n21. *See also gymnasion*, antitemple; Hanukkah story; Jason, disrupter; Judas Maccabee, his first temple refoundation & his second refoundation; Judas's time unit (in 1 Maccabees); Nikanor's Day story

temple foundation (refoundation) narrative pattern, 38, 43–44, 45, 61–62, 64, 69, 72, 73, 75–76, 82, 83, 91, 92, 93, 94, 95–118, 119–41, 147–77; in 1 and 2 Maccabees, 38, 43–44, 67–69, 83, 94, 97–118, 119–41, 146, 148–77, 208, 456n48; alien to the Greek tradition, 43, 67, 96, 115–17; in the ancient Near Eastern literary traditions, 38, 43, 67, 96, 97, 99–102; its adaptation to changes in political organization, 43, 96, 98–99, 106–15, 118, 119, 133, 148, 166, 167, 180, 445n88; its duplication in 1 and 2 Maccabees, 94, 98, 119–20, 121, 148–77, 189; its function of ruler's legitimation, 38, 39, 43, 68–69, 72, 82, 92, 96, 98–99, 117–18, 120, 130, 135–36, 148, 160, 175, 190; in the Judahite/Judean literary tradition, 38, 72, 97, 106–15, 123, 129–30, 132–33, 133–34, 445n91, 449n7, 450n21; literary structure of, 43, 96, 97–98, 102–3, 104, 112–14, 119, 121, 122–24, 125–27, 128, 129, 136–38, 154, 157, 158–59, 162, 166–67, 224, 264, 449n7, 450n21; and other items of urban architecture, 96, 97, 98, 100–101, 103, 106, 115, 164–69, 170, 174, 222, 224, 439n6, 454n7; and political support for the Hasmoneans, 38, 69, 82–83, 84, 85, 94, 118, 119–20, 175, 185, 189; and ruler's ideology, 38, 43, 68–69, 96, 103–6, 117, 167, 440n7. *See also* Akra, Simon's liberation and purification of; Hanukkah story; Judas's time unit (in 1 Maccabees); Nehemiah; Nikanor's Day story; palace building account; Solomon; Zerubbabel and Joshua

temple liberation, 9, 36–37, 153, 160, 223

temple liberation accounts, 37, 67, 84, 95–96; in 2 Maccabees, 9, 34, 36, 38, 66, 78, 79, 80–82, 82, 83, 95, 117, 154, 160, 436n65, 436n71; Greek, 34, 72, 73, 77, 78–80, 96. *See also* Hanukkah story; Heliodoros story; Nikanor's Day story; temple propaganda

temple, of Gerizim. *See* Gerizim

temple, of Jerusalem (in historical view, selected): and Antiochos IV's reforms, 263, 264, 363, 367
center of tax collection, 307, 350–54, 493n115; its fate during Antiochos IV's repression, 16, 17–18, 56, 153, 232–33, 238, 241, 243, 245–46, 251–52, 256, 281, 285, 307, 387, 390, 392, 394, 397–403; its revenues, 209, 335–43, 485n14; its status, 47, 107, 180–81, 241, 268, 309, 312, 342; and royal control and taxation, 46, 268, 269, 308–10, 329–35, 339, 342–44, 345–47, 349, 359–61, 363, 368, 369, 383, 493n115, 497n58; royal subsidies to, 241, 248, 268, 308–9, 324, 333–34, 335, 336–37, 402, 466n80, 474n24, 488n38; and various economic matters, 12, 313–14, 324, 345, 346. *See also agoranomia;* Antiochos IV, his plunder; Simon (temple *prostatēs*); temple desecration

temple plundering, 232, 319, 321, 326–27, 489n48, 492n98; stories of, 32, 162, 279, 319, 321, 326–27, 489n45. *See also* Heliodoros story

temple propaganda, 34–35, 37, 66, 67, 93, 185, 193, 194, 195, 418n18, 418n24, 419n30, 439n1

temple, purification of, 37, 38, 66, 70–71, 72, 79, 96–97, 98, 124, 125, 126, 127, 128–29, 135, 138, 160, 166, 167, 284, 434n36. *See also* temple foundation (refoundation)

temple-state, 12, 13, 14, 19, 61, 116, 421n139, 425n147

temple, temples (in historical view, selected): centers of tax collection, 326–27, 350; and royal control and taxation, 46, 59, 226, 321–25, 326–27, 330–31, 342, 344, 345, 354–59, 369, 383, 473n20, 492n98, 492n100, 494n1; royal subsidies to, 268, 308, 324–25, 330, 336, 344, 345, 354–55, 466n86, 473n20, 492n92, 494n1, 497n45; t. revenues, 337–39, 343, 492n93. *See also* Antiochos III's decree; *epi tōn hierōn; epistatēs;* high priests, appointment of; high priests, of Jerusalem; high priests, other; *paqdu; prostatēs;* Ptolemy II; Seleukos IV, his administrative and fiscal reform; Simon (temple *prostatēs*); state culture

temple vessels. *See* holy vessels

Testament of Levi, 251, 471n75

theokratia, 106, 115–17, 143

time, construction of, 84–91, 93–94, 183, 326, 328, 436n71, 436n74, 436n75, 436n76, 436n79, 437n81, 438n92; and cyclical composition of 1 and 2 Maccabees, 37, 43, 68, 70, 84, 94, 161, 170, 183, 186; as cyclical, 43, 68, 70, 85–86, 87, 89. *See also* 1 and 2 Maccabees, their value, compositional montages; chronology of events; disruption, time of; high priests, paired with kings

Tobiads. *See* Hyrkanos; Joseph; Oniads

tribute, 31–32, 40, 46, 226, 268, 278–80, 292, 308–10, 320, 326–27, 329, 349, 350–59, 368,

tribute *(continued)*
377, 468n18, 475n46, 485n14, 488n38, 489n49, 490n61; exemption from, 134, 160, 161, 174, 176, 266, 279, 474n26; high priests responsible for payment of, 46, 107, 343, 346, 350, 352, 353–54, 360–61, 365, 377, 496n36; levied on behalf of the Ptolemies, 46, 342–43, 345, 346, 350, 352, 353, 378–79, 399n78. *See also* Antiochos III's decree; Antiochos IV; Joseph the Tobiad, story of; *philanthropa basilika*; Seleukos IV; semantic concatenation
tribute increase, 162, 163, 164, 262–66, 267, 268, 269, 270, 274, 278, 285, 292, 293, 310, 318, 334, 346, 353, 360, 368, 377; and Antiochos IV, 39, 346, 347, 349–50, 361, 379, 499n81; and deposition of Onias III, 46, 263, 276, 277, 346, 347, 349–50, 360, 364–65, 377, 379; its instigator, 12, 46, 275, 277–78, 333, 349–59, 379; and Jason, 32, 263, 264, 266, 268, 274, 275–77, 291, 294, 350, 499n81; and Menelaos, 15, 20, 30, 219, 274, 276, 291, 390, 392; and Seleukid interference with appointments of high priests, 261, 270, 273, 274, 275, 276, 278, 280, 288, 334, 346, 349–60, 359–61, 364–65, 379. *See also* rebellion, causes of
Tyriaion inscription, 19, 29–30, 46, 212, 268, 277, 340–41, 347, 362, 363–66, 370, 375, 422n92, 465n63, 465n65, 473n12, 488n39, 493n111, 499n87, 500n92

Uruk prophecy, 89, 206, 438n93, 438n99, 462n31
usurpation, usurpers, 38, 91, 92, 96, 105, 142, 145, 150, 153, 177, 193, 349, 440n8, 443n58, 475n41

victory, victories (selected), 18, 58, 124, 127, 128, 136–41, 142, 146, 152, 168, 172–73, 257, 403, 436n65, 455n29, 456n43, 470n51, 506n38; consequence of temple foundation, 83, 91, 92, 104, 124, 136, 138, 139; cosmic, of deities, 100, 101, 103, 104, 108–9, 137, 441n34, 463n65; entitling v. and temple foundation, 79, 103, 104–5, 110, 124, 128, 135, 137, 138, 139–41, 146, 150–51, 153, 156, 160, 161, 443n55; and Judas's kinglike status, 145, 146, 149, 150, 152–53, 155–56; Judas's v., 7, 66–67, 83, 91, 138, 139, 149, 456n47, 456n48, 511n111; and kings, kingship, 103, 104–5, 109, 137, 138, 139–40, 145, 146, 155–56, 172–73, 243, 279, 455n27, 455n29; and military defeats, 168; sign of divine approval, 36, 78, 104, 136, 137, 138, 141, 149, 164. *See also* battle; war

wall, of Jerusalem, 199, 341, 384, 393, 400, 439n6, 446n103, 457n61; and Alkimos, 190, 198, 220–21, 222, 224, 226, 292; and Nehemiah, 96, 97, 101, 106, 111–14, 128, 148, 160, 167, 168, 176, 180, 222, 444n79; and Simon, 160, 176, 180; and Solomon, 148, 160, 162, 163, 180, 189, 190, 198, 222, 292
war, warfare (selected), 17, 32–33, 139, 170, 179, 283–84, 383–84, 387–88, 389, 391, 511n111; illegitimate, impious, 214, 220, 222, 224, 226, 274, 278–79, 454n17; Judas's w. and Antiochos V's time unit, 7, 8, 9, 71, 79, 124; and kingship, 167, 170, 171–73, 176, 179; legitimate, 139, 214, 222, 255, 391, 435n52; pious, 139–41, 142, 149, 151, 155, 163, 164, 276, 279, 452n52, 454n13; war versus peace (ideological aspects), 125, 127–28, 166–67, 176, 224, 449n16. *See also* altars, unlawful, mediating synecdoche; battle; *Ioudaïsmos*; Sabbath, mediating synecdoche & war on; victory
war indemnity, 12, 15, 30, 279, 317, 318, 319–21. *See also* Apamea, treaty of
warriors, 152, 227; pious, 138, 140, 141–42, 144, 151, 152, 204, 222, 397. *See also* few against the many; *Ioudaioi*; *Ioudaïsmos*
wicked: king, 60, 62, 89, 96, 120, 142, 170, 206, 214, 217, 219, 229–31, 233, 244–45, 246, 253, 254; punishment of, as reconciliation, 73, 91, 127, 139, 151. *See also allophyloi*; impious
wickedness, 38, 57–58, 60–61, 62–63, 70, 145, 223. *See also allophylismos*; *Hellēnismos*; piety, and impiety; righteousness
widows and orphans, 140, 141, 142, 149, 276, 340, 452n50, 454n14

Zechariah, 104–5, 114, 154–55, 341, 351, 444n85, 449n16
Zerubbabel and Joshua, 86, 87, 102, 106–11, 113, 123, 128, 129–33, 134, 154, 217, 218, 444n85, 445n96
Zeus, 301, 400, 419n45, 421n92, 466n86, 470n45, 509n95, 509n97, 510n99; Z. Olympios, 21–22, 153, 240, 250–51, 256, 399–400, 401, 423n116, 509n96; Z. Xenios, 250–51, 256, 386

www.ingramcontent.com/pod-product-compliance
Lightning Source LLC
Chambersburg PA
CBHW031408230426
43668CB00007B/239